Quick, Simple, and
Main-Course Vegetarian Pleasures

Also by Jeanne Lemlin

Quick Vegetarian Pleasures
Vegetarian Pleasures: A Menu Cookbook
Main-Course Vegetarian Pleasures
Simple Vegetarian Pleasures

Quick, Simple, and Main-Course Vegetarian Pleasures

By
Jeanne Lemlin

ISBN 0060533501
02 03 04 05 RRD 10 9 8 7 6 5 4 3 2 1

CONTENTS

QUICK VEGETARIAN PLEASURES

SIMPLE VEGETARIAN PLEASURES

MAIN-COURSE VEGETARIAN PLEASURES

Quick Vegetarian Pleasures

Jeanne Lemlin

HarperPerennial
A Division of HarperCollinsPublishers

To my husband, Ed, whose unending help with typing, grocery shopping, dishwashing, and the care of our son, allowed me to write this book

and

to my mother, who let me, from a very early age, totally overrun her kitchen.

INTRODUCTION

Shortly after the publication of my first book, Vegetarian Pleasures: A Menu Cookbook, *my son Daniel was born. His wondrous arrival precipitated a host of changes in our household, the way only an infant can turn your life upside down. Some of these changes I was prepared for; others were completely unexpected.*

I had always taken for granted my habit of spending long hours in the kitchen experimenting with new foods and recipes. The more complex and time-consuming a task was, the more I would be drawn to it. No matter how busy my day, I would find myself inexorably gravitating toward the kitchen to seek some new culinary challenge. This all came to an abrupt halt. Although my love of cooking has continued unabated, I now wish to create only dishes that can be assembled quickly. *If a recipe looks like it might take more than thirty minutes of my time, I lose all interest. Quickness has gained a whole new appeal.*

Many people think of vegetarian cooking as being more time-consuming than traditional fare. In many cases it is. But I knew from developing a chapter on quick menus in Vegetarian Pleasures: A Menu Cookbook *that, with a good dose of imagination, meatless cooking can be fast and easy. Without sacrificing quality for convenience, I have been able to wed my love of adventurous eating with speed in the kitchen. An abundant use of fresh vegetables, grains, herbs, semi-exotic ingredients, and new items on the market still are the staples of my cooking, but I have learned to handle them with a quick hand.*

Some ready-made products have found their way into my repertoire, but none at the expense of flavor. For example, I searched for and found a commercial tomato sauce that I like, and I can spruce it up with red wine, herbs, and garlic if I desire. Salsa is another store-bought item that can vary greatly by brand, and I have found some exceptionally good ones that free me from concocting my own in the kitchen. And canned cooked beans have more often than not replaced freshly cooked dried beans in my meal planning, enabling me to incorporate more beans in my diet. Many canned beans contain a preservative—their one drawback—but I avoid preservatives in most other foods, so I allow myself this shortcut. Again, brands vary, so I have searched for and found a product with firm beans, and I always rinse them thoroughly before using them in a recipe.

My idea of a quick recipe is one that takes less than thirty minutes to prepare, though it might demand additional cooking time. If a soup has to simmer one hour on the stove, I overlook that time because I don't have to tend to the soup. Many recipes, such as Capellini with Tomato Pesto (page 116), take just ten minutes to prepare, and they taste as wonderful as many more-involved dishes. If the quality of ingredients is high, I have found, then elaborate preparations aren't necessary for noteworthy results. (Incidentally, the length of recipe directions is not necessarily an indication of the time needed to prepare a dish. Detailed instructions are a reflection of my background as a cooking instructor and my desire to be precise rather than a measure of how involved a particular recipe is.)

Although I am a vegetarian and convinced of the link between diet and health, I have always tried to maintain a relaxed stance toward meal planning. When meat is removed from our diets, we must find other sources such as beans, grains, dairy products, and soy foods to replace the lost protein and iron. And it is not only essential to eat a lot of these important foods, but also to seek variety in our diets.

But I don't believe in meticulously calculating nutritional needs and planning our meals according to these calculations. I think this approach to eating hampers pleasure at the table, and pleasure is what good eating is all about. Once eating is turned into a mathematics problem, then drudgery sets in. (Of course, there are people who, for extreme health reasons, must be very calculating about their diets. But these are special cases that require medical guidance.)

I also maintain this approach to the amount of fat in my diet. It is very important to avoid the misconception that fat intake is not a concern for vegetarians because meat is missing from our diets and we therefore can consume all the dairy products we want. We still must restrict our use of cream, milk, cheese, and eggs because of their unusually high fat content.

Rather than try to meet a set of exact dietary guidelines, I prefer to alternate richer meals with lighter meals, making lighter dishes a more frequent part of my diet. I have found that whenever I take an extreme approach to eating, there is a backlash. If I eat very light meals for too long a period of time, I inevitably crave an ultrarich dessert as compensation (like those outrageously good Häagen-Dazs hot fudge sundaes served at our local drugstore!). So moderation is also a sensible approach to take with menu planning. If a particular entrée appeals to you and it is on the rich side, choose a light accompaniment and dessert to maintain a balance.

This relaxed yet thoughtful approach to diet might sound slack to some readers, but I am not encouraging negligence. It's just that too often health-conscious people turn eating into a regimen, and because eating then loses much of its appeal, the rigid approach soon gets dropped in search of a new routine.

The general guidelines that I follow are to seek protein complementarity, restrict fats and sugar, and include a wide variety of high-fiber foods. (Protein complementarity means combining different nonmeat sources of protein in the same meal to make them complete, thereby enhancing their quality and accessibility. The foods that best complement each other are: grains and legumes; grains and dairy products; and seeds and legumes.) By keeping these basic principles in mind, I can balance my diet in an easygoing manner. Rather than make each meal a model of nutritional perfection, I can remember which foods I should include—and do so often but not always.

We should be informed about nutrition, strive to eat sensibly, and be concerned about our health. But eating must not become a religion; that's no way to feed our souls. Instead, let's approach eating with a cautious but relaxed spirit. I hope these recipes enable you to prepare delectable food in a short time and inspire you to be adventurous. Above all, I hope they enhance your cooking pleasures, quick though they may be.

TIPS FOR THE BUSY COOK

☛ Whenever you prepare rice or pasta, cook an extra batch. Chill, tossing pasta with a little oil beforehand. Use in stir-fried or skillet dishes; marinate as a salad; or sprinkle with a few tablespoons of water, cover with foil, and reheat in the oven.

☛ On weekends, make an extra-large pot of soup. Doubling a recipe doesn't mean double work. Undercook the soup, then spoon out a portion to serve later in the week or freeze a batch.

☛ Don't shy away from recipes that serve six, even though there may be just one or two people in your household. Leftovers are the salvation of the busy person.

☛ Keep your pantry and refrigerator well stocked. It's easier to assemble a quick meal if you've got plenty of ingredients on hand.

☛ Go out to dinner.

APPETIZERS

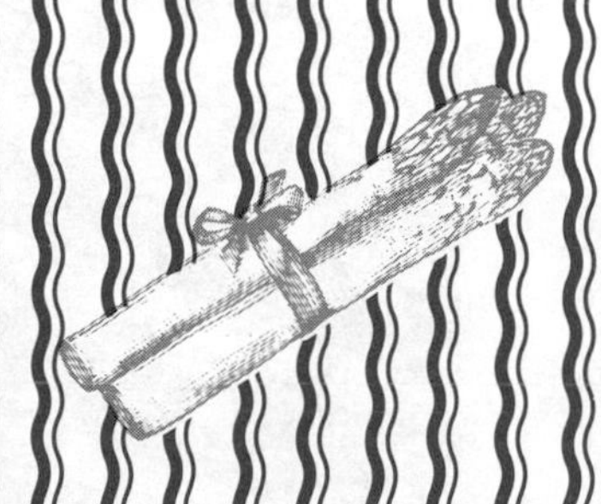

Appetizers play a special role in menu planning, especially when you are entertaining and want to stimulate guests' appetites with an intriguing prelude to the meal. Presenting a tempting hors d'oeuvre before your guests sit down to dinner can set the tone for the evening while enabling them to nibble while conversing. But these dishes need not be reserved for entertaining. Many are simple enough to put together quickly to precede an informal family dinner. Whether the occasion is special or not, the same rules for selection should be taken into account. If your main course contains cheese or is on the rich side, select a dairy free appetizer such as Marinated Roasted Peppers (page 14) or Spicy Mixed Nuts (page 11). If you are serving a meal free of dairy products or on the light side, then a cheesy appetizer beforehand would strike a nice balance. Hors d'oeuvres should awaken, not satisfy, the appetite, so small portions suffice.

Everyone enjoys a party in

which there is a large assortment of appetizers artfully laid out on a table. For the cook, this can be a somewhat relaxed approach to entertaining because so much of the work can be done in advance. Strive for contrasting flavors, textures, and colors to provide a tantalizing selection (see Appetizer Party menu, page 238).

CHÈVRE TOASTS WITH ASSORTED TOPPINGS

These are richly flavored and irresistible with wine. A great appetizer for a special or simple meal.

12 thin slices narrow-loaf French bread

Olive oil

¼ pound chèvre (goat cheese)

ASSORTED TOPPINGS

Marinated roasted red peppers (page 14, or use store-bought)

Capers

Black olives (preferably small, oil-cured)

Chopped fresh herbs

Cherry tomato slices

Makes 1 dozen toasts

❶ Place the bread on a baking sheet and broil on both sides until golden and crisp.

❷ Remove from the oven. Using a pastry brush, coat 1 side of each slice with some olive oil. Spread some chèvre on top of each slice, then garnish with your choice of toppings. Here are some suggestions: marinated roasted red peppers cut into strips, rolled, and placed in the center; 3 capers placed in the center; a whole black olive with a sprig of a fresh herb such as dill or parsley; overlapping cherry tomato slices; chopped fresh herbs such as chives, thyme, parsley, dill, or chervil.

CRISPY GARLIC TOASTS
(CROSTINI)

Here is one case in which garlic powder works better than fresh garlic. These toasts are light and buttery, with an assertive garlic flavor. Serve them with soup or relish them as an appetizer.

1 narrow loaf French bread (about ½ pound)

½ cup olive oil

Garlic powder

Salt

Makes about 40 toasts

❶ Preheat the oven to 350°F. Cut the French bread into ¼- to ½-inch-thick slices. With a pastry brush, lightly coat each slice on both sides with olive oil and lay it on a baking sheet.

❷ Generously sprinkle garlic powder on top of each slice, then lightly season with some salt.

❸ Bake 5 to 7 minutes, or until *bottoms* are lightly golden. Turn the slices over and sprinkle again with garlic powder and salt. Bake 5 minutes more, or until golden all over.

❹ Place the baking sheet on a wire rack and let the toasts cool completely, about 30 minutes. Store in a covered tin or plastic bag at room temperature for up to 1 week, or freeze for up to 2 weeks.

HERB CHEESE TOASTS
(CROSTINI)

It's best to let these toasts sit for twenty-four hours before serving, to let the wonderful mingling of flavors develop fully. Also, dried herbs work better than fresh in this recipe.

1 narrow loaf French bread (about ½ pound), *or* grinder rolls

½ cup olive oil

2 tablespoons grated Parmesan cheese

½ teaspoon dried oregano

½ teaspoon dried basil

½ teaspoon dried dill

¼ teaspoon dried thyme

Makes about 40 toasts

❶ Preheat the oven to 350°F. Cut the French bread into ¼-inch-thick slices. With a pastry brush, lightly and evenly coat both sides of each slice with olive oil, then lay the slices on a baking sheet. Bake 5 minutes, then remove from the oven. Turn each slice over.

❷ In a small bowl combine the cheese with the herbs. Sprinkle the mixture evenly on top of each toast, then press down lightly with your fingertips to help stick it to the bread. Return to the oven and bake 7 to 10 minutes more, or until the cheese is golden brown and the toasts appear crisp (they will harden more upon cooling). Be careful not to burn the toasts. Cool completely on a wire rack. Store in a covered tin or plastic bag at room temperature for up to 3 days, or refrigerate up to 1 week, or freeze up to 2 weeks.

STUFFED CHERRY TOMATOES

These little tomato cups stuffed with a ricotta cheese–scallion mixture are pretty enough for an elegant party, yet simple enough for an informal occasion.

½ cup ricotta cheese (preferably part skim)

2 tablespoons grated Parmesan cheese

1½ tablespoons very thinly sliced scallions

Freshly ground black pepper to taste

20 to 25 cherry tomatoes, stems removed

2 teaspoons minced scallions (green parts only)

Fresh parsley sprigs

Makes 20 to 25

❶ In a small bowl, beat together the ricotta and Parmesan cheeses, sliced scallions, and pepper. Cover and chill while preparing the tomato cups.

❷ Slice off ¼ of the bottom of a tomato (it will sit more securely on its stem end). With the tip of a knife, scoop out the pulp and gently squeeze out the seeds and juice. Discard the sliced-off cap, juice, and seeds. Repeat with the remaining tomatoes.

❸ Using the handle of a teaspoon, stuff each tomato with some of the ricotta mixture. To garnish, sprinkle a few minced scallion pieces on top of each tomato. Chill the tomatoes at least 30 minutes so the flavors can blend, then let sit at room temperature for 20 minutes or so before serving (cold tomatoes lose their flavor). For a striking presentation, serve on an attractive platter and garnish with bunches of parsley sprigs.

CHEESE CRACKERS

The flavor of your cheese will determine the quality of these mouth-watering crackers. Choose the best cheddar you can get, and you'll be well rewarded. Serve the crackers as an appetizer or alongside a steaming bowl of soup.

½ cup (1 stick) unsalted butter, softened

2 cups (½ pound) grated extra-sharp cheddar cheese

1¼ cups unbleached flour

¼ teaspoon salt

⅛ teaspoon cayenne pepper

1 to 2 tablespoons water

Makes 4 dozen crackers

❶ In a large bowl, cream the butter with an electric mixer until soft and smooth. Beat in the cheese until blended.

❷ In a small bowl, mix together the flour, salt, and cayenne. Sprinkle into the butter mixture and beat just until combined. Pour in 1 to 2 tablespoons water, or just enough to help the dough cohere (it will be crumbly). Do not overbeat.

❸ Gather the dough into 2 balls, knead 2 or 3 times, then roll each ball into a cylinder 1½ inches in diameter. Wrap in wax paper or plastic wrap and chill the logs at least 30 minutes and up to 24 hours. Or wrap in plastic wrap and freeze for up to 2 weeks. If frozen, thaw the logs for 1 hour before using.

❹ Preheat the oven to 350°F. Slice the logs into rounds a little less than ¼ inch thick. Place on an ungreased baking sheet and bake 12 to 15 minutes, or until the edges are golden. Cool thoroughly on a wire rack. To store, place in a tin and keep at room temperature for up to 3 days. Or wrap in plastic and refrigerate for up to 2 weeks or freeze for up to 1 month.

TAMARI ALMONDS

Salty but not too salty, and with an alluring overtone of spiciness. Great for nibbling.

3 tablespoons tamari soy sauce

1½ tablespoons vegetable oil

¼ teaspoon cayenne pepper

¾ teaspoon salt

4 cups (about 1¼ pounds) whole, unblanched almonds

Makes 4 cups

❶ Combine the tamari, oil, cayenne, and salt in a large bowl. Stir in the almonds and coat well. Let sit 1 hour, stirring often.

❷ Preheat the oven to 300°F. With a slotted spoon, remove the almonds from the bowl and spread in a baking sheet in a single layer. Discard any remaining marinade. Bake 20 minutes, removing the baking sheet from the oven every 5 minutes or so and tossing the almonds with a spatula. (When done, the almonds will be somewhat dry and crusty looking and have a dark coating, but they should not be burnt.)

❸ Spoon the almonds into another baking sheet or onto a few plates, and let them cool completely. Store in an airtight container for up to 2 weeks, or wrap well and freeze up to 1 month.

SPICY MIXED NUTS

2 tablespoons unsalted butter

1 teaspoon chili powder

1 teaspoon ground cumin

½ teaspoon paprika

¼ teaspoon cayenne pepper

1 teaspoon salt

1 cup almonds

1 cup walnuts

1 cup raw or dry-roasted cashews *(see Note)*

1 cup pecans

Makes 4 cups

❶ Preheat the oven to 350°F.

❷ Melt the butter in a large skillet over medium heat. Add the spices and cook 30 seconds. Stir in the nuts and toss to coat well. Cook 2 minutes.

❸ Spread the nuts in one layer on a baking sheet. Bake 8 minutes. Remove from the oven and cool completely. Store in a tin or jar for up to 2 weeks, or freeze for up to 1 month.

☛***Note:*** Raw cashews can be purchased in natural foods stores.

RUSSIAN-STYLE MARINATED MUSHROOMS

My friend Sally Patterson, a Russian translator, introduced me to some memorable Russian dishes that she discovered while living in the Soviet Union. Here's one of my favorites: a tantalizing way of preparing mushrooms that doesn't involve any cooking. The mushrooms soak up the garlicky marinade and turn a rich, brown color. These make a popular hors d'oeuvre, served with toothpicks for nibbling, or a tasty first course, served on lettuce leaves.

½ cup olive oil

1 tablespoon red wine vinegar

3 garlic cloves, minced

⅓ cup minced fresh parsley

¼ teaspoon salt

Freshly ground black pepper to taste

1 pound very fresh mushrooms, rinsed and patted dry

Serves 4

❶ In a large bowl, whisk together the olive oil, vinegar, garlic, parsley, salt, and a liberal amount of pepper until blended.

❷ Cut any large mushrooms in half, and leave the others whole. Stir the mushrooms into the marinade and coat well. Cover and let sit at least 8 hours, but preferably for 24 hours. Stir periodically to coat with the marinade. (If marinating for a lengthy period, refrigerate after the first 8 hours.) Serve at room temperature.

EGGPLANT CAVIAR

Here's another recipe Sally Patterson brought back from the Soviet Union. It's so delicious that my husband and I inevitably eat the entire bowlful in one sitting. Serve it Russian style with party-size pumpernickel bread or toasts.

¼ cup olive oil

1 medium onion, finely diced

1 16-ounce can tomatoes, finely chopped and well drained

1 medium eggplant (about 1 pound), peeled and finely diced

1 green bell pepper, finely diced

2 tablespoons lemon juice

½ teaspoon salt

½ teaspoon sugar

Freshly ground black pepper to taste

Serves 6 to 8

❶ Heat the oil in a large skillet over medium-high heat. Add the onion and sauté 5 minutes. Add the drained tomatoes and sauté 5 minutes more, stirring often.

❷ Lower the heat to medium, then stir in the remaining ingredients. Cover the pan and cook about 20 minutes, or until the eggplant is very tender. Stir periodically. Remove the cover of the pan and cook until all the juices have evaporated, another 5 minutes or so.

❸ Puree half the eggplant mixture in a blender or food processor and return to the pan. Stir very well to mix, then scrape into a serving bowl. Serve at room temperature.

MARINATED ROASTED PEPPERS

Spoon these garlic-soaked peppers on slices of French bread for a divine appetizer — and be sure to fill the wine glasses. If red bell peppers are not available or are too expensive you can substitute additional green peppers, although the mixture is more striking if both colors are used.

1 pound (about 2 extra-large) red bell peppers

1 pound (about 2 extra-large) green bell peppers

⅓ cup olive oil

2 garlic cloves, pressed or minced

½ teaspoon salt

Freshly ground black pepper to taste

Makes 2 cups

❶ Place the peppers on a baking sheet and broil 1 to 3 inches from the flame or heating element until the peppers are blackened all over (this could take up to 20 minutes). You will have to turn the peppers every so often to char them evenly.

❷ When done, place the peppers in a paper or plastic bag and close it tight. Let the peppers sit 10 minutes; the steam they release will loosen the skins. Remove the peppers from the bag, then slip off the skins under cold running water. Pat the peppers very dry with paper towels.

❸ Core each pepper, then scrape out and discard the seeds. Cut the peppers into 1-inch squares and place in a bowl or jar.

❹ Add the remaining ingredients and toss to coat well. Marinate at least 2 hours before serving. These peppers can be refrigerated for up to 1 week, but be sure to bring them to room temperature before serving.

BLUE CHEESE LOG

8 ounces Neufchâtel or cream cheese, at room temperature

1 cup (about 4 ounces) crumbled blue cheese

2 tablespoons finely chopped walnuts

2 tablespoons minced fresh parsley

Serves 6 to 8

❶ Mash the cream cheese and blue cheese together with a fork until blended. Scrape the mixture onto a piece of wax paper and shape into a log 1½ inches in diameter. (The wax paper will help you roll the cheese into a cylinder. If the cheese mixture is too soft to handle, chill 20 minutes or so and shape again.)

❷ Combine the walnuts and the parsley in a small bowl. Sprinkle over the top and sides of the log. Slip the log onto a serving plate and serve at room temperature surrounded by crackers.

JALAPEÑO CHEESE NACHOS

These delicate crisps are made with flour tortillas instead of the corn variety, and this accounts for their unusual lightness. You can cook the tortillas up to three days in advance, but don't broil them with the cheese until you are ready to serve.

2 tablespoons vegetable oil

3 8-inch flour tortillas, cut into six wedges

1½ cups grated Monterey Jack cheese with jalapeño peppers

Serves 4

❶ With a pastry brush, lightly coat both sides of each tortilla wedge with oil. Place on cookie sheets and broil on both sides until lightly golden. (Do not let the tortillas get too brown.)

❷ When ready to serve the nachos, neatly sprinkle some of the grated cheese on each wedge. Broil just until melted. Serve immediately.

NACHOS WITH SOUR CREAM

***P**lace this dish of nachos in the center of the table and let everyone dip in. So simple, yet downright addictive.*

6 cups (about 4 ounces) corn chips

1½ cups grated Monterey Jack cheese

1 tablespoon minced fresh cilantro (optional)

1 cup salsa

½ cup sour cream

Serves 4

❶ Preheat the oven to 400°F. Place the corn chips in one layer in a large shallow baking dish. Sprinkle on the cheese and cilantro. Bake 10 minutes, or until the cheese is melted.

❷ Remove from the oven, then drizzle the salsa all over the corn chips. Place little spoonfuls of sour cream all over the tops of the nachos, and serve immediately.

POTATO SKINS WITH HORSERADISH DIP

***C**hildren love these "fried potatoes," and they are much more nutritious than French fries or potato chips.*

4 large baking potatoes, scrubbed

1 cup sour cream

1 tablespoon prepared horseradish

Dash salt

Chili powder

❶ Prick each potato in a few spots with a fork or knife and place in the oven. Set the oven at 400°F. (you don't have to preheat), and cook about 1 hour, or until tender.

❷ Meanwhile make the dip. Combine the sour cream, horseradish, and salt in a small bowl and mix to blend. Sprinkle on some chili powder, then chill the dip until ready to serve.

2½ tablespoons tamari soy sauce

¼ cup plus 2 tablespoons vegetable oil

Serves 4

❸ When the potatoes are done, remove them from the oven, then raise the temperature to 500°F. Let the potatoes cool until you can handle them. Cut each in half crosswise, then cut each half lengthwise into 4 pieces (each potato will yield 8 wedges). Slice some potato from each wedge, leaving about ¼ inch of potato on the skins. (Save the leftover potato flesh for potato pancakes. *See Note.*)

❹ Combine the tamari and oil in a small dish and, with a pastry brush, brush some of the mixture all over each potato wedge. Lay the wedges skin side down on a cookie sheet as you complete them. Liberally sprinkle chili powder on top of each wedge.

❺ Bake 15 to 20 minutes, or until crisp and golden brown. Serve on a platter surrounding the horseradish dip.

☛***Note:*** To make potato pancakes, mix some melted butter, salt, and pepper into the potatoes and beat well with a fork. Form into patties and coat on both sides with flour. Fry over medium heat in a hot skillet that has been coated with some oil.

CHEESY POTATO SKINS WITH SALSA DIP

Here is another enticing version of potato skins. These are extra crisp and match well with a spicy salsa.

4 baking potatoes

4 tablespoons unsalted butter, melted

1 cup grated extra-sharp cheddar cheese

Salsa

Serves 4

❶ Prick the potatoes, then bake them in a 400°F. oven until tender, about 1 hour. Remove from the oven and let cool a few minutes until easier to handle.

❷ Raise the oven temperature to 500°F. Slice the potatoes in half lengthwise, then in half again crosswise. Scoop out the potato flesh, leaving about 1/4 inch on the skins. (Save the flesh for another use, such as potato pancakes. *See Note,* page 17.)

❸ Brush each potato shell—inside and out—with the melted butter, then place skin side down on a baking sheet. Bake 8 minutes, or until the wedges begin to brown.

❹ Remove the wedges from the oven, then place some grated cheese on each. Return to the oven and cook 5 minutes more, or until the cheese is bubbly. Serve warm with a bowl of salsa.

STUFFED MUSHROOMS

Sherry and thyme accent these juicy mushrooms. Be certain to cook them so that they are tender throughout and have rendered their juices.

12 large fresh mushrooms

3 tablespoons unsalted butter

2 garlic cloves, minced

1 small onion, minced

4 slices good-quality white bread

2 tablespoons minced fresh parsley

3 tablespoons dry sherry

½ teaspoon dried thyme

¼ teaspoon poultry seasoning

¼ teaspoon salt

Freshly ground black pepper to taste

Serves 3 to 4

❶ Preheat the oven to 350°F. Wipe the mushrooms clean with damp paper towels. Snap off the stems and mince them. Generously butter a pie plate or other shallow baking pan.

❷ Melt 2 tablespoons of the butter in a medium skillet over medium heat. Add the garlic and onion and sauté 10 minutes, stirring often. Add the minced mushroom stems and sauté 5 minutes more. Remove the pan from the heat.

❸ Toast the bread until golden. Let cool a few minutes, then tear it into tiny pieces and stir it into the onion mixture, pressing it to help it absorb the juices. Stir in the parsley, sherry, thyme, poultry seasoning, salt, and pepper.

❹ Place the mushroom caps in the prepared pie plate. Place a bit of the remaining tablespoon of butter inside each mushroom cap. Mound some stuffing in the caps, pressing it in firmly with your fingers.

❺ Bake 45 minutes, or until the mushrooms are brown, tender, and juicy.

STUFFED MUSHROOMS WITH SPINACH, FETA CHEESE, AND PINE NUTS

I like to make these aromatic mushrooms bite size so they can be eaten easily with the fingers.

24 medium fresh mushrooms

1 10-ounce package frozen chopped spinach, thawed

⅓ cup crumbled feta cheese

1 tablespoon grated Parmesan cheese

3 tablespoons pine nuts

1½ tablespoons cold unsalted butter, cut into bits

Serves 4 to 6

❶ Preheat the oven to 375°F. Butter a shallow baking dish large enough to hold the mushrooms.

❷ Wipe the mushrooms clean with damp paper towels. Remove the stems and discard, or save for another use.

❸ With your hands, squeeze the spinach to remove all the moisture. When dry, place in a bowl, then stir in the feta and Parmesan cheeses. Set aside 24 of the pine nuts, then stir in the remainder.

❹ Stuff each mushroom with some of the spinach mixture. Press one pine nut into the top of each stuffed mushroom as a garnish. Press one bit of butter on top of each mushroom.

❺ Bake 30 minutes, or until brown and juicy. Serve warm.

CHEESE STRAWS

These delicate puff pastry twists pair perfectly with wine or cocktails and are equally suitable as a snack for an informal occasion. They are easy to prepare and can be made up to one week in advance. Try standing them upright in a pretty glass tumbler.

1 sheet (about ½ pound) frozen store-bought puff pastry

¼ cup grated Parmesan cheese

¼ teaspoon dry mustard

A few pinches cayenne pepper

Makes 4 dozen cheese straws

❶ Thaw the puff pastry at room temperature until thoroughly defrosted but still cold, about 30 minutes. Carefully unroll it. Mix the Parmesan cheese, mustard, and cayenne together, then sprinkle half of it over the top of the pastry. With a rolling pin, lightly roll the cheese into the surface (the pastry will stretch a bit). Turn the pastry over and repeat.

❷ Preheat the oven to 350°F. Cut the dough in half (each half will now be about 5½ inches long). Using a ruler as a guide, cut the pastry into ⅓-inch-wide strips. (You should have about 48 5½ × ⅓-inch strips.)

❸ Twist each strip lengthwise to create a slight spiral, then place it on a baking sheet. Press the ends onto the sheet to help hold the spiral in place. Repeat with the remaining strips.

❹ Bake 15 minutes, or until puffed and golden brown. (The straws should not be dark brown, but they must be cooked through.) Transfer to a rack and cool to room temperature. The straws can be stored in an airtight tin for up to 1 week, or refrigerated or frozen for a few weeks.

CHOPPED BLACK OLIVE SPREAD

(OLIVADA)

This dark, lusty spread makes a wonderful appetizer spooned on toasted French bread slices and served with a heady red wine. In this version I use two types of olives because I have found that the bland-tasting canned olives pair beautifully with the pungent oil-cured variety.

Try spreading a thin layer of Olivada on sandwich bread or a hard roll. Top with sliced tomato and Swiss cheese for a superlative sandwich.

4 ounces (about 1 cup) oil-cured black olives *(see Note)*

1 6-ounce can pitted black olives

2½ tablespoons olive oil

1 to 2 garlic cloves, pressed

Pinch each dried oregano, basil, rosemary, and thyme

Freshly ground black pepper to taste

Makes about 1 cup

❶ Pit the oil-cured olives one at a time by placing each on a cutting board and resting the flat side of a large knife on it. Thump the knife with the heel of your hand—the olive will split and the pit can be removed easily. When done, you should have a generous ½ cup of pulp.

❷ Drain the canned olives in a strainer and shake out all the liquid.

❸ Combine the olive oil and garlic in a blender or processor and process until smooth and creamy or cloudy in appearance.

❹ Add the olives and herbs and blend just until the mixture reaches a nice spreading consistency. The *Olivada* should not be perfectly smooth. (Turn off the machine and scrape down the sides as necessary if you're using a blender.) Scrape the paste into a serving bowl and season with black pepper. Let sit 20 minutes before serving, or cover and chill for up to 1 week. Bring to room temperature before using.

☞***Note:*** If oil-cured olives are unavailable, you can substitute a more assertive brine-cured variety such as Greek Kalamata olives.

MOLDED WHITE BEAN PÂTÉ

Pretty enough for entertaining and quick enough for a last-minute appetizer, this pâté has a wonderful blend of Mediterranean flavors.

2 15-ounce cans cannellini (white kidney) beans, rinsed and thoroughly drained

2 garlic cloves, pressed or minced

2 tablespoons olive oil

¾ teaspoon dried thyme

¼ teaspoon good-quality Hungarian paprika

½ teaspoon tamari soy sauce

Freshly ground black pepper to taste

2 tablespoons grated Parmesan cheese

2 tablespoons minced fresh parsley

Toasted French bread slices, or other toast

Serves 4 to 6

❶ Place the drained cannellini beans in a medium bowl and thoroughly mash them with a fork.

❷ Sauté the garlic in the olive oil just until lightly golden, about 30 seconds. Do not let it brown. Mix the garlic into the beans, along with all the other ingredients *except* 1 tablespoon parsley and the bread.

❸ Line a 1½-cup mold or bowl with wax paper. Scrape the pâté into it and press it down with the flat side of a knife. Cover with wax paper and chill at least 30 minutes. Unmold onto a plate and sprinkle on the remaining tablespoon of parsley, pressing it lightly into the pâté. Surround the pâté with the toast. (I like to let the pâté sit at room temperature for a while so that it's served cool, not cold.)

GREEN GODDESS DIP

This pretty, pale-green dip has a cottage cheese base, making it a low-calorie alternative to the traditional mayonnaise-laden version. When pureed in a blender or food processor, cottage cheese assumes a perfectly smooth texture that makes it ideal for dips. Serve this in an attractive bowl and surround it with a bright assortment of crudités such as carrots, celery, red peppers, and cauliflower.

1 cup cottage cheese

¼ cup milk

1 tablespoon fresh lemon juice

1 tablespoon mayonnaise

½ cup thinly sliced scallions (mostly green parts)

¼ cup finely chopped fresh parsley

Salt

Freshly ground black pepper

Fresh parsley sprig, for garnish

Makes 1⅓ cups

❶ Put the cottage cheese, milk, lemon juice, mayonnaise, scallions, and parsley in the container of a blender or food processor and blend until perfectly smooth. If you are using a blender, you will have to turn if off frequently and scrape down the sides.

❷ Scrape the dip into a serving bowl and season to taste with salt and pepper. Cover and chill at least 1 hour before serving, to allow the flavors to meld. Just before serving, stir the dip to smooth out the consistency. If the dip is too thick, stir in a few drops of milk. Serve garnished with the parsley sprig. The dip will keep 3 days in the refrigerator.

CREAMY CURRY DIP

A pale-yellow dip with a smooth cottage cheese base, this mildly spicy version looks pretty served in a contrasting bowl surrounded by colorful crudités.

1 cup cottage cheese

¼ cup milk

¼ cup sour cream

1 garlic clove, minced

½ teaspoon minced fresh ginger

1 teaspoon turmeric

¼ teaspoon ground cumin

¼ teaspoon ground coriander

½ teaspoon sugar

Makes 1½ cups

❶ Combine all of the ingredients in a blender or food processor and blend until perfectly smooth. Turn off the machine and scrape down the sides as necessary.

❷ Scrape the dip into a serving bowl. Cover and chill for 30 minutes before serving to allow the flavors to blend. This dip will keep, refrigerated, for up to 3 days.

SPICY PEANUT DIP

Peanuts have a natural affinity with spices, as many Asian and African cuisines attest. Try this feisty dip with a colorful assortment of raw vegetables surrounding it.

1 cup crunchy natural-style peanut butter

¾ cup water

2 tablespoons fresh lemon juice

1 teaspoon soy sauce

3 garlic cloves, minced

2 teaspoons minced fresh ginger

Dash cayenne pepper

Fresh parsley or cilantro sprig, for garnish

Makes 2 cups

❶ Combine all of the ingredients except the herb sprig in a large bowl and stir with a fork until blended. If the mixture is too thick, add ¼ cup water, or enough to create a good dipping consistency.

❷ Scrape the dip into a serving bowl, cover, and let sit at room temperature at least 30 minutes before serving. If you must chill the dip, bring it to room temperature before serving. (If it becomes very thick, thin it with a little more water.) Garnish with the parsley or coriander sprig. The peanut dip will keep in the refrigerator for 3 days.

☞***Variations:*** Leftover Spicy Peanut Dip is delicious served with steamed or sautéed mixed vegetables (or sliced, raw salad vegetables such as cucumber, crunchy lettuce, green pepper, onion, and tomato). Stuff them into pita bread halves, then pour the dip over them.

BEAN AND SALSA DIP

You can control the spiciness of this dip by using mild, medium, or hot salsa (I prefer hot). Hot pita triangles are my favorite accompaniment, but corn chips or your favorite crackers will also be delicious with this robust dip.

2 cups freshly cooked kidney beans (page 161), or 1 16-ounce can kidney beans, rinsed and drained

2 tablespoons olive oil

2 to 3 tablespoons water

4 tablespoons salsa

1 teaspoon chili powder

¼ teaspoon ground cumin

Fresh parsley or cilantro sprigs, for garnish

Hot pita triangles

Makes 1½ cups

❶ Combine the beans, oil, and 2 tablespoons of the water in a blender or food processor and blend until almost smooth. (You will have to turn off the machine and scrape down the sides a few times.) Add the remaining tablespoon water if necessary, but be careful not to thin the mixture too much; it should be somewhat like thick mashed potatoes.

❷ Scrape the mixture into a serving bowl and stir in 3 tablespoons of the salsa, the chili powder, and the cumin until well mixed. Spoon the remaining tablespoon salsa on top of the dip, and gently swirl it into the surface to make a decorative look. Cover and chill at least 1 hour to develop the flavors. Just before serving, garnish with the parsley or coriander sprigs. Serve on a platter and surround with hot pita triangles.

SOUPS

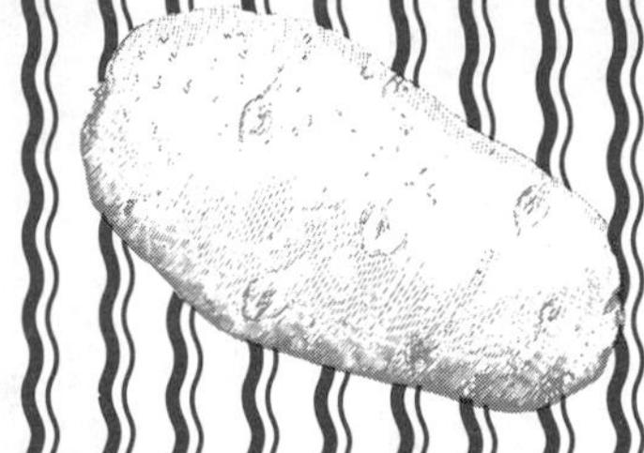

To my mind, a savory pot of homemade soup is a creation worthy of center stage. I often serve generous bowlfuls as a main course, accompanied by soup's natural mates: salad and bread. The soup, salad, and bread trio makes a wonderfully complete meal, both nutritionally and aesthetically (see Soup Meals, page 236).

For the busy cook, soup can be a godsend. All the recipes in this chapter can be doubled easily, and the extra portion can be refrigerated and served within a week. Freezing a batch of soup is another smart approach, one that you'll be thankful for when a hectic day comes along and you have no time at all to cook. The following soups freeze well: Curried Zucchini Soup (page 33), Mexican Vegetable Stew (page 35), Split Pea Soup (page 38), and Lentil Soup with Garlic (page 40). Undercook them slightly, cool completely before freezing for up to one month, and adjust the seasoning after thawing and reheating.

MUSHROOM SOUP WITH HERBS

This light version of mushroom soup is a luscious change from the more common cream of mushroom soup.

3 tablespoons unsalted butter

2 medium onions, finely chopped

2 garlic cloves, minced

1 pound (about 6 cups) thinly sliced fresh mushrooms

1 carrot, minced

1 celery rib, very thinly sliced

3 tablespoons unbleached flour

7 cups vegetable stock *(see Note)*

½ teaspoon salt

Freshly ground black pepper to taste

¾ cup heavy cream

2 tablespoons minced fresh chives

½ teaspoon minced fresh thyme, or ¼ teaspoon dried thyme

Dash cayenne pepper

3 tablespoons sherry

Serves 4 as a main course

❶ Melt the butter in a large stockpot over medium heat. Add the onions and garlic and sauté 10 minutes, or until very tender. Stir often.

❷ Raise the heat to medium-high. Stir in the mushrooms, carrot, and celery and cook until the mushrooms are tender and juicy, about 10 minutes.

❸ Sprinkle on the flour and stir to mix. Cook 2 minutes, stirring frequently. Stir in the vegetable stock, salt, and pepper and bring the soup to a boil, scraping the bottom of the pot with your spoon to remove any flour bits that have stuck. Cook 30 minutes at a lively simmer, stirring often. Remove 2 cups soup from the pot and puree in a blender or food processor, then return to the pot.

❹ Mix in the cream, chives, thyme, cayenne, and sherry. Bring to a boil again, then remove from the heat. Serve immediately, or reheat when ready to serve.

☛***Note:*** Vegetable stock can be made with powdered vegetable stock base, available at health food stores.

CURRIED ZUCCHINI SOUP

The base of this spicy soup has an almost satinlike consistency, with chunks of zucchini throughout. Its apparent richness belies the fact that it's very low in calories.

3 tablespoons vegetable oil

2 large onions, diced

2 garlic cloves, minced

1 teaspoon minced fresh ginger

1 teaspoon turmeric

1 teaspoon ground cumin

1 teaspoon ground coriander

Few dashes cayenne pepper

5 cups vegetable stock *(see Note,* page 32)

5 medium zucchini (about 2 pounds), quartered lengthwise and finely diced

½ teaspoon salt

Plain yogurt, for garnish

Serves 4 as a main course

❶ Heat the oil in a large stockpot over medium heat. Add the onions, garlic, and ginger and sauté 10 minutes, stirring often. Sprinkle on the turmeric, cumin, coriander, and cayenne and cook 2 minutes.

❷ Pour in the stock and bring to a boil. Add the zucchini and salt and cook, partially covered, 30 minutes, or until the zucchini is very tender. Remove the cover and let the soup cool 10 minutes.

❸ Puree half the soup in a blender or food processor, then return it to the pot. Reheat until hot, then serve in bowls with a generous spoonful of yogurt on each serving.

CURRY. The word kari in Tamil means sauce, but in the West we use the word curry as a catchall term to describe Indian food prepared with a mixture of spices. Many Westerners erroneously think curry powder is a spice in itself. Rather, it is a blend of between three and twenty spices, including turmeric, coriander seed, cumin seed, cayenne pepper, mustard seed, cardamom, ginger, black pepper, fennel seed, fenugreek, cloves, and cinnamon. Curry powder is not used in India; it is an item packaged for Western cooks. Indian cooks artfully combine many of the above spices in varying proportions to season each dish. On rare occasions I use curry powder to accent a simple dip or cream soup, but most often I toast a mélange of spices in oil or butter to achieve the multidimensional character for which Indian dishes are renowned.

The amount of cayenne pepper in a recipe determines how hot your curry will be. The heat can be adjusted easily to suit your taste. Start off with 1/8 teaspoon cayenne pepper, taste the finished dish, then sprinkle on more if needed.

MEXICAN VEGETABLE STEW

This fragrant stew, unlike most vegetable soups and stews, doesn't demand much chopping and so can be prepared quickly and easily. Like most soups, it tastes even better when served the next day, so don't hesitate to make it in advance. I like to sprinkle cheddar cheese and broken corn chips on top.

¼ cup olive oil

4 garlic cloves, minced

2 large onions, diced

1 teaspoon ground cumin

1 28-ounce can imported plum tomatoes (about 3 cups), roughly chopped, with their juice

8 cups vegetable stock *(see Note,* page 32)

½ teaspoon salt

Freshly ground black pepper to taste

2 carrots, thinly sliced

3 medium zucchini, cut lengthwise into sixths, then into 1-inch chunks

2 cups freshly cooked kidney beans (page 161), or 1 15-ounce can kidney beans, rinsed and drained

2 cups fresh or frozen corn kernels

Grated cheddar cheese (optional)

Corn chips (optional)

Serves 4 as a main course

❶ In a 6- to 8-quart pot, heat the olive oil over medium heat. Sauté the garlic, onions, and cumin 10 minutes, stirring often.

❷ Add the tomatoes with their juice, the vegetable stock, salt, and pepper and bring to a boil.

❸ Add the carrots and cook 15 minutes, then add the zucchini and cook 5 to 10 minutes, or until the zucchini is tender, not mushy.

❹ Add the kidney beans and corn and cook 2 minutes. Remove 2 cups of the stew, puree it in the blender or food processor, then return it to the pot. This will nicely thicken the stew. Taste to adjust the seasoning. If desired, sprinkle on grated cheese and break a few corn chips over each serving.

CHILLED AVOCADO SOUP

Here is a creamy, delicious soup for avocado lovers. It is the quickest soup I know of — particularly wonderful on a hot summer day because it doesn't require any cooking.

1 medium ripe Haas avocado (black pebble-skinned variety)

2 cups buttermilk

2 tablespoons lemon juice

½ teaspoon salt

Few dashes cayenne pepper

1 medium tomato, seeded and finely diced

1 small scallion, very thinly sliced

Serves 4 as a first course

❶ Cut the avocado in half lengthwise and discard the pit. Insert the handle of a teaspoon between the flesh and the skin and move it around until the flesh is released from the skin.

❷ Combine the avocado flesh, buttermilk, lemon juice, salt, and cayenne in a blender or food processor and puree until smooth. Pour into a medium bowl.

❸ Set aside about a tablespoon each of the tomato and scallion. Stir the remaining tomato and scallion into the soup. Cover the bowl and chill at least 1 hour before serving.

❹ Serve with some of the reserved tomato and scallions topping each serving.

CURRIED BARLEY AND MUSHROOM SOUP

If you prefer this soup only slightly spicy, reduce the amount of cayenne to a few dashes.

- 3 tablespoons vegetable oil
- 2 medium onions, diced
- 2 garlic cloves, minced
- 2 teaspoons minced fresh ginger
- 12 ounces (about 4½ cups) chopped mushrooms
- 2 teaspoons ground coriander
- 1½ teaspoons ground cumin
- 1 teaspoon turmeric
- ½ teaspoon ground cardamom
- ⅛ teaspoon cayenne pepper
- 1 bay leaf
- Freshly ground black pepper to taste
- 1 cup uncooked barley
- 8 cups water
- 1 teaspoon salt
- 1 tablespoon tamari soy sauce
- 1 tablespoon unsalted butter
- 2 egg yolks
- ½ cup milk
- Minced fresh chives, scallions, parsley, or cilantro

Serves 4 as a main course

❶ Heat the oil in a large stockpot over medium heat. Sauté the onions, garlic, and ginger 3 minutes. Add the mushrooms and sauté 5 minutes.

❷ Sprinkle in the spices and the bay leaf and mix well. Cook 1 minute, stirring often. Add the barley and cook another 2 minutes, stirring all the while. Add the water, salt, and tamari, then cover the pot. Cook the soup at a lively simmer 1 hour, or until the barley is tender. Discard the bay leaf.

❸ Remove the pot from the heat, then swirl in the butter. Mix the egg yolks with the milk, then slowly stir the mixture into the soup *(see Note)*. Serve immediately, garnished with your choice of herbs.

☞***Note:*** If you want to prepare this soup in advance, add the yolk mixture just before serving. The soup can be reheated once it has been thickened with the yolks, but it must not boil.

SPLIT PEA SOUP

Cumin lends a delicious nuance to this delectable soup. However, you can omit it and still have a full-flavored soup.

2 cups (1 pound) green split peas

10 cups water

2 bay leaves

3 tablespoons olive oil

3 medium onions, finely diced

3 garlic cloves, minced

2 teaspoons ground cumin

2 celery ribs, finely diced

3 carrots, finely diced

2 tablespoons tamari soy sauce

Freshly ground black pepper to taste

Salt

2 tablespoons unsalted butter

Serves 4 as a main course

❶ In a large stockpot, combine the split peas, water, bay leaves, and 1 tablespoon of the olive oil. Cover the pot, bring to a boil (watch for overflowing foam), then reduce the heat to a lively simmer. Cook 1 hour, stirring occasionally.

❷ Meanwhile, heat the remaining 2 tablespoons olive oil in a medium skillet. Add the onions and garlic and sauté 10 minutes, or until tender. Stir in the cumin and cook, stirring frequently, 2 additional minutes.

❸ After the peas have cooked 1 hour, stir in the onion mixture and all of the remaining ingredients except the butter. Cook, uncovered, an additional 30 to 35 minutes, or until the soup has a somewhat smooth consistency and the vegetables are tender. Be aware that the soup will thicken in each serving bowl as it cools, so don't let it get too thick. Remove the bay leaves. Just before serving, taste for salt, then stir in the butter.

SPINACH SOUP WITH SEMOLINA CHEESE DUMPLINGS

The most widely available semolina is packaged farina, easily found in supermarkets.

DUMPLINGS

1 cup milk

2 tablespoons unsalted butter

½ cup semolina (farina)

3 tablespoons grated Parmesan cheese

¼ teaspoon freshly grated nutmeg

½ teaspoon salt

1 egg, beaten

SOUP

3 tablespoons olive oil

2 medium onions, finely diced

10 cups vegetable stock *(see Note,* page 32)

1 pound loose fresh spinach (stems removed), finely chopped, *or* 1 10-ounce package frozen chopped spinach, thawed and squeezed dry

1 teaspoon salt

Freshly ground black pepper to taste

1 tablespoon unsalted butter

Grated Parmesan cheese

Serves 4 as a main course

❶ To make the dumplings: In a medium saucepan bring the milk and butter to a boil. Lower the heat to simmer, then slowly sprinkle in the semolina, stirring all the while with a wire whisk. Whisk in the Parmesan cheese, nutmeg, and salt and cook just until the mixture begins to clump, about 2 minutes. Remove from the heat and whisk in the egg. Scrape the mixture into a medium bowl, cover, and chill at least 2 hours or overnight.

❷ To make the soup: Heat the olive oil in a large stockpot and sauté the onions until very tender, about 10 minutes. Add the stock and bring to a boil.

❸ Meanwhile, form the dumplings into compact ½-inch balls by squeezing some of the chilled dough between your hands, then rolling it between your palms. You should have about 20 dumplings. Set aside on a platter.

❹ Add the chopped spinach to the boiling stock. When the soup returns to a boil, drop in the dumplings. Cover the pot and cook 15 minutes. Remove the cover and stir in the salt, pepper, and butter. Serve with Parmesan cheese sprinkled over each bowl.

LENTIL SOUP WITH GARLIC

This is my sister-in-law Beth's memorable version of lentil soup. Its deep, lingering flavor soothes the soul.

¼ cup olive oil

4 garlic cloves, minced

3 large onions, diced

7½ cups water

1 cup lentils, picked over and rinsed

4 carrots, thinly sliced

3 celery ribs, thinly sliced

¼ cup tomato paste mixed with ½ cup water

1 tablespoon tamari soy sauce

½ teaspoon salt

Freshly ground black pepper to taste

2 tablespoons unsalted butter

Serves 4 as a main course

❶ Heat the olive oil in a large stockpot over medium heat. Add the garlic and onions and sauté 10 minutes, or until the onions are very soft and begin to brown. Stir often.

❷ Add all of the remaining ingredients except the butter. Raise the heat and bring the soup to a boil, stirring often. Reduce the heat to simmer and cook 45 minutes, or until the carrots are very tender and the soup has thickened.

❸ Just before serving, add the butter and stir until melted.

BILLIE'S FRESH PEA SOUP

My friend Billie Chernicoff, a highly inventive cook, created this soup. The use of sweet peas rather than dried, split peas lends this soup a special flavor. Mint and lemon also give it a refreshing spring accent, although it can be made during any season.

3 tablespoons olive oil

2 medium onions, diced

2 garlic cloves, minced

5 cups vegetable stock *(see Note,* page 32)

1 large potato, peeled and diced

6 cups (3 10-ounce packages) frozen peas

⅛ teaspoon cayenne pepper

½ teaspoon salt

Juice of ½ lemon

½ cup heavy cream

1 teaspoon minced fresh dill

1 tablespoon minced fresh mint

Additional fresh dill or mint, for garnish

Serves 4 as a main course

❶ Combine the olive oil, onions, and garlic in a large stockpot and sauté over medium heat until the onions begin to get tender, about 10 minutes.

❷ Pour in the vegetable stock, add the potatoes, then bring to a boil. Reduce the heat to simmer and cook until the potatoes are tender, about 20 minutes.

❸ Stir in the peas, cayenne, and salt and cook 5 minutes more. Remove 1 cup of the soup and set aside. Let the rest of the soup cool a bit, then puree in batches until perfectly smooth. Return the pureed soup to the pot, then stir in the reserved cup of soup, lemon juice, cream, dill, and mint. Reheat until piping hot but not boiling. Serve garnished with mint or dill.

CORN CHOWDER

Scallions greatly enhance the flavor of this thick soup, so be certain to include them. Making the soup a few hours in advance will allow the flavors to meld.

1 tablespoon unsalted butter

2 tablespoons olive oil

2 medium onions, finely diced

2 garlic cloves, minced

1 teaspoon good-quality sweet paprika

4 cups vegetable stock *(see Note,* page 32)

2 large potatoes, peeled and finely diced (about 2½ cups)

1 celery rib, very thinly sliced

1 bay leaf

½ teaspoon salt

1 teaspoon sugar

Freshly ground black pepper to taste

4 cups frozen corn kernels

5 scallions, very thinly sliced

1 cup milk

¼ teaspoon dried thyme

Few dashes cayenne pepper

¼ cup sour cream

Serves 4 as a main course

❶ In a large stockpot, combine the butter, olive oil, onions, and garlic and sauté over medium heat until the onions are tender but not brown, about 10 minutes. Sprinkle on the paprika, toss, and cook 1 minute.

❷ Add the stock, potatoes, celery, bay leaf, salt, sugar, and pepper. Cook, partially covered, until the potatoes are tender, about 15 minutes. Stir in the corn and scallions, and cook 2 minutes more. Remove the bay leaf.

❸ Scoop out 2 cups of the chowder and set it aside. Puree the remainder and return it to the pot. Stir in the reserved chowder, the milk, thyme, and cayenne pepper. Cook 5 minutes more. Serve in bowls with a spoonful of sour cream on top.

BREADS, MUFFINS, ETC.

No matter how delicious the bread at the corner bakery, there is nothing quite so satisfying as a loaf of homemade bread or a batch of warm, fragrant muffins fresh from the oven. The kitchen abounds with inviting aromas, conveying a delightful feeling of comfort.

For the cook who is pressed for time, bread baking can be quick and simple if quick leavenings such as baking powder and baking soda are used instead of yeast. Quick breads don't always have to be sweet, although the popular zucchini, pumpkin, or banana breads are great served for breakfast, snacks, or teatime. Savory breads such as Herb Oat Bread (page 48), Jalapeño Cheddar Soda Bread (page 54), Irish Brown Bread (page 53), and Rich Cream Cheese Biscuits (page 59) make wonderful accompaniments to steaming bowls of homemade soup and fresh, colorful salads.

When I'm busy but want to make bread, scones, or muffins, I approach the recipe in stages.

First I prepare the pan, at some other time I combine the dry ingredients, and later on I mix together the wet ingredients. When I'm ready to bake, I preheat the oven. About twenty minutes later I combine the wet and dry ingredients, then pop the batter into the oven. When approached in this way, bread baking is a breeze.

WHOLE WHEAT MOLASSES BREAD

Spread softened butter on this ultraquick, nutritious bread and serve it for breakfast or tea, or alongside soup for supper. This is also a good choice for parents seeking a wholesome snack for their kids.

2 cups whole wheat flour

1½ teaspoons baking powder

½ teaspoon baking soda

1½ teaspoons caraway seeds (optional)

¾ teaspoon salt

1 large egg

1 cup buttermilk, or plain low-fat yogurt

½ cup molasses

¼ cup vegetable oil

Makes one 9 × 5-inch loaf

❶ Preheat the oven to 350°F., then butter a 9 × 5-inch (1½-quart) loaf pan.

❷ In a large bowl, thoroughly combine the flour, baking powder, baking soda, caraway seeds, and salt.

❸ In a medium bowl, beat the egg, then beat in the buttermilk or yogurt, molasses, and oil. Scrape this into the flour mixture and stir just until combined.

❹ Pour the batter into the prepared loaf pan and bake 40 minutes, or until a knife inserted in the center of the loaf comes out dry. Cool on a rack 10 minutes, then remove the loaf from the pan and cool at least 1 hour before slicing.

HERB OAT BREAD

1¼ cups rolled oats
1 cup unbleached flour
¼ cup whole wheat flour
2 teaspoons baking powder
½ teaspoon baking soda
¾ teaspoon salt
½ teaspoon dried basil
½ teaspoon dried oregano
½ teaspoon dried dill
⅛ teaspoon crumbled dried rosemary
¼ cup vegetable oil
¼ cup honey
1¼ cups plain low-fat yogurt
2 large eggs, beaten

Makes one 9×5-inch loaf

❶ Preheat the oven to 375°F. Butter and flour a 9×5-inch (1½-quart) loaf pan.

❷ Place the oats in a blender or food processor and grind until almost powdery. Pour into a large bowl and mix in the flours, baking powder, baking soda, salt, and herbs.

❸ In a small saucepan, combine the oil and the honey and heat just until blended. Remove from the heat and stir in the yogurt and beaten eggs.

❹ Pour into the flour mixture and stir just until evenly moistened. Do not overbeat. Scrape into the prepared pan.

❺ Bake 40 minutes, or until a knife inserted in the center of the bread comes out clean. (If the top of the bread begins to darken before it finishes cooking, lay a sheet of foil over the top of the pan and bake until done.) Cool on a wire rack 10 minutes before removing from the pan. Cool completely before slicing.

☛***Variations:*** A great gift idea is to bake this bread 25 minutes in 3 5×3×2-inch baby loaf pans (disposable aluminum ones work well). Cool thoroughly when done, and wrap individually. To make Sage Onion Bread, substitute ¼ teaspoon powdered sage and ¼ cup fresh minced onion instead of the basil, dill, and rosemary.

MUFFIN AND QUICK-BREAD TIPS

☛ Preheat your oven for at least fifteen minutes to be certain it is hot enough. A hot oven ensures high rising.

☛ Generously butter your loaf pan. Butter the insides *and* the top of your muffin pan.

☛ Mix dry ingredients thoroughly, then mix wet ingredients thoroughly. Combine just until evenly moistened. Don't overbeat.

☛ You can't make muffin or quick-bread batter ahead of time because once the leavening (baking powder or baking soda) begins to work—which is almost instantly upon the addition of a liquid—the batter must be baked immediately. But you can do a few steps in advance: butter the pan; mix all of the dry ingredients in one bowl and the wet ingredients in another, keeping them separate. Just be certain not to let the leavening come in contact with the wet ingredients until you are ready to bake.

☛ Although bread, muffins, scones, and biscuits always taste best when fresh, they can be frozen with good results. After they have cooled completely, wrap them in aluminum foil, then place in a plastic bag. Freeze for up to one month. Defrost at room temperature.

ZUCCHINI BRAN BREAD

A moist and not-too-sweet version of zucchini bread with added bran. Freeze one of the loaves for a future treat.

3 large eggs

1½ cups sugar

1 tablespoon vanilla extract

1 cup vegetable oil

4 cups (about 2 large) grated zucchini

2 cups unbleached flour

½ cup whole wheat flour

½ cup bran

1 teaspoon baking powder

1 teaspoon baking soda

1 teaspoon salt

2 teaspoons cinnamon

1 cup finely chopped walnuts

Makes two 9×5-inch loaves

❶ Preheat the oven to 350°F. Butter and flour 2 9×5-inch (1½-quart) loaf pans.

❷ In a large bowl, beat the eggs and sugar until light and fluffy. Beat in the vanilla and the oil, then stir in the zucchini.

❸ In a medium bowl, thoroughly combine the remaining ingredients. Stir into the zucchini mixture just until evenly moistened. Scrape into the prepared pans. Bake 50 minutes, or until a knife inserted in the center of a loaf comes out clean. Let sit 5 minutes before turning out onto a wire rack. Cool completely before slicing.

OATMEAL RAISIN BREAD

This moist and buttery bread is excellent spread with cream cheese and served either open faced or made into bite-size sandwiches.

1½ cups rolled oats

1 cup unbleached flour

2 teaspoons baking powder

½ teaspoon baking soda

1 teaspoon cinnamon

¾ teaspoon salt

1 cup raisins

¼ cup vegetable oil

⅓ cup honey

1¼ cups buttermilk, or plain low-fat yogurt

2 large eggs, beaten

Makes one 9 × 5-inch loaf

❶ Preheat the oven to 375°F. Butter and flour a 9 × 5-inch (1½-quart) loaf pan.

❷ Grind the oats in a blender or food processor until almost powdery. Pour into a large bowl and thoroughly mix in the flour, baking powder, baking soda, cinnamon, and salt. Stir in the raisins.

❸ Combine the oil and honey in a small saucepan and heat until just blended. Stir in the buttermilk or yogurt and the beaten eggs, then pour into the flour mixture and stir until just blended. Do not overmix. Scrape into the prepared pan.

❹ Bake 45 to 50 minutes, or until a knife inserted in the center comes out clean. (If the bread begins to get too brown before it has finished cooking, lay a sheet of foil over the top of the pan and continue baking.) Cool on a wire rack 10 minutes, then slide a knife around the periphery of the bread and slip it out of the pan. Cool at least 1½ hours before slicing.

APPLE BREAD

Almond extract gives this bread a wonderful accent without overpowering the fresh taste of the apples.

- **1½ cups unbleached flour**
- **½ cup whole wheat flour**
- **1 teaspoon baking powder**
- **1 teaspoon baking soda**
- **½ teaspoon salt**
- **2 large eggs**
- **½ cup vegetable oil**
- **⅔ cup firmly packed light brown sugar**
- **½ cup orange juice**
- **¾ teaspoon almond extract**
- **⅔ cup raisins**
- **2 cups finely chopped peeled apple (about 3 apples)**

Makes one 9×5-inch loaf

❶ Preheat the oven to 350°F. Butter and flour a 9×5-inch (1½-quart) loaf pan. In a medium bowl, thoroughly combine the flours, baking powder, baking soda, and salt.

❷ Beat the eggs in a large bowl, then beat in the oil, brown sugar, orange juice, and almond extract.

❸ Stir in the flour mixture, then mix in the raisins and apples until evenly coated. Scrape into the prepared pan. Bake 70 minutes, or until a knife inserted in the center of the loaf comes out clean. (If the bread begins to get dark on top before it has finished cooking, place a sheet of foil over it and continue baking.) Let cool on a rack 10 minutes before removing from the pan. Cool completely before slicing, about 2 hours.

IRISH BROWN BREAD

In Ireland, brown bread is made with a unique whole meal flour that is unmatched in this country for both its flavor and texture. I have discovered that a combination of oats, wheat germ, and whole wheat flour produces an almost identical loaf that is as hauntingly good.

1¼ cups unbleached flour, plus additional for sprinkling

1 cup whole wheat flour

½ cup rolled oats

¼ cup toasted wheat germ

1½ teaspoons baking soda

¾ teaspoon salt

4 tablespoons cold unsalted butter

1⅓ cups buttermilk, or plain low-fat yogurt

Makes one 7-inch round loaf

❶ Preheat the oven to 425°F. Lightly dust a baking sheet with flour and set it aside.

❷ In a large bowl, very thoroughly mix together the flours, oats, wheat germ, baking soda, and salt.

❸ Cut the butter into bits, then rub it into the flour mixture with your fingertips until it is evenly incorporated.

❹ Stir in the buttermilk or yogurt until blended, then turn the dough onto a lightly floured surface and knead for 1 minute. Sprinkle on more flour as necessary to prevent sticking, but let the dough remain soft.

❺ Roll the dough into a ball, then flatten into a 7-inch circle. Sprinkle some unbleached flour on top of the circle, then lightly spread it around with your hand. With a sharp knife cut a shallow X on top. Bake 30 minutes, then cool on a wire rack at least 2 hours before slicing.

JALAPEÑO CHEDDAR SODA BREAD

A delicate, buttery texture and hint of spiciness make this bread absolutely delicious.

2¼ cups unbleached flour

¼ cup whole wheat flour

1 teaspoon baking soda

1 teaspoon baking powder

¾ teaspoon salt

4 tablespoons cold unsalted butter, cut into bits

2 cups grated extra-sharp cheddar cheese

4 fresh or canned jalapeño peppers, seeded and minced *(see Note)*

1 large egg, beaten

1¼ cups buttermilk, *or* plain low-fat yogurt

Makes one 7-inch round loaf

❶ Preheat the oven to 400°F. Rub a little flour into an 8-inch circle on a baking pan and set aside.

❷ In a large bowl, thoroughly combine the flours, baking soda, baking powder, and salt. Drop in the butter bits, and rub them into the flour mixture with your fingertips until coarse crumbs are formed.

❸ Stir in the cheese and jalapeño peppers until evenly distributed. Combine the egg with the yogurt and stir it into the mixture until just evenly moistened.

❹ Scrape the dough onto a lightly floured surface and knead for 1 minute, or until the dough is just smooth and pliable. Pat it into a 7-inch circle, then place on the floured baking sheet. Cut a shallow X in the top.

❺ Bake 35 minutes, or until golden brown. For best results, let cool about 1 hour and serve warm.

☛ ***Note:*** Wear rubber gloves when handling hot peppers so that the volatile oils don't get on your fingers and later come into contact with your eyes. Jalapeños burn!

IRISH GOLDEN RAISIN BREAD

Golden raisins impart a special flavor to this raisin-filled version of Irish soda bread.

2 cups unbleached flour, plus extra for sprinkling

¼ cup bran or toasted wheat germ

1 teaspoon baking soda

½ teaspoon salt

4 tablespoons cold unsalted butter

1 cup golden raisins

1 cup buttermilk, *or* plain low-fat yogurt

Makes one 6-inch round loaf

❶ Preheat the oven to 400°F. Lightly sprinkle some flour on a baking sheet and rub it into an 8-inch circle.

❷ In a large bowl, mix together the flour, bran or wheat germ, baking soda, and salt. Cut the butter into bits, letting it drop into the flour. Stir in the butter to coat it, then rub it into the flour mixture with your fingertips until it is the consistency of coarse meal.

❸ Toss in the raisins and thoroughly coat them with flour. Stir in the buttermilk or yogurt and mix until incorporated. Turn the dough onto a lightly floured surface and knead for a full 1 minute, sprinkling on more flour as necessary to prevent sticking.

❹ Shape the dough into a ball, then flatten it into a 6-inch circle. Place on the floured baking sheet and sprinkle on a teaspoon or so of flour, spreading it evenly over the top. Cut a shallow X on top of the dough. Bake 35 minutes, or until the bread is a rich golden brown.

❺ Wrap the bread in a cotton kitchen towel (this softens the crust) and let cool 1 hour. Unwrap the loaf and continue to cool on a wire rack. This bread is best if allowed to sit for a few hours before slicing.

APPLESAUCE OATMEAL BREAD

Oatmeal is the source of this bread's intriguing nubby texture.

1½ cups rolled oats

1¼ cups unbleached flour

1 teaspoon baking powder

¾ teaspoon baking soda

½ teaspoon cinnamon

½ teaspoon freshly grated nutmeg

⅔ teaspoon salt

⅔ cup raisins

2 large eggs

½ cup firmly packed light brown sugar

¼ cup vegetable oil

1 cup applesauce

Makes one 9×5-inch loaf

❶ Preheat the oven to 350°F. Butter and flour a 9×5-inch (1½-quart) loaf pan.

❷ In a large bowl, thoroughly combine the oats, flour, baking powder, baking soda, cinnamon, nutmeg, salt, and raisins.

❸ In a medium bowl, beat the eggs. Beat in the brown sugar, oil, and applesauce. Pour this into the oat mixture and stir until just evenly moistened. Scrape into the prepared loaf pan.

❹ Bake 50 minutes, or until a knife inserted in the center of the loaf comes out dry. Let sit 5 minutes, then remove from the pan and cool completely on a wire rack, at least 2 hours.

PUMPKIN BREAD WITH STREUSEL TOPPING

Freeze one of these loaves for a ready-made breakfast or snack.

½ cup vegetable oil

¾ cup sugar

¾ cup firmly packed light brown sugar

3 large eggs

1 teaspoon vanilla extract

1 15- to 16-ounce can solid-packed pumpkin

2½ cups unbleached flour

1½ teaspoons baking powder

1½ teaspoons baking soda

¾ teaspoon salt

1½ teaspoons cinnamon

½ teaspoon freshly grated nutmeg

1 cup finely chopped walnuts or pecans

⅔ cup raisins

STREUSEL TOPPING

⅓ cup unbleached flour

⅓ cup sugar

4 tablespoons cold unsalted butter, cut into bits

Makes two 9 × 5-inch loaves

❶ Preheat the oven to 350°F. Butter and flour two 9 × 5-inch (1½-quart) loaf pans.

❷ In a large bowl, beat together the oil, sugars, eggs, and vanilla using an electric mixer. Beat in the pumpkin until thoroughly blended. Beat in the remaining bread ingredients until evenly moistened. Scrape into the prepared pans.

❸ To make the topping: Combine the flour and sugar in a small bowl. With your fingers, rub the butter into the flour mixture until coarse crumbs are formed. Sprinkle the crumbs on top of each loaf. Bake 50 to 55 minutes, or until a knife inserted in the center of a loaf comes out clean. Cool on a wire rack 10 minutes before removing from the pans. Cool thoroughly before slicing.

BANANA DATE BREAD

A favorite in our house, this dark, gutsy banana bread filled with dates and walnuts is delicious plain or slathered with cream cheese.

1 cup whole wheat flour

1 cup unbleached flour

1 teaspoon baking soda

½ teaspoon baking powder

¼ teaspoon salt

½ teaspoon cinnamon

¼ teaspoon ground cloves

¼ teaspoon freshly grated nutmeg

1 cup chopped pitted dates

1 cup finely chopped walnuts

½ cup vegetable oil

½ cup honey

2 large eggs

1 cup mashed banana (about 3 small bananas)

1 teaspoon vanilla extract

Makes one 9×5-inch loaf

❶ Preheat the oven to 350°F. Butter and flour a 9×5-inch (1½-quart) loaf pan.

❷ In a large bowl thoroughly combine the flours, baking soda, baking powder, salt, cinnamon, cloves, and nutmeg. Stir in the dates and walnuts.

❸ In a medium bowl, beat the oil and honey together until smooth. Beat in the eggs, banana, and vanilla until well mixed. Pour into the flour mixture and stir just until evenly moistened. Scrape the batter into the prepared loaf pan.

❹ Bake 60 to 70 minutes, or until a knife inserted in the center of the loaf comes out clean. (If the loaf begins to get too dark before it has finished cooking, lay a sheet of aluminum foil over the top and continue baking.) Let stand on a wire rack 10 minutes before removing from the pan. Cool completely before slicing, about 2 hours.

RICH CREAM CHEESE BISCUITS

Buttery, flaky, and unforgettable — everything you could want in a biscuit.

1¾ cups unbleached flour

¼ cup whole wheat flour

1 tablespoon baking powder

½ teaspoon salt

4 tablespoons cold unsalted butter

2 tablespoons cold cream cheese

1 large egg, beaten

¾ cup milk

Makes 12 biscuits

❶ In a large bowl combine the flours, baking powder, and salt and mix very well. Cut the butter and cream cheese into bits and mix into the flour mixture to coat. With a pastry cutter or your fingers, rub the bits into the flour until coarse crumbs are formed.

❷ Stir in the beaten egg with a fork, then slowly pour in the milk, stirring all the while. Let the dough sit for 1 minute to absorb the liquid.

❸ Turn the dough onto a slightly floured surface and knead 5 or 6 times to make it pliable.

❹ Pat the dough into a round or oblong shape ½ to ¾ inch thick (measure it). With a 2½-inch biscuit cutter or cup, cut out the biscuits and place them, with edges touching, on an ungreased cookie sheet. You should have about 12 biscuits.

❺ Preheat the oven to 375°F. Place the cookie sheet in the freezer for 10 minutes, or in the refrigerator for at least 15 minutes and up to 4 hours before baking. (Cold biscuits in a hot oven ensure flakiness.) Bake 20 to 25 minutes, or until lightly golden. Serve immediately.

CHEESE SCONES

Cheese inside and out accounts for the sharp flavor of these Scottish "biscuits."

1¾ cups unbleached flour

¼ cup whole wheat flour

2 teaspoons baking powder

1 teaspoon dry mustard

¼ teaspoon salt

Dash cayenne pepper

3 tablespoons cold unsalted butter

1 cup grated extra-sharp cheddar cheese

1 large egg, beaten

½ cup milk, plus extra for brushing

Makes 8 large scones

❶ Preheat the oven to 400°F. Lightly butter a baking sheet.

❷ In a large bowl, thoroughly combine the flours, baking powder, mustard, salt, and cayenne. Cut the butter into bits and rub it into the mixture until it resembles coarse crumbs.

❸ Stir in all but 2 tablespoons of the grated cheese. Mix the egg with the milk and stir in until just evenly moistened.

❹ Turn the dough onto a lightly floured surface, and knead a few times, or just until pliable. Pat into a ½-inch-thick circle and cut the circle into 8 triangles. Place the scones on the baking sheet. Brush the tops lightly with some milk, then sprinkle on the reserved cheese.

❺ Bake 17 minutes, or until golden brown. Serve warm, not hot.

ORANGE CURRANT SCONES

These scones are incredibly delicate and flavorful. Try them with a steamy pot of Earl Grey tea.

1¾ cups unbleached flour

¼ cup whole wheat flour

2 tablespoons sugar

1½ teaspoons baking powder

½ teaspoon baking soda

¼ teaspoon salt

4 tablespoons cold unsalted butter

½ cup currants

1 large egg

Grated rind of 1 orange

⅔ cup buttermilk, *or* plain low-fat yogurt

Milk for brushing on tops

Makes 10 scones

❶ Preheat the oven to 400°F. Lightly butter a baking sheet.

❷ In a large bowl, combine the flours, sugar, baking powder, baking soda, and salt. Cut the butter into bits and with your fingertips work it into the mixture until it resembles coarse meal. Stir in the currants.

❸ Beat the eggs with the orange rind. Beat in the buttermilk or yogurt. Stir this into the flour mixture just until evenly moistened.

❹ Turn the dough onto a lightly floured surface and knead a few seconds. Pat it into a circle ¾ inch thick. With a 2½-inch biscuit cutter, form the scones. Place them on the prepared baking sheet and lightly brush the tops with some milk.

❺ Bake 15 minutes, or until the scones are a rich golden brown. Serve warm.

APPLESAUCE WHEAT GERM MUFFINS

These are big, fat, impressive muffins, exceptionally moist and light.

1½ cups unbleached flour
1 cup toasted wheat germ
2 teaspoons baking powder
½ teaspoon baking soda
¾ teaspoon salt
1 teaspoon cinnamon
¼ teaspoon freshly grated nutmeg
½ cup raisins
1 large egg
½ cup firmly packed light brown sugar
⅓ cup vegetable oil
1 cup applesauce
½ cup milk

TOPPING

2 teaspoons sugar
¼ teaspoon cinnamon

Makes 12 muffins

❶ Preheat the oven to 425°F. Generously butter the insides and top of a regular-size (⅓-cup) muffin pan.

❷ In a large bowl, thoroughly combine the flour, wheat germ, baking powder, baking soda, salt, cinnamon, nutmeg, and raisins.

❸ In a medium bowl, beat the egg, then beat in the brown sugar, oil, applesauce, and milk. Mix with the dry ingredients just until evenly moistened. Spoon the batter into the muffin cups.

❹ For the topping, combine the sugar and cinnamon, and sprinkle on top of each muffin.

❺ Bake 17 minutes, or until a knife inserted in the center of a muffin comes out clean. Let sit a few minutes before removing from pan. Serve warm, not hot.

CHEDDAR CORN MUFFINS

These are light and moist, with a mild but irresistible cheese accent. They are equally good served for breakfast or with chili. If you want a more traditional corn muffin, just leave out the cheese.

1 cup unbleached flour

1 cup yellow cornmeal

1 tablespoon baking powder

½ teaspoon salt

¼ cup sugar

1 large egg

1 cup milk

4 tablespoons unsalted butter, melted

1¼ cups grated extra-sharp cheddar cheese

Makes 12 muffins

❶ Preheat the oven to 425°F. Butter the insides and the top of a regular-size (⅓-cup) muffin pan.

❷ In a large bowl, thoroughly combine the flour, cornmeal, baking powder, salt, and sugar.

❸ In a medium bowl, beat the egg. Beat in the milk, and the melted butter. Combine with the dry ingredients until just evenly moistened. Do not overmix. Stir in 1 cup of the cheese.

❹ Immediately spoon the batter into the muffin cups. Evenly sprinkle the remaining ¼ cup of cheese on top of the muffins.

❺ Bake 17 minutes, or until a knife inserted in the center of a muffin comes out clean. Serve hot or warm.

CARROT BRAN MUFFINS

These bran muffins are grainy but light and have just the right amount of molasses to make their flavor deep but not overbearing. Grated carrots add flavor and texture.

1½ cups bran

1½ cups whole wheat pastry flour, or ¾ cup whole wheat flour plus ¾ cup unbleached white flour

2 teaspoons baking powder

¼ teaspoon cinnamon

½ teaspoon salt

⅔ cup raisins

2 medium carrots, grated

1 large egg

⅓ cup vegetable oil

½ cup unsulphured molasses

⅓ cup honey

¾ cup milk

Makes 12 muffins

❶ Preheat the oven to 400°F. Generously butter the insides and top of a regular-size (⅓-cup) muffin pan.

❷ In a large bowl, combine the bran, flour, baking powder, cinnamon, and salt and mix very well. Stir in the raisins and carrots to coat evenly.

❸ Beat the egg in a medium bowl, then beat in the oil, molasses, honey, and milk. Combine with the dry ingredients until just evenly moistened. Do not overstir.

❹ Spoon the batter into the prepared muffin pan and bake 17 minutes, or until a knife inserted in the center of a muffin comes out clean. Cool 5 minutes before removing from pan.

OATMEAL MUFFINS

The irresistible brown sugar–oatmeal flavor of these muffins is heightened by the crunchy topping. A favorite with children.

1¼ cups rolled oats

1¼ cups buttermilk, *or* plain low-fat yogurt

1 cup unbleached flour

1½ teaspoons baking powder

½ teaspoon baking soda

½ teaspoon cinnamon

½ teaspoon salt

½ cup raisins

1 large egg

½ cup firmly packed light brown sugar

5 tablespoons unsalted butter, melted

TOPPING

1 tablespoon unsalted butter, melted

1 tablespoon firmly packed light brown sugar

¼ cup rolled oats

⅛ teaspoon cinnamon

Makes 12 muffins

❶ Preheat the oven to 400°F. In a large bowl, beat together the oats and buttermilk or yogurt, and let sit 15 minutes. Meanwhile, butter the insides and top of a regular-size (⅓-cup) muffin pan.

❷ In a small bowl, thoroughly combine the flour, baking powder, baking soda, cinnamon, salt, and raisins.

❸ Beat the egg, brown sugar, and melted butter into the oat mixture. Stir in the dry ingredients until just evenly combined. Spoon the batter into the muffin pan.

❹ Combine the ingredients for the topping and sprinkle some on top of each muffin. Bake 17 minutes, or until a knife inserted in the center of a muffin comes out clean. Let sit 5 minutes before removing from the pan. Serve warm, not hot.

SPICY PUMPKIN MUFFINS

Remember these moist, flavorful muffins at Halloween. Top them with cream cheese icing for a great kids' treat.

1½ cups unbleached flour

½ cup whole wheat flour

1 tablespoon baking powder

½ teaspoon salt

2 teaspoons cinnamon

½ teaspoon ground ginger

½ teaspoon freshly grated nutmeg

¼ teaspoon ground cloves

1 large egg

½ cup firmly packed light brown sugar

1 cup fresh or canned pumpkin puree *(see Note)*

½ cup vegetable oil

½ cup milk

¾ cup raisins

½ cup finely chopped walnuts

Makes 12 muffins

❶ Preheat the oven to 400°F. Butter the insides and top of a regular-size (⅓-cup) muffin pan.

❷ In a large bowl, thoroughly combine the first 8 ingredients.

❸ In a medium bowl, beat the egg. Beat in the brown sugar, then stir in the pumpkin, oil, and milk until well mixed.

❹ Mix the pumpkin mixture into the dry ingredients until just combined. Don't overmix. Stir in the raisins and all but 2 tablespoons of the walnuts.

❺ Spoon the batter into the muffin cups, then sprinkle the remaining walnuts on top of the muffins. Bake 15 to 17 minutes, or until a knife inserted in the center of a muffin comes out clean. Let sit 2 minutes before removing from pan. Serve warm or at room temperature, not hot.

☛***Note:*** Leftover pumpkin puree can be frozen in 1-cup portions for future use.

FRUIT JUICE MUFFINS

Only frozen apple juice concentrate, grated apple, and raisins sweeten these light, fruity muffins.

1½ cups unbleached flour

½ cup whole wheat flour

2 teaspoons baking powder

½ teaspoon baking soda

½ teaspoon salt

½ teaspoon cinnamon

½ cup raisins

½ cup finely chopped walnuts

1 medium apple, peeled and grated

1 large egg

⅓ cup vegetable oil

½ cup frozen apple juice concentrate

½ cup water

Makes 12 muffins

❶ Preheat the oven to 425°F. Butter the insides and top of a regular-size (⅓-cup) muffin pan.

❷ In a large bowl, thoroughly combine the flours, baking powder, baking soda, salt, and cinnamon. Stir in the raisins, walnuts, and grated apple.

❸ In a medium bowl, beat the egg, then beat in the oil, apple juice concentrate, and water. Stir this into the dry mixture until just evenly moistened. Spoon the batter into the muffin pan.

❹ Bake 15 minutes, or until a knife inserted in the center of a muffin comes out clean. Cool for a few minutes before removing from the pan. Serve warm, not hot.

SUBSTANTIAL SALADS AND SALAD DRESSINGS

A favorite quick meal in our house that allows advance preparation is a hearty grain or pasta salad. These one-dish meals need little to accompany them because they are composed of so many satisfying ingredients. An appetizer beforehand and some delicious bread served alongside the salad is enough to complete the meal.

Although I serve these substantial salads year round, I particularly enjoy them during the warm-weather months when I can appreciate the minimal amount of cooking they require. Sometimes I cook the pasta or grain the night before or in the early morning, to keep my kitchen cool throughout the day. Then I finish the salad making later on. (If you cook pasta in advance, be certain to coat it with a little oil after draining, to prevent sticking.)

Spread on a bed of sprightly greens such as red- or green-leaf lettuce or lightly dressed bite-size spinach leaves, these salads make attractive buffet or potluck supper dishes. They are also an appealing way to introduce less adventurous eaters to unfamiliar grains such as bulghur, kasha, and couscous.

The salad dressings in this chapter are intended for mixed green salads. Creamy dressings mate well with crisp, sturdy greens such as romaine and iceberg lettuces and fresh spinach, while vinaigrette-style dressings work well with the aforementioned greens, and also with lighter-textured lettuces such as Boston, green-leaf, and red-leaf varieties.

You can pour oil-and-vinegar-based dressings on the entire salad, toss, and serve immediately. Creamy dressings should be served at the table in a sauceboat so that each person can pour on the amount he or she desires.

WILD RICE SALAD WITH APPLES AND WALNUTS

This crunchy, nutty salad is surprisingly light and has a tantalizing flavor. Serve it on a bed of curly green-leaf lettuce.

1 cup wild rice

2 cups water

1 tablespoon vegetable oil

¼ teaspoon salt

1 cup coarsely chopped walnuts

1 celery rib, sliced

4 scallions, thinly sliced

1 cup raisins

1 medium red apple (not Delicious), cored and diced

Grated rind of 1 lemon

....

3 tablespoons fresh lemon juice

2 garlic cloves, pressed

½ teaspoon salt

Freshly ground black pepper to taste

⅓ cup olive oil

....

Green-leaf lettuce (optional)

Serves 4 as a main course

❶ Put the wild rice in a strainer and rinse under cold water. Place it in a medium saucepan along with the water, oil, and salt. Cover, bring to a boil, and reduce the heat to simmer. Cook 50 minutes, or until the rice is tender and all the water has been absorbed. (When wild rice is done, it has a tender yet nubby texture.)

❷ Meanwhile, combine the walnuts, celery, scallions, raisins, apple, and lemon rind in a large bowl. In a jar with a tight-fitting lid, combine the lemon juice, garlic, salt, pepper, and olive oil and shake vigorously. Pour half of this dressing on the apple mixture and toss well.

❸ When the rice is done, let it cool until just warm. Combine with the fruit mixture and pour on the remaining dressing. Let sit at least 1 hour before serving at room temperature, on a bed of lettuce if desired.

COUSCOUS AND VEGETABLE SALAD WITH ORANGE AND GARLIC

The mingling of flavors and colors in this salad is hypnotic. The orange, garlic, and basil are an unforgettable combination. Paired with the raisins and toasted almonds, these ingredients result in a triumphant blending of flavors that will gratify the most discerning palate. On a sultry summer day, what better than a memorable dish that requires barely any cooking?

1½ cups couscous

½ cup raisins

1 teaspoon turmeric

2 cups boiling water

⅔ cup sliced almonds

2 cups chick-peas (page 161), *or* 1 15-ounce can chick-peas, rinsed and drained

3 scallions, thinly sliced

2 medium tomatoes, halved, seeded and diced

....

⅓ cup fresh lemon juice

⅓ cup olive oil

2 garlic cloves, minced

Grated rind of 1 orange

2 tablespoons minced fresh basil, *or* 2 teaspoons dried

½ teaspoon salt

Freshly ground black pepper to taste

Green-leaf lettuce

Serves 4 as a main course

❶ Place the couscous, raisins, and turmeric in a large bowl, then pour the boiling water over them and stir well. Cover with foil or a large plate and let sit 5 minutes. Fluff with a fork, cover again, and let sit 10 minutes longer.

❷ Stir in the almonds, chick-peas, scallions, and tomatoes.

❸ Combine the lemon juice, olive oil, garlic, orange rind, basil, salt, and pepper and beat to blend. Pour over the couscous mixture and toss. Cover and chill at least 30 minutes, or up to 24 hours, before serving. Serve mounded on leaves of green-leaf lettuce.

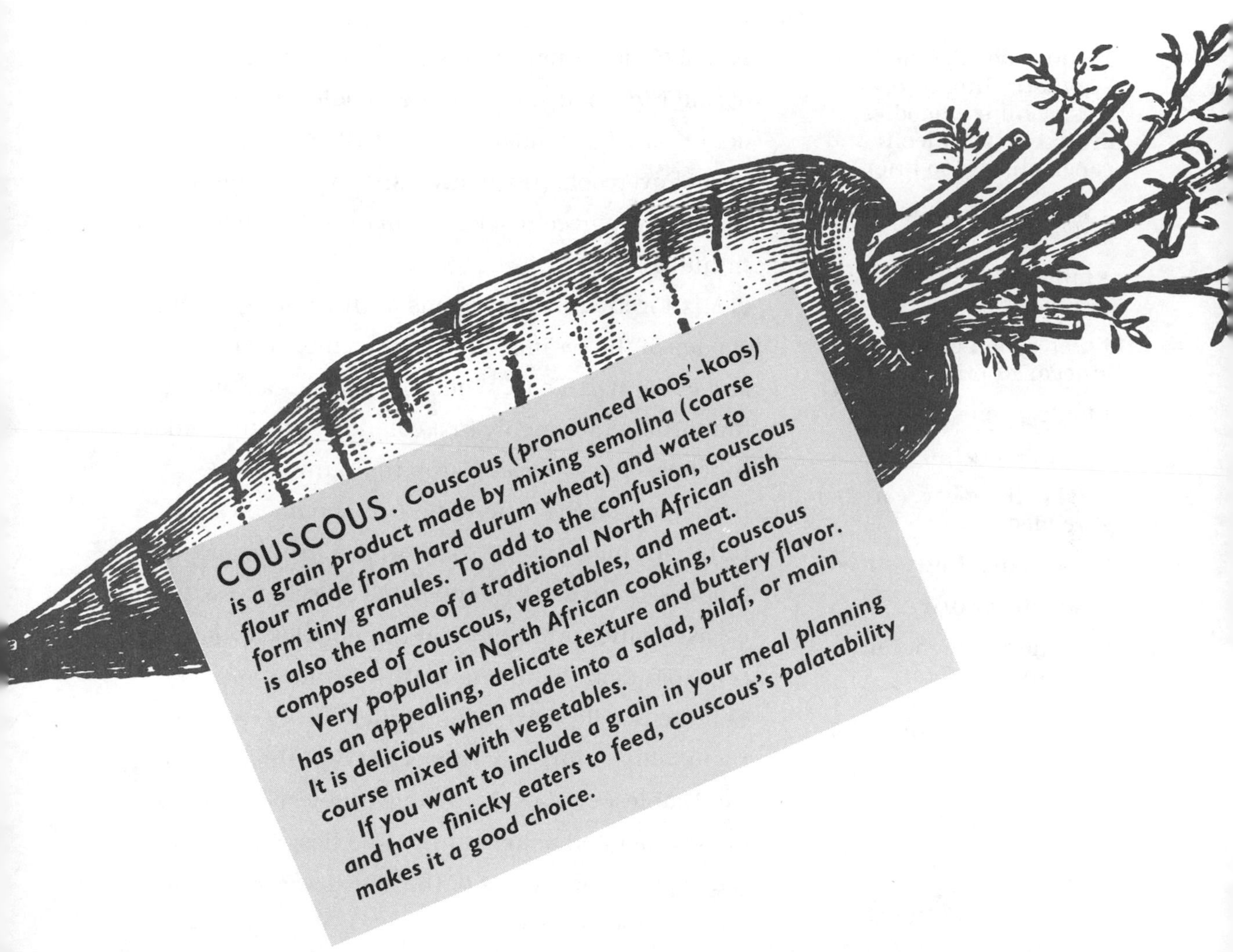

COUSCOUS. Couscous (pronounced koos'-koos) is a grain product made by mixing semolina (coarse flour made from hard durum wheat) and water to form tiny granules. To add to the confusion, couscous is also the name of a traditional North African dish composed of couscous, vegetables, and meat.

Very popular in North African cooking, couscous has an appealing, delicate texture and buttery flavor. It is delicious when made into a salad, pilaf, or main course mixed with vegetables.

If you want to include a grain in your meal planning and have finicky eaters to feed, couscous's palatability makes it a good choice.

COLD SZECHUAN NOODLES WITH SHREDDED VEGETABLES

Marinated Chinese noodle dishes have such a delicious flavor and texture that few people can resist their appeal. This is an excellent main course for a hot day because the noodles can be cooked early in the morning (or the night before) when it is cool and left to marinate until serving time.

This is the kind of dish that begs for improvisation. Try different vegetables — whatever is freshest at the market.

1 pound noodles such as spaghetti, linguine, or fresh Chinese noodles, if available (vermicelli and capellini are too fine)

4 tablespoons tamari soy sauce

4 tablespoons oriental sesame oil

1 tablespoon Chinese rice vinegar *or* other vinegar

1 tablespoon sugar

½ teaspoon chili oil

1 red bell pepper, cored and shredded

3 scallions, thinly sliced

2 carrots, grated

1 scallion branch, for garnish *(see Note)*

Serves 4 as a main course

❶ In a (6- to 8-quart) stockpot, bring several quarts of water to a boil and cook the noodles until al dente — that is, tender yet slightly firm to the bite. Do not overcook. (If you are using fresh Chinese noodles, you need to cook them only for a few minutes.)

❷ Mix together 3 tablespoons of the tamari, 3 tablespoons of the sesame oil, and the vinegar, sugar, and chili oil in a cup. When the noodles are done, drain them thoroughly in a colander, shaking out as much water as you can. Drop them into a large bowl, pour on the sauce, and toss the noodles carefully with tongs to coat them well. Marinate at least 2 hours, or up to 24 hours, before serving, tossing occasionally. Cover and chill the noodles if they are prepared more than 4 hours in advance.

❸ If the noodles have been chilled, bring them to room temperature before serving. Mix the remaining 1 tablespoon soy sauce and 1 tablespoon sesame oil together and pour over the noodles. Stir in the red peppers, two-thirds of the sliced scallions, and half the grated carrots.

ORIENTAL SESAME OIL. Do not confuse this strong-tasting oil with mild, cold-pressed sesame oil that is usually sold in natural foods stores. Oriental sesame oil, dark brown in color, is made from roasted sesame seeds and has a distinct toasted sesame aroma. Just a few teaspoons will enliven the flavors of any Chinese dish. Unlike light-colored sesame oil, oriental sesame oil will keep indefinitely and need not be refrigerated.

❹ To serve, mound the noodles on a serving platter and sprinkle on the remaining scallions and carrots. Place the scallion branch on top.

☛***Note:*** To make a scallion branch, trim the top from a scallion so that the remaining white-and-pale-green piece is about 3 inches long. Cut off the root section. Insert the tip of a small, sharp knife about ¼ inch from the center of the scallion and slice upward. Repeat 3 or 4 times to create thin strips. Turn the branch and repeat with the other end. The point is to leave about ½ inch in the center intact and shred the ends. Drop the branch into ice water for about 30 minutes so the ends will curl. Remove the branch and shake out any water before placing it on the noodles.

CRUNCHY LENTIL SALAD

Keeping the lentils slightly crunchy and dressing them with a small amount of olive oil, lemon juice, and spices contributes to this salad's light consistency. I often serve this alongside a baked potato for a quick, complete meal.

1 cup lentils, picked over and rinsed

5 cups water

1 bay leaf

1 celery rib, finely diced

1 carrot, minced

¼ cup finely diced red onion

2 tablespoons minced fresh parsley

¼ cup fruity olive oil

2 tablespoons fresh lemon juice

1 garlic clove, pressed or minced

¼ teaspoon dried thyme

¼ teaspoon ground cumin

Salt to taste

Freshly ground black pepper to taste

Serves 4 as a main course

❶ In a medium saucepan, combine the lentils, water, and bay leaf. Bring to a boil and cook, uncovered, 15 minutes, or until the lentils are tender but still crunchy. Stir occasionally. Pour into a colander and discard the bay leaf. Drain the lentils very well, and let them sit 5 minutes or so to be certain all the water has drained out.

❷ Place the lentils in a serving bowl and gently stir in the celery, carrot, onion, and parsley.

❸ Mix together the olive oil, lemon juice, garlic, thyme, cumin, salt, and pepper. Pour onto the lentil mixture, and carefully toss. Serve at room temperature.

PENNE AND BROCCOLI SALAD WITH CREAMY GARLIC DRESSING

The Parmesan cheese and creamy dressing that coat this salad are a welcome change from the more common vinaigrette that usually dresses pasta salads.

1 bunch broccoli, cut into small flowerets and stalks peeled and diced (about 5 cups)

½ pound (3 cups) *penne* (quill-shaped pasta)

1 medium tomato, seeded and cubed

⅓ cup pine nuts

1 tablespoon minced fresh basil, or 1 teaspoon dry

⅔ cup Creamy Garlic Dressing (page 93)

2 tablespoons grated Parmesan cheese

Salt to taste

Freshly ground black pepper to taste

Serves 4 as a main course

❶ Bring a large stockpot of water to a boil. Drop in the broccoli and blanch until tender but still crunchy, about 2 minutes. Remove with a slotted spoon and place in a bowl. Rinse under cold running water until chilled. Drain thoroughly, then pat dry with paper towels. Place in a large serving bowl.

❷ Cook the *penne* in the boiling water until al dente. Drain in a colander, then chill under cold water. Drain again, then pat with paper towels to absorb moisture. Place in the bowl with the broccoli.

❸ Stir in the tomato, pine nuts, and basil. Mix the dressing with the Parmesan cheese and pour on the salad. Season with salt and pepper. Let sit at least 30 minutes before serving. If you are going to wait longer, cover and chill until 30 minutes before serving, then bring to room temperature.

BULGHUR SALAD WITH CORN, ZUCCHINI, AND SHREDDED BASIL

I prefer to use dark, coarse-grain American bulghur for this salad because its color is more appealing and harmonious with corn than that of the lighter-colored Middle Eastern variety.

The inimitable flavor of fresh basil stands tall in this dish and mates wonderfully with the corn, zucchini, and tomatoes.

1½ cups coarse-grain bulghur

1½ cups frozen corn kernels, thawed

1 tomato, cut into small cubes

1 cup very thinly sliced zucchini rounds, cut into sixths

3 tablespoons finely shredded fresh basil

¼ cup thinly slivered red onion

⅓ cup olive oil

¼ cup lemon juice

2 garlic cloves, pressed

½ teaspoon salt

Freshly ground black pepper to taste

Lettuce leaves, for garnish

Serves 4 as a main course

❶ Place the bulghur in a large bowl. Pour boiling water over it to cover by 2 inches. Let soak 30 minutes, or until tender. Remove all of the soaking liquid by placing the bulghur, in batches, in cheesecloth or a cotton towel and squeezing it dry. Or place it in a strainer and press out the liquid with the back of a large spoon. Place the strained bulghur in a large serving bowl.

❷ Stir in the corn, tomato, zucchini, basil, and onion. In a separate bowl, beat together the olive oil, lemon juice, garlic, salt, and pepper. Pour it over the salad and mix well. Let sit 30 minutes, or cover and chill for up to 24 hours, then bring to room temperature before serving. Place lettuce leaves on individual plates and spoon the salad on top.

BASIL ICE CUBES. Have too much fresh basil and don't want to stuff any more pesto into your freezer? Try pureeing fresh basil leaves with a little water in your blender or food processor, then pouring the mixture into an ice cube tray. Freeze until solid, then pop out the cubes and store them in a plastic bag in the freezer. Basil ice cubes can be dropped into soups or sauces to imbue them with that fresh basil flavor.

MEDITERRANEAN PASTA SALAD WITH CHICK-PEAS AND ROASTED PEPPERS

Roasted peppers, chick-peas, olives, tomatoes, and herbs fill this salad in which the pasta serves only as a backdrop. A good crusty bread would add the right touch.

½ pound *rotini* (short corkscrew pasta)

1 large green bell pepper

1 large red bell pepper

1 19-ounce can chick-peas, rinsed and well drained

1 medium tomato, diced

16 oil-cured black olives

2 tablespoons minced fresh parsley

½ cup slivered red onion

DRESSING

⅓ cup olive oil

2 tablespoons red wine vinegar

1 teaspoon Dijon mustard

3 garlic cloves, pressed

½ teaspoon dried oregano

¼ teaspoon crushed red pepper flakes

½ teaspoon salt

Freshly ground black pepper to taste

Serves 4 to 6 as a main course

❶ Roast, peel, seed, and chop the peppers as described through step 3 on page 14.

❷ Meanwhile, cook the *rotini* until al dente in a large stockpot of boiling water. Drain the pasta in a colander and shake vigorously to remove all the water. Place in a large bowl. Stir in the peppers, chick-peas, tomato, olives, parsley, and onion.

❸ In a jar with a tight-fitting lid, combine all the ingredients for the dressing. Shake vigorously, then pour over the pasta mixture and toss well. Serve the salad warm or at room temperature.

BROCCOLI AND RICE SALAD

Raisins are a surprise ingredient in a number of savory Italian dishes. In this light salad they add a welcome sweetness in counterpoint to the broccoli and garlic. Remember this salad when you have leftover cooked rice.

½ cup long-grain brown rice

1½ cups water

1 teaspoon vegetable oil

¼ teaspoon salt

1 bunch broccoli (flowerets cut into small pieces and stems discarded) (about 3½ cups)

⅓ cup raisins

1 carrot, minced

⅓ cup slivered red onion

2 tablespoons minced fresh basil, *or* 1 teaspoon dried

DRESSING

2 garlic cloves, pressed

2 tablespoons red wine vinegar

1 teaspoon Dijon mustard

⅓ cup olive oil

¼ teaspoon salt

Freshly ground black pepper to taste

Serves 2 to 3 as a main course

❶ In a small saucepan, combine the rice, water, oil, and salt. Cover the pan, bring to a boil, and reduce the heat to a low simmer. Cook undisturbed until all of the water is absorbed, about 45 minutes. Spoon the rice into a large serving bowl and let cool to warm; refrigerate until cold.

❷ Steam the broccoli flowerets until tender yet still bright green. Immediately immerse them in cold water to stop further cooking. Drain and pat dry with a cotton or paper towel. Stir into the rice along with the raisins, carrot, onion, and basil.

❸ Combine the ingredients for the dressing in a jar with a tight-fitting lid. Shake vigorously, then pour over the salad. Toss to coat. Let the salad marinate 30 minutes or so before serving. Serve at room temperature.

TORTELLINI SALAD PRIMAVERA

Let your imagination and the season's bounty determine your vegetable selection; just be sure not to overcook any of the vegetables, and strive for contrasting colors.

8 asparagus stalks, peeled and cut into 1-inch lengths

1 carrot, thinly sliced

1 cup small broccoli flowerets

1 cup sliced yellow squash

1 medium tomato, seeded and cubed

½ cup frozen peas, thawed

1 celery rib, thinly sliced

2 scallions, thinly sliced

⅓ cup pine nuts

2 tablespoons minced dill

1 pound fresh or frozen cheese tortellini

DRESSING

2 garlic cloves, pressed

3 tablespoons fresh lemon juice

1 tablespoon red wine vinegar

½ cup olive oil

¼ teaspoon sugar

½ teaspoon salt

Freshly ground black pepper to taste

Lettuce leaves (optional)

Serves 4 as a main course

❶ Bring a large stockpot of water to a boil. Drop in the asparagus, carrot, and broccoli and let sit 1 minute. Remove with a slotted spoon and drop into a bowl of ice water. Drain and dry on paper towels.

❷ Drop the yellow squash into the boiling water for 30 seconds, then remove, cool, and dry as above. Place the blanched vegetables in a serving bowl large enough to hold the tortellini also. Mix in the tomato, peas, celery, scallions, pine nuts, and dill.

❸ Drop the tortellini into the boiling water and cook until just al dente, not mushy, about 3 minutes for fresh tortellini and 5 minutes for frozen. Drain in a colander, then run cold water over the tortellini. Drain again very well. Stir the tortellini into the vegetables.

❹ To make the dressing, combine all of the dressing ingredients in a jar with a screw-on top. Shake very well. The dressing can be made up to 8 hours before using. Pour over the tortellini and vegetables and coat thoroughly. Chill until ready to serve. For a pretty presentation, serve on a bed of curly lettuce leaves.

MARINATED KASHA AND VEGETABLE SALAD

A light, attractive salad in which the nutty flavor of kasha marries perfectly with lemon and thyme. Try this on a hot day when you crave something fresh and flavorful that requires minimal cooking.

3 cups vegetable stock *(see Note), or* water

½ teaspoon salt

1½ cups medium-granulation kasha

½ cup plus 1 tablespoon olive oil

12 ounces (about 4½ cups) mushrooms, quartered

Grated rind of 1 lemon

3 tablespoons fresh lemon juice

1 garlic clove, minced

1 teaspoon dried thyme

Freshly ground black pepper to taste

½ cup minced fresh parsley

1 celery rib, thinly sliced

2 carrots, minced

3 scallions, very thinly sliced

⅔ cup finely chopped walnuts

1 cup frozen peas, thawed

Lettuce leaves (optional)

Serves 4 to 6 as a main course

❶ Bring the vegetable stock or water to a boil in a medium pot. Pour in the salt and the kasha, cover the pot, and reduce the heat to a simmer. Cook until all of the water is absorbed, about 10 minutes. Spoon the kasha into a large bowl and let it cool. Stir it occasionally to break up any lumps that might form.

❷ Heat 1 tablespoon of the olive oil in a large skillet over medium-high heat. Add the mushrooms and sauté until the juices rendered evaporate and the mushrooms begin to stick to the pan. Spoon the mushrooms into a bowl and stir in the remaining ½ cup olive oil, lemon rind, lemon juice, garlic, thyme, and pepper.

❸ Mix the parsley, celery, carrots, scallions, walnuts, and peas into the kasha. Pour in the mushrooms and their marinade and toss thoroughly. Cover and chill 30 minutes, or up to 24 hours, before serving. Serve at room temperature on lettuce leaves, if desired.

☛ ***Note:*** Vegetable stock can be made with powdered vegetable stock base, available at health food stores.

CAPONATA

Try serving this cold Sicilian eggplant salad on lettuce leaves as a salad course, or surrounded by French bread pieces for a robust appetizer. And remember it for your next picnic.

¼ cup plus 2 tablespoons olive oil

1 medium (1¼-pound) eggplant, peeled and cut into ½-inch cubes

2 celery ribs, thinly sliced

2 large onions, finely diced

2 tablespoons capers

½ cup (about 8 large) chopped green olives

2 tablespoons tomato paste

½ cup water

¼ cup red wine vinegar, *or* balsamic vinegar

2 teaspoons sugar

Serves 6 to 8 as an appetizer and 4 as a main course

❶ Heat ¼ cup of the olive oil in a large skillet over medium-high heat. Add the eggplant and cook, tossing often, until tender, about 10 minutes. (The eggplant will absorb the oil and begin to stick, but don't add any more oil, just keep tossing.) When done, the eggplant will be cooked through but not mushy. Scoop it out of the pan and onto a platter. Reduce the heat to medium.

❷ Pour the remaining 2 tablespoons olive oil into the skillet and stir in the celery and onions. Sauté until tender, about 10 minutes, scraping up any crusty bits of eggplant that may have stuck to the pan.

❸ Return the eggplant to the skillet, then toss in the capers and olives. In a small bowl, combine the tomato paste, water, vinegar, and sugar and stir into the eggplant mixture. Simmer 10 minutes, stirring occasionally. Scrape the eggplant mixture into a large bowl, and chill at least 2 hours. Bring to room temperature before serving. Caponata can be kept refrigerated for up to 3 days.

TORTELLINI SALAD WITH PESTO

Serve this salad, always popular at cookouts and informal parties, in a pretty bowl or on an attractive platter to brighten it up.

PESTO

1 cup moderately well-packed basil leaves, well rinsed and drained

⅓ cup olive oil

2 garlic cloves, chopped

¼ cup grated Parmesan cheese

1 tablespoon unsalted butter, softened

1 pound fresh or frozen cheese tortellini

1 tablespoon pine nuts

Few sprigs fresh basil, for garnish

Serves 4 as a main course

❶ To make the pesto: Combine the basil, olive oil, and garlic in a blender or food processor and process until smooth. Scrape into a bowl, then stir in the cheese and butter. (You can make this in advance and refrigerate for 2 weeks.)

❷ Bring a large stockpot of water to a boil. Cook the tortellini until tender but not mushy. Taste to be certain the tortellini is done. Drain thoroughly in a colander, then place in a serving bowl. Spoon on the pesto *(see Note)* and toss very well. Sprinkle on the pine nuts and toss again. Serve the salad at room temperature with one or two sprigs of basil as garnish.

☛***Note:*** If the pesto is cold and firm, you can thin it with a few drops of the hot pasta cooking water.

COLD ORIENTAL NOODLES WITH PEANUT SAUCE

Like so many of life's delicacies, the flavors in this captivating sauce linger long after the thrill is gone!

1 pound spaghettini

4 tablespoons oriental sesame oil

. . . .

½ cup natural-style peanut butter

⅓ cup tamari soy sauce

3 tablespoons Chinese rice wine, *or* sherry

1 tablespoon water

1½ tablespoon rice vinegar, *or* other vinegar

1 tablespoon vegetable oil

1 tablespoon firmly packed light brown sugar

3 garlic cloves, minced

1 teaspoon minced fresh ginger

½ teaspoon crushed red pepper flakes (or less for a milder version)

. . . .

1 cucumber, peeled, cut lengthwise, seeded, and julienned

4 scallions, thinly sliced

Serves 4 as a main course

❶ Cook the spaghettini al dente. Drain and rinse under cold water. Drain very well again. With your hands, toss the noodles with 2 tablespoons of the sesame oil. Cover and chill until ready to combine with the peanut sauce, or up to 24 hours.

❷ To make the sauce, combine the remaining 2 tablespoons sesame oil with all the other ingredients except the cucumber and scallions. Beat until well mixed. The sauce can be kept in the refrigerator, covered, up to 24 hours before using.

❸ Just before serving, gently toss the noodles with the sauce, cucumbers, and half the scallions. Garnish with the remaining scallions.

ORZO AND VEGETABLE SALAD

Josef Oszuscik, an adventurous cook in a California monastery, gave me the idea for this tasty salad. It has a light, creamy dressing and a potpourri of Mediterranean flavors. Great as a main course or side dish.

1½ cups orzo (rice-shaped pasta)

1 medium zucchini, quartered lengthwise and thinly sliced

10 Kalamata (Greek) olives, pitted and sliced

4 scallions, thinly sliced

1 celery rib, thinly sliced

1 medium tomato, seeded and cubed

1 green or red bell pepper, seeded and finely diced

⅓ cup minced fresh parsley

⅓ cup olive oil

2 tablespoons red wine vinegar

3 garlic cloves, minced

1 teaspoon dried oregano

1 tablespoon minced fresh dill, *or* 1 teaspoon dried

¼ teaspoon salt

Freshly ground black pepper to taste

4 ounces (⅔ cup) crumbled feta cheese

2 tablespoons mayonnaise

Serves 4 as a main course

❶ Bring a large stockpot of water to a boil. Add the orzo and cook until tender but not mushy, 6 to 8 minutes. Drain in a colander and rinse under cold water. Drain again very thoroughly. Place in a large bowl.

❷ Stir in the zucchini, olives, scallions, celery, tomato, bell pepper, and parsley.

❸ In a small bowl, beat together the olive oil, vinegar, garlic, oregano, dill, salt, and pepper. Pour over the salad and toss to coat well. Sprinkle on the feta cheese and toss again. Spoon on the mayonnaise and gently toss to coat evenly. Chill at least 2 hours, then bring to room temperature before serving. This salad can be stored in the refrigerator up to 8 hours before serving.

MISO DRESSING

This creamy, tangy dressing is made for a crunchy lettuce such as Romaine.

3 tablespoons rice (white) miso, *or* barley (red) miso

2 garlic cloves, chopped

2 tablespoons apple cider vinegar, *or* red wine vinegar

1½ tablespoons oriental sesame oil

¾ cup vegetable oil

⅓ cup plus 1 tablespoon water

Makes 1½ cups

❶ Blend the miso, garlic, vinegar, and sesame oil in a blender or food processor until smooth.

❷ With the machine still running, very slowly pour in the oil. When the mixture has emulsified, slowly pour in the water and blend 10 seconds or so. The finished dressing should have a smooth, mayonnaiselike consistency. Scrape into a serving dish, cover, and chill until ready to use. The dressing can be kept refrigerated for up to 4 days.

☛***Note:*** If by chance your dressing separates, try scraping the dressing into a bowl. Clean and dry the processor or blender, put 1 tablespoon cold water in the container, and turn on the machine. With the cover off, pour in 1 tablespoon of the dressing. Once incorporated, add another 1 tablespoon dressing. Repeat until all the dressing has been added. It should rebind to a thick, creamy consistency.

TAHINI SALAD DRESSING

Serve a crunchy lettuce such as romaine with this savory garlic- and lemon-spiked dressing, and garnish with sesame seeds.

⅔ cup tahini

2 garlic cloves, pressed

6 tablespoons fresh lemon juice

½ teaspoon salt

5 to 7 tablespoons water

Makes 1¼ cups

❶ In a medium bowl, beat the tahini, garlic, lemon juice, and salt together until smooth. Slowly beat in the water, using just the amount needed to give the dressing a nice pouring consistency. Let sit 20 minutes before serving. The dressing will thicken slightly. Leftovers can be stored in refrigerator up to 4 days.

MISO. This fermented soy food has a pastelike consistency and usually is diluted with water to make stocks, sauces, and dressings. A highly concentrated source of protein, vitamin B-12, and minerals, miso is devoid of cholesterol and low in fat. Generally speaking, the darker the color of miso, the stronger the flavor and the more intense the saltiness. White or yellow miso is sweet, creamy, and ideal for dishes requiring a light touch. Choose unpasteurized miso sold refrigerated in health food stores. The unpasteurized product is filled with lactobacillus bacteria and enzymes, which aid digestion.

CREAMY HERB VINAIGRETTE

This is a wonderful way to use leftover egg white; it makes this dressing thick and creamy, and the emulsion will hold together for a number of days. Serve this on romaine lettuce with a generous handful of Parmesan cheese, and top with croutons.

2 garlic cloves, chopped

1 cup olive oil

1 teaspoon Dijon mustard

1 tablespoon water

1 egg white

⅓ cup red wine vinegar

¼ teaspoon dried oregano

¼ teaspoon dried basil

Pinch dried marjoram

Salt to taste

Freshly ground black pepper to taste

Makes 1¾ cups

❶ Combine all the ingredients in a blender or food processor and process 15 seconds, or until the dressing binds and is smooth. Scrape into a pitcher or jar. If the dressing is too thick, stir in a bit of water to thin. Cover and chill until serving time. It will keep for up to 3 days.

DOUBLE SESAME DRESSING

The dark, bewitching flavor of sesame comes from both the seeds and the oil in this dressing. It pairs especially well with spinach salads and with lettuce-based salads that have a handful of watercress or arugula tossed in.

- 1 tablespoon sesame seeds
- ½ cup peanut oil *or* vegetable oil
- 1½ tablespoons oriental sesame oil
- 2½ tablespoons red wine vinegar *or* cider vinegar
- ½ teaspoon tamari soy sauce
- 1 garlic clove, pressed
- Salt to taste
- Freshly ground black pepper to taste

Makes ¾ cup

❶ Place the sesame seeds in a small saucepan over medium-high heat and toast until they begin to smoke and become fragrant, about 3 minutes. Shake the pan around while the seeds are cooking to toast them evenly. Pour the seeds into a small bowl and cool.

❷ Combine all of the remaining ingredients in a jar with a screw-on top, then pour in the sesame seeds. Shake vigorously and chill. This dressing can be kept in the refrigerator for up to 4 days.

CREAMY GARLIC DRESSING

This pungent dressing can enliven a salad of greens or serve as a marinade for cold blanched vegetables.

- ½ cup mayonnaise
- ½ cup plain low-fat yogurt
- 2 garlic cloves, pressed
- 1 teaspoon Dijon mustard
- 2 tablespoons fresh lemon juice

Makes about 1 cup

❶ In a bowl or glass measuring cup, beat the mayonnaise and yogurt together until smooth.

❷ Beat in the garlic, mustard, and lemon juice until blended. Cover and chill until ready to use, up to 4 days.

BLUE CHEESE VINAIGRETTE

Soft lettuces such as Boston or green- or red-leaf lettuce mixed with some watercress and red onion slivers pair well with this vinaigrette.

2 tablespoons red wine vinegar

1 tablespoon Dijon mustard

1 garlic clove, pressed

Salt to taste

Freshly ground black pepper to taste

Pinch sugar

6 tablespoons olive oil

½ cup (2 ounces) crumbled blue cheese

Makes ⅔ cup

❶ In a small bowl, thoroughly beat together the vinegar, mustard, garlic, salt, pepper, and sugar. Slowly beat in the olive oil, then stir in the blue cheese. Chill. Toss with the salad just before serving. This vinaigrette will keep, refrigerated, for up to 4 days.

SANDWICHES AND SPREADS

Vegetarians have clearly been at a disadvantage when lunchtime rolled around. Cold cuts and tuna, the staples of most nonvegetarian sandwiches, have always made sandwich making simple and effortless for meat eaters. But for vegetarians, sandwiches have been problematic.

The sandwiches presented here range from the sophisticated to the simple. A number of them, such as Provençal Eggplant and Tomato Sandwiches with Garlic Mayonnaise (page 105) and Vegetable Melt with Wasabi Mayonnaise (page 103), could make a satisfying and delicious supper.

Sandwich making invites improvisation; therefore, I hope these recipes will inspire you to invent your own combinations, expanding your lunch repertoire. Always work with high-quality ingredients: nicely textured breads; ripe, juicy tomatoes; fresh, crisp greens; good-quality mayonnaise and mustard; and thinly sliced, savory cheese. This will get you off to the right start.

MEDITERRANEAN VEGETABLE SANDWICH

The intoxicating flavors of the Mediterranean are wedded in this aromatic "stuffed" sandwich. French breads vary greatly in width and texture. For this sandwich a wide, soft loaf works best.

1 wide, soft loaf French bread, cut into 4 pieces

10 tablespoons fruity olive oil

4 garlic cloves, minced

Freshly ground black pepper to taste

1 teaspoon dried oregano

2 tablespoons minced fresh basil, *or* 1½ teaspoons dried

1 green bell pepper, thinly sliced into rings

1 small red onion, thinly sliced

2 large tomatoes, thickly sliced

10 ounces sliced provolone cheese (preferably smoked)

5 to 6 ounces (28 to 30) Kalamata (Greek) olives

Serves 4

❶ Slice each French bread section in half horizontally and pull some of the inner bread from each half-section to make a cavity. Drizzle an equal amount of olive oil on each half-section and spread it around with a knife to coat the bread. Sprinkle equal amounts of the garlic, black pepper, oregano, and basil on each piece of bread.

❷ Layer the bell pepper, onion, tomato, and provolone cheese in one half of each bread section.

❸ One at a time, place an olive on a cutting board and rest the flat side of a cutting knife on it. Thump it with the heel of your hand, the olive will split and the pit will fall out. Discard the pits and place the olives on the sandwich bottoms. Cover the sandwich with the remaining bread halves.

❹ Tightly wrap each sandwich with plastic wrap and let sit at least 1 hour, or up to 4 hours, before serving. Sandwiches can sit for 1 hour unrefrigerated, on in the refrigerator if longer. Return to room temperature before serving.

PITA BREAD STUFFED WITH GREEN SALAD

Serve this aromatic salad sandwich with black olives to nibble.

3 tablespoons olive oil

2 teaspoons red wine vinegar

1 teaspoon dried oregano

Freshly ground black pepper to taste

1 green bell pepper, cored and cut into 1-inch dice

1 cucumber, peeled, seeded, and cut into 1-inch dice

½ cup slivered red onion

¼ pound (about ¾ cup) feta cheese, cut into ½-inch cubes

12 cherry tomatoes, halved, *or* 2 small tomatoes, cubed

1½ cups diced romaine or iceberg lettuce

4 pita breads, halved

Serves 4

❶ In a large bowl, whisk together the olive oil, vinegar, oregano, and pepper. Stir in the bell pepper, cucumber, onion, feta cheese, tomatoes, and lettuce until coated.

❷ Heat the pita bread halves in a 350°F. oven until just heated through, then cool. (You can omit this step, but I find that it enhances the texture of the bread.) Stuff some salad in each pita half and serve immediately.

☛***Note:*** You can prepare the salad mixture up to 30 minutes in advance, but don't combine with the dressing until just before serving.

PITA BREAD PIZZAS

Here is the most popular lunch in my house, served at least three times a week! These pizzas are excellent plain or dressed with a favorite topping such as sliced black olives, mushrooms, or red pepper flakes. I love the combination of mozzarella and Muenster cheese; mozzarella alone is too firm and stringy, and Muenster adds a wonderful creaminess.

The proportions in this recipe are for 6-inch pita. You can easily adjust the amounts if your bread is a different size.

4 6-inch pita breads

½ cup tomato sauce

¾ cup grated mozzarella cheese

¾ cup grated Muenster cheese

Toppings of your choice (optional)

Makes four 6-inch pizzas

❶ Preheat the broiler. Lay the pita breads on a baking sheet and lightly toast on both sides. (You don't want them brown, just hot throughout and barely toasted.)

❷ Remove the pan from the oven and place each pita concave side up so the sauce and cheese won't run down the edges. Evenly divide the sauce and spread it on top of each bread. Sprinkle on the cheeses and any toppings.

❸ Place the baking sheet under the broiler and cook until the cheese begins to bubble. At this point, I usually remove the pan and spread the cheese more evenly with a knife. Return to the broiler and cook another minute or so, or until the cheese begins to brown.

❹ Place the pizzas one by one on a cutting board and cut in half with a large knife. Serve immediately.

GREEK PIZZA

This is simplicity itself, yet very aromatic and flavorful. A good-quality, fruity olive oil can really stand out in this recipe. If you have some on hand, by all means use it lavishly.

4 6-inch pita breads

6 ounces (about 1¼ cups) crumbled feta cheese

1¼ teaspoons dried oregano

4 paper-thin slices onion, separated into rings

2 tablespoons fruity olive oil

Makes four 6-inch pizzas

❶ Preheat the broiler. Place the pita breads on a baking sheet concave sides up. Sprinkle the feta cheese on top of the bread. Sprinkle on the oregano, and top with the onion rings. Drizzle the olive oil over all.

❷ Broil 5 minutes, or until the cheese softens and the edges of the bread begin to brown. Place the pizzas on a cutting board and slice in half. Serve immediately.

TOFU "EGGLESS" SALAD

This sandwich filling is similar in taste, texture, and appearance to egg salad. Spread on a good-quality whole wheat bread and top with romaine lettuce for a delicious sandwich combination. You can also serve it on toasted French bread slices as an appetizer.

½ pound extra-firm or firm tofu, patted very dry

¼ teaspoon turmeric

2 tablespoons mayonnaise

1 tablespoon finely diced red onion

Fills 4 sandwiches

❶ Place the tofu in a medium bowl and mash it with a fork until crumbs the size of small peas are formed.

❷ Stir in the turmeric and mix well, then stir in the remaining ingredients. Let sit 30 minutes before using, or cover and chill for up to 24 hours.

WASABI. Wasabi is green horseradish that is sold in powdered form. When mixed with a few drops of water, it makes a paste that is used as a condiment in Japanese cooking. Wasabi's fiery flavor goes a long way, so only a small amount is needed to enliven a dish.

Wasabi can be purchased in health food stores, specialty food shops, and the oriental section of some supermarkets.

VEGETABLE MELT WITH *WASABI* MAYONNAISE

Almost any sautéed vegetable mixture will do on this open-faced sandwich. Just season it with tamari, sprinkle on Muenster cheese, broil until melted, and top with a generous spoonful of this spunky wasabi mayonnaise.

1 teaspoon *wasabi* powder (see opposite page)

3 tablespoons mayonnaise

1 tablespoon olive oil

12 ounces (4½ cups) sliced mushrooms

1 large red bell pepper, cored and cut into thin strips

1 bunch broccoli, cut into small pieces and stalks peeled (about 5 cups)

2 teaspoons tamari soy sauce

2 7-inch pita breads

1¼ cups grated Muenster cheese

Serves 4

❶ Mix the *wasabi* with about 1 teaspoon water, or just enough to make a paste the consistency of mustard. Let sit 10 minutes to develop the flavor. Place the mayonnaise in a small bowl and stir until smooth, then stir in the *wasabi* paste. Set aside.

❷ Heat the olive oil in a large skillet over medium-high heat. Add the mushrooms and sauté 5 minutes, tossing often. Stir in the bell pepper and broccoli, then sprinkle on about 1 tablespoon water. Cover and cook until the broccoli is crisp-tender, about 5 minutes.

❸ Remove the cover from the pan. If there is any water remaining, raise the heat to high to evaporate it. Stir the mixture frequently. Pour on the tamari and toss to coat. Remove from the heat.

❹ Preheat the broiler. Meanwhile, split the pitas in half to make 4 disks. Place them on a baking sheet, then spoon on the vegetable mixture. Sprinkle on the cheese, and broil until melted, about 3 minutes. Slip onto serving plates. Spoon an equal portion of the *wasabi* mayonnaise in the center of each sandwich, and let each person spread it.

VEGETABLE CREAM CHEESE SPREAD

Garlic and scallions spark this pretty, salmon-colored crunchy spread that will please the palates of children and adults alike. This spread is a good choice when sandwiches are to be transported because they will hold together well.

1 large carrot, peeled

8 ounces Neufchâtel or cream cheese, softened

1 small garlic clove, pressed or minced

Salt

Freshly ground black pepper to taste

½ cucumber

2 scallions, very thinly sliced

¼ cup finely diced green bell pepper

Fills 4 sandwiches

❶ Cut the carrot into chunks and mince in a blender or food processor. Scrape it into a medium bowl and thoroughly mix the cream cheese into it with a fork. Mix in the garlic, salt, and pepper.

❷ Peel the cucumber half, then cut it in half lengthwise. Scrape out the seeds and discard them. Cut the cucumber into thin strips and then into small dice.

❸ Stir the cucumber, scallions, and bell pepper into the cream cheese mixture.

☛***Note:*** This spread will keep up to 3 days if well wrapped and refrigerated.

☛***Variations:*** Spread on pumpernickel bread and top with lettuce or alfalfa sprouts and another slice of bread. Or spread on a toasted or untoasted bagel and serve open-faced.

PROVENÇAL EGGPLANT AND TOMATO SANDWICHES WITH GARLIC MAYONNAISE

¾ cup mayonnaise

1 medium eggplant, peeled and sliced into ½-inch-thick rounds

⅓ cup plus 2 tablespoons grated Parmesan cheese

1 teaspoon Dijon mustard

2 garlic cloves, minced

1 loaf crusty French or Italian bread, *or* 4 crusty sandwich rolls

2 medium tomatoes, sliced

Makes 4 sandwiches

❶ Preheat the broiler. Using a pastry brush and ¼ cup of the mayonnaise, brush a thin layer of mayonnaise on both sides of the eggplant slices. Dip the slices in the Parmesan cheese to coat. Place the slices in one layer on a baking sheet and broil on both sides until a rich golden brown and very tender, about 10 minutes. Let cool to room temperature. (If you want to do this step up to 24 hours in advance, cover and chill the cooled eggplant slices. Before serving, bring to room temperature.)

❷ Mix the remaining ½ cup mayonnaise with the mustard and garlic.

❸ Halve the bread lengthwise and then cut the entire loaf into 4 sections. Brush each side generously with the garlic mayonnaise, then layer the bottom half of each bread section with the eggplant and tomato slices. Top with the remaining bread.

TEMPEH HEROS

After the tempeh slices are sautéed, a drizzling of tamari gives them a deep, rich, roasted flavor somewhat reminiscent of bacon. Layered with lettuce, tomato, and Russian dressing, the result is a satisfying sandwich that could be served as a quick dinner.

10 ounces tempeh (see opposite page)

2 tablespoons vegetable oil

2 teaspoons tamari soy sauce

RUSSIAN DRESSING

¼ cup mayonnaise

2½ tablespoons ketchup

1½ tablespoons sweet relish (optional)

4 submarine or hero rolls

4 romaine lettuce leaves

8 tomato slices

4 red onion slices

Makes 4 sandwiches

❶ Cut the tempeh into 4 slices, then cut each piece in half crosswise to make 8 thin slices.

❷ Heat the oil in a large skillet. When it is hot, add the tempeh and fry until golden brown on both sides. Remove the tempeh to a platter, then drizzle about ⅛ teaspoon tamari on top of each slice and rub it in with your fingers (the tempeh will quickly absorb it). Turn over the slices and repeat. Let the slices cool to room temperature or until slightly warm.

❸ Mix the mayonnaise, ketchup, and relish together to make the Russian dressing. Slice each roll lengthwise to open. Generously spread both sides of each roll with the Russian dressing, then layer with the tempeh, lettuce, and sliced onion.

TEMPEH. Tempeh is a fermented soybean product made by mixing cooked soybeans with a rhizopus culture and pressing the mixture into flat cakes. It has a beanier flavor and texture than tofu, and, unlike tofu, contains vitamin B-12, the vitamin most likely to be absent from a vegetarian or vegan diet. Tempeh is very high in protein, rich in calcium and iron, low in fat, and free of cholesterol. In Indonesia, where it originated, and in the West, tempeh is always cooked before it is eaten.

Fried tempeh cubes have a crisp but tender texture, and are delicious mixed with vegetables and coated with a marinara sauce or a Chinese sweet-and-sour sauce. The black specks found in tempeh are spores of the rhizopus culture and are not a sign of spoilage. Spoiled tempeh will smell bad, feel slimy, and have pink, green, or yellow discolorations.

TEMPEH SPREAD SANDWICHES

The flavor of this spread is reminiscent of chicken salad and bacon. I like to serve it on hard rolls with lettuce and tomato, but it is also delicious on toasted French bread or crackers.

10 ounces tempeh (see page 107)

1 tablespoon vegetable oil

2 teaspoons tamari soy sauce

¼ cup mayonnaise, plus extra for the bread

1 scallion, thinly sliced

1 celery rib, finely chopped

⅛ teaspoon celery seed

3 hard sandwich rolls

Romaine or iceberg lettuce leaves

Tomato slices

Makes 3 sandwiches

❶ Finely chop the tempeh, then heat the oil in a large skillet over medium-high heat. Sauté the tempeh until golden all over, about 7 minutes.

❷ Scrape the tempeh into a medium bowl, then mash with a fork until it resembles large crumbs. Pour on the tamari and mix well. Let cool to room temperature. Stir in the mayonnaise, scallion, celery, and celery seed. Cover and chill at least 30 minutes.

❸ To make sandwiches, spread some mayonnaise on sliced hard rolls. Spoon on the tempeh spread, then top with lettuce and sliced tomatoes.

GINGERED TOFU PEANUT SPREAD

Serve this ultracreamy spread as a sandwich filling and top with cucumber slices to provide a delicious contrast in texture and filling.

½ pound firm or extra-firm tofu, patted very dry

1 tablespoon tamari soy sauce

⅔ cup natural-style peanut butter

1 tablespoon lemon juice

1½ teaspoons minced fresh ginger

1 garlic clove, minced

2 tablespoons water

Fills 6 sandwiches

❶ Put the tofu and tamari in a blender or food processor and puree until a smooth, thick paste forms. Turn off the blender and scrape down the sides as necessary. Scrape the tofu into a medium bowl.

❷ With a fork, vigorously beat in all of the remaining ingredients. Let sit 30 minutes at room temperature before serving. This spread will keep 3 days, covered and refrigerated.

ASSORTED TEA SANDWICHES

Make a platter of these for your next party or get-together; they'll disappear in a flash. The bread slices and fillings are all different colors and look quite lovely when artfully arranged.

CUCUMBER AND DILL SANDWICHES

1 large cucumber

¼ teaspoon salt

¼ cup mayonnaise

1 teaspoon minced fresh dill

10 slices whole wheat bread, crusts removed

1 teaspoon white vinegar

Freshly ground black pepper to taste

SCALLION CREAM CHEESE SANDWICHES

3 scallions, thinly sliced

¼ cup minced fresh parsley

4 tablespoons unsalted butter, softened

4 ounces cream cheese, softened

Freshly ground black pepper to taste

10 slices good-quality white bread, crusts removed

CURRIED EGG SALAD SANDWICHES

4 hard-boiled eggs, peeled

1½ tablespoons mayonnaise, plus extra for bread

¼ teaspoon curry powder

❶ To make the cucumber and dill sandwiches: Peel the cucumber, then cut in half lengthwise. With a spoon, scrape out the seeds and discard them. Cut the cucumber into paper-thin half-moon slices. Toss with salt in a bowl and let sit 15 minutes.

❷ Meanwhile, mix the mayonnaise with the dill and spread on each bread slice. Drain the cucumber slices on paper towels. Return them to the bowl and toss with the vinegar and black pepper. Arrange the cucumbers over half of the bread slices, then top with the remaining bread slices. Cut each sandwich into 4 squares. Arrange neatly in the center of a large platter.

❸ To make the scallion and cream cheese sandwiches: In the container of a blender or food processor, combine the scallions and parsley and process until very fine. Add the butter, cream cheese, and pepper and blend until the mixture turns green. Scrape into a bowl, then spread on half the bread slices. Top with the remaining slices, then cut each sandwich into 4 triangles. Arrange the triangles standing up, next to the cucumber sandwiches.

❹ To make the curried egg salad sandwiches: Mince the hard-boiled eggs. Mix with the mayonnaise, curry powder, celery, onion, salt, and pepper. Lightly spread mayonnaise on each bread slice.

1½ tablespoons very thinly sliced celery

1 tablespoon finely chopped onion

Salt to taste

Freshly ground black pepper to taste

10 slices good-quality pumpernickel bread, crusts removed

....

Fresh parsley and dill sprigs or nasturtiums, for garnish

Makes 60 tea sandwiches

Spread the egg salad on half the slices, then top with the remaining slices. Cut the sandwiches into 4 triangles. Place these triangles, standing up, on the other side of the cucumber sandwiches.

❺ Cover the sandwich platter with a slightly damp towel and plastic wrap. Chill until serving time. Garnish the platter with parsley and dill sprigs or nasturtiums.

GARLIC AND HERB TOFU SPREAD

Here's a richly flavored, smooth spread that is very low in fat and calories. This has become my favorite quick lunch, especially if I've overindulged the night before!

½ pound firm tofu, patted dry

1 garlic clove, pressed

2 teaspoons tamari soy sauce

¼ teaspoon dried basil

¼ teaspoon dried oregano

¼ teaspoon minced fresh dill

Fills 3 sandwiches

❶ Place the tofu, garlic, and tamari in a blender or food processor and blend until smooth. Turn off the machine and scrape down the sides as necessary. Scrape the spread into a bowl.

❷ Stir in the herbs, then cover and chill 30 minutes. Spread will keep 3 days in the refrigerator.

☞***Variations:*** Spread between 2 slices of bread and top with sliced cucumbers and sprouts or lettuce. Or fill pita bread halves with raw vegetables and top with the spread.

ENTREES

PASTA PRONTO

Pasta has become the shining member of the complex-carbohydrate family. Because complex carbohydrates are metabolized slowly, they curb the appetite and have been singled out as the best source of fuel for the body. In addition, complex carbohydrates (grains, vegetables, legumes, and fruits) have not been linked to any fatal diseases, as have fats and sugar.

Pasta is one of the most versatile foods known to man. It can be prepared in limitless ways and is one of the most satisfying foods to eat. For vegetarians, pasta offers the means to create countless dishes, from the simple to the elegant.

The only drawback to many pasta dishes is the heavy reliance on rich sauces. Here, I have kept the use of cream, butter, and olive oil to a minimum without sacrificing flavor and consistency. If you are serving a pasta dish with cream in the sauce, balance the remainder of the meal by serving a light salad and a low-fat dessert.

Always cook pasta al dente, that is, tender yet slightly chewy to the bite. Overcooked pasta becomes mushy and doesn't react well with sauce. Although dried pasta has cooking instructions on the package, it is best to taste a piece to test for doneness, then drain it thoroughly in a colander before mixing with a sauce. If you anticipate that your pasta will be done before you are ready to serve it, try the following trick: A few minutes before the pasta reaches the desired degree of doneness, remove the pot from the heat and let the pasta sit in the hot water until you are ready to serve. You'll probably have about 7 minutes leeway, since the pasta will still be cooking in the hot water, but at a much slower rate.

CAPELLINI WITH TOMATO PESTO

When I want to make an ultraquick pasta dish that will be a surefire winner, I choose this favorite recipe. The assertive tomato-based sauce is richly infused with garlic, basil, and olive oil, and like other pestos, it clings doggedly to the pasta. You won't be satisfied with traditional marinara sauce once you've tried this tomato pesto.

⅓ cup pine nuts

6 ounce can good-quality tomato paste

½ cup minced fresh parsley

¼ cup finely chopped fresh basil, *or* 2 teaspoons dried

½ cup olive oil

½ cup grated Parmesan cheese

2 garlic cloves, pressed or minced

½ teaspoon salt

Freshly ground black pepper to taste

1 pound capellini, *or* vermicelli or spaghettini

Serves 4

❶ Lightly toast the pine nuts in a 350°F. oven until golden, about 5 minutes.

❷ To make the sauce, combine the pine nuts with all the remaining ingredients except the pasta in a medium bowl. (This step may be completed up to 24 hours in advance, covered, and chilled. Bring to room temperature before mixing it with the pasta.)

❸ Bring a 6-quart pot of water to a boil. Add the pasta and cook until al dente. Before draining the pasta, beat 2 tablespoons of the boiling pasta water into the sauce. Drain the pasta and return it to the pot or drop it into a large bowl. Spoon on the sauce and toss quickly. Serve immediately.

TORTELLINI WITH SOUR CREAM SAUCE

A strikingly pretty presentation: Tortellini coated with a simple sour cream sauce is topped with a vivid mixture of bright-red diced tomatoes and green scallion slices.

1 pound fresh or frozen cheese tortellini

2 teaspoons unsalted butter

4 to 6 scallions, thinly sliced

2 medium tomatoes, cored, seeded, and diced

⅔ cup sour cream

2 tablespoons grated Parmesan cheese

½ teaspoon salt

Freshly ground black pepper to taste

Serves 4

❶ Bring a large pot of water to a boil and cook the tortellini until tender but not mushy. (It's a good idea to taste one to judge accurately.)

❷ Meanwhile, melt the butter in a medium skillet, add the scallions and tomatoes, and sauté 2 minutes, or until the vegetables are hot throughout. Set aside.

❸ In a small bowl mix together the sour cream, Parmesan cheese, salt, and pepper.

❹ Drain the tortellini thoroughly, then return it to the pot. Pour on the sour cream mixture and toss quickly to coat. Spoon the tortellini onto serving plates, and spoon some of the tomato mixture in the center of each serving.

VEGETABLE LO MEIN

I find the following unconventional method an easy and relaxing alternative to stir-frying pasta.

½ pound linguine *or* spaghettini

1 tablespoon oriental sesame oil

2 tablespoons tamari soy sauce

VEGETABLES

3 tablespoons vegetable oil

1 pound extra-firm or firm tofu, cut into ½-inch cubes and patted very dry

2 garlic cloves, minced

1 teaspoon minced fresh ginger

4½ cups (about 12 ounces) thinly sliced mushrooms

2 scallions, thinly sliced

1 tablespoon tamari soy sauce

2 teaspoons oriental sesame oil

Serves 3 to 4

❶ Cook the pasta al dente in a large pot of boiling water. The noodles should remain a little chewy in texture. Drain very well in a colander. Mix the sesame oil and soy sauce together, pour over the noodles, and toss to coat. Place in a baking dish and cover with foil. Keep warm in a 300°F. oven while stir-frying the vegetables. (The noodles can be prepared up to 24 hours in advance and chilled. To reheat, sprinkle with 2 tablespoons of water, then cover and reheat in a 300°F. oven till hot, about 15 minutes.)

❷ In a wok or large skillet, heat 2 tablespoons of the oil over high heat until hot but not smoking. Add the tofu and stir-fry until golden all over. Remove to a platter. Reduce the heat to medium and add the remaining 1 tablespoon of the oil. Stir-fry the garlic and ginger 30 seconds. Add the mushrooms and stir-fry until brown and juicy, about 7 minutes. Return the tofu to the pan and toss. Add the scallions and stir-fry 2 minutes. Sprinkle on the soy sauce and sesame oil and toss again.

❸ Remove the noodles from the oven. Spoon on the vegetable mixture and toss thoroughly. Serve immediately, or cover and keep warm in the oven for up to 20 minutes.

ULTRAQUICK LASAGNA

Preparing this lasagna takes just 10 minutes because the noodles are not precooked. Raw noodles are layered with ricotta and mozzarella cheeses and surrounded with a thin tomato-wine sauce that cooks the noodles until tender. It's delicious and it works!

1 32-ounce jar (4 cups) tomato sauce

1 garlic clove, pressed

½ cup dry red wine

1½ cups water

1 teaspoon dried oregano

2 large eggs

2 cups (about 15 ounces) part-skim ricotta cheese

¼ cup grated Parmesan cheese

¼ teaspoon freshly ground nutmeg

1 pound uncooked lasagna

1 pound (about 5 cups) grated mozzarella cheese

Serves 6

❶ Preheat the oven to 350°F. In a large bowl, combine the tomato sauce, garlic, wine, water, and oregano.

❷ In a medium bowl, beat the eggs. Beat in the ricotta and Parmesan cheeses and the nutmeg.

❸ Pour a generous amount of sauce on the bottom of a 9 × 13-inch pan or baking dish, or on the bottoms of 2 smaller baking dishes. (You must give the lasagna enough room to swell during cooking.) Alternating the lasagna, sauce, ricotta mixture, and mozzarella, make about three layers, ending with the mozzarella.

❹ Cover the pan(s) tightly with aluminum foil. (The lasagna may be prepared to this point and refrigerated up to 24 hours in advance. Bring to room temperature before baking.) Bake 1 hour, remove the foil, and continue baking 15 minutes, or until the sauce has thickened and the noodles are tender. Let sit 10 minutes before cutting.

LINGUINE WITH CAULIFLOWER IN A TOMATO CREAM SAUCE

Tomato cream is one of the most seductive pasta sauces. Combined with cauliflower and hot peppers, it transforms pasta into a truly elegant creation.

1 pound linguine

2 tablespoons olive oil

4 garlic cloves, minced

¼ teaspoon crushed red pepper flakes

1 large cauliflower, cut into small flowerets (about 7 cups)

1 cup tomato puree

1 cup light cream, *or* ½ cup heavy cream mixed with ½ cup milk

¼ teaspoon freshly grated nutmeg

½ teaspoon salt

Freshly ground black pepper to taste

¼ cup minced fresh parsley

Grated Parmesan cheese

Serves 4

❶ Bring a large stockpot of water to a boil. Drop in the linguine and cook until al dente.

❷ Meanwhile, heat the olive oil in a large skillet over medium heat. Add the garlic and red pepper flakes and cook 2 minutes. Do not let the garlic brown. Stir in the cauliflower and toss to coat well. Pour in ⅓ cup water and cover the pan. Cook 10 minutes, or until the cauliflower is tender but not mushy. Remove the cover and toss occasionally.

❸ Mix together the tomato puree, cream, nutmeg, salt, and pepper. Pour over the cauliflower and toss well. Bring to a boil, then turn off the heat.

❹ Drain the linguine in a colander. Place some linguine on each serving plate. Spoon on the sauce, then garnish with the minced parsley. Pass the Parmesan cheese at the table.

ZITI WITH BROCCOLI AND RICOTTA SAUCE

Part-skim ricotta cheese is the base for this creamy sauce, making it relatively low in fat.

½ pound ziti, *or penne,* rigatoni, or *rotini*

1 tablespoon unsalted butter

1 tablespoon olive oil

3 garlic cloves, minced

⅛ teaspoon crushed red pepper flakes

3 scallions, thinly sliced

1 bunch broccoli, stalks peeled and cut into small pieces (about 5 cups)

1 cup part-skim ricotta cheese, at room temperature

¼ cup milk

¼ cup grated Parmesan cheese

¼ teaspoon dried basil

¼ teaspoon dried oregano

¼ teaspoon salt

Freshly ground black pepper to taste

Serves 2 to 3

❶ Bring a large pot of water to a boil, then cook the ziti until al dente, about 15 minutes.

❷ Meanwhile, heat the butter and olive oil in a large skillet over medium heat. Add the garlic, red pepper flakes, and scallions; sauté 2 minutes, stirring frequently. Add the broccoli, toss, then add a few tablespoons of water. Cover the pan and cook just until the broccoli is tender but still bright green, about 5 minutes. Keep warm over low heat.

❸ In a medium bowl beat together the ricotta, milk, Parmesan, basil, oregano, salt, and pepper, along with 2 tablespoons of the boiling pasta water.

❹ Drain the ziti in a colander. Place in a large serving bowl or return to the pot. Stir in the ricotta mixture to coat, then toss with the broccoli. Serve immediately.

RAVIOLI WITH GARLIC, PEPPERS, AND TOMATOES

Olive oil, garlic, bell pepper strips, and diced tomatoes combine to make a spicy, chunky sauce that suits the bulky texture of ravioli perfectly.

1 pound fresh or frozen cheese ravioli

¼ cup olive oil

3 garlic cloves, minced

¼ teaspoon crushed red pepper flakes

3 medium green bell peppers, cored and cut into ½-inch strips

3 medium tomatoes, cored, seeded, and diced

½ teaspoon dried oregano

¼ teaspoon dried thyme

Salt to taste

Freshly ground black pepper to taste

Grated Parmesan cheese

Serves 4

❶ Bring a large pot of water to a boil and cook the ravioli until tender.

❷ Meanwhile, make the sauce. In a large skillet, heat the olive oil over medium heat. Add the garlic and the red pepper flakes and cook 2 minutes. Do not let the garlic brown.

❸ Toss in the pepper strips and sauté, stirring often, for 10 minutes, or until the peppers are almost tender. Raise the heat to medium-high. Add the tomatoes, oregano, thyme, salt, and pepper and cook 5 minutes more, or until the peppers are tender and the tomatoes are heated through. (The tomatoes will have rendered their juices and made a light sauce.)

❹ Drain the ravioli and return to the pot or place in a large pasta serving bowl. Spoon on the sauce and toss lightly. Pass the Parmesan cheese at the table.

BABY RAVIOLI WITH CREAM, MUSHROOMS, AND PEAS

The small ravioli known as raviolini are available in many supermarkets in the frozen-foods section. If you cannot find them, substitute cheese tortellini or regular-size ravioli.

1 pound fresh or frozen cheese raviolini

2 tablespoons olive oil

4½ cups (about 12 ounces) fresh mushrooms, sliced

2 cups (about 1 pound) frozen peas

½ cup heavy cream

Salt to taste

Freshly ground black pepper to taste

2 tablespoons unsalted butter, cut into bits

Grated Parmesan cheese

Serves 4

❶ In a large stockpot, cook the raviolini in boiling water until tender, about 10 to 15 minutes.

❷ Meanwhile, make the sauce. In a large skillet, heat the olive oil over medium heat. Add the mushrooms and cook until brown and juices evaporate, about 10 minutes. Add the peas and cook 3 minutes more, or until heated through. Stir in the cream and bring to a boil. Season with salt and pepper, then remove from the heat.

❸ Drain the ravioli thoroughly. Meanwhile, melt the butter in the stockpot, then return the ravioli to the pot and toss to coat. Pour on the sauce and heat until bubbly, about 1 minute. Serve with some Parmesan cheese sprinkled on each serving.

PENNE WITH SPINACH AND CHICK-PEAS IN GARLIC SAUCE

A light, flavorful way to serve pasta that is also nutritious and low in fat. This sauce goes well with a short, tubular pasta, so if you cannot get* penne, *or* mostaccioli, *try* ziti, rigatoni, *or* rotini *(short spirals).

1 10-ounce package loose fresh spinach, *or* 1 10-ounce package frozen chopped spinach, thawed

1 pound *penne* or *mostaccioli* (short, quill-shaped pasta)

⅓ cup olive oil

6 garlic cloves, minced

¼ teaspoon crushed red pepper flakes

2 medium tomatoes, cored, seeded, and cut into ½-inch dice

2 cups freshly cooked chick-peas (see page 161), *or* 1 15-ounce can chick-peas, rinsed and drained

¼ teaspoon salt

¼ cup grated Parmesan cheese

Serves 4

❶ Clean the fresh spinach and discard the stems. Place the spinach in a large skillet with just the water that clings to it, cover, and cook over medium heat just until wilted, about 5 minutes. Drain, cool, then squeeze dry with your hands. (If you are using frozen spinach, just squeeze out all of the moisture with your hands.) Set aside.

❷ Bring a 6-quart pot of water to a boil and add the *penne.* Cook until al dente, 12 to 15 minutes.

❸ Meanwhile, make the sauce. Heat the olive oil in a large skillet over medium heat. Add the garlic and red pepper flakes and cook 2 minutes. Add the tomatoes and chick-peas and cook 2 minutes more. Add the spinach, salt, and ¼ cup of the boiling pasta water and stir well. Cook until heated through, about 3 minutes.

❹ When the pasta is done, drain it thoroughly in a colander. Return it to the pot or put it in a large serving bowl. Spoon on the sauce and toss well. Sprinkle on the Parmesan cheese, toss again, and serve with additional cheese to pass at the table.

SPAGHETTINI WITH CRUMBLED BLUE CHEESE

This is simplicity itself, yet intensely flavorful and appealing.

1 pound spaghettini

3 tablespoons unsalted butter

¼ cup olive oil

1 cup minced fresh parsley

1 cup (about 4 ounces) crumbled blue cheese

Serves 4

❶ Cook the spaghettini until al dente in a large pot of boiling water.

❷ Meanwhile, melt the butter with the olive oil in a small saucepan. Remove from the heat and stir in the parsley.

❸ Drain the spaghettini and place in a large bowl. Pour on the parsley sauce and toss very well. Sprinkle on the crumbled blue cheese and toss again. Serve immediately.

FETTUCCINE MARGHERITA

After having this dish in Montreal one summer, the lingering memory of the sauce followed me home. I experimented with this dish until I captured the original's earthy blend of mushrooms, tangy tomatoes, and silky cream. A superb pasta dish with great panache.

1 pound fettuccine

2 tablespoons olive oil

2 tablespoons unsalted butter

12 ounces (about 4½ cups) sliced mushrooms

4 garlic cloves, minced

¼ teaspoon crushed red pepper flakes

1 28-ounce can imported plum tomatoes, well drained and chopped

¼ cup white wine

½ cup heavy cream

½ teaspoon salt

⅓ cup grated Parmesan cheese

Serves 4

❶ Cook the fettuccine until al dente in a large pot of boiling water.

❷ Meanwhile, in a large skillet heat the olive oil and butter over medium-high heat. Add the mushrooms and sauté until they brown and the juices begin to evaporate, about 7 minutes.

❸ Add the garlic and red pepper and cook for 2 minutes, stirring frequently. Add the tomatoes and wine and boil 2 minutes, stirring often. Add the cream and salt and boil 1 minute.

❹ Drain the fettuccine thoroughly. Return to the pot or place in a large bowl, then pour on the sauce and sprinkle on the Parmesan cheese. Toss quickly and serve immediately.

FETTUCCINE WITH ASPARAGUS IN LEMON CREAM SAUCE

A rich—but not too rich—
way to celebrate spring's asparagus crop.

¾ pound fettuccine

1 tablespoon olive oil

2 garlic cloves, minced

¾ pound asparagus, stalks peeled and cut into 1-inch pieces

½ cup heavy cream

½ cup milk

Grated rind of 1 lemon

¼ teaspoon freshly grated nutmeg

½ teaspoon salt

Freshly ground black pepper to taste

⅓ cup grated Parmesan cheese

Serves 4

❶ Cook the fettuccine until al dente in a large pot of boiling water.

❷ Meanwhile, heat the oil in a large skillet over medium heat. Add the garlic and asparagus and sauté, tossing constantly, 2 minutes. Pour in about 2 tablespoons water and cover the pan. Cook until the asparagus are just tender, about 5 minutes. Combine the cream, milk, lemon rind, nutmeg, salt, and pepper. Pour over the asparagus and bring to a boil.

❸ Drain the fettuccine and return to the pot. Pour on the asparagus sauce, toss, and stir in the Parmesan cheese. Serve immediately.

SOBA WITH BROCCOLI AND *WASABI*

Soba (buckwheat noodles) is especially suited to being served in broth, Japanese fashion. Here, wasabi, a Japanese green horseradish paste, is used to spike the broth and give it a wonderful pungency.

This dish is particularly light and contains almost no fat, so it serves two, allowing two bowlfuls per person.

1 bunch broccoli, stalks peeled and cut into small pieces (about 5 cups)

8 ounces *soba* (buckwheat noodles)

1 teaspoon *wasabi* powder (see page 102)

1¾ cups vegetable stock (*see Note*)

3 tablespoons *mirin* (sweet sake) *or* pale dry sherry

3 tablespoons tamari soy sauce

2 scallions, very thinly sliced

Serves 2

❶ Bring a large stockpot of water to a boil. Drop in the broccoli, cover the pot, and cook 5 minutes, or until the broccoli is tender but still bright green. Remove with a slotted spoon and set aside.

❷ Let the water return to a rapid boil. Drop in the *soba* and cook until tender, about 10 minutes.

❸ Mix the *wasabi* and 1 teaspoon water together in a small dish (the resulting paste should have the consistency of smooth mustard; add a few more drops of water if necessary). Let sit 10 minutes to develop the flavor.

❹ While the *soba* is cooking, combine the stock, *mirin* or sherry, and tamari in a medium saucepan and bring to a boil.

❺ Drain the *soba* in a colander. Divide between 2 large bowls or 4 medium bowls. Place equal amounts of broccoli on top of each bowlful. Pour boiling stock into each bowl. Sprinkle on the scallions. Serve with the *wasabi* paste at the table, to spoon on as desired.

☛***Note:*** Vegetable stock can be made with powdered vegetable stock base, available at health food stores.

PASTA FRITTATA

I'm indebted to Marcella Hazan, noted Italian cookbook author, for the marvelous idea of using leftover pasta in a frittata. I have become so enamored of this dish that I hope family or guests don't finish all the pasta so I can make this frittata the following evening.

For the filling, you can use plain spaghetti that has been coated with butter, parsley, and cheese. Elaborate preparations such as Fettuccine Margherita (page 126) or Capellini with Tomato Pesto (page 116) will be even more savory. Improvisation is the key. This is the type of "pie" that is rarely the same twice but is always good. Serve it with Green Bean Salad with Lemon, Dill, and Feta Cheese (page 178), a colorful side dish.

5 large eggs

⅓ cup grated Parmesan cheese

¼ cup milk

4 cups cooked pasta

¼ teaspoon salt

Freshly ground black pepper to taste

½ tablespoon unsalted butter

Serves 3 to 4

❶ Preheat the oven to 350°F. Butter a pie plate and set it aside.

❷ Beat the eggs in a large bowl until well mixed. Stir in all of the remaining ingredients except the butter. Pour the mixture into the pie plate. Cut the butter into bits and distribute all over the top.

❸ Bake 10 minutes, then remove from the oven and very lightly stir the mixture. Return to the oven and bake an additional 10 to 15 minutes, or until a knife inserted in the center comes out almost dry. Cut into wedges and serve immediately.

PASTA AND VEGETABLE GRATIN

This baked pasta dish with a thin cheese sauce is much lighter than traditional macaroni and cheese and, to my mind, more appetizing. You can prepare much of this in advance, but don't pour on the sauce until you are ready to bake the gratin.

8 ounces (2 to 3 cups) *rotini*, macaroni, or ziti

1 medium yellow squash, cut into ½-inch dice

1 small red bell pepper, finely diced

2 scallions, thinly sliced

1 cup grated extra-sharp cheddar cheese

1 tablespoon unsalted butter

1 tablespoon unbleached flour

2¼ cups low-fat milk

¼ cup grated Parmesan cheese

⅛ teaspoon freshly grated nutmeg

¼ teaspoon dried dill

½ teaspoon salt

Freshly ground black pepper to taste

2 tablespoons bread crumbs

Serves 4

❶ Cook the *rotini* until al dente in a large pot of boiling water. Drain in a colander, then rinse under cold running water and drain again very thoroughly. Pour the pasta into a shallow dish such as a 2-quart oval gratin or a 12 × 7 × 2-inch baking dish.

❷ Stir in the yellow squash, red pepper, and scallions. Sprinkle on the cheddar cheese and lightly mix.

❸ Preheat the oven to 400°F. To make the sauce, melt the butter in a medium saucepan over medium heat. Whisk in the flour and let bubble, whisking constantly, until it begins to turn beige. Immediately whisk in the milk, and bring to a boil, whisking constantly. Remove from the heat and whisk in the Parmesan cheese, nutmeg, dill, salt, and pepper.

❹ Pour the sauce over the pasta mixture and toss lightly. Sprinkle on the bread crumbs. Bake 30 minutes, or until bubbly and brown on top.

GREAT GRAINS

With so much attention turned toward the importance of fiber in our diets, grains cookery has gained a new prominence. Although side dishes such as rice and bulghur pilafs have been around for some time, the use of grains in main courses has been less common.

Once you taste the delicious entrées in this chapter, you'll want to make grains a regular part of your diet. They are economical; highly nutritious, providing protein, vitamins, and much-needed fiber; and satisfying.

Many of the recipes in this chapter are low in fat and therefore a good choice if you have been indulging in rich foods recently. Because these entrées are complete in themselves, all you'll need is a fresh green salad to round off your meal.

BAKED STUFFED TOMATOES WITH COUSCOUS, PEAS, AND FETA CHEESE

A choice dish at the end of the summer when fat, juicy tomatoes are abundant. Serve this with a green salad and French bread.

4 large tomatoes

1 cup couscous

1½ cups boiling water

¼ cup plus 1 tablespoon olive oil

3 garlic cloves, minced

1 cup frozen peas, thawed

½ cup grated Parmesan cheese

1 cup (about 5 ounces) crumbled feta cheese

¼ cup minced fresh parsley

½ teaspoon dried oregano

Freshly ground black pepper to taste

Serves 4

❶ Slice the tomatoes in half horizontally. With a teaspoon, scoop out the pulp and seeds and discard. Drain the tomatoes upside down for 30 minutes.

❷ Meanwhile, make the stuffing. Place the couscous in a large bowl and stir in the boiling water. Cover and let sit 10 minutes. Preheat the oven to 375°F. Spread one tablespoon of the olive oil on the bottom of a large, shallow 2½-quart baking dish such as a 10 × 10 × 2-inch or other baking dish.

❸ In a small pan, heat the remaining ¼ cup of the olive oil and sauté the garlic until barely golden. Don't let it brown. Fluff the couscous with a fork and stir in the olive oil and garlic mixture and all the remaining ingredients.

❹ Divide the stuffing evenly among the tomato shells, pressing it in firmly. Bake 30 minutes. Pour the accumulated juices over the top when serving.

VEGETABLE COUSCOUS

A colorful medley of vegetables in a spicy sauce tops a mound of delicate couscous.

2 tablespoons olive oil

2 garlic cloves, minced

1 medium onion, diced

2 teaspoons ground cumin

½ teaspoon turmeric

1 teaspoon paprika

⅛ teaspoon cayenne pepper

2 medium zucchini, cut into ½-inch cubes

1 15-ounce can chick-peas, rinsed and drained, *or* 2 cups freshly cooked chick-peas (page 161)

1 16-ounce can tomatoes, finely chopped, with their juice

½ cup raisins

1½ cups vegetable stock *(see Note)*

½ teaspoon salt

2 tablespoons unsalted butter

1 cup couscous

Serves 3 to 4

❶ Heat the olive oil in a large skillet over medium-high heat. Add the garlic and onion and sauté 2 minutes. Sprinkle in the cumin, turmeric, paprika, and cayenne and cook 2 minutes more, stirring often.

❷ Stir in the zucchini, chick-peas, tomatoes, and raisins. Cover the pan and lower the heat to medium. Cook, stirring occasionally, until the zucchini is tender, about 10 minutes. (The juices should be thickened at this point. If they are not, remove the cover and boil a few minutes until thick.) You may prepare the dish to this point up to 8 hours in advance (cover and refrigerate, and reheat before proceeding with step 3).

❸ Meanwhile, prepare the couscous. Bring the stock, salt, and butter to a boil. Stir in the couscous, cover, remove from the heat, and let sit 5 minutes, or for up to 20 minutes. Fluff with a fork before serving.

❹ Serve the couscous with the vegetable mixture mounded in the center.

☞***Note:*** Vegetable stock can be made with powdered vegetable stock base, available at health food stores.

BAKED COUSCOUS WITH SPINACH AND PINE NUTS

The fresh spinach in this garlic- and basil-scented concoction retains its vivid color and has a delightful texture because it is baked only for a short time. The entire dish can be assembled up to 24 hours in advance and is particularly good served with hot, crusty bread.

1 cup couscous

1½ cups boiling vegetable stock *(see Note,* page 133), *or* water

½ teaspoon salt

¼ cup olive oil

3 garlic cloves, minced

1 large onion, diced

1 28-ounce can tomatoes, chopped and drained (reserve ⅓ cup juice)

1½ tablespoons minced fresh basil, *or* 1 teaspoon dried

⅓ cup pine nuts

5 cups (about 5 ounces) loosely packed fresh spinach, stems removed and leaves torn into small pieces

Freshly ground black pepper to taste

1 cup grated Muenster cheese

Serves 4

❶ Combine the couscous, boiling stock or water, and salt in a large bowl; cover with a plate. Let sit 5 minutes, then fluff with a fork.

❷ Preheat the oven to 375°F. Heat the olive oil in a large skillet over medium heat. Sauté the garlic and onion 10 minutes, or until tender. Add the drained tomatoes and cook 10 minutes more, stirring frequently.

❸ Stir the tomato mixture into the couscous and mix in the reserved tomato juice, basil, pine nuts, raw spinach, and pepper.

❹ Spread half the couscous mixture in a 12 × 7 × 2-inch or other shallow (2½-quart) baking dish. Sprinkle on the cheese, then top with the remaining couscous. Cover the dish with foil and bake 25 minutes, or until hot and bubbly.

CURRIED BULGHUR WITH CHICK-PEAS AND VEGETABLES

Serve this with plain yogurt to provide a contrasting flavor and texture.

1½ cups bulghur

3 tablespoons vegetable oil

3 large scallions, thinly sliced, white and green parts separated

1 teaspoon turmeric

2 teaspoons ground coriander

1 tablespoon ground cumin

⅛ teaspoon ground cloves *or* allspice

¼ teaspoon cayenne pepper, or to taste

2 cups freshly cooked chick-peas (page 161), or 1 15-ounce can chick-peas, rinsed and drained

2 medium carrots, grated

1 16-ounce can plum tomatoes, seeded, well drained, and diced

1 tablespoon tamari soy sauce

Serves 4

❶ Rinse the bulghur in a sieve. Put the bulghur in a medium bowl and cover with boiling water by 2 inches. Soak uncovered for 30 minutes, or until tender when tasted. Drain thoroughly by spooning batches into a sieve and pressing out all of the liquid with the back of a spoon. Or put batches of the bulghur in a cotton kitchen towel or piece of cheesecloth and squeeze out the liquid. As the batches are completed put them in another medium bowl.

❷ Heat the oil in a large skillet over medium heat. Add the white parts of the scallions and sauté 3 minutes, tossing often.

❸ Sprinkle on the turmeric, coriander, cumin, cloves, and cayenne and cook 1 minute, stirring frequently. Add the drained chick-peas, the carrots, and the drained diced tomatoes, toss to mix, and cook 2 minutes.

❹ Stir in the drained bulghur, the green tops of the scallions, and the tamari and mix thoroughly. Cook, tossing occasionally, 10 minutes or until piping hot.

POLENTA WITH SPICY EGGPLANT SAUCE

Simmering eggplant in this tasty sauce rather than frying it reduces the amount of fat needed and cuts down on time spent in front of the stove. Here, the eggplant sauce is spooned onto slices of slightly firm polenta to make a colorful and substantial dish.

SAUCE

3 tablespoons olive oil

3 garlic cloves, minced

⅛ to ¼ teaspoon crushed red pepper flakes

1 28-ounce can plum tomatoes, roughly chopped, with their juice

1 tablespoon tomato paste

2 teaspoons red wine vinegar

½ teaspoon salt

Freshly ground black pepper to taste

1 medium eggplant, peeled and cut into ½-inch dice

1 green bell pepper, diced

....

1¼ cups cornmeal

3½ cups water

½ teaspoon salt

1 tablespoon unsalted butter

¼ cup grated Parmesan cheese

Minced fresh parsley

Serves 4 to 6

❶ To make the sauce, heat the olive oil in a large skillet over medium heat. Add the garlic and red pepper flakes and cook 30 seconds. Do not let the garlic brown. Stir in the tomatoes and their juice. Mix the tomato paste with the vinegar, stir it in, then stir in the salt and pepper. Bring to a boil.

❷ Add the eggplant and cover the pan. Cook 10 minutes, stirring occasionally. Add the bell pepper, cover again, and cook 10 minutes more, or until the eggplant and pepper are tender. If the sauce is watery, remove the cover and boil a few minutes more until thickened. Keep warm while making the polenta. (The recipe may be prepared up to 24 hours in advance to this point and the sauce chilled. If too thick when reheated, add a few tablespoons water.)

❸ To make the polenta, combine the cornmeal, water, and salt in a medium heavy saucepan. Place over medium-high heat and bring to a boil, whisking often. When the cornmeal mixture begins to boil, whisk constantly until the polenta is the consistency of mashed potatoes and begins to pull away from the pot.

❹ Remove from the heat and stir in the butter and

cheese. Pour onto an oiled platter or large cutting board (about 10 × 8 inches) and let sit 20 minutes, or until firm enough to cut into 3-inch squares.

❺ Place the polenta squares on serving plates and spoon piping hot eggplant sauce over them. Garnish with parsley.

☛***Note:*** Leftover polenta squares can be refrigerated up to 4 days, then reheated in the oven when needed.

CHEESE POLENTA

Here is a variation of a polenta dish created by my friend, cookbook author Richard Sax. If you are not familiar with polenta (boiled cornmeal), choose this recipe to make its acquaintance. It has a wonderfully cheesy, creamy consistency, and you'll find that you want to have cornmeal on hand to put this together at a moment's notice. Serve this polenta with Green Bean and Red Pepper Sauté (page 187) for a pleasing match.

2 cups low-fat milk

2 cups water

¼ teaspoon freshly grated nutmeg

½ teaspoon salt

1¼ cups cornmeal

2 tablespoons cold unsalted butter, cut into bits

4 tablespoons grated Parmesan cheese

½ cup grated sharp cheddar cheese

½ cup grated Monterey Jack cheese, *or* Muenster cheese

Serves 4

❶ Generously butter a 9-inch pie plate or shallow 1-quart baking dish and set aside.

❷ Combine the milk, water, nutmeg, and salt in a heavy medium saucepan and bring to a boil. Reduce the heat to a simmer and very slowly sprinkle in the cornmeal, whisking continuously. Cook 5 minutes, or until the cornmeal mixture pulls away from the sides of pan.

❸ Remove the pan from the heat. Whisk in 1½ tablespoons of the butter and 2 tablespoons of the Parmesan cheese.

❹ With a rubber spatula, spread half the polenta mixture in the prepared pie plate or baking dish, then top with the grated cheddar and Monterey Jack cheeses. Spread on the remaining polenta, then sprinkle on the remaining 2 tablespoons Parmesan cheese and dot with the remaining ½ tablespoon of butter.

❺ Let the polenta sit at least 15 minutes, or cover and chill for up to 24 hours. When ready to cook, preheat the oven to 400°F. Bake uncovered 30 minutes, or until golden brown and bubbly.

BARLEY MUSHROOM CASSEROLE

The woodsy flavor of mushrooms permeates this dish and will fill your house with an irresistible aroma. Mashed butternut squash makes a wonderful accompaniment, both in color and texture.

5 tablespoons unsalted butter

2 medium onions, diced

4½ cups (12 ounces) sliced fresh mushrooms

1½ cups barley

¾ teaspoon dried thyme

½ teaspoon salt

Freshly ground black pepper to taste

4½ cups boiling vegetable stock *(see Note,* page 133)

Serves 4

❶ Preheat the oven to 350°F.

❷ Melt the butter in a large skillet over medium-high heat, and add all of the ingredients except the stock. Sauté, stirring frequently, until the mushrooms begin to brown, about 10 minutes.

❸ Scrape the mixture into a deep 2-quart baking dish and pour in the vegetable stock. Cover tightly and bake 60 to 75 minutes, or until all of the liquid is absorbed. (Be careful of the steam when removing the cover.) The barley should have a slightly crunchy texture when done. If it is too hard after all of the stock has been absorbed, add some boiling water and cook 10 to 15 minutes more.

BAKED RICE AND VEGETABLE PILAF WITH CASHEWS

Cinnamon and cloves spike this vibrantly colored Indian dish, creating a wonderfully aromatic blend of flavors. Serve this with hot, buttered pita bread.

- ½ cup raw cashews *(see Note)*
- 2 tablespoons unsalted butter
- 1 tablespoon vegetable oil
- 1 medium onion, finely diced
- 1 garlic clove, minced
- ½ teaspoon minced fresh ginger
- ½ teaspoon turmeric
- ⅛ teaspoon cayenne pepper
- 1 cinnamon stick
- 2 cloves
- 1 bay leaf
- 1 cup white basmati rice *or* converted rice
- 1 pound green beans, cut into 1-inch lengths, *or* 1 10-ounce package frozen cut green beans
- 1 carrot, very thinly diced
- ⅓ cup raisins
- ½ teaspoon salt
- 1¾ cups boiling water

Serves 3 to 4

❶ Preheat the oven to 400°F. Spread the cashews on a baking sheet and lightly toast, stirring occasionally, until golden and fragrant, about 7 minutes.

❷ Melt the butter with the oil in a large skillet over medium heat. Add the onion, garlic, and ginger, and sauté 2 minutes. Mix in the turmeric, cayenne, cinnamon stick, cloves, and bay leaf and cook 1 minute longer, stirring constantly. Mix in the rice and toss to coat.

❸ Scrape the rice mixture into a 2-quart baking dish. Stir in the green beans, carrot, raisins, cashews, and salt. (You can prepare the dish to this point up to 4 hours in advance, refrigerating it.) Pour in the boiling water and tightly cover the dish.

❹ Bake about 40 minutes, or until all of the liquid is absorbed. (Be careful when you remove the cover; there will be a lot of steam.) Remove the cinnamon stick and bay leaf, fluff with a fork, and let sit, covered, 5 minutes before serving.

☛ ***Note:*** Raw cashews can be purchased at any natural foods store.

RICE, BROCCOLI, AND FETA CHEESE SAUTÉ

The tang of feta cheese gives this simple dish character. For a pleasing accompaniment, try sliced tomatoes drizzled with vinaigrette.

1 cup white or brown rice

2 cups water

½ teaspoon salt

2 teaspoons vegetable oil

¼ cup olive oil

4 garlic cloves, minced

2 medium tomatoes, cored, seeded, and diced

1 bunch broccoli, stalks peeled and cut into bite-size pieces (about 5 cups)

½ teaspoon dried oregano

¼ cup water

1 cup (about 5 ounces) crumbled feta cheese

Freshly ground black pepper

Serves 2 to 3

❶ Combine the rice, water, salt, and oil in a small saucepan and bring to a boil over high heat. Lower the heat to simmer and cook until all of the water is absorbed (20 minutes for white rice and 45 minutes for brown rice). When done, remove from the heat and keep covered.

❷ In a large skillet, heat the olive oil over medium heat. Sauté the garlic 2 minutes, stirring frequently. Do not brown. Add the tomatoes and sauté 2 minutes more. Add the broccoli and oregano, toss well, pour in the water, and cover the pan. Raise the heat to medium-high and cook 5 minutes, or until the broccoli is tender but not mushy. (Remove the cover occasionally and toss the mixture.)

❸ Stir in the hot rice, feta cheese, and black pepper to taste. Serve immediately.

RICE WITH CHICK-PEAS, HERBS, AND SUN-DRIED TOMATOES

A wonderful blending of flavors and textures makes this simple dish special. A steamed vegetable such as broccoli, zucchini, or green beans is all you need for a side dish.

2 tablespoons unsalted butter

1 tablespoon olive oil

2 cups freshly cooked chick-peas (page 161), *or* 1 15-ounce can chick-peas, rinsed and drained

1½ tablespoons chopped, drained sun-dried tomatoes packed in oil *(see Note)*

⅓ cup minced fresh parsley

2½ to 3 cups cold cooked white or brown rice

1 teaspoon minced fresh basil, *or* ¼ teaspoon dried

¼ teaspoon dried oregano

Salt to taste

Freshly ground black pepper to taste

¼ cup grated Parmesan cheese

Serves 3

❶ Heat 1 tablespoon of the butter with the olive oil in a large skillet over medium heat. Add the chick-peas, sun-dried tomatoes, and parsley and cook 3 minutes.

❷ Add the rice, basil, oregano, salt, and pepper and toss well. Sprinkle on 2 tablespoons water. Cook, tossing frequently, until the rice is hot, about 10 minutes.

❸ Cut the remaining 1 tablespoon butter into bits and mix it into the rice. Sprinkle on the Parmesan cheese, toss, and serve.

☞***Note:*** If you do not have sun-dried tomatoes on hand, try substituting one seeded and minced fresh medium tomato.

ESSENTIALLY VEGETABLES

Fresh vegetables are such an important part of a healthful diet that they deserve special treatment that enables them to play more than a supporting role.

Many people avoid using fresh vegetables when they need to be quick in the kitchen. I have found a way around this tendency by doing prep work well in advance of cooking. That is, I peel, chop, or slice my vegetables at an earlier time; then, when I'm ready to cook, it's a snap.

A tip about storage: Never wash fresh vegetables before you store them in the refrigerator. The extra moisture encourages decay and cuts down considerably on their storage life. Most vegetables should be kept in a plastic bag with a few holes to allow some air circulation. Potatoes, onions, and garlic should remain at room temperature.

ZUCCHINI, TOMATO, AND SWISS CHEESE PIE

The flavors in this pie are fantastic, so do follow the recipe exactly. The crust is made by sprinkling bread crumbs in a buttered pie plate, keeping preparation quick. It's important to use Swiss cheese because its firmness helps hold the pie together. Serve this pie with Provençal Potatoes (page 179) for a great combination.

1 tablespoon unsalted butter

¼ cup bread crumbs

1½ tablespoons olive oil

1 medium onion, diced

2 garlic cloves, minced

2 medium tomatoes, seeded and diced

3 medium zucchini, quartered lengthwise and thinly sliced

½ teaspoon fennel seed, crushed

¼ teaspoon salt

Freshly ground black pepper to taste

3 large eggs

⅓ cup milk

¼ pound grated or sliced (about 1⅓ cups) Swiss cheese

3 tablespoons grated Parmesan cheese

Serves 4

❶ Preheat the oven to 375°F. Using ½ tablespoon of the butter, grease a pie plate, then sprinkle the bread crumbs over the bottom and sides.

❷ Heat the olive oil in a large skillet over medium heat. Add the onion and garlic and sauté 10 minutes. Stir in the diced tomatoes and sauté 5 minutes. Raise the heat to high. Mix in the zucchini, fennel seed, salt, and pepper. Cook until the zucchini is barely tender, about 5 minutes. (The mixture should begin to stick to the pan.) Remove the pan from the heat and cool 5 minutes. (The recipe may be prepared in advance to this point and chilled up to 24 hours. Bring to room temperature before proceeding.)

❸ Beat the eggs in a large bowl. Stir in the milk, then mix in the zucchini mixture. Pour half into the prepared pie plate, top with the Swiss cheese, then pour on the remaining vegetable mixture. Sprinkle the Parmesan cheese all over the top and dot with the remaining ½ tablespoon of the butter.

❹ Bake 30 minutes, or until a knife inserted in the center comes out clean and the top is golden brown. Let sit 10 minutes before cutting.

MUSHROOM PIE

Savory, juicy mushrooms stand supreme in this pie, which is made with a crumb crust. Try serving it with something colorful but not overpowering, such as Couscous Pilaf with Peas (page 176).

½ tablespoon unsalted butter, softened

⅓ cup bread crumbs

2 tablespoons olive oil

2 garlic cloves, minced

2 medium onions, diced

4 celery ribs, thinly sliced

1½ pounds (about 8 cups) finely chopped (not minced) fresh mushrooms

½ teaspoon dried thyme

½ teaspoon paprika

Dash cayenne pepper

2 tablespoons unbleached flour

¾ cup milk

½ teaspoon salt

2 large eggs, beaten

Serves 4

❶ Preheat the oven to 375°F. Grease a 9-inch pie plate with the butter, sprinkle in the bread crumbs, and rotate the plate until the bottom and sides are coated (there will be a loose layer of crumbs remaining on the bottom).

❷ Heat the olive oil in a large skillet over medium-high heat, then sauté the garlic, onions, and celery 5 minutes.

❸ Raise the heat to high, stir in the mushrooms, thyme, paprika, and cayenne. Cook, stirring often, 10 minutes, or until the juices have almost completely evaporated.

❹ Sprinkle on the flour, stir to coat the mixture, and cook 1 minute. Stir in the milk and salt and cook 1 minute more. Scrape into a large bowl and let cool until just warm.

❺ Stir the beaten eggs into the mushroom mixture and spoon into the prepared pie plate. Bake 30 minutes, or until a knife comes out clean when inserted in the sides of the pie or almost clean when inserted in the center. Let the pie sit on a cooling rack 10 minutes before cutting into wedges.

BROCCOLI CALZONES

A calzone is like a miniature pizza folded in half to make a filled turnover. Here broccoli, tomatoes, provolone cheese, and mozzarella are combined to make a delicious stuffing with a slightly smoky flavor.

Frozen pizza dough is a great find for cooks who are seeking shortcuts but want to cook with additive-free ingredients. Most supermarkets carry frozen pizza dough that contains only flour, water, yeast, and salt, so choose this type if available.

1 pound frozen pizza dough, thawed

2 tablespoons olive oil plus additional for dough

4 cups finely chopped broccoli

2 garlic cloves, minced

2 medium tomatoes, cored, seeded, and finely diced

¼ teaspoon dried oregano

¼ teaspoon dried basil

Freshly ground black pepper to taste

6 ounces smoked provolone cheese, cut into 6 slices

6 ounces mozzarella cheese, cut into 6 slices

1 large egg

Makes 6 calzones

❶ While the dough is thawing, heat 2 tablespoons of the olive oil in a large skillet over medium heat. Add the broccoli and sauté 2 minutes, then add 2 tablespoons water and cover the pan. Cook 5 minutes, or until the broccoli is tender.

❷ Remove the cover, stir in the garlic, tomatoes, oregano, basil, and pepper. Raise the heat to high and cook, uncovered, until all the liquid evaporates, about 2 minutes. Scrape into a bowl and let cool to room temperature.

❸ Preheat the oven to 375°F. Divide the pizza dough into 6 pieces of equal size. Roll each piece into a ball, and use a rolling pin to flatten each ball into a 6-inch circle. Brush the top of each round with olive oil to within ½ inch of the edges. With your finger, rub the outer edges of the dough circles with some water to help the calzone seal.

❹ On the bottom half of each round of dough, place 1 slice of provolone, top it with ⅙ of the broccoli filling, and add 1 slice of mozzarella. Fold the dough over to make a half-moon and pinch the edges to seal.

❺ Beat the egg with 1 teaspoon water. Brush the top of each calzone with some of this egg wash. Place the calzones on a baking sheet and cook 25 minutes, or until golden.

Let the calzones sit for 10 minutes before serving. Be careful when you bite into the calzones because the filling is very hot.

CRUSTY POTATOES, TOMATOES, AND ONIONS BAKED WITH OLIVE OIL AND GARLIC

The onions and tomatoes caramelize and create an irresistible crust in this peasant-style casserole. All you need is a salad to round off the meal.

6 medium (about 2 pounds) potatoes, peeled, halved, and very thinly sliced

3 large onions, halved vertically and thinly sliced

4 garlic cloves, minced

1 28-ounce can plum tomatoes, chopped and drained

¼ cup tomato paste

½ cup fruity olive oil

3 tablespoons water

2 teaspoons dried oregano

Salt to taste

Freshly ground black pepper to taste

Serves 4

❶ Preheat the oven to 400°F. In a large bowl, combine the potatoes, onions, garlic, and tomatoes.

❷ In a small bowl, beat together the tomato paste, olive oil, water, oregano, salt, and pepper. Pour over the vegetable mixture and toss to coat well. Spread this mixture in a 12 × 7 × 2-inch baking dish or other 2½-quart ovenproof shallow dish. Cover tightly with aluminum foil and bake 30 minutes. Remove the foil and bake 45 minutes longer, or until the potatoes are tender.

SCALLOPED KALE AND POTATOES

Kale, garlic, and potatoes are a distinctly harmonious blending of flavors, each enhancing the other. This crusty-coated casserole is hearty enough to stand as a main course, yet could also be a delightful side dish if served with a light entrée.

1 pound fresh kale, *or* 1 10-ounce package frozen kale, thawed

5 medium-large potatoes, peeled and very thinly sliced

2 garlic cloves, minced

1½ cups grated Swiss cheese

6 tablespoons cold unsalted butter, cut into bits

½ teaspoon salt

Freshly ground black pepper to taste

1¼ cups milk

Serves 2 to 3 as a main course

❶ If using fresh kale, thoroughly rinse it and shake off the excess water. Pull the leaves from the stems and discard the stems. Stuff the kale into a medium pot and add about ½ cup water. Cook until the kale just wilts, about 7 minutes. Drain and cool the kale. Squeeze out the remaining water with your hands. Roughly chop the kale and set aside. (If using frozen kale, simply squeeze it dry with your hands and set aside.)

❷ Preheat the oven to 425°F. Generously butter a 10 × 10 × 2-inch baking dish or other large shallow baking dish. Spread half the potato slices on the bottom of the dish. Spread on all of the kale, then sprinkle on the garlic and half of the cheese, butter, salt, and pepper. Top with the remaining potato slices, cheese, butter, salt, and pepper.

❸ Carefully pour in the milk and gently shake the dish to distribute. Bake 50 minutes, or until the potatoes are tender and the top is nicely browned.

VEGETABLE CURRY

There are many different versions of vegetable curry, and this one is my favorite. Its richly flavored sauce, made with coconut milk, is particularly good served on rice, with plain yogurt on the side to provide a soothing contrast. Warm pita bread would be the perfect finishing touch.

1½ cups unsweetened dessicated coconut *(see Note)*

2 cups hot water

3 tablespoons unsalted butter

2 medium onions, diced

2 teaspoons minced ginger

4 garlic cloves, minced

1½ teaspoons turmeric

2 teaspoons ground cumin

2 tablespoons ground coriander

⅛ teaspoon cayenne pepper, or more to taste

2 carrots, very thinly sliced

1 small (1½-pound) cauliflower, broken into bite-size flowerets (about 4 cups)

1 cup diced green beans, fresh or frozen

1 cup freshly cooked (page 161) or canned chick-peas, rinsed and drained

½ teaspoon salt

Hot cooked white or brown rice

Serves 4

❶ To make the coconut milk, combine the coconut and hot water in a blender or food processor and blend 2 minutes. Strain the coconut milk in batches through a sieve, pressing out all the liquid from the pulp with the back of a large spoon. Discard the coconut. You should have about 1½ cups coconut milk.

❷ Melt the butter in a large skillet over medium heat. Add the onions, ginger, and garlic and sauté, tossing often, 10 minutes, or until the onions begin to brown.

❸ Sprinkle on the spices and stir to mix thoroughly. Cook this mixture 2 minutes to blend the flavors.

❹ Stir in the coconut milk and bring to a boil. Add the carrots, cauliflower, green beans, chick-peas, and salt, and toss to coat the vegetables with the sauce. Cover the pan and cook 5 minutes. Remove the cover and continue to cook the curry, tossing often, until the vegetables are tender and the sauce has thickened, about 10 minutes more.

❺ Serve with some rice on the side, and drizzle a spoonful of sauce over the rice.

☛***Note:*** Unsweetened dessicated coconut can be purchased in health food stores.

☛***Variations:*** Try substituting different vegetables

such as zucchini, peas, or even chopped fresh spinach. (Just mound the spinach on top of the cooked curry and cover the pan. In a few minutes it will be wilted, and it can then be mixed into the vegetables and the sauce.)

CHEESY STUFFED POTATOES

This is one of my family's favorite easy meals. Because it is so substantial, I like to serve only a light salad as an accompaniment. Try these potatoes the next time you have a child who is a fussy eater joining you for dinner.

4 large baking potatoes, well scrubbed

1 tablespoon cold unsalted butter, cut into bits

½ cup sour cream

1 cup finely cubed Muenster cheese

½ cup finely cubed cheddar cheese

1 tablespoon minced fresh parsley

Paprika

Serves 4

❶ Prick the potatoes in a few places, place in the oven, and set the temperature at 400°F. Bake 1 hour, or until tender throughout.

❷ Slice the potatoes in half lengthwise and let cool a few minutes. With a spoon, scoop the flesh into a large bowl, leaving ¼ inch of the flesh in the shell. Divide the butter bits and place in the shells.

❸ Mash the potato flesh with a fork, then stir in the sour cream, cheese, and parsley. Spoon back into the shells, then sprinkle paprika on each stuffed potato. Place the potatoes on a baking sheet. Return to the oven and bake 20 minutes, or until hot and bubbly.

POTATO AND ONION FRITTATA

Frittatas are often cooked in skillets on the stovetop, but I have had equally good results baking them in the oven. I have come to prefer this method because it is more relaxed. I like to precede fritattas with a salad, and serve thick slices of toasted Italian or Portuguese bread or bagels alongside.

¼ cup olive oil

2 medium-large potatoes, peeled and cut into ¼-inch cubes

4 medium onions, finely diced

6 large eggs

¼ cup grated Parmesan cheese

¼ teaspoon salt

Freshly ground black pepper to taste

Serves 3 to 4

❶ Heat the oil in a large, preferably cast-iron or nonstick skillet over medium-high heat until hot but not smoking. Fry the potatoes in one layer until golden and tender all over. Remove with a slotted spoon to a plate.

❷ Place the onions in the pan and cook about 15 minutes, tossing frequently, until the onions are very tender. Meanwhile, preheat the oven to 350°F. Butter a 9-inch pie plate and set aside.

❸ In a large bowl, beat the eggs well. Beat in the cheese, salt, and pepper.

❹ When the onions are done, stir them into the egg mixture along with the potatoes. (If you are not ready to cook the frittata, let the onions and potatoes cool before mixing them with the eggs. The mixture can be refrigerated up to 4 hours. Return to room temperature before baking.) Scrape the egg mixture into the pie plate and bake 15 to 25 minutes, or until a knife inserted in the center of the frittata comes out almost clean. Be careful not to overcook the frittata. (The frittata will take longer to cook if the onions and potatoes cool before being mixed with the eggs.) Cut into wedges and serve.

CRUSTY CAULIFLOWER AND RICOTTA CASSEROLE

The pretty pink hue of this savory dish looks lovely with a spinach salad accompaniment. Try mixing the salad with Double Sesame Dressing (page 93).

2 tablespoons olive oil

2 garlic cloves, minced

½ cup finely diced, drained tomatoes

1 medium (2½-pound) cauliflower, cut into small flowerets (about 6 cups)

3 large eggs

1 cup part-skim ricotta cheese

¾ cup milk

¼ cup grated Parmesan cheese

1 tablespoon minced fresh parsley

¼ teaspoon freshly grated nutmeg

Dash cayenne pepper

Freshly ground black pepper to taste

1 cup grated Muenster cheese

¼ cup bread crumbs

Serves 4

❶ Heat the oil in a large skillet over medium heat. Add the garlic and cook 30 seconds. Do not brown. Add the tomatoes and cook 5 minutes, stirring often. Stir in the cauliflower and toss to coat all over with the tomato mixture. Pour in a few tablespoons water and cover the pan. Cook until the cauliflower is tender, about 7 minutes. Take the pan off the heat and let cool to warm or room temperature.

❷ Preheat the oven to 375°F. Butter a 12 × 7 × 2-inch ovenproof dish or other shallow 2½-quart baking dish.

❸ Beat the eggs in a large bowl. Beat in the ricotta, milk, Parmesan cheese, parsley, nutmeg, cayenne, pepper, and Muenster cheese. Stir in the cauliflower mixture. Spread in the prepared dish and sprinkle on the bread crumbs.

❹ Bake 20 minutes, or until hot and bubbly. Do not overcook, or the casserole will dry out.

WILD MUSHROOM TART IN PUFF PASTRY

This elegant entrée would make a sensational centerpiece for a vegetarian Thanksgiving feast. Although the directions are lengthy, it is not very time-consuming. Couscous Pilaf with Peas (page 176) would be an ideal side dish.

2 tablespoons olive oil

4 garlic cloves, minced

1 medium onion, finely diced

1 medium tomato, seeded and very finely chopped

12 ounces cultivated mushrooms, wiped clean and thinly sliced (about 4½ cups)

4 ounces wild mushrooms (such as shiitake, cèpes, or porcini), stems discarded, wiped clean, and thinly sliced *(see Note)*

¼ teaspoon dried thyme

A few dashes cayenne pepper

⅛ teaspoon freshly grated nutmeg

2 tablespoons dry white wine

2 large eggs

¼ cup heavy cream

2 tablespoons minced fresh parsley

¼ teaspoon salt

Freshly ground black pepper to taste

❶ Heat the oil in a large skillet over medium-high heat. Add the garlic and onion and sauté 5 minutes. Add the tomato and cook 10 minutes, stirring frequently. Stir in all the mushrooms, thyme, cayenne, and nutmeg. Cook, stirring often, until the mushrooms are tender and most of the juices have evaporated, about 7 minutes. Stir in the wine and cook 5 minutes more, or until mostly evaporated.

❷ Scrape the mushroom mixture into a large bowl and let cool to room temperature. Beat 1 of the eggs and stir in, then mix in the cream, parsley, salt, and pepper. (The recipe may be prepared to this point up to 24 hours in advance. Cover and chill if holding more than 2 hours. Bring to room temperature before proceeding with the next step.)

❸ To prepare the puff pastry, thaw at room temperature 20 to 30 minutes. Preheat the oven to 400°F. Gently unfold the pastry on a lightly floured surface. Roll into an 11 × 14-inch rectangle. Cut a 1-inch-wide strip from each side of the rectangle to make 4 strips. Place the rectangle on an ungreased baking sheet. Beat the remaining egg with 1 tablespoon water. Brush the egg wash evenly over the rectangle. Place the strips along the edges of the

1 sheet (about ½ pound) frozen store-bought puff pastry

Serves 4 generously

rectangle to form walls. Trim as necessary. Brush the strips with some egg wash. Prick the bottom of the pastry all over with a fork.

❹ Bake the crust 7 minutes. Remove from the oven and gently prick the bottom of the crust again to deflate it. Let cool. Reduce the oven temperature to 350°F.

❺ Spoon the mushroom mixture into the tart shell. Bake 25 minutes, or until the filling is set. Let cool 5 minutes before cutting.

☛***Note:*** 1 ounce dried wild mushrooms can be substituted. Soak in warm water 30 minutes. Rinse clean. Discard the stems and slice the mushroom caps. If you cannot get fresh or dried wild mushrooms, substitute 4 ounces cultivated mushrooms.

ZUCCHINI TOSTADAS

Juicy pieces of tender zucchini and kidney beans are coated with salsa, spread on crispy flour tortillas, and covered with melted cheese. A simple Mexican treat.

3 tablespoons vegetable oil

8 8-inch flour tortillas *(see Note)*

¼ cup olive oil

8 cups thinly sliced zucchini (from about 4 medium-size, quartered lengthwise)

½ teaspoon dried oregano

2 cups freshly cooked kidney beans (page 161), *or* 1 15-ounce can kidney beans, rinsed and drained

1¼ cups salsa (hot, medium, or mild)

Salt to taste

Freshly ground black pepper to taste

4 cups (about 12 ounces) grated extra-sharp cheddar cheese

Serves 4 generously

❶ Preheat the broiler. With a pastry brush, lightly coat both sides of each tortilla with the oil and place on a baking sheet (this will have to be done in batches). Broil on both sides until lightly golden and crisp. Cool completely. (The tortillas can be prepared up to 2 days in advance and stored in a plastic bag or tin.)

❷ Reduce the oven heat to 450°F. Heat the olive oil in a large skillet over medium-high heat. Add the zucchini and oregano and sauté, tossing frequently, until the zucchini is tender but still slightly crisp, about 7 minutes. Stir in the kidney beans and salsa and toss to blend. Season with salt and pepper, and remove from the heat.

❸ Using 2 baking sheets, place 2 tortillas on each sheet. Spread one eighth of the zucchini mixture on each tortilla. Sprinkle about ½ cup cheese over each tostada.

❹ Bake 5 minutes, or until the cheese melts and begins to bubble. Serve immediately. Repeat with the remaining ingredients.

☛***Note:*** Flour tortillas can be found in the dairy section of most supermarkets.

STUFFED POTATOES WITH CHEESE AND SCALLIONS

The creamy filling in this high-protein version of twice-baked potatoes bubbles and oozes with cheese. As with Cheesy Stuffed Potatoes (page 151), this hearty dish needs only a salad to round off the meal.

4 large baking potatoes, well scrubbed

1 tablespoon cold unsalted butter, cut into bits

1 cup cottage cheese

3 tablespoons low-fat milk

⅓ cup grated Parmesan cheese, plus extra for sprinkling

1 cup (about 5 ounces) diced part-skim mozzarella cheese

2 scallions, thinly sliced

Freshly ground black pepper to taste

Serves 4

❶ Cook and prepare the potatoes, following steps 1 and 2 of Cheesy Stuffed Potatoes (page 151).

❷ In a blender or food processor, combine the cottage cheese and milk and blend until very smooth. Turn off the blender and scrape down the sides as necessary. Scrape the cottage cheese into a bowl; stir in the Parmesan, mozzarella, scallions, and pepper.

❸ Mash the potato pulp with a fork. Stir it into the cheese mixture. Spoon the mixture into the potato shells, then sprinkle the tops with some Parmesan cheese. Place the stuffed potatoes on a cookie sheet and bake 20 minutes, or until bubbly and golden brown.

EGGPLANT PARMESAN WITH RICOTTA AND FRESH BASIL

***I** have always disliked the process of breading and frying eggplant slices because it's messy and time-consuming. No alternative method was satisfactory, until I learned a clever trick. I now brush a thin layer of mayonnaise on both sides of each eggplant slice, coat them with bread crumbs, and broil until golden brown. It's very quick and easy, and this step can be done a day in advance.*

This version of Eggplant Parmesan contains ricotta and fresh basil, making it both creamy and flavorful.

2 medium eggplants (about 2 pounds total)

1⁄3 cup mayonnaise

3⁄4 cup bread crumbs

1½ cups tomato sauce

1 garlic clove, pressed

2 tablespoons dry red wine

1 cup part-skim ricotta cheese

½ cup grated Parmesan cheese

½ pound (about 2½ cups) grated mozzarella cheese

2 tablespoons minced fresh basil, *or* 1 teaspoon dried basil

Serves 4 to 6

❶ Peel the eggplant and slice it ½ inch thick. Place the mayonnaise in a dish and the bread crumbs on a plate. With a pastry brush, lightly coat both sides of each eggplant slice with mayonnaise, then dip in the bread crumbs to coat both sides. Place the slices on a baking sheet and broil on both sides until golden brown and tender but not mushy. Place the eggplant on a platter and let cool.

❷ Preheat the oven to 375°F. Combine the tomato sauce, garlic, and red wine in a medium bowl. In a separate bowl, beat together the ricotta and Parmesan cheeses.

❸ Pour half the sauce into a 12 × 7 × 2-inch baking dish or other 2½-quart baking dish. Cover with half the eggplant slices, then spoon on all the ricotta mixture. Sprinkle on half the mozzarella, then top with all the basil. Place the remaining eggplant slices on top, pour on the remaining sauce, then top with the remaining mozzarella cheese.

❹ Cover the baking dish with aluminum foil. (The recipe may be prepared to this point and chilled up to 8 hours in advance. Bring to room temperature before baking.) Bake, covered, 15 minutes; remove the foil and bake 15 minutes more, or until hot and bubbly. Remove from the oven and let sit 10 minutes before serving.

☛***Variation:*** Leftover Eggplant Parmesan makes delicious submarine sandwiches. Reheat it in the oven, then place on heated submarine, grinder, or hero rolls.

FULL OF BEANS

Beans are the best nonmeat source of protein. They also are low in fat, high in fiber, and a great source of B vitamins and iron. In addition, the protein in beans has been shown to help lower cholesterol levels in the blood. With all of these benefits, beans have become an indispensable part of the vegetarian diet.

When used in entrées, as they are in this chapter, beans make highly nutritious dishes and need only a salad to complete the meal. As a general rule, if you want to bolster the protein quality of a bean dish, add either grains, seeds, or some form of dairy products to the meal if these aren't already present in the recipe.

With so many health risks attributed to eating meat, beans—once thought of as poor man's food—are rightfully gaining prominence because they offer so much to the health-conscious diet. (To learn how to cook dried beans, see Freshly Cooked Beans on the opposite page.)

FRESHLY COOKED BEANS

Cooking dried beans at home, rather than purchasing canned, cooked beans, is not a quick method for incorporating beans into meals. But with a little forethought, you can cook a large batch of beans and freeze them in small containers to have them on hand when needed. Cooking beans doesn't take much preparation, just the time necessary for them to cook.

There are two ways to prepare beans for cooking. The first is to soak them overnight; the alternative is to boil them for two minutes, then let them soak for one hour. In both cases the beans should be drained and covered with fresh water before cooking.

The following method applies to kidney beans, chickpeas, cannellini, pinto beans, black beans, navy beans, and black-eyed peas. Lentils and split peas do not have to be precooked.

☛ Pick over the beans to remove any stones, twigs, etc.

☛ Rinse the beans in a strainer under cold running water.

☛ Place the beans in a large bowl and fill with cold water to cover by 2 inches. Cover the bowl and soak overnight. Alternatively, place the beans in a large pot and cover with water by 2 inches. Bring to a boil and cook 2 minutes. Cover the pot, remove from the heat, and soak 1 hour.

☛ Thoroughly drain the beans and discard the soaking liquid. Place beans in a large pot. Cover them with plenty of fresh water, and cook at a lively simmer, partly covered, until tender, 1 to 1½ hours, depending on the size of the bean. If you plan to freeze the beans, slightly undercook them because freezing will make them softer. Drain very well and bring to room temperature before refrigerating or freezing. Use in any recipe that calls for cooked beans.

LENTILS WITH BALSAMIC VINEGAR

Here's one of my favorite ways to eat lentils. The vinegar adds a subtle tang to this dish, and it's an old trick for aiding digestion. Serve with a steamed vegetable.

1½ cups lentils

½ cup white basmati rice, *or* converted white rice

5 cups water

1 bay leaf

½ teaspoon dried thyme

½ teaspoon salt

Freshly ground black pepper to taste

2 tablespoons fruity olive oil

2 large onions, diced

2 garlic cloves, minced

1 carrot, thinly sliced

1 tablespoon balsamic vinegar, *or* red wine vinegar

Serves 4 to 6

❶ Pick over the lentils and discard any stones. Rinse in a strainer and place in a heavy saucepan with the rice, water, bay leaf, thyme, salt, and pepper. Cover, bring to a boil, and cook at a lively simmer 20 to 25 minutes, or until tender but not mushy. (The lentils should retain a very slight crunch.)

❷ Meanwhile, heat the olive oil in a medium skillet. Add the onions, garlic, and carrot and cook over medium-low heat 20 minutes, or until the onions are brown and the carrot is tender.

❸ Drain the lentils and rice very well and return to the pot. Discard the bay leaf. Gently stir the carrot mixture into the lentils along with the vinegar and cook 2 minutes to blend the flavors. Serve immediately.

CHILAQUILES

This dish is best described as a Mexican lasagna. Corn tortilla layers alternated with kidney beans, tomatoes, chiles, sour cream, and cheese are baked in a casserole. Very quick and flavorful.

1½ tablespoons olive oil

2 onions, finely diced

2 garlic cloves, minced

1 28-ounce can tomatoes, finely chopped, with their juice

1 16-ounce can kidney beans, rinsed and drained

1 4-ounce can mild green chiles, minced and drained

12 corn tortillas *(see Note)*, cut into 1-inch strips

1 cup sour cream

2½ cups (about 8 ounces) grated Monterey Jack cheese

Serves 4

❶ Preheat the oven to 350°F. Heat the oil in a large skillet over medium-high heat, add the onions and garlic, and sauté 10 minutes, or until the onions are tender.

❷ Stir in the tomatoes and juice, the kidney beans, and chiles. Boil 5 minutes, stirring occasionally, until the juices begin to thicken. Remove from the heat.

❸ Spread half the sauce in a 10 × 10 × 2-inch or 12 × 7 × 2-inch casserole. Top with half the tortilla strips, half the sour cream, and half the cheese. Complete with the remaining tortillas, then the remaining sauce, sour cream, and cheese.

❹ Bake 35 minutes, or until hot and bubbly.

☛***Note:*** Corn tortillas usually can be found in the dairy department of most supermarkets.

MEXICAN RED BEANS AND RICE

If you use canned beans or leftover home-cooked beans, this dish is so easy to prepare that it almost seems like cheating.

1½ cups brown rice, *or* converted white rice

3 cups water

1 tablespoon vegetable oil

½ teaspoon salt

BEANS

2 tablespoons olive oil

2 large onions, finely diced

1 tablespoon chili powder

2 15-ounce cans red kidney beans, rinsed and drained, *or* 4 cups freshly cooked kidney beans (page 161)

1 cup salsa (mild, medium, or hot)

¼ cup water

⅔ cup sour cream

Minced fresh parsley, for garnish

Serves 4

❶ Combine the rice, water, oil, and salt in a medium saucepan, cover, and bring to a boil. Reduce to a simmer, and cook the rice, undisturbed, 45 minutes for brown rice or 20 minutes for white rice, or until all the water is absorbed and the rice begins to stick to the pot.

❷ Meanwhile, prepare the beans. Heat the olive oil in a large skillet over medium-high heat. Add the onions and sauté 10 minutes, or until tender. Sprinkle on the chili powder and cook 1 minute. Toss frequently.

❸ Add the beans, salsa, and water, and cook about 5 minutes, or until the mixture is piping hot. To serve, spread some of the hot rice on each serving plate, and top with a mound of the bean mixture. Place a spoonful of sour cream on top of the beans, and garnish with parsley.

VEGETABLE ENCHILADAS

The heavenly tomato-cream mixture that coats these enchiladas is one of my all-time favorite sauces, and here it gives a delicate touch to a hearty, stick-to-your-ribs Mexican dish.

2 tablespoons olive oil

1 medium onion, diced

2 medium zucchini, quartered lengthwise and thinly sliced

1 teaspoon dried oregano

1 4-ounce can chopped green chiles, drained

1½ cups cooked kidney beans, fresh or canned, rinsed and drained

Salt to taste

Freshly ground black pepper to taste

SAUCE

1 28-ounce can tomato puree

½ cup heavy cream

⅓ cup finely chopped cilantro

1 large garlic clove, pressed

¼ teaspoon salt

Freshly ground black pepper to taste

....

8 8-inch flour tortillas

2 cups grated Monterey Jack cheese

Serves 4

❶ Heat the oil in a large skillet over medium-high heat. Add the onion and sauté 5 minutes. Stir in the zucchini and oregano and cook until tender but not mushy, about 7 minutes. Remove the pan from the heat and stir in the chiles, kidney beans, salt, and pepper. Let the mixture cool.

❷ Preheat the oven to 350°F. To make the sauce, combine the tomato puree, heavy cream, cilantro, garlic, salt, and pepper.

❸ To assemble the enchiladas, pour a layer of sauce on the bottom of 2 large casseroles such as a 12 × 7 × 2-inch baking dish (you don't want to crowd the enchiladas). Spoon one eighth of the bean mixture along the center of a tortilla, then sprinkle on 2 tablespoons of the cheese. Roll the enchilada and place seam-side down in a baking dish (don't worry if the tortilla breaks a bit). Repeat with the remaining tortillas.

❹ Spoon the remaining sauce over all of the enchiladas, and sprinkle some of the remaining 1 cup of the cheese on each enchilada. (The enchiladas may be prepared to this point up to 2 hours in advance, refrigerated, and returned to room temperature before baking.)

❺ Bake 25 minutes, or until hot and bubbly. Let sit 5 minutes before serving.

SPICY STIR-FRIED TOFU, PEPPERS, AND MANDARIN ORANGES

Cook about 1½ cups brown rice approximately 1 hour before (or the same amount of white rice for 30 minutes before) you stir-fry the vegetables, and keep warm.

SAUCE

3 tablespoons tamari soy sauce

¼ cup Chinese rice wine

¼ cup syrup from mandarin oranges (see below)

2 teaspoons cornstarch

½ teaspoon sesame oil

1 teaspoon chili oil

....

3 tablespoons peanut oil

1 pound firm tofu, cut into ½-inch cubes and patted dry

2 garlic cloves, minced

2 teaspoons minced ginger

2 green bell peppers, cored and cut into ¾-inch squares

1 red bell pepper, cored and cut into ¾-inch squares

2 tablespoons water

2 11-ounce cans mandarin oranges in light syrup, well drained and ¼ cup syrup reserved

....

Hot cooked rice

Serves 4

❶ Combine all of the sauce ingredients in a cup and set aside. Make sure all of the remaining ingredients are prepared before you begin stir-frying.

❷ Heat a large skillet or wok over high heat. When hot, pour in 2 tablespoons of the peanut oil. When the oil is hot, add the tofu. Stir-fry until golden all over, about 10 minutes. Remove the tofu from the pan and set aside on a platter. Reduce the heat to medium-high.

❸ Pour in the remaining 1 tablespoon of the oil and add the garlic and ginger. Cook 10 seconds, tossing constantly, then add the green and red peppers. Stir-fry 2 minutes, pour in the water, and cover the pan. Cook 5 minutes, occasionally removing the cover to give the mixture a toss. After 5 minutes, remove the cover and stir-fry until most of the liquid has evaporated.

❹ Return the tofu to the pan and stir-fry 1 minute. Give the sauce a stir, then pour it over the mixture and cook 30 seconds. Place some hot cooked rice on each plate and immediately spoon the tofu and vegetables on the rice. Put equal amounts of mandarin oranges on top of each serving, and let each person gently mix them in.

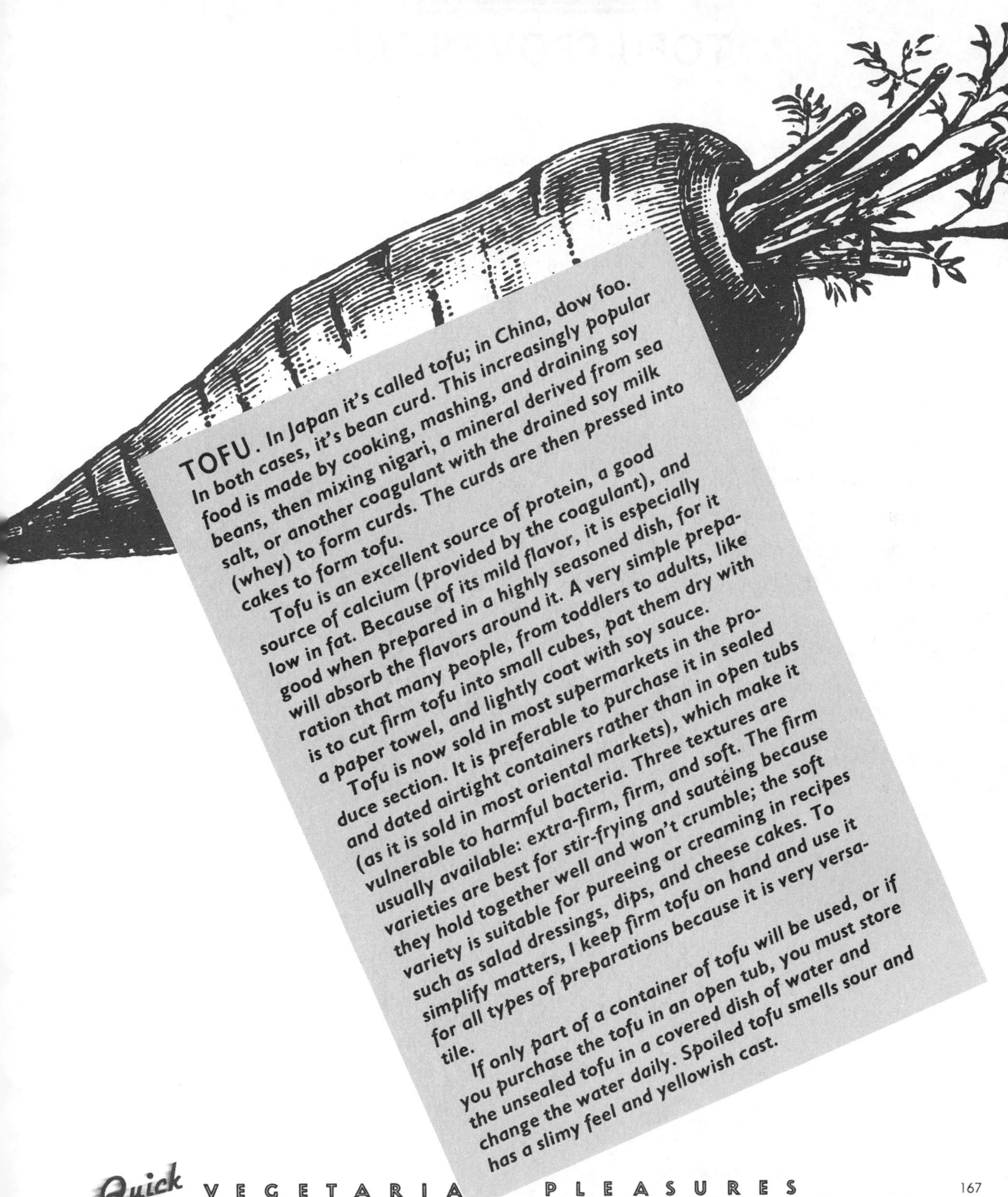

TOFU. In Japan it's called tofu; in China, dow foo. In both cases, it's bean curd. This increasingly popular food is made by cooking, mashing, and draining soy beans, then mixing nigari, a mineral derived from sea salt, or another coagulant with the drained soy milk (whey) to form curds. The curds are then pressed into cakes to form tofu.

Tofu is an excellent source of protein, a good source of calcium (provided by the coagulant), and low in fat. Because of its mild flavor, it is especially good when prepared in a highly seasoned dish, for it will absorb the flavors around it. A very simple preparation that many people, from toddlers to adults, like is to cut firm tofu into small cubes, pat them dry with a paper towel, and lightly coat with soy sauce.

Tofu is now sold in most supermarkets in the produce section. It is preferable to purchase it in sealed and dated airtight containers rather than in open tubs (as it is sold in most oriental markets), which make it vulnerable to harmful bacteria. Three textures are usually available: extra-firm, firm, and soft. The firm varieties are best for stir-frying and sautéing because they hold together well and won't crumble; the soft variety is suitable for pureeing or creaming in recipes such as salad dressings, dips, and cheese cakes. To simplify matters, I keep firm tofu on hand and use it for all types of preparations because it is very versatile.

If only part of a container of tofu will be used, or if you purchase the tofu in an open tub, you must store the unsealed tofu in a covered dish of water and change the water daily. Spoiled tofu smells sour and has a slimy feel and yellowish cast.

TOFU PROVENÇAL

Try this low-fat dish served with Bulghur Mushroom Pilaf (page 177).

3 tablespoons olive oil

1 pound firm tofu, cut into ½-inch cubes and patted very dry

3 garlic cloves, minced

2 medium onions, diced

3 cups (almost 1 35-ounce can) plum tomatoes, coarsely chopped with their juice

1 tablespoon tomato paste

2 cups diced green beans

½ teaspoon dried basil

½ teaspoon dried oregano

1 bay leaf

Salt to taste

Freshly ground black pepper to taste

Serves 4

❶ Heat the oil in a large skillet over high heat until hot but not smoking. Add the tofu and stir-fry until golden all over. Remove to a platter and lower the heat to medium.

❷ If the pan is dry, pour in a little more oil. Add the garlic and onions and sauté 5 minutes. Pour the tomatoes and their juice into the onion and garlic mixture, along with the tomato paste, stirring until blended.

❸ Return the tofu to the skillet, toss, and add the green beans, basil, oregano, bay leaf, salt, and pepper. Toss thoroughly, reduce the heat to simmer, and cover the pan. Cook 15 minutes, or until the green beans are tender. If at this point the sauce is too thin, cook uncovered a few minutes, or until it boils down and thickens somewhat. Remove the bay leaf before serving.

TOFU *HOISIN* WITH CASHEWS AND VEGETABLES

To keep this a relaxed meal, completely cook 1½ cups brown or white rice before you begin stir-frying, then keep the rice warm on the back burner or in the oven while you prepare the dish.

4 tablespoons peanut oil

1 pound firm tofu, cut into ½-inch cubes and patted very dry

5 carrots, thinly sliced on the diagonal

3 tablespoons water

½ pound snow peas, tips and strings removed

¾ cup (about 4 ounces) roasted *(see Note)* cashews

1 teaspoon minced fresh ginger

SAUCE

⅓ cup *hoisin* sauce

2 tablespoons tamari soy sauce

2 tablespoons Chinese rice wine, *or* dry sherry

1 tablespoon oriental sesame oil

....

Hot cooked rice

Serves 4

❶ Place all of the ingredients in front of you before you begin stir-frying. Mix the sauce ingredients together in a small cup and keep nearby. Heat 2 tablespoons of the peanut oil in a wok or large skillet over high heat until hot but not smoking. Add the tofu and stir-fry until evenly golden, about 10 minutes. Remove the tofu to a platter and keep it near the stove; reduce the heat to medium high.

❷ Put the carrots in the pan or wok, toss, then pour in the 3 tablespoons water. Immediately cover the pan and cook 3 minutes. Remove the cover. (The water should have evaporated; if not, cook uncovered for a few seconds.) Push the carrots to the sides of the pan to make a well, then pour the remaining 2 tablespoons of the peanut oil into the center of the pan. Let it heat for a few seconds, then toss it onto the carrots.

❸ Add the snow peas, cashews, and ginger and stir-fry 2 minutes. Return the tofu to the pan and stir-fry 1 minute more.

❹ Give the sauce mixture a quick stir and pour it over the tofu and vegetables. Toss to coat and immediately spoon the vegetables onto a platter or into a serving bowl. Serve over rice.

(continued)

☛*Note:* If the roasted cashews are salted, rinse with water in a strainer and pat dry. You can substitute raw cashews from the health food store, but toast them in a 350°F. oven until golden, about 7 minutes, before beginning to cook.

HOISIN SAUCE. Hoisin sauce is a delicious, sweetened soybean-based sauce that also contains garlic and chiles. Avoid brands that include red and yellow dyes and other additives. I often use the China Bowl brand found in many supermarkets and specialty food shops.

SPICY RAGOUT OF VEGETABLES AND TOFU

The traditional French method of gently cooking a mélange of vegetables (with tofu instead of meat, in this case) in a small amount of seasoned liquid makes this ragout a very tasty, low-fat entree. Serve this alongside hot brown rice that has been drizzled with olive oil and sprinkled with Parmesan cheese.

4 tablespoons olive oil

1 pound firm tofu, cut into ½-inch cubes and patted very dry

6 garlic cloves, minced

¼ teaspoon crushed red pepper flakes

1 28-ounce can plum tomatoes, roughly chopped, with their juice

1 tablespoon minced fresh basil, *or* ½ teaspoon dried basil

Salt to taste

Freshly ground black pepper to taste

1 medium head cauliflower, cut into bite-size flowerets (about 5 cups)

2 cups frozen peas, thawed

Serves 4

❶ In a 6-quart pot, heat 3 tablespoons olive oil over medium-high heat. Fry the tofu until golden all over and remove to a platter.

❷ Pour in the remaining 1 tablespoon of the oil, reduce the heat to medium, and sauté the garlic and red pepper flakes until the garlic just begins to get golden, about 2 minutes. Immediately add the chopped tomatoes and their juice, the basil, salt, and pepper and bring to a boil. Cook 3 minutes, then add the cauliflower. Tossing occasionally, cook until the cauliflower is tender but not mushy, about 15 minutes.

❸ Return the tofu to the pot, and stir in the peas. Cook just until both are heated through, about 3 minutes.

SKILLET TOFU, YELLOW SQUASH, AND PEPPERS WITH MELTED CHEESE

This colorful stir-fry has just a hint of tomato sauce that clings to the vegetables with the creamy melted cheese. Serve with rice, Bulghur Mushroom Pilaf (page 177), or buttered egg noodles.

3 tablespoons vegetable oil

1 pound firm tofu, cut into ½-inch cubes and patted very dry

2 medium onions, diced

2 yellow squash, halved lengthwise and thinly sliced

1 green bell pepper, seeded and cubed

½ cup tomato sauce

Freshly ground black pepper to taste

1 cup (about 4 ounces) grated Muenster cheese

Serves 4

❶ Heat the oil in a large skillet over medium-high heat until hot but not smoking. Stir-fry the tofu until golden, about 10 minutes. Remove from the pan with a slotted spoon and set aside on a platter.

❷ If the pan has no oil left, add a little more, and sauté the onions, squash, and pepper until crisp-tender, about 10 minutes.

❸ Return the tofu to the pan, toss, and stir in the tomato sauce. Season with pepper and cook 2 minutes, or until hot and bubbly.

❹ Sprinkle on the cheese, and cover the pan. Cook 1 to 2 minutes, or until the cheese has melted. Serve immediately.

SIDE DISHES

The side dish recipes in this chapter will assist you in menu planning when you lack a certain something to accompany your main course. Or, as I often like to do, you can make a meal of a combination of dishes, such as a tasty prepared vegetable accompanied by buttered egg noodles or brown rice, or select a pilaf or potato recipe and serve it with steamed vegetables.

At the height of summer, when a plentiful supply of all sorts of vegetables is available, turn to this chapter to discover new ways of preparing them.

COUSCOUS PILAF WITH PEAS

Fresh dill enlivens this light pilaf and gives it a distinctive flavor.

1 tablespoon olive oil

1 medium onion, finely diced

1 garlic clove, minced

1 cup couscous

1 cup frozen peas, thawed

1 tablespoon minced fresh dill, *or* 1 teaspoon dried

¼ teaspoon salt

Freshly ground black pepper to taste

1½ cups vegetable stock *(see Note)*

1 tablespoon cold unsalted butter, cut into bits

Serves 4

❶ Heat the oil in a medium saucepan over medium heat. Sauté the onion and garlic, stirring often, until very tender, about 10 minutes.

❷ Stir in the couscous, peas, dill, salt, pepper, and vegetable stock. Cover, bring to a boil, and remove from the heat. Let sit until all of the water is absorbed, about 5 minutes. Fluff with a fork, then stir in the butter bits. Serve immediately, or cover again and let sit up to 10 minutes more.

☞***Note:*** Vegetable stock can be made with powdered vegetable stock base, available at health food stores.

BULGHUR MUSHROOM PILAF

Golden, medium-textured bulghur, as opposed to the dark, coarse-grain variety, is especially good in this pilaf. Its buttery flavor is enhanced by the mushrooms and scallions.

1 tablespoon unsalted butter

1½ cups (about 4 ounces) finely chopped mushrooms

1 carrot, minced

1 cup golden bulghur

¼ teaspoon dried thyme

¼ teaspoon salt

Freshly ground black pepper to taste

2 cups vegetable stock *(see Note,* page 176)

2 scallions, very thinly sliced

Serves 4

❶ Over medium-high heat, melt the butter in a heavy, medium saucepan. Add the mushrooms and cook, stirring often, 10 minutes. The juices that accumulate will enhance the vegetable stock.

❷ Stir in the carrot, bulghur, thyme, salt, pepper, and vegetable stock. Cover the pan, reduce the heat to a simmer, and cook, undisturbed, 20 minutes, or until all of the liquid has been absorbed.

❸ Remove the pan from the heat, sprinkle on the scallions, and fluff the mixture with a fork. Cover the pan again and let sit 10 minutes. Serve hot as a side dish with a steamed vegetable.

GREEN BEAN SALAD WITH LEMON, DILL, AND FETA CHEESE

This tasty treatment of green beans works well with delicate summer beans as well as mature green beans.

1 pound green beans, tips removed

3 tablespoons olive oil

2 tablespoons fresh lemon juice

Freshly ground black pepper to taste

2 tablespoons minced fresh dill, *or* 1 teaspoon dried dill weed

3 tablespoons slivered red onion

¼ cup crumbled feta cheese

Salt

Serves 4

❶ Steam the green beans until crisp-tender. Rinse under cold running water until cold throughout. Drain very well, and pat dry with a paper or cotton towel.

❷ Combine the olive oil, lemon juice, and pepper in a serving bowl. Stir in the green beans and toss. Sprinkle on the dill and onion and toss again. Let sit 30 minutes, or cover and chill for up to 4 hours. Serve at room temperature. Just before serving, sprinkle on the feta cheese and toss again. Taste for salt.

PROVENÇAL POTATOES

If I had to choose one potato dish from among them all, it would be Provençal potatoes.

4 medium (about 1 pound) red-skinned boiling potatoes

3 tablespoons olive oil

2 garlic cloves, finely chopped

1 scallion, very thinly sliced

Salt to taste

Freshly ground black pepper to taste

Serves 2 to 3

❶ Peel the potatoes and slice them in half lengthwise. Slice each half into ¼-inch-thick half-moons.

❷ Heat the olive oil in a large, heavy skillet over medium-high heat. Add the potatoes and cook, tossing frequently, about 15 minutes, or until tender and evenly browned.

❸ Reduce the heat to medium, then sprinkle on the garlic and scallion. Cook, tossing constantly, about 2 minutes more, or until the scallions are hot and tender. Season with salt and pepper and serve immediately.

☛***Note:*** If you want to double this recipe, use two large skillets to avoid overcrowding.

SWEET POTATOES ANNA

This treatment of sweet potatoes makes a crusty "pie." Cut it into wedges and serve it alongside steamed vegetables for a simple, delicious meal.

6 tablespoons unsalted butter, melted

2 pounds (about 4 medium) sweet potatoes or yams

4 tablespoons grated Parmesan cheese

¼ teaspoon freshly ground nutmeg

Salt

Freshly ground black pepper to taste

Serves 4

❶ Preheat the oven to 425°F. Pour 1 tablespoon of the melted butter in an 8-inch round cake pan and brush it all over the bottom and sides with a pastry brush.

❷ Peel the potatoes and cut them into paper-thin slices. Layer one-quarter of the potato slices in concentric circles in the prepared pan, then dab on one-quarter of the melted butter with the pastry brush. Mix the cheese with the nutmeg. Sprinkle on one-quarter of the cheese mixture and season lightly with salt and pepper. Repeat 3 times, ending with the cheese mixture. The potatoes will have risen above the pan slightly; push them down with your hand to flatten. Cover the pan with foil. (The recipe to this point may be prepared up to 24 hours in advance and refrigerated. Return to room temperature before baking.)

❸ Bake 45 minutes, then uncover and bake 30 to 40 minutes longer, or until tender. Let sit 5 minutes. Drain off any excess butter.

❹ Run a knife around the edges of the potatoes and invert onto a platter. Cut into wedges to serve.

SCALLOPED SWEET POTATOES

I prefer to use yams— bright-orange sweet potatoes—for their attractive color. Serve this at your next Thanksgiving feast as a welcome change from traditional sugary sweet potato dishes.

6 medium-large (about 2½–3 pounds) sweet potatoes or yams

4 tablespoons cold unsalted butter, cut into bits

1½ cups grated sharp cheddar cheese

Salt to taste

Freshly ground black pepper to taste

1¼ cups low-fat milk

Serves 4 to 6

❶ Preheat the oven to 425°F. Lightly butter a 10 × 10 × 2-inch or other large, shallow baking dish. Peel the sweet potatoes and cut them in half lengthwise, then slice them into paper-thin half-moons.

❷ Spread half the sliced potatoes in the bottom of the baking dish. Sprinkle with half the butter bits and grated cheese, and season with salt and pepper. Spread the remaining sweet potato slices on top, then the remaining butter and grated cheese.

❸ Slowly pour the milk into the corner of the dish, then gently shake the dish to distribute the milk. Cook, uncovered, 45 minutes, or until the potatoes are tender when pierced with a knife. Let sit 10 minutes before serving.

YELLOW SQUASH AU GRATIN

This buttery gratin with an overtone of onion has become my favorite way to serve yellow squash.

2 pounds (about 4 medium) yellow summer squash, thinly sliced

1 medium onion, minced

⅓ cup sour cream

1 large egg, beaten

4 tablespoons butter, melted

2 teaspoons sugar

½ teaspoon salt

⅓ cup bread crumbs

Serves 4 to 6

❶ Steam the squash until very tender. Mash it in a large bowl until almost smooth. Drain out any liquid.

❷ Preheat the oven to 375°F. Mix the onion, sour cream, egg, 2 tablespoons of the melted butter, sugar, and salt into the mashed squash.

❸ Scrape the mixture into a medium gratin dish or an 8-inch square baking dish. Sprinkle the bread crumbs on top and drizzle on the remaining melted butter. Bake 45 minutes. Let sit 10 minutes before serving.

BRAISED FENNEL

Try this aromatic dish with some hot buttered rice and crusty French bread for a simple meal.

2 medium fennel bulbs, with tops

3 tablespoons olive oil

3 large shallots, finely diced

1 14-ounce can plum tomatoes, finely chopped, with their juice

3 tablespoons water

Salt to taste

Freshly ground black pepper to taste

2 tablespoons grated Parmesan cheese

Serves 4

❶ Wash the fennel and pat very dry. Remove about 1 cup of the feathery tops and set aside. Cut the stalks from the fennel bulbs. Remove the 2 tough outer leaves from each bulb and discard. Cut each bulb into quarters vertically, making sure to keep the core intact on each piece.

❷ Heat the olive oil in a flameproof baking dish over medium heat. When hot, sauté the fennel quarters 10 minutes, turning them frequently. They should begin to brown.

❸ Add the shallots and toss to mix. Cook 10 minutes more.

❹ Roughly chop the reserved tops and add to the pan. Stir in the chopped tomatoes and their juice, the water, salt, and pepper.

❺ Cover the dish and reduce the heat to simmer. Cook 30 minutes, or until the bulbs are tender when pierced with a knife. Turn the fennel occasionally while it cooks. At this point, the sauce should be nice and thick; if it is watery, boil uncovered until it thickens.

❻ Sprinkle the Parmesan cheese on each fennel quarter. For a nice brown crust, put the dish under the broiler for 1 to 2 minutes, or until golden brown.

GRATED ZUCCHINI SAUTÉ

Grated zucchini with the juices squeezed out can be sautéed very quickly and keep its crunchy texture.

3 medium zucchini

1 tablespoon olive oil

1 tablespoon minced fresh basil, *or* ½ teaspoon dried

Salt to taste

Freshly ground black pepper to taste

2 teaspoons cold unsalted butter, cut into bits

1 tablespoon grated Parmesan cheese

Serves 4

❶ Cut the ends from the zucchini and discard. Shred the zucchini using a hand grater. Place the zucchini in a cotton kitchen towel and gather it into a ball. Twist hard to remove all the juices. Scrape the grated zucchini into a bowl.

❷ Heat the oil in a large skillet over medium-high heat. Add the zucchini, basil, salt, and pepper and sauté, tossing often, until crisp-tender, about 5 minutes. Sprinkle on the butter and Parmesan cheese, toss, and serve.

TOMATOES PROVENÇAL

Tomatoes are halved and topped with bread crumbs spiked with garlic and herbs, then drizzled with olive oil and baked until juicy.

2 large firm ripe tomatoes

2 slices white bread

2 garlic cloves, minced

1 tablespoon minced fresh basil, *or* 1 teaspoon dried basil

2 tablespoons minced fresh parsley

2 teaspoons minced fresh chives

Salt to taste

Freshly ground black pepper to taste

6 tablespoons olive oil

Serves 2 to 4

❶ Preheat the oven to 375°F. With a small pointed knife, core each tomato, cutting only as deep as necessary. Cut each tomato in half horizontally and gently squeeze each half to remove the seeds and juice. Use your fingertip to help push out the seeds.

❷ Lightly toast the bread. Tear it into pieces and process in a blender or food processor to make crumbs. In a small bowl, combine the crumbs, garlic, basil, parsley, chives, salt, and pepper. Moisten with 4 tablespoons of the olive oil to make the mixture sticky.

❸ Fill each tomato half with the crumb mixture, pushing it into the cavities and mounding it on top. Place the stuffed tomatoes in a lightly oiled shallow baking dish. Drizzle the remaining 2 tablespoons of the olive oil over the tomatoes. Bake 20 to 30 minutes, or until the stuffing is golden on top and the tomatoes are juicy.

OVEN FRIES

Here's an easy, low-fat method for making French fries (see Note). Cut potatoes are tossed in a little oil, then placed on a baking sheet and cooked in a hot oven to produce crisp, tender fries.

3 medium baking potatoes
1 tablespoon vegetable oil
Salt

Serves 2 to 4

❶ Leaving the skins on, scrub the potatoes thoroughly and pat dry. Cut each potato lengthwise into 16 wedges about ¼ inch thick. Place the potatoes in a large bowl, cover with cold water, and soak 30 minutes. Meanwhile, preheat the oven to 475°F.

❷ Thoroughly drain the potatoes and pat very dry with a cotton or paper towel. Return to the bowl. Pour on the oil and toss to coat evenly.

❸ Lightly oil a baking sheet. Spread the potatoes in one layer. Bake 15 minutes. Turn the potatoes over and bake 10 to 15 minutes more, or until golden and tender. Season with salt and serve immediately.

☞***Note:*** You can also make home fries using this low-fat method. Peel waxy boiling potatoes and cut them into pieces the size of a half-dollar. Toss with oil (olive oil is delicious), and bake as directed. (Chopped onion and a generous sprinkling of chili powder mixed with the potato slices before baking add a spunky flavor.)

GREEN BEAN AND RED PEPPER SAUTÉ

¾ pound green beans

¼ cup water

1 large red bell pepper, cored and cut into ½-inch-wide strips

1 tablespoon olive oil

1 garlic clove, pressed

½ tablespoon unsalted butter

Serves 4

❶ Snap the ends of the green beans and discard. Leave the beans whole and place in a large skillet. Pour in the water, cover the pan, and bring to a boil over medium-high heat. Cook 5 to 7 minutes, or until almost tender. Drain out all the water.

❷ Lower the heat to medium. Stir in the red pepper, olive oil, and garlic. Sauté 2 minutes, stirring frequently. Cover the pan and cook 3 minutes more, or until the red peppers are crisp but tender. Stir in the butter and serve immediately.

THE VEGETARIAN BARBECUE

Vegetarians finally can be included in snazzy outdoor cookouts with dishes that transcend the old standbys of corn-on-the-cob and potato salad. Grilled vegetables are a splendid contribution to barbecues, freeing the imaginations of meat-eaters and vegetarians alike.

One of the great appeals of cooking on the grill is its ease, and the simplistic approach works well with vegetables. Marinades requiring little or no cooking saturate vegetables, tofu, and tempeh, the main components of the vegetarian barbecue, to make satisfying main courses. The smoky flavor produced by the hot coals enhances these ingredients in a special way, unlike any indoor cooking method.

LEMON-SOY MARINADE

Here is a tasty marinade for grilling — one that will have you shamelessly licking your fingers.

½ cup peanut oil *or* vegetable oil

3 tablespoons fresh lemon juice

4½ tablespoons tamari soy sauce

2½ tablespoons oriental sesame oil

1 scallion, very thinly sliced

3 garlic cloves, pressed

1½ teaspoons ground ginger

Makes about 1¼ cups

❶ Combine all the ingredients in a jar with a screw-on top and shake vigorously. Use for Tofu Shish Kebab (page 193), Grilled Mushrooms (below), and Grilled Eggplant Slices (page 198).

GRILLED MUSHROOMS

These mouth-watering mushrooms are so delectable you can serve a whole skewer to each person as a side dish.

1 recipe Lemon-Soy Marinade (above)

1½ pounds mushrooms, rinsed and patted dry

1 teaspoon minced fresh parsley

Serves 4

❶ Prepare the marinade and pour into a large bowl. Stir in the mushrooms and toss to coat well. Let sit 4 to 6 hours, tossing occasionally.

❷ Thread the mushrooms on skewers, running the skewers through the stems and out the caps.

❸ Grill over hot coals 15 minutes, turning every 5 minutes or so. Brush with some of the leftover marinade while cooking. Brush with marinade and sprinkle the minced parsley over the mushrooms just before serving.

TOFU SHISH KEBAB WITH LEMON-SOY MARINADE

1 recipe Lemon-Soy Marinade (page 192)

1 pound extra-firm or firm tofu, cut into ¾-inch cubes and patted very dry

16 cherry tomatoes

1 large green bell pepper, cored and cut into 1-inch squares

½ large red onion, cut vertically into thirds and chunks separated

12 fresh mushrooms, rinsed and patted dry

Serves 4

❶ Prepare the marinade. Place the tofu in a medium bowl, pour on ⅓ of the marinade, and toss gently to coat. Cover and refrigerate 4 to 8 hours.

❷ In a large bowl, combine the tomatoes, pepper, onions, and mushrooms. Pour on the remaining marinade and toss well. Let sit for 4 to 8 hours. (Cover and refrigerate if making longer than 4 hours in advance.)

❸ Alternately thread the tofu and vegetables on skewers. Cook over hot coals about 15 minutes, turning the skewers every 5 minutes. Brush with some of the leftover marinade a few times while cooking, and again just before serving.

TEMPEH TERIYAKI SHISH KEBAB

This sweet and spicy sauce is great for barbecuing; it coats well and superbly enhances the charcoal flavor.

MARINADE

¼ cup peanut oil *or* vegetable oil

¼ cup tamari soy sauce

¼ cup sherry

2 garlic cloves, pressed

1 teaspoon ground ginger

2 tablespoons molasses

10 ounces tempeh, cut into 1-inch cubes

1 red bell pepper, cored and cut into 1-inch squares

1 small yellow squash, quartered lengthwise and cut into 1-inch chunks

½ large red onion, cut vertically into thirds and chunks separated

Serves 4

❶ In a large bowl, combine the ingredients for the marinade and whisk together until blended. (The marinade can be made up to 24 hours in advance and refrigerated.)

❷ Stir in the tempeh, red pepper, squash, and red onion. Let sit 4 to 8 hours. (If holding longer than 4 hours, cover and refrigerate.) Stir occasionally to coat everything well.

❸ Alternately thread the tempeh and vegetables on skewers. Cook on a hot grill 15 minutes, turning the skewers every 5 minutes. Occasionally brush some of the leftover marinade on the skewers while cooking, and again just before serving.

GRILLED EGGPLANT WITH SPICY PEANUT SAUCE

This spicy Indonesian sauce is the perfect foil for the mild taste of eggplant. For a colorful accompaniment, serve this with Smoked Vegetables with Cumin Dressing (page 196).

2 teaspoons oriental sesame oil

2 garlic cloves, minced

⅛ teaspoon crushed red pepper flakes

⅓ cup crunchy natural-style peanut butter

2 teaspoons tamari soy sauce

2 teaspoons fresh lime juice

1½ teaspoons sugar

⅓ cup water

. . . .

2 medium eggplants

Vegetable oil for brushing

Serves 4

❶ In a small saucepan, heat the sesame oil over medium heat. Add the garlic and red pepper and cook 30 seconds.

❷ With a whisk or fork, beat in the peanut butter, soy sauce, lime juice, sugar, and water. The sauce should be the consistency of hot fudge sauce. Add a few drops water if necessary. Keep barely warm while cooking the eggplant. (You can make this sauce in advance and chill it for up to 24 hours. Warm over low heat.)

❸ Slice the eggplant ½ inch thick. Brush both sides of each slice with oil, then grill on a rack over hot coals 7 to 10 minutes, turning once. The eggplant should be tender, not mushy. (I like to grill with the cover closed for extra-smoky flavor.) Serve with a spoonful of warm peanut sauce on each slice.

SMOKED VEGETABLES WITH CUMIN DRESSING

Serve this delicious concoction at your next barbecue, and it will be a glowing success (pun intended!). A colorful assortment of vegetables grilled with the cover closed acquire a deep, smoky flavor. If you have more dishes to grill, prepare this first; it can sit for a few hours.

DRESSING

½ teaspoon cumin seeds

2 garlic cloves, minced

2 tablespoons fresh lemon juice

1 teaspoon tamari soy sauce

⅓ cup olive oil

Salt to taste

Freshly ground black pepper to taste

VEGETABLES

1 medium yellow squash, cut lengthwise ½ inch thick

1 medium zucchini, cut lengthwise ½ inch thick

1 medium onion, cut into ¾-inch-thick slices

1 large red bell pepper

Serves 4

❶ To make the dressing, toast the cumin seeds in a small skillet over medium heat. Shake the pan a few times to prevent burning. Pour the seeds into a small bowl and let cool. Crush them a bit with a mortar and pestle, or roll with a rolling pin. Return them to the bowl. Whisk in the remaining dressing ingredients.

❷ Brush the yellow squash, zucchini, and onion slices on both sides with some of the dressing. Place on a grill over hot coals, along with the whole bell pepper. Close the cover and cook about 10 minutes, turning the vegetables after 5 minutes. (The bell pepper should be turned frequently to char it evenly. It will cook 15 to 20 minutes.) When done, the vegetables should be tender but still crunchy.

❸ Place the vegetables on a platter and let cool. When the bell pepper is done, place it in a paper or plastic bag, close tightly, and steam for 10 minutes. Cut the yellow squash, zucchini, and onion into large chunks and stir them into the remaining dressing. Peel the bell pepper under cold running water, core it, and pat dry. Cut the pepper into large chunks and stir it into the vegetable mixture. Serve warm or at room temperature.

GARLICKY GRILLED TOMATOES

These tomatoes are extra-juicy and flavorful, and are a wonderful addition to a meal cooked on the grill.

2 large firm ripe tomatoes

1 garlic clove, pressed

1 teaspoon minced fresh basil, *or* 1/4 teaspoon dried basil

Salt to taste

Freshly ground black pepper to taste

2 tablespoons olive oil

Serves 2 to 4

❶ With a very shallow cut, remove the cores from the tomatoes. Cut each tomato in half horizontally, then gently squeeze out the juice and seeds.

❷ Place 2 tomato halves on each of 2 double sheets of aluminum foil large enough to enclose them. Sprinkle the garlic, basil, salt, and pepper over each tomato. Drizzle on the olive oil. Fold the foil over the tomatoes to form well-sealed packets.

❸ Place the packets on a hot grill and cook about 15 minutes. Check one of the packets; when done, the tomatoes will be juicy and tender but not mushy. Serve with the accumulated juices poured over them.

GRILLED EGGPLANT SLICES

The eggplant slices soak up the Lemon-Soy Marinade and become nice and juicy.

1 medium eggplant

1 recipe Lemon-Soy Marinade (page 192)

Serves 4

❶ Keeping the skin on, slice the eggplant ½ inch thick.

❷ Prepare the Lemon-Soy Marinade and pour into a large bowl.

❸ One by one, dip the eggplant slices in the marinade, then place on a hot grill. Cook 15 minutes, turning the eggplant after 7 minutes. Brush the slices with marinade throughout the cooking time, and again just before serving.

GRILLED CORN-ON-THE-COB

This ultrasimple method produces very tender, tasty corn. Simplicity at its best.

Fresh sweet corn

Butter

Salt

❶ Soak the desired amount of corn in the husk in a sink or tub full of cold water for 15 minutes.

❷ Remove the corn from the water, shake off the excess, and place on the grill over hot coals. Cover the grill and cook 30 minutes, rotating the corn one-third of a turn every 10 minutes. The husks will blacken, but the corn inside will not burn.

❸ Let cool a few minutes, or until easy to handle. Peel off the husks and the silk (the silk should come off easily in clumps). Serve immediately with butter and salt.

CORN-ON-THE-COB WITH CHILI-GARLIC BUTTER

The cornhusks are pulled back halfway to slather on a flavored butter, then closed to let the corn steam. A delicious method of grilling corn.

3 tablespoons unsalted butter, softened

1 garlic clove, pressed

1 teaspoon chili powder

6 ears fresh sweet corn

Makes 6 ears of corn

❶ Thoroughly combine the butter, garlic, and chili powder in a small bowl. Set aside.

❷ Soak the corn in the husk in a sink or tub filled with cold water 15 minutes. Remove the corn from the water, shake off the excess, and pull the husks back halfway. Remove as much silk as you can. Rub the flavored butter all over the exposed corn. Pull the husks back over the corn and twist shut. Tightly wrap each ear of corn in foil.

❸ Immediately place the corn on the grill over hot coals (don't delay, or the wet husks will dry out). Close the cover and cook 35 minutes, rotating each ear one-third of a turn every 10 minutes.

❹ Remove the foil from each ear. Cool a few minutes until easy to handle, then remove the husks. Serve immediately.

DESSERTS

Dessert, for me, is not an everyday affair but an occasional treat that I relish without guilt. I avoid sweets on a regular basis and allow myself a pleasurable concoction from time to time.

When planning menus, the choice of a dessert should always depend on how rich the other courses are. Not only will the dessert taste better if it is in balance with the rest of the meal, but your guests will feel better as well. If you choose to serve a pasta dish with a cream-based sauce, then a light dessert such as Strawberry and Peach Compote (page 225) will be refreshing and satisfying. On the other hand, if your dinner includes a light entrée such as Bulghur Salad with Corn, Zucchini, and Shredded Basil (page 80), then a seductive dessert such as Toasted Almond Mocha Ice Cream Torte (page 204) would be very welcome.

Sensible eating allows you to splurge occasionally, and you'll be none the worse for such indulgences.

ICE CREAM TRUFFLE PIE WITH RASPBERRY SAUCE

I can easily say that this is one of the best desserts I've ever tasted. A dense chocolate truffle layer sandwiched between vanilla and chocolate ice cream gives this pie a captivating texture, while the tartness of the raspberry sauce beautifully offsets its sweetness.

⅔ cup chocolate wafer crumbs (about 14 wafers; *see Note,* page 206)

3 tablespoons unsalted butter, melted

1 pint chocolate ice cream

1 cup (6 ounces) semisweet chocolate chips

⅓ cup heavy cream

1 pint vanilla ice cream

2 tablespoons finely chopped walnuts

1 10-ounce package frozen raspberries in syrup, thawed

1 tablespoon Grand Marnier (optional)

Serves 8

❶ Lightly oil the bottom and sides of a 9-inch pie plate. With a fork, mix the crumbs with the melted butter until evenly moistened. Sprinkle evenly over the bottom of the pie plate, then press firmly into place. Freeze at least 30 minutes.

❷ Meanwhile, thaw the chocolate ice cream in a large bowl until it is soft enough to spread. With a rubber spatula, spread the ice cream over the frozen crust and smooth the top. Freeze at least 1 hour.

❸ To make the truffle layer, combine the chocolate chips and cream in a saucepan over medium heat. Stir until the chocolate begins to melt, then remove from the heat and stir until very smooth. Spread evenly over the frozen pie. Freeze for 30 minutes, or until firm.

❹ Soften the vanilla ice cream in a large bowl. Spread it over the pie, then sprinkle on the walnuts. Freeze at least 1 hour, or covered up to 2 weeks.

❺ To make the raspberry sauce, place the thawed raspberries and their juice in the blender. Puree until smooth. Press through a strainer, discard the seeds, and stir in the Grand Marnier.

❻ Serve the pie in small wedges with raspberry sauce poured over each portion. Cut the pie by dipping a knife in hot water.

TOASTED ALMOND MOCHA ICE CREAM TORTE

This is the kind of dessert culinary memories are made of. It's rich, has an incredible marriage of flavors, and it looks striking. Although this torte is of formidable size, don't be dissuaded from making it even if there are only two people in your household. It keeps well and will be just as good one to two weeks later.

1 cup chocolate wafer crumbs (about 20 wafers; *see Note*)

4 tablespoons unsalted butter, melted

3 pints coffee ice cream

1 cup whole, unblanched almonds

3 pints vanilla ice cream

½ teaspoon almond extract

MOCHA SAUCE

1 cup firmly packed light brown sugar

½ cup light corn syrup

1½ tablespoons instant coffee powder

⅔ cup heavy cream

3 ounces (3 squares) unsweetened baking chocolate, coarsely chopped

2½ tablespoons coffee liqueur

Dash salt

Serves 8

❶ Lightly oil the sides and bottom of an 8- or 9-inch springform pan. In a small bowl, combine the cookie crumbs and melted butter with a fork. Sprinkle them on the bottom of the pan, and press them in to form a bottom crust. Freeze at least 30 minutes.

❷ Soften the coffee ice cream just until you can spread it evenly on the crust. Freeze 30 minutes, or until firm.

❸ Meanwhile, roughly chop ½ cup of the almonds. Place the other ½ cup in a blender or food processor and grind to a fine powder. Combine with the chopped almonds in a pie tin or other shallow ovenproof dish and toast in a 350°F oven until fragrant and golden, 7 to 8 minutes. (Stir occasionally to prevent uneven toasting.) Let cool. Set aside 1 tablespoon of the toasted almonds.

❹ Soften the vanilla ice cream and stir in the toasted almonds and the almond extract. Spread over the coffee ice cream and smooth the top. Sprinkle on the reserved 1 tablespoon of the almonds. Cover with foil or plastic wrap and freeze 2 hours, or overnight.

(continued)

❺ To make the sauce: In a medium saucepan, combine the brown sugar, corn syrup, instant coffee, and heavy cream. Bring to a boil over medium heat, stirring constantly, and boil 5 minutes. Remove the pan from the heat. Stir in the chocolate until melted, then stir in the coffee liqueur and the salt. Keep warm or at room temperature; the sauce will thicken as it cools. (If chilled, reheat the sauce in a bowl of hot tap water and stir until of pouring consistency. Store leftover sauce in the refrigerator up to 2 weeks in a jar with a screw-on cap).

❻ Just before serving, wrap a warm, dampened kitchen towel around the sides of the springform pan and remove the rim. With a large knife dipped in hot water, cut the torte into wedges. Serve with the mocha sauce.

☛***Note:*** The best wafers for making a crumb crust are a plain variety such as Nabisco's Famous Chocolate Wafers. Place wafers in a plastic bag, seal, and crush with a rolling pin.

ORANGE POPPY SEED CAKE

A rich, buttery cake drizzled with a creamy white glaze — simple, yet utterly seductive. I bake this in a bundt pan because it looks so impressive, but any tube pan will do.

3 cups unbleached flour

1½ teaspoons baking powder

1½ teaspoons baking soda

¾ teaspoon salt

3 tablespoons poppy seeds

1 cup (2 sticks) unsalted butter, softened

1½ cups sugar

3 large eggs

1½ cups sour cream *or* **plain yogurt**

1 tablespoon pure orange extract ***(see Note)***

GLAZE

1 cup confectioners' sugar

1½ tablespoons warm water

½ teaspoon pure orange extract

Serves 12 to 16

❶ Preheat the oven to 350°F. Butter and flour a bundt pan or other 10-cup tube pan.

❷ In a medium bowl, thoroughly combine the flour, baking powder, baking soda, salt, and poppy seeds.

❸ In a large mixing bowl, cream together the butter and sugar with an electric mixer until light and fluffy. Beat in the eggs until mixed, then beat in the sour cream and orange extract.

❹ Beat in the flour mixture until combined, scraping the sides of the bowl as necessary. Scrape the batter into the prepared pan. Bake 50 to 55 minutes, or until a cake tester inserted in the center of the cake comes out dry. Cool 10 minutes on a wire rack before turning out. Cool completely before making the glaze.

❺ To make the glaze: Combine the confectioners' sugar, water, and orange extract in a small bowl. With a spoon, drizzle the glaze over the top of the cake. Let harden before serving, about 20 minutes.

☛***Note:*** This cake freezes very well. Wrap in plastic, and cover again with foil or seal in a plastic bag. Orange extract can be purchased in most supermarkets. If necessary, you could substitute 1½ tablespoons grated orange rind and 1 tablespoon orange juice in the cake, and omit the orange extract in the glaze.

FRESH APPLE CAKE

Here is a very different apple-filled cake — the best one I know. It will still be moist and fresh-tasting 5 days after baking if well wrapped and refrigerated.

CAKE

5 medium apples, peeled, cored, and thinly sliced

1½ cups plus 2 tablespoons sugar

2 teaspoons cinnamon

3 large eggs

¾ cup vegetable oil

¼ cup plus 2 tablespoons orange juice

2¼ cups unbleached flour

2¼ teaspoons baking powder

2 teaspoons vanilla extract

GLAZE

½ cup apricot preserves

1½ tablespoons water

· ·

2 tablespoons sliced almonds

· ·

Sweetened whipped cream (optional)

Serves 10 to 12

❶ Preheat the oven to 350°F. Butter and flour a 9-inch tube pan.

❷ Place the apple slices in a medium bowl. Sprinkle on 2 tablespoons of the sugar and the cinnamon, and toss very well to coat. Set aside.

❸ In a large bowl, beat the eggs with an electric mixer. Add the remaining 1½ cups sugar and beat until pale and creamy. Beat in the remaining cake ingredients until well blended.

❹ Pour one-third of the batter into the prepared pan, give the apple mixture a quick toss, and spread half the apples on top of the batter. Pour on half the remaining batter (don't worry if the apples aren't completely covered), and top with the remaining apples. Pour on the remaining batter and spread to cover the apples as best you can.

❺ Bake 60 to 70 minutes, or until a knife inserted in the center of the cake comes out clean. Cool on a wire rack 10 minutes, invert onto a plate, and invert again onto a serving plate to cool right side up.

❻ To make the glaze: Heat the apricot preserves and water together until the mixture is very hot. Pour through a strainer, pressing the solid pieces through. With a pastry brush, coat the entire cake with the glaze. Sprinkle the sliced almonds on top. Let the cake cool thoroughly before serving plain or with sweetened whipped cream.

OATMEAL CAKE WITH PENUCHE FROSTING

The idea of oats in a cake may sound unusual, but in fact this buttery, light cake is one of the most delicious I've tasted. Be sure to include the cardamom, for the flavor marries superbly with the oats and brown sugar.

8 tablespoons (1 stick) unsalted butter, softened

1 cup sugar

2 large eggs, room temperature

1 teaspoon vanilla extract

1½ cups unbleached flour

1 cup oats, ground fine in a blender

3 teaspoons baking powder

1 teaspoon ground cardamom

½ teaspoon salt

1 cup milk

PENUCHE FROSTING

6 tablespoons unsalted butter

½ cup packed light brown sugar

1½ tablespoons milk

1 cup confectioners' sugar

½ teaspoon vanilla extract

....

⅓ cup very finely ground pecans *or* walnuts

Serves 8

❶ Preheat the oven to 350°F. Butter and flour a 9-inch springform cake pan, or use an 8 × 8-inch square cake pan. (If your pan is made of glass, set the oven at 325°F.)

❷ In a large mixing bowl, cream the butter with an electric mixer until soft. Add the sugar and beat until well blended. Add the eggs and vanilla and beat again until light and creamy.

❸ Thoroughly combine the flour, ground oats, baking powder, cardamom, and salt in a medium bowl. Beat these ingredients into the butter mixture, alternating with the milk, until well blended. Scrape into the prepared pan and smooth the top. Bake 50 to 55 minutes, or until a knife inserted in the center of the cake comes out clean. Cool on a wire rack 15 minutes, then loosen the edges of the cake, invert onto a platter, and invert again onto the rack so the cake is right side up. Let the cake cool completely, about 2 hours.

❹ When the cake is cool, make the frosting: In a small saucepan, melt the butter over medium-low heat. Add the brown sugar and stir until melted and blended with the butter. Slowly pour in the milk, mix well, and bring the mixture to a boil. Scrape it into a medium bowl and cool 10 minutes. Add the

(continued)

confectioners' sugar and vanilla and beat with an electric mixer until smooth. Spread all over the cooled cake. Decorate the cake by sprinkling the ground nuts on top, leaving a ¾ inch border bare. Wait at least 15 minutes before serving, to allow the frosting to set.

OLD-FASHIONED POUND CAKE

This cake is great to have on hand because it's so popular and versatile. Freeze a portion to serve at a moment's notice — plain, with sliced fresh fruit, or with Strawberry and Peach Compote (page 225). Try varying the flavor by following any of the suggestions below.

1 cup (2 sticks) unsalted butter, softened

2 cups sugar

5 large eggs

2 teaspoons vanilla extract

2 cups cake flour *(see Note)*

½ teaspoon salt

Serves 10 to 12

❶ Preheat the oven to 325°F. Butter and flour a 10-cup bundt pan. In a large mixing bowl, cream the butter until smooth, using an electric mixer. Add the sugar and beat until light. Add the eggs one at a time, beating well after each addition. Beat in the vanilla extract.

❷ Add the flour and salt and beat until the batter is very smooth. Scrape the batter into the prepared pan and bake 1 hour, or until a knife inserted in the center of the cake comes out clean. Cool on a wire rack 10 minutes before removing from the pan. Cool completely (at least 2 hours) before serving.

☛***Note:*** If you don't have cake flour, substitute 1¾ cups unbleached white and ¼ cup cornstarch.

☛***Variations:*** For Lemon Pound Cake, use 1 teaspoon vanilla extract, plus the grated rind of 1 lemon. For Almond Pound Cake, use ½ teaspoon vanilla extract plus ½ teaspoon almond extract. For Orange Pound Cake, use ½ teaspoon vanilla extract plus the grated rind of 1 orange or 1 teaspoon pure orange extract.

POACHED PEARS IN GINGER SYRUP

These succulent sweet-and-spicy pears are the perfect finale for a rich meal.

2 cups water

⅔ cup sugar

7 quarter-size slices fresh ginger

4 firm ripe pears, peeled, halved, and cored

Serves 4

❶ In a large stockpot, combine the water, sugar, and ginger. Bring to a boil and stir until the sugar dissolves, about 2 minutes.

❷ Add the pears and reduce the heat to a lively simmer. Cook, basting occasionally, 15 minutes. Remove from the heat and let the pears cool in the syrup 30 minutes.

❸ With a slotted spoon, remove the pears from the liquid and place them in a bowl. Boil the syrup briskly 2 minutes, or until it thickens slightly. Pour it through a strainer onto the pears. Discard the ginger. Chill the fruit in its syrup until cold, about 2 hours. Serve in pretty bowls.

BLUEBERRY KUCHEN

***Kuchen** (pronounced **koo'-kin**) is a type of low coffee cake topped with fruit. Here, blueberries cover an almond-flavored cake that has a cookielike texture. Great for dessert, for teatime, or to pack on a picnic and eat with your fingers.*

8 tablespoons (1 stick) unsalted butter, softened

⅔ cup sugar

1 large egg

1 teaspoon vanilla extract

½ teaspoon almond extract

1¼ cups unbleached flour

½ teaspoon baking powder

¼ teaspoon salt

2 cups fresh blueberries

1 tablespoon sugar

¼ teaspoon cinnamon

Serves 8

❶ In a large bowl, cream the butter with the sugar until blended. Beat in the egg, vanilla, and almond extract until pale and creamy.

❷ Add the flour, baking powder, and salt and beat until well mixed. Don't overwork the batter. Chill 30 minutes, or until the batter is no longer wet and sticky. Meanwhile, preheat the oven to 350°F. Butter a 9- or 10-inch tart pan with a removable rim.

❸ Press the batter into the bottom and sides of the tart pan. Mix the blueberries with the 1 tablespoon sugar and the cinnamon. Fill the tart shell. Bake 40 minutes, or until the cake is a rich golden brown. Cool 5 minutes on a wire rack, then place the tart pan on an inverted bowl and pull down the rim. Return the pan to the rack and cool completely before serving, about 1½ hours.

☛***Note:*** This kuchen freezes exceptionally well when wrapped well in foil and sealed in a plastic bag. Thaw at room temperature a few hours before serving.

APPLE WALNUT KUCHEN

This kuchen has a buttery crust and is topped with cinnamon-coated apple slices arranged in concentric circles. Very delicious and attractive. It's rich, so small slices suffice.

8 tablespoons (1 stick) unsalted butter, softened

⅔ cup plus 1½ teaspoons sugar

1 large egg yolk

1 teaspoon vanilla extract

1 cup unbleached flour

¼ teaspoon salt

1 tablespoon milk

¼ cup finely chopped walnuts

3 large apples (not Delicious), peeled, cored, and very thinly sliced

2 tablespoons unsalted butter, melted

½ teaspoon cinnamon

Serves 8

❶ Cream the butter and the ⅔ cup sugar together in a large bowl until it is well mixed. Add the egg yolk and vanilla extract and beat until blended. Sprinkle in the flour and salt and beat just until evenly mixed. Pour in the milk and beat just until the dough begins to clump together. Chill 15 minutes.

❷ Generously butter an 8- or 9-inch tart pan with a removable rim. Pat the dough into the bottom and sides of the tart pan. Chill 30 minutes.

❸ Preheat the oven to 350°F. Sprinkle the walnuts evenly over the bottom of the crust. Place the apple slices in the crust in concentric circles; you probably will have 2 layers. Brush the top layer with the melted butter.

❹ Mix the remaining 1½ teaspoons sugar with the cinnamon and sprinkle evenly over the apples. Bake 40 minutes, or until the crust is a rich golden brown and the apples are tender. Cool on a wire rack 10 minutes, then remove the rim of the tart pan. Cool completely before serving.

THE BEST CHOCOLATE CAKE

Many arrogant cooks think they have the best chocolate cake recipe. They're all wrong; I have it!

The basis of this recipe is what is known as a wacky cake: such a cake has no eggs, and everything is quickly mixed in one bowl. For some marvelous reason, it creates an ultramoist, rich, memorable two-layer cake, which I frost with the silkiest chocolate buttercream icing you've ever tasted.

CAKE

2¼ cups unbleached white flour

1½ cups sugar

½ cup cocoa

1½ teaspoons baking soda

¾ teaspoon salt

1½ cups warm water

½ cup vegetable oil

1½ teaspoons vanilla extract

1½ teaspoons white vinegar

ICING

1 cup semisweet chocolate chips

8 tablespoons (1 stick) unsalted butter, softened

1 large egg

Serves 8

❶ Preheat the oven to 350°F. Wait 10 minutes before starting to make the cake. Meanwhile, butter and flour 2 8-inch layer pans and set aside. When the 10 minutes are up, thoroughly combine the flour, sugar, cocoa, baking soda, and salt in a bowl.

❷ Pour in the water, oil, vanilla, and vinegar and stir until well combined. Pour into the prepared pans. Bake 30 minutes, or until a knife inserted in the center of the cake comes out clean. Cool on a wire rack 10 minutes, then remove the cakes from the pans and cool completely.

❸ To make the buttercream: Melt the chocolate in a double boiler, then remove the top pan. Let the chocolate cool until tepid. In a medium bowl, cream the butter, using an electric mixer. Add the egg and beat until blended but not smooth. Pour in the chocolate and beat just until combined.

❹ When the cake is completely cool, spread some icing on one layer. Top with the other layer, then spread the remaining icing all over the cake. Chill the cake at least 30 minutes, then bring to room temperature before serving.

DEEP-DISH PEAR PIE

A thick and flaky clove-scented crust covers succulent pears bathed in their own juices. A splendid dessert for fruit lovers.

6 ripe Bosc, Anjou, or Comice pears

½ cup sugar

1 tablespoon fresh lemon juice

1 teaspoon pure vanilla extract

2 tablespoons cornstarch

CRUST

1 cup unbleached flour

¼ teaspoon ground cloves

Dash salt

5 tablespoons cold unsalted butter

1 tablespoon vegetable oil

2 tablespoons water

1 large egg, beaten

Serves 4 to 6

❶ Preheat the oven to 425°F. Peel and core the pears and slice them into bite-size pieces. Drop them into a 1½-quart baking dish and mix in the sugar, lemon juice, vanilla extract, and cornstarch.

❷ To make the crust: Mix the flour, cloves, and salt in a medium bowl. Cut the butter into small bits and work it into the flour with your fingers or a pastry cutter until it resembles coarse meal. Pour on the oil, stir, and sprinkle on the water. Work the mixture until you can gather it in a ball, then knead the dough 2 or 3 times to blend.

❸ Roll the dough on a floured surface into a circle large enough to cover the pear mixture. Drape it over the pears, cut a vent in the center, and brush the crust with the beaten egg.

❹ Bake 10 minutes, then reduce the heat to 350°F. Cook 40 minutes longer, or until the crust is a nice golden brown. Cool on a rack and serve warm.

FRESH STRAWBERRY TART

This glorious tart is rather quick to assemble because you don't have to roll out the crust or cook the filling. Other summer fruit works well; try blueberries, raspberries, peaches, or plums.

ALMOND CRUST

5 tablespoons unsalted butter, softened

1 large egg yolk

½ teaspoon vanilla extract

3 tablespoons sugar

⅔ cup almonds

1 cup unbleached flour

FILLING

8 ounces Neufchâtel or cream cheese, at room temperature

¼ cup sugar

2 tablespoons fresh lemon juice

¼ cup heavy cream

1 to 1½ pints fresh strawberries, hulled

¼ cup apricot preserves

1 tablespoon water

Serves 6

❶ Preheat the oven to 350°F. Butter the sides of a 9- to 10-inch tart pan with a removable rim or set aside a 9-inch pie plate.

❷ To make the crust: In a large bowl, beat the butter, egg yolk, vanilla, and sugar until smooth and creamy. Finely grind the almonds, then combine with the flour and beat in just until mixed. The dough will be crumbly; don't overwork. Gather the dough into a ball, then break off pieces and press it into the bottom and sides of the tart pan or pie plate. Prick the crust all over with a fork. Chill 1 hour, or cover and freeze for up to 2 weeks.

❸ Line the crust with foil, then cover the bottom with dried beans or pie weights. Bake 12 minutes. Remove the foil and beans and bake 10 minutes longer, or until golden all over. Cool completely on a wire rack. If using a tart pan, remove the outer rim.

❹ To make the filling: Beat the cream cheese, sugar, and lemon juice together. Pour in the cream and beat until very smooth. Spread on the bottom of the tart.

❺ Cover the tart with strawberries in a decorative manner. Heat the preserves and water together until blended. Strain out any bits of pulp through a mesh strainer. Brush the glaze on the strawberries with a pastry brush. Chill the tart 4 hours, or overnight, before serving. Serve cool, not cold.

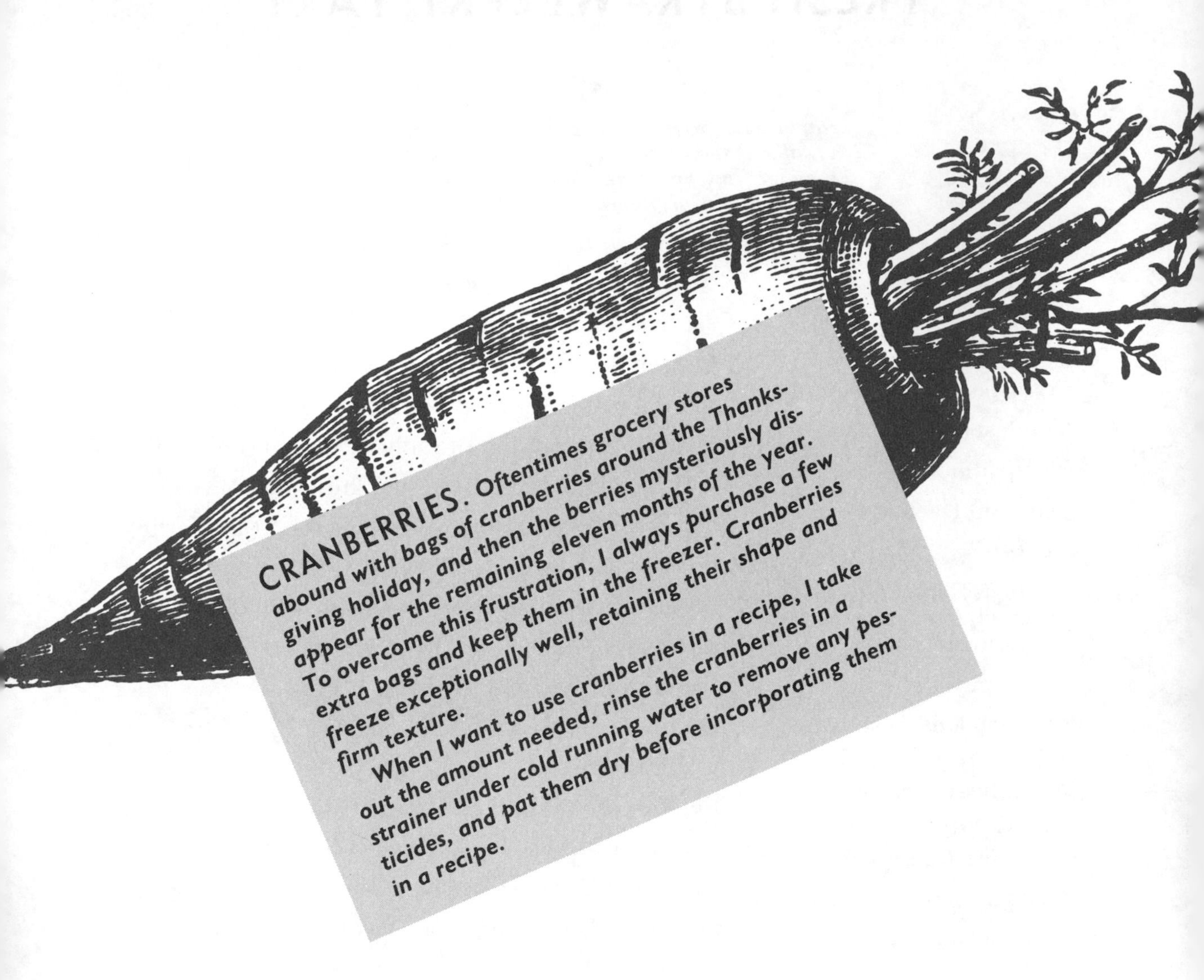

CRANBERRIES. Oftentimes grocery stores abound with bags of cranberries around the Thanksgiving holiday, and then the berries mysteriously disappear for the remaining eleven months of the year. To overcome this frustration, I always purchase a few extra bags and keep them in the freezer. Cranberries freeze exceptionally well, retaining their shape and firm texture.

When I want to use cranberries in a recipe, I take out the amount needed, rinse the cranberries in a strainer under cold running water to remove any pesticides, and pat them dry before incorporating them in a recipe.

MAPLE FRUIT CRISP

Maple syrup sweetens this winter fruit dessert. It's great for conquering the winter doldrums.

5 medium apples (any type but Delicious), peeled, cored, and thinly sliced

2 firm ripe Anjou, Comice, or Bartlett pears, peeled, cored, and thinly sliced

⅔ cup fresh or frozen cranberries

2 tablespoons golden raisins

3 tablespoons pure maple syrup

1 tablespoon unbleached flour

TOPPING

¼ cup unbleached flour

¼ cup oats

2 tablespoons finely chopped walnuts

¼ cup firmly packed light brown sugar

1 teaspoon ground cinnamon

¼ teaspoon salt

5 tablespoons cold unsalted butter, cut into bits

3 tablespoons pure maple syrup

Serves 4 to 6

❶ Preheat the oven to 350°F. In a large bowl, combine the apples, pears, cranberries, raisins, and maple syrup. Toss to coat well. Sprinkle on the flour and toss again. Scrape the fruit into an 8 × 8-inch pan and smooth the top.

❷ To make the topping: Combine the flour, oats, walnuts, brown sugar, cinnamon, and salt in a medium bowl. With your fingertips, rub in the butter bits until coarse crumbs form. Stir in the maple syrup just until the crumbs are evenly moistened (the mixture will be a little gooey). With your fingers, sprinkle the mixture on top of the fruit, breaking up any large chunks.

❸ Bake 40 to 50 minutes, or until the filling is bubbly and the apples are tender. Serve warm or at room temperature.

RHUBARB CRUMBLE

The cardamom flavor is outstanding in this absolutely delicious dessert. The apples give the rhubarb filling some body, and it all turns a beautiful rosy hue.

4 cups (about 1¼ pounds) diced rhubarb

3 Granny Smith apples, peeled, cored, and thinly sliced

¾ cup honey

1½ tablespoons cornstarch

½ teaspoon ground cardamom

TOPPING

½ cup unbleached flour

½ cup firmly packed light brown sugar

½ teaspoon cinnamon

¼ teaspoon salt

5 tablespoons cold unsalted butter, cut into bits

2 tablespoons slivered almonds

Serves 6

❶ Preheat the oven to 350°F. In a large bowl, combine the rhubarb, apples, honey, cornstarch, and cardamom. Pour the fruit into an 8 × 8 × 2-inch baking pan and smooth the top.

❷ To make the topping: Combine the flour, brown sugar, cinnamon, and salt in a medium bowl. Add the butter bits and stir to coat. With your fingertips, rub the butter into the mixture until coarse crumbs form. Stir in the almonds. Sprinkle the crumbs all over the top of the rhubarb filling.

❸ Bake 50 minutes, or until the topping is brown and the filling is bubbly. Serve slightly warm or at room temperature.

FRUIT COUPE

This is a very pretty, light dessert. It's worthwhile investing in some decorative dessert goblets so that with a dessert such as this you can make a stunning presentation with little effort. Below is my favorite combination of fruit. Feel free to improvise as desired.

2/3 cup heavy cream, well chilled

1½ tablespoons confectioners' sugar

¼ teaspoon almond extract

1½ cups fresh blueberries

2 peaches, peeled and sliced

1 ripe banana, cut into ½-inch slices

1 tablespoon sliced almonds, lightly toasted

Serves 4

❶ Whip the cream with the sugar and almond extract until stiff. (This can be done up to 2 hours in advance and the whipped cream refrigerated.)

❷ Set 4 decorative goblets in front of you. Using half the fruit, divide it evenly among the goblets. Spoon on half the whipped cream. Top with the remaining fruit, then with the remaining whipped cream. Sprinkle some almonds on each portion. Serve immediately.

PEACH MELBA

Each summer my family eagerly awaits raspberry season so we can savor this memorable dessert. Many people poach fresh peaches in sugar syrup when they make Peach Melba, but I find this step unnecessary with really ripe, sweet, juicy peaches. I think this dessert looks stunning in pretty dessert goblets that show off its striking colors, but small dessert dishes will do.

1⅔ cups fresh raspberries

3 tablespoons plus 2 teaspoons sugar

½ cup heavy cream, chilled

2 ripe peaches

1⅓ pints rich vanilla ice cream

12 whole raspberries, for garnish

Serves 4

❶ Put the raspberries in a blender or food processor and puree until smooth. Strain through a medium-mesh strainer into a small bowl and press out all the juice from the pulp. Discard the seeds. (Alternatively, lay a piece of cheesecloth over a medium bowl so that it hangs over the edges, and pour a small amount of the puree into it. Gather up the sides and gently squeeze out the juice. Discard the seeds and repeat with the rest of the puree.) Stir 2 tablespoons plus 2 teaspoons of the sugar into the sauce, cover, and chill at least 2 hours.

❷ Whip the cream (it is a good idea to chill the bowl and beaters beforehand) until it begins to thicken, then sprinkle on the remaining 1 tablespoon of the sugar and whip until stiff. Cover and chill until ready to use.

❸ To assemble: Peel the peaches, cut them in half lengthwise, and discard the stone. Scoop ¼ of the ice cream into each dish, then gently press a peach half—cut side down—into the ice cream. Spoon on equal portions of the raspberry sauce. Top with the whipped cream (I like to use a pastry bag and pipe the cream using a star tip). Decorate each serving with 3 whole raspberries.

FRESH BLUEBERRIES WITH STRAWBERRY CREAM

Strawberry jam gives whipped cream a pink caste that contrasts beautifully with blueberries layered in goblets.

1 pint fresh blueberries

3 tablespoons strawberry jam

⅔ cup heavy cream, well chilled

Serves 4

❶ Rinse the blueberries in a colander and drain very well. Pick out and discard any blemished berries.

❷ Place the jam in a large mixing bowl and beat a few seconds with an electric mixer. Pour in the heavy cream and whip until stiff.

❸ In attractive goblets, layer the blueberries with the strawberry cream, making 3 layers of blueberries and two layers of cream. Chill until ready to serve, but no longer than 2 hours.

EGGNOG DIP FOR FRUIT

Here is a very different idea given me by my friend Billie Chernicoff: an eggnog-flavored dessert dip for fresh fruit. I've taken a rich, rum-and-nutmeg-spiked pastry cream and folded whipped cream into it.

Serve the dip in a beautiful bowl surrounded with a striking assortment of fruit that includes strawberries; banana, apple, and pear slices; and an attractively carved pineapple.

3 large egg yolks

⅓ cup plus 1 tablespoon sugar

1½ tablespoons cornstarch

2 tablespoons plus 1 teaspoon rum

⅛ teaspoon freshly grated nutmeg

1½ cups milk

½ teaspoon vanilla extract

½ cup heavy cream, well chilled

1 strawberry, for garnish

Serves 8

❶ In a large bowl, whisk the egg yolks and sugar until well blended. Whisk in the cornstarch until smooth, then whisk in 2 tablespoons of the rum and the nutmeg. Place a medium bowl on the counter for use in Step 3.

❷ Heat the milk in a medium saucepan over medium-high heat until very hot but not boiling. Slowly whisk the milk into the egg yolk mixture, then return the mixture to the saucepan. Whisking constantly, bring the mixture to a boil. Boil 1 minute, or until thickened like a custard.

❸ With a rubber spatula, immediately scrape the custard into the reserved bowl. Whisk in the vanilla. (If for some reason the custard is not smooth, pour it through a strainer.) Cover with plastic wrap, pressing it directly onto the custard to prevent a skin from forming. Chill until cold, at least 2 hours and up to 24 hours.

❹ No more than 4 hours before serving, whip the cream until very stiff. Gently but thoroughly fold it into the custard, along with the remaining 1 teaspoon rum. Scrape the dip into a serving bowl and garnish with the strawberry. Chill until serving time.

STRAWBERRY AND PEACH COMPOTE

Strawberries and peaches swim in a heavenly wine-flavored syrup that accentuates their flavors. Because the alcohol is boiled away, this dessert is suitable for children and is always popular with them.

¾ cup water

¾ cup dry white or red wine

½ cup sugar

2 cups fresh strawberries, hulled and halved

4 fresh peaches (about 2 cups), peeled and sliced

Serves 4 to 6

❶ In a small saucepan, combine the water, wine, and sugar and bring to a boil. Boil 30 seconds. Refrigerate until cold, about 1 hour.

❷ Combine the strawberries and peaches in a bowl and pour the syrup over them. Chill 4 to 12 hours. Serve cold in decorative goblets with a sprig of fresh mint.

GLAZED CARDAMOM PEARS

Juicy, sweet pears don't need much embellishment. These are baked with a brown sugar–cardamom syrup and served with sweetened sour cream.

1½ tablespoons unsalted butter

2 tablespoons firmly packed light brown sugar

2 ripe pears, peeled, halved, and cored

½ teaspoon ground cardamom

¼ cup water

¼ cup sour cream

2 teaspoons firmly packed light brown sugar

Serves 2

❶ Preheat the oven to 400°F. Grease the bottom of a 9-inch pie plate or shallow baking dish with 1 tablespoon of the butter and sprinkle on 1 tablespoon of the brown sugar. Place the pears in the dish cut side down, and sprinkle on the cardamom and the remaining 1 tablespoon brown sugar. Pour the water into the dish. Bake 30 minutes, turning the pears twice.

❷ Meanwhile, mix the sour cream with the brown sugar and chill until ready to serve.

❸ Serve the pears warm or at room temperature, with any remaining syrup drizzled over them. Top each serving with a few spoonfuls of the sweetened sour cream.

COFFEE MOUSSE

Coffee lovers take note! This silken mousse layered with bits of semisweet chocolate makes a rich but delicate finale for a special meal.

1 cup strong coffee

1 cup milk

4 large egg yolks

½ cup plus 2 tablespoons sugar

3 tablespoons cornstarch

½ tablespoon unsalted butter, melted

½ cup heavy cream, well chilled

4 teaspoons minced semisweet chocolate

Serves 4 to 6

❶ Combine the coffee and milk in a heavy saucepan and heat until hot but not boiling.

❷ Meanwhile, place the egg yolks, ½ cup of the sugar, and the cornstarch in a large bowl and whisk until pale and creamy.

❸ Slowly whisk the hot milk into the egg mixture until blended, and return to the saucepan, setting aside the bowl. Whisking constantly, bring the mixture to a boil. Boil 1 minute, whisking often. Pour into the bowl, then whisk in the butter. Cover by placing plastic wrap directly on the custard to prevent a skin from forming. Refrigerate until cold, about 2 hours.

❹ The custard will now be firm, so whisk gently to smooth and lighten it. Whip the cream with the remaining 2 tablespoons sugar until stiff but not buttery. With a rubber spatula, fold the cream into the custard until evenly incorporated.

❺ Spoon half the mousse into 4 8-ounce dessert goblets (or 6 smaller goblets). Divide half the minced chocolate among the portions. Spoon the remaining mousse on top of the chocolate, and sprinkle the remaining chocolate on top of each portion. Chill 30 minutes before serving. Cover each dish with plastic wrap if chilling longer. These can be stored in the refrigerator for up to 24 hours.

ALMOND RICE PUDDING

I've experimented with many versions of rice pudding in order to develop the perfect one — easy to prepare, very creamy, and unusually delicious. I think you'll agree that this is it.

4 cups low-fat milk, scalded

½ cup converted white rice

½ cup plus 3 tablespoons sugar

1 cinnamon stick

½ teaspoon salt

2 large egg yolks

½ cup milk

½ cup raisins

1 teaspoon vanilla extract

¼ teaspoon almond extract

⅔ cup heavy cream, well chilled

Sliced almonds, for garnish

Serves 6 generously

❶ Bring water to a boil in the bottom of a double boiler. In the top, combine the scalded milk, rice, ½ cup of the sugar, the cinnamon stick, and the salt. Cook, covered, over medium heat 45 to 50 minutes, or until the rice is tender. Stir occasionally to prevent sticking.

❷ In a medium bowl, whisk together the egg yolks and the ½ cup milk. Ladle in some of the hot rice mixture, stir, and carefully pour the yolk mixture into the pudding. Stir to blend. Cover and cook 10 minutes, stirring occasionally. Mix in the raisins and cook, covered, 20 minutes longer, or until the pudding thickens. Continue to stir periodically to prevent sticking.

❸ Remove the cinnamon stick and discard. Stir in the vanilla and almond extracts. Scrape the pudding into a large bowl, cover, and chill until cold, at least 2 hours. (It is a good idea to put your beaters in the freezer at this time.)

❹ Whip the cream until it begins to stiffen, then sprinkle in the remaining 3 tablespoons sugar and whip until stiff. Fold the cream into the cold pudding and spoon individual portions into 6 decorative goblets or dishes. Garnish with the sliced almonds. Serve immediately, or cover and chill for up to 24 hours before serving.

BREAD PUDDING WITH BOURBON SAUCE

I had this unforgettable bread pudding in New Orleans and was finally able to duplicate it in my kitchen.

PUDDING

1 8-ounce loaf day-old French or Italian bread, torn into small pieces (about 8 cups)

3 cups low-fat milk

2 large eggs, beaten

1 cup sugar

½ cup raisins

2 tablespoons vanilla extract

1 tablespoon cold unsalted butter, cut into bits

BOURBON SAUCE

6 tablespoons unsalted butter

1 large egg

¾ cup confectioners' sugar

3 tablespoons bourbon whiskey

Serves 8

❶ Butter a deep 2-quart baking dish and set aside.

❷ Tear the bread into small pieces and drop them into a large bowl. Pour the milk over them and stir to moisten. Soak 30 minutes. (About 20 minutes after beginning to soak the bread, preheat the oven to 350°F.) When finished soaking, break up the bread into bits with a large spoon.

❸ Beat together the eggs, sugar, raisins, and vanilla. Pour into the bread mixture and stir thoroughly, breaking up any large chunks of bread that surface. Scrape the pudding into the prepared baking dish, smooth the top, and dot with the butter. Place the baking dish in a large pan and fill the outer pan halfway with hot water. Place both pans in the oven and bake 70 minutes, or until a knife inserted in the center of the pudding comes out clean.

❹ Meanwhile, make the sauce: Melt the butter in a double boiler. In a small bowl, beat the egg, and beat in the confectioners' sugar. Stir into the melted butter, and whisk the mixture until it becomes very hot, about 7 minutes. Do not boil. Remove from the heat and scrape into a bowl. Let cool to room temperature, stirring occasionally. The sauce will thicken as it cools. Stir in the bourbon.

❺ Serve the pudding hot or warm in small custard cups. Spoon some sauce over each serving.

SWEET POTATO PUDDING WITH CRYSTALLIZED GINGER

This nutritious, spicy pudding is cooked in individual custard or soufflé cups, inverted, and topped with whipped cream and crystallized ginger. If you cannot get crystallized ginger, preserved ginger in syrup can be substituted. Try to get yams for their bright color, although regular sweet potatoes will still be delicious.

3 medium-large (about 1¼ pounds) yams or sweet potatoes

1¼ cups low-fat milk

¾ cup pure maple syrup, *or* ⅔ cup honey

3 large eggs

¼ cup unbleached flour

2 teaspoons cinnamon

1 teaspoon ground allspice

¼ teaspoon salt

2 tablespoons finely chopped crystallized ginger, plus 2 teaspoons, for garnish *(see Note)*

Lightly sweetened whipped cream

Serves 8

❶ Butter 8 ¾-cup custard cups or small soufflé dishes and set aside.

❷ Scrub the sweet potatoes, and cut each in half. Bring a medium saucepan of water to a boil, and cook the sweet potatoes until very tender, about 25 minutes. About 10 minutes before the sweet potatoes are done, preheat the oven to 350°F.

❸ Drain the sweet potatoes thoroughly. When cool enough to handle, peel off the skins and mash the flesh. Measure out 2¼ cups mashed sweet potato. (Any remaining sweet potato can be reheated and served with butter.)

❹ Put the mashed sweet potato, milk, maple syrup or honey, eggs, flour, cinnamon, allspice, and salt in a blender or food processor and blend until very smooth. Turn off the processor and stir in the 2 tablespoons crystallized ginger by hand.

❺ Pour the mixture into the prepared custard cups (it's OK to fill them almost to the tops). Place the cups in a large pan, and fill the outside pan with enough hot water to reach halfway up the sides of the cups.

❻ Bake 1 hour, or until the pudding pulls away from the sides of the cups and a knife inserted in the center of the pudding comes out almost clean. Remove the cups from the water bath, and cool on a wire rack at least 20 minutes, but no longer than 45 minutes. Run a knife around the edge of each pudding, and invert onto individual small plates or a large platter. Serve at room temperature, or chilled slightly, with spoonfuls of whipped cream and a few pieces of chopped crystallized ginger topping the cream.

☛***Note:*** Crystallized ginger can be purchased in most specialty food shops and in many supermarkets, often in the Chinese-food section.

MENUS

An asterisk indicates a recipe not given in the text.

EASY DINNERS

MIXED GREEN SALAD WITH ARUGULA * AND BLUE CHEESE VINAIGRETTE

CAPELLINI WITH TOMATO PESTO

FRENCH BREAD *

POACHED PEARS IN GINGER SYRUP

SPICY MIXED NUTS

VEGETABLE CURRY

BASMATI RICE *

WARM PITA BREAD *

OATMEAL CAKE WITH PENUCHE FROSTING

MIXED GREEN SALAD OF BOSTON LETTUCE AND WATERCRESS * WITH DOUBLE SESAME DRESSING

ZUCCHINI, TOMATO, AND SWISS CHEESE PIE

BULGHUR MUSHROOM PILAF

FRUIT COUPE

CRUDITÉS * WITH CREAMY CURRY DIP

MUSHROOM PIE

COUSCOUS PILAF WITH PEAS

COFFEE MOUSSE

GREEN SALAD * WITH TAHINI SALAD DRESSING

PASTA AND VEGETABLE GRATIN

GARLIC BREAD *

MAPLE FRUIT CRISP

MIXED GREEN SALAD * WITH CREAMY HERB VINAIGRETTE

RAVIOLI WITH GARLIC, PEPPERS, AND TOMATOES

FRENCH BREAD *

ALMOND RICE PUDDING

MARINATED ROASTED PEPPERS ON FRENCH BREAD TOASTS

CHILAQUILES

STEAMED GREEN BEANS *

THE BEST CHOCOLATE CAKE

CRUDITÉS * WITH SPICY PEANUT DIP

SPICY STIR-FRIED TOFU, PEPPERS, AND MANDARIN ORANGES

RICE *

OLD-FASHIONED POUND CAKE

OLIVADA WITH FRENCH BREAD TOASTS

SPICY RAGOUT OF VEGETABLES AND TOFU

BROWN RICE WITH OLIVE OIL AND PARMESAN CHEESE *

BREAD PUDDING WITH BOURBON SAUCE

JALAPEÑO CHEESE NACHOS

BAKED STUFFED TOMATOES WITH COUSCOUS, PEAS, AND FETA CHEESE

STEAMED GREEN BEANS *

FRENCH BREAD *

BLUEBERRY KUCHEN

GREEN SALAD WITH ROMAINE LETTUCE, RED ONION, AND CROUTONS * AND CREAMY GARLIC DRESSING

BARLEY MUSHROOM CASSEROLE

MASHED BUTTERNUT SQUASH *

MAPLE FRUIT CRISP

GREEN BEAN SALAD WITH LEMON, DILL, AND FETA CHEESE

BAKED COUSCOUS WITH SPINACH AND PINE NUTS

FRENCH BREAD *

OLD-FASHIONED POUND CAKE

SOUP MEALS

MIXED GREEN SALAD OF ROMAINE LETTUCE, CUCUMBERS, GRATED CARROT, AND SCALLIONS * WITH MISO DRESSING

MUSHROOM SOUP WITH HERBS

IRISH BROWN BREAD

OATMEAL CAKE WITH PENUCHE FROSTING

GREEN BEAN SALAD WITH LEMON, DILL, AND FETA CHEESE

CORN CHOWDER

HERB OAT BREAD

DEEP-DISH PEAR PIE

JALAPEÑO CHEESE NACHOS

SPINACH SALAD WITH GRATED CARROT, MUSHROOMS, AND RED ONION * WITH CREAMY GARLIC DRESSING

MEXICAN VEGETABLE STEW

MAPLE FRUIT CRISP

MIXED GREEN SALAD OF ROMAINE LETTUCE, SPINACH, RED ONION, AND SESAME SEEDS * WITH TAHINI SALAD DRESSING

CURRIED BARLEY AND MUSHROOM SOUP

RICH CREAM CHEESE BISCUITS

COFFEE MOUSSE OR POACHED PEARS IN GINGER SYRUP

SUMMER MENUS

BLUE CHEESE LOG

COUSCOUS AND VEGETABLE SALAD WITH ORANGE AND GARLIC

FRENCH BREAD *

PEACH MELBA

CRUDITÉS * WITH SPICY PEANUT DIP

COLD SZECHUAN NOODLES WITH SHREDDED VEGETABLES

CRISPY GARLIC TOASTS

ALMOND RICE PUDDING

CHÈVRE TOASTS WITH ASSORTED TOPPINGS

WILD RICE SALAD WITH APPLES AND WALNUTS

RUSSIAN-STYLE MARINATED MUSHROOMS

ICE CREAM TRUFFLE PIE WITH RASPBERRY SAUCE OR STRAWBERRY AND PEACH COMPOTE

CHILLED AVOCADO SOUP

TORTELLINI SALAD PRIMAVERA

FRENCH BREAD *

TOASTED ALMOND MOCHA ICE CREAM TORTE OR RHUBARB CRUMBLE

EGGPLANT CAVIAR

MEDITERRANEAN PASTA SALAD WITH CHICK-PEAS AND ROASTED PEPPERS

FRESH STRAWBERRY TART

VEGETARIAN BARBECUES

CORN-ON-THE-COB WITH CHILI-GARLIC BUTTER

TEMPEH TERIYAKI SHISH KEBAB

GRILLED MUSHROOMS

COLD ORIENTAL NOODLES WITH PEANUT SAUCE

ORANGE POPPY SEED CAKE

GRILLED CORN-ON-THE-COB

TOFU SHISH KEBAB WITH LEMON-SOY MARINADE

GRILLED EGGPLANT WITH SPICY PEANUT SAUCE

CRISPY GARLIC TOASTS

BLUEBERRY KUCHEN

APPETIZER PARTY

FOR 15 PEOPLE

STUFFED CHERRY TOMATOES (DOUBLE RECIPE)

CHEESE CRACKERS

CRISPY GARLIC TOASTS (CROSTINI)

CRUDITÉS * WITH GREEN GODDESS DIP (DOUBLE RECIPE)

STUFFED MUSHROOMS WITH SPINACH, FETA CHEESE, AND PINE NUTS (DOUBLE RECIPE)

EGGPLANT CAVIAR

MEDITERRANEAN PASTA SALAD WITH CHICK-PEAS AND ROASTED PEPPERS

BULGHUR SALAD WITH CORN, ZUCCHINI, AND SHREDDED BASIL

ASSORTED TEA SANDWICHES

FRESH APPLE CAKE

EGGNOG DIP WITH FRESH FRUIT

A VEGETARIAN BUFFET

FOR 10 PEOPLE

CHÈVRE TOASTS WITH ASSORTED TOPPINGS

VEGETABLE ENCHILADAS (USE 10 TORTILLAS)

BAKED STUFFED TOMATOES WITH COUSCOUS, PEAS, AND FETA CHEESE (USE 5 MEDIUM TOMATOES)

WILD RICE SALAD WITH APPLES AND WALNUTS

PENNE AND BROCCOLI SALAD WITH CREAMY GARLIC DRESSING

ORANGE POPPY SEED CAKE

FRUIT SALAD *

A THANKSGIVING FEAST

MOLDED WHITE BEAN PÂTÉ

SPINACH SOUP WITH SEMOLINA CHEESE DUMPLINGS

HERB OAT BREAD

MIXED GREEN SALAD OF RED-LEAF LETTUCE, WATERCRESS, AND RED ONION * WITH DOUBLE SESAME DRESSING

WILD MUSHROOM TART IN PUFF PASTRY

COUSCOUS PILAF WITH PEAS

TOMATOES PROVENÇAL

SWEET POTATO PUDDING WITH CRYSTALLIZED GINGER OR MAPLE FRUIT CRISP

Simple Vegetarian Pleasures

JEANNE LEMLIN

I am so fortunate to have two great sisters, Jackie Lemlin and Julianne Lemlin-Dufresne

It is to them that this book is lovingly dedicated

In cooking, as in all the arts, simplicity is the sign of perfection.
— Curnonsky

The greatest dishes are very simple dishes.
— Escoffier

Acknowledgments

More than any of my previous titles, this work has depended on the kindness of many people—none of them strangers.

To help conceptualize this book, I have been fortunate to exchange ideas, visions, and dreams with a number of friends who helped me in more ways than they know. My heartfelt gratitude goes to my editor, Susan Friedland, who makes me laugh, feel appreciated, and gives me room to maneuver; Lisa Ekus, my publicist, who is generous with her warmth, wisdom, and support; Darra Goldstein, whose insight and judgment I greatly value; Susan Lescher, my agent, who helped launch this book; and Nach Waxman of Kitchen Arts and Letters, for his astute observations and help with the title. Special thanks to my friends in Great Barrington, who have given me invaluable support: Jane Walsh, who shares my passion for cooking and loves to "talk food"; Geri Rybacki, whose enthusiasm for discovery has inspired me many a time; Jean Whitehead, who encouraged me to keep focused on quick cooking; Elisabeth Rhodes, who helped me with culinary history; and Debbie Reed and the staff at the Bookloft, who supply me with precious tidbits about the book industry and loyally promote me whenever they can. To the women at BCC, who have helped me tame that computer when I swore it was a Goliath: Becky Couch and Patti White, two teachers whose patience and expertise make them two in a million; and Cathy Dargi and Phylene Farrell, who generously made me feel welcomed. A special thanks to Alan Wallach of Interlaken Computers, who kept my laptop—and peace of mind—in good shape.

My family has bestowed on me much love and support. I want to especially thank my husband, Ed Curtin, for his fine judgment in critiquing dishes and his editorial skills; my son, Daniel, for his unbridled enthusiasm for the dessert chapter; my stepdaughter, Susanne, for her growing interest in using my recipes to cook for her college friends; and my mother and two sisters, for their encouragement, humor, and love of excellent vegetarian food.

Introduction

The Pleasures of Simplicity

There is a reason why the call to simplify our lives is echoed throughout modern history, and that is because chosen simplicity is inextricably linked to *enjoyment*. This, many of us are grateful to learn, is no less true in the kitchen. What a wonderful realization when we discover that a simplified approach to cooking can actually heighten the pleasures we derive from preparing food. Complex, labor-intensive recipes are welcome when the cook has time to play leisurely in the kitchen, but for the busy person who is juggling armloads, simplified cooking is essential.

How do we learn to cook quickly so that it reflects simplicity at its highest form, that is, the delivery of intensely flavored, yet uncomplicated food, rather than fare that is dull and uninspired, though also simple? We must develop a new orientation in the kitchen so that a little advance planning will take us a long way. Everyday cooking is most successful and enjoyable when it arises out of some organization. If you don't want to rely on frozen or packaged convenience foods, and you have a busy schedule, then you'll benefit tremendously by developing some new habits to make your time in the kitchen easier and more productive. Practicing the simple art of "thinking ahead" will transform your cooking. Let's examine some key elements that I have learned are crucial to creating a new strategy for simplified, sophisticated meals.

Selecting Recipes

Before you do your grocery shopping, choose a few recipes that you'd like to prepare in the upcoming week. What are you in the mood to eat? What's in season? Is there a new food that you'd like to become familiar with? Do you anticipate company coming? Will you need some do-ahead meals or would last-minute preparations suit you better? I highly recommend that you often include soup as one of your weekly choices. It's a helpful strategy to make the soup on the weekend when you have some extra time, and then reach for it on an evening when putting some heat under a pot is about all you can manage.

Make a note of the recipes that you select and hold on to it. It will be invaluable when you put together your shopping list, and will be a reminder of what you are equipped to cook throughout the week. It's a great feeling to approach a recipe and know you have everything you need.

The Shopping List

Although it can be fun and prudent to shop by spontaneously selecting what's in season or on sale, or by what grabs your attention, the shopping list is, without a doubt, salvation for the busy cook. I always have a running list on my counter so that I can immediately jot down an ingredient that I need or must replace. Shortly before I go shopping I select a few recipes for the week (as I have described above), and add those ingredients to the list. Refer to the items in "A Well-Stocked Kitchen" (opposite), and include any staples that are missing from your pantry. Now you have a truly useful shopping list, and you'll soon see how much easier this will make your cooking.

What's for Dinner

With some recipes for the week and all the ingredients you need to prepare them, you are left with the not-so-onerous task of choosing what you want each day for dinner. Don't wait until late in the day or when you come home from work to make this decision; settle this early in the morning or even the night before. Cultivating this habit will relieve you of pressure throughout the day because you'll know dinner has been decided, and you have all you need to create it. It might seem awkward at first to be thinking of dinner while you are eating breakfast, but you'll soon see how much you'll benefit from this advance planning.

Furthermore, if you can complete one recipe-related task before you leave the house in the morning, you'll be so appreciative when you return. It's amazing how just chopping a few vegetables, washing greens, cooking some rice (which takes 2 minutes of your attention and can be cooking while you're eating breakfast), or grating some cheese can significantly lessen your load at dinnertime.

Keeping Track

Have you ever prepared a fabulous recipe a few times and then, not too long thereafter, forgotten about its very existence? It's easy to lose track of old favorites when you enjoy experimenting and discovering new dishes.

To easily remember these treasures, keep an updated list of quick recipes that you love (and note where each one can be found), and tack this list to the inside of a cabinet or onto your refrigerator, or anywhere else you can easily read it. When you are making your shopping list or are in need of an idea for a quick meal, refer to your list and you'll be pleased to remember these old friends.

A Well-Stocked Kitchen

The items on this list are basic to the well-supplied kitchen and are easy to store. Do strive to keep these ingredients on hand; they will make your meal planning much easier.

On nights when you don't have a particular recipe planned, you can reach into your pantry and create an impromptu meal. Nonperishable items and those that have a long refrigerator life are easy to keep stocked because they require no attention. So refer to this itemization when you make your shopping list and you'll find it will significantly simplify your meal planning.

Cupboards or Pantry

- vegetable oil
- olive oil
- oriental sesame oil
- vinegars (red wine, balsamic, Chinese rice wine, apple cider)
- assorted pastas
- roasted red peppers
- canned plum tomatoes
- tomato sauce
- tomato puree
- tomato paste
- canned beans (chickpeas, black beans, kidney beans, small white beans)
- salsa
- lentils (brown and red)
- oats (regular and quick)
- cornmeal
- couscous
- bulghur
- rice (converted white, brown, Arborio)
- peanut butter
- unbleached flour
- sugar (white and brown)
- honey
- baking powder
- baking soda

onions (yellow and red)
garlic

Refrigerator

powdered vegetable stock base
celery
carrots
lemons
parsley
olives
whole wheat flour
tamari soy sauce
Parmesan cheese
Cheddar cheese
feta cheese
Monterey Jack cheese
nuts (almonds, walnuts, pine nuts, and pecans)
gingerroot

Freezer

peas
corn
chopped spinach
ravioli
tortellini
pita bread
tortillas

Health Issues for the Vegetarian

I have been a vegetarian for nearly 30 years and, consequently, have followed many health issues, both the benefits and pitfalls, related to maintaining a vegetarian diet.

What I have concluded after reading numerous scientific studies, hearing many unfounded claims, using common sense, and heeding my own physiological messages is that the challenge of adopting a sound vegetarian diet has been grossly exaggerated. If we eat a wide variety of foods, that is, plenty of fresh vegetables, fruits, grains, and legumes, and go easy on fats (dairy products) and sugar, then it would be virtually impossible not to thrive on a vegetarian diet. It is also crucial to acknowledge that diet is not the only factor in achieving good health; exercise and emotional well-being are key elements as well. It's a mistake to overemphasize the role food plays in making us healthy while underplaying those salient considerations.

It is my hope that after reading about the nutritional issues outlined below, you will learn to *relax* about keeping a vegetarian kitchen, and begin to *enjoy* a diet rich in plant foods. If you always bear in mind that "variety" is the one indispensable feature of a sensible meatless regimen, you will have grasped the crux of the matter and will now be able to focus on having fun cooking with these diverse ingredients.

Protein and Calcium: The Hidden Link

The number one dietary concern that has been inextricably linked to vegetarianism over the years has been adequate protein consumption. No other question has been asked of vegetarians more than "What do you do for protein?" But is there a real danger of not getting sufficient protein, or is it a pseudo concern?

America's love affair with protein, and especially meat-based protein, is a relatively recent trend. Up until 1900, 70 percent of our protein was derived from plants and 30 percent from animals. Today those figures are reversed. We all grew up with admonitions to eat enough protein, so much so that protein and health have almost become synonymous. Not only have we been told to get enough protein but to get our protein from meat. This advice seems to have been grossly off-target. Many recent studies have shown that Americans now eat twice the amount of protein they need, and that too much protein is linked to "diseases of affluence," that is, heart disease, cancers, and diabetes. This is also true for Europeans and increasingly the Japanese.

Another very interesting correlation that has recently come to light is the link between high protein intake and the loss of calcium from the bones. Calcium is an important health concern, especially for menopausal and postmenopausal women, because of the high incidence of osteoporosis in our society. Now here's where it becomes very interesting. People in many Asian and African countries, where lactose intolerance is common, consume relatively few dairy products and eat a small percentage of meat, yet have *low* rates of osteoporosis. North American and northern European populations, known to have dairy and protein-rich diets, have the greatest number of hip fractures in the world (the way we measure osteoporosis). Protein and calcium intake are high, yet as a society we have weak bones. What is going on here?

Numerous studies have suggested that excessive protein consumption may create a potentially dangerous level of urea in the blood. Minerals, including calcium, are then leached out into our urine in order for the body to rid itself of this imbalance. Osteoporosis thus appears to be a disease of excess, not deficiency. The central issue now becomes one of preventing calcium loss rather than increasing calcium intake. Avoiding a high-protein, meat-centered diet and substituting a vegetable-filled, high-fiber regimen along with vigorous daily exercise seems to be the wisest approach.

Note: For further reading on the protein/calcium connection, I'd like to refer you to two books that I have found extremely illuminating: May All Be Fed *by John Robbins (William Morrow, 1992) and* The Vegetarian Way *by Virginia Messina, M.P.H., R.D., and Mark Messina, Ph.D. (Crown Trade Paperbacks, 1996).*

Watch Those Fats

The other dietary issue that is in the foreground of vegetarianism is fat intake. Many vegetarians used to think that eliminating meat allowed us to eat liberal amounts of cheese, cream, nuts, and other high-fat foods without worry. Now we know that those fats can be just as threatening to our health, and we must watch our consumption of fat from non-meat sources as well.

I have always resisted a nutritional breakdown of recipes because I think it is counterproductive. We should be informed about which foods are high in fats and which are not, and then learn to balance our eating habits by choosing lower-fat foods the majority of time. We know when we've had rich food, and the sensible reaction is to take it easy on fats for a while. By learning to balance our eating habits this way, we never feel deprived or at war with food. Once we start calculating everything and turn our kitchens into veritable laboratories, then certain foods become forbidden and the battle begins. It's a fight few people win, I'm afraid. Success with weight control and health are much more likely when we eat good food consistently, enjoy what we eat, and adopt these habits as part of our daily life.

This relaxed approach to maintaining a healthful vegetarian diet might seem surprisingly general to those looking for detailed guidance; however, it is meant to demystify the kitchen once meat is removed from our meals so that we can approach vegetarianism with less fear.

It is important to learn about nutrition in a broad sense, e.g., good plant sources of protein, calcium, and iron, and to be aware of which foods are rich in key nutrients, but beyond that our time in the kitchen is best spent learning to cook with a diverse array of vegetables, grains, beans, and fruits, and to have fun doing so. Again, the more variety we embrace, the better off we will be.

Protein-Rich Foods

- beans and legumes
- dairy products (preferably low-fat)
- grains (especially wheat, oats, and buckwheat)
- tofu
- tempeh
- nuts
- seeds (sunflower and sesame)
- eggs

Calcium-Rich Foods

- dairy products (preferably low-fat)
- fortified soy milk
- sesame seeds and tahini
- tofu
- dark green vegetables: broccoli, kale, collards, turnip greens

Iron-Rich Foods

- seeds (sunflower and sesame)
- beans and legumes
- dried fruits
- tofu
- eggs
- raw oats
- molasses
- bran

The Basics

About Vegetable Stocks

There is probably nothing more important in the vegetarian's cache of staple ingredients than good vegetable stock, but acquiring it can be very frustrating for the busy cook. Vegetable stock is the foundation of soups, sauces, and many grain dishes such as risottos, polentas, and pilafs, and its savoriness, or lack thereof, can make or break a recipe.

I have provided a few favorite vegetable stock recipes below for the cook who has time to make these wonderful broths, but I think it would be presumptuous and unfair to expect the average person who works outside the home to have homemade stock on hand all the time. I have found a great-flavored, powdered vegetable stock base that I use when I don't have a homemade batch available (more often than not, I'll admit), and it passes my test, which is: If it's delicious enough to drink on its own, then it will be good enough for your recipe. The brand I use is Morga Vegetable Broth Mix. It's made in Switzerland, it's additive-free, and it has a wonderful flavor. There are also canned and frozen vegetable stocks available, but keep an eye on their ingredients—you don't want them to be filled with artificial flavors or preservatives.

Vegetable Stock

Here is an all-purpose vegetable stock with a light, pleasant flavor. These vegetables work well together, but others such as leeks, cauliflower, cabbage, red bell pepper, and zucchini could be included with good results. Stronger-flavored vegetables like turnips, broccoli stalks, fennel, and Swiss chard can enhance your stock, but bear in mind you should use these with a light hand so they don't dominate the final result.

Makes 7 cups

1 tablespoon olive oil
6 garlic cloves, roughly chopped
3 onions, roughly chopped
6 mushrooms, roughly chopped
3 celery ribs, roughly chopped
3 unpeeled carrots, roughly chopped
1 potato, scrubbed and diced
2 cups roughly chopped parsley (stems included)
2 bay leaves
2 tablespoons tamari soy sauce
10 cups water
Freshly ground pepper

1. Heat the oil in a large stockpot over medium heat. Add the garlic, onions, and mushrooms and sauté 10 minutes, stirring often.
2. Add all the remaining ingredients and bring the stock to a boil. Reduce the heat to a simmer and cook 1 hour, stirring occasionally. Strain the stock through a large strainer or colander set over a large bowl, and with the back of a spoon, press out as much liquid as possible from the vegetables. Discard the vegetables. Let the stock cool to room temperature, then store in the refrigerator for up to 1 week, or the freezer for up to 3 months.

Tomato-Scallion Stock

This light broth is excellent with soups that contain tomato and with risottos that are laced with spring vegetables. The tomato flavor is subtle, so it won't overpower other flavors.

Makes 7 cups

1 tablespoon olive oil
4 garlic cloves, chopped
10 scallions, chopped
2 1/4 cups (6 ounces) chopped mushrooms
2 carrots, unpeeled and chopped
2 celery ribs, chopped
1 (16-ounce) can tomatoes, chopped with their juice
10 cups water
1/2 teaspoon salt
Liberal seasoning freshly ground pepper
1 sprig fresh thyme, or 1/2 teaspoon dried
1 bay leaf
1/2 cup chopped fresh parsley (stems included)
1 sprig fresh marjoram, or 1/4 teaspoon dried

1. Heat the oil in a large stockpot over medium-high heat. Add the garlic and scallions and cook 1 minute. Stir in the mushrooms, carrots, and celery and sauté 5 minutes, stirring often.
2. Add all the remaining ingredients and bring to a boil. Reduce to a simmer and cook 45 minutes. In batches strain the stock through a sieve, or place a colander over a large bowl and strain. With a large spoon press out all the liquid from the vegetables. Discard the vegetables. Cool completely. Refrigerate until needed for up to 1 week. If after a week you still have some stock, bring it to a boil and simmer 10 minutes. You will now be able to keep it 1 more week. Alternatively, this stock can be frozen up to 3 months.

Mushroom Stock

This stock is richly infused with the essence of mushrooms and is wonderful with risottos, pilafs, and mushroom-based soups.

Makes 8 cups

1 tablespoon olive oil
4 garlic cloves, chopped
2 onions, quartered
4 ½ cups (¾ pound) chopped mushrooms
2 carrots, unpeeled and chopped
2 celery ribs, chopped
1 tomato, cored and chopped
11 cups water
1 bay leaf
1 sprig fresh thyme, or ½ teaspoon dried
½ cup chopped fresh parsley (stems included)
½ teaspoon salt
Liberal seasoning freshly ground black pepper

1. Heat the oil in a large stockpot over medium-high heat. Add the garlic, onions, mushrooms, carrots, and celery and cook, stirring often, until the vegetables begin to brown, about 10 minutes.
2. Stir in all the remaining ingredients and bring to a boil. Reduce to a simmer and cook gently for 45 minutes.
3. In batches strain through a sieve, or place a colander over a large bowl and strain the stock. Use a large spoon and press out all the liquid from the vegetables. Discard the vegetables. Cool the stock completely. Refrigerate the stock until needed for up to 1 week. If you have any stock remaining after a week, bring it to a boil, then simmer it for 10 minutes. Now you can keep the stock 1 more week. Alternatively, freeze the stock up to 3 months.

Crostini

(Crisp Toasts)

Sometimes a basic, plain crostini is just the right vehicle for an assertive topping that might otherwise pale when spread on crackers. I prefer to use cheap, light, supermarket French bread or grinder rolls for crostini because chewy, good-quality baguettes oftentimes make hard crostini that threaten to break your teeth. Do a comparison and you'll readily see how the airiness of commercial French bread becomes an asset when toasts are created from bread you might otherwise avoid.

Makes about 20 toasts

½ narrow loaf French bread (about ¼ pound), or 2 grinder rolls
¼ cup olive oil

1. Preheat the oven to 350 degrees. With a serrated knife slice the bread into ¼-inch-thick slices. Using a pastry brush very lightly brush each side of the bread with some olive oil. Place the bread on a baking sheet in one layer.
2. Bake 5 minutes, turn each slice over, bake about 5–7 more minutes, or until lightly golden all over. Cool completely before storing in a plastic bag or tin. If stored in a refrigerator, they will keep at least 1 week.

Cooking Beans

Although I'm in favor of using canned beans when I'm pressed for time (I buy a brand made by a manufacturer that doesn't overcook its beans, and I rinse them thoroughly in a strainer before using them), cooking dry beans from scratch is, undoubtedly, the most economical and savory way to add beans to your meal planning.

It's not that cooking beans demands any skill of the cook (nothing could be easier), it's that you must think ahead if you want cooked beans to be available when you need them for a recipe. That's the hard part for most busy cooks.

If you've jumped that hurdle and are ready to cook a pot of beans, you won't regret having a batch in the refrigerator to use throughout the week. They can be marinated in a vinaigrette and used as a salad, or used in dips, in soups, with pasta, or in gratins. (See the Index under "Beans.")

Here's how you do it: Rinse the dry beans in a strainer and finger through them to locate any stones or other foreign particles. Now you can either put them in a pot and cover them with water (about 3 inches above the bean line), then let them soak overnight at room temperature, or you can use the quick-soak method: Bring the mixture to a boil and cook it 2 minutes, then let it soak (covered) for 1 hour. Both procedures will bring you to the same point—presoaked beans. Now you'll be ready to cook them.

Drain off all the soaking liquid and cover the beans with fresh, cold water to 3 inches or so above the beans. (Discarding the soaking liquid will help you digest the beans more easily.) If you like, you can flavor the cooking water with a bay leaf and a whole small onion. Bring the pot to a boil, then reduce the heat to a simmer. Cook, uncovered, until the beans are tender—this can take from about 60 minutes for small black beans or white navy beans, to 1 ½ hours for chickpeas. (Skim off any foam that rises during cooking.) I always taste the beans at various points to check on their tenderness. You don't want them at all mushy; however, they should be cooked throughout, that is, not "crunchy." When the beans are done, drain them of any remaining liquid, then let them come to room temperature. Store them in a covered bowl in the refrigerator.

Washing and Storing Greens

Assorted greens have become such a bedrock of the vegetarian and semi-vegetarian diet—whether raw in salads or cooked in soups, casseroles, or sautés—that it is imperative that we know how to properly clean and handle them.

There is really only one way to thoroughly rid these leafy gems of hidden dirt and sand, and that is by dunking them in copious amounts of cold water. Greens cannot be properly cleaned in a colander or the basket of a salad spinner; particles of grit remain lodged when rinsed this way.

Here's how to do it the right way: Fill a large pot or the base of a salad spinner with plenty of cold water. Remove the stems or cut off the core of your vegetable (depending on whether it's individual leaves or a head of something like lettuce or radicchio). Drop the leaves in the cold water and move them around with your hands. The dirt will fall to the bottom. Now here's the decisive moment: Do *not* pour the water out while the greens are in the container, or else you'll get them dirty again. Remove the greens with your hands *before* the water is dumped out, and place them in a colander or the basket part of your salad spinner. Get rid of the dirty water. Repeat this procedure a few more times, or until the soaking water is no longer dirty. You can now shake the washed greens dry in a colander, or preferably spin them in a salad spinner. If these greens are intended for a salad, then you'll have to spin them to get them sufficiently dry.

Washed greens do not store well and therefore you should clean them on the day you plan to use them. However, if you must do this step the day before you plan to work with them, the best way to store them is to roll them up in a linen kitchen towel and place the towel in the refrigerator. If you don't have a suitable towel on hand, you can place some paper towel in the bottom of a plastic bag, then put in half of the greens, then another layer of paper towel, then the remaining greens, finally ending with some paper towel. This method will also absorb any excess water clinging to the leaves, which could promote rapid decay.

Some vegetables are a lot dirtier than others. Boston lettuce, spinach, basil, leaf lettuces, and escarole harbor nuggets of dirt; whereas kale, mustard greens, and Swiss chard are relatively easy to clean. Get to know the peculiarities of different greens and handle them accordingly. There's nothing like biting into some particles of sand to ruin your meal. Once you develop a good technique for cleaning them, you'll find you can prepare leafy vegetables quite quickly and efficiently.

Roasting Peppers

Rather than roasting peppers whole, I have found that it is much easier if you cut peppers in half vertically, remove the seeds and fibrous membranes, then lay them skin side up on a baking sheet. Place an oven rack as close to the broiling element as possible, then broil the peppers until charred all over. Put the peppers in a bowl and cover the bowl with a plate or plastic wrap to trap the steam, or place the peppers in a paper or plastic bag and close tightly. Let the peppers sit 10 minutes. It is easiest to remove the skins from the peppers by peeling them in the sink under gently running water. Don't worry; this will not wash away their flavor. Pat the peppers dry with some paper towel before you proceed with your recipe.

Making Fresh Bread Crumbs

There are, undoubtedly, some instances when using commercial bread crumbs is acceptable. It is a convenience that I allow myself when the results will not be affected by the consistency of these dry, fine crumbs. However, there are also times when the success of a recipe hinges upon freshly made, coarse bread crumbs (as in Spaghettini with Garlic, Hot Peppers, and Toasted Bread Crumbs, page 239), and no substitution will do.

Tear slices of bread and process them in a food processor until they become coarse crumbs. The longer you process them the finer they become, so keep an eye on them. Certain dishes, such as the pasta dish mentioned above, require *coarse* crumbs because of their preferred texture, so you don't want to process them too long. Some recipes call for toasted fresh bread crumbs. The only difference here is that you toast the bread before you process it.

In my freezer I always keep a bag of white bread slices that are odds and ends from different loaves, and make bread crumbs as I need them; however, you can make the crumbs in advance and freeze those so that they'll be ready when you want them.

Although I generally prefer to make bread crumbs in a food processor, you can get satisfactory results with a blender. Again, just keep an eye on them.

Breakfast Is Ready

You don't need to spend hours creating a tempting breakfast table. One homemade item, such as muffins or scones, can be extended by the addition of fresh berries in season, or a simple fruit salad, and a steaming pot of perfectly brewed coffee or tea. If you choose to make French toast or pancakes, something as simple as grapefruit or a perfectly ripe melon is a fitting addition and barely increases your time in the kitchen. Perhaps you would prefer to focus on creating a glorious fruit salad; in that case, supplement it with some freshly made, store-bought bagels and you will have a well-rounded, delicious breakfast that will be relaxing for all.

See also: Frittatas and Omelets, pages 413-431

Crispy French Toast

I am indebted to my mother for a trick she learned years ago for making French toast with a crispy exterior: Coat it in flour. This produces a crust-like surface when the slices cook, and simultaneously preserves a moist interior. Children love this French toast because its texture is less eggy than the traditional variety.

Serves 4

4 large eggs
1 teaspoon cinnamon
2 cups milk
1 tablespoon vanilla extract
1 tablespoon rum, or 1½ tablespoons sugar
Oil for frying
8 slices good-quality white loaf bread, or 12 slices French bread, cut 1 inch thick on the diagonal
½ cup unbleached flour (approximately)

1. In a large bowl whisk the eggs and cinnamon together. Whisk in the milk, vanilla, and rum. Pour this mixture into an 8 × 8-inch pan or similar medium-size shallow dish. Place a baking sheet in the oven, then preheat the oven to 250 degrees.
2. Pour a thin layer of oil into a large skillet and heat it over medium heat until hot but not smoking.
3. Place another baking sheet on the counter next to you. One by one dip the bread slices in the egg mixture and let them soak 30 seconds or so, or just until moistened. Flip over and soak again. Carefully remove the bread, letting any excess liquid drip off. Place the soaked bread in two rows on the baking sheet. Place the flour in a sieve. Shaking the sieve, sprinkle flour evenly over the bread slices. With a spatula, flip the bread over, then coat this side with flour.

4. Cook 2 slices at a time in the skillet until golden brown and crispy, about 5 minutes, then flip over and cook on the second side until golden. Keep the cooked slices hot in the oven on the baking sheet until you are ready to serve them. Continue with the remaining bread, being certain to oil the skillet in between batches. Serve with warm maple syrup.

Overnight Breakfast Casserole

No one would describe this quiche-style breakfast dish as low-fat; however, everyone will want to come back for seconds.

My sister Julianne introduced me to the idea of this delectable casserole, and I now make it two different ways. Both versions are great. The first interpretation has a bacon flavor from the inclusion of smoked tempeh strips that can be purchased in natural foods stores. These look like bacon and are cooked in a similar way. The final result of this version is reminiscent of bacon and eggs (or quiche Lorraine, I suppose). The second way I like to prepare this dish is with sautéed mushrooms, which also gives flavorful results. You choose; I'm sure you'll love both versions.

For an accompaniment, Roasted Home Fries (page 159) or Sweet Potato and Red Pepper Home Fries (page 160) are ideal. To cook them, just place the baking sheet on a lower rack in the oven (set at 350 degrees) while you bake this casserole and everything will be ready about the same time.

Serves 6

---

2 teaspoons canola oil

3 slices smoked tempeh strips (tempeh "bacon"), *or* 12 ounces (4 ½ cups) thinly sliced mushrooms

1 ½ tablespoons unsalted butter, softened

6 slices good-quality white bread

1 ½ cups grated Swiss or mild Cheddar cheese

5 large eggs

Dash nutmeg

½ teaspoon salt

1 ½ cups low-fat milk

½ cup heavy cream

---

1. Heat the oil in a large, preferably non-stick, skillet over medium heat. If you are using the tempeh bacon, fry it in the oil until it is golden brown on both sides. Place the strips on a plate and let cool. Cut it into ½-inch pieces. If you are using mushrooms, sauté them until their juices are rendered and then evaporated, and the mushrooms begin to brown.
2. Lightly butter a 12 × 7 × 2-inch (Pyrex) baking dish. With the 1½ tablespoons of butter, very lightly butter one side of each bread slice, then cut the bread into 1-inch cubes. Spread the cubes on the bottom of the baking dish.
3. Sprinkle the "bacon" or mushrooms on the bread cubes. Top with the grated cheese.
4. By hand or in a food processor, beat the eggs with the nutmeg and salt. Beat in the milk and cream. Pour this custard all over the bread mixture. Cover the dish and chill overnight.
5. Let the casserole stand at room temperature for 30 minutes before baking. Meanwhile, preheat the oven to 350 degrees. Bake the casserole uncovered 30–35 minutes, or until golden on top and a knife inserted in the center comes out dry. Let sit 10 minutes before cutting. As with quiche, I prefer to eat this warm, rather than piping hot.

Mixed Grain Pancakes

These scrumptious pancakes are great for breakfast or a quick, nutritious supper. The whole wheat flour and oats give them an extra boost yet still keep these pancakes light.

Serves 4

1 3/4 cups unbleached flour
1/2 cup whole wheat flour
1/4 cup quick oats or wheat germ
2 1/2 teaspoons baking powder
1/4 cup sugar
1 teaspoon salt
2 large eggs, beaten
2 1/2 cups low-fat milk
4 tablespoons melted butter, cooled slightly
Oil for pan

1. In a large bowl thoroughly combine the first six (the dry) ingredients.
2. In a medium-size bowl beat the eggs, then beat in the milk and butter.
3. Pour the wet ingredients into the flour mixture and stir just until evenly moistened, about 10 strokes. It's okay if there are some lumps; in fact, there should be some if you haven't overbeaten it. Let the batter rest 10 minutes.
4. Lightly oil a skillet, and heat it over medium heat until a drop of water splatters when flicked onto the pan. Pour on 2 tablespoons of batter and wait until the surface of the pancake is filled with bubbles. (Regulate the heat so the pancakes are golden underneath and covered with bubbles at the same time.) Flip and cook until golden. Serve with warm maple syrup.

Buttermilk Pancakes

Buttermilk is a tenderizer in baked goods, and in these pancakes it serves to make them light and moist. You can add blueberries to make America's favorite pancakes; just be sure to cook them throughout because they hold a tad more moisture than traditional pancakes.

Serves 3

2 large eggs
1 ½ cups buttermilk*
3 tablespoons butter, melted
1 ½ cups unbleached flour
1 ½ tablespoons sugar
1 ½ teaspoons baking powder
½ teaspoon baking soda
½ teaspoon salt
Oil for pan

1. In a large bowl thoroughly whisk the eggs. Add the buttermilk and butter and whisk until well blended.
2. Sprinkle in the flour, sugar, baking powder, baking soda, and salt and whisk just until the dry ingredients are evenly moistened. The batter will look somewhat like a yeast batter rather than standard pancake batter.
3. Pour a thin film of oil on a griddle or large skillet and heat over medium heat until a fleck of water dropped on it sizzles. Make 3-inch pancakes using a few tablespoons of batter per pancake. These won't bubble up as easily as traditional pancakes, but should have some bubbles and golden edges when they are ready to be flipped. Cook until golden brown on each side. Regulate the heat so the pancakes have time to cook throughout. Serve with warm maple syrup.

**Use leftover buttermilk to make some scones (pages 32–37 in this chapter).*

Summer Fruit Salad with Yogurt and Granola

This breakfast salad is the quintessential sixties dish, and has stayed around for good reason. Served with a muffin alongside it, it is one of my favorite breakfasts both at home and when traveling. The pleasing contrasts in textures and flavors and the abundance of juicy, fresh fruit make this healthful salad the ideal food with which to start the day.

Below is one of my favorite combinations of summer fruits, but peaches, blueberries, kiwis, plums, raspberries, blackberries, and honeydew melon are all wonderful additions. Just steer clear of apples and grapefruit; they clash with these delicate fruits.

Serves 4

1 small cantaloupe, diced (3 cups diced)
1 pint strawberries, each one halved
2 cups diced seeded watermelon
1 banana, thinly sliced

Yogurt Sauce
3/4 cup plain low-fat yogurt
1 1/2 tablespoons honey
Dash cinnamon

4 tablespoons granola, homemade (opposite page) or store-bought

1. Combine the fruit in a large bowl. (If you are assembling this in advance, wait until the last minute to add the banana.)
2. To make the yogurt sauce combine the yogurt, honey, and cinnamon in a small bowl. Cover and chill until ready to use, up to 24 hours ahead.
3. Just before serving divide the fruit among 4 serving bowls. Drizzle some yogurt sauce all over the top in a haphazard design. Sprinkle 1 tablespoon of granola on each serving.

Dried Cranberry and Almond Granola

Many granolas are so sweet they seem more like dessert than breakfast food. This cereal has just the right degree of sweetness, and is equally good mixed with milk or plain yogurt.

Packaged in an attractive container, Dried Cranberry and Almond Granola would be a good choice for a holiday gift.

Makes about 12 cups

½ cup canola oil
½ cup honey
6 cups oats (regular cut)
1 cup unsweetened coconut (see Note)
1 ½ cups finely chopped almonds
⅔ cup bran or wheat germ
½ cup sunflower seeds
1 tablespoon cinnamon
½ teaspoon salt
1 ¼ cups dried cranberries

1. Preheat the oven to 350 degrees.
2. In a large stockpot combine the oil and honey and heat over medium heat just until blended. Do not let it boil. Remove the pot from the heat and stir in all the remaining ingredients *except* the dried cranberries.
3. Spread one third of the granola on a large baking sheet. Bake 10 minutes. Remove from the oven and, with a spatula, toss the granola, paying special attention to the sides of the pan, which brown more quickly. Return to the oven and cook 5–10 more minutes, tossing a few more times. Do not let the granola burn; it should be a light golden brown

when done. It will get crisp when it cools. Pour the granola into a large bowl and let cool. Repeat with the remaining two batches of granola.

4. When the granola is completely cool, mix in the dried cranberries. Store in a covered container up to 3 months in the refrigerator. (You can keep a portion at room temperature during the cool-weather months, but in the summer it should be refrigerated.)

Note: Unsweetened coconut can be purchased in natural foods stores.

Muesli

Muesli is a Swiss cereal made of raw oats, dried fruit, and nuts. Admittedly, muesli isn't for everybody. Some people dislike the texture once it is mixed with milk, but I love it. I do, however, prefer to let it soak for 10–20 minutes, rather than the customary overnight soaking. It's a breeze to assemble; the only cooking involved is the toasting of the nuts. You can keep muesli at room temperature if it is in a tightly sealed container, but during the hot-weather season, you should refrigerate it.

Makes 9–10 cups

1 ½ cups finely chopped almonds or hazelnuts
3 cups regular oats
3 cups quick oats
1 cup bran
¾ cup minced dates, *or* 1 cup raisins
½ cup (1 ounce) minced dried apple (snipped with scissors)

1. Preheat the oven to 300 degrees. Spread the chopped nuts on a baking sheet and toast in the oven until lightly golden, about 5 minutes. Keep an eye on them so they don't burn. Let the nuts cool completely.
2. In a large container with a tight-fitting lid mix the nuts with all the remaining ingredients. Serve the muesli in bowls with milk and honey or brown sugar, and let sit 10–20 minutes before eating it so the mixture can soften and thicken.

Lemon–Poppy Seed Scones

Light and pillowy, these delicate scones were inspired by my reading of Phyllis Richman's *The Butter Did It*, a charming murder mystery set in the world of four-star chefs and restaurants. At one point the exhausted main character is soothed by a gift of her favorite lemon–poppy seed scones, and that sent me right into my kitchen to develop a recipe for them. The butter does it here, too.

Makes 8 scones

2 cups unbleached flour
1/3 cup sugar
1 tablespoon baking powder
1/2 teaspoon salt
1 tablespoon poppy seeds
5 tablespoons chilled unsalted butter
1 large egg
Grated zest of 1 lemon
2 tablespoons lemon juice
2/3 cup buttermilk or plain yogurt thinned with a little milk
Milk for brushing

1. Raise an oven rack to the top position in the oven. Preheat the oven to 400 degrees. Lightly butter a baking sheet and set it aside. (If you stack 2 baking sheets together you will get lighter bottoms on your scones. Invert the bottom baking sheet so that it is bottom side up, then place the baking sheet with the scones on top.)
2. In a large bowl thoroughly combine the flour, sugar, baking powder, salt, and poppy seeds.
3. Cut the 5 tablespoons butter into bits and drop them into the flour mixture. Toss to coat them, then, with the tips of your fingers or a pastry cutter, rub the butter into the flour mixture to form coarse crumbs.

4. In a medium-size bowl beat the egg. Beat in the lemon zest, lemon juice, and buttermilk. Pour this into the flour mixture and stir with a fork until the dough is evenly moistened.

5. Lightly flour your work surface. Drop the dough onto it and knead it 3 or 4 times. If it is too sticky, add a bit more flour to your work surface. Pat the dough into a disk 3/4 inch thick (no thicker), then cut it into 8 wedges (or you can cut it with a round or scalloped biscuit cutter into smaller shapes). Brush them lightly with milk to create a sheen during baking. Place the wedges on the prepared baking sheet.

6. Bake 15–17 minutes, or until golden brown. Serve warm or at room temperature, but not hot.

Oatmeal Scones

These scones are at once grainy, nubby, and tender—a wonderful combination of textures producing superior scones. Coupled with blackberry jam, they're a knockout.

Makes 8 scones

3/4 cup unbleached flour
1/4 cup whole wheat flour
1 cup quick oats, plus extra for sprinkling
2 tablespoons firmly packed light brown sugar
1 1/2 teaspoons baking powder
1/2 teaspoon baking soda
1/4 teaspoon salt
4 tablespoons unsalted butter, chilled
1 large egg
2/3 cup buttermilk or plain yogurt thinned with a little milk
Milk for brushing

1. Raise an oven rack to its highest position. Preheat the oven to 400 degrees. Lightly butter a baking sheet. (If you stack 2 baking sheets together, you will be less likely to get dark bottoms on your scones. Invert the bottom baking sheet so that it is bottom side up, then place the baking sheet that contains the scones on top.)
2. In a large bowl thoroughly combine the unbleached flour, whole wheat flour, oats, brown sugar, baking powder, baking soda, and salt.
3. Cut the 4 tablespoons butter into bits and drop them into the flour mixture. Toss to coat the bits, then, using your fingers, rub the butter into the flour mixture until coarse crumbs form, like little pellets.
4. Beat the egg in a small bowl. Beat in the buttermilk or thinned yogurt. Pour this into the flour mixture, then stir until evenly moistened.
5. Lightly flour your work surface. Dump the dough onto it and knead 3 or 4 times.

Gather the dough into a ball, then pat it into a disk 3/4 inch thick. Cut the disk into 8 wedges. To make an attractive topping, lightly brush the top of each wedge with some milk and sprinkle on some oats, patting the oats down with your fingers to help them adhere.

6. Place the scones on the prepared baking sheet. Bake 15 minutes, or until golden brown. Serve warm or at room temperature.

Dried Cranberry–Orange Scones

The tangy, chewy character of dried cranberries is delightful in these colorful scones. Dried cranberries, also called craisins, can be purchased in most natural foods stores and specialty food shops.

Makes 8 scones

2 cups unbleached flour
1/3 cup sugar
1 tablespoon baking powder
1/2 teaspoon salt
5 tablespoons unsalted butter, chilled
1/2 cup dried cranberries
1 large egg
Grated zest of 1 orange, or 1/2 teaspoon orange extract
2/3 cup buttermilk or plain yogurt thinned with a little milk
Milk for brushing

1. Raise an oven rack to its highest position. Preheat the oven to 400 degrees. Lightly butter a baking sheet and set it aside. (If you stack 2 baking sheets together, you will be less likely to get dark bottoms on your scones. Invert the bottom baking sheet so that it is bottom side up, then place the baking sheet that contains the scones on top.)
2. In a large bowl combine the flour, sugar, baking powder, and salt and mix well.
3. Cut the 5 tablespoons butter into small bits and drop it into the flour mixture, tossing thoroughly to coat the bits. With your fingers or a pastry cutter, rub the butter into the flour mixture until coarse crumbs are formed.
4. In a medium-size bowl beat the egg, then beat in the orange zest and buttermilk. Pour this into the flour mixture and stir with a large spoon just until the dough is evenly moistened.
5. Lightly flour a work surface. Drop the dough onto the flour and knead it 2 or 3 times,

or just until it is smooth. Keeping the surface lightly floured to prevent sticking, pat the dough into a 3/4-inch-thick disk, making sure it doesn't stick to the counter. Cut the disk into 8 wedges, and place them on the prepared baking sheet. Brush the scones lightly with milk.

6. Bake 15–17 minutes, or until golden brown. Serve warm or at room temperature, but not piping hot.

Preventing Burned Bottoms

Do you sometimes have a problem with keeping the bottoms of biscuits and scones from becoming too dark? If you don't have heavy-duty, high-quality baking sheets, this can be a challenge, especially with baked goods containing sugar, which will cause them to brown quicker. Even parchment paper won't prevent some scones from getting too dark.

Here are a few tricks that I have found solve the problem: When you are baking small items like biscuits and scones, raise your oven rack to its highest position; keeping the baking sheet farther from the heating element deters burning. The second thing you should do is to stack 2 baking sheets together to further insulate your baked goods. If your baking sheets are the same size, you can invert the bottom one to create a sort of platform for the top sheet. If the pan you have your biscuits or scones on is larger than your extra baking sheet, you can place the smaller one down first—right side up—and then rest the larger one on top. This will trap hot air and also shield the top baking sheet from the heating element in your oven. However you choose to do it, the idea is to add another layer of insulation that will prevent the bottom of your baking sheet from becoming too hot.

Flaky Wheat Biscuits

I used to make these biscuits only on special holidays such as Thanksgiving, but now my son requests them for breakfast, and so they have become a household staple.

You can turn these into herbed biscuits by adding a few tablespoons of minced fresh herbs to the flour mixture before you mix in the milk. The key to delicate biscuits is in a minimal handling of the dough.

Makes about 12 biscuits

1 ½ cups unbleached flour
½ cup whole wheat flour
4 teaspoons baking powder
½ teaspoon salt
5 tablespoons chilled unsalted butter
1 cup whole milk

1. Line a baking sheet with parchment paper or lightly butter the baking sheet.
2. In a large bowl thoroughly combine the two flours, baking powder, and salt. Cut the 5 tablespoons butter into bits, then toss it with the flour to coat the pieces. Using your fingers or a pastry cutter, rub the butter into the flour until coarse crumbs form. Pour in the milk and mix it into the flour just until a ball of dough can be formed. Don't overbeat.
3. Lightly flour your work surface. Drop the dough onto the surface and knead it 2 or 3 times. Pat it into a ½-inch-thick disk.
4. Using a 2-inch biscuit cutter, cut out about 12 biscuits and place them on the prepared baking sheet. Place the baking sheet in the freezer for 15 minutes, or in the refrigerator for at least 30 minutes or up to 4 hours. (Placing cold biscuits in a hot oven ensures flakiness.)
5. Meanwhile raise an oven rack to the highest position possible. Preheat the oven to 425 degrees. (If you stack 2 baking sheets together, you will less likely get dark bottoms on your biscuits—see page 37.)
6. Cook the biscuits on the top rack for 10–12 minutes, or until golden brown.

Blueberry Oat Muffins

I am not enamored of cakey blueberry muffins, but I do like them light and moist. The oats in these muffins enhance their texture and flavor so that they contain just the right balance of heft and delicacy. A sprinkling of oats and sugar on top of each muffin adds to its charm.

Makes 12 muffins

1 1/2 cups unbleached flour
1/2 cup quick oats, plus extra for sprinkling
1/2 cup sugar, plus extra for sprinkling
1 tablespoon baking powder
3/4 teaspoon salt
1 1/2 cups fresh or frozen blueberries (if frozen, unthawed, and preferably tiny wild blueberries)
1 egg
1/2 teaspoon vanilla extract
1/4 cup canola oil
1 cup low-fat milk

1. Preheat the oven to 400 degrees. Butter the insides and top of a regular-size (1/3-cup) muffin pan.
2. In a large bowl combine the flour, oats, sugar, baking powder, and salt. Add the blueberries and toss to evenly coat them.
3. In a medium-size bowl beat the egg. Beat in the vanilla, oil, and milk. Immediately pour this into the flour mixture and stir just until blended, only a few strokes.
4. Fill each prepared muffin cup with the batter. Sprinkle some oats on top of each muffin, then sprinkle on some sugar. Bake 20 minutes, or until the muffins are golden and a knife inserted in the center of a muffin comes out clean. Pop them out of the pan and cool on a wire rack. Serve warm or at room temperature.

Multi-Grain Muffins

When you want a nutrient-packed muffin that's also moist and flavorful, choose these muffins for breakfast or a snack.

Makes 12 muffins

1 1/4 cups unbleached flour
1/4 cup whole wheat flour
1/2 cup quick oats
2 tablespoons toasted wheat germ or bran
2 tablespoons cornmeal
1 tablespoon baking powder
1 teaspoon cinnamon
1/2 teaspoon salt
1/2 cup raisins or chopped dates
1/4 cup finely chopped walnuts
1 small carrot, peeled and grated
1 medium apple, peeled and grated
1 egg
1/2 cup canola oil
1/2 cup honey
1 cup low-fat milk

1. Preheat the oven to 400 degrees. Butter the tops and insides of a regular-size (1/3-cup) muffin pan.
2. In a large bowl combine all the ingredients up to and including the grated apple.
3. In another large bowl whisk the egg, oil, honey, and milk until the mixture is smooth. Mix in the dry ingredients and stir just until blended. Do not overbeat the batter. Let it sit undisturbed for 1 minute so the grains can absorb the liquid. Fill the prepared muffin cups with the batter. Bake 17–18 minutes, or until a knife inserted in the center of a muffin comes out clean. Serve warm or at room temperature, but not hot.

Banana Wheat Germ Muffins

These tender muffins are the perfect solution for overripe bananas that are too soft to eat. The riper they are, the more they'll enhance this batter.

Makes 12 muffins

1 ½ cups unbleached flour
1 cup toasted wheat germ
½ cup finely chopped walnuts
½ cup firmly packed light brown sugar
2 ½ teaspoons baking powder
¼ teaspoon ground nutmeg
½ teaspoon salt
2 large eggs
1 cup mashed ripe banana (2–3 bananas)
½ cup low-fat milk
¼ cup canola oil

1. Preheat the oven to 400 degrees. Butter the top and insides of a regular-size (1/3-cup) muffin pan.
2. In a medium-size bowl thoroughly combine the flour, wheat germ, walnuts, sugar, baking powder, nutmeg, and salt.
3. Beat the eggs in a large bowl. Beat in the mashed banana, being certain to break up any large lumps. Beat in the milk and oil until smooth. Add the dry mixture to this bowl and stir just until it is evenly moistened. Do not overbeat it.
4. Spoon the batter into the prepared muffin pan. Bake about 17 minutes, or until a knife inserted in the center of a muffin comes out dry. Cool the muffins on a rack a few minutes before serving. They are better warm, not hot.

Blueberry Almond Bread

The "almond" in this bread comes from almond extract, not chopped nuts. My son Daniel begged me not to "ruin the bread" by putting nuts in it, and so I capitulated (intending, though, to include them in the written recipe). To my surprise, he was absolutely right. The delicate, buttery texture of this marvelous bread would be compromised by the nuts, and so once again, out of the mouth of babes . . .

Makes 1 loaf

1 3/4 cups unbleached flour
1/4 cup wheat germ or bran
1 tablespoon baking powder
1/2 teaspoon salt
1 1/4 cups fresh or frozen blueberries (if frozen, unthawed, and preferably tiny wild blueberries)
6 tablespoons unsalted butter, very soft
1/2 cup sugar
2 eggs
1 teaspoon vanilla extract
1/2 teaspoon almond extract
1 cup low-fat milk

1. Preheat the oven to 350 degrees. Butter a 9 × 5-inch (1 1/2-quart) loaf pan.
2. Thoroughly combine the flour, wheat germ, baking powder, and salt in a medium-size bowl. Place the blueberries in a small bowl. Sprinkle about 2 tablespoons of the flour mixture on the blueberries and toss to evenly coat them. (This will prevent the blueberries from sinking in the batter to the bottom of the bread.)
3. Place the 6 tablespoons butter and the sugar in a large bowl. With an electric mixer beat the butter and sugar until fluffy. Beat in the eggs and vanilla and almond extracts until well blended. (It's okay if the mixture separates.)

4. Sprinkle in the flour mixture and the milk, and beat until well incorporated. *By hand* stir in the blueberries.

5. Scrape the batter into the prepared loaf pan. Bake 55 minutes, or until a knife inserted in the center of the loaf comes out clean. If the bread begins to get dark before it is finished, lay a flat piece of foil over the top and continue baking. Cool on a wire rack for 10 minutes before removing it from the pan. Let cool at least 2 hours before slicing. Do not attempt to slice this bread while it is at all warm. If well wrapped in foil and placed in a plastic bag, this bread can be frozen up to 1 week.

For Starters

The main function of hors d'oeuvres, aside from their purely pleasurable contribution, is to provide guests with some palate teasers that will gently lead them into the main meal without quelling their appetites. In addition, these nibbles allow the cook some extra time while guests chat leisurely and contentedly.

Unless the dinner is an extra-special occasion that calls for elaborate fare, I usually serve a spread of some sort, with crackers, Crostini (page 16), or pita bread triangles alongside it. This can always be extended by including olives, mini carrots, cucumbers, red pepper strips, etc., as tidbits that provide contrasting texture and color. I like to cluster individual hors d'oeuvres, such as Spinach Balls with

Honey-Mustard Dipping Sauce or Pan-Fried Ravioli with Sun-Dried Tomato Pesto, with other finger foods to create an appetizer menu. (Christmas Eve is my favorite time to do this.)

When you are going to select an appetizer to precede a carefully planned dinner, take care to match compatible flavors and ingredients. If the main course is rich with cheese, avoid a cheese-based starter. If red peppers are a salient ingredient in the entree, select an appetizer without them.

All these recipes can be prepared in advance (or at least a number of their steps can), so take advantage of this feature to enjoy your guests, and save last-minute prep time for other courses that need your attention.

Tiny Eggplant Turnovers

The idea for this hors d'oeuvre came to me one night in bed, and I couldn't wait to get up the next morning to try it out. Thin slices of breaded eggplant are spread with a goat cheese–red pepper filling and then folded over to make half moons. You could even use small Japanese eggplants and make little sandwiches instead of the turnovers, or if you can only get a large eggplant, cut each slice in half before you turn it over. Whichever method you choose, you'll find that this appetizer is addictive.

Makes about 24 turnovers

1 medium (about 1 $\frac{1}{4}$ pounds) eggplant (skin left on), sliced into $\frac{1}{3}$-inch-thick slices (no thicker)
$\frac{1}{4}$ cup mayonnaise (approximately)
$\frac{1}{3}$ cup dry bread crumbs (approximately)
$\frac{1}{2}$ teaspoon dried basil
Salt
Freshly ground pepper to taste

The Filling
5 ounces soft mild goat cheese (chèvre)
1 small garlic clove, put through a press
2 tablespoons very finely diced roasted red pepper, freshly roasted (page 19) or store-bought
$\frac{1}{2}$ teaspoon dried oregano
$\frac{1}{4}$ teaspoon dried thyme
Salt
Freshly ground black pepper to taste

Minced parsley for garnish

1. Preheat the broiler.
2. Place the eggplant slices in front of you. Put the mayonnaise in a small bowl. Mix the bread crumbs, basil, salt, and pepper together on a small plate.
3. With a pastry brush very lightly coat both sides of each eggplant slice with some

mayonnaise, then press each slice into the bread crumbs to coat it evenly. Place the slices on a baking sheet in one layer. Broil until golden brown on each side. Let the eggplant cool to room temperature. Do not fill it while it is at all warm.

4. To make the filling combine the filling ingredients in a small bowl. When the eggplant is cool spread a *thin* layer of filling on each slice. Fold the slices over to make turnovers. Arrange decoratively on a platter, then sprinkle on some minced parsley to garnish them. Serve at room temperature.

Note: You can prepare and chill these up to 24 hours in advance. Bring to room temperature before serving.

Cheesy Polenta Disks with Assorted Toppings

Because these little disks of polenta are just the right size and firmness to be grasped easily while holding a glass of wine in the other hand, they can be a great hors d'oeuvres for a party. The bright yellow polenta lends itself to whimsical, colorful toppings. I like to use slices of plum tomatoes on some, and chopped black olives on others; however, you can try: paper-thin slices of sautéed red, green, and yellow bell peppers; sliced cherry tomatoes and capers; sautéed diced red onion; and sautéed mushrooms, just to name a few possibilities. Just be certain to place some cheese on the polenta disks before garnishing them so that the toppings will have something to adhere to.

You can also be playful with the *shapes* of these tidbits. My preference is to use a 2½-inch fluted biscuit cutter, but you can use other cutters such as hearts, ovals, diamonds, etc.

If you have a big crowd, don't hesitate to multiply this recipe; it's very easy to handle.

Serves 4

1¾ cups vegetable stock, store-bought or homemade (page 13)
¼ teaspoon salt
½ teaspoon finely chopped fresh rosemary, or ⅛ teaspoon dried, crumbled
½ cup cornmeal
1 tablespoon unsalted butter
2 tablespoons grated Parmesan cheese
½ cup grated part-skim mozzarella cheese
1 tablespoon olive oil

The Toppings
⅓ cup grated part-skim mozzarella cheese
1 plum tomato, cut into 6 thin slices
6 pitted black olives (your favorite kind), each cut into quarters

1. Place a baking sheet in front of you to pour the polenta on. Combine the vegetable

stock, salt, and rosemary in a medium-size, heavy-bottomed saucepan and bring to a boil. Reduce the heat to a simmer, then slowly drizzle in the cornmeal, whisking all the while with a wire whisk. Continue to whisk until the polenta tears away from the sides of the pot, about 5 minutes. Whisk in the butter, and the Parmesan and mozzarella cheeses. Pour the polenta onto the baking sheet so that it is ½ inch thick. Use a rubber spatula to spread it around evenly; it should fill about one third of the pan. Let the polenta cool. Cover it with plastic wrap, and chill for at least 30 minutes, or up to 2 days.

2. Preheat the oven to 425 degrees. Using the tablespoon of olive oil, grease a baking sheet. With a 2½-inch fluted biscuit cutter or other shape of your choice, cut out polenta disks. Lift the disks with a narrow spatula and place them on the prepared baking sheet. You should have about 12.

3. Place a teaspoon or so of the grated mozzarella on each disk. Place a slice of tomato on 6 of the disks, and the quartered olives on the other 6 disks. Bake 10 minutes, or until the cheese has melted and the disks are sizzling. Let sit 2 minutes before removing them from the pan. (They tend to stick a bit but are manageable.) Place on a decorative platter, and serve warm, not piping hot.

Pan-Fried Ravioli with Sun-Dried Tomato Pesto

My son Daniel can't get enough of these crisp ravioli. Although I like to serve them as hors d'oeuvres, he prefers them for his main course (minus the sauce). In our house they have become a perfect quick, staple dinner to fix for our selective ten-year-old. Fresh ravioli work best with this treatment because they remain tender and delicate; however, defrosted frozen ravioli will be just fine if that's what you have on hand. For entertaining I arrange them decoratively on a platter with a tiny spoonful of pesto on top of each one.

Serves 4–6 as an hors d'oeuvre

The Pesto
1 ½ ounces (about 10) loose sun-dried tomatoes
¼ cup olive oil
2 small garlic cloves, chopped
1 tablespoon lemon juice
2 tablespoons pine nuts
½ cup chopped fresh parsley
¼ teaspoon salt
Freshly ground pepper
1 tablespoon grated Parmesan cheese

⅓ cup milk (approximately)
5 tablespoons dry bread crumbs (approximately)
20 cheese ravioli, defrosted if frozen
Oil for frying

1. To make the pesto, steam the tomatoes in a vegetable steamer until soft, about 10 minutes. Remove and let cool.
2. In a food processor combine the tomatoes, oil, garlic, and lemon juice and process until smooth. Add the pine nuts, parsley, salt, and pepper and pulse until the mixture is

almost smooth but has tiny bits of these last ingredients visible. Scrape the pesto into a small bowl, then stir in the cheese by hand.

3. To prepare the ravioli put the milk in a small bowl and the bread crumbs on a small plate and place them in front of you. Dip each ravioli in the milk, then coat both sides with bread crumbs, being careful to cover them completely. Place all the ravioli on a large plate or platter.

4. Cover the bottom of a large skillet with a little oil. Heat it over medium heat until hot but not smoking. Fry the ravioli in one layer (you'll probably have to do this in batches) until golden brown on both sides. Use tongs to flip them over as needed. Place on a paper towel–covered plate to drain. Serve on a platter with ½ teaspoon of tomato pesto on top of each one.

Note: If there is any leftover pesto, you can cover and refrigerate it for a few days, then serve it on toasted French bread slices, on leftover pasta, in an omelet, or in a vegetable soup.

Leek Puff Pastries

For entertaining I like to cook these elegant, bite-sized puffs in advance and then reheat them a few minutes prior to serving. This method keeps the pace relaxed by eliminating any last-minute fussing. This hors d'oeuvre is not difficult or time-consuming, but you must poke the pastries a few times while they are baking. I like to get this step over with before the guests arrive.

Don't let the length of these instructions dissuade you from trying these flaky pastries; the recipe is not painstaking at all.

Makes 40 puffs

2 large leeks
1 tablespoon plus 2 teaspoons unsalted butter
¼ cup heavy cream
Two pinches dried thyme
Pinch sugar
Salt
Generous seasoning freshly ground black pepper
⅔ cup (2 ounces) grated Gruyère or other Swiss cheese
1 (17-ounce) box frozen puff pastry sheets, thawed
Flour for dusting

1. Cut the roots off the leeks plus everything but 2 inches of the green tops. Cut the leeks in half lengthwise. Under cold running water rinse the leeks, thumbing through all the leaves to wash away any hidden dirt. Thinly slice the leeks, discarding any thick, dark green pieces that look tough. You should get about 2 ½ cups sliced leeks.

2. Melt 1 tablespoon of the butter in a large skillet over medium heat. Add the leeks and sauté until very tender, about 10 minutes. Do not let the leeks get at all brown. Mix in the cream, thyme, sugar, salt, and pepper and cook just until the cream is very thick and

coats the leeks, about 3 minutes. Scrape the mixture into a bowl and let cool to room temperature. Stir in the cheese.

3. Unfold the puff pastry sheets. Lightly flour your work surface, then roll each sheet into a 10 × 10-inch square. With a 2-inch biscuit cutter cut out as many rounds as possible, probably 20 per sheet. Use your thumb to make a few indentations in the center of each round. This will cause the sides to raise up a bit, like a saucer.

4. Melt the remaining 2 teaspoons of butter. With a pastry brush lightly coat the edge of each round. Using a measuring teaspoon, place 1 teaspoon of filling in the center of each round. Place the rounds on ungreased baking sheets.

5. Now you can proceed in the following ways: Freeze the pastries for 30 minutes, then when hard, cover them with plastic wrap and cook within 1 week; or chill them up to 4 hours, then bake; or bake as directed (below) and reheat before serving.

6. To bake them preheat the oven to 400 degrees. Bake the pastries about 4 minutes, or until they begin to rise. To prevent them from toppling over, which they sometimes do if they rise too high, remove the baking sheets from the oven and, with a sharp, pointed knife, poke a few holes in the sides of the pastries to let steam escape. Return to the oven and bake 6 more minutes, or until golden, checking and poking them as necessary. Serve warm, not hot, or let cool completely, then reheat in a 350-degree oven for 4–5 minutes.

Spinach Balls with Honey-Mustard Dipping Sauce

These tender, green morsels are very quick to prepare, and because you can freeze the balls uncooked, they are ideal for entertaining. I use frozen rather than fresh spinach here because it all gets pureed and you can't tell the difference.

Makes about 40 balls

2 (10-ounce) packages frozen chopped spinach, thawed
1 medium onion, minced
½ cup dry bread crumbs
1 teaspoon poultry seasoning
¾ cup grated Parmesan cheese
6 tablespoons unsalted butter, melted
3 eggs
¼ teaspoon salt
Oil for baking sheet

Honey-Mustard Dipping Sauce
½ cup plain yogurt
2 tablespoons Dijon-style mustard
4 teaspoons honey

1. Squeeze all the water out of the spinach with your hands, or by placing it in a strainer and pressing out the liquid with the back of a large spoon. Place the spinach and onion in a food processor and process until the onion is fine.
2. Stop the machine and add the bread crumbs, poultry seasoning, cheese, butter, eggs, and salt. Process until perfectly pureed. Scrape the mixture into a bowl and chill until cold, at least 1 hour.
3. Lightly oil a baking sheet. Roll the mixture into balls 1 to 1½ inches in diameter, and place them on the baking sheet. At this point you can place the baking sheet in the refrigerator and chill the balls until you are ready to bake them, or place the baking

sheet in the freezer for about 1 hour, or until the balls are frozen. With a spatula remove the frozen balls and place them in a plastic bag. Freeze up to 1 month.

4. Preheat the oven to 350 degrees. Bake the spinach balls 10–15 minutes (unthawed if frozen), or until they are hot throughout and lightly golden. Don't overcook them or they will get dry. Serve them warm, not hot, around a bowl of Honey-Mustard Dipping Sauce.

5. To make the sauce combine the ingredients in a small bowl. Chill until ready to use.

Caramelized Onion, Gorgonzola, and Walnut Bruschetta

I once tasted this magical combination of caramelized onion, Gorgonzola cheese, and walnuts on a pizza that was created by Joyce Goldstein, chef of the now defunct Square One restaurant in San Francisco, and I was totally captivated by the fantastic interplay of flavors. Here it is repeated on a bruschetta (grilled or toasted bread) and it retains all the charm of the original combination.

Makes 8 bruschetta

½ tablespoon unsalted butter
1 large onion, halved vertically and very thinly sliced
Pinch sugar
4 tablespoons crumbled Gorgonzola or other blue cheese
2 ½ tablespoons finely chopped walnuts
8 slices baguette, each ½ inch thick
Fruity olive oil for brushing

1. Heat the butter in a medium-size skillet over medium heat. Add the onion and, with the tip of a spoon or spatula, break the onion slices into rings. Sauté 5 minutes, tossing occasionally.
2. Add the pinch of sugar, cover the pan, and lower the heat. Cook until the onion is evenly caramelized and soft, about 15 minutes. Stir repeatedly. Scrape the onion into a bowl and let cool. Mix in the Gorgonzola and walnuts.
3. Preheat the oven to 400 degrees. Place the bread on the baking sheet and toast until golden on both sides. Lightly brush some olive oil on one side of the toast.
4. Spoon an equal portion of the Gorgonzola mixture onto the oiled side of each toast. Pat it down firmly with your fingers. (You can assemble the bruschetta up to an hour before cooking them.) Bake until hot and melted, about 7 minutes. Serve warm.

Bruschetta

(pronounced broos-KAYT-tah)

Peasant cooks worldwide have found ingenious, yet simple, uses for stale bread. That these treatments are born of necessity and frugality only adds to their rustic charm, for it is no small feat to avoid waste.

Roman peasants created bruschetta as one answer to the prevalence of stale bread. Thick slices of chewy bread are grilled over a wood fire; they are then sometimes rubbed with garlic, and always drizzled with olive oil. This is the essence of bruschetta, and from here, many offshoots extend.

For the contemporary cook, toasting often has to replace grilling if no grill is available. And bruschetta are now widely used as a base for many delectable toppings, which makes them ideal hors d'oeuvres, especially when served with some robust wine. But the two characteristics of bruschetta that must never be tampered with in order to preserve its distinctiveness are the use of chewy, crusty bread, and fruity, extra-virgin olive oil. That aside, you can have fun with endless toppings.

Triple Pepper Bruschetta

These colorful little morsels are just the thing to serve with some wine when the guests arrive. This topping is so tasty that I oftentimes use it as a sandwich filling with some sliced cheese, all atop some chewy Tuscan-style bread.

About 12 small bruschetta

2 tablespoons fruity olive oil, plus extra for brushing
½ red bell pepper, cut into ⅛ × 2-inch strips
½ yellow bell pepper, cut into ⅛ × 2-inch strips
½ green bell pepper, cut into ⅛ × 2-inch strips
1 medium onion, halved vertically and very thinly sliced
1 tablespoon minced fresh basil
Salt
Freshly ground black pepper
12 slices baguette, cut ¾ inch thick

1. Heat the 2 tablespoons olive oil in a large skillet over medium heat. Add the 3 peppers and the onion and sauté, tossing often, for 10 minutes. Cover the pan and cook about 20 minutes more, or until the mixture is very soft and almost caramelized. Stir it occasionally. Remove from the heat and let cool to warm. Stir in the basil, salt, and pepper.
2. Grill or toast the bread slices until they are lightly browned. (You can toast them in a toaster or in a 400-degree oven.) Lightly brush some olive oil on each toast. Neatly arrange some of the pepper mixture on each one. Arrange the bruschetta on a decorative plate. You can let the bruschetta sit up to 20 minutes before serving them.

Spinach Dip with Pita Crisps

These sturdy crisps are just what is needed to scoop up this bulky, delectable dip.

Serves 4–6

The Dip

½ (10-ounce) package frozen chopped spinach, thoroughly defrosted (see Note)
1 cup sour cream
1 large scallion, very thinly sliced
2 tablespoons pine nuts, toasted
2 teaspoons lemon juice
1 tablespoon milk
¼ teaspoon salt
Generous seasoning freshly ground black pepper

The Pita Crisps

2 (6-inch) pita breads
2 tablespoons olive oil

1. Place the half portion of defrosted spinach in a strainer and press out *all* the liquid with the back of a large spoon. Place the spinach in a medium-size bowl. Stir in all the remaining dip ingredients. Cover and chill for at least 2 hours to blend the flavors.
2. To make the pita crisps, preheat the oven to 300 degrees. Cut both pita breads in half to make 4 pockets, then, with a small knife, carefully separate each pocket into single layers. Using a pastry brush, coat each piece of bread on the rough (inner) side with the olive oil. Cut each piece into 3 or 4 triangles.
3. Place the pita triangles on a baking sheet, then bake until golden and crisp, about 12–15 minutes. Let cool completely. Store in a plastic container until ready to use. Serve surrounding the bowl of spinach. Serve the dip cool or at room temperature, not cold.

Note: The remaining half box of spinach can be used to fill an omelet, mix with pasta, or stuff into a baked potato with some cheese.

Two White Bean Spreads

Both these spreads are teeming with flavor and are delightful spread on toasts, especially those made from French bread slices (see Crostini, page 16).

The first version is enlivened with basil and roasted red peppers, the second spread has a dominant scallion-onion theme. I had a hard time choosing which one I preferred, so I have included both.

Makes about 1 ½ cups (each)

Spread #1

½ cup chopped fresh parsley
1 (16-ounce) can small white beans, rinsed well and drained
1 tablespoon olive oil
2 tablespoons finely diced roasted red peppers, freshly roasted (page 19) or store-bought
2 tablespoons minced fresh basil
1 garlic clove, put through a press
Salt
Freshly ground black pepper

Spread #2

½ cup chopped fresh parsley
1 (16-ounce) can small white beans, rinsed well and drained
1 tablespoon olive oil
1 garlic clove, put through a press
2 tablespoons minced scallion, white and green parts
1 tablespoon minced red onion
Salt
Freshly ground black pepper

1. For each spread proceed in the same manner. Place the parsley in a food processor and process until fine. Scrape it into a medium-size bowl. Don't worry about getting it

all out of the processor. Place the beans and olive oil in the processor and process until smooth. Mix the beans into the parsley.

2. In either case, whether you're making spread #1 or #2, mix in all the remaining ingredients. Cover and chill for at least 1 hour before serving so the flavors can blend. Bring to room temperature before serving.

Vegetarian Chopped Liver

The transformation of these ingredients into a sensational mock chopped liver spread is just short of magical. Spread it on room temperature toast points, preferably made from good-quality white bread.

Makes 2 1/2 cups

1 cup walnuts
1 1/2 tablespoons canola oil
2 medium onions, diced
2 cups (1/2 pound) fresh or frozen diced green beans
3 hard-boiled eggs, chopped
4 teaspoons tomato paste
2 tablespoons mayonnaise
1/2 teaspoon salt
Generous seasoning freshly ground black pepper

1. Preheat the oven to 350 degrees. Place the walnuts in a shallow pan and toast until fragrant and golden, about 5–7 minutes. Let cool.
2. Heat the oil in a small skillet. Sauté the onions until very tender and deep brown, about 15 minutes. Set aside to cool.
3. Steam the fresh or frozen green beans until they are very tender and begin to turn olive green in color. (You don't want bright, crunchy green beans for this recipe.) Set aside to cool.
4. In a food processor combine all the ingredients and process until perfectly smooth, almost 5 minutes of processing. Turn off the machine and scrape down the sides as necessary. Scrape into a bowl, cover, and chill at least 4 hours or up to 3 days before serving. Serve at room temperature.

Hummus

Hummus recipes are everywhere, but I can guarantee you that few are as luscious as this one. The secret is in the generous use of tahini. Tahini (sesame butter), a great non-dairy source of calcium, gives this hummus its silken consistency and rich flavor.
For busy cooks (our numbers are legion), this hummus can be a godsend, for it can be used throughout the week in a variety of ways, and this recipe makes an ample amount to provide for that. (See "Uses" below.) When company is coming it is the perfect recipe to reach for because it is so delicious and versatile, and you can prepare it well in advance. Have I convinced you to try this captivating spread? It's bound to become one of your favorites.

Makes 2 ½ cups

2 cups freshly cooked or canned chickpeas, drained and well rinsed if canned
3 garlic cloves, minced
½ cup fresh lemon juice (about 3 lemons)
1 cup tahini*
½ teaspoon salt
½–1 cup water
Paprika for garnish

1. Combine the chickpeas and garlic in a food processor and process until a mealy texture is formed. Stop the machine and add the lemon juice, tahini, salt, and ½ cup of the water. Process until very smooth and creamy, at least 2 minutes.

**Tahini is sesame butter made from untoasted sesame seeds. It is different from Chinese sesame paste, which is dark and roasted. Stir the tahini well before measuring it because its oil will most likely have risen to the top.*

2. Stop the machine and check the consistency. It should be like soft mashed potatoes, not thick and pasty. With the machine running add more water if necessary until it is smooth and creamy. Scrape into a bowl and garnish with some paprika. This hummus will last a week if well covered and refrigerated.

Uses for hummus:

✣ As an appetizer: Serve as a spread with hot pita triangles or Pita Crisps (page 60).

✣ For sandwiches: Place raw, crisp vegetables, such as cucumbers, peppers, Romaine lettuce, and some tomato wedges or cherry tomatoes, in pita bread halves and spoon on some hummus.

✣ Spread it on bagels.

✣ Make an open-faced sandwich by spreading hummus on whole grain bread, then topping it with some red onion, thin cucumber slices, and alfalfa sprouts.

Roasted Red Pepper Spread

I love to pipe this rosy spread onto cucumber rounds and serve them as hors d'oeuvres. It is equally delicious, though, spread on Crostini (page 16) or crackers. Whichever you choose, it will be a hit at any gathering.

Makes about 1 ½ cups

½ cup roasted red peppers, store-bought or freshly roasted (page 19), patted *very* dry
1 small garlic clove, put through a press or minced*
8 ounces Neufchâtel cheese (light cream cheese), at room temperature
2 tablespoons lemon juice
Salt to taste
2 teaspoons minced fresh parsley
1 teaspoon minced fresh basil, or ¼ teaspoon dried

1. Process the peppers and garlic in a food processor just until very finely chopped.
2. Add the Neufchâtel and lemon juice and process just until smooth. Scrape the mixture into a bowl, then stir in the salt, parsley, and basil. Cover and chill at least 1 hour.

Note: To pipe it onto cucumber rounds, place the spread in a pastry bag with a large star tube. Keeping the skin on, slice an English (seedless) cucumber into ¼-inch-thick slices. Pat them dry with paper towels. Pipe a thick row of the spread on each slice. Garnish the top of the row with a parsley leaf.

**You must mince the garlic before adding it to the processor or else the blade could miss it and it will remain whole.*

Goat Cheese Spread with Pistachios and Mint

My friend Jane Walsh put mint in a cheese mixture once and I loved the fresh nuance it lent the spread. Here, mixed with pistachio nuts, you have an appetizer with simple elegance. After the cheese mixture is unmolded onto a platter, you can create a Moroccan theme by surrounding it with black olives, orange wedges, and raw fennel slices—all exciting and compatible flavors. Oh, and don't forget the crackers!

Serves 6

5 ounces soft mild goat cheese
2 tablespoons coarsely chopped shelled pistachio nuts
1 tablespoon minced fresh mint, or 1 teaspoon dried

1. In a medium-size bowl mash the goat cheese with a fork. Stir in the nuts and mint.
2. Line a 6-ounce custard cup or other ramekin with a piece of plastic wrap that's big enough to extend over the sides. Pack in the goat cheese mixture and smooth over the top. Fold over the plastic to cover the cheese. Chill at least 1 hour or up to 8 hours before serving. To serve, invert the cup onto a large serving plate, then remove the cup and plastic. Let the cheese come close to room temperature so that it isn't ice cold. Surround the cheese with crackers or Crostini (page 16), and perhaps some olives, sliced raw fennel, and orange slices.

Special Dinner Salads

It's easy to get into a rut serving the same salad meal after meal. When we find a harmonious combination of leafy vegetables that match well with a favorite dressing, that oftentimes becomes one course that we are grateful *not* to have to think about.

But upon further reflection, the salad course is more important than many of us imagine. It is the prelude to our meal (in the United States, at least, where it is customary to serve the salad before the entree rather than after it, as many Europeans do), and can set a tone that makes our guests or family eager to taste what will follow.

To make a memorable salad doesn't demand any more time than your everyday salad, just a good dose of imagination.

Salad of Baby Greens with Baked Goat Cheese

Here's a variation of the salad made famous at the restaurant Chez Panisse in Berkeley, California. The little rounds of creamy goat cheese encased in buttery bread crumbs are truly irresistible, and inevitably make the salad a hit at any dinner party.

Serves 4

The Dressing
1 ½ tablespoons lemon juice
2 teaspoons red wine vinegar
1 small garlic clove, minced
Salt
Freshly ground black pepper
5 tablespoons olive oil

Olive oil for greasing

The Salad
½ cup toasted fresh bread crumbs (from about 1 slice toast)
1 teaspoon chopped fresh thyme, or ¼ teaspoon dried
Salt
Freshly ground black pepper
1 (4-ounce) log soft mild goat cheese (such as Montrachet), cut into 4 rounds
8 cups mesclun (mixed baby greens)

1. Combine the ingredients for the salad dressing in a jar with a tight-fitting lid and shake vigorously. Set aside.
2. Very lightly oil the center portion of a baking sheet. Place the bread crumbs in a small bowl and mix in the thyme, salt, and pepper. Using a pastry brush or your fingers, one by one lightly coat each goat cheese round with some olive oil, then press the rounds into the bread crumbs to coat them with a thick crust. Lay them on the center portion of the baking sheet. You can cook them now, or chill them until you are ready, up to 4 hours.

3. Preheat the oven to 425 degrees. Bake the cheese until golden on the outside and hot on the inside, about 5 minutes. Keep an eye on it so it doesn't become so hot that it melts.
4. Toss the greens with the dressing. Divide them among 4 salad plates. Place 1 goat cheese round on top of each serving of greens. Serve immediately.

Goat Cheeses
(Chèvres)

A new appreciation for goat cheeses is sweeping the United States, and these once uncommon little parcels can now be found in most supermarkets. Technically chèvre refers to a French cheese made from goat's milk; Montrachet and Boucheron are two of the most well known. But the United States is now producing some wonderful goat cheeses, and it seems appropriate to drop the French designation and refer to them as "goat cheese."

Goat cheeses range in texture from soft and creamy to hard and shrunken, and in flavor from mild to strong. In this book soft, fresh, mild goat cheese is the cheese of preference when goat cheese is called for. Montrachet is the mildest chèvre from France, and the United States has many to choose from. Check your local cheese store or the cheese section of a top-notch supermarket to become familiar with what's available to you. Where I live in the Berkshires, we have wonderful goat cheese that's made locally. See if you do.

Green Leaf Salad with Fennel, Apple, and Pecans

Here's a special salad that has lots of crunch and a great variety of flavors. Because it has no cheese or dairy in it, it's a good choice for a meal that's on the rich side.

Serves 4

Balsamic Vinaigrette
2 tablespoons balsamic vinegar
1 garlic clove, put through a press or minced
1/4 teaspoon salt
Freshly ground black pepper
5 tablespoons olive oil

6 cups torn-up green leaf lettuce, washed and spun dry
1 cup torn-up radicchio, washed and spun dry
1/2 large Granny Smith apple, cut into 12 thin slices
2/3 cup thinly sliced fennel (see Note)
1/2 cup chopped toasted pecans

1. Combine all the ingredients for the dressing in a medium-size bowl and whisk until blended.
2. Mix the lettuce and radicchio in a salad bowl. Just before serving pour on the dressing and toss. Divide salad among 4 salad plates.
3. Place 3 apple slices on one side of each salad, and one quarter of the fennel on the other side. Sprinkle the pecans all over the salads. Serve immediately.

Note: Leftover fennel can be used in Chickpea Salad with Fennel, Tomatoes, and Olives (page 94), or Leek, Fennel, and Goat Cheese Frittata (page 170), or Tortellini with Fennel, Tomatoes, and Spinach (page 229).

Mixed Greens with Pears, Walnuts, and Blue Cheese

This salad is so delicious that I sometimes serve double portions to create a luncheon entree. For the greens I especially love Boston lettuce and watercress to dominate, with a touch of Romaine for crunch and radicchio for color. Because it is a tad on the rich side, I like to match it with a light entree for balance when I serve it as a salad course.

Serves 4

6 cups bite-size mixed greens, such as Boston lettuce, Romaine, and radicchio
1 bunch watercress, tough stems discarded and large pieces torn in half

The Dressing
1 tablespoon lemon juice
2 teaspoons red wine vinegar
1 small garlic clove, minced
Salt
Freshly ground black pepper
5 tablespoons olive oil

1 ripe pear (preferably D'Anjou), cored and cut into 12 slices
4 tablespoons crumbled blue cheese
3 tablespoons chopped toasted walnuts

1. Wash and spin dry all the greens, then place them in a large salad bowl.
2. To make the dressing combine the lemon juice, vinegar, garlic, salt, pepper, and olive oil in a jar with a tight-fitting lid and shake vigorously.
3. Place the pear slices in a medium-size bowl, and mix with 1 tablespoon of dressing. Toss to coat evenly and prevent the pear from discoloring.
4. Pour the remaining dressing on the salad greens and toss. Divide the salad among 4 salad plates. Place 3 slices of pear in the center of each salad. Sprinkle on the blue cheese and walnuts. Serve immediately.

Mesclun Salad with Dried Apricots and Spiced Nuts

The tiny bursts of spiciness from the nuts are a pleasing counterpoint to the sweet and tangy bits of dried apricot, together making this a superlative prelude to a special meal. The recipe might look lengthy, but it's a breeze to prepare.

Serves 4

Spiced Nuts
1 teaspoon unsalted butter
¼ teaspoon chili powder
¼ teaspoon ground cumin
Dash cayenne
A few dashes salt
½ cup roughly chopped walnuts

The Salad
5 cups mesclun (baby greens), washed and spun dry
5 cups torn Boston lettuce, washed and spun dry
½ cup slivered red onion
8 dried apricots, snipped with scissors into quarters

The Dressing
1½ tablespoons balsamic vinegar
½ teaspoon Dijon-style mustard
¼ teaspoon sugar
¼ teaspoon salt
Freshly ground black pepper
5 tablespoons olive oil

1. To make the spiced nuts, melt the butter in a medium-size skillet over medium heat. Sprinkle in the chili powder, cumin, cayenne, and salt and, using a spatula, blend it together. Cook 1 minute. Add the walnuts, toss to coat well, and cook 3–5 minutes, toss-

ing frequently. The nuts should be toasted when done. Set aside to cool completely.
2. Combine the salad ingredients in a large salad bowl.
3. Whisk together the dressing ingredients in a small bowl until smooth and emulsified, or place them in a jar with a tight-fitting lid and shake vigorously.
4. Just before serving pour three quarters of the dressing on the salad. Toss to coat well. If you need more, then add it, but be careful not to overdress the greens; they are soft and delicate. Arrange the salad on 4 salad plates, and sprinkle 1/4 of the nuts on each portion.

Boston Lettuce and Arugula Salad with Dried Cranberries and Walnuts

A delicate, pretty salad that's a good choice when your meal is hearty and you want a light salad to balance it. I especially like this salad for the holidays.

Serves 4

Lemon-Soy Dressing

1 ½ tablespoons lemon juice
1 ½ teaspoons red wine vinegar
1 garlic clove, put through a press or minced
1 ½ teaspoons tamari soy sauce
Salt
Freshly ground black pepper
5 tablespoons olive oil

3 tablespoons dried cranberries
2 tablespoons chopped walnuts
6 cups bite-size pieces Boston lettuce, well washed and spun dry (from about 1 ½ heads)
2 cups torn-up arugula, washed and spun dry
1 scallion, thinly sliced

1. Combine all the ingredients for the dressing in a jar with a tight-fitting lid and shake vigorously. Place the cranberries and walnuts in a small bowl, then pour on a tiny bit of dressing to moisten them and soften the cranberries a bit.
2. Combine the salad greens and scallion in a large salad bowl.
3. Just before serving pour on the dressing and toss well. Serve on individual salad plates with some of the cranberries and walnuts sprinkled on each portion.

Red Leaf Lettuce with Crumbled Goat Cheese and Honey-Mustard Dressing

The array of flavors in this tantalizing salad is a study of harmonious contrasts—sweet, pungent dressing, tangy goat cheese, salty olives, and spicy onion. It all comes together to delightfully whet the appetite for the next course.

Serves 4

Honey-Mustard Dressing

1 ½ tablespoons red wine vinegar
2 tablespoons honey
2 teaspoons Dijon-style mustard
2 tablespoons minced red onion
Dash salt
5 tablespoons mild olive oil

The Salad

4 cups bite-size pieces red leaf lettuce, washed and spun dry
4 cups bite-size pieces Romaine lettuce
⅔ cup slivered red onion
12 black olives, Niçoise, Kalamata, or other favorites
4 tablespoons crumbled soft mild goat cheese

1. To make the dressing, combine the vinegar and honey in a small bowl or jar and whisk to blend. This will take a minute or so. Whisk in all of the remaining dressing ingredients and set aside. If you are using a jar with a tight-fitting lid, add the remaining dressing ingredients and shake vigorously.

2. Combine the two lettuces and onion in a large salad bowl. Spoon on most of the dressing and toss well. Check to see if you need more dressing. Serve the salad on 4 salad plates. Place three olives on each portion, then place 1 tablespoon of crumbled goat cheese on each portion as well. Serve immediately.

Orange, Red Onion, and Black Olive Salad

This spectacular winter salad has become popular in recent years with good reason. The contrasting flavors and brilliant colors make it a perfect antidote to the winter blahs. Mediterranean in origin, it goes especially well with meals from that region, including most pasta dishes. Choose the sweetest and juiciest seedless oranges you can get. In New England that means navel oranges available in February, March, and April.

Serves 4

The Dressing

2 tablespoons red wine vinegar
1 small garlic clove, put through a press or minced
1/4 teaspoon salt
5 tablespoons olive oil

The Salad

4 large navel oranges, peeled
4 paper-thin slices red onion
16 oil-cured black olives, Niçoise olives, or other favorite olives

1. To make the dressing, combine its ingredients in a jar with a tight-fitting lid and shake vigorously.
2. To make the salad, slice the oranges crosswise into about 6 slices per orange. Arrange the slices by overlapping them around the rims of four plates. Separate the onion slices into rings and scatter them on top of the oranges. Place 4 olives on each plate. Drizzle some dressing over each portion. Let sit 30 minutes before serving.

Summer Tomato Salad

Perfectly ripe, juicy tomatoes are spotlighted in this seasonal salad, which is a delightful change of pace from more common salads based on leafy greens. Be certain to use only tomatoes that are at their prime; second-rate tomatoes just won't carry the dish.

Serves 4

The Dressing
1/4 cup olive oil
1 tablespoon balsamic vinegar
1 large garlic clove, put through a press or minced
Salt
Generous seasoning freshly ground black pepper

The Salad
3 medium, perfectly ripe summer tomatoes, each cut into about 10 wedges
1 1/2 cups torn arugula
2/3 cup freshly cooked or canned small white beans, well rinsed if canned
2/3 cup slivered red onion

1. To make the dressing, combine the olive oil, vinegar, garlic, salt to taste, and pepper in a jar with a tight-fitting lid and shake vigorously.
2. Combine the salad ingredients in a large bowl. Just before serving pour on the dressing and toss gently. Serve on salad plates.

Mushroom Salad with Sun-Dried Tomato Vinaigrette

Thinly sliced mushrooms soak up a rosy-hued, garlicky dressing which makes them succulent and tender. Just wipe the mushrooms clean with paper towel; washing them will add too much moisture to these fabulous fungi.

Serves 4

The Dressing

3 loose sun-dried tomatoes (see Note)
1 large garlic clove, finely chopped
1/3 cup olive oil
3 tablespoons red wine vinegar
1/4 teaspoon salt
Generous seasoning freshly ground black pepper

1 pound very fresh white button mushrooms, wiped clean and thinly sliced
1/4 cup finely chopped flat-leaf parsley
Lettuce leaves

1. Place the sun-dried tomatoes in a small bowl and cover them with boiling water. Let soak 30 minutes. Drain the tomatoes and pat dry with paper towel. Cut the tomatoes into pieces, and put them in a blender along with the remaining dressing ingredients. Blend until smooth.
2. Place the mushrooms in a large bowl. Pour on the dressing and toss to coat well. Marinate the mushrooms for at least 4 hours or up to 24 hours. Cover and refrigerate if longer than 4 hours. Bring to room temperature before serving.
3. Just before serving mix the parsley into the mushrooms. Place some lettuce leaves on 4 salad plates. Serve a mound of mushrooms on each plate.

Note: If your sun-dried tomatoes are packed in oil, omit soaking them.

Spinach Salad with Sesame Dressing

Though it has an Asian accent, this salad goes well with many European-style entrees.

Serves 4

1 tablespoon sesame seeds

Sesame Dressing
1 ½ tablespoons red wine vinegar
1 small garlic clove, minced
½ teaspoon tamari soy sauce
Freshly ground black pepper
1 tablespoon oriental sesame oil
5 tablespoons canola oil

The Salad
8 cups well-washed spinach leaves, torn into small pieces, preferably from 1 large bunch flat-leaf spinach
2 scallions, very thinly sliced
4 large mushrooms, very thinly sliced
½ yellow or orange bell pepper, cut into thin slivers

1. Place a small bowl near the stove. Place the sesame seeds in a small saucepan and heat them over medium heat, swirling them around the pan continuously until they begin to get fragrant and just start to smoke. Don't take your eyes off them for one second! Immediately drop them into the bowl and let them cool.
2. To make the dressing, combine all the dressing ingredients in a jar with a tight-fitting lid and shake vigorously.
3. Combine the salad ingredients in a large salad bowl. Pour on the dressing and toss. Place a portion of salad on each salad plate, artfully arranging some pieces of pepper and mushroom on top. Sprinkle some sesame seeds on each portion.

Spinach Salad with Oranges and Toasted Pecans

Bursts of sweet, juicy oranges contrast splendidly with the slightly spicy dressing to make this salad a real charmer. If possible, purchase young delicate spinach in a bunch rather than thicker-leafed spinach packaged in a bag.

Serves 4

Creamy Orange-Cumin Dressing
1 tablespoon mayonnaise
1 tablespoon plain low-fat yogurt
2 teaspoons frozen orange juice concentrate
3 tablespoons olive oil
1 tablespoon red wine vinegar
1 small garlic clove, put through a press or minced
1/4 teaspoon ground cumin
Salt
Freshly ground black pepper to taste

The Salad
8 cups torn tender spinach leaves, well washed and spun dry
1 navel orange, peeled and separated into sections, then each section cut in half
4 thin slices red onion, separated into rings
20 pecan halves, toasted

1. To make the dressing, place the mayonnaise in a small bowl and beat it with a fork (this prevents any lumps from forming when the other ingredients are beaten in). Beat in the yogurt and orange juice concentrate, then briskly stir in the remaining dressing ingredients. Cover and chill the dressing for at least an hour for the flavors to develop.
2. Place the spinach on 4 salad plates. Drizzle one quarter of the dressing over each spinach portion. Top with the orange sections, onion rings, and pecans. Serve immediately.

Weekly Batch of Salad Dressing

I love having some vinaigrette in the refrigerator to fall back on when I want to quickly throw together a salad. I can modify a portion of it with some herbs or sesame oil to vary its original flavor, or just keep it as is—which is a delicious "all-purpose" dressing with garlic and lemon overtones. If you are pressed for time during the week, make a batch of this on the weekend and it will keep 7–10 days. You can use it on green salads, as well as marinated pasta salads, or cold bean or grain concoctions.

Makes 1 ¼ cups

3 tablespoons lemon juice
2 tablespoons red wine vinegar
2 garlic cloves, put through a press
2 teaspoons tamari soy sauce
¼ teaspoon salt
Generous seasoning freshly ground black pepper
1 cup olive oil

1. Combine all the ingredients in a jar with a tight-fitting lid and shake vigorously. Store in the refrigerator, but remove it at least 30 minutes before using it because the olive oil will solidify and, therefore, need to melt at room temperature.

Main-Course Salads

Summertime brings many seasonal pleasures, including the profusion of glorious, locally grown vegetables and herbs that, in their perfection, remind us of what is lost when food travels too far and for too long a time. With the emergence of hot weather comes a change in my kitchen that I readily welcome, and that is the reliance on main-course salads for many of our meals. I do make these dishes throughout the year, but nowhere near as often as I do when the temperature rises both outdoors and indoors. These salads benefit from being made in advance, and that works well with my desire to cook early in the day when it's cooler, and have a one-dish meal ready in the evening when I'm hot and sluggish.

If you have family members or friends who are hesitant to include various grains in their diets, these salads are a clever way to introduce them to ingredients they might otherwise shun. Garlicky vinaigrettes bring these medleys to life, and almost guarantee their widespread appeal. To extend these main-course salads into mini feasts, include some excellent crusty bread, a cheese platter, and some olives, and you've got an impressive spread with little work involved.

See also: Marinated Fried Tofu and Vegetable Salad with Mesclun (page 206)
Bow-Tie Pasta and Fried Tofu Salad with Sesame Dressing (page 210)
Soba and Fried Tofu Salad with Shredded Spinach (page 208)

Couscous Salad with Dried Cranberries and Pecans

Tangy, crimson-colored dried cranberries and toasted pecans are a dynamic combination in this special salad. If you plan to make it more than 2 hours in advance, hold back on adding the cucumbers until serving time so they will retain their special crunch.

Serves 4 as a main course

1 cup shelled pecans
1 ½ cups couscous
1 cup dried cranberries
½ teaspoon turmeric
2 cups boiling water
1 cup thawed frozen peas
3 scallions, very thinly sliced
2 medium cucumbers, peeled, seeded, and diced
¼ cup shredded fresh basil

Lemon Dressing
Zest of 1 lemon
⅓ cup lemon juice
3 garlic cloves, minced
½ teaspoon salt
Freshly ground black pepper
⅓ cup olive oil

1. Toast the pecans in a shallow pan in a preheated 350-degree oven until very fragrant, about 7 minutes. Set aside to cool.
2. Place the couscous, cranberries, and turmeric in a large bowl. Pour in the boiling water, stir, then cover the bowl with a large plate or foil. Let sit for 10 minutes. Remove the cover, then fluff the couscous with a fork. Cover again and let sit 5 more minutes.
3. Stir in the pecans, peas, scallions, cucumbers, and basil.

4. Combine the dressing ingredients in a jar with a tight-fitting lid and shake vigorously. Pour onto the couscous mixture and stir to blend. Let the salad sit at least 1 hour before serving to allow the flavors to blend. If longer than 1 hour, cover and chill, but then bring the salad to room temperature before serving. (Don't forget—if you make the salad more than an hour before you intend to serve it, hold back on adding the cucumbers until serving time or thereabouts.)

Rice Salad with Roasted Red Peppers, Chickpeas, and Feta Cheese

This piquant Greek-style salad is jam-packed with vegetables and flavor. I oftentimes cook the rice the night before or early in the day if I know the weather is going to be hot, then all I have to do is assemble it later on with no further cooking needed.

Serves 4 as a main course

2 1/2–3 cups cold cooked converted white rice or other long-grain white rice (made from 1 cup rice boiled in 2 1/4 cups water)
1 (16-ounce) can chickpeas, rinsed well and drained
3/4 cup finely diced feta cheese
2/3 cup diced roasted red peppers, store-bought or freshly roasted (page 19)
1/2 cup chopped fresh parsley
1/4 cup chopped fresh dill, or 2 teaspoons dried
3 scallions, very thinly sliced

The Dressing
1/4 cup fresh lemon juice
2 garlic cloves, put through a press or minced
Generous seasoning freshly ground black pepper
Salt
1/4 cup olive oil

1. Combine the rice, chickpeas, feta cheese, peppers, parsley, dill, and scallions in a large bowl and toss well.
2. Combine all the dressing ingredients in a jar with a tight-fitting lid and shake vigorously. Pour the dressing on the rice mixture and mix thoroughly. Let sit at least 1 hour or up to 8 hours before serving. Serve at room temperature.

Curried Rice Salad

This delicious salad is easy to assemble, and the result is an eye-catching palette of yellows and greens which looks quite lovely as a summer entree when served on a contrasting plate. Brown rice is preferable to white rice here because its nutty flavor enhances all the other components of this favorite salad.

Serves 4 as a main course

2½–3 cups cold cooked long-grain brown rice (made from 1 cup rice boiled in 2 cups water)
½ cup raisins
1 red-skinned apple, cut into ½-inch dice
⅓ cup chopped dry roasted peanuts
1 cup thawed frozen peas
3 scallions, thinly sliced
10 snow peas, cut in half diagonally

The Dressing
3 tablespoons fresh lemon juice
2 teaspoons minced gingerroot
2 garlic cloves, minced
2 teaspoons curry powder
½ teaspoon salt
Generous seasoning freshly ground pepper
¼ cup olive oil

1. Combine the rice, raisins, apple, peanuts, peas, scallions, and snow peas in a large bowl and toss well.
2. Combine all the dressing ingredients in a jar with a tight-fitting lid and shake vigorously. Pour the dressing on the salad and toss to coat well. Chill at least 1 hour or up to 8 hours, then bring to room temperature before serving.

Triple Rice Salad with Dried Fruits and Nuts

Second to wheat in worldwide importance, rice has been the mainstay of the diet of millions of people across many cultures. I love to turn it into a main course, and the use of three types of rice here provides the full impact of this delicious, versatile grain. Chock full of color and texture, this salad is the perfect choice when you crave something wholesome yet light.

Serves 4 as a main course

3 cups water
1/4 teaspoon salt
1 teaspoon olive oil
1/2 cup wild rice, rinsed
1/2 cup long-grain brown rice, rinsed
1/2 cup converted or basmati white rice, rinsed
1 cup dried cranberries
1/3 cup currants
1/2 cup diced dried apricots (snip apricots with scissors into sixths)

The Dressing
1/4 cup fresh lemon juice
3 garlic cloves, minced
2 shallots, minced
1/2 teaspoon salt
Generous seasoning freshly ground black pepper
1/3 cup olive oil

2/3 cup whole pecans
3 scallions, very thinly sliced
1/2 cup chopped fresh parsley
2 tablespoons chopped fresh mint, or 2 teaspoons dried
1 tablespoon chopped fresh basil, or 1/2 teaspoon dried

1. In a medium-size saucepan over high heat combine the water, salt, olive oil, wild rice, and brown rice. Cover the pan and bring to a boil. Reduce the heat to a simmer and cook 30 minutes.

2. Remove the cover and sprinkle in the white rice, being careful not to disturb the rice below. Cover the pan and cook about 20 minutes, or until all the water has been absorbed and the rice is just about to start sticking to the pot.

3. Meanwhile combine the dried cranberries, currants, and apricots in a large serving bowl. When the rice is cooked, carefully spoon it onto the dried fruit and toss just enough to incorporate it without making it gummy, a few strokes. Let the mixture cool completely. (The heat from the rice will plump up the dried fruit.)

4. Meanwhile make the dressing. Combine the lemon juice, garlic, shallots, salt, pepper, and olive oil in a jar with a tight-fitting lid and shake vigorously.

5. Gently stir the pecans, scallions, parsley, mint, and basil into the rice mixture. Pour on the dressing and toss. Chill and let marinate a few hours before serving. Serve at room temperature.

Asian Barley and Mushroom Salad

Barley's nubbiness is accentuated in this crunchy, yet light salad.

Serves 4 as a main course

1 cup barley, rinsed in a strainer
1 teaspoon plus 1 tablespoon canola oil
12 ounces thinly sliced mushrooms (4 ½ cups)

The Dressing
2 ½ tablespoons tamari soy sauce
1 ½ tablespoons oriental sesame oil
1 tablespoon Chinese rice wine or dry sherry
1 small garlic clove, minced

2 carrots, finely diced
2 scallions, very thinly sliced
Salt
Freshly ground black pepper

1. Fill a stockpot half full with water and bring it to a boil. Drop in the barley and 1 teaspoon of the canola oil. Reduce the heat to a lively simmer and cook 40 minutes.
2. Meanwhile heat the remaining tablespoon of canola oil in a large skillet over medium-high heat. Add the mushrooms and sauté until they are brown and their juices are rendered, then evaporated, about 10 minutes. Set aside to cool.
3. Drain the barley in a colander or large strainer. Place the barley in a large bowl.
4. Make the dressing by combining the soy sauce, sesame oil, rice wine, and garlic. Pour *half* the dressing on the barley and toss. Let the barley cool to room temperature.
5. Stir the mushrooms, carrots, and scallions into the barley along with the remaining dressing. Season with salt and pepper and toss well. Let marinate at least 1 hour before serving, or cover and chill up to 24 hours. Bring to room temperature before serving.

Chickpea Salad with Fennel, Tomatoes, and Olives

This is an ideal dish for a hot summer day because you can assemble it with no cooking at all. To complete the Mediterranean theme, serve this savory salad with French bread and goat cheese for a fabulous combination.

Serves 2–3 as a main course

The Dressing
1 tablespoon red wine vinegar
1 garlic clove, minced
½ teaspoon Dijon-style mustard
Salt
Generous seasoning freshly ground black pepper
3 tablespoons fruity olive oil

2 cups freshly cooked or canned chickpeas, rinsed thoroughly if canned
1 small fennel bulb, halved vertically and thinly sliced (1½ cups sliced); reserve feathery sprigs for garnish
2 ripe tomatoes, diced
10 black olives (your favorite kind), pitted and halved (see sidebar, opposite page)
½ cup thinly sliced red onion
⅓ cup chopped fresh parsley
2 tablespoons chopped fennel sprigs for garnish (see above)

1. To make the dressing, combine the vinegar, garlic, mustard, salt, and pepper in a large serving bowl and whisk to blend. Slowly whisk in the olive oil.
2. Stir in all the remaining ingredients except the fennel sprigs. Let the salad marinate at least 1 hour or up to 4 hours before serving. Garnish with fennel when ready to serve.

Olives

There are so many olives available that one can become dizzy from the choices. It seems pointless to list all the different varieties of olives because most stores don't label their olives with specific names.

When it comes to olives, you must find ones that suit your palate. What is wonderfully pungent to one person can be overwhelmingly caustic to another. I have found a fabulous black olive (sold locally) that I believe has been cured in brine but packed in a fruity, herb-laced olive oil. I can't get any information on these olives except from the huge can they are shipped in, which states only, "Greek Olives Packed in Oil." They are juicy, sweet, and meaty. To my taste, all other olives pale in comparison.

The best approach is to sample as many olives as you can, and stick to your favorites. If an olive is too dry, or salty, or pungent when you nibble on it, then chances are you won't enjoy it in a recipe.

Pitting Olives

It is not at all difficult to pit olives if you do it the following way: Put 1 olive on a heavy cutting board or other steady surface. Place the flat side of a large knife on the olive, then with your fist, thump the flat surface of the knife (the way you would remove the skin off garlic). This will loosen the pit, and now you can split the olive open with your fingers and remove the pit. Repeat this with the remaining olives, and you can count the pits to help you keep track of the number of olives you have prepared.

Tabbouli with Feta and Cucumbers

Bolstering traditional bulghur wheat salad with feta cheese and cucumber makes it into a substantial main-course salad teeming with flavor, color, and texture. There might appear to be an inordinate amount of parsley in this interpretation, but actually, classic tabbouli is a parsley salad with a little bulghur added, not the other way around.

Serves 4 as a main course

1 1/2 cups golden bulghur wheat (preferably coarse-cut), rinsed in a strainer
1/2 cucumber, peeled, seeded, and finely diced
2 scallions, very thinly sliced
1 1/2 cups very finely chopped fresh parsley
1 1/2 tablespoons minced fresh mint
3/4 cup (4 ounces) finely diced feta cheese

The Dressing
1/4 cup fresh lemon juice
1/3 cup olive oil
1/2 teaspoon salt
Generous seasoning freshly ground black pepper

1. Place the bulghur in a medium-size bowl. Pour enough boiling water over it to cover by about 1 inch. Cover the bowl with a plate and let the bulghur sit for 30 minutes. In batches, scoop up some bulghur into a strainer, then press out all of its liquid with the back of a large spoon. Dump this bulghur into a large bowl. Repeat with the remaining bulghur. (Alternatively, you can place batches of bulghur in a cotton kitchen towel, twist the towel into a ball, then squeeze out all the liquid.) Let the bulghur cool completely.
2. Stir the vegetables, herbs, and feta cheese into the bulghur.
3. Whisk the lemon juice, olive oil, salt, and pepper together in a medium-size bowl. Pour onto the tabbouli and toss to coat. Chill at least 1 hour or up to 8 hours before serving. Serve cool, not cold.

Mediterranean White Bean Salad

The sun-drenched flavors of tomatoes, yellow peppers, and arugula dazzle when this salad is made during the peak of summer with homegrown or local produce. If you are using canned beans, choose a small, firm, white variety such as Great Northern or navy beans because canned cannellini (white kidney beans) are too soft for this salad. Crusty Tuscan-style bread is the ideal accompaniment.

Serves 4 as a main course

4 cups freshly cooked or canned small white beans (such as navy or Great Northern), rinsed and well drained if canned (2 [16-ounce] cans)
2 perfectly ripe tomatoes, cored and finely diced
½ cup slivered red onion
1 yellow bell pepper, cut into thin 2-inch-long strips

The Dressing
¼ cup olive oil
2 tablespoons lemon juice
1 large garlic clove, put through a press or minced
¼ teaspoon salt
Generous seasoning freshly ground black pepper

2 cups torn-up pieces arugula

1. Place the beans, tomatoes, onion, and pepper in a large bowl.
2. Combine the dressing ingredients in a jar with a tight-fitting lid and shake vigorously. Pour the dressing on the salad and toss well. Let sit 1–4 hours to marinate.
3. Just before serving, add the arugula and toss to thoroughly coat with the dressing. Serve immediately.

Lentil and Arugula Salad with Feta Cheese

The slightly sweet tone of the balsamic dressing is a pleasing counterpoint to the peppery arugula and tangy feta cheese. This salad is wonderful as an entree with some crusty bread, or as a first course for a soup-centered meal.

Serves 4 as a main course

1 cup lentils

Balsamic Dressing
2 tablespoons balsamic vinegar
1 teaspoon Dijon-style mustard
1 large garlic clove, put through a press or minced
1/4 teaspoon salt
Generous seasoning freshly ground black pepper
1/4 cup olive oil

1 cup (5 ounces) finely cubed feta cheese
1/2 cup slivered red onion
1 cucumber, peeled, cut lengthwise and seeded, and cut into small dice
2 cups bite-size pieces arugula

1. Fill a medium-size saucepan with water and bring to a boil. Drop in the lentils and return the water to a boil, stirring occasionally. Reduce the heat a bit and cook the lentils about 20 minutes, or until tender but still slightly crunchy. Taste a few to be certain because you don't want mushy lentils.
2. Meanwhile combine the dressing ingredients in a jar with a tight-fitting lid and shake vigorously.
3. Drain the lentils in a colander and shake it a few times to remove all the liquid. Scrape the lentils into a large serving bowl, then pour on *half* the dressing. Toss to coat well.

Let the lentils cool to room temperature. (The lentils may be prepared to this point up to 8 hours in advance, covered, and chilled. Bring to room temperature before proceeding with the next step.)

4. Mix in the feta, onion, cucumber, arugula, and remaining dressing. Let sit at least 10 minutes but no more than 30 minutes before serving.

Soba Salad with Spicy Peanut Sauce

This spicy sauce has sweet overtones that go well with the nutty flavor of soba.

Serves 3–4 as a main course

1 pound soba (buckwheat spaghetti)

Peanut Sauce
1/3 cup natural-style peanut butter
1/4 cup tamari soy sauce
1 1/2 tablespoons pale dry sherry
3 tablespoons brown sugar
2 1/2 tablespoons oriental sesame oil
1 tablespoon water
2 teaspoons minced gingerroot
A few dashes cayenne

1 carrot, very finely chopped
2 scallions, very thinly sliced

1. Bring a large stockpot of water to a boil for the soba.
2. Meanwhile make the sauce. Combine the peanut butter and soy sauce in a medium-size bowl, and, using a fork, beat them together until smooth. Beat in all the remaining sauce ingredients.
3. Cook the soba until al dente, about 5 minutes. Taste a strand at about 4 minutes so you don't overcook it. It should still be chewy when done. You have to be careful not to overcook soba because the noodles will break into small pieces when you toss them with the sauce; on the other hand, you don't want them hard. Drain in a colander, then rinse the soba under cold running water. Drain again thoroughly.
4. Place the soba in a large serving bowl. Spoon on the sauce and toss thoroughly. Sprinkle the carrot and scallions over the top and serve.

Summer Spaghetti Salad

At the peak of summer when tomatoes and basil boast their glory by dazzling us with their splendid perfumes, that is the time to make this classic marinated salad. I like to start this early in the day so the flavors get a chance to meld.

Serves 4 as a main course

The Dressing
2 tablespoons red wine vinegar
3 large garlic cloves, minced
½ teaspoon salt
Generous seasoning freshly ground black pepper
⅓ cup olive oil

1 pound spaghetti
3 medium ripe tomatoes, cored, seeded, and finely diced
1 cup finely shredded fresh basil
1 cup chopped arugula *or* chopped fresh parsley
¼ cup toasted pine nuts

1. Bring a large stockpot of water to a boil.
2. Meanwhile combine the ingredients for the dressing in a jar with a tight-fitting lid and shake vigorously.
3. Drop the spaghetti into the boiling water and cook until al dente. Taste a strand to avoid overcooking. Drain very well in a colander, then place the spaghetti in a very large serving bowl. Pour on *half* the dressing and toss to thoroughly coat the strands. Let cool to room temperature, tossing occasionally.
4. Mix in the tomatoes, basil, arugula, pine nuts, and the remaining dressing and let marinate at least one hour or up to 8 hours before serving. If you chill the salad, bring it to room temperature before serving, then taste to see if it needs more salt.

Thai Noodle and Green Bean Salad

Mint, basil, and cilantro come together to create an enchanting backdrop to this sesame-flavored dish. I love all Asian-style noodles, but this is among my favorites for its intriguing blend of flavors.

Serves 4 as a main course

1 pound spaghetti

The Marinade

3 tablespoons peanut or canola oil
3 tablespoons oriental sesame oil
3 tablespoons lime juice
3 tablespoons tamari soy sauce
2 tablespoons brown sugar
3 garlic cloves, minced
2 teaspoons minced gingerroot
½ teaspoon crushed red pepper flakes
½ teaspoon salt

1 pound green beans, each cut in half
3 scallions, very thinly sliced
2 tablespoons finely shredded fresh basil
2 tablespoons finely chopped fresh mint
1 tablespoon finely chopped cilantro

1. Bring a large stockpot of water to a boil for the noodles. Meanwhile combine the marinade ingredients in a medium-size bowl and set aside.
2. Drop the green beans in the boiling water and cook just until tender yet still slightly crunchy, about 5 minutes. Taste one to test. Scoop out the green beans with a strainer or slotted spoon and place in a bowl filled with ice-cold water to stop any further cooking. Dump out the water and repeat until the green beans are cold throughout. (Taste one.)

Drain thoroughly and place the green beans in a large serving bowl. Stir in the scallions, basil, mint, and cilantro.

3. Drop the spaghetti into the boiling water and cook until al dente. Drain thoroughly in a colander, then rinse under cold water. Shake the colander vigorously to remove all excess water. Mix the spaghetti with the green bean mixture.

4. Pour the marinade on the noodles and toss gently with tongs. Tossing occasionally to coat it with sauce, let marinate at room temperature at least 2 hours or up to 24 hours before serving. (Cover and chill the noodles if longer than 4 hours, then bring to room temperature before serving.)

Mint

Mint has moseyed its way into my kitchen recently, mostly via Thai and Middle Eastern cooking, and I'm finding that it's an herb I now always want to have on hand. It lends such a cool, vibrant tone and harmonizes well with many other flavors. I grow spearmint in my garden, or rather this persistent, hardy herb grows itself. From the spring through the fall I can snip mint as I please.

But what about the winter? I have found a source for dried mint at my local health food store. It sells peppermint and spearmint in bulk, the latter almost always being my choice. In desperation I have even ripped open mint tea bags, and have, consequently, saved a recipe or two.

Add mint to the selection of herbs you cook with, and it won't be long before you find it indispensable to the dishes it enhances.

Ziti and Broccoli Salad with Sun-Dried Tomato Pesto

This is a hearty pasta salad with a robust sauce—just the thing you want when your "salad" is the main event.

Serves 4–6

1 pound ziti

The Pesto
2 ounces (about 13) loose sun-dried tomatoes
⅓ cup olive oil
2 garlic cloves, finely chopped
2 tablespoons chopped fresh basil, or 1 teaspoon dried
½ cup chopped fresh parsley
3 tablespoons finely chopped walnuts
2 tablespoons grated Parmesan cheese
½ teaspoon salt
Generous seasoning freshly ground black pepper

4–5 cups tiny broccoli florets (from 1 bunch broccoli)

1. Bring a large stockpot of water to a boil for the pasta.
2. To make the pesto, steam the sun-dried tomatoes in a vegetable steamer until they are soft, about 7 minutes. Remove and let cool to room temperature.
3. In a food processor combine the sun-dried tomatoes, olive oil, and garlic and process until smooth. Add the basil and parsley and pulse a few times to finely chop. Scrape the pesto into a bowl, then stir in the walnuts, Parmesan cheese, salt, and pepper by hand.
4. When the water comes to a boil, drop in the broccoli. Cook 2–3 minutes, or until crisp yet tender. Scoop out with a strainer and immerse it in a bowl of cold water to stop any further cooking. Drain the broccoli, then drop it onto a cotton kitchen towel and pat dry. Place in a large serving bowl.

5. Cook the ziti until al dente. Before you drain it, remove 1 tablespoon of the pasta water and stir it into the pesto. Drain the ziti in a colander, then rinse under cold running water. Shake the colander vigorously to remove all the water. Mix the ziti together with the broccoli.

6. Scrape the pesto onto the pasta and broccoli. Toss thoroughly to evenly coat it. Serve immediately or chill and let marinate up to 48 hours. Serve at room temperature.

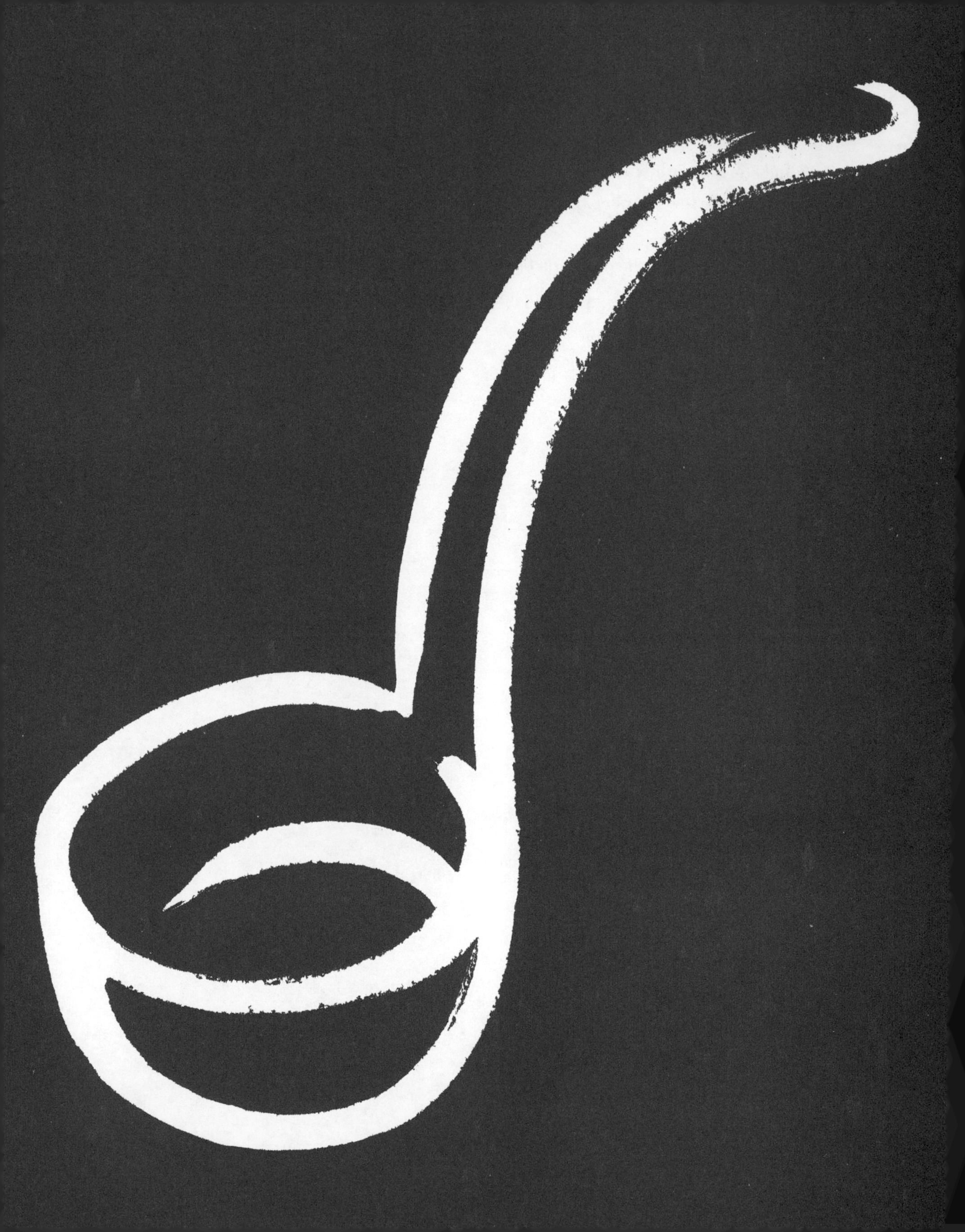

Substantial Soups

For the busy cook who wants to eat fresh, wholesome foods yet often finds herself in a last-minute crunch, few things in the kitchen can be more of a godsend than a pot of homemade soup in her refrigerator or freezer. Making soup is a task that all food lovers should embrace because it uses time at the stove so efficiently, while producing a one-pot meal that is nutritionally sound and restorative.

Furthermore, not many dishes we prepare actually benefit from sitting around a few days, but herein lies soup's greatest asset. If the busy cook can cultivate the habit of preparing a pot of soup when time allows, e.g., the weekend, then the reward for this advance thinking can be enjoyed throughout the week when time is in short supply. One can also easily multiply these benefits by doubling soup recipes and freezing a portion. It doesn't take twice the amount of time, perhaps only 10 extra minutes of chopping vegetables, yet the results of our efforts are significantly increased.

Because stock is the foundation of most soups and provides a layer of flavor upon which other flavors build, its value cannot be overestimated. This does not mean, however, that you must create your own stocks from scratch in order to have a delicious soup, but it does mean that you should search for a good-quality stock if you are going to use a store-bought product. (Read About Vegetable Stocks, page 11.)

So with a favorite soup stock in hand, a large pot, and a commitment to a bit of advance planning, let's make some soup!

Chickpea and Swiss Chard Soup with Parmesan Crostini

The building of layers of flavor in thick vegetable stews makes them especially inviting, but equally appealing to me are simple soups with just a few ingredients whose flavors are transported in a tasty broth. Although you can enjoy this soup just after you make it, it will benefit from being made a few hours in advance so the stock can really develop the garlicky undertones.

Serves 4 as a main course

1/4 cup olive oil
1 medium onion, very finely diced
8 garlic cloves, minced
1/4 teaspoon crushed red pepper flakes
8 cups vegetable stock, store-bought or homemade (page 13)
2 tablespoons tomato paste mixed with 1/2 cup water
4 cups freshly cooked or canned chickpeas, well rinsed and drained if canned (2 [16-ounce] cans)
8 cups (about 3/4 pound) finely shredded Swiss chard leaves
1 teaspoon salt

Parmesan Crostini
8 thin slices French bread
1 tablespoon olive oil
1 1/2 tablespoons grated Parmesan cheese

1. Heat the oil in a large stockpot over medium heat. Add the onion and cook, stirring often, for 3 minutes. Mix in the garlic and crushed pepper flakes and sauté 5 minutes, or until the onion is tender.
2. Add the stock, tomato paste mixture, and chickpeas and bring to a boil. Reduce the heat to a lively simmer and cook 10 minutes. Stir in the Swiss chard and salt and simmer 10 minutes.

3. Remove 2 cups of the soup and puree it in a blender or food processor. Return it to the pot.

4. To make the crostini, preheat the oven to 300 degrees. Using a pastry brush, lightly brush both sides of each French bread slice with some olive oil. Place them on a baking sheet and bake 5 minutes. Turn them over and bake 5 more minutes. Sprinkle the Parmesan cheese on top of each crostini, and return the crostini to the oven. Bake 5 minutes or until golden all over. Let cool completely before serving alongside the soup.

Mediterranean Vegetable Soup with Feta Cheese

As odd as it may sound, this soup's hauntingly good flavor is reminiscent of bouillabaisse, even though that soup is based on seafood. The interplay of fennel, tomato, and white wine creates a sensational broth that begs for crusty French bread to be dipped into it. Leftover fennel can be used another day in such recipes as Green Leaf Salad with Fennel, Apple, and Pecans (page 72), or Chickpea Salad with Fennel, Tomatoes, and Olives (page 94), or Leek, Fennel, and Goat Cheese Frittata (page 170).

Serves 4 as a main course

3 tablespoons olive oil
2 onions, very finely diced
6 garlic cloves, minced
1/4 teaspoon crushed red pepper flakes
1 cup dry white wine
1 (16-ounce) can tomatoes, very finely chopped with their juice
6 cups vegetable stock, store-bought or homemade (page 13)
1 1/2 cups thinly sliced fennel (from 1/2 medium bulb), reserve feathery sprigs
1/2 teaspoon dried oregano
1/2 teaspoon salt
Generous seasoning freshly ground black pepper
1/3 cup orzo (rice-shaped pasta)
1/2 cup chopped fresh parsley
1/2–3/4 cup crumbled feta cheese
1/3 cup chopped fennel sprigs (see above)

1. Heat the oil in a large stockpot over medium heat. Add the onions, garlic, and red pepper flakes and sauté, stirring frequently, until the onions are tender, about 10 minutes.
2. Pour in the wine and boil until reduced by half. Stir in the tomatoes, stock, fennel, oregano, salt, and pepper and bring to a boil. Cook the soup 20 minutes, stirring occasionally.

3. Mix in the orzo and parsley and cook 10 minutes more. Serve the stew in bowls with about 1 tablespoon of feta cheese sprinkled on top of each serving, then top with some chopped fennel sprigs.

Don't Skip the Parsley

We are all guilty of allowing little bundles of fresh herbs to wilt and perish in our refrigerators because of neglect and forgetfulness. But this should never happen to parsley. It has such a fresh and compatible flavor that it can enhance almost anything, and so should disappear rather quickly.

Before the days when fresh herbs were readily available in the United States, dried parsley was used as a garnish and flavor was not an expectation. One could easily omit the parsley and the dish wouldn't suffer. This has all changed with the availability of fresh herbs in the American kitchen. We can now appreciate parsley as the ancient Greeks did, who prized it for medicinal purposes; the Romans enjoyed it as a culinary herb.

The vivid, harmonious flavor of fresh parsley enhances any dish in which it's included. Parsley doesn't usually define the character of a dish the way basil or other assertive herbs can; however, it accents the surrounding flavors with a welcome piquancy while providing a tone of freshness.

I purchase or grow flat-leaf Italian parsley rather than the curly-leaf variety because I prefer its appearance and find that it chops into more attractive pieces. I doubt that one could discern a difference in flavor between the two, although many cooks claim they can. Parsley is one green that I wash before storing in the refrigerator; that way it is readily available to use in soups, salads, sandwich spreads, and sauces. It will store better than most greens and herbs if it is spun dry in a salad spinner, then stored in a plastic bag with a paper towel placed at the bottom of the bag to absorb any excess moisture.

So don't skip the parsley; it adds a delicious supporting flavor to your dish.

Kale, Butternut Squash, and White Bean Soup

Three highly nutritious foods come together in this soup, lending it vibrant color and flavor. For a fitting accompaniment, try Crostini (page 16) spread with goat cheese.

Serves 4–6 as a main course

1/3 cup olive oil
2 large onions, diced
10 cups vegetable stock, store-bought or homemade (page 13)
1 cup finely diced canned tomatoes, with their liquid
2 teaspoons finely chopped fresh rosemary, or 1/2 teaspoon dried
1/2 teaspoon salt
Generous seasoning freshly ground black pepper
1 tiny butternut squash (1 pound), peeled, seeded, and diced (2 cups diced)
2 cups freshly cooked or canned small white beans, well rinsed if canned
1/2 pound kale (weight with stems), ripped off its stems and leaves cut into shreds (chiffonade) (4 cups shredded leaves)
Grated Parmesan cheese (optional)

1. Heat the oil in a large stockpot over medium heat. Add the onions and sauté until tender, about 10 minutes.

2. Stir in the stock, tomatoes, rosemary, salt, and pepper and bring to a boil. Add the squash and reduce the heat to a lively simmer. Cook 30 minutes, or until the squash is tender.

3. Add the beans and kale and cook 15 more minutes. Serve with grated Parmesan cheese, if desired.

Split Pea and Barley Soup

My neighbor, Clare Ward, gave me the idea of adding barley to split pea soup and it has proven to be just one more demonstration of her finely tuned palate. The creamy backdrop of pea soup is delightful with the nubbiness of barley. This soup has become a cold-weather favorite in our house, its appeal further enhanced by the fact that I always seem to have these ingredients on hand.

Serves 4

14 cups water
1 pound green split peas
½ cup barley, rinsed in a strainer
1 tablespoon olive oil
1 bay leaf
2 tablespoons unsalted butter
2 medium onions, diced
4 garlic cloves, minced
2 carrots, finely diced
1 celery rib, finely diced
1 teaspoon fresh thyme, or ½ teaspoon dried
1 teaspoon salt
Freshly ground black pepper to taste

1. In a large stockpot combine the water, split peas, barley, olive oil, and bay leaf. Bring to a boil, stirring occasionally, then reduce the heat to a lively simmer. Cook the soup, continuing to stir periodically, for 30 minutes.
2. Meanwhile melt the butter in a medium-size skillet over medium heat. Add the onions and garlic and sauté until the onions are golden brown, about 10 minutes.

3. Stir the onions into the soup along with the carrots, celery, thyme, salt, and pepper. Cook, now stirring frequently to prevent the soup from sticking as it thickens, for 30 more minutes. The soup is ready when the peas have almost totally dissolved and the barley and vegetables are tender. The soup will thicken as it cools in the serving bowls, so thin it with more water if necessary so that its consistency resembles heavy cream. Remove and discard the bay leaf before serving the soup.

Creamy White Bean Soup with Red Pepper Swirl

This luscious soup has a rich, silken texture. The red pepper swirl is achieved by spooning a small amount of red pepper puree on the center of each portion and using a knife to swirl it around.

I prefer to use a blender rather than a food processor for both the red peppers and the soup because it produces a perfectly smooth texture—just what you want for this graceful soup.

Serves 4 as a main course

3 tablespoons fruity olive oil
2 large onions, diced
2 celery ribs, thinly sliced*
6 garlic cloves, minced
6 cups vegetable stock, store-bought or homemade (page 13)
6 cups freshly cooked or canned cannellini (white kidney beans), rinsed well in a strainer if canned (3 [15-ounce] cans)
1 tablespoon red wine vinegar
½ teaspoon chopped fresh rosemary, or ¼ teaspoon dried, crumbled
½ teaspoon salt
Generous seasoning freshly ground black pepper

Red Pepper Puree

1 cup roasted red peppers, freshly roasted (page 19) or from 1 (7-ounce) jar, drained
1 garlic clove, minced

1. Heat the oil in a large stockpot over medium-high heat. Add the onions and celery and sauté until they begin to brown, about 10 minutes. Stir in the garlic and cook 5 minutes, stirring often. (The browning of these vegetables will flavor the soup, so keep the heat high enough to achieve that color.)

**Celery is an essential flavor in this soup, so don't omit it.*

2. Add the stock, beans, vinegar, rosemary, salt, and pepper. Bring the soup to a boil, then reduce the heat to a simmer. Cook 20 minutes, or until the celery is very soft.

3. Meanwhile make the red pepper puree by combining the red peppers and garlic in a blender and pureeing them. Scrape the mixture into a small bowl. Rinse out the blender container.

4. In batches puree the soup until it is perfectly smooth. You can pour the pureed batches into a smaller saucepan at this point. The thickness of the finished soup should be like heavy cream; thin with some stock if it is too thick.

5. To serve, ladle the soup into bowls. Spoon a generous mound of red pepper puree in the center. Using a knife, swirl the puree to make a lovely design, such as irregular radiating lines from the center.

Butternut Squash Soup

I created this delicious soup on an unforgiving day in March when it seemed as if spring would never come. It was a burst of sunshine in a bowl, bolstered by that savory trio of parsley, garlic, and Parmesan cheese. This is not a smooth soup, as are most versions with butternut squash, but rather cubes of squash with rice and a generous amount of parsley afloat in a delicious broth. The ginger only slightly accents the soup without dominating it, so be sure to include it.

Serves 4 as a main course

¼ cup olive oil
2 large onions, finely diced
6 garlic cloves, minced
1 teaspoon minced gingerroot
10 cups vegetable stock, store-bought or homemade (page 13)
6 cups (2½ pounds) diced butternut squash (½-inch dice)
½ cup white rice, preferably converted or basmati
1 teaspoon salt
Generous seasoning freshly ground black pepper
1 cup minced fresh parsley
Grated Parmesan cheese

1. Heat the oil in a large stockpot over medium heat. Add the onions, garlic, and gingerroot and sauté until the onions are golden, about 10 minutes.
2. Pour in the stock and bring it to a boil. Stir in the squash, rice, salt, and pepper and bring the soup again to a boil, stirring often. Reduce it to a simmer, then cook it about 45 minutes, or until the squash and rice are very tender.
3. Remove about 2 cups of the soup and puree it in a blender or processor. Return it to the soup pot. Taste to correct the seasoning. Just before serving, stir in the parsley. Serve in bowls with a generous spoonful of grated Parmesan sprinkled on top.

Kale and Potato Soup

Such a simple soup yet so satisfying and flavorful. Caldo verde, the classic Portuguese soup, is very similar to this version; however, I've omitted the common addition of sausage and mimicked its flavor with this light garlic broth, which wonderfully enhances the kale and potatoes without overpowering them.

When I've been overindulging because of a long stretch of company, or holiday festivities, or too many restaurant meals in a row, I inevitably turn to this soup for its restorative qualities. Kale simmered in broth tenderizes that leafy green—one of my all-time favorite vegetables—and brings out its best qualities.

Serves 3–4 as a main course

3 tablespoons olive oil
4 garlic cloves, minced
1/4 teaspoon crushed red pepper flakes
8 cups vegetable stock, store-bought or homemade (page 13)
2 medium boiling (waxy) potatoes, peeled and finely diced (2 cups diced)
1/2 pound kale (weight with stems), leaves ripped off stems and finely shredded (about 7 cups shredded)
1/2 teaspoon salt

1. Heat the oil in a large stockpot over medium heat. Add the garlic and red pepper flakes and cook 1 minute. Do not let the garlic get at all brown. Pour in the stock, raise the heat to high, then bring to a boil.

2. Add the potatoes, lower the heat to a lively simmer, and cook 15 minutes. Stir in the kale and salt and cook the soup 15 more minutes.

Fresh Tomato Corn Soup

This is a splendid summer soup whose success is completely dependent upon juicy, ripe tomatoes at their peak and sweet ears of fresh corn. It will fill your house with an irresistible aroma, yet all it needs is about a half hour of cooking. Although it is not at all fussy to prepare this low-fat soup, you will need a food mill to puree and strain it. And don't hesitate to try this recipe if you've never cut corn off its cob; it couldn't be easier to do.

Serves 4 as a main course

2 tablespoons unsalted butter
2 large onions, chopped
4 garlic cloves, chopped
1 celery rib (preferably with leaves attached), chopped
1 carrot, finely chopped
½ cup chopped parsley
3 pounds (5 very large) ripe tomatoes, cored and chopped
4 cups Tomato-Scallion Stock (page 14), or vegetable stock, store-bought or homemade (page 13)
½ teaspoon sugar
1 teaspoon salt
Generous seasoning freshly ground black pepper
2 ears corn, shucked
Shredded basil for garnish

1. Melt the butter in a large stockpot over medium-high heat. Add the onions, garlic, celery, and carrot and sauté, tossing frequently, until the vegetables begin to get brown, about 10 minutes.
2. Stir in the parsley, tomatoes, stock, sugar, salt, and pepper. Bring the soup to a boil, then reduce the heat to a lively simmer, and cook the soup 20 minutes. Let the soup cool.

3. While the soup is cooling, cut the kernels off the cob by standing the cob on its wide end and slicing the kernels off from the tip of the cob to the bottom.
4. In batches put the soup through a food mill, then discard the solids that remain. Drop the corn in the soup, then return it to a boil. Cook 10 minutes, or until the corn is tender yet still slightly crunchy. Serve in bowls, with a few shreds of basil as a garnish.

Curried Red Lentil Soup with Coconut Milk

Two of my other cookbooks have recipes for curried red lentil soup because I am so enamored of this delicious legume and its natural mating with curry. This version contains coconut milk and lime juice, which make it an even more spectacular soup. You'll love this triumphant blending of flavors.

Serves 4 as a main course

4 cups water
1 tablespoon vegetable oil
1 1/2 cups red lentils, rinsed in a strainer
3/4 teaspoon salt
4 cups very hot water
2 1/2 cups unsweetened desiccated coconut (see Note)
1 tablespoon unsalted butter
1 onion, diced
4 garlic cloves, minced
1 teaspoon minced fresh gingerroot
1 teaspoon turmeric
1 teaspoon ground coriander
1 teaspoon ground cumin
Dash cayenne
Juice of 1 lime

1. Combine the water, oil, lentils, and salt in a 3-quart saucepan and bring to a boil, stirring occasionally. Reduce the heat to a simmer and cook 20 minutes, stirring often.
2. Meanwhile make the coconut milk by combining the hot water and coconut in a blender or food processor and blending it for 2 minutes. In batches, pour it through a strainer over a large bowl and press out as much milk as you can from the coconut by

using the back of a large spoon. Discard the coconut pulp. Mix the coconut milk into the lentil mixture and simmer 20 minutes, stirring frequently.

3. Melt the butter in a medium-size skillet over medium heat. Add the onion, garlic, and ginger and sauté until the onion is golden brown, about 10 minutes. Sprinkle in the spices and "toast" them 2 minutes. Scrape this mixture into the soup, then add the juice of the lime. Cook the soup 10 more minutes, stirring often. The soup is done when the lentils have dissolved. (If you make the soup in advance—a good idea to help develop the flavors—it will get thick when it cools. After reheating it over low heat, check the consistency. If it is too thick, thin it with a little water.)

Note: Unsweetened desiccated coconut can be purchased at natural foods stores and some specialty shops. It will last up to a year in the refrigerator.

Leek and Potato Chowder

In the fall and winter when the price of leeks goes down, I am eager to make this simple yet delicious chowder because it so splendidly spotlights the incomparable sweet flavor of leeks, one of my favorite vegetables. This recipe doubles or triples easily, so don't hesitate to make it for a crowd, if the occasion arises.

Serves 3 as a main course

3 large leeks
2 tablespoons unsalted butter
3 cups light vegetable stock, store-bought or homemade (page 13)
3 medium-large boiling (waxy) potatoes, peeled and finely cubed
1 teaspoon salt
Generous seasoning freshly ground black pepper
1 1/4 cups milk
1/4 cup sour cream
Minced parsley or chives for garnish

1. To clean the leeks, cut off and discard their root ends plus all the dark green leaves except for 2 inches closest to the white part. Cut the leeks in half lengthwise, then rinse them thoroughly under cold running water, flipping through the leaves to rid them of *all* sand. Thinly slice the leeks.
2. Heat the butter in a large stockpot over medium heat. Sauté the leeks until tender, about 10 minutes. Do not let them get brown. Add the stock, potatoes, salt, and pepper and bring to a boil. Partially cover the pot and cook the soup about 20 minutes, or until the potatoes are tender.
3. Puree about two thirds of the soup in a food processor or blender and return it to the pot. Stir in the milk and sour cream. Reheat until hot, but do not let the soup boil. Serve in bowls with parsley or chives sprinkled on top.

Mixed Mushroom and Barley Soup

Mushroom lovers take note—a mixture of exotic and common mushrooms creates a tantalizing broth that becomes a veritable balm on a frosty evening. Do try to make this soup in advance—at least 6 hours or preferably 1–2 days—because the mushroom flavor will be intensified, and that can only mean more of a good thing.

Serves 4 as a main course

3 tablespoons olive oil
2 medium onions, finely diced
4 garlic cloves, minced
½ pound common white button mushrooms, coarsely chopped into almond-size pieces
½ pound exotic mushrooms, such as shiitake, portobello, and oyster mushrooms, coarsely chopped into almond-size pieces
10 cups Mushroom Stock (page 15) or vegetable stock, either store-bought or homemade (page 13)
½ cup barley, rinsed in a strainer
2 carrots, finely chopped
2 tablespoons tamari soy sauce
2 tablespoons dry sherry
1 teaspoon fresh thyme, or ½ teaspoon dried
½ teaspoon salt
Generous seasoning freshly ground pepper

1. In a large stockpot heat the oil over medium-high heat. Add the onions and garlic and sauté until the onions turn golden brown, at least 10 minutes.
2. Stir in the mushrooms and sauté until they become brown, about 10 minutes. Stir often and scrape the bottom of the pot to loosen those tasty bits that adhere to the pot.
3. Mix in all the remaining ingredients and bring to a boil. Lower the heat to a lively simmer, cover the pan, and cook 45–60 minutes, or until the barley is tender. If the soup is too thick, thin with a little stock.

Peanut Soup

Here's a delicious African-inspired, non-dairy soup with a lot of flavor. I prefer to puree it in a food processor rather than in a blender because the processor allows the peanut butter to retain a little texture.

Serves 4–6

2 tablespoons canola oil
6 garlic cloves, minced
3 medium onions, finely diced
2 celery ribs, thinly sliced
3 carrots, finely diced
A few dashes cayenne pepper (or more to taste)
6 cups vegetable stock, store-bought or homemade (page 13)
½ teaspoon salt
Generous seasoning freshly ground pepper
1 cup plus 2 tablespoons natural-style peanut butter
1 ½ teaspoons tamari soy sauce
Juice of 1 lemon
1 ½ teaspoons brown sugar
Minced cilantro or fresh parsley for garnish

1. Heat the oil in a large stockpot over medium heat. Add the garlic and onions and sauté until the onions begin to soften, about 5 minutes. Add the celery and carrots and sauté, stirring often, until the vegetables begin to brown, about 10 minutes.
2. Stir in the cayenne, stock, salt, and pepper and bring to a boil. Lower the heat and simmer 10 minutes. Whisk in the peanut butter, then remove the soup from the heat.
3. In batches, puree the soup in a food processor until somewhat smooth, but with a little texture remaining. Return it to the pot. Stir in the soy sauce, lemon juice, and brown sugar. Serve in bowls with a little cilantro or parsley as a garnish.

Sweet Potato and Peanut Soup

The peanuts are barely discernible in this savory soup, yet provide an important layer of flavoring. Both fresh ginger and ground ginger bolster it all to make this a tonic on a chilly fall or winter night.

Serves 4 as a main course

2 tablespoons olive oil
4 garlic cloves, minced
1 tablespoon minced gingerroot
3 large onions, diced
2 tablespoons dry-roasted unsalted peanuts, plus finely chopped peanuts for garnish
½ teaspoon ground (powdered) ginger
6 cups vegetable stock (plus extra for thinning), store-bought or homemade (page 13)
3 large yams or sweet potatoes (2½ pounds), peeled and cut into ½-inch dice
1 tablespoon brown sugar
Pinch cinnamon
1 teaspoon salt
Generous seasoning freshly ground black pepper
1 tablespoon unsalted butter

1. In a large stockpot heat the oil over medium-high heat. Add the garlic, gingerroot, onions, and peanuts and sauté, stirring often, until the onions begin to brown, at least 10 minutes. Sprinkle on the ground ginger, toss, and cook 1 minute.
2. Stir in the stock, yams, brown sugar, cinnamon, salt, and pepper. Partially cover the pot, and cook the soup until the yams are soft, about 20 minutes.
3. Let the soup cool slightly, then remove about 2 cups of it and set that portion aside. Puree the soup in a few batches and return it to the pot. Stir in the reserved soup and the butter. Reheat the soup and check its consistency; it should be like heavy cream. Serve in bowls and garnish with some chopped peanuts.

Spinach Soup with Couscous and Lemon

The tender, fluffy texture of couscous lends a delicate touch to this tasty soup. If possible, make it early in the day so the flavors have a chance to develop.

Serves 4–6 as a main course

2 tablespoons olive oil
4 garlic cloves, minced
2 shallots, finely diced
10 cups vegetable stock, store-bought or homemade (page 13)
½ cup couscous
2 cups freshly cooked or canned chickpeas, rinsed thoroughly and well drained if canned
1 (1-pound) bunch or 1 (10-ounce) package fresh spinach, washed, stems discarded, and leaves torn into small pieces, about 10 cups
1 cup chopped fresh parsley
6 scallions, very thinly sliced
1 tablespoon chopped fresh dill, or 1 teaspoon dried
1 teaspoon salt
Generous seasoning freshly ground black pepper
Juice of 1 lemon
1 tablespoon unsalted butter

1. Heat the oil in a large stockpot over medium heat. Add the garlic and shallots and cook 2 minutes, stirring often. Pour in the stock and bring it to a boil.
2. Stir in the couscous and chickpeas and cook at medium heat for 10 minutes, stirring often. Add the spinach, parsley, *half* the scallions, the dill, salt, and pepper. Cook the soup 10 more minutes, stirring frequently. (The soup can be prepared to this point up to 2 days in advance.)
3. Just before serving stir in the lemon juice, butter, and remaining scallions.

Black Bean Chili

This gutsy chili, which is so easy to prepare, could be the perfect antidote to a chilly (no pun intended) evening. Hot buttered corn bread could only make things better.

Serves 6

2 tablespoons olive oil
6 garlic cloves, minced
2 onions, very finely diced
1/4 teaspoon crushed red pepper flakes
1 tablespoon chili powder
1 tablespoon ground cumin
1 teaspoon dried oregano
1 bay leaf
1 (28-ounce) can imported plum tomatoes, finely chopped with their juice
1 tablespoon tamari soy sauce
3 cups water
3 tablespoons tomato paste
3/4 teaspoon salt
8 cups freshly cooked (1 1/2 pounds dry) or 4 (15-ounce) cans black beans, rinsed and well drained if canned
1 tablespoon red wine vinegar
Minced parsley for garnish

1. Heat the oil in a large stockpot over medium heat. Add the garlic, onions, and red pepper flakes and cook 1 minute. Stir in the chili powder and cumin and cook 2 minutes, stirring often.
2. Stir in all the remaining ingredients except the parsley and bring to a boil. Reduce the heat to a lively simmer and cook about 30 minutes, or until the chili is thick but not pasty. Remove the bay leaf. Serve in bowls and garnish with the parsley.

Sweet Potato Chili

I'm sure many Tex-Mex aficionados are appalled by the liberties cooks have taken with chili in recent years, but I find the temptation to experiment with new versions hard to resist. Here, sweet potatoes provide a lively contrast in flavor to the spicy backdrop of chili, and together with the vegetables and beans create a dazzling palette of color. Because the sweet potatoes take the place of a portion of beans that would normally be in this amount of chili, you'll find this version lighter than the traditional bean-laden rendition, but just as infused with flavor.

Serves 4–6

3 tablespoons canola oil
2 large onions, finely diced
6 garlic cloves, minced
1 red bell pepper, finely diced
1 green bell pepper, finely diced
1 ½ tablespoons chili powder
1 ½ teaspoons ground cumin
1 teaspoon dried oregano
5 cups water
1 (28-ounce) can imported plum tomatoes, finely chopped with their juice
¼ cup tomato paste, thinned with ¼ cup water
2 medium-large sweet potatoes (preferably yams), peeled and cut into ½-inch dice
2 (15-ounce) cans black beans, rinsed and well drained in a strainer
¾ teaspoon salt
Chopped cilantro or Sofrito (page 152) to taste for garnish (optional)

1. Heat the oil in a large stockpot over medium heat. Add the onions and garlic and sauté, stirring frequently, until the onions begin to brown, at least 10 minutes. Stir in the 2 bell peppers and cook 10 minutes, stirring often.

2. Sprinkle on the chili powder and cumin and cook the spices 2 minutes, stirring continuously. Stir in all the remaining ingredients—except the cilantro or Sofrito—and bring the mixture to a boil. Cook 15 minutes or so, or just until the sweet potatoes are tender. Stir the soup occasionally and be certain to scrape the bottom of the pot to dislodge any flavorful food bits that might be stuck there. Serve with some cilantro or Sofrito sprinkled on top, if desired.

P
B
S
Q

Pizzas, Burgers, Sandwiches, Quesadillas, Etc.

Here is a hodgepodge of collations that can be just the right solution to those times when a full dinner seems too heavy and a salad is not quite enough. These are casual, fun foods that are eaten handheld. They can be extended with a salad or followed by a special dessert if you have the time and desire to make them, but could also suffice on their own. If you are having a friend over for lunch, choose something from this chapter to make it simple but special. What these meals lack in formality they make up in flavor.

See also: *Mock Chicken Salad (page* 458*)*
Curried Tofu "Eggless" Salad (page 459*)*
Barbecued Tempeh Spread (page 466*)*
Hummus (page 310*)*

Thin Crisp Tortilla Pizzas with Tomatoes and Goat Cheese

Using a flour tortilla as a base for pizza gives you an ultra-thin crust.

Serves 2–4

4 (8-inch) flour (wheat) tortillas
1½ tablespoons olive oil

The Topping
2½ cups grated part-skim mozzarella cheese
4 plum tomatoes, sliced
2 garlic cloves, minced
2 tablespoons olive oil
½ teaspoon dried basil
½ cup crumbled soft mild goat cheese

1. Preheat the oven to 375 degrees. Using 2 baking sheets, place 2 tortillas side by side on each sheet. With a pastry brush, lightly brush each tortilla with some of the olive oil. Flip the tortillas over and brush again. Bake 8–10 minutes, flipping over the tortillas and alternating the placement of the baking sheets halfway through the cooking time. Also, during the first few minutes, use a knife point to pop any air bubbles that might develop. The tortillas should be golden and crisp when done. (The tortillas may be prepared to this point up to 3 days in advance. Cool completely. Seal in a plastic bag and refrigerate until ready to use.)
2. Sprinkle the mozzarella evenly over the 4 tortillas. Place the tomatoes over the cheese.
3. Combine the garlic, olive oil, and basil and drizzle the mixture over the tomatoes.
4. Bake about 12 minutes, or until the cheese is bubbly. Alternate the placement of the baking sheets halfway during the cooking time. Remove the pizzas from the oven, then sprinkle bits of goat cheese all over their tops. Cut and serve immediately.

Tortilla Pizzas with Jalapeño Cheese and Roasted Peppers

The double impact of jalapeño peppers and blazing roasted red peppers electrifies these pizzas. A glass of cold beer alongside them would be welcome.

Serves 2–4

4 (8-inch) flour (wheat) tortillas
1½ tablespoons olive oil

The Topping
3 cups grated Monterey Jack cheese with jalapeño peppers
20 black olives (your favorite kind), pitted and halved (see page 95)
½ cup diced roasted red peppers, store-bought or freshly roasted (page 19)

1. Preheat the oven to 375 degrees. Prepare and precook the tortillas as for Thin Crisp Tortilla Pizzas with Tomatoes and Goat Cheese (step 1, opposite page).
2. Sprinkle the cheese on the tortillas. Top with the olives and peppers. Bake about 12 minutes, or until the cheese is bubbly. Alternate the placement of the baking sheets halfway during the cooking time. Cut and serve immediately.

Tortilla Pizzas with Feta Cheese, Zucchini, and Tomatoes

This could become a United Nations favorite—a Greek-style pizza on a tortilla! Three cultures represented in harmony.

Serves 2–4

4 (8-inch) flour (wheat) tortillas
1½ tablespoons olive oil

The Topping
4 plum tomatoes, thinly sliced
2 small zucchini, very thinly sliced
6 ounces (about 1⅓ cups) finely crumbled feta cheese
2 teaspoons dried oregano
3 tablespoons olive oil
Generous seasoning freshly ground black pepper

1. Preheat the oven to 375 degrees. Prepare and precook the tortillas as for Thin Crisp Tortilla Pizzas with Tomatoes and Goat Cheese (step 1, page 134).
2. Lay the tomato slices in one layer all over each tortilla. Spread the zucchini slices in one layer over the tomatoes (you might have some leftover zucchini slices).
3. In a medium-size bowl combine the feta cheese, oregano, olive oil, and pepper. Toss gently. With your fingers sprinkle the mixture evenly over the zucchini and tomato slices.
4. Bake about 12 minutes, or until the feta is sizzling and the zucchini is softened. Alternate the placement of the baking sheets halfway during the cooking time. Cut and serve immediately.

Beer Pizza

This pizza crust is a riot! My friend Geri Rybacki told me about this crust and I'm always amazed that it works so well. The beer lends the dough a yeasty flavor and contributes to its lightness. Just be certain to roll or pat it very thinly and cook it until golden brown.

Makes 2 (11–12-inch) pizzas

3 cups unbleached flour, plus extra for dusting
1 tablespoon baking powder
½ teaspoon salt
1 (12-ounce) bottle or can light or dark beer
Olive oil for greasing
3 cups grated part-skim mozzarella cheese
Toppings of your choice: diced tomatoes, garlic, sliced olives, mushrooms, peppers, etc.

1. Preheat the oven to 450 degrees. Combine the flour, baking powder, and salt in a large bowl and mix thoroughly. Pour in the beer and mix well. The dough will be sticky.
2. Spread a handful of flour on your work surface and dump the dough onto it. Toss the dough around to coat with the flour and prevent it from sticking. Knead it 2 or 3 times to make it pliable. Shape the dough into a ball, then divide it to make 2.
3. Lightly grease 2 baking sheets. Use a rolling pin to roll each ball into an 11- or 12-inch circle, or place the balls on the baking sheets and use your hands to flatten them into 11- or 12-inch circles. (If you are not ready to cook the pizza now, you can place the pans directly in the freezer to stop any rising action in the dough. Remove from the freezer about 30 minutes before cooking.)
4. I like to cook 1 pizza at a time, but you can cook the pizzas on 2 different oven racks and alternate them halfway through the cooking. Sprinkle 1½ cups of cheese on each crust. Top with the toppings of your choice. (Alternatively, you can make a traditional version with pizza sauce underneath the cheese—just be certain to spread a *thin* layer.)
5. Bake 12–15 minutes, or until golden brown on top and underneath.

Mixed Pepper Calzones

Calzones are essentially stuffed pizza turnovers. Frozen pizza dough works very well as a wrapping because it has a chance to get brown and chewy and so its texture is enhanced. If you can't get your hands on goat cheese, ricotta cheese is also delicious in these piquant calzones.

Makes 4 calzones

1 tablespoon olive oil, plus extra for brushing
1/8 teaspoon crushed red pepper flakes
1 green bell pepper, cut into thin 2-inch strips
1 red bell pepper, cut into thin 2-inch strips
1 medium onion, halved vertically and very thinly sliced
1/4 teaspoon dried thyme
Salt
Freshly ground black pepper to taste
1 cup (4 ounces) finely cubed part-skim mozzarella cheese
5 ounces soft mild goat cheese, crumbled
1 pound frozen bread (pizza) dough, thawed
Flour for dusting

1. Heat the tablespoon of oil in a large skillet over medium heat. Add the pepper flakes and cook 30 seconds. Mix in the 2 peppers, onion, thyme, salt, and pepper. Sauté the mixture, tossing often, until the vegetables are soft and brown, about 15 minutes. Scrape into a medium-size bowl and let cool completely. You can put it in the refrigerator or freezer to hasten the cooling, but keep an eye on it if you put it in the freezer so that it doesn't freeze.
2. When the mixture is cooled stir in the 2 cheeses. Preheat the oven to 375 degrees. Lightly grease a baking sheet.
3. Divide the pizza dough in four and roll each portion into a ball. Place a small bowl of

water in front of you. Dust your work surface with a little flour. With a rolling pin roll a ball of dough into a 7-inch circle, dusting the dough with flour as necessary. Dip your finger in the water and moisten the outer edge of the dough circle. Place one quarter of the pepper-cheese mixture on half of the dough, then fold the remaining dough over to make a turnover. Carefully pinch together and fold over the edges of the dough to make a tight seal. Repeat with the remaining 3 portions.

4. Place the calzones on the baking sheet. With your fingers lightly coat the top of each calzone with a little oil. Bake 25 minutes, or until golden brown. Let sit at least 10 minutes before serving, for they will be too hot to eat before then.

Spicy Garlic and Potato Calzones

Potatoes and garlic are a match made in heaven. The potatoes soak up this garlicky sauté and come to life, making a delectable filling. Calzones reheat extremely well, so if you have any left over, you can look forward to them for another lunch or dinner.

Makes 4

2 1/4 cups diced (1/4 inch) peeled boiling potatoes (about 2 medium-large)
2 tablespoons olive oil, plus extra for brushing
4 fat garlic cloves, minced
1/4 teaspoon crushed red pepper flakes
1 tomato, cored, seeded, and finely cubed
Generous seasoning salt
1 cup (4 ounces) finely cubed part-skim mozzarella cheese
Flour for dusting
1 pound frozen bread (pizza) dough, thawed

1. Place the potatoes in a large skillet with about 2 inches of water. Cover the pan and bring to a boil. Reduce to a simmer and cook until the potatoes are tender, about 10 minutes. Drain the potatoes in a colander.
2. Wipe the skillet clean, then pour in the 2 tablespoons olive oil. Place over medium heat. Add the garlic and crushed red pepper flakes and cook 30 seconds. Mix in the tomato and cook, tossing often, until the tomato is soft, about 2 minutes. Stir in the potatoes, season generously with salt, and cook another 2 minutes, or until the mixture is hot and sizzling. Remove from the heat and cool completely. (This mixture can be prepared up to 8 hours in advance.)
3. When the mixture is cool stir in the mozzarella cheese. Preheat the oven to 375 degrees. Lightly grease a baking sheet.
4. Lightly flour your work surface. Place a small bowl of water in front of you. Divide the pizza dough into 4 and roll each portion into a ball. With a rolling pin roll a ball of dough

into a 7-inch circle, lightly dusting the dough with some flour as necessary to prevent sticking. Dip your finger in the water and moisten the edge of the circle. Place one quarter of the potato mixture on half the circle, then fold the remaining dough over the mixture to make a turnover. Carefully pinch and fold over the edges of the dough to make a tight seal. Repeat with the remaining 3 portions.

5. Place the calzones on the baking sheet. With your fingers lightly coat the top of each calzone with a little oil. Bake 30 minutes, or until deep golden brown. Let sit at least 10 minutes before biting into one because otherwise it will release a blast of hot steam and scald you.

Black Bean and Red Onion Burgers

Salsa mayonnaise is the perfect topping for these delicious burgers, but if you want to go the whole hog, add sliced red onion and lettuce for an extra kick.

Makes 3 burgers

2 cups freshly cooked or canned black beans, rinsed and well drained if canned
1 egg, beaten
⅓ cup minced red onion
1 teaspoon chili powder
⅓ cup dry bread crumbs
⅓ cup mayonnaise
⅓ cup salsa (mild, medium, or hot)
Oil for frying
3 burger rolls

1. Place the beans in a medium-size bowl and mash about two thirds of them with a fork. Stir in the egg, onion, chili powder, and bread crumbs. Cover and chill for 30 minutes, or up to 24 hours.
2. Meanwhile place the mayonnaise in a small cup and stir until smooth. (This advance stirring prevents lumps from forming when the salsa is stirred in.) Stir in the salsa. Chill 30 minutes.
3. Form the burger mixture into 3 patties. Cook in a lightly oiled frying pan until golden brown on each side and piping hot throughout, at least 10 minutes total.
4. Serve the burgers on rolls with some salsa mayonnaise spread on each half.

Herbed Bean Burgers

Poultry seasoning lends these burgers a flavor reminiscent of traditional stuffing. They pair well with Russian dressing (mayonnaise with a little ketchup and relish) as a topping; however, mayonnaise alone is also a good match. And for the crowning touch? Lettuce and tomato, of course, to make an impressive, towering burger.

Makes 3 burgers

2 cups freshly cooked or canned white beans (such as navy, Great Northern, or cannellini), rinsed and well drained if canned
1/4 cup minced celery
1/4 cup minced red onion
1 garlic clove, put through a press or minced
1/2 cup dry bread crumbs
1/2 teaspoon poultry seasoning
1 teaspoon red wine vinegar
1 teaspoon tamari soy sauce
Salt
Generous seasoning freshly ground black pepper
Oil for frying or grilling
3 burger rolls

1. Place the beans in a medium-size bowl and mash half of them with a fork. Stir in all the remaining ingredients, except the oil and burger rolls, then use your hands to knead it all together into a ball.
2. Form the mixture into 3 burgers. If you are not going to cook them right away, you can wrap them individually in plastic wrap and refrigerate up to 4 days. Grill or fry them on a lightly oiled grill or skillet over medium heat until golden on both sides and hot throughout. Serve them on round rolls with Russian dressing, lettuce, and sliced tomato.

Shiitake Mushroom, Roasted Red Pepper, and Arugula Sandwiches

I had a sandwich with this combination at The Union Bar and Grill in Great Barrington, Massachusetts, and I knew I had to re-create it at home. The wedding of these ingredients is a triumph of flavor, texture, and color, but you must use high-quality, homemade-type bread to successfully hold it all together. I "roast" the shiitakes and onion in a hot oven; however, if you have a grill, by all means cook them on that.

Makes 2 sandwiches

2 tablespoons olive oil
1 teaspoon tamari soy sauce
1 medium red onion, sliced into ½-inch-thick slices and separated into rings
8 medium shiitake mushrooms, stems discarded and caps wiped clean
Salt
Freshly ground black pepper
4 slices homemade-type bread, such as sourdough, Tuscan, or semolina bread
1 roasted red pepper, cut in half, either freshly roasted (page 19) or store-bought
8 large arugula leaves (approximately)

1. Preheat the oven to 450 degrees. In a medium-size bowl combine the oil and tamari. Add the onion rings, shiitakes, salt, and pepper and toss to coat. Lay the vegetables on a roasting pan or baking sheet in one layer. Roast until brown and juicy, about 10–15 minutes. Flip the mushrooms over halfway during the cooking time.
2. Top 2 of the bread slices with the mushroom-onion mixture. Lay a red pepper half and some of the arugula on each sandwich. Top with the remaining bread, then slice each sandwich in half.

Portobello Mushroom, Smothered Onion, and Feta Cheese Sandwiches

The onions and mushrooms in this sandwich are natural mates. Choose a good-quality baguette to make this a sensational sandwich.

Serves 2

½ tablespoon unsalted butter
2 large portobello mushrooms, stems discarded and caps wiped clean
2 (¼-inch-thick) red onion slices
2 tablespoons olive oil
1 teaspoon red wine vinegar
Salt
Generous seasoning freshly ground black pepper
2 pieces French bread, each approximately 5 inches long
3 tablespoons crumbled feta cheese

1. Melt the butter in a large skillet over medium heat. Add the mushroom caps and cook 10 minutes or so, or until they begin to get juicy.
2. Separate the onion slices into rings and add to the mushrooms. Cover the pan, then cook until the onions are very soft and the mushrooms are juicy throughout, about 10 minutes. Occasionally remove the cover and toss the ingredients so they cook evenly. Remove from the heat.
3. In a small bowl mix together the olive oil, vinegar, salt, and pepper.
4. Slice the French bread horizontally. Spoon the olive oil mixture on both sides of each pair. Sprinkle the feta cheese on the bottom halves. Top with the mushrooms and onions, then the remaining bread.

Fried Green Tomato, Basil, and Smoked Cheese Sandwiches

Cornmeal-encrusted fried-tomato slices have a semblance of meatiness that reminds me of eggplant. Paired with basil and smoked cheese you have the workings of a vegetarian BLT—albeit, totally transformed!

Makes 2 sandwiches

2 tablespoons cornmeal
Salt
Freshly ground black pepper
1 medium green tomato, cut into 1/4-inch-thick slices
Oil for frying
Mayonnaise
4 slices crusty white bread (preferably Tuscan-style or sourdough)
2 thin slices (about 1 ounce) smoked cheese (such as mozzarella or Gouda)
8 basil leaves

1. Combine the cornmeal, salt, and pepper on a small plate. Dip the green tomato slices in the mixture and thoroughly coat both sides of each slice.
2. Heat just enough oil over moderate heat in a medium-size skillet to coat the bottom of the pan. Fry the tomato slices until they are golden brown on each side and tender, about 10 minutes. Let cool to warm.
3. Spread a thin layer of mayonnaise on each bread slice and top two of the slices with some cheese, basil leaves, and the fried tomatoes. Form into 2 sandwiches and slice each in half.

Broccoli and Jalapeño Cheese Quesadillas

You'll love these scrumptious quesadillas and the fact that they are assembled with so few ingredients. They can be easily doubled, tripled, etc., so don't hesitate to serve them to a crowd.

Serves 2

2 stalks broccoli (to yield 3½ cups chopped broccoli)
4 (8-inch) flour (wheat) tortillas
1½ cups grated Monterey Jack cheese with jalapeño peppers

1. Peel the stalks of the broccoli, then finely chop the stalks and florets.
2. Steam the broccoli until tender—neither crunchy nor mushy. Drain well and let cool.
3. To assemble, place 2 tortillas on a counter. Sprinkle one quarter of the cheese on each tortilla, leaving empty a 1-inch border around the tortilla. Spread *half* the broccoli on each tortilla. Sprinkle the remaining cheese on the broccoli, then place the remaining tortillas on top to create a sandwich. Press down with your hands to help the quesadillas stick together.
4. You can either cook the quesadillas on the stove top or in the oven. To cook them on the stove top, place 1 quesadilla on a large, ungreased skillet (if your tortillas are fresh and moist) or on a lightly buttered skillet (if the tortillas are on the dry side) and cook, over medium heat, for about 10 minutes, flipping with a spatula after the first 5 minutes. If you prefer to bake your quesadillas, place them on an ungreased baking sheet (or a lightly buttered one if your tortillas are somewhat dry), and bake in a preheated 375-degree oven for about 10 minutes, flipping the quesadillas over after 5 minutes. Whether cooked in a skillet or oven, the quesadillas are done when they begin to get brown flecks on them and the cheese is melted. Place the quesadillas on a cutting board and cut into 4 wedges. Let them rest a little before serving because they will be piping hot.

Corn, Black Bean, and Red Onion Quesadillas

I always have these ingredients on hand, and so these quesadillas are often what come to mind when I'm searching for a quick lunch or dinner. Kidney beans work just as well as black beans so don't hesitate to make that substitution if it suits you.

Serves 2

4 (8-inch) flour (wheat) tortillas
1/2 cup frozen corn, thawed
1/2 cup freshly cooked or canned black beans, rinsed and well drained if canned
1/3 cup paper-thin slivers of red onion
1 cup grated Monterey Jack cheese
1/2 teaspoon chili powder

1. Place 2 tortillas in front of you on a work surface. Sprinkle *half* the corn, beans, onion, cheese, and chili powder evenly on *each* tortilla, leaving a 1-inch border around the tortilla. Top with the remaining tortillas to create "sandwiches," and press down on the quesadillas to help them stick together.
2. You can either cook the quesadillas on the stove top or in the oven. To cook them on the stove top, place 1 quesadilla on a large, ungreased skillet (if your tortillas are fresh and moist) or on a lightly buttered skillet (if the tortillas are on the dry side) and cook, over medium heat, for about 10 minutes, flipping with a spatula after the first 5 minutes. If you prefer to bake your quesadillas, place them on an ungreased baking sheet (or a lightly buttered one if your tortillas are somewhat dry), and bake in a preheated 375-degree oven for about 10 minutes, flipping the quesadillas over after 5 minutes. Whether cooked in a skillet or oven, the quesadillas are done when they begin to get brown flecks on them and the cheese is melted. Place the quesadillas on a cutting board and cut into 4 wedges. Let them rest a little before serving because they will be piping hot.

Zucchini, Tomato, and Mozzarella Quesadillas

I choose a plum tomato for this filling because it is less juicy and more meaty than a round tomato. If your tomato is too ripe and juicy (a problem that is conceivable only in August or September), it could make these quesadillas a tad messy to eat. However, I'm sure you'll love them nonetheless.

Serves 2

4 (8-inch) flour (wheat) tortillas
1 1/4 cups grated part-skim mozzarella cheese
1 small zucchini, very thinly sliced
1 plum tomato, very thinly sliced
2 tablespoons shredded basil, or 1/2 teaspoon dried

1. Place two tortillas side by side on a countertop. Sprinkle one quarter of the cheese on each tortilla. Layer *half* the zucchini slices, tomato slices, and basil onto each tortilla, then sprinkle on the remaining cheese. Top with the remaining tortillas to make a "sandwich."
2. You can either cook the quesadillas on the stove top or in the oven. To cook them on the stove top, place 1 quesadilla on a large, ungreased skillet (if your tortillas are fresh and moist) or on a lightly buttered skillet (if the tortillas are on the dry side) and cook, over medium heat, for about 10 minutes, flipping with a spatula after the first 5 minutes. If you prefer to bake your quesadillas, place them on an ungreased baking sheet (or a lightly buttered one if your tortillas are somewhat dry), and bake in a preheated 375-degree oven for about 10 minutes, flipping the quesadillas over after 5 minutes. Whether cooked in a skillet or oven, the quesadillas are done when they begin to get brown flecks on them and the cheese is melted. Place the quesadillas on a cutting board and cut into 4 wedges. Let them rest a little before serving because they will be piping hot.

Portobello Mushroom Quesadillas

The pure experience of chewy, meaty portobellos comes through in these simple yet distinguished quesadillas. Think of these the next time you want an easy finger food for an appetizer. For such an occasion, just cut them into 8 instead of 4 portions.

Serves 2

1 tablespoon unsalted butter
3 medium-large (1 pound weight with stems) portobello mushrooms, stems discarded and caps thinly sliced
2 scallions, very thinly sliced
Salt
Freshly ground black pepper
4 (8-inch) flour (wheat) tortillas
1¼ cups grated Muenster cheese

1. Melt the butter in a large skillet over medium heat. Add the mushrooms and sauté them, tossing often, until they are brown and juicy and their juices begin to evaporate, at least 10 minutes. Make certain they are cooked throughout. Remove the pan from the heat, mix in the scallions, salt, and pepper. Let the mixture cool to room temperature.
2. To assemble the quesadillas, place 2 tortillas on a counter. Sprinkle one quarter of the cheese on *each* tortilla, leaving an empty 1-inch border around the edges. Spread *half* the mushroom filling on each tortilla, then top with the remaining cheese. Place the remaining tortillas on top to create "sandwiches." Press down with your hands to help the quesadillas stick together.
3. You can either cook the quesadillas on the stove top or in the oven. To cook them on the stove top, place 1 quesadilla on a large, ungreased skillet (if your tortillas are fresh and moist) or on a lightly buttered skillet (if the tortillas are on the dry side) and cook, over medium heat, for about 10 minutes, flipping with a spatula after the first 5 minutes. If you prefer to bake your quesadillas, place them on an ungreased baking sheet (or a

lightly buttered one if your tortillas are somewhat dry), and bake in a preheated 375-degree oven for about 10 minutes, flipping the quesadillas over after 5 minutes. Whether cooked in a skillet or oven, the quesadillas are done when they begin to get brown flecks on them and the cheese is melted. Place the quesadillas on a cutting board and cut into 4 wedges. Let them rest a little before serving because they will be piping hot.

Quesadillas

Quesadillas are best described as Mexican grilled cheese sandwiches made with 2 flour tortillas or 1 tortilla folded in half. They are usually fried in oil, butter, or lard, but I find them much more delicious and less greasy if cooked on a dry pan. (If you are not able to find flaky, supple tortillas, however, you will probably need to put a little butter in the skillet or on your baking pan when cooking your quesadilla to help soften the tortillas.)

Quesadillas can be the ideal vehicle for a quick supper or lunch because you can improvise with different cheeses and vegetables and come up with delectable fillings. There is one caveat, however, and that is you *must* use high-quality tortillas if you want good results. All flour tortillas are *not* alike; in fact, some are more like cardboard than bread. I have found a brand, called Maria and Ricardo's (from Jamaica Plain, Massachusetts), that is fantastic. Their tortillas are chewy and flaky, and delicious just heated and eaten with a little butter. So do experiment with different brands until you find a good one, then always keep a few packages in your freezer for convenience.

The next time you have an informal party or large get-together consider making a few different fillings and serving quesadillas at the gathering. Use 2 baking sheets at once and reverse their positions in the oven midway through the cooking time. Serve with a tossed salad and you have a delicious meal for a crowd.

Bean Tostadas with Sofrito

I have always been lukewarm toward cilantro; I could take it or leave it. Then a friend of mine, Geri Rybacki, dropped off a container of what she called "Puerto Rican sofrito," and my taste buds have never been the same. Geri pureed her sofrito to the point where it resembled a pesto, and we liked it so much in its raw state that we never got to use it in the traditional manner.

The point of departure from more familiar pestos is the addition of vinegar. This makes all the flavors come alive and lends a special "pickled" nuance to the sauce.

Serves 3

Sofrito

3–4 cups lightly packed cilantro, stems included, washed and spun dry
1 small jalapeño pepper, seeded and chopped (wear rubber gloves)
1 small green bell pepper, cored and chopped
2 garlic cloves, minced
1 small onion, chopped
1/3 cup olive oil
1/4 cup cider vinegar
1/2 teaspoon salt

The Beans

1 (16-ounce) can pinto or kidney beans, rinsed well and drained
1 teaspoon chili powder
1/4 cup water
1/4 teaspoon salt

The Tortillas

6 small (6-inch) soft corn tortillas
2–3 tablespoons canola oil
2/3 cup grated Monterey Jack cheese

1. To make the sofrito, combine all of the sofrito ingredients in a food processor or blender and puree until smooth. Pour into a container with a cover and set aside.

2. To prepare the beans, combine them with the chili powder, water, and salt in the container of a food processor and puree. Scrape into a bowl.

3. Preheat the broiler. Brush both sides of each tortilla with some of the oil, and place the tortillas on a baking sheet. (You'll probably have to do this in batches.) Broil on both sides until golden and crisp. (The tortillas may be prepared to this point up to 24 hours in advance.)

4. Divide the bean mixture and spread some on each tortilla. Top each with some of the grated cheese. Broil the tostadas until the cheese has melted and they are hot throughout. Serve with little spoonfuls of sofrito dotted on the top of each tostada.

Note: This recipe makes an ample amount of sofrito. Use the leftover sauce on rice dishes, in soups and chilis, and on other Mexican-style bean creations.

Side Dishes

There are occasions when a special side dish would nicely round out the meal, such as alongside savory tarts, egg dishes, or as part of a large holiday spread. But why wait for the need to arise to serve a sumptuous potato dish such as Garlic Mashed Potatoes (page 156) or Scalloped Potatoes and Onions (page 158)? You can always accompany it with some Roasted Vegetables (page 163), for example, and fashion a meal out of two smashing side dishes, with perhaps a salad and some bread to precede them.

So whether you are looking for that "extra something" to balance a menu, or want to bring together favorite side dishes to create an entree, these memorable accompaniments will help you with your meal planning.

Garlic Mashed Potatoes

Some people prefer "baking" potatoes for mashed potato dishes because they are light in texture; however, I like the creaminess that results from using starchy, boiling potatoes. Also, I like to whip my potatoes using an electric hand mixer, although some have claimed this makes them gummy. I have never found this to be true. *Chacun à son goût.* This version of garlic mashed potatoes calls for simmering the garlic in the milk that is added when whipping the potatoes. It mellows the garlic while still imparting its unmistakable flavor. You won't have any leftovers with these luscious potatoes.

Serves 4 very generously (as they should be served)

1¼ cups milk, plus more if necessary
6 large garlic cloves, peeled and coarsely chopped
5 large (3 pounds) boiling (waxy) potatoes, peeled and quartered
2 tablespoons unsalted butter
½ teaspoon salt
Freshly ground black pepper

1. Combine the milk and garlic in a medium-size, heavy-bottomed saucepan and bring it to a simmer. Simmer about 20 minutes, or until the garlic is very soft. Keep an eye on the pot to prevent the milk from swelling and boiling over; it should cook at just a simmer.
2. Meanwhile boil the potatoes in a large pot of water until they are tender when pierced with a knife.
3. While the potatoes are cooking puree the garlic and milk in a blender just until smooth. Return the garlic cream to the pot. (You can do this step up to a few hours before cooking the potatoes.)
4. Drain the potatoes in a colander, then return them to the pot over low heat. Add the garlic cream, butter, salt, and pepper. With an electric mixer whip the potatoes until creamy. Serve immediately or cover and keep warm over low heat.

Baked Chive and Mashed Potato Casserole

So many mashed potato dishes need to be served immediately because they suffer from reheating. This version is ideal for entertaining because not only is it exceptionally light and savory but it can be made up to 8 hours in advance of baking it.

Serves 8

3 pounds (5 large) boiling (waxy) potatoes, peeled and quartered
2 tablespoons unsalted butter cut into bits, plus extra for greasing
6 ounces whipped cream cheese with chives
2 eggs
1/2 teaspoon salt
Freshly ground black pepper
2 tablespoons grated Parmesan cheese

1. Boil the potatoes in a large stockpot until they are tender when pierced with a knife. Drain thoroughly and return them to the pot.
2. Add the butter and stir to melt. Drop in the cream cheese, eggs, salt, and pepper. With an electric mixer whip the potatoes until fluffy.
3. Lightly butter a 2-quart shallow casserole. Spoon the potato mixture into it and smooth over the top. Sprinkle with the Parmesan cheese. (The casserole may be prepared to this point up to 8 hours in advance. If made more than 2 hours in advance, cover with foil and refrigerate it. Bring to room temperature before baking.)
4. Preheat the oven to 400 degrees. Bake the casserole, uncovered, for 40 minutes, or until golden on top and sizzling.

Scalloped Potatoes and Onions

Here's a light version of scalloped potatoes that's just as delicious as the traditional dish. Serve it as a side dish or as a hearty, main-course casserole, accompanied by a salad to round out the meal. The onions will be brown and caramelized, the top of the dish golden and crusty—just as you would expect of that classic potato gratin.

Serves 6

3 tablespoons unsalted butter, plus extra for greasing
2 large onions, halved vertically and thinly sliced
1 1/2 cups vegetable stock, store-bought or homemade (page 13)
5 large (3 pounds) boiling potatoes
1 1/2 cups grated cheese, preferably Swiss or Cheddar
Salt and freshly ground pepper to taste

1. Melt 1 tablespoon butter in a large skillet over medium heat. Add the onions and sauté, stirring often, until they begin to get brown, about 10 minutes. Set aside.
2. Lightly butter a shallow 2 1/2-quart ovenproof casserole or oval gratin dish. Set it aside. Place the vegetable stock in a large bowl. Peel, then rinse, the potatoes. Slice each potato in half vertically, then very thinly into half moons. Drop them into the vegetable stock as you slice them. This prevents them from turning brown and allows you to postpone cooking the casserole. You can keep them in the stock, stirring occasionally, for up to 4 hours .
3. Preheat the oven to 425 degrees. Spoon half the potatoes into the prepared casserole in an even layer. Spread the onions on top. Cut 1 tablespoon of the butter into bits and layer on top of the onion. Sprinkle on *half* of the grated cheese. Add salt and pepper.
4. Spoon on the remaining potatoes, then pour all the stock over everything. Top with the remaining tablespoon of butter cut into bits, then season again with salt and pepper.
5. Bake 30 minutes. Remove the casserole from the oven and flatten the top with the back of a spatula. Sprinkle on the remaining cheese. Bake 30 more minutes, or until the potatoes are tender, and the top is brown and crusty. Let sit 10 minutes before serving.

Roasted Home Fries

These little roasted potato disks are so quick and easy to prepare, they're bound to become your favorite method of making home fries. I have had great results baking these potatoes at different temperatures, depending on whether or not the oven needed to be set at a specific temperature for another dish. Just don't go lower than 350 degrees because you need that much heat to brown them. If you have another dish baking at the time you want to cook these, bake these home fries on the lower rack.

Serves 4–6

6 medium-large red-skinned potatoes
2 tablespoons olive oil
Salt

1. Preheat the oven to 425 degrees. Peel the potatoes, then slice them 1/4 inch thick. Cut the slices in half so that each piece is about the size of a half dollar. Place the potatoes on a large baking sheet. Drizzle the oil all over them, then with your hands, toss to coat them thoroughly with the oil.
2. Bake about 25 minutes (or longer if the oven is at a lower setting), tossing them once after the first 15 minutes. When done, they will be tender and golden all over. Season with salt before serving.

Sweet Potato and Red Pepper Home Fries

Roasting these "home fries" causes their sugars to caramelize and make them brown and crispy on the edges. The vibrant splash of color this combination provides looks terrific next to a slice of frittata or simple scrambled eggs.

Although I usually cook these vegetables at a high oven setting, they are successful in an oven as low as 350 degrees; you'll just have to cook them about 10 minutes longer. This sometimes is necessary if you are baking something simultaneously that requires the lower oven setting.

Serves 4–6

3 medium sweet potatoes or yams, peeled, quartered, and sliced 1/4 inch thick
1 medium red bell pepper, cut into pieces 2 × 1/2 inch
1 large onion, halved vertically and sliced 1/4 inch thick
2 tablespoons olive oil
1 tablespoon tamari soy sauce
Freshly ground black pepper

1. Preheat the oven to 425 degrees. Combine all the ingredients in a large bowl and toss well to evenly coat with the oil and soy sauce.
2. Spread the vegetables on a large baking sheet or roasting pan so that they rest in one layer. When the oven is thoroughly preheated, bake the vegetables for 30 minutes, removing the pan from the oven and tossing them once at the halfway point. When done, the vegetables should be tender and brown.

Whipped Sweet Potatoes

A satin-like consistency and spicy flavor make these sweet potatoes an outstanding side dish. Remember them for your next Thanksgiving feast.

Serves 4 generously

4 medium-large (2 pounds) yams or sweet potatoes
3 tablespoons unsalted butter
1/4 cup pure maple syrup
1/4 cup heavy cream
1/4 teaspoon ground cinnamon
1/8 teaspoon ground allspice
Salt
Freshly ground black pepper

1. Peel the yams or sweet potatoes and cut them into 1-inch dice. Place them in a 3-quart saucepan and fill with water to cover. Partly cover the pan and bring to a boil. Cook until the sweet potatoes are very tender, about 15 minutes. Drain in a colander.
2. While the potatoes are draining, quickly heat the remaining ingredients in the same saucepan until the mixture is hot and the ingredients are combined. Remove the pan from the heat and stir in the sweet potatoes.
3. With a handheld electric mixer whip the sweet potatoes until smooth. (You could, alternatively, do this step in a food processor and then reheat the potatoes until hot.)
4. Serve immediately, or keep covered over low heat until serving time.

Roasted Vegetables

This side dish of roasted vegetables is quite versatile. It can be made in advance and reheated; used as a sandwich filling on French bread; incorporated into a frittata or omelet; or just served alongside Garlic Mashed Potatoes (page 156) for a dynamic combination.

Serves 4 generously

1 green or red bell pepper, cored and cut into ½-inch dice
2 small–medium zucchini, quartered lengthwise and cut into ½-inch dice
1 small (1 pound) eggplant, sliced lengthwise and cut into ½-inch dice
1 large onion, cut into ½-inch dice
2 plum tomatoes, cored, seeded, and cut into 1-inch dice
3 garlic cloves, minced
¼ teaspoon dried rosemary, finely crumbled
2 tablespoons olive oil
1 teaspoon tamari soy sauce
Generous seasoning freshly ground black pepper
Salt

1. Preheat the oven to 425 degrees. Combine all the vegetables plus the garlic and rosemary in a large bowl. Mix together the olive oil and tamari and pour over the vegetables. Toss well.
2. Spread the vegetables on a large baking sheet in one layer. Season generously with pepper. Bake 30 minutes, tossing once after 15 minutes. The vegetables will be very tender when done, not crunchy. Season with salt just before serving.

Roasted Asparagus

I thought I had tried every conceivable way to cook asparagus until my friend Jane Walsh told me how fabulous they are when roasted. If you want a side dish of plain asparagus that is highly flavorful without any doctoring, choose this method. Just be sure to remove the tough bottoms of the asparagus by cutting off the white part, then peeling the bottom 2 inches. This will produce perfectly tender, succulent asparagus.

Serves 4

1 pound asparagus
1½ tablespoons olive oil (approximately)
Salt (preferably coarse kosher salt)

1. Preheat the oven to 425 degrees. Cut off the white bottoms of the asparagus and discard them. With a sharp paring knife peel the bottom 2–3 inches of the asparagus to remove any tough skin.
2. Place the asparagus in a roasting pan or on a baking sheet and drizzle the olive oil all over them. With your hands roll the asparagus around so they are evenly coated with the oil. Sprinkle with salt to taste.
3. Bake about 10 minutes, or until tender when pierced with a knife.

Couscous Pilaf with Pistachio Nuts and Scallions

This light and flavorsome side dish of couscous goes well with assertive entrees, such as Baked Thai-Style Tofu (page 215). You can successfully make this pilaf in advance and reheat it in the oven in a foil-covered dish. Just sprinkle it with a few teaspoons of water to help create steam.

Serves 4

1 tablespoon unsalted butter
1 large scallion, thinly sliced
1 1/2 cups vegetable stock, store-bought or homemade (page 13)
1/4 teaspoon salt
1 cup couscous
1/3 cup shelled pistachio nuts

1. Melt the butter in a small- or medium-size saucepan over medium heat. Add the scallion and sauté 30 seconds. Pour in the vegetable stock and salt and bring to a boil.
2. Mix in the couscous and pistachio nuts and cover the pan. Remove it from the heat and let sit 5 minutes. Fluff with a fork, cover, and let sit 2–10 minutes more.

Coconut Lime Rice

I am quite fond of this aromatic pilaf and so sometimes make a simple meal by just serving it alongside a steamed vegetable, such as green beans.

Serves 4

2 tablespoons unsalted butter
1 onion, very finely diced
1 cup basmati rice or converted white rice
1 3/4 cups water
1/2 teaspoon salt
2 tablespoons sliced almonds
2 tablespoons desiccated unsweetened coconut (see Note)
1/4 teaspoon ground cardamom
Juice of 1/2 lime

1. Melt 1 tablespoon of the butter in a medium-size saucepan over medium heat. Add the onion and sauté until tender, about 5 minutes.
2. Stir in the rice and cook 1 minute, stirring continuously, then add the water and salt. Raise the heat to high, cover the pan, and bring the contents to a boil. Reduce the heat to a simmer and cook until all the water is absorbed, about 18–20 minutes.
3. Meanwhile melt the remaining tablespoon of butter in a small skillet over medium heat. Stir in the almonds and sauté 2 minutes, or just until the almonds are faintly colored. Add the coconut and cardamom and cook until the coconut begins to get a light golden color, about 1 minute. Remove from the heat.
4. When the rice has absorbed all the water, very gently stir in the almond mixture and lime juice. Remove from the heat and let sit, covered, 5–10 minutes.

Note: Desiccated unsweetened coconut can be purchased at natural foods stores and some specialty markets.

Frittatas and Omelets

The debate continues on whether eggs are a perfect food, that is, a good source of protein, vitamins, and minerals, or whether they should be marked with a scarlet letter and shunned because of their high cholesterol content. Depending on when and where you read the latest research, you'll hear many conflicting perspectives. Several recent comprehensive scientific studies indicate that blood cholesterol is not elevated by dietary cholesterol, and therefore a moderate consumption of eggs poses no problem for generally healthy adults.

I suspect this is the most reasonable approach to take toward the much maligned egg, and so a couple of times a month I serve an omelet or frittata to my family for dinner and we enjoy it wholeheartedly. I do always purchase organic eggs, however, because I don't want the hormones and antibiotics that factory-farmed chickens ingest. Eggs are an inexpensive food to begin with, so I don't mind the extra cost of purchasing eggs that come from free-range chickens.

Making an omelet is one of the simplest and quickest of tasks to perform at the stove, yet it is also quite easy to make a mess of it. A non-stick skillet will help things considerably; however, a heavy-bottomed omelet pan will work well if enough oil or butter is used to prevent the omelet from sticking.

It's a good idea to make 1 omelet at a time because you'll have more control of the process. With 40 seconds the average time it takes to complete the task, individual omelet making will not delay your dinner.

The key to a tender, delicate omelet is to use high heat and a quick hand. When your pan is hot and the oil or butter starts to sizzle, it is ready for the eggs. Pour in the beaten eggs and watch them immediately begin to set at the edges. Use an inverted spatula to push in the edges and cause the uncooked eggs to spill over onto the pan. When very little uncooked egg remains visible, spoon on your *hot* filling, then fold over the omelet and slide it onto your plate. This should all take under 1 minute.

If the filling for your omelet is more than grated cheese, that is, a cooked vegetable concoction, make certain it is hot when you spoon it onto the omelet. You can keep it warm on the back burner while you cook your eggs.

A tiny bit of water is beaten into the eggs to lighten their texture and help steam them during cooking; however, you can also use club soda or white wine to do the trick.

Frittatas

The Italian version of an omelet, known as a frittata, combines the filling ingredients with the beaten eggs and cooks them together to form a firm, pie-shaped egg dish. In contrast to the French omelet, frittatas should be cooked slowly over low or medium-low heat.

A non-stick skillet is ideal because the frittata will be easy to remove from the pan. Heating a small amount of butter or oil in the pan before the egg mixture is poured in will add flavor and facilitate the removal of the frittata. I used to bemoan the fact that my skillet had a plastic handle and, therefore, was unsafe to put under the broiler. Now I know a handy trick that cleverly solves the problem: Just wrap a double layer of foil around the handle to protect it from the heating element and broil away!

Frittatas can also be successfully baked rather than cooked on the stove top. This method can be a lifesaver if you are preparing a brunch, for example, where a number of dishes will be cooked on the burners. To bake a frittata, butter a pie plate (such as a Pyrex 9-inch pie dish) and pour in the egg mixture. Bake it in a preheated 350-degree oven for 20–30 minutes, or until it is no longer runny on top. (The temperature of the added vegetable mixture affects the cooking time. If the vegetables are quite warm rather than at room temperature, the frittata won't take as long to cook.) Keep an eye on it to prevent overcooking. You don't need to broil the top of the frittata when you use the baking method.

Think of frittatas when you are planning a picnic, as the French and Italians do. They are delicious cold or at room temperature, and they travel well.

Leek, Fennel, and Goat Cheese Frittata

Here's a frittata that's fit for a special occasion. The creamy pockets of goat cheese along with this triumphant blending of flavors make this egg dish ideal for a no-fuss, yet memorable meal. It can be easily doubled, and in that case, you'd need a 10-inch skillet. Just be certain to cook the frittata on low heat as directed; this will produce very tender results.

Serves 2

1 tablespoon unsalted butter
1½ cups thinly sliced fennel (about ½ large bulb)
1 leek, halved lengthwise, washed thoroughly, and thinly sliced
1 plum tomato, diced
4 large eggs
¼ teaspoon salt
Generous seasoning freshly ground black pepper
2 ounces soft mild goat cheese, crumbled

1. Over medium heat melt the butter in an 8-inch non-stick skillet, and roll it around so the butter coats the sides. Add the fennel and sauté until tender, about 10 minutes.
2. Stir in the leek and tomato and cook, stirring often, until the leek is soft, about 10 minutes. At first the vegetables will crowd the pan, but they will shrink once cooked. You can prepare the vegetables in advance to this point, then reheat before beginning step 3.
3. Meanwhile beat the eggs thoroughly. Add the salt, pepper, and crumbled goat cheese and stir very gently to keep the goat cheese in separate pieces rather than completely blended into the egg mixture.
4. When the vegetables are cooked, reduce the heat to a low setting. Carefully pour in the egg mixture and stir gently to incorporate it. Cook slowly until the eggs are almost set, about 15 minutes. During this time use a rubber spatula to loosen the edges of the

frittata and let some of the liquid egg fall over the sides onto the pan. This will help it cook more evenly. Meanwhile turn on the broiler.

5. When the frittata is about 80 percent set and there is just a film of uncooked egg on top, broil it for 1 minute or so, or until set. Do not overcook it. (If your skillet doesn't have an ovenproof handle, wrap a double layer of foil around it before placing it under the broiler.) Cut the frittata in half and serve immediately.

Spinach, Potato, and Feta Cheese Frittata

The saltiness of the feta cheese becomes subdued in this frittata yet retains its tangy character to give this frittata some spunk. Serve hot pita bread alongside it for a good match.

Serves 2

½ pound fresh spinach in a bunch, or ½ (10-ounce) bag fresh spinach, stems removed and leaves torn (5 cups leaves)
1 tablespoon olive oil
1 medium boiling (waxy) potato, peeled, quartered lengthwise, and thinly sliced
1 scallion, thinly sliced
5 large eggs
½ cup crumbled feta cheese
Pinch salt
Generous seasoning freshly ground black pepper
½ tablespoon butter

1. Wash the spinach and drain it well. Crowd it into an 8- to 10-inch non-stick skillet and cook, covered, over medium heat just until it wilts. Place the spinach in a strainer and press out any liquid with the back of a large spoon. Let it cool.
2. Wipe the skillet clean, and pour in the olive oil. Heat it over medium heat, then add the potato and fry it until tender and golden, about 10 minutes. Stir in the scallion and cook 1 minute. Tip the vegetables onto a plate and let cool.
3. Thoroughly beat the eggs in a medium-size bowl. Stir in the feta cheese, salt, pepper, spinach, and potato mixture.
4. Melt the ½ tablespoon of butter in the skillet over medium-low heat and swirl it around to coat the sides. Pour in the egg mixture. After about 5 minutes when the edges begin to set, help the liquid egg pour over the sides of the frittata by occasionally loosen-

ing the edges with a rubber spatula and tilting the pan. It should take about 15 minutes for the frittata to become almost completely set.

5. Preheat the broiler. When the frittata is about 80 percent cooked, slide it under the broiler for a minute or so until the top is set. (If the handle of your pan isn't ovenproof, wrap a few layers of foil around it before placing the pan under the broiler.) Cut the frittata and place it on plates, but let it cool a little before serving it.

Roasted Vegetable Frittata

Although this recipe technically takes more than 30 minutes of cooking, I count it among my quick meals because it is so easy to prepare. Think of this frittata when you plan a picnic; it is also delicious cold or at room temperature.

Serves 4

1 medium-large boiling (waxy) potato, peeled, quartered, and very thinly sliced
1 red bell pepper, cored and cut into ¼-inch-thick strips
1 green bell pepper, cored and cut into ¼-inch-thick strips
2 medium-large tomatoes, cored and cut into sixths
1 medium red onion, cut into sixths and sections separated
6 garlic cloves, each halved
Salt
Freshly ground black pepper to taste
2½ tablespoons olive oil
1½ teaspoons chopped fresh rosemary, or ¼ teaspoon crumbled dried
8 black olives (Kalamata or oil-cured), pitted and halved (page 95)
8 large eggs
½ cup (3 ounces) finely cubed mozzarella cheese

1. Preheat the oven to 425 degrees. Combine the potato, peppers, tomatoes, red onion, garlic, and salt and pepper to taste in a large bowl. Pour on 1½ tablespoons of the olive oil and toss to coat well. (This mixture can be prepared up to 4 hours in advance.)
2. Spread the vegetables onto a baking sheet and cook 20–30 minutes, or until they are very soft and brown. (You don't want crisp vegetables for this frittata.) Remove from the oven and sprinkle on the rosemary and black olives. Let cool to warm or room temperature.
3. Meanwhile beat the eggs in a large bowl with ¼ teaspoon salt. Stir in the mozzarella cheese and then the roasted vegetables.

4. Place the remaining tablespoon of olive oil in a 10-inch non-stick skillet and heat over medium-low heat, tilting the pan to coat the sides with oil. Pour in the egg mixture and cook about 5 minutes. At this point the edges will have begun to set. You can help the liquid egg pour over the sides of the frittata by occasionally running a rubber spatula around the edges of the frittata and tilting the pan. It should take about 15–20 minutes for the frittata to become almost completely set.

5. Preheat the broiler. When the frittata is about 80 percent set, place it under the broiler to finish cooking the top layer. (If the handle of your pan isn't ovenproof, wrap a few layers of foil around it before placing the pan under the broiler.) Cut the frittata into wedges and place on serving plates, but let cool somewhat before serving. It is better when not piping hot.

Broccoli and Smoked Cheese Frittata

Broccoli and smoked cheese animate this simple frittata with their highly compatible flavors. To create a tender frittata that also has a fresh look, you must precook the broccoli to just the right stage—no longer crunchy yet still bright green. Be attentive!
Sweet Potato and Red Pepper Home Fries (page 160) would be a tantalizing match with this frittata.

Serves 2

1 tablespoon olive oil
2 garlic cloves, minced
4–5 cups tiny broccoli florets (from about 1 bunch broccoli)
1/4 cup water
5 large eggs
1/4 teaspoon salt
Generous seasoning freshly ground black pepper
1/2 cup grated smoked Gouda or mozzarella cheese
1/2 tablespoon butter

1. Heat the oil in an 8- to 10-inch non-stick skillet over medium heat. Add the garlic and cook 30 seconds. Stir in the broccoli florets and the 1/4 cup of water. Cover the pan and cook the broccoli until it is tender but still bright green. Taste one to be sure it is cooked; you don't want crunchy broccoli in this frittata. If the water has not completely evaporated, cook, uncovered, until it evaporates. Place the broccoli on a plate and let cool. Wipe the pan clean.
2. Beat the eggs in a large bowl. Mix in the salt, pepper, smoked cheese, and cooled broccoli.
3. Melt the butter in the skillet over medium-low heat and swirl it around to coat the sides of the pan. Pour in the egg mixture. After about 5 minutes when the edges begin to set, let the liquid egg pour over the sides of the frittata by occasionally loosening the

edges of the frittata with a rubber spatula and tilting the pan. It should take about 15 minutes for the frittata to become almost completely set.

4. Preheat the broiler. When the frittata is about 80 percent set, slide it under the broiler for a minute or so until the top is cooked. (If the handle of your pan isn't oven-proof, wrap a few layers of foil around it before placing the pan under the broiler.) Cut the frittata and place it on serving plates, but let cool a few minutes before serving.

Zucchini, Red Pepper, and Onion Frittata

I cook the onion and red pepper until they are very soft, almost caramelized, because they render a wonderful flavor this way. At first the vegetables will take up a lot of room in the sauté pan, so it is easier to use a large skillet for this step, then switch to a medium-size non-stick pan for the cooking of the frittata.

Serves 2–3

1 tablespoon olive oil
1 medium onion, halved vertically and thinly sliced
1 red bell pepper, cut into very thin strips
1 medium zucchini, quartered lengthwise and very thinly sliced
5 large eggs
3 tablespoons grated Parmesan cheese
½ cup finely chopped fresh parsley
¼ teaspoon salt
Generous seasoning freshly ground black pepper
½ tablespoon unsalted butter

1. Heat the oil in a large skillet over medium heat. Add the onion and red pepper and cook, tossing often, for 10 minutes. Cover the pan and cook 10 more minutes, or until the vegetables are soft and beginning to brown. Toss occasionally.
2. Mix in the zucchini and cook until tender yet slightly crisp, about 5 minutes. Remove the pan from the heat.
3. Meanwhile thoroughly beat the eggs in a large bowl. Beat in the Parmesan cheese, parsley, salt, and pepper. If you are going to cook the frittata immediately, then stir in the vegetable mixture; otherwise, let the vegetables cool before mixing them into the eggs.
4. Melt the butter in a 10-inch non-stick skillet over medium-low heat and swirl it around to coat the sides of the pan. Pour in the egg mixture. After about 5 minutes when

the edges begin to set, help the liquid egg pour over the sides of the frittata by occasionally loosening the edges with a rubber spatula and tilting the pan. It should take about 15 minutes for the frittata to become almost completely set.

5. Preheat the broiler. When the frittata is about 80 percent set, slide it under the broiler for a minute or so until the top is cooked. (If the handle of your pan isn't ovenproof, wrap a few layers of foil around it before placing the pan under the broiler.) Cut the frittata and place it on plates, but let it cool a little before serving it.

Shiitake Mushroom and Roasted Red Pepper Omelet

You'll only need about 3 ounces of these fabulous fungi to treat yourself to this savory omelet. The rich flavor and chewy texture of shiitakes make them one of the preeminent mushrooms, so do add them to your repertoire if you haven't done so already.

Serves 2

4 teaspoons olive oil
1 medium onion, halved and thinly sliced
8 medium (3 ounces) shiitake mushrooms, stems discarded, tops wiped clean and thinly sliced
1/4 cup roasted red peppers, store-bought or freshly roasted (page 19), cut into thin strips
1/2 teaspoon minced fresh thyme, or 1/4 teaspoon dried
1/4 cup finely chopped fresh parsley
Salt
Freshly ground black pepper to taste
2 tablespoons sour cream
4 large eggs
2 tablespoons water

1. To make the filling, heat 2 teaspoons of the olive oil in a medium-size skillet over medium heat. Add the onion and sauté until they begin to get tender, about 10 minutes. Stir in the mushrooms and cook until tender and juicy, about 10 more minutes.
2. Mix in the red peppers, thyme, parsley, salt, pepper, and sour cream, and keep hot.
3. Beat the eggs with the water and 1/4 teaspoon salt in a medium-size bowl.
4. Make the omelets one at a time. Heat 1 teaspoon of the oil in an 8-inch, preferably non-stick, skillet over medium-high heat. When the pan is very hot, pour in half of the egg mixture. It should immediately set at the edges. With an inverted spatula push the cooked edges toward the center while tipping the pan to let the liquid egg run out to the hot pan. When very little uncooked egg remains, spoon half of the hot filling onto one side of the omelet. Immediately fold the omelet in half and flip it onto a plate.

Caramelized Onion Omelet

I love to make this omelet when I don't have much on hand for dinner. Little can beat the flavor of caramelized onions, and they are so easy to prepare. Cook the onions slowly (you'll be able to accomplish other tasks during that time), and you'll have an incomparable omelet filling.

Serves 2

4 teaspoons olive oil
2 large onions, halved vertically and thinly sliced
Pinch sugar
4 large eggs
2 tablespoons water
1/4 teaspoon salt
Freshly ground black pepper to taste
2/3 cup grated sharp Cheddar cheese

1. Heat 2 teaspoons of the oil in a large skillet over medium-low heat. Add the onions and sugar and cook slowly, stirring frequently, until the onions are very soft and a deep caramel color, about 20 minutes. Keep hot over low heat.
2. Beat the eggs with the water, salt, and pepper in a medium-size bowl. Have the cheese ready and near the stove.
3. Make the omelets one at a time for maximum control. Heat 1 teaspoon of the oil over medium-high heat in a medium-size non-stick skillet and swirl it around to coat the sides of the pan. When the pan is very hot, pour in *half* the egg mixture. It should set immediately at the edges. With an inverted spatula push the cooked edges toward the center while tipping the pan to let the uncooked egg run out to the hot pan. When very little liquid egg remains, spoon *half* the onions onto one side of the omelet, then sprinkle on half the cheese. Immediately fold the omelet in half, then flip it onto a plate. This should all take less than one minute. Repeat to make another omelet.

Leek and Ricotta Omelet

Leeks and ricotta cheese both have a natural sweetness and delightfully enhance one another in this toothsome filling.

Serves 2

2 large leeks (to yield 2 ½ cups sliced leeks)
4 teaspoons unsalted butter
Salt
Freshly ground black pepper
¼ cup part-skim ricotta cheese
4 large eggs
2 tablespoons water

1. Cut the root ends off the leeks plus all but 2 inches of the green tops. Slice the leeks in half lengthwise. Under cold running water rinse the leeks, fingering through all the leaves to dislodge any hidden dirt. Do this thoroughly to rid them of *all* their sand. Thinly slice the leeks, discarding any thick, dark green pieces.
2. Heat 2 teaspoons of the butter in a medium-size skillet over medium heat. Add the leeks and sauté until soft and tender, about 10 minutes. Season generously with salt and pepper, then stir in the ricotta cheese. Heat until the ricotta gets hot, then keep the mixture hot over low heat.
3. In a medium-size bowl beat the eggs with ¼ teaspoon of salt and the water.
4. Make the omelets one at a time. Heat 1 teaspoon of the butter in an 8-inch, preferably non-stick, skillet over medium-high heat. When the pan is very hot, pour in half of the egg mixture. It should immediately set at the edges. With an inverted spatula push the cooked edges toward the center while tipping the pan to let the liquid egg run out to the hot pan. When very little uncooked egg remains, spoon half of the hot filling onto one side of the omelet. Immediately fold the omelet in half and flip it onto a plate. Repeat to make one more omelet.

Potato, Pepper, and Tomato Omelet

Here's a mélange of flavors that were meant for each other. I like this filling to be soft, almost jam-like, so I don't aim for crunchy, crisp vegetables here (and neither should you!). If you don't want a spicy dimension, use plain Monterey Jack cheese rather than the one with the jalapeños added. In either case, you'll love this homey omelet.

Serves 2

1 tablespoon plus 2 teaspoons olive oil
1 medium boiling (waxy) potato, peeled, quartered, and thinly sliced
1/2 green bell pepper, very thinly sliced into 1-inch strips
1 medium onion, quartered and very thinly sliced
2 plum tomatoes, cored, seeded, and finely diced
1/4 teaspoon dried oregano
Salt
Freshly ground black pepper
4 large eggs
2 tablespoons water
2/3 cup grated Monterey Jack cheese with jalapeño peppers (see Headnote)

1. Heat the tablespoon of oil in a medium-size, preferably non-stick, skillet over medium heat. Add the potato and cook, tossing often, until tender, about 10 minutes.
2. Add the green pepper and onion and sauté about 5 minutes, then cover the pan and cook 5 more minutes, or until the vegetables are very tender. Add the tomatoes and oregano, season generously with salt and pepper, and cook 5 more minutes, or until the tomatoes are soft and the mixture is somewhat like jam. Keep hot while you prepare the eggs.
3. Beat the eggs with the water and 1/4 teaspoon salt. Have the cheese ready and near the stove.
4. Make two omelets, one at a time. Heat 1 teaspoon of the oil in an 8-inch, preferably

non-stick, skillet over medium-high heat. When the pan is very hot, pour in *half* of the egg mixture. It should immediately set at the edges. With an inverted spatula push the cooked edges toward the center while tipping the pan to let the uncooked egg run out to the hot pan. When very little uncooked egg remains, spoon half of the hot filling onto one side of the omelet. Sprinkle on half the cheese. Immediately fold the omelet in half, then flip it onto a plate. Repeat to make one more omelet.

Portobello Mushroom and Caramelized Shallot Omelet

Here is another filling that creates a special meal out of an omelet. Keep the shallots in chunks when you cook them for soft pockets of caramelized shallots in your filling.

Serves 2

6 teaspoons unsalted butter, divided
4 golf-ball-size shallots, each quartered
Pinch sugar
4 portobello mushrooms (3-inch diameter), stems discarded and caps sliced ¼ inch thick
Salt
Freshly ground black pepper to taste
½ teaspoon minced fresh or 1 teaspoon dried tarragon
3 tablespoons soft mild goat cheese
4 large eggs
2 tablespoons water

1. Melt 2 teaspoons butter in a medium-size skillet over medium heat. Add the shallots and sugar and toss. Lower the heat to medium-low and cover the pan. Cook the shallots until they are soft and brown, about 10 minutes. Remove the cover and toss occasionally. Scrape the shallots into a bowl, then wash the pan.
2. Melt 2 teaspoons of the butter over medium heat in the same skillet. Add the mushrooms and sauté until brown and juicy, about 10 minutes. Stir in the shallots, salt, pepper, and tarragon. Gently stir in the goat cheese. Keep the mixture hot.
3. In a medium-size bowl beat the eggs with the water and some salt to taste.
4. Make the omelets one at a time. Heat 1 teaspoon of the oil in an 8-inch non-stick skillet over medium-high heat. When the pan is very hot, pour in *half* of the egg mixture. It should immediately set at the edges. With an inverted spatula push the set egg toward the center and tip the pan to let the liquid run back to the edge. When most of egg is cooked, spoon half of the hot filling onto one side of the omelet. Immediately fold the omelet in half and flip it onto a plate.

Stove-Top Dinners

Tasty combinations of ingredients cooked together in a skillet characterize these wholesome meals. Polenta or couscous may be an accompaniment, or sometimes a stew-like mixture such as White Bean, Sweet Potato, and Pepper Ragout (page 200) can stand on its own. Whatever the case, these hearty dinners are easy to prepare, and most can be made in advance and reheated.

Potato and Vegetable Curry

The flavor and silken consistency of this sauce are unsurpassed. This could be an ideal dish for quick entertaining (it doubles easily), with a spread of side dishes to add to the festiveness: Hot pita bread, chutney, and a cucumber raita (yogurt and grated cucumber salad) are ideal. Take time to cut the vegetables into small pieces to keep the cooking time down to a minimum.

Canned coconut milk is a boon for the quick cook because it is made only of coconut and water (without additives), and is a close second to freshly made coconut milk. Don't worry if it is very thick in the can; it will "melt" when heated.

Serves 2–3

2 tablespoons canola oil
1 onion, minced
3 garlic cloves, minced
1 teaspoon minced fresh gingerroot
2 teaspoons curry powder
1 teaspoon ground cumin
1/4 teaspoon ground cardamom
1 cinnamon stick
1 cup seeded and finely diced tomato, fresh or canned
1 (14-ounce) can unsweetened coconut milk
1/2 teaspoon salt
2 medium red-skinned potatoes, cut into 1/2-inch dice (no bigger)
1 large sweet potato or yam, peeled and cut into 1/2- inch dice
3 cups finely chopped cabbage
1 cup frozen peas, thawed

1. In a large skillet heat the oil over medium heat. Add the onion and cook, stirring often, for 5 minutes. Add the garlic and gingerroot and cook 2 minutes. Stir in the spices and cinnamon stick and "toast" them for 30 seconds, stirring continuously.

2. Stir in the tomato, coconut milk, and salt, and mix well. Mix in the potatoes, sweet potato, and cabbage, and cover the pan. Bring to a boil, then reduce the heat to a simmer. Cook about 20 minutes, or until the potatoes are tender. Stir in the peas and cook 1 more minute, or until the peas are hot throughout. Remove the cinnamon stick before serving.

Note: If you make the curry in advance, don't add the peas until you reheat it. Also, the sauce will thicken when cooled, so you might need to sprinkle in a tablespoon or so of water upon reheating.

Couscous Topped with White Beans, Tomatoes, and Zucchini

This dish has a tasty and satisfying sauce that captures the flavors of southern France. To make this quickly, I use canned beans. Cannellini (white kidney beans) would be my bean of choice if I were to cook them from scratch; however, canned cannellini are usually overcooked and too soft, so I prefer a small white bean, such as Great Northern or navy beans, when I choose to use canned beans.

Serves 3–4

The Vegetables
2 tablespoons olive oil
1 onion, finely diced
4 garlic cloves, minced
1 medium zucchini, quartered lengthwise and thinly sliced on the diagonal
1 (16-ounce) can tomatoes, finely chopped with their juice
1 (16-ounce) can small white beans, well rinsed and drained
1 tablespoon chopped fresh basil, or 1/2 teaspoon dried
1 teaspoon chopped fresh rosemary, or 1/4 teaspoon dried, crumbled
Salt
Generous seasoning freshly ground black pepper

The Couscous
1 1/2 cups water
1/4 teaspoon salt
1 tablespoon unsalted butter
1 cup couscous

1. Heat the oil in a large skillet over medium heat. Add the onion and sauté until tender but not brown, about 10 minutes. Add the garlic and zucchini and cook 5 minutes, or until the zucchini is beginning to get tender but is still crisp.
2. Stir in the tomatoes, beans, herbs, salt, and pepper and cook, tossing occasionally,

until the zucchini is tender and the sauce has thickened slightly, about 5 minutes. (The vegetables may be prepared to this point up to 4 hours in advance and reheated.)

3. Meanwhile cook the couscous. Bring the water, salt, and butter to a boil in a small saucepan. Pour in the couscous, cover the pot, and remove it from the heat. Let sit 5 minutes, fluff with a fork, then cover again and let sit 5 more minutes. Serve a portion on each plate and top with a mound of the vegetable mixture.

Thai Fried Rice

Fried rice requires a little forethought because you have to begin with *cold,* cooked rice to obtain fluffy results, but it's worth the effort when you are in the mood for a grain-based dish that's teeming with flavor. This recipe benefits from reheating, so don't hesitate to make the entire dish in advance and reheat it over low heat or in the oven. Cold, leftover fried rice is delicious as a salad; if you need to pack a lunch for work, take a container of this rice.

Serves 4 as a main course

1 teaspoon plus 1 tablespoon canola oil
2 eggs, well beaten
1 red bell pepper, cut into small dice
1 teaspoon minced gingerroot
2 garlic cloves, minced
1/4 teaspoon crushed red pepper flakes
3 scallions, thinly sliced
6 cups cold cooked brown rice (made from 2 cups raw rice boiled with 5 1/2 cups water)
1/4 cup tamari soy sauce
1 tablespoon tomato paste
1 tablespoon lime juice
2 tablespoons oriental sesame oil
2 cups bean sprouts
1 tablespoon minced fresh basil, or 1/2 teaspoon dried
1 tablespoon minced fresh mint, or 1 teaspoon dried

1. To make shredded egg for the rice, heat the teaspoon of oil in a small skillet over medium-high heat. Pour in the eggs and scramble a bit with a fork. Let the eggs cook into a "pancake," then flip over and cook on the other side. This should all take about 1 minute. Place the pancake on a plate and let cool slightly. Cut the pancake into small strips and set aside.

2. Heat the remaining tablespoon of oil in a large, preferably non-stick, skillet over medium heat. Add the bell pepper and sauté 3 minutes. Stir in the ginger, garlic, and red pepper flakes and cook 2 minutes, tossing often. Stir in the scallions and cook 30 seconds.
3. Break up the cold rice if it is clumpy, then mix it into the vegetable mixture.
4. In a small bowl mix together the soy sauce, tomato paste, lime juice, and sesame oil. Pour over the rice and toss gently to coat with the sauce.
5. Stir in the bean sprouts, basil, mint, and shredded egg. Heat until hot throughout, about 3 minutes. Serve immediately, or cool and reheat it within 2 days.

Polenta with Broccoli and Garlic

Few vegetables can compete with broccoli from a nutritional standpoint, and I think the same is true regarding flavor. The fact that it is commonplace doesn't diminish its appeal. Bolstered by garlic and hot pepper flakes, it's a delicious match for this cheesy polenta.

Serves 3–4

The Polenta
4 cups light vegetable stock, store-bought or homemade (page 13)
1/4 teaspoon salt
1 1/4 cups cornmeal
1/3 cup grated Parmesan cheese
2 tablespoons unsalted butter, cut into bits

The Vegetables
2 tablespoons olive oil
6 garlic cloves, minced
1/4 teaspoon crushed red pepper flakes
1 large bunch broccoli, cut into tiny florets, stalks peeled and diced (5–6 cups total)
1/3 cup water
3 plum tomatoes, seeded and finely diced
Salt

1. To make the polenta, bring the vegetable stock and salt to a boil in a medium-size, heavy-bottomed saucepan. Meanwhile prepare all the ingredients for this dish and set them out in front of you.
2. When the stock boils, reduce the heat to low and very slowly drizzle in the cornmeal, whisking constantly with a wire whisk. Continue to cook the polenta, whisking continuously, until it is thick like mashed potatoes and begins to tear away from the sides of the pot, about 5 minutes. Whisk in the cheese and butter, cover the pot, then remove it

from the heat. The polenta can be kept like this for 10 minutes or so.

3. Heat the oil in a large skillet over medium heat. Add the garlic and red pepper flakes and cook 1 minute. Mix in the broccoli, toss well, then pour in the water. Cover the pan and cook the broccoli until tender, about 5 minutes. Remove the cover and stir in the tomatoes and salt to taste. Cook, uncovered, for about 2 minutes, or until the tomatoes are soft and most of the liquid has evaporated.

4. To serve, spoon a mound of polenta on each dinner plate. Top with the broccoli mixture.

Gorgonzola Polenta with Spinach and Exotic Mushrooms

If you don't have access to assorted, exotic mushrooms (technically they are no longer "wild," since they are cultivated), common white button mushrooms will also be delicious here, lending their juices and buttery flavor.

You can make the sautéed vegetables a bit in advance and quickly reheat them; however, the polenta should be prepared at the last minute.

Serves 4

3½ cups water
2 tablespoons olive oil
6 garlic cloves, minced
¼ teaspoon crushed red pepper flakes
¾ pound assorted exotic and common mushrooms (such as shiitake, oyster, cremini, and white button), wiped clean and sliced (about 4½ cups sliced)
1 (1-pound) bunch fresh spinach, or 1 (10-ounce) bag fresh spinach, stems discarded and leaves washed
Salt to taste

The Polenta
¼ teaspoon salt
1¼ cups cornmeal
1 tablespoon unsalted butter
2 tablespoons grated Parmesan cheese
3 ounces Gorgonzola or other blue cheese, finely diced (about ¾ cup diced)

1. Bring the water to a boil in a medium-size, heavy-bottomed saucepan.
2. Meanwhile heat the oil in a large skillet over medium-high heat. Add the garlic and red pepper flakes and cook 30 seconds. Immediately drop in the mushrooms and toss well. Cook, tossing often, until the mushrooms render their juices and begin to brown.
3. Pile on the spinach, toss, then cover the pan. Cook just until the spinach wilts, about

3 minutes. Remove the cover, then season with salt to taste. Keep the vegetables warm while you make the polenta. (The vegetables may be prepared to this point up to 4 hours in advance and reheated.)

4. When the water boils, add the 1/4 teaspoon salt, then reduce the heat to medium-low. Very slowly drizzle in the cornmeal, whisking all the while with a wire whisk. Cook the polenta about 5 minutes, or until it pulls away from the sides of the pan. Keep whisking often while it cooks to keep it smooth.

5. Drop in the butter, Parmesan cheese, and Gorgonzola and stir just until blended.

6. Spoon some polenta onto each serving plate, then top with some of the vegetable mixture and its juices.

Polenta with Spicy Tomato-Garlic Sauce

Such a simple topping but with so much punch! This is bound to become one of your favorites.

Serves 3–4

The Sauce

2 tablespoons olive oil
8 garlic cloves, coarsely chopped (no less!)
1/4 teaspoon crushed red pepper flakes
1 (28-ounce) can imported plum tomatoes, drained and very finely diced
2 tablespoons mixed chopped fresh herbs (such as basil, rosemary, and parsley), or 1 teaspoon dried
1/4 teaspoon salt
Pinch sugar
Freshly ground black pepper to taste

The Polenta

3 1/2 cups water
1/4 teaspoon salt
1 cup cornmeal
1 tablespoon unsalted butter
1/4 cup grated Parmesan cheese
1/2 cup grated cheese (such as mozzarella, Fontina, Monterey Jack, or Muenster)

1. To make the sauce, heat the oil in a medium-size skillet over medium heat. Add the garlic and pepper flakes and cook 1 minute.
2. Stir in the tomatoes, herbs, salt, sugar, and pepper. Simmer just until the juices thicken, about 10 minutes. (The sauce may be prepared to this point up to 4 hours in advance. Reheat and keep warm while making the polenta.)
3. To make the polenta, bring the water and salt to a boil in a 2 1/2- to 3-quart heavy-

bottomed saucepan. Reduce the heat to a simmer, then very slowly drizzle in the cornmeal, whisking all the while with a wire whisk. Whisk continuously until the polenta is the consistency of mashed potatoes and begins to tear away from the sides of the pan, about 5 minutes. Whisk in the butter and both cheeses. (At this point you can cover the polenta, turn off the heat, and keep it hot for up to 10 minutes before serving.)

4. Pour some polenta on each dinner plate, then spoon some sauce on the center of the polenta. Serve immediately.

White Bean, Sweet Potato, and Pepper Ragout

The great marriage of colors and flavors in this peasant-style mélange calls for some crusty French or Italian bread to wipe up the tantalizing juices that will accumulate on your plate.

Serves 2–3

2 tablespoons olive oil
1 red bell pepper, cut into strips 2 × ½ inch
1 green bell pepper, cut into strips 2 × ½ inch
1 large sweet potato or yam, peeled, cut in half lengthwise, and sliced ¼ inch thick
4 garlic cloves, minced
½ teaspoon finely chopped fresh rosemary, or ¼ teaspoon dried, crumbled
1 (14-ounce) can diced tomatoes with their juice
2 cups freshly cooked or canned small white beans, well rinsed and drained if canned
¼ cup water
Salt and generous seasoning freshly ground black pepper

1. Heat the oil in a large skillet over medium heat. Add the red and green peppers and sauté 5 minutes, tossing frequently. The peppers should begin to get tender.
2. Stir in the sweet potato, garlic, and rosemary, and cook, stirring often, for 10 minutes. The mixture will begin to brown and bits of it will stick to the pan—this is good, for the scrapings will later be incorporated into the sauce and add flavor.
3. Mix in the tomatoes, white beans, water, salt, and pepper. Cover the pan and simmer everything for about 15 minutes, or until the sweet potatoes are tender. Periodically remove the cover and scrape the bottom of the skillet to loosen those tasty bits that have stuck to the pan. There should be some thickened juices remaining when the dish is ready to be served. If it seems dry, add a bit more water and cook a few minutes until thickened. (The ragout may be prepared to this point up to 4 hours in advance and reheated.) Serve on dinner plates or in shallow pasta bowls with some bread alongside it.

White Beans with Spinach, Garlic, and Tomatoes

There is a recent enthusiasm for most things Mediterranean. And with good reason. These stewed white beans are an example of the simplicity and quality that one finds in rustic dishes of the Italian home cook. Garlic permeates the thick sauce that is created, which of course makes you want to clean your plate with some crusty Tuscan-style bread.

I have had good results making these stewed beans with canned small white beans (find a brand that offers firm, not mushy, beans), so don't hesitate to make this dish if you are pressed for time.

Serves 4

¼ cup fruity olive oil
6 garlic cloves, minced
3 plum tomatoes, seeded and diced
6 cups freshly cooked or canned small white beans, well rinsed and drained if canned
⅓ cup vegetable stock, store-bought or homemade (page 13)
5 cups torn spinach leaves (torn into small pieces)
Generous seasoning freshly ground black pepper

1. Heat the oil in a large skillet over medium heat. Add the garlic and cook 30 seconds. Stir in the tomatoes and sauté, tossing often, until the tomatoes are soft, about 7 minutes.

2. Stir in the beans and stock and bring to a simmer. Pile on the spinach, cover the pan, and cook just until wilted, about 3 minutes. Season generously with pepper. When done, the mixture should have thickened, sauce-like juices, not watery, not dry. If it's too soupy, cook a few minutes more; if too dry, add a bit more stock. Serve on flat dinner plates or in large, shallow pasta bowls with a good chunk of bread on the side.

Tofu and Tempeh Favorites

Tofu

Tofu, also called soybean curd, is made in a similar way as cheese. Soybeans are cooked and mashed, then their liquid is pressed out of them. This soy milk is mixed with a coagulant to cause the curds to separate from the whey. The curds are then pressed into cakes to form tofu. Tofu is an excellent source of protein and iron and a good source of calcium. It is widely used throughout China and Japan.

I buy tofu in sealed packages rather than out of open bins because tofu can be a haven for bacteria when it is exposed to dust and dirt in a store. Once the package of tofu is opened and a portion remains to be stored, place it in some fresh water in a covered container in the refrigerator.

Change the water daily until you use the tofu. Spoiled tofu will have a slimy feel to it, take on a yellowish tinge, and taste sour.

Cooking with Tofu

Have you ever wondered why tofu can be so appealing at times (like in Chinese restaurants), and at other times be off-putting? It's all in the texture; it will make or break a tofu dish.

When tofu is cooked *properly,* that is, fried or roasted so that it is golden all over, it retains a chewy consistency. If this tofu is then cooled, as in Marinated Fried Tofu and Vegetable Salad with Mesclun (page 206), Bow-Tie Pasta and Fried Tofu Salad with Sesame Dressing (page 210), Mock Chicken Salad (page 212), and Roasted Marinated Tofu (page 214), the tofu becomes even firmer and more palatable. Although tofu aficionados enjoy tofu fixed many different ways—even uncooked—I have found that a crisply cooked treatment is the best way to introduce tofu to newcomers. If you spot a tofu recipe (in another cookbook) that calls for stir-frying a few ingredients and then adding the tofu—beware! The tofu will not become sufficiently crispy if other ingredients in the pan give off moisture, etc. Soft, wobbly tofu has turned off many an eager novice.

I always use extra-firm tofu because I want it to retain its shape when I cook it, and I prefer its texture. Even in salad dressings that require pureeing I use the extra-firm variety because it will become creamy, and this allows me to purchase one variety of tofu for all purposes.

Tofu and other soy products have gotten a lot of attention recently because Asian women who consume ample amounts of these foods have been found to have noticeably lower mortality rates from breast cancer, and significantly weaker menopausal symptoms, such as hot flashes and night sweats. Soy is a plant source of phytoestrogens, which help compensate women for natural estrogen losses.

So if you not only want to increase your tofu consumption but also *enjoy* eating it, try it in the following recipes and you'll see that tofu doesn't deserve to be the brunt of all those food jokes, unless, of course, it gets improperly cooked—as in those *other* cookbooks!

Pan-Frying and Roasting Tofu

In order to pan-fry (cook in a skillet with a minimal amount of oil) or roast (bake in the oven at high heat) tofu properly, that is, create a crisp, uniformly golden exterior, you must begin with dry tofu. Oil and water don't mix, and the moisture from the tofu will interfere with the oil's ability to brown the tofu.

You can "dry" tofu a number of ways. Here are two: I have found that the easiest and quickest way to rid tofu of its excess moisture is to cut it into slices, lay them on one half of a cotton or linen kitchen towel, then fold over the other half of the towel to cover the tofu. Now gently press on the tofu to release its moisture into the towel. You can also use paper towels to pat the tofu dry. Repeat this "patting" a few times until the tofu no longer feels wet—just moist. Cut the tofu into cubes (or whatever shape the recipe calls for), and pat them dry once again. This might sound like a lot of patting, but it is actually quite quick and hassle-free. Wash the towel(s) you used, and keep them available for this and other kitchen tasks.

The other method of draining tofu is to place the tofu on a dinner plate. Put a salad-size plate on top of the tofu, and weigh it down with a heavy can (such as a 32-ounce can of tomatoes). Place a teaspoon under one end of the dinner plate to slightly tilt it; this will drain the released liquid to one end of the plate. Pour off the liquid as it accumulates. It will take about an hour to thoroughly drain the tofu. After you cut the tofu into slices or cubes, you will still have to pat them dry, but because you are starting with a drier tofu than in the first method, you won't have to pat them as much.

Now you are ready to fry or roast the tofu. If you use a non-stick skillet for pan-frying, you'll be amazed at how easily you can achieve a golden crust on the tofu. If your skillet isn't a non-stick pan, you'll have to toss the tofu frequently to prevent it from sticking. In either case, heat the amount of oil specified in the recipe until it is very hot but not yet smoking. You don't want to add tofu to warm oil. Keep the pan hot and fry the tofu until it is evenly golden all over. To roast tofu properly (see Roasted Marinated Tofu, page 214), make sure your oven is sufficiently preheated, and use a heavy ceramic or Corning Ware baking dish. A roasting pan might cause the tofu to stick. Both methods of cooking tofu will produce wonderful results.

Marinated Fried Tofu and Vegetable Salad with Mesclun

Cold, fried tofu, as in this very special salad, is the best way to introduce tofu to a hesitant newcomer. By frying the tofu first, it gets crispy and chewy, and then absorbs the garlicky marinade, making it resemble chicken in flavor and texture. (Lest it sound odd to you that I would mention chicken in a vegetarian cookbook, I should explain that although I've been a vegetarian for nearly 30 years, I never said that chicken doesn't taste good!)

Using fried tofu rather than raw tofu in a salad was a revelation to me. I've always loved the way tofu is transformed when it is cooked in a little oil, but until recently I never thought it would be good cold. Now I can't get enough of it.

A non-stick skillet makes frying tofu infinitely easier than when cooked in other pans because moist tofu tends to stick when fried. If you don't have such a pan, use the heaviest skillet you have and make sure the tofu is patted *very dry* before frying.

Serves 3–4

1 tablespoon canola oil
1 pound extra-firm tofu, cut into ½-inch cubes and patted *very dry*

The Dressing
3 tablespoons lemon juice
2 large garlic cloves, minced
1 teaspoon tamari soy sauce
½ teaspoon salt
Generous seasoning freshly ground black pepper
¼ cup olive oil

4–5 cups tiny broccoli florets
2 large scallions, very thinly sliced
1 red bell pepper, cut into ¾-inch dice
4 cups mesclun (baby salad greens), washed and spun dry

1. Heat the oil in a large, preferably non-stick, skillet over high heat until it is very hot but not smoking. Add the tofu and spread it out so that it is in one layer. Fry it, shaking the pan often to prevent sticking, until it is a rich golden color all over. With a spatula flip it over occasionally so it gets evenly browned. Place it in a large bowl. Set the skillet aside.

2. Combine all the ingredients for the dressing in a jar with a tight-fitting lid and shake vigorously. Pour half the dressing on the hot tofu and toss well. Chill the tofu until it is very cold, about 2 hours.

3. Meanwhile place the broccoli in the skillet, add a little water, and cover the pan. Cook it until it is crisp yet tender, about 4 minutes. Immerse it in a bowl of cold water to stop any further cooking. Drain the broccoli thoroughly, then place it on a cotton or linen kitchen towel and pat it dry.

4. Mix the broccoli, scallions, red pepper, and remaining dressing into the cold tofu. Toss well. Let sit at least 30 minutes to marinate, or chill up to 4 hours then bring close to room temperature so it's cool, not cold.

5. Just before serving, mix in the mesclun. Serve on large plates.

Soba and Fried Tofu Salad with Shredded Spinach

This salad contains a perfectly harmonious blending of ingredients that seem made for each other. Don't hesitate to make it 1–2 days before you intend to serve it because it will be just as good as the day it was made. Hold off mixing in the spinach, though, until serving time.

I grate the ginger for this salad because I prefer the thin strands. All you have to do is use a knife to scrape the skin off the gingerroot, then grate it on the *coarse* side of the grater (it clogs the finer side). If the pieces are a bit too big, use a large knife to mince them.

A note about soba—try to find a store that sells soba loosely by the pound, instead of in packages. It is considerably cheaper when purchased in bulk. In our town the natural foods store and our upscale marketplace sell them this way.

Serves 4 as a main course

1 pound extra-firm tofu
1 tablespoon canola oil
1 tablespoon tamari soy sauce
1 pound soba (buckwheat noodles)

The Dressing
3 tablespoons tamari soy sauce
3 tablespoons oriental sesame oil
2 tablespoons brown sugar
1 teaspoon hot chili oil
1 tablespoon rice vinegar or red wine vinegar
2 teaspoons scraped then coarsely grated gingerroot

1 tablespoon sesame seeds
2 large scallions, very thinly sliced
4 cups spinach leaves, washed, then stacked and julienned

1. Cut the tofu into ¼-inch-thick slices and pat them *very* dry with a kitchen towel or paper towels. Cut each slice into 4 triangles by cutting a big "X" from corner to corner.

2. Heat the oil in a large, preferably non-stick, skillet over high heat. Add half of the tofu triangles and fry them on both sides until golden brown. Keep the heat high. Remove the tofu and place it in a large bowl. Repeat with the remaining tofu. Pour the tablespoon of tamari on the tofu, toss well, then chill it until it is very cold, about 1½ hours.

3. Meanwhile bring a large stockpot of water to a boil. Drop in the soba and cook until al dente, about 7 minutes. You must watch soba carefully because if it is overcooked it will fall apart, yet you don't want it too firm either. Keep tasting a strand to be certain it is cooked properly. Drain the soba in a colander, then rinse under cold running water. Vigorously shake out all the water, then place the noodles in a large bowl. (Once the noodles are rinsed, they become firmer. Don't worry, though, they will get tender again once they marinate.)

4. Make the dressing by combining all the ingredients in a bowl. Set it aside.

5. Toast the sesame seeds by placing them in a small pot over medium heat. Swirl the pan around until the seeds become fragrant and start to smoke, about 4 minutes. Do not take your eyes off them. When lightly golden, pour them into a small bowl and let them cool.

6. When the tofu is cold, mix it into the noodles along with the sesame seeds and scallions. Pour on the dressing and toss well. Marinate the salad at least 1 hour or up to 2 days before serving. Cover and chill it if it is longer than 2 hours. It is best served cool or at room temperature, so remove it from the refrigerator a half hour or so before serving time. Just before serving, mix in the spinach.

Bow-Tie Pasta and Fried Tofu Salad with Sesame Dressing

Tofu again resembles chicken in this savory marinated pasta salad with Sesame-Ginger Dressing. Farfalle (bow-tie noodles) are especially good here and worth making a special trip for because their delightful shape pairs well with the tofu chunks. This is a great salad for picnics, potlucks, and traveling lunches.

Serves 4 as a main course

Sesame-Ginger Dressing
2 tablespoons tamari soy sauce
2 tablespoons red wine vinegar
1 tablespoon brown sugar
1 large garlic clove, put through a press or minced
1 teaspoon minced gingerroot
1/4 teaspoon salt
Freshly ground black pepper
2 tablespoons oriental sesame oil
1/4 cup canola oil

1 tablespoon canola oil
1 pound extra-firm tofu, cut into 1/2-inch cubes and patted *very* dry
1 pound farfalle (bow-tie pasta)
4 large scallions, very thinly sliced

1. To make the dressing, combine all its ingredients in a jar with a tight-fitting lid and shake vigorously. Set aside.
2. Bring a large stockpot of water to a boil for the pasta. Meanwhile cook the tofu. Place the tablespoon of canola oil in a large, preferably non-stick, skillet and heat the pan over high heat until very hot but not smoking. Add the tofu and let sit in one layer. Shaking the pan to prevent the tofu from sticking, cook the tofu until it is golden underneath,

then with a spatula, toss it around until it is a deep golden color all over. Drop the tofu into a deep, large bowl.

3. Pour about one quarter of the dressing on the tofu and toss well. Let cool.

4. Drop the farfalle into the boiling water and cook until al dente, about 12 minutes. Drain in a colander, then rinse under cold running water. Drain again thoroughly.

5. Mix the farfalle into the tofu. Pour on the remaining dressing and toss well. Sprinkle on the scallions and toss again. Chill the salad at least 2 hours before serving. Serve at room temperature or slightly cool, but not cold.

Mock Chicken Salad

When small bits of cold, fried, chewy tofu get mixed with celery and mayonnaise, a tantalizing sandwich spread is created that is remarkably like chicken salad in flavor and texture. Fried tempeh makes a similar mock chicken salad but has a stronger flavor. Try it with leaf lettuce on a good-quality whole grain bread.

For 4–5 sandwiches

1 pound extra-firm tofu
1 tablespoon canola oil
1 tablespoon tamari soy sauce
1 large scallion, very thinly sliced
1 medium celery rib, very thinly sliced
3 tablespoons mayonnaise
Freshly ground black pepper to taste

1. Place the tofu in a cotton or linen kitchen towel and gather up the sides of the towel to create a pouch of tofu. Twist the ball of tofu until a lot of liquid is released. Drop the tofu ball onto a cutting board, then with a large knife, finely chop it so the pieces are the size of small peas.
2. Heat the oil in a large, non-stick skillet over high heat until it is very hot but not yet smoking. Add the tofu and shake the pan to prevent it from sticking, then, using a spatula, flip it around until it gets evenly golden brown. This should take at least 10 minutes. Keep the heat high. The pan might start to smoke but that's okay; just keep flipping the tofu. When done, drop it into a medium-size bowl and drizzle the soy sauce all over it. Toss well. Let cool 10 minutes, then refrigerate it until very cold, at least 1 hour.
3. Stir in the remaining ingredients. Keep covered and chilled until ready to use.

Curried Tofu "Eggless" Salad

I have a basic version of this sandwich spread in *Quick Vegetarian Pleasures* and I am so fond of it that creating an equally delicious variation seemed an inevitable challenge. The crunchy vegetables, mild spiciness of the curry, and contrasting sweetness of the raisins make this rendition a tough competitor.

For 4 sandwiches

½ pound extra-firm tofu
3 tablespoons mayonnaise
¾ teaspoon curry powder
1 celery rib, very finely diced
1 small carrot, grated
1½ tablespoons raisins
1 scallion, very thinly sliced
¼ teaspoon salt
Generous seasoning freshly ground black pepper

1. To rid it of excess moisture, place the block of tofu on a linen or cotton kitchen towel and gather up the sides of the towel. Twist the ball of tofu over the sink, letting the released liquid drip into the sink. Open up the towel and drop the tofu into a medium-size bowl. Mash it with a fork until its texture is fine, that is, resembling coarse bread crumbs.
2. Stir in all the remaining ingredients. Cover and chill at least 1 hour so that the flavors can develop. Use as a sandwich spread. It is particularly delicious on toasted bread.

Roasted Marinated Tofu

Here is a treatment of tofu that is an alternative to pan-frying and also produces fabulous results. I love to chill this tofu and add it to salads or just eat it alone. Packed in a plastic container, it makes the perfect portable lunch.

Serves 2–4

1 pound extra-firm tofu
1½ tablespoons tamari soy sauce
1 tablespoon oriental sesame oil
1 teaspoon canola oil
1 tablespoon dry sherry

1. Slice the tofu into ½-inch-thick slices. Lay them on a clean cotton kitchen towel or on paper towels and pat *very* dry. Cut the tofu into cubes, triangles, or any shape of your choice.
2. Combine the soy sauce, sesame oil, canola oil, and sherry in a large bowl. Add the tofu, and very gently toss it with the marinade. Let marinate at least 30 minutes, or cover and chill up to 24 hours.
3. Preheat the oven to 450 degrees. Place the tofu, and its marinade in a single layer in a large, shallow baking dish. Bake 25–30 minutes, or until golden all over. Shake the pan after 15 minutes to prevent the tofu from sticking. Serve warm, or, better yet, cool the tofu, then refrigerate until very cold, at least 2 hours.

Baked Thai-Style Tofu

This method of baking marinated tofu gives it a crispy coating and intensifies all the flavors in the "sauce." You'll also love the ease with which this dish can be put together. A side portion of rice, plain couscous, or Couscous Pilaf with Pistachio Nuts and Scallions (page 164) is the best accompaniment.

Don't hesitate to serve this dynamic tofu dish cold; it would make a great lunch to take to work.

Serves 3

The Marinade

2 tablespoons tamari soy sauce
1 tablespoon oriental sesame oil
1 tablespoon canola oil
1/2 teaspoon minced gingerroot
1 garlic clove, minced
1/4 teaspoon crushed red pepper flakes

1 pound extra-firm tofu, cut into 3/4-inch cubes and patted *very* dry
1 red bell pepper, cut into thin strips, 1/4 × 2 inches

The Sauce

1 tablespoon natural-style peanut butter
2 tablespoons lime juice
1 scallion, very thinly sliced
2 teaspoons finely chopped fresh basil, or 1/4 teaspoon dried
2 teaspoons finely chopped fresh mint, or 1/2 teaspoon dried

1. Combine the marinade ingredients in a large bowl. Using a rubber spatula, gently fold in the tofu and red pepper to coat them evenly with the marinade. Let sit 30 minutes at room temperature, or up to 8 hours chilled. Toss occasionally.

2. Preheat the oven to 450 degrees. Place the tofu mixture and any remaining marinade in a large shallow baking dish so that the tofu rests in one layer. Bake 15 minutes, tossing once with a spatula after about 7 minutes.

3. Meanwhile make the sauce by stirring all its ingredients together with a fork. Remove the tofu from the oven. Spoon on the sauce, then, using a spatula, toss the ingredients together until everything is well coated. Return the dish to the oven and bake undisturbed for 10 minutes. Let the tofu sit at least 10 minutes before serving it, for it is better when warm, not piping hot.

Baked Tofu and Mushrooms Hoisin

Serves 3

The Marinade

2 tablespoons tamari soy sauce
1 tablespoon oriental sesame oil
1 tablespoon vegetable oil
½ teaspoon minced gingerroot
2 garlic cloves, minced

1 pound extra-firm tofu, cut into ¾-inch cubes and patted *very* dry
½ pound mushrooms, each quartered, large ones cut into sixths

The Sauce

1½ teaspoons tamari soy sauce
1 tablespoon natural-style peanut butter, smooth or chunky
1 tablespoon hoisin sauce
1 tablespoon dry sherry
1 scallion, very thinly sliced

1. Combine the marinade ingredients in a large bowl. Add the tofu and mushrooms and, using a rubber spatula, gently toss to coat evenly. Let sit 30 minutes, or up to 8 hours, tossing occasionally. If marinating longer than 8 hours, cover and chill. Bring to room temperature before cooking.
2. Preheat the oven to 425 degrees. Combine all of the sauce ingredients—except the scallion—in a small bowl.
3. Place the tofu mixture and its marinade in a shallow baking dish so that it all rests in one layer. Bake 15 minutes, tossing once with a spatula.
4. Remove the dish from the oven, then pour the sauce over the tofu mixture. Toss gently, then sprinkle on the scallion. Return the dish to the oven and bake 10 more minutes. Let sit 10–15 minutes before serving. It should be served warm, not hot.

Penne with Fried Tofu, Roasted Peppers, and Olives

Here's another great way to introduce newcomers to the charm of fried tofu, although in this case the tofu is hot and therefore slightly softer, but still delicious. The Mediterranean flavors of peppers, olives, and basil are an enticing backdrop to these chunks of crispy, fried tofu, which soak up the garlicky sauce and lend this hearty dish some bulk and character.

Serves 4

1 tablespoon canola oil
1 pound extra-firm tofu, cut into ½-inch cubes and patted *very* dry
1 tablespoon tamari soy sauce
1 pound penne
3 tablespoons olive oil
6 garlic cloves, minced
1 (7-ounce jar) roasted red peppers, drained and cut into ½-inch dice (1 cup diced)
10 black olives (your favorite kind), pitted and halved (see page 95)
½ cup chopped fresh parsley
¼ cup chopped fresh basil
½ teaspoon salt
Generous seasoning freshly ground black pepper
¼ cup grated Parmesan cheese

1. Fill a large pot with water and bring to a boil.
2. Heat the oil in a large, preferably non-stick, skillet over high heat until it is very hot but not smoking. Add the tofu and, making sure it is in one layer and not overcrowded, fry it until golden brown all over. Shake the pan to keep it from sticking, and with a spatula flip the tofu around occasionally so it cooks evenly. Drop the tofu into a large bowl, then drizzle on the soy sauce. Toss well. Set the tofu aside.
3. Drop the penne into the boiling water and cook until al dente. Do not overcook it.

4. Meanwhile make the sauce. Heat the olive oil in a large skillet over medium heat. Add the garlic and cook 30 seconds. Do not let it get at all brown. Add the peppers and cook 2 minutes. Stir in the olives, parsley, basil, salt, pepper, and tofu. Toss well. Remove ½ cup of the starchy pasta water and stir it into the sauce. Cook 1 minute.
5. Drain the penne in a colander and shake to remove all the water. Return it to the pot or place it in a large bowl. Pour on the sauce and mix well. Sprinkle on the Parmesan cheese, toss, and serve.

Tempeh

Indonesian in origin, tempeh is a fermented soybean product that is made from chopped soybeans mixed with a rhizopus culture which are then pressed together to form a cake. In this state it is considered raw, and it must be cooked before being eaten. Because tempeh has a strong flavor, it doesn't depend on potent seasonings the way tofu does.

High in protein and a good source of iron, tempeh also contains vitamin B_{12}, the one vitamin vegans can have difficulty getting enough of.

Tempeh is sold in tightly sealed packages that display an expiration date. Unlike tofu, it can easily be frozen by just placing the package in the freezer. Fresh tempeh often has black spots on it. These are not a sign of decay, but rather spores of the culture that was mixed with the soybeans. Spoiled tempeh is unmistakable—it will smell foul, feel slimy, and have pink or yellow mold on it.

Cooking with tempeh is easy. It doesn't require any special handling—just chop it into small pieces and sauté them in a skillet until hot throughout.

Barbecued Tempeh Spread

Many people feel that the texture and flavor of tempeh spread are reminiscent of chicken salad. Mixed with this spicy barbecue dressing, it makes a delicious and satisfying sandwich filling that is packed with protein.

Enough for 3–4 sandwiches

1 tablespoon vegetable oil
1½ teaspoons chili powder
8 ounces tempeh, finely chopped
1 celery rib, finely diced
¼ cup minced red onion
¼ cup mayonnaise
2 tablespoons ketchup
½ teaspoon red wine vinegar
1 teaspoon Dijon-style mustard
1 teaspoon molasses
1 small garlic clove, put through a press or minced
Salt
Freshly ground black pepper to taste

1. Heat the oil in a medium-size, preferably non-stick, skillet over medium heat. Stir in the chili powder and cook 10 seconds, then stir in the tempeh and toss to coat it with the chili powder. Cook, tossing frequently, until the tempeh is golden, about 7 minutes.
2. Scrape the tempeh into a bowl and let cool. Stir in the celery and onion.
3. In a small bowl combine all the remaining ingredients. Pour it over the tempeh mixture and toss well. Cover and chill at least 30 minutes, or up to 3 days. Serve as a sandwich spread.

Garlicky Tempeh and Potato Ragout

Tender chunks of tempeh and potatoes simmer in an aromatic, garlic-spiked tomato sauce to make a hearty, one-dish meal that is dairy-free. I prefer red-skinned potatoes in this case because they hold together so well when cooked. A salad and some crusty bread would nicely round out the meal.

Serves 2–3

2 large red-skinned potatoes, cut into small (1/2-inch) dice
3 tablespoons olive oil
6 garlic cloves, minced
1/4 teaspoon crushed red pepper flakes
1 (8-ounce) package tempeh, cut into 1/2-inch dice
1 (16-ounce) can tomatoes, finely diced with their juice
1/2 teaspoon salt
Freshly ground black pepper to taste
1/4 cup water
1/4 cup finely chopped fresh parsley

1. Place the potatoes in a large skillet and add about 1/2 inch of water. Cover the pan and cook the potatoes over medium heat until tender when gently pierced with a knife, about 7 minutes. Drain the potatoes in a colander and let them sit while proceeding with the next step.
2. Wipe the skillet clean. Pour the oil in the skillet and heat it over medium heat. Add the garlic and red pepper flakes and cook 30 seconds. Stir in the tempeh, toss, and cook 1 minute.
3. Mix in the tomatoes, salt, pepper, and 1/4 cup of water. Cover the pan and simmer 5 minutes. Remove the cover and check the thickness of the sauce. If it seems watery, cook a few more minutes uncovered. Just before serving, stir in the parsley.

Pasta and Noodles

No cuisine has helped vegetarian meal planning more than Italy's, most especially with its contribution of pasta. Everyone loves pasta, and its popularity shows no sign of abating.

But what is it that makes some pasta preparations spectacular and others undistinguished? Though plain buttered or oiled noodles can be satisfying, it's really the sauce that makes the dish. It needn't be complex to be delicious; sometimes just a few ingredients like olive oil, garlic, and hot peppers can create a humble yet seductive dressing for pasta. The ingredients must, above all, be intensely flavorful to bring pasta to life. This is equally true of Asian noodles, which are also a fantastic contribution to the vegetarian's repertoire.

The quantity of sauce is another important factor in its ability to enhance pasta. There is a limit to how much we can cut back on fat without destroying our final creation. For a pound of dried pasta, a minimum of 1/4 cup of olive oil is required to adequately coat the noodles. We can extend our sauce using a tried-and-true trick—adding some starchy pasta water to it—but the 1/4 cup minimum of olive oil still stands.

Although the importance of a zesty sauce cannot be overemphasized, the *texture* of the pasta is equally significant in producing a superlative pasta dish. If you overcook pasta, no sauce can save it. Pasta should be cooked to the "al dente" stage, which means "firm to the bite." Taste a piece a few minutes before it approaches the recommended cooking time to ensure that it has some chewiness to it. Don't rely just on appearance or the clock. Sample a piece.

And finally, if you can get your hands on some fresh pasta, do so. (Fortunately, it can be found increasingly in towns across the United States.) There is nothing quite like the texture of fresh noodles, and they take only a few minutes to cook. A pound of fresh pasta equals about 3/4 pound dried (see page 226).

Matching a noodle shape to a sauce can be summed up easily: Thick, chunky-style sauces generally go well with bulky noodles, such as penne, rigatoni, ziti, and lasagne. More delicate, finely textured sauces pair better with strands of pasta, such as spaghetti, linguine, vermicelli, and angel hair. There are sauces whose heaviness lies somewhere in between, and you can have more latitude with these.

See also: Penne with Fried Tofu, Roasted Peppers, and Olives (page 464)

Fresh Fettuccine with Spinach, Red Peppers, and Smoked Cheese

This pasta dish is a knockout, and one of my favorite recipes to serve when company's arriving on short notice. Even a die-hard vegetarian like myself will readily admit that the bacon-like flavor of smoked cheese is hard to resist, and here, it weaves magic. If you can't get fresh pasta, 3/4 pound dried linguine could be substituted (odd as it may seem, fresh fettuccine and dried linguine are the same width), but a little character will be lost.

Serves 3–4

1/4 cup olive oil
4 garlic cloves, minced
1 red bell pepper, cut into thin 2-inch-long strips
1 (1-pound) bunch or 1 (10-ounce) package fresh spinach, stems discarded and leaves washed
1/2 teaspoon salt
Generous seasoning freshly ground pepper
1 pound fresh fettuccine
1 cup grated smoked Gouda cheese

1. Bring a large stockpot of water to a boil.
2. Meanwhile heat the olive oil in a large skillet over medium heat. Add the garlic and cook 1 minute. Stir in the pepper and sauté until tender yet crisp, about 7 minutes.
3. Pile on the spinach, and cover the pan. Cook until wilted, about 3 minutes. Stir in the salt and ground pepper. Keep the sauce warm over very low heat.
4. Drop the fresh pasta into the boiling water and cook about 3 minutes, or until al dente. (If you are using dried pasta it will take 7–10 minutes.) Remove 1/4 cup of the starchy pasta water and stir it into the sauce. Drain the pasta and toss it with the sauce. Mix in the cheese and serve immediately.

Pasta Equivalents

A pound of uncooked fresh pasta and a pound of uncooked dried pasta are not equivalent because, when cooked, their yield will be different. Uncooked fresh pasta contains moisture and consequently weighs more than dried pasta, cup for cup. Because fresh pasta weighs more, you get less volume per pound. The best way to determine equivalents is by measuring volume. Use the guide below to help you substitute accurately.

Dried linguine	Fresh fettuccine	Yield (volume)
½ pound	10.5 ounces	3½ cups cooked
¾ pound	1 pound	5 cups cooked
1 pound	1 pound 5 ounces	7 cups cooked

Fresh Fettuccine with Uncooked Tomato Sauce and Goat Cheese

In the summer months when fat, juicy tomatoes are abundant, nothing beats this pasta dish for flavor and quickness.

Serves 4

6 ripe plum tomatoes, cored and cut into small dice
3 garlic cloves, minced
1 cup chopped fresh basil
½ teaspoon salt
Generous seasoning freshly ground black pepper
⅓ cup olive oil
4 ounces soft mild goat cheese, crumbled
1 pound fresh fettuccine (or ¾ pound dry linguine)

1. Combine the tomatoes, garlic, basil, salt, pepper, olive oil, and goat cheese in a very large bowl and toss gently. Let sit 30–60 minutes.
2. Bring a large stockpot of water to a boil. Drop in the fresh pasta and cook about 3 minutes. Taste to check its texture. It should be al dente, that is, still chewy. (If you are using dried pasta, it will take considerably longer.) Drain thoroughly in a colander.
3. Drop the pasta into the sauce and toss well. Serve immediately.

Linguine with Roasted Red Peppers, Peas, and Pine Nuts

I love the array of colors and textures in this sauce. In a well-stocked kitchen, these ingredients will all be on hand and you can put this sauce together in just a couple of minutes. If Romano cheese is available, you'll find that its assertiveness is delightful with these flavors.

Serves 4

1 pound linguine
1/3 cup olive oil
4 garlic cloves, minced
3/4 cup diced roasted red peppers, store-bought or freshly roasted (page 19)
2 tablespoons pine nuts
1 1/2 cups frozen peas, thawed
1/2 teaspoon salt
Generous seasoning freshly ground pepper
1/2 cup chopped fresh parsley
1/3 cup grated Romano (pecorino) (preferably) or Parmesan cheese

1. Bring a large stockpot of water to a boil. Drop in the linguine and cook until al dente, about 7 minutes.
2. Meanwhile heat the olive oil in a medium-size skillet over medium heat. Add the garlic and cook 1 minute. Stir in the red peppers, pine nuts, peas, salt, and pepper and cook 1 minute, stirring often.
3. Remove 1/4 cup of the starchy pasta water and add it to the sauce along with the parsley.
4. Drain the linguine in a colander and place it in a large bowl or return it to the pot. Pour on the sauce, then sprinkle on the cheese. Toss thoroughly and serve.

Tortellini with Fennel, Tomatoes, and Spinach

The mild licorice flavor in fennel is highlighted by this garlicky mélange of vegetables to create a wonderful sauce with a pleasing palette of colors.

Serves 4

1/4 cup olive oil
6 garlic cloves, minced
1/8 teaspoon crushed red pepper flakes
1 fennel bulb, halved vertically and thinly sliced (reserve feathery sprigs)
2 plum tomatoes, seeded and cubed
5 cups (5 ounces) fresh spinach, stems discarded
1/4 teaspoon salt
Generous seasoning freshly ground black pepper
1 pound frozen cheese tortellini
1/4 cup grated Parmesan cheese
1 tablespoon finely chopped fennel sprigs (see above)

1. Bring a large stockpot of water to a boil.
2. Heat the oil in a large skillet over medium heat. Add the garlic and red pepper flakes and cook 1 minute. Stir in the fennel and sauté 5 minutes, or until crisp but tender. Add the tomatoes, toss well, and cook 5 minutes, or until the tomato pieces begin to soften.
3. Stir in the spinach, salt, and pepper and toss just until wilted, about 1 minute. Keep the sauce warm over low heat.
4. Drop the tortellini into the boiling water and cook until al dente, that is, tender yet firm, about 5 minutes. Meanwhile check the consistency of the sauce. Depending on the juiciness of your tomatoes, it might need some liquid. If so, remove 2 tablespoons of the starchy pasta water and add it to the sauce. Drain the tortellini thoroughly, then mix it into the sauce along with the cheese. Serve with the chopped fennel sprigs sprinkled on top.

Tortellini with Kale and Garlicky Bread Crumbs

Toasted, buttery bread crumbs mixed with garlic and herbs become a perfect vehicle for flavor when quickly tossed with pasta. Here, with tender juicy kale as a companion, we have a great match.

Serves 4

The Crumbs
1 tablespoon olive oil
2 garlic cloves, minced
1 cup coarse fresh bread crumbs (from about 2 slices bread; see page 19)
1 tablespoon mixed chopped fresh herbs (such as rosemary, thyme, basil, tarragon, parsley)

1 pound kale
3 tablespoons olive oil
4 garlic cloves, minced
1/4 teaspoon crushed red pepper flakes
1 pound frozen cheese tortellini
2 teaspoons balsamic vinegar
1/4 teaspoon salt
Freshly ground black pepper
2 tablespoons grated Parmesan cheese

1. To prepare the crumbs, heat the oil in a large skillet over medium heat. Add the garlic and cook 30 seconds. Stir in the bread crumbs and toss continuously until the crumbs become golden, about 5 minutes. Stir in the herbs, toss a few times, then scrape the crumbs into a medium-size bowl. Let them cool. Hold on to the skillet for the next step. (The crumbs can be prepared up to 24 hours in advance.)
2. Bring a large stockpot of water to a boil. Prepare the kale by ripping the leafy part off the stems. Gather the leaves into tight bunches and cut them into shreds (chiffonade). Wash them by dunking them in a large bowl of cold water. Remove and drain in a colander.

3. In the skillet in which the crumbs cooked, heat 2 tablespoons of the olive oil over medium heat. Add the garlic and red pepper flakes and cook 30 seconds. In batches add the kale with the water that clings to it and toss to mix with the garlic. Cover the pan tightly and cook, stirring occasionally, until the kale wilts and becomes tender, about 5–7 minutes. Taste the kale for tenderness. There should be a few tablespoons of liquid in the bottom of the pan when done. If it is dry, add a few tablespoons of boiling pasta water.

4. Meanwhile drop the tortellini into the boiling water and cook until tender, about 5 minutes. Drain in a colander.

5. Sprinkle the balsamic vinegar, salt, and pepper on the kale. Mix the tortellini into the kale along with the Parmesan cheese and remaining tablespoon of olive oil. Serve with a generous handful of crumbs on each serving.

Tortellini with Leeks and Cream

This sauce is very simple and elegant. You don't need much cheese or any other additions because the wonderful flavor of leeks carries the dish.

Serves 3–4

2 large leeks
1 tablespoon unsalted butter
½ cup heavy cream
¼ teaspoon salt
Freshly ground black pepper to taste
1 pound frozen cheese tortellini
1 tablespoon grated Parmesan cheese

1. Bring a large stockpot of water to a boil.
2. Meanwhile slice the roots off the leeks, plus all but 2 inches of the green tops. Slice the leeks in half lengthwise. Under cold running water rinse the leeks, thumbing through all the leaves to dislodge any hidden dirt. Do this thoroughly to rid them of *all* their dirt. Thinly slice the leeks. You can use the light green tops, but discard any dark green pieces. You should get about 2½ cups sliced leeks.
3. Melt the butter over medium heat in a large skillet. Add the leeks and sauté until tender, about 10 minutes. Stir frequently, and keep an eye on the leeks so they don't get at all brown.
4. Pour in the cream, salt, and pepper. Heat just until it boils, then turn the heat very low to keep the sauce warm.
5. Drop the tortellini in the boiling water and cook until al dente, about 5 minutes. Drain in a colander, then mix into the sauce along with the Parmesan cheese. Toss and serve.

Rigatoni with Potatoes, Arugula, and Tomatoes

Pairing pasta with potatoes, as the Genoese do in their regional dish Trenette with Pesto and Potatoes, makes a hearty dish. The potatoes soak up the garlicky sauce and thereby provide little bursts of flavor. This rustic treatment of pasta is utterly satisfying.

Serves 4

1/4 cup olive oil
1 large boiling (waxy) potato, peeled and cut into 1/2-inch dice
1 pound rigatoni
6 garlic cloves, minced
1 (16-ounce) can tomatoes with their juice, finely diced
1/2 teaspoon salt
Generous seasoning freshly ground black pepper
1 bunch arugula, coarse stems discarded and leaves cut in half (3–4 cups lightly packed)
1/4 cup grated Romano (pecorino) cheese

---

1. Bring a large stockpot of water to a boil.
2. Meanwhile heat the oil in a medium-size, preferably non-stick, skillet over medium heat. Add the potato and cook until tender and golden, about 10 minutes.
3. When the water boils, drop in the rigatoni. Cook until al dente, about 10 minutes.
4. Meanwhile add the garlic to the potatoes and cook 1 minute. Do not let it color. Stir in the tomatoes, salt, and pepper and cook 2 minutes. Mix in the arugula and cook 1 minute, or until wilted.
5. Drain the rigatoni and place it in a large pasta bowl or return it to the pot. Pour on the sauce, then sprinkle on the cheese. Toss and serve.

Ziti with Cauliflower, Tomatoes, and Hot Peppers

Tomatoes, garlic, and hot peppers bring out the best in cauliflower. This is an electrifying and delicious pasta dish.

Serves 4

3 tablespoons olive oil
6 garlic cloves, minced
1/4 teaspoon crushed red pepper flakes
1 (16-ounce) can tomatoes, finely diced with their juice
1 small (about 1 1/2 pounds) cauliflower, cut into tiny florets
1/2 teaspoon salt
1 pound ziti
2 tablespoons minced fresh parsley
3 tablespoons grated Parmesan cheese

1. Bring a large stockpot of water to a boil.
2. Heat the olive oil in a large skillet over medium heat. Add the garlic and hot pepper flakes and cook 1 minute. Do not let the garlic brown at all. Mix in the tomatoes and their juice, then stir in the cauliflower and salt. Toss well and cover the pan. Cook until the cauliflower is tender, about 5 minutes.
3. Drop the ziti into the boiling water and cook until al dente. Taste one to test it.
4. Drain the ziti in a colander and return it to the pot, or place it in a large pasta bowl. Pour on the sauce, toss, then sprinkle on the parsley and Parmesan cheese. Serve immediately.

Penne with Chunky Sun-Dried Tomato and Black Olive Pesto

Choose your favorite olives to mix into this pesto. In a pinch I have even used canned, "California-style" black olives and had good results. This pesto packs a punch, so all you need for this simply delicious, yet hearty sauce is some pasta to toss it on.

Serves 4

2 ounces (about 13) loose sun-dried tomatoes
1/3 cup olive oil
2 garlic cloves, finely chopped
3 tablespoons pine nuts
2/3 cup chopped fresh parsley
1/2 teaspoon salt
Freshly ground black pepper to taste
1/2 cup pitted black olives (page 95)
3 tablespoons grated Parmesan cheese
1 pound penne

1. Steam thc tomatoes in a vegetable steamer until they are soft and tender, about 10 minutes. Remove from the pot and let cool.
2. In a food processor combine the tomatoes, oil, and garlic and process until it is the texture of coarse crumbs. Add the pine nuts, parsley, salt, and pepper and process until somewhat smooth but with bits still visible. Add the olives and pulse just a few times to chop them into small pieces. Scrape the pesto into a bowl, then stir in the cheese by hand. (You can prepare the pesto up to 4 days in advance. Cover and chill until ready to use.)
3. Bring a large stockpot of water to a boil. Drop in the penne and cook until al dente. Remove 1/2 cup of the starchy pasta water and stir it into the pesto.
4. Drain the penne. Toss it with the pesto and serve. I prefer it served warm, not piping hot.)

Penne with Yellow Peppers, Tomatoes, and Black Olives

If it's true that we also eat with our eyes, then both the colors and flavors in this striking treatment will wonderfully satisfy us. The "bite" of Romano cheese juxtaposed with the sweetness of the yellow peppers works well here.

Serves 4

1/3 cup olive oil
1 yellow bell pepper, cut into strips 2 × 1/2 inch
6 garlic cloves, minced
1/4 teaspoon crushed red pepper flakes
4 plum tomatoes, cut into 1-inch cubes
15–20 black olives (your favorite kind), pitted and halved (page 95)
1 pound penne
1/2 cup chopped fresh basil or parsley
1/4 teaspoon salt
1/4 cup grated Romano cheese plus extra for serving

1. Bring a large stockpot of water to a boil.
2. Heat the oil in a large skillet over medium heat. Add the yellow pepper and sauté 5 minutes, or until tender yet still crunchy.
3. Add the garlic and hot pepper flakes and cook 2 minutes. Stir in the tomatoes and olives and cook 5 minutes, stirring often. Keep warm over low heat while the pasta cooks.
4. Drop the penne into the boiling water and cook until al dente, about 10 minutes. Remove 2 tablespoons of the starchy pasta water and stir it into the tomatoes along with the basil and salt.
5. Drain the penne thoroughly and return it to the pot, or place it in a large bowl. Stir in the vegetable mixture and Romano cheese. Serve with extra cheese to pass at the table.

Penne with Portobello Mushrooms

Slices of juicy portobello mushrooms make this pasta dish both substantial and elegant. Choose portobellos that are very firm and fresh for best results.

Serves 4 generously

1 pound penne
2 tablespoons olive oil
3/4 pound portobello mushrooms, sliced 1/2 inch thick
4 garlic cloves, minced
3 plum tomatoes, seeded and diced
1 cup frozen peas, thawed
1/2 cup heavy cream
1 tablespoon chopped fresh basil, or 1/2 teaspoon dried
1/4 teaspoon salt
Generous seasoning freshly ground black pepper
1/4 cup grated Parmesan cheese

1. Bring a large stockpot of water to a boil. Drop in the penne and cook until al dente, about 10 minutes.
2. Meanwhile heat the oil in a large skillet over medium heat. Add the mushrooms and sauté until brown, juicy, and cooked throughout, about 10 minutes. Stir often.
3. Add the garlic, toss, and cook 2 minutes. Stir in the tomatoes and peas and cook 2 minutes, or until the tomatoes are hot throughout. Mix in the cream, basil, salt, and pepper and boil 1 minute.
4. Drain the penne and return it to the pot, or place it in a large pasta bowl. Pour on the sauce, sprinkle on the Parmesan cheese, then toss. Serve immediately.

Angel Hair with Spinach and Feta Cheese in Garlic Sauce

Garlic lovers, take note of this captivating sauce, which also features feta cheese in a notable, but not overpowering way.

Serves 4

- 1/4 cup olive oil
- 8 garlic cloves, minced
- 1/2 teaspoon crushed red pepper flakes
- 3 tablespoons finely chopped walnuts
- 1 (1-pound) bunch or 1 (10-ounce) package fresh spinach, washed thoroughly, stems discarded, and leaves torn into small pieces, or 1 (10-ounce) package frozen chopped spinach, thawed and squeezed dry
- 1/2 teaspoon salt
- 3/4 cup milk
- 1 pound angel hair pasta
- 4 ounces crumbled feta cheese (about 3/4 cup)
- 2 tablespoons Romano (pecorino)cheese

1. Bring a large stockpot of water to a boil.
2. Meanwhile heat the oil in a large skillet over medium heat. Add the garlic, red pepper flakes, and walnuts and cook 1 minute, stirring frequently.
3. Pile on the spinach and immediately cover the pan. Cook just until the spinach wilts, about 3 minutes. (If you are using frozen spinach, just stir it into the garlic mixture.) Use tongs to toss the spinach with the garlic mixture. Mix in the salt and milk and keep the sauce warm over low heat.
4. Drop the angel hair into the pot and cook until al dente. Drain thoroughly and return it to the pot or place it in a large pasta bowl. Pour on the sauce, then sprinkle on the feta and Romano cheeses. Toss and serve.

Spaghettini with Garlic, Hot Peppers, and Toasted Bread Crumbs

The garlicky sauce in this humble pasta rendition will have you licking your lips and asking for more. You don't need Parmesan cheese in this case because the bread crumbs do the trick.

Serves 2

4 tablespoons olive oil
1 cup coarse fresh bread crumbs (from about 2 slices bread; see page 19)
½ pound spaghettini
6 garlic cloves, finely chopped
¼ teaspoon crushed red pepper flakes
2 plum tomatoes, cored and diced
1 cup chopped fresh parsley
¼ teaspoon salt

1. Bring a large stockpot of water to a boil.
2. Meanwhile heat 1 tablespoon of the oil in a medium or large skillet over medium heat. Add the bread crumbs and cook, tossing frequently, until they begin to get golden, about 5 minutes. Scrape them into a bowl and set aside.
3. Drop the spaghettini into the boiling water and cook until al dente, about 8–9 minutes. Heat the remaining 3 tablespoons of oil in the same skillet the bread crumbs were cooked in. Add the garlic and crushed red pepper flakes and cook 1 minute. Stir in the tomatoes and sauté 1 minute. Mix in the parsley, salt, and ¼ cup of the starchy pasta water. Remove from the heat.
4. Drain the spaghettini and return it to the pot or place it in a large bowl. Pour on the sauce and toss well. Serve with half the bread crumbs sprinkled on each serving.

Macaroni and Cheese

This is a stove-top version of the favorite American classic. It is just as kids would want it—smooth, creamy, and untouched by any adult embellishments—just macaroni and a silky cheese sauce. Do not turn this into a casserole and bake it, for the cheese will clump and lose its creaminess.

Serves 4

2 large eggs
1/2 teaspoon Dijon-style mustard
A few dashes cayenne
3/4 teaspoon salt
1 (12-ounce) can evaporated milk
1 pound elbow macaroni
2 tablespoons unsalted butter, cut into bits
8 ounces (2 1/2–3 cups) grated extra-sharp Cheddar cheese
1/4 cup grated Parmesan cheese

1. Bring a large stockpot of water to a boil.
2. Meanwhile beat the eggs, mustard, cayenne, and salt together in a large measuring cup or bowl. Beat in the evaporated milk.
3. Cook the macaroni until al dente. Taste one to be sure. Drain it in a colander and shake well to remove all the water. Return the macaroni to the pot and place it over low heat. Add the butter and stir until it has melted.
4. Pour on the milk mixture, sprinkle on the cheeses, then stir until the cheeses have melted and the sauce has thickened slightly. Serve immediately. The sauce will get too firm if left too long.

Note: To reheat any leftover macaroni and cheese, heat a bit of milk in a saucepan until very hot. Add the leftover macaroni and stir until piping hot.

Potato Gnocchi and Mushrooms in Gorgonzola Sauce

A little Gorgonzola (or other blue cheese) goes a long way to create a robust sauce for these hearty gnocchi. Look for potato gnocchi in the frozen pasta section of your supermarket; they are usually additive-free, and made with only a few simple ingredients.

Serves 2–3

1 tablespoon olive oil
12 ounces mushrooms, thinly sliced (about 4½ cups)
1 pound frozen potato gnocchi
2 garlic cloves, minced
¼ cup milk
3 ounces Gorgonzola or other blue cheese, cut into small dice
2 tablespoons minced fresh parsley
¼ teaspoon salt
Generous seasoning freshly ground black pepper

1. Bring a large stockpot of water to a boil.
2. Meanwhile heat the oil in a large skillet over medium-high heat. Add the mushrooms and sauté until they render their juices, then reabsorb them and begin to get dry, about 10 minutes. Stir often.
3. Drop the gnocchi into the boiling water and cook until tender, about 7 minutes.
4. Add the garlic to the mushrooms and cook 2 minutes, tossing frequently. Pour in the milk and bring to a boil. Stir in the blue cheese, parsley, salt, and pepper and toss.
5. Drain the gnocchi and add it to the skillet. Toss 1 minute, or just until the cheese melts. Serve immediately.

Potato Gnocchi with Swiss Chard and Garlic

Garlic and greens were made for each other, as this aromatic sauce demonstrates. Feel free to substitute spinach, kale, escarole, or broccoli rabe and you'll still have a winner.

Serves 2–3

1 pound Swiss chard (weight with stems)
3 tablespoons olive oil
4 garlic cloves, minced
1/4 teaspoon crushed red pepper flakes
1/4 teaspoon salt
Freshly ground black pepper
1 pound frozen potato gnocchi (see Potato Gnocchi and Mushrooms in Gorgonzola Sauce, page 241)
2 tablespoons grated Parmesan cheese

1. Bring a large stockpot of water to a boil.
2. Meanwhile chop the stems off the chard. Rinse the stems under cold running water to rid them of any sand. Chop them into 1/2-inch pieces and set them aside. Wash the greens by dunking them in a large bowl of cold water. Remove the leaves, then dump out the water. Repeat until there is no sandy sediment in the water. Drain the greens. Gather the leaves into bunches and slice them into 1/2-inch-wide strips.
3. Heat the olive oil in a large skillet over medium heat. Add the garlic and hot pepper flakes and cook 1 minute. Add the chard stems and leaves with just the water that clings to them. Toss with the garlic, then cover the pan. Cook, tossing occasionally, just until the chard is wilted, about 3 minutes. Season with the salt and pepper.
4. Drop the gnocchi into the boiling water. Cook according to the package directions, probably about 5 minutes. Drain thoroughly, then mix into the chard. Sprinkle on the cheese, toss, and serve.

Spicy Thai-Style Noodles

Thai cooking is noted for its contrasting combinations of sweet, hot, sour, salty, and bitter flavors. These forces come together to make a beguiling sauce in this special noodle dish, which is one of my all-time favorites.

Although the list of ingredients is long, these noodles are very easy to prepare and are a great choice for entertaining because of their noteworthy flavor and vivid color.

Serves 4

The Sauce

1/4 cup natural-style peanut butter, chunky or smooth
3 tablespoons tamari soy sauce
3 tablespoons tomato sauce or tomato puree
3 tablespoons dry sherry
Grated zest of 1 lime
2 tablespoons lime juice
2 tablespoons brown sugar
1/2–1 teaspoon chili paste with garlic (see Note)
2 tablespoons canola oil
4 garlic cloves, minced

The Vegetable Mixture

2 tablespoons finely chopped roasted peanuts
2 scallions, very thinly sliced
1 small red bell pepper, very finely diced
10 snow peas, cut diagonally into thin shreds
1 pound spaghetti

1. Bring a large stockpot of water to a boil.
2. Place the peanut butter in a medium-size bowl. With a whisk or fork stir in the soy sauce, tomato sauce, sherry, lime zest, lime juice, brown sugar, and chili paste.

3. Heat the oil in a small saucepan over medium heat. Add the garlic and cook 1 minute. Stir in the peanut sauce and keep warm over low heat. Do not let the sauce in any way simmer or boil or it will get too thick; it just needs to be slightly warmed. (The sauce may be prepared to this point up to 6 hours in advance. Reheat when ready to combine with the pasta.)

4. Combine the peanuts, scallions, red pepper, and snow peas in a small bowl and set aside.

5. Drop the spaghetti into the boiling water and cook until the noodles are tender yet still chewy and slightly firm, about 7 minutes. Drain in a colander and return to the pot or place in a large bowl. Pour on the sauce and toss with the noodles. Sprinkle on the vegetable mixture and mix again. Serve immediately.

Note: Chili paste with garlic is a Chinese condiment available in specialty stores, health food stores, and many supermarkets.

Noodles with Cashews in Curried Coconut Sauce

This wondrous sauce takes only a few minutes to make, yet has great depth and complexity. You can prepare the sauce well in advance and come dinnertime, all you'll need to do is cook the pasta. Do serve these noodles in bowls, Asian-style; it adds to their charm.

Serves 4

1 tablespoon canola oil
3 garlic cloves, minced
2 teaspoons minced gingerroot
2 teaspoons ground coriander
1 1/2 teaspoons ground cumin
1/2 teaspoon turmeric
1/4 teaspoon ground cardamom
1/8 teaspoon cayenne pepper
1 (14-ounce) can unsweetened coconut milk (see Note)
2 tablespoons lemon juice
1 teaspoon salt
1 pound spaghettini
4 scallions, very thinly sliced
1/2 cup coarsely chopped dry-roasted cashews
1 1/2 tablespoons minced cilantro (optional)

1. Bring a large stockpot of water to a boil.
2. To make the sauce, heat the oil in a small saucepan over medium heat. Add the garlic and gingerroot and cook 1 minute. Do not let the garlic get brown. Stir in the coriander, cumin, turmeric, and cayenne and cook 1 minute.
3. Slowly whisk in the coconut milk until it is smooth and well blended. Stir in the lemon juice and salt and heat until hot.
4. Cook the spaghettini until al dente, that is, still somewhat chewy. Drain thoroughly

and return it to the pot. Pour on the sauce, then sprinkle on the scallions and cashews. With tongs toss to evenly coat the noodles. Serve in bowls with some cilantro sprinkled on top, if desired.

Note: Coconut milks vary in thickness. The final sauce should be the consistency of heavy cream, no thicker. If the sauce is too thick, add a few tablespoons of water.

Spicy Peanut Noodles

My friend Darra Goldstein, in her wonderful cookbook *The Vegetarian Hearth,* has a fabulous recipe for Spicy Soba that haunted me for days after I prepared it. Here is my rendition with a few changes from the original. You are likely to have all these ingredients on hand and will be able to put this together in minutes. If you happen to have soba (buckwheat noodles) in your larder, however, try it with them for a tantalizing marriage of flavors.

This has become a staple dish in our house because it's so quick to prepare and utterly satisfying.

Serves 3–4

1/4 cup natural-style peanut butter
1/3 cup tamari soy sauce
2 tablespoons water
1/3 cup firmly packed light brown sugar
1/4 cup oriental sesame oil
2 garlic cloves, put through a press or minced
1 teaspoon minced gingerroot
1/2 teaspoon crushed red pepper flakes
6 scallions, thinly sliced (set aside 2 tablespoons for garnish)
1 pound thin spaghetti

1. Bring a large stockpot of water to a boil.
2. Meanwhile whisk together the peanut butter and tamari in a small saucepan. Stir in all of the remaining ingredients—except the reserved scallions and the spaghetti—until smooth. Put a low heat under the pot to warm the sauce.
3. Drop the spaghetti into the boiling water and cook until al dente. Don't overcook the pasta; it should remain chewy. Drain thoroughly in a colander and return it to the pot. Pour on the sauce and toss. Serve in bowls and garnish with the remaining scallions.

Do-Ahead Casseroles, Gratins, and Tians

Often a one-dish meal that has been made well in advance and needs only to be popped in the oven come mealtime is the perfect solution for your busy schedule. So if the end of the day is when the crunch is on, and you have some time to cook earlier in the day, you'll benefit from selecting a do-ahead recipe out of this chapter.

Some of these casseroles are composed of raw vegetables with little or no precooking involved (tians), and some require more attention, like cooking pasta or making a sauce, but whatever the case, these are ideal cool-weather dishes that will fill your house with warmth and aroma.

White Bean and Vegetable Gratin

This aromatic gratin has become my favorite bean dish. Under a blanket of buttery crumbs is a brightly colored concoction of beans, vegetables, and herbs that creates delectable juices to be sopped up with some crusty French bread. To get these juices you must use ripe tomatoes and very tender white beans; home-cooked beans that are too firm will absorb all the rendered juices and make the mixture dry. Keep an eye on the gratin during the last 15 minutes of cooking. If it appears dry, add a little vegetable stock or thin tomato liquid (the liquid present in canned tomatoes is good) and let it bake with the bean mixture for the remaining 15 minutes. This will thicken the liquid and allow it to blend with the other flavors.

Serves 3–4

2 cups (6 ounces) green beans, each cut in half
4 cups freshly cooked or canned small white beans, such as navy or Great Northern (rinsed thoroughly and well drained if canned)
3 ripe tomatoes, seeded and quartered
1 small red onion, quartered vertically, sections separated
1 yellow bell pepper, cored and cut into 1½-inch chunks
2 small jalapeño peppers (see Note), seeded and minced, or ¼ teaspoon crushed red pepper flakes
5 garlic cloves, roughly chopped
¼ cup olive oil
1 teaspoon chopped fresh thyme, or ½ teaspoon dried
Salt
Generous seasoning freshly ground black pepper

The Topping
1 cup fresh bread crumbs (from about 2 slices bread; see page 19)
1 tablespoon olive oil

1. Preheat the oven to 375 degrees.
2. Steam the green beans until crunchy and bright green, though not yet tender, about 5 minutes.
3. In a large bowl combine the green beans with all the remaining ingredients *except* those for the topping. Toss well, then place in a 2½-quart gratin dish or other shallow casserole. Pat down the top to make it smooth.
4. In a small bowl combine the bread crumbs with the 1 tablespoon oil and mix to coat evenly. Sprinkle the crumbs all over the casserole, then cover the dish with foil. (The gratin may be prepared to this point up to 8 hours in advance.)
5. Bake, covered, for 30 minutes. Remove the foil and bake 30 more minutes. Let sit 10 minutes before serving.

Note: Wear rubber gloves when handling chili peppers.

Gratins

In the United States "au gratin" has become synonymous with cheese sauce, but this is a misuse of the words. In French cooking, gratin simply means "crusted." (In colloquial French *le gratin* refers to the "upper crust" of society.)

A gratin is several ingredients that are placed in a shallow baking dish so that there is a lot of surface exposed. The ingredients are then sprinkled with bread crumbs, or cheese, or are mixed into a white sauce and baked until the characteristic "crust" is formed. Even a fruit dessert can be cooked "au gratin," with sugar and butter or cream melding to form a crunchy topping. Few people can resist a sizzling, golden-topped dish fresh out of the oven, and that accounts for the great appeal of something "gratinéed."

A gratin is also the name of the oval, earthenware baking dish that these crusty creations have been cooked in, so that a "gratin" refers to the preparation inside the dish as well as the baking dish itself.

Penne and Cauliflower Gratin in Tomato-Cream Sauce

Here's an upscale yet homey version of macaroni and cheese with a lighter touch and deeper flavor. The sauce is unusually quick to prepare and the final result very tasty.

Serves 4

1 small cauliflower, cut into small florets (about 4 cups florets)
½ pound penne
1 ¼ cups chunky tomato sauce, store-bought or homemade
1 cup light cream (or ½ cup heavy cream and ½ cup low-fat milk)
1 garlic clove, put through a press or minced
¼ teaspoon crushed red pepper flakes
½ cup finely chopped fresh basil or parsley
¼ cup grated Parmesan cheese
¼ teaspoon salt
½ cup fresh bread crumbs (made from 1 slice bread)
1 tablespoon olive oil

1. Bring a large pot of water to a boil. Drop in the cauliflower and cook 5 minutes, or just until tender. Scoop it out with a strainer and drop it into a 2½-quart casserole.
2. Drop the penne into the water and cook until al dente, about 10 minutes. Drain it in a colander and shake to remove all the moisture. Mix it into the cauliflower.
3. Preheat the oven to 400 degrees. In a large bowl mix together the tomato sauce, cream, garlic, red pepper flakes, basil or parsley, cheese, and salt. Pour the sauce on the pasta and toss well. (If you don't plan to bake the gratin right away, pour on just one third of the sauce and toss. You can prepare it to this point up to 4 hours in advance. Just before baking pour on the remaining sauce and toss again.)
4. Combine the bread crumbs and olive oil in a small bowl and mix until evenly moistened. Sprinkle all over the gratin. Bake 20–25 minutes, or until hot, bubbly, and golden on top. Let sit 5 minutes before serving.

Potato, Spinach, and Feta Cheese Gratin

Here's a good choice for a blustery evening when you want a hearty casserole that will warm your bones.

Serves 4

1 (1-pound) bunch or 1 (10-ounce) bag fresh spinach, well washed and stems removed, or
  1 (10-ounce) package frozen chopped spinach, thawed
Unsalted butter for greasing dish plus 2 tablespoons
5 medium-large (2½ pounds) boiling (waxy) potatoes, peeled and *very* thinly sliced
Salt
Freshly ground black pepper to taste
4 ounces (about ¾ cup) crumbled feta cheese
2 scallions, very thinly sliced
1 tablespoon minced fresh dill, or 1 teaspoon dried
1¼ cups low-fat milk

1. Place the washed, fresh spinach in a large pot. Cover the pot and cook the spinach over medium heat just until it begins to wilt and is still slightly firm, about 1 minute. (You want to cook it as little as possible because it will bake later.) Put the spinach in a strainer and press out as much liquid as possible with the back of a large spoon. Set the spinach aside. If you are using frozen spinach, just place it in the strainer and extract the liquid.
2. Preheat the oven to 425 degrees. Butter a 2½-quart shallow baking dish.
3. Spread half the potatoes in the baking dish. Season with salt and pepper, then top with the spinach, feta cheese, scallions, and dill. Layer on the remaining potato slices, pour the milk all over the potatoes, then dot the gratin with the remaining 2 tablespoons of butter cut into bits.
4. Cover the dish with foil. Bake 30 minutes. Remove the foil and bake 30 more minutes, or until the potatoes are tender and golden brown on top.

Rice and Leek Gratin

If you have leftover rice, this dish is especially easy to prepare. If you must cook the rice for it, do all the preparatory work in the recipe while the rice is cooking and you'll be able to assemble the casserole by the time the rice is cooled.

Serves 4

The Rice
2¼ cups vegetable stock, store-bought or homemade (page 13)
1 cup basmati or converted white rice
Dash salt
1 teaspoon canola oil

3 large leeks
Unsalted butter for greasing dish, plus 1 tablespoon
1 teaspoon sugar
1 tomato, seeded and very finely diced
½ teaspoon chopped fresh thyme, or ¼ teaspoon dried
½ teaspoon salt
Freshly ground black pepper to taste
1 egg, beaten
1 cup whole milk
1 cup (3 ounces) grated Gruyère or other Swiss cheese
1 slice bread
1 tablespoon olive oil

1. To cook the rice, bring the vegetable stock to a boil in a medium-size saucepan. Add the rice, salt, and oil and lower the heat to a simmer. Cook, uncovered, until all the liquid is absorbed, about 20 minutes. Place the rice in a large bowl and let cool to room temperature.
2. Meanwhile chop almost all of the green tops off the leeks, except for about 2 inches.

Discard the tops. Cut the roots off the leeks, then slice the leeks in half vertically. Under cold running water wash all the sand from the leeks, flipping through each leaf with your fingers to find any hidden dirt. Be thorough; leeks harbor a lot of dirt. Thinly slice the leeks.

3. In a large skillet heat the butter over medium heat. Add the leeks and sauté until tender, about 10 minutes. Stir in the sugar, tomato, and thyme and cook 2 minutes. Let cool to room temperature.

4. Combine the leek mixture with the rice. Mix in the salt, pepper, egg, and milk.

5. Butter a 2- to 2½-quart shallow gratin dish. Spread half of the rice mixture in the bottom of the dish. Top with the cheese. Spread on the remaining rice mixture and smooth over the top.

6. Put the bread in the blender or food processor to make crumbs. Pour them into a small bowl, then stir in the tablespoon of oil to coat them. Sprinkle them all over the casserole. (The gratin may be prepared to this point up to 8 hours in advance. Cover and chill until ready to bake. Bring to room temperature before cooking.)

7. Preheat the oven to 375 degrees. Bake the gratin 35 minutes, or until sizzling and brown on top. Let sit 5 minutes before serving.

Sweet Potato and Vegetable Tian

One of the wonderful by-products of a slow-cooking tian is that your house will be permeated with intoxicating aromas that can help set the stage for a sumptuous peasant-style meal. Crusty Tuscan-style bread will continue the theme.

Rosemary is the herb of choice in this tian because of its compatibility with sweet potatoes. Do go out of your way to include it because it works so well here.

A tian is a Provençal earthenware baking dish and also the name of the finished product of slowly baked vegetables. You can have successful results with any shallow casserole, but the heavier the better.

Serves 4

1 red onion, cut vertically into sixths, sections separated
1 green bell pepper, cut into 1 ½-inch chunks
12 ounces mushrooms, large ones quartered, medium ones halved
2 plum tomatoes, cored and cut into sixths
3 medium-large sweet potatoes or yams, peeled, quartered lengthwise, and sliced ¼ inch thick
4 garlic cloves, thinly sliced
2 teaspoons chopped fresh rosemary, or ¾ teaspoon crumbled dried
½ teaspoon salt
Generous seasoning freshly ground black pepper
⅓ cup olive oil

The Topping
3 slices homemade-type white bread
1 tablespoon olive oil

1. Preheat the oven to 375 degrees. Combine all the vegetables, garlic, and rosemary in a large mixing bowl. Sprinkle on the salt, pepper, and ⅓ cup olive oil and toss to coat thoroughly. (The vegetables may be prepared to this point up to 4 hours in advance.)

2. Drop the vegetables into a shallow 2½-quart ovenproof casserole and press them down evenly. Bake 45 minutes.
3. To make the topping, break up the bread and make coarse crumbs in a food processor. Scrape them into a small bowl and drizzle on the 1 tablespoon of olive oil. Use your fingers to rub the oil evenly into the crumbs.
4. Remove the tian from the oven. Sprinkle the crumbs all over the top. Return the dish to the oven and bake 15 more minutes, or until the vegetables are very tender. Let sit 10 minutes before serving.

Tians

A tian (pronounced TEE-ahn) is a Provençal specialty of vegetables and seasonings cloaked in olive oil and cooked slowly in a hot oven until succulent and tender. "Tian" refers to the method of cooking as well as the heavy baking dish that contains the mélange of ingredients.

In the past, French village bakers would allow home cooks to place their heavy, vegetable-filled tians into still-hot ovens once the last breads were removed. The remaining heat became trapped in the earthenware casseroles and gently cooked the vegetables until they were suffused with the surrounding flavors of a fruity olive oil and aromatic herbs.

When warm weather sets in, it is not uncommon for the French to serve this versatile dish cold, and to tote it along on a picnic. And although it is customary to prepare a simplified tian as a side dish, I love to expand them into one-dish meals. Served with a crusty baguette and some great wine, it's a feast both rustic and sublime.

Cauliflower and Potato Tian

When winter is howling at your door and you want to fill your house with the warmth and bewitching aromas of a slow-cooked, garlicky casserole, choose this homey dish. In India, cauliflower and potatoes are often paired in side dishes and main courses because they enhance each other. Here, a tomato, olive oil, and basil coating gives them a pink hue and a seductive flavor.

Serves 3–4

1 medium (2 pounds) cauliflower, separated into small florets (6 cups florets)
3 medium red-skinned potatoes, quartered lengthwise and sliced 1/4 inch thick
4 garlic cloves, finely chopped
1/4 cup finely chopped fresh parsley
1 tablespoon finely chopped fresh basil, or 1/2 teaspoon dried
1/4 cup tomato paste
1/4 cup olive oil
1/4 cup dry white wine or vegetable stock, store-bought or homemade (page 13)
1/4 cup water
1/4 teaspoon salt
Generous seasoning freshly ground black pepper

The Topping
2 slices homemade-style white bread
1 tablespoon olive oil
1/4 cup grated Parmesan cheese

1. Preheat the oven to 400 degrees.
2. In a large bowl combine the cauliflower, potatoes, garlic, parsley, and basil.
3. In a small bowl beat together the tomato paste, olive oil, wine, water, salt, and pepper. Pour it on the vegetables and toss thoroughly to evenly coat them. Scrape this mixture into a 2 1/2-quart shallow ovenproof casserole. Cover with foil. Bake 45 minutes.

4. Meanwhile make the topping by placing the bread in a food processor or blender and processing to make fresh bread crumbs. Pour them into a bowl, then drizzle on the tablespoon of olive oil. Toss thoroughly to distribute the oil.

5. After the casserole has cooked for 45 minutes, remove it from the oven and discard the foil. Sprinkle on the Parmesan cheese, then distribute the bread crumbs all over the top. Bake 15 more minutes, or until golden brown.

Greens and Bulghur Tian

The contrasting textures of the greens are intriguing and delightful here. Kale has a coarse texture, while escarole and spinach are soft and tender. If you love garlicky greens, this casserole is for you, and the bonus is it's filled with calcium and iron. I was surprised to discover how delicious this tian is cold, so consider taking leftovers to work for lunch, or bringing the tian on a picnic.

A note on organization: If you wash the greens early in the day or at least a few hours before you prepare the entire recipe, you'll find this simplifies the whole process considerably.

Serves 4 as a main course

½ cup bulghur, preferably coarse- cut
2 pounds mixed fresh greens, such as kale, escarole, spinach, and Swiss chard
3 tablespoons olive oil, plus extra for greasing dish
6 garlic cloves, minced
Salt
Freshly ground black pepper to taste
¼ cup grated Parmesan cheese
1 cup grated part-skim mozzarella cheese

The Topping
½ cup fresh bread crumbs (from about 1 slice bread; see page 19)
1 tablespoon olive oil

1. Place the bulghur in a medium-size bowl and pour in enough boiling water to cover the bulghur by 1 inch. Cover the bowl with a plate and let sit 20 minutes. Strain the bulghur, pressing out the excess liquid with the back of a large spoon. Set the bulghur aside.

2. Tear the greens into bite-size pieces and discard the stems. Keep the different greens in separate piles. Thoroughly wash the greens by dunking them in a large pot of cold

water. Remove the greens with your hands, place them in a large bowl or other container, then pour out the sandy water. Repeat until the water no longer has any sandy residue.

3. Place the coarser greens, such as kale, in a large stockpot with only the water that clings to them. Cover and cook just until they begin to wilt. Add the more delicate greens, cover the pot, and cook just until wilted. Drain the greens in a colander, and press out any excess liquid with the back of a large spoon.

4. Heat the olive oil in a large skillet over medium heat. Add the garlic and cook 2 minutes. Do not let it brown. Stir in the greens and bulghur. Season generously with salt and pepper, then stir in the Parmesan cheese. Remove from the heat.

5. Preheat the oven to 400 degrees. Oil a 1½-quart tian, gratin dish, or other similar shallow casserole. Spoon in half of the greens mixture. Sprinkle on the mozzarella cheese. Spread on the remaining greens mixture and smooth over the surface. Combine the topping ingredients and sprinkle over the tian. (The tian may be prepared to this point up to 8 hours in advance. Cover and refrigerate if longer than 1 hour, and bring to room temperature before baking.) Bake, uncovered, for 30 minutes, or until sizzling and brown on top.

Baked Goat Cheese and Tomato Polenta

The essence of tomato is a wonderful counterpoint to the creamy layer of goat cheese in this colorful do-ahead casserole.

Serves 6

The Tomato Filling
1 tablespoon olive oil
4 garlic cloves, minced
1 onion, minced
1 (28-ounce) can whole tomatoes, well drained and finely chopped
Generous seasoning freshly ground black pepper
½ cup chopped fresh basil, or 1 teaspoon dried

The Polenta
Unsalted butter for greasing the dish, plus ½ tablespoon cut into bits
2½ cups vegetable stock, store-bought or homemade (page 13)
1½ cups cornmeal
2 cups cold water
½ teaspoon salt
¼ cup plus 1 tablespoon grated Parmesan cheese
½ cup grated part-skim mozzarella cheese
4 ounces soft mild goat cheese, chilled

1. To make the filling, heat the oil in a medium-size skillet over medium heat. Add the garlic and onion and sauté until soft and golden, about 10 minutes. Stir in the tomatoes, season with the pepper, and cook until the juices thicken and are almost evaporated, about 10 minutes. Stir in the basil, and remove the pan from the heat.
2. To make the polenta, preheat the oven to 400 degrees. Butter a 2- to 2½-quart shallow baking dish and set aside.
3. Bring the vegetable stock to a boil in a 3½-quart saucepan over high heat. Place the

cornmeal in a large bowl and whisk in the cold water. (This method ensures lump-free polenta.) Continue to whisk this mixture while pouring it into the boiling stock. Bring the entire contents to a boil, whisking almost constantly. Once the polenta begins to boil, reduce the heat to medium. Whisk the polenta continuously until it begins to tear away from the sides of the pan, about 5 minutes. Whisk in the salt, 1/4 cup of the grated Parmesan cheese, and the mozzarella cheese.

4. Immediately pour half the polenta into the prepared baking dish. Quickly spread on the tomato mixture. Crumble the goat cheese evenly over the tomatoes. Immediately spoon on the remaining polenta, covering the entire surface. Sprinkle the top with the remaining tablespoon of Parmesan cheese. Dot with the butter bits.

5. Let the polenta rest at least 15 minutes, or up to 24 hours. If longer than 1 hour, cover and refrigerate. Bring to room temperature before baking. Bake 25 minutes, or until hot and bubbly, and golden on top. Let the polenta sit 15 minutes before serving.

Baked Cheese Polenta with Swiss Chard

Although I'm partial to chard in this melt-in-your-mouth casserole, other greens would work, such as spinach, kale, escarole, or broccoli rabe. Have everything laid out in front of you before you begin cooking to allow you to smoothly run through these steps.

Serves 4

1 tablespoon olive oil
6 garlic cloves, minced
8–10 cups chopped Swiss chard, stems and leaves kept separate

The Polenta
Butter for greasing dish, plus 1 tablespoon butter
2 cups low-fat milk
1½ cups water
½ teaspoon salt
1 cup cornmeal
3 tablespoons grated Parmesan cheese
1 cup grated part-skim mozzarella cheese
⅓ cup sour cream

1. Heat the oil in a large skillet over medium heat. Add the garlic and cook 30 seconds, then stir in the Swiss chard stems. Pour in a few tablespoons of water and cover the pan. Cook the stems 2 minutes. Remove the cover, then mix in the Swiss chard leaves. Cover the pan again and cook until the leaves wilt, about 3 minutes. Toss occasionally. Remove the pan from the heat and let cool, uncovered.
2. To make the polenta, preheat the oven to 400 degrees.
3. Butter a 2- to 2½-quart shallow baking dish and set it nearby. Combine the milk, water, and salt in a medium-size saucepan and bring to a boil. Reduce the heat to medium-low and slowly drizzle in the cornmeal, whisking all the while with a wire whisk. Continue to cook and whisk the polenta until it is the consistency of mashed

potatoes and tears away from the sides of the pan, about 5 minutes. Whisk in 2 tablespoons of the Parmesan cheese, the 1 tablespoon butter, and the mozzarella cheese.

4. Spread half of the polenta in the baking dish. Spoon on the Swiss chard and distribute it evenly. Drop on small spoonfuls of the sour cream and spread it with the back of a spoon. Spoon on the remaining polenta and spread it out. Sprinkle on the remaining tablespoon of Parmesan cheese. (The casserole may be prepared to this point and refrigerated up to 24 hours in advance. Bring to room temperature before baking.)

5. Bake the polenta for 20–25 minutes, or until golden on top and sizzling. Do not overcook it because you want to retain its creamy interior.

Foolproof Polenta

Despite its reputation, polenta can be one of the quickest and easiest dishes to whip up. You don't always need to use stone-ground or coarse cornmeal; a finer grind of cornmeal makes a delicious polenta with a more satiny texture. (Although it is slightly less nutritious because it is degerminated.)

There are two foolproof methods that I use to make polenta. The quickest approach is to bring water or stock to a boil, then *very slowly* drizzle or sprinkle in some fine cornmeal (Quaker Oats is okay), whisking all the while with a wire whisk. Reduce the heat to a simmer, and keep whisking until the polenta has the consistency of soft mashed potatoes and pulls away from the sides of the pot. This will take 5–10 minutes. This is the point to add butter and cheese.

Another method, which takes a bit longer and also guarantees smooth polenta, is to place the cornmeal in your saucepan, then whisk in the required amount of cold water. Turn the heat on under the pot, and whisk the mixture almost constantly until it comes to a boil. Lower the heat, and keep whisking until it is as described above, like soft mashed potatoes.

Baked Pasta Shells with Eggplant

A non-stick skillet allows you to fry eggplant with just a little oil rather than the generous amounts normally used to brown it. While the eggplant is frying and the pasta water is coming to a boil, use this time to prepare the remaining ingredients and you'll have it all ready to assemble by the time the shells are cooked.

Serves 4

4 tablespoons olive oil
1 medium (1 1/4 pounds) eggplant, peeled and diced (3/4-inch dice)
1/2 pound small pasta shells
6 garlic cloves, minced
1/4 teaspoon crushed red pepper flakes
1 1/2 cups canned crushed tomatoes (or tomato puree)
2 tablespoons dry red wine
1/2 teaspoon salt
1/2 cup chopped fresh parsley
1/4 cup chopped fresh basil, or 1 teaspoon dried
1/2 cup diced roasted red peppers, store-bought or freshly roasted (page 19)
4 tablespoons grated Parmesan cheese
1 1/2 cups grated part-skim mozzarella cheese

1. Bring a large stockpot of water to a boil. Heat 1 tablespoon of the oil in a large non-stick skillet over medium-high heat. Fry *half* the eggplant, tossing often, until it begins to brown and appears somewhat translucent or shiny. Initially the eggplant will absorb the oil and look dry; don't add any more oil, just keep frying and tossing until its juices are released. When done, the eggplant should be still somewhat firm because it will bake further in the oven. Don't overcook it.
2. Remove the eggplant and place it in a shallow 2 1/2-quart baking dish. Using 1 tablespoon of the oil, fry the second batch of eggplant in the same way.
3. When the pasta water is ready, drop in the shells. Cook until al dente, not mushy.

Drain in a colander, then return to the pot.

4. Place the remaining 2 tablespoons of the oil in the skillet. Add the garlic and hot pepper flakes and cook 1–2 minutes, just until fragrant but not colored. Stir in the tomatoes, wine, salt, parsley, basil, and red peppers. Cook 2 minutes, and remove from the heat.

5. Preheat the oven to 375 degrees.

6. Stir the eggplant, sauce, and 2 tablespoons of the Parmesan cheese into the pasta shells. Place *half* of this mixture in the casserole dish that held the eggplant (you don't need to dirty another dish this way). Top with the mozzarella cheese. Spread the remaining pasta mixture on top, then sprinkle on the remaining 2 tablespoons of Parmesan cheese. Cover the dish with foil. (The casserole can be prepared to this point, covered, and refrigerated up to 24 hours in advance.)

7. Bake 30 minutes, or until hot and bubbly. Remove the foil and bake 5 more minutes.

Spinach, Roasted Red Pepper, and Corn Enchiladas

The wonderfully appealing flavor of cumin enhances the filling in these delicious enchiladas. There is little cooking involved in the assembling of the dish, so you'll be able to put these together quite effortlessly.

Serves 4

The Filling
1 cup low-fat cottage cheese
1 (10-ounce) box frozen chopped spinach, thawed
1 tablespoon olive oil
1 medium onion, minced
½ teaspoon ground cumin
1½ cups frozen corn, thawed
1 (7-ounce) jar roasted red peppers, patted dry and diced (1 cup diced)
2 tablespoons grated Parmesan cheese
¼ teaspoon salt
Freshly ground pepper to taste
½ teaspoon dried oregano

Butter for greasing dish
8 (8-inch) flour (wheat) tortillas

The Sauce
1¼ cups mild or medium salsa
½ cup heavy cream
¼ cup milk

1¼ cups grated Monterey Jack cheese

1. Puree the cottage cheese in a food processor or blender until perfectly smooth. Scrape it into a medium-size bowl.

2. Place the spinach in a strainer and press out all its liquid with the back of a large spoon. Set the spinach aside.

3. Heat the olive oil in a large skillet over medium heat. Add the onion and sauté, stirring frequently, until golden brown and soft, about 10 minutes. Add the cumin and cook 2 minutes to "toast it." Stir in the spinach and cook 2 minutes, tossing frequently. Let the mixture cool, then stir it into the cottage cheese along with all the remaining filling ingredients. (The filling may be prepared and chilled up to 24 hours in advance.)

4. Preheat the oven to 375 degrees. Butter a 9 × 13-inch baking dish, or 2 smaller similar baking dishes. If your tortillas seem dry and might tear easily, use a pastry brush and lightly brush each one on both sides with some water. Divide the spinach mixture into 8 portions and place a portion along the bottom of each tortilla and roll tightly. Place the enchiladas on the counter as you complete them.

5. To make the sauce, combine the salsa, cream, and milk in a small bowl. Spoon a thin layer of the sauce on the bottom of the baking dish. Place the enchiladas in the dish, then spoon on the remaining sauce. Sprinkle some cheese along each enchilada. (The enchiladas may be prepared to this point up to 8 hours in advance. Cover and chill if longer than 1 hour. Bring to room temperature before baking.) Bake, covered, 25 minutes. Remove the cover and bake 5 more minutes, or until golden and bubbly. Let sit 5 minutes before serving.

Desserts

Serving a homemade dessert is a special treat, not a daily occurrence, and so to my mind it better be well worth the time and calories. These sumptuous finales surely are. Here is a selection of desserts to suit every occasion—from elegant entertaining to casual after-school snacks. When choosing a dessert for a menu, keep in mind the structure of the meal. Richness is almost always a primary consideration. If the entree has cheese or cream in it, then select a dessert that is fruit-based or on the light side. If you're serving an Asian-style main course that is dairy-free and low-fat, then this is the time to present a buttery cake or rich, flaky tart. As with so much in life, it's a question of balance.

Caramelized Pear and Ginger Upside-Down Cake

The caramelized layer of pears spiked with candied ginger gives this superb cake its hauntingly good flavor. I prefer Bosc pears because they are so sweet; however, D'Anjou or Comice are acceptable. This is one of my favorite desserts.

Serves 6–8

4 tablespoons unsalted butter
½ cup firmly packed light brown sugar
2 tablespoons finely diced candied (crystallized) ginger
3 small firm but ripe Bosc pears, peeled, cored, and cut into sixths

The Cake
4 tablespoons unsalted butter, softened
1 cup sugar
2 teaspoons vanilla extract
2 eggs
1¼ cups unbleached white flour
1½ teaspoons baking powder
½ teaspoon salt
½ cup milk

Sweetened whipped cream (optional)

1. Preheat the oven to 350 degrees. Melt 4 tablespoons butter in a small saucepan over low heat. Brush some of it on the sides of a 9-inch round cake pan (not a springform). Mix the brown sugar into the butter in the saucepan and stir until melted. Pour the mixture into the cake pan and spread evenly.
2. Place pieces of the candied ginger evenly over the pan. Arrange the pear slices in a circle around the pan in the following way: Lay them on their rounded exteriors with the top tip of each slice pointing toward the center. Chop any remaining pear slices and use the pieces to fill the center of the circle.

3. To make the cake, place the 4 tablespoons of butter plus the sugar and vanilla in a large bowl. With an electric beater cream the mixture until very smooth. Add the eggs and beat until fluffy.

4. Add the flour, baking powder, and salt and beat until combined. Add the milk and beat until smooth. Scrape the batter over the pears and smooth over the top.

5. Place the pan in the oven; place a baking sheet on the rack beneath it to catch any juices that might overflow. Bake 45–55 minutes, or until a knife inserted in the cake comes out clean. The cake will be a deep golden brown when done. Don't worry if the top of the cake isn't picture perfect—it will be turned upside down.

6. Cool on a wire rack for 10 minutes, then loosen the edges by running a knife all around the cake. Lay a platter over the cake and invert. Cool to room temperature before serving as is or with a spoonful of whipped cream beside each piece.

Unsalted Butter

I am frequently asked why I specify unsalted butter in my recipes, then include salt as an ingredient. The reason unsalted butter is preferred is not that I am limiting my salt intake, but that unsalted butter is fresher than the salted variety. Because salt masks rancidity, salted butter has a much longer shelf life than unsalted (sweet) butter, which must always be fresh.

Orange Almond Cake

There are few flavors more beguiling in combination than orange and almond. In addition to this cake's sensational flavor, its texture is so delicate and moist that it practically melts in your mouth. Almond paste greatly contributes to this cake's wonderful character. The final result is a luxurious 1-layer butter cake that needs just a dusting of powdered sugar to finish it off. Simple elegance at its best.

Serves 8

¼ pound (1 stick) unsalted butter, very soft
1 cup sugar
7-8 ounces almond paste (see Note)
2 tablespoons orange liqueur (such as Grand Marnier or triple sec)
Grated zest of 1 orange, or ½ teaspoon orange extract
5 large eggs
½ cup cake flour
1 teaspoon baking powder
Confectioners' sugar for dusting

1. Preheat the oven to 325 degrees. Butter and flour a 9-inch springform pan and set it aside.

2. In a large bowl, using an electric mixer, beat the butter and sugar together until very fluffy, at least 3 minutes. Finely crumble up the almond paste with your fingers, and add it to the bowl along with the orange liqueur and orange zest. Beat until perfectly blended, another 2 minutes or so.

3. One by one beat in the eggs until the mixture is very smooth and fluffy, about 2 minutes. Sprinkle on the flour and baking powder and beat just until combined, 30 seconds or so.

4. Scrape the batter into the prepared pan. Bake 55 minutes, or until a knife inserted in the center of the cake comes out clean and the sides have begun to shrink away from the

pan. Cool on a wire rack for 10 minutes. (The cake might sink a little in the center.)

5. Remove the outer ring of the pan. Place a plate over the cake and invert it. Remove the bottom of the pan. Invert again onto a wire rack. Cool the cake completely. Serve dusted with confectioners' sugar.

Note: Almond paste, usually sold in a log similar to marzipan, can be purchased in most supermarkets and specialty food shops. Almond paste, which has less sugar and more almonds than marzipan, is intended for cooking, while marzipan is intended for icings and confections that don't require baking.

If your almond paste is not easily malleable at room temperature, process it in a food processor until it is the texture of cracked wheat, then add it to your recipe.

Nantucket Cranberry Cake

This delicious cake is a spin-off of a dessert called Nantucket Cranberry Pie. Both desserts are made in a pie plate or quiche dish in which a thin, buttery cake sits atop a layer of sweetened cranberries and walnuts. In my version the topping is lighter in texture and more cake-like, which I feel is an improvement on the original.

You cannot use a springform pan for this dessert because the juices will leak out. Any pie plate or ceramic (or Pyrex) quiche dish that holds 1½ quarts of liquid will do. It should be shallow and about 10 inches in diameter.

This is an ideal dessert for Thanksgiving or Christmas. Dusted with confectioners' sugar and served with espresso, coffee, or tea, you have a sumptuous and easy dessert.

Serves 8

Butter for greasing the dish

The Bottom Layer

2 cups cranberries
½ cup finely chopped (not ground) walnuts
½ cup sugar

The Batter

¼ pound (1 stick) unsalted butter, softened
¾ cup sugar
1 egg
½ teaspoon vanilla extract
¼ teaspoon almond extract
1 cup unbleached flour
1 teaspoon baking powder
¼ teaspoon salt
½ cup milk

Confectioners' sugar for dusting

1. Preheat the oven to 350 degrees. Lightly butter a 1½-quart-capacity pie plate or quiche dish (not with a removable bottom).

2. Arrange the cranberries evenly on the bottom of the dish. Sprinkle on the walnuts and sugar.

3. To make the batter, in a large bowl use an electric mixer to beat the butter and sugar together until light and somewhat fluffy. Add the egg and the vanilla and almond extracts and beat until very smooth and fluffy. Be patient.

4. Sprinkle in the flour, baking powder, and salt and beat a few seconds. Pour in the milk and beat just until incorporated.

5. Using a spoon, drop small mounds of batter all over the cranberries. With a narrow metal icing spatula spread the batter around to evenly cover the berries.

6. Bake 45 minutes, or until the cake springs back when you gently press the center with your finger. (The cake will be a rich golden color.) Cool completely before serving. Place confectioners' sugar in a sieve and dust the top of the cake with it. Cut into wedges and serve.

Chocolate Orange Almond Torte

Favorite ingredients that are highly compatible go beyond the sum of their good flavors to create another dimension in taste. The trinity of chocolate, orange, and almond is one such example of mutually enhancing flavors that excite the palate and linger in one's memory.

This rich, sophisticated, European-style cake, which is about 1-inch high, is a superlative example of that magic in action. Served in small portions with a spoonful of whipped cream on the side, it is a dessert that is utterly gratifying.

Serves 8

6 ounces semi-sweet chocolate, chopped, or 1 cup semi-sweet chocolate chips
3 tablespoons water
1/4 pound (1 stick) unsalted butter, cut into small chunks
2/3 cup whole almonds
3 eggs
Pinch salt
2/3 cup sugar
2 tablespoons Grand Marnier or triple sec
3 1/2 tablespoons unbleached flour
Grated zest of 1 orange
Confectioners' sugar
Unsweetened or barely sweetened whipped cream (optional)

1. Preheat the oven to 375 degrees. Butter and flour a 9-inch layer pan.
2. Combine the chocolate and water in a medium-size, heavy-bottomed saucepan over medium-low heat and stir almost continuously until melted and blended. Do not let the mixture get too hot or scorch; chocolate does not like high heat. Remove the pan from the heat. Drop in the pieces of butter and stir until blended. Set aside.
3. Finely grind the almonds in a blender or processor. You should get about 3/4 cup.

4. Separate the eggs, placing the whites in 1 large bowl and the yolks in another large bowl. Beat the egg whites with a pinch of salt until stiff but not dry.
5. Without cleaning the beaters beat the yolks with the sugar until pale and creamy, a good 3 minutes. Beat in the cooled melted chocolate until blended. Beat in the almonds, Grand Marnier, flour, and orange zest just until blended, about 1 minute.
6. With a rubber spatula *stir* one third of the egg whites into the batter to lighten it. Carefully *fold* the remaining egg whites into the batter until they are incorporated. (Do this with a light hand so that the batter isn't overbeaten yet no streaks remain.)
7. Scrape the batter into the prepared pan and bake for 28–30 minutes, or until a knife inserted in the center of the cake comes out almost, but not completely, dry. Do not overbake the cake.
8. Cool on a wire rack for 10 minutes, then invert the cake onto a plate and remove the pan. Let cool completely before serving. Dust lightly with powdered sugar. If desired, serve with a spoonful of whipped cream next to each portion.

Strawberry Almond Cream Cake

This is the perfect summer cake—light and fresh-tasting while amply filled with berries and whipped cream. It's quick to make and its texture is moist and delicate. I prefer to use a blender rather than a food processor for the batter because it grinds the almonds very fine; however, if a food processor is all you have, you'll still get great results. For the strawberries, you'll need about 1 quart total: 2 cups sliced and the remainder for decorating.

Serves 8

7 eggs
1 teaspoon almond extract
1/2 teaspoon vanilla extract
1 1/2 cups sugar
1 1/4 cups whole skinless almonds, or 1 3/4 cups slivered almonds, or a scant 2 cups sliced almonds
1/4 cup plus 2 tablespoons unbleached flour
3 3/4 teaspoons baking powder

The Filling
2 cups thinly sliced fresh strawberries
2 tablespoons strawberry jam
1 teaspoon Grand Marnier, rum, or kirsch

The Topping
1 1/2 cups well-chilled heavy cream
1/4 cup sugar
1 teaspoon vanilla extract
1/4 teaspoon almond extract

About 2 cups halved strawberries for decorating

1. Preheat the oven to 350 degrees. Butter 2 (9-inch) cake pans. Line the bottoms with parchment or wax paper and butter the paper. Place your beaters and bowl in the freezer, so they are well chilled for whipping the cream.
2. In a blender combine the eggs, the almond and vanilla extracts, and the sugar and blend until creamy and smooth. Turn off the blender and add the almonds. Blend until very fine, at least 1 minute. Add the flour and baking powder and blend until smooth.
3. Divide the batter between the 2 prepared pans. Bake about 17–18 minutes, or until the cakes are golden brown on top and have begun to shrink from the sides of the pan. The cakes will puff while cooking, and then collapse. When done, they will no longer be "jiggly," but will spring back when touched with your index finger. They'll be only about 1¼ inches high.
4. Cool on a wire rack for 5 minutes. Invert the cakes, then remove the pans and parchment paper. Let cool completely.
5. To make the filling, place the 2 cups of sliced strawberries in a large bowl. With a fork mash about one quarter of the berries. Mix in the jam and liqueur. Let sit until you are ready to assemble the cake.
6. When the cake is completely cool, remove the beaters and bowl from the freezer. Place the heavy cream in the cold bowl and whip on high speed until it begins to thicken. Sprinkle in the sugar and vanilla and almond extracts and whip until stiff but not buttery.
7. To assemble the cake, place a layer on a large plate. Spoon the strawberries all over the top, plus about ½ cup of the accumulated liquid. (Discard the remaining liquid.) Place the remaining cake layer on top. Cover the entire cake with the whipped cream. Decorate the cake with the strawberry halves. I like to place them on top of the cake along the edge, then create an inner circle in the center, plus a row along the outside bottom edge of the cake.
8. Chill until ready to serve. You can make the entire cake 1 day in advance. Cover it with a cake dome or large inverted pot and refrigerate.

Cassata Siciliana

There are many versions of cassata. What they share is a sweetened ricotta filling and chocolate icing. This easy 3-layer loaf cake resembles a cross between a cannoli and a rum cake. There's virtually no cooking involved and the final product looks stunning. Great for a party.

Do start the cake early in the day so that it has time to chill.

Serves 8

The Syrup
1/4 cup light rum
1/4 cup sugar
3 tablespoons water

The Filling
1 1/2 cups part-skim ricotta cheese
2/3 cup confectioners' sugar
2 tablespoons semi-sweet chocolate chips, finely chopped
Grated zest of 1 orange

The Ganache (Chocolate Cream Icing)
3/4 cup heavy cream
1/2 cup (about 3 ounces) semi-sweet chocolate chips
1 tablespoon sugar

1 (10-ounce) frozen pound cake, thawed
1/3 cup sliced almonds for decorating

1. To make the syrup, combine the rum, sugar, and water in a small saucepan and bring to a boil, stirring to make sure the sugar has melted. Pour it into a small bowl and let cool.
2. In a medium-size bowl whisk together the ricotta and confectioners' sugar until very smooth. Whisk in the chocolate chips and grated orange zest. Cover and chill until it

becomes a spreadable consistency, not soupy, about 30 minutes.

3. To make the ganache, combine the cream, chocolate, and sugar in a medium-size saucepan. Heat over medium heat, stirring frequently, until the chocolate is blended with the cream. Do not boil the mixture. Pour it into a metal bowl and chill until ice cold, about 2 hours. Stir it occasionally to speed up the process.

4. To assemble the cake, slice the pound cake *lengthwise* into 3 layers. Place the bottom layer on a platter. With a small spoon drizzle one third of the rum syrup all over the layer. Spread on *half* of the ricotta mixture. Top with the second layer of cake and drizzle on one third of the syrup. Spread on the remaining ricotta mixture. Top with the final layer of cake, but flip it over so that the crusted layer is underneath. Spoon on the remaining rum syrup. Cover the cake with plastic wrap and chill a few hours or overnight.

5. To ice the cake, use an electric mixer and whip the icing just until it is spreadable—not soupy or like butter. This will happen rather quickly. Spread the ganache all over the loaf cake. Make an attractive, continuous "S" or "ribbon" pattern on the top of the cake using a knife or thin metal spatula. Press the almonds into the sides of the cake. Chill at least 1 hour or until the icing gets firm. Serve thinly sliced.

Quick Strawberry Shortcake

Here is a fabulous dessert that always gets raves in my house. To make shortcakes quickly, I have developed a method whereby one big almond-flavored "biscuit" is baked and then cut into individual portions, rather than rolling and cutting out separate shortcakes. Although the biscuit is cut into 9 portions, the strawberry and whipped cream amounts are for 4–5 servings. I did this because I imagine most people won't be serving 9 people, and would prefer to freeze the leftover shortcakes for another day. However, if you are serving a large group, just double the strawberry filling and whipped cream topping.

Serves 4–5

2 pints strawberries, hulled and thinly sliced
¼–⅓ cup sugar (depending on the sweetness of the berries)

The Shortcake
1⅔ cups unbleached flour
⅓ cup plus 1 tablespoon sugar
1 teaspoon baking powder
½ teaspoon baking soda
¼ teaspoon salt
4 tablespoons chilled unsalted butter, cut into bits
1 large egg
⅔ cup buttermilk or yogurt thinned with a little milk
½ teaspoon vanilla extract
¼ teaspoon almond extract

¾ cup chilled heavy cream
1½ tablespoons sugar
½ teaspoon vanilla extract

1. Combine the strawberries and sugar in a large bowl, and set aside for at least 1 hour to extract the juices. If longer than an hour, cover and chill.
2. Preheat the oven to 400 degrees. Generously butter an 8 × 8-inch baking pan. To make the shortcake, thoroughly combine the flour, ⅓ cup sugar, baking powder, baking soda, and salt in a large bowl. Drop in the butter, toss to coat it with the flour, then rub it between your fingertips until pea-size crumbs form.
3. Beat the egg in a medium-size bowl. Beat in the buttermilk and the vanilla and almond extracts. Scrape this mixture into the flour mixture, then stir it quickly with a fork just until the flour is evenly moistened. Don't overbeat it. Scrape the dough into the prepared pan and smooth over the top. Sprinkle on the remaining tablespoon of sugar.
4. Bake about 17 minutes, or until a knife inserted in the center of the shortcake comes out clean, and the top is golden. Cool completely on a wire rack.
5. Meanwhile whip the cream with the sugar and vanilla until thick but still somewhat soupy.
6. To serve the strawberry shortcake, cut the biscuit into 9 squares. Freeze 4–5 of them for future use, if desired. Split each biscuit in half horizontally. Spoon some of the strawberries and syrup in the bottom of each serving dish. Place the bottom of the biscuit on the strawberries, then cover with some more strawberries and some whipped cream. Place the top of the biscuit on the berries, and finish with a dollop of whipped cream on top.

Wacky Cake

"Wacky" cake is so called because it has no eggs in it and is mixed together in an unusual way. I have a 2-layer version in *Quick Vegetarian Pleasures* and offer you this adaptation because it is even quicker, and is the ideal chocolate cake to make at a moment's notice when you want something for the family that will go well with a glass of ice-cold milk. It is made in an 8 × 8-inch pan, and covered with a fantastic chocolate glaze. Chocolate cake doesn't get any quicker—or better—than this. Enjoy!

Because it takes only a few minutes to make this cake batter (you don't even have to butter the pan beforehand), you must turn your oven on at least 10 minutes before you begin so it has enough time to preheat.

Serves 6–9

1 1/4 cups unbleached flour
1 cup sugar
1/3 cup unsweetened cocoa powder
1 teaspoon baking soda
1/2 teaspoon salt
1 cup warm water
1 teaspoon vanilla extract
1/3 cup vegetable oil
1 teaspoon distilled white or apple cider vinegar

The Chocolate Glaze
1/2 cup sugar
4 tablespoons unsalted butter
2 tablespoons milk
2 tablespoons unsweetened cocoa powder
2 teaspoons vanilla extract

1. Preheat the oven to 350 degrees.(If you are using a Pyrex baking dish, preheat it to 325 degrees.) A good 10 minutes later, begin to make the cake. Place the flour, sugar,

cocoa, baking soda, and salt in an 8 × 8-inch cake pan. Using a fork, stir the dry ingredients together until *completely* blended and uniform in color with no visible streaks.

2. Pour on the water, vanilla, oil, and vinegar and immediately stir with the fork until completely blended. It's a good idea to use a rubber spatula at this point to help mix the batter that's lodged in the corners.

3. Place the cake in the oven and bake 30 minutes, or until a knife inserted in the center of the cake comes out clean. Cool the cake completely on a wire rack, about 2 hours. (This cake is meant to be served out of the pan, not unmolded.)

4. To make the glaze, combine the sugar, butter, milk, and cocoa in a small saucepan and bring to a boil, stirring frequently. Reduce the heat to a lively simmer and cook 2 minutes, stirring constantly. Remove the pan from the heat and stir until cool, about 5 minutes. Add the vanilla extract, then pour the glaze on the cake. Let cool completely before serving, about 1 hour.

Variations

✣ For a 9 × 13-inch rectangular cake pan, use 1½ times the recipe and cook about 25 minutes.

✣ For a 9-inch round springform pan use 1½ times the recipe and cook about 50 minutes. (Butter and flour the pan beforehand, mix the batter in a large bowl, then pour in the pan. Unmold after baking.)

✣ For a sheet cake use a 17 × 11-inch jelly roll pan that has been buttered and floured beforehand. Mix 3 times the batter in a large bowl, then pour into the prepared pan. Bake about 35 minutes. Unmold after baking.

✣ For cupcakes this recipe will make a dozen. Place 12 paper liners in a muffin pan. Mix the batter in a bowl, then fill the liners. Bake about 22 minutes.

Almond Pound Cake

Pound cake doesn't get any better than this.

Serves 10–12

2 cups unbleached flour
1 teaspoon baking powder
2 sticks (1 cup) unsalted butter, softened
1½ cups sugar
7 ounces almond paste (see Note)
4 large eggs
½ cup milk
Confectioners' sugar for dusting

1. Preheat the oven to 350 degrees. Butter and flour a 10-inch tube pan. Combine the flour and baking powder in a medium-size bowl and set aside.
2. In a large bowl, using an electric mixer, cream together the butter and sugar until very fluffy and smooth.
3. Using your fingers, break up the almond paste into small bits and soften it by rubbing it between your fingers. Drop it into the butter mixture and beat until well incorporated.
4. One by one add the eggs, beating well after each addition.
5. Add a portion of the flour alternately with some of the milk and beat until well incorporated. Repeat until all the flour and milk have been added.
6. Scrape the batter into the prepared pan. Bake about 55 minutes, or until a knife inserted in the center of the cake comes out clean. Cool on a wire rack for 10 minutes, then remove the cake from the pan. Let cool completely, about 2 hours. Sprinkle confectioners' sugar over the top of the cake before serving. To serve, cut into thin slices.

Note: If your almond paste is not malleable at room temperature, process it in a food processor for a minute or so, or until it is the texture of cracked wheat, then add it to your recipe.

Easy Tarte Tatin

This classic French dessert, which is essentially an upside-down caramelized apple tart, is one of the most delicious fruit concoctions ever. By using frozen puff pastry instead of a homemade piecrust, your work is cut down considerably while preserving this dessert's wonderful panache.

Using the right skillet for this dish is essential. I use a 10-inch non-stick ovenproof skillet, which produces perfect results. A cast-iron skillet would work equally well.

Serves 6

1 sheet (1/2 [17-ounce] box) frozen puff pastry, thawed
Flour for dusting
5 tablespoons unsalted butter
2/3 cup sugar
5 medium-large apples (such as Golden Delicious, Cortland, or Macoun), peeled, quartered, and cored
1/4 teaspoon ground cinnamon

1. Once the pastry is thawed, gently unfold it on a lightly floured work surface. Now cook the apples.

2. Melt the butter in a 10-inch ovenproof, non-stick or cast-iron skillet over medium heat. Mix in all but 2 tablespoons of the sugar. Boil gently for 2 minutes, or until the sugar dissolves.

3. Remove the pan from the heat. Place the apple quarters—rounded-side down—all around the pan in concentric circles, also filling in the center. Be sure to pack the apples tightly, as they will shrink when cooled.

4. Mix the remaining 2 tablespoons of sugar with the cinnamon, and sprinkle all over the apples. Return the pan to the heat, set at medium, and cook 15 minutes. The syrup should boil briskly, but not violently. Shake the pan occasionally to distribute the syrup and allow everything to cook evenly.

5. Preheat the oven to 400 degrees. Roll out the puff pastry a tiny bit, just so you can cut out a 10-inch circle. Use a large stainless steel bowl or other 10-inch circle as a guide, then place it on the pastry and cut around it to get a 10-inch circle. Cut 4 slits in the center of the pastry for steam vents.

6. Remove the skillet from the heat and lay the pastry directly over the apples. Carefully push the edges of the pastry down to tuck around the apples.

7. Place the skillet in the preheated oven and bake 15–17 minutes, or until the pastry is a deep golden brown. Remove the pan from the oven and let sit on a rack for 3 minutes. Place a large plate (at least 12 inches in diameter) over the pastry. With one hand resting on the center of the plate and one hand grasping the handle of the pan, quickly invert the pan and let the tart drop onto the plate. Remove the pan. Let the tart cool until it is warm or at room temperature before serving.

Plum Walnut Crisp

Tender chunks of plum simmer in thickened scarlet-colored juices—all under a canopy of clove-spiked crumbs. This crisp is as delicious as it is pretty.

Serves 4–6

2 pounds ripe plums (about 12), pitted and cut into sixths
½ cup firmly packed light brown sugar
1 tablespoon unbleached flour
2 tablespoons orange juice

The Topping
½ cup unbleached flour
⅓ cup finely chopped walnuts
½ cup firmly packed light brown sugar
¼ teaspoon ground cloves
4 tablespoons chilled unsalted butter, cut into bits

1. Preheat the oven to 375 degrees.
2. Place the plums in a shallow 1½- to 2-quart baking dish. Sprinkle on the sugar, flour, and orange juice, then toss lightly.
3. To make the topping, combine the flour, walnuts, sugar, and cloves in a medium-size bowl. Drop in the butter bits and toss to coat with the flour. With your fingertips rub the butter into the flour mixture until evenly moist crumbs form. Sprinkle all over the plums.
4. Bake 35 minutes, or until juices bubble energetically and the top is brown. Cool on a wire rack until at room temperature. Serve plain, with vanilla ice cream, or with whipped cream flavored with a splash of cassis.

Rhubarb Bars

The incomparable tang of rhubarb is the perfect foil for the rich, flaky crust that underlies these sumptuous bars. This dessert would work equally well as an informal treat, or served after a special meal. For the latter, place a bar on a pretty dessert plate and sift confectioners' sugar over the bar *and* around the plate. Serve with espresso.

Makes 20 bars

The Crust
1½ sticks (12 tablespoons) unsalted butter, very soft
⅓ cup sugar
1 large egg
1 teaspoon vanilla extract
2 cups unbleached flour
¼ teaspoon salt

The Topping
2 large eggs
5 cups (about 1½ pounds) thinly sliced rhubarb
1½ cups sugar
½ cup unbleached flour
½ teaspoon allspice
½ teaspoon cinnamon
½ teaspoon salt

Confectioners' sugar for dusting

1. Preheat the oven to 350 degrees. Set aside a 9 × 13-inch Pyrex baking dish, or similar size pan.
2. To make the crust, combine the butter, sugar, egg, and vanilla in a large bowl and beat with an electric mixer until *very* smooth. Add the flour and salt and beat just until the dough is evenly moistened, about 1 minute. Don't overbeat it. Scrape the crumbly

dough into the baking dish and, using your fingertips, press it evenly onto the bottom of the dish. Place the dish in the oven and precook the crust for 15 minutes.

3. Meanwhile prepare the topping. Beat the eggs in a large bowl. Stir in the remaining topping ingredients.

4. When the crust is done, remove the pan from the oven. Pour on the topping and spread evenly. Bake 45 minutes. Cool completely on a wire rack. Cut the bars into 20 pieces. Serve dusted with confectioners' sugar. Cover and chill any leftover bars. Bring to room temperature before serving.

Date Crumb Squares

These sweet morsels were the delight of my elementary school years in New Bedford, Massachusetts. After attending midweek early morning mass by myself, I would have a half hour or so before the other kids arrived at school. This would be the time I'd walk a few blocks over to Worthington's Bakery, in a state of peaceful reverie, and select a treat. More often than not it would be a Date Crumb Square, so concentrated in flavor that I could take little bites and have it last for the duration of the walk back to school.

These squares would make an ideal sweet for a buffet, for they can be made a few days in advance and taste just as fresh as the day they were made. Because they are best cut into small squares, you'll have an ample amount and you can freeze a portion for another day.

Makes about 35 (2-inch) squares

The Filling

3/4 pound pitted dates
1/2 cup firmly packed light brown sugar
2/3 cup water
1 teaspoon vanilla extract

The Crust

1 1/2 cups unbleached flour
1 1/2 cups quick oats
1 cup firmly packed light brown sugar
1/2 teaspoon baking soda
1 1/2 sticks (12 tablespoons) cold unsalted butter

1. Combine the filling ingredients in a medium-size saucepan and bring to a simmer over medium heat. Cook 1 minute, stirring to dissolve the sugar. Let the mixture cool to room temperature.
2. Preheat the oven to 350 degrees. Butter a 9 × 13-inch baking dish.

3. Puree the date mixture in a food processor and set aside.
4. To make the crust, combine the flour, oats, brown sugar, and baking soda in a large bowl. Stir to evenly mix it. Cut the butter into bits, drop it into the mixture, and toss to coat it. Using your fingertips, rub the butter into the flour mixture until even crumbs form.
5. Pour half the contents into the baking dish and pat it down evenly. Spoon the date mixture on it and spread it out evenly with a spatula. Crumble the remaining flour mixture over the date layer and press it down lightly.
6. Bake 30–35 minutes, or until evenly golden. Cool completely before cutting it into 2-inch squares. Store well wrapped at room temperature, or freeze up to 1 month and bring to room temperature before serving.

Chocolate Almond Macaroons

Chewy and almost candy-like, these fabulous macaroons are sure to draw raves. Buttered parchment paper works best to prevent the macaroons from sticking, but buttered aluminum foil will do an adequate job if parchment paper is unavailable.

Makes 24 large cookies

1 2/3 cups (8 ounces) whole almonds
4 ounces semi-sweet chocolate, chopped, or 2/3 cup semi-sweet chocolate chips
1 cup sugar
Pinch salt
1 large egg, at room temperature
2 egg whites, at room temperature
1/2 teaspoon almond extract

1. Preheat the oven to 325 degrees. Place the almonds on a baking sheet and toast for 5–7 minutes, or until fragrant. Let cool completely. Raise the oven heat to 350 degrees.
2. Place the chocolate in a small saucepan over low heat and melt it, stirring constantly. Do not let it get too hot. Let cool to room temperature.
3. Place the almonds, sugar, and salt in a food processor and process until very fine.
4. Add the egg, egg whites, almond extract, and melted chocolate and process just until combined. Scrape the mixture into a medium-size bowl.
5. Line 1 or 2 baking sheets—you can make this with 2 baking sheets or use 1 baking sheet and bake the cookies in 2 batches—with lightly buttered parchment paper or aluminum foil. Place a bowl of water in front of you next to the cookie batter. Moisten your hands and then form balls of dough the size of a walnut, rolling the dough in your palms. Place 12 on each baking sheet, making sure to keep your hands moistened at all times. (This mixture will be soft but should be workable with the moistened-hand method. If for some reason it is too soft to form a ball, chill the mixture for 5 minutes to firm up the chocolate somewhat.)

6. If you are using 2 baking sheets, arrange the oven racks so that one is in the center of the oven, and one is *above* the center rack. Otherwise, just use the center placement if you are baking one batch at a time. Bake the macaroons 12–14 minutes, alternating the baking sheets halfway during cooking. When done, the macaroons will have puffed up but will still be soft. Do not overcook them. With a spatula immediately remove the cookies and cool completely on a wire rack. You can store them at room temperature in a covered tin if you haven't eaten them all, but it is best to store them in the refrigerator, then bring them to room temperature before eating. These macaroons also freeze very well—up to 1 month—if well wrapped.

Mixed Berry Frozen Yogurt

I use frozen berries for this smashing frozen yogurt because the dessert is frozen anyway, and they are exceptionally convenient. You can buy mixed frozen berries in one bag in the freezer section of most supermarkets. They'll produce the vivid, fruity flavor that marks this refreshing dessert, along with an irresistible rosy hue.

Even though this frozen yogurt is a snap to prepare, you must start it early in the day to provide sufficient time for freezing.

Serves 8

2 (12-ounce) bags (4 generous cups) frozen mixed berries (strawberries, raspberries, blueberries, and blackberries), thawed
1 cup firmly packed light brown sugar
½ cup frozen orange juice concentrate
2 cups plain yogurt

1. Puree the berries in a food processor. Place a strainer over a large bowl, and, in batches, pour the mixture through the strainer to filter out the seeds. Use a large spoon to continuously tap the rim of the strainer—this will help the liquid shake through the strainer. Discard the seeds, and return the fruit puree to the processor. (I know what you're thinking, "Hmmm, maybe I could skip this step . . ." But you can't; the seeds will spoil the silken texture.)
2. Add the sugar and orange juice concentrate and process until mixed. Add the yogurt and process just until combined.
3. Pour the mixture into a shallow, metal baking pan (such as an 8 × 8-inch pan) and freeze until solid, about 3 hours. Break up the mass into chunks and process them in the food processor until smooth. Return the mixture to the pan and freeze until scoopable, not slushy, about 4 more hours. If it gets frozen too long and is too firm to scoop, let it sit in the refrigerator until the right consistency is achieved. Store leftover frozen yogurt in the freezer in a tightly covered plastic container for up to 4 days.

Cappuccino Ice

Homemade desserts don't come much easier than this, yet it has all the flavor and charm of something that's been labored over. This frozen dessert is technically an "ice"—not a sorbet—because it has cream in it; however, the word "ice" often conjures up an image of something with ice crystals and a grainy texture, and this dessert is smooth and delicate, as a properly made ice should be. The creamy texture will develop when the mixture is aerated in the food processor, creating a final product that will literally melt in your mouth.

Another fun way to serve this is to skip the second freezing that normally takes place after the "ice" has been processed, and instead pour the slushy mixture into tall glasses and serve with straws and long-handled spoons. You have now made "granitas."

Serves 6–8

3 cups prepared espresso or other strong coffee, with or without caffeine
1 1/4 cups sugar
1 cup light cream (or half milk, half heavy cream)
1 tablespoon Kahlúa (or other coffee liqueur)

1. Combine the coffee and sugar in a medium-size saucepan and heat, stirring frequently, until the sugar melts. Remove from the heat and pour in the cream and Kahlúa. Stir to blend. Let cool.
2. Pour the mixture into an 8 × 8-inch metal pan (or similar shallow pan), and freeze until hard, about 4 hours.
3. Break into chunks and process in a food processor until smooth and slushy. Scrape it into a plastic container and cover tightly. Freeze again until scoopable and no longer slushy, about 1 hour. If it gets too hard, let it thaw in the refrigerator until it is the right consistency to scoop. Serve in decorative glass goblets. Leftover cappuccino ice will keep up to 4 days or so.

Menus

Green Leaf Salad with Fennel, Apple, and Pecans
Fresh Fettuccine with Spinach, Red Peppers, and Smoked Cheese
Chocolate Orange Almond Torte

Spinach Salad with Sesame Dressing
Couscous Pilaf with Pistachios and Scallions
Easy Tarte Tatin

Red Leaf Lettuce with Crumbled Goat Cheese and Honey-Mustard Dressing
Sweet Potato and Vegetable Tian
Nantucket Cranberry Cake

Salad of Baby Greens with Baked Goat Cheese
Spicy Thai-Style Noodles
Caramelized Pear and Ginger Upside-Down Cake

Green Leaf Salad with Fennel, Apple, and Pecans
Polenta with Spicy Tomato-Garlic Sauce
Nantucket Cranberry Cake

Orange, Red Onion, and Black Olive Salad
Cauliflower and Potato Tian
Chocolate Almond Macaroons

Mixed Greens with Pears, Walnuts, and Blue Cheese
White Bean and Vegetable Gratin
Orange Almond Cake

Red Leaf Lettuce with Crumbled Goat Cheese and Honey-Mustard Dressing
Penne with Fried Tofu, Roasted Peppers, and Olives
Cappuccino Ice

Spinach Salad with Sesame Dressing
Noodles with Cashews in Curried Coconut Sauce
Almond Pound Cake

Mushroom Salad with Sun-Dried Tomato Vinaigrette
Baked Cheese Polenta with Swiss Chard
Cappuccino Ice

Spinach Salad with Oranges and Toasted Pecans
Penne and Cauliflower Gratin in Tomato-Cream Sauce
Mixed Berry Frozen Yogurt

Orange, Red Onion, and Black Olive Salad
Spinach, Roasted Red Pepper, and Corn Enchiladas
Chocolate Almond Macaroons

Mixed Greens with Pears, Walnuts, and Blue Cheese
Ziti with Cauliflower, Tomatoes, and Hot Peppers
Cassata Siciliana

Boston Lettuce and Arugula Salad with Dried Cranberries and Walnuts
Baked Pasta Shells with Eggplant
Rhubarb Bars

Spinach Salad with Oranges and Toasted Pecans
Spicy Peanut Noodles
Date Crumb Squares

Mesclun Salad with Dried Apricots and Spiced Nuts
Rigatoni with Potatoes, Arugula, and Tomatoes
Almond Pound Cake

Mesclun Salad with Dried Apricots and Spiced Nuts
Tortellini with Fennel, Tomatoes, and Spinach
Chocolate Orange Almond Torte

Especially for Summer

Tiny Eggplant Turnovers
Marinated Fried Tofu and Vegetable Salad with Mesclun
Cassata Siciliana

Goat Cheese Spread with Pistachios and Mint
Summer Spaghetti Salad
Quick Strawberry Shortcake

Triple Pepper Bruschetta
Bow-Tie Pasta and Fried Tofu Salad with Sesame Dressing
Strawberry Almond Cream Cake

Spinach Dip with Pita Crisps
Tabbouli with Feta and Cucumbers
Quick Strawberry Shortcake

Hummus with Pita Triangles
Soba and Fried Tofu Salad with Shredded Spinach
Mixed Berry Frozen Yogurt

Goat Cheese Spread with Pistachios and Mint
Thai Noodle and Green Bean Salad
Plum Walnut Crisp

Soup Suppers

Red Leaf Lettuce with Crumbled Goat Cheese and Honey-Mustard Dressing
Sweet Potato Chili
Wacky Cake

Salad of Baby Greens with Baked Goat Cheese
Leek and Potato Chowder
Chocolate Orange Almond Torte

Mushroom Salad with Sun-Dried Tomato Vinaigrette
Creamy White Bean Soup with Red Pepper Swirl
Caramelized Pear and Ginger Upside-Down Cake

Boston Lettuce and Arugula Salad with Dried Cranberries and Walnuts
Chickpea and Swiss Chard Soup with Parmesan Crostini
Easy Tarte Tatin

Orange, Red Onion, and Black Olive Salad
Mediterranean Vegetable Soup with Feta Cheese
Orange Almond Cake

MAIN-COURSE VEGETARIAN PLEASURES

MAIN-COURSE VEGETARIAN PLEASURES

Jeanne Lemlin

HarperPerennial
A Division of HarperCollins*Publishers*

To Susanne and Daniel,

two wonderful children who have given me so much joy

ACKNOWLEDGMENTS

Many friends have given me suggestions and ideas that have been brought to play in the development of my recipes. Trips to restaurants recounted, new recipes discovered, dishes that they fantasized about, have all been food for my imagination. I would like to thank the following people who have contributed to this book, sometimes unbeknownst to them: Bonnie and Bob Benson for use of their "library," Stephanie Blumenthal, Billie Chernicoff, Julianne Lemlin, Rita Lemlin, Sally Patterson, Geri Rybacki, Mary Jane Simigan, David Tucker, Jane Walsh, and Christine Ward.

And a special thanks to my editor, Susan Friedland, for her continuous support.

INTRODUCTION

When it comes to preparing a vegetarian meal, the entrée is the biggest challenge. Favorite recipes for meatless appetizers, soups, salads, and, of course, breads and desserts are discovered in all types of cookbooks, as well as in magazines or from friends. But an exceptional vegetarian main course, that's a rarer bird. For many cooks, vegetarian and nonvegetarian alike, the meatless centerpiece that is outstanding and memorable is a real find.

So I have decided, in this third book of mine, to face the challenge head-on and offer you 125 recipes for vegetarian main courses. Most are quick and easy, and are so designated. Although my passion for cooking has not diminished over the years, I do have less time for it now with a young child to care for. Quickness, without sacrificing quality, has become the pace in my kitchen. My idea of a quick meal is preparation time of less than thirty minutes. I don't include baking or marinating time because nothing is demanded of me except waiting.

There are occasions, however, when I want to extend myself and prepare an elaborate meal for guests. I've included these more involved dishes in the Especially for Entertaining chapter. Although they demand more attention, they are generally not difficult to prepare. And in many instances you can prepare some of the steps in advance.

As in my second book, *Quick Vegetarian Pleasures,* I have maintained a cautious but relaxed approach to health and diet. Although I am watchful of my fat intake, and I cook with a plentiful assortment of fresh vegetables, grains, and legumes, I have avoided turning my recipes into mathematical problems by calculating all the nutrients and fats. I lament the trend in today's cooking where the kitchen no longer seems a place of joy, comfort, and fun but instead a laboratory in which food has become a problem to be solved. In so many kitchens, cans of vegetable-oil spray now take up counter space next to the calculator.

Sometimes it feels as though the "fat patrol" is out there ready to flagellate those food writers who don't provide nutritional breakdowns with their recipes. Some writers have become so intimidated by this expectation that they artificially keep these figures down by increasing the number of portions a recipe will serve. Smaller portions mean lower fat figures. This is deceptive.

The servings in this book are generous. For example, a large pizza, a pound of pasta, a main-course grain or pasta salad usually will serve four people in my family. Most cookbooks, however, would say these dishes serve six. Six mouselike portions, perhaps, not genuinely satisfying ones.

The moderate approach to eating has always worked well for me. I choose lower-fat meals most of the time and allow myself to indulge in richer foods on occasion. Dessert is not an everyday treat; instead, I eat it only occasionally and make certain that it is worth waiting for. Brunch is another time when I allow myself to splurge. It is not a meal I often prepare, but when I do, richer foods seem to suit the occasion. Foods very low in fat just don't provide the comforting touch one expects from a brunch, and so in those rare instances I relax my guard. With this approach I never feel deprived of the pleasures of eating, and the kitchen doesn't become a battlefield. But each person has to decide what works best for him or her and carry out that plan.

Eating and cooking are highly personal matters. Tastes are like fingerprints—no two are exactly alike. But one's tastes can change with education and exposure to new foods. The best way to develop an appreciation for fresh, wholesome food is to cook with these ingredients using adventurous, well-tested recipes that put flavor above all else. Once you begin to prepare meatless meals with grains, vegetables, and/or beans taking center stage, then any mystery surrounding them dissolves, and they soon become familiar additions to your cooking repertory. Couscous, polenta, assorted beans and lentils, lots of fresh vegetables, and sundry pastas can become the building blocks for a new way of eating, providing seemingly endless variety and enjoyment.

If our diets are composed principally of generous amounts of fresh, healthful foods, then allowing ourselves a shortcut here and there does not compromise our standards in any significant measure. For example, frozen vegetables such as kale, spinach, peas, and corn can be great time-savers for the busy cook without sacrificing flavor or texture. Canned beans are another example. If I allowed myself only freshly cooked beans rather than canned versions when pressed for time, I would eat far fewer beans. Cooking beans from scratch takes time and forethought, and with my busy schedule I know I would, more often than not, seek other, quicker recipes if I had to begin a recipe by cooking beans. So this is an allowance I grant myself, and I eat a lot more beans as a result. I do recommend, however, that you snoop around and find brands that don't have a preservative in them. They do exist (at both supermarkets and natural foods stores), and you'll find they are just as good, if not better, than those with disodium EDTA added.

Above all, I want you to enjoy your time in the kitchen. My three books have kept the words "Vegetarian Pleasures" in their titles because the pleasurable aspect of cooking is what is most in danger of being lost with the waxing and waning of so many cooking trends. Preserving that pleasure is of central importance to me. Whether you are a vegetarian or are just tired of having meat as the center of each meal, these recipes are meant to awaken your palate to a new sense of vegetable-based cookery. So with an eye on good health and with pleasure as our guide, let's begin to cook.

A NOTE ON ORGANIZATION

Many of the recipes in this book would fit equally well in different chapters, and so I would like to explain why they are where they are. For example, Baked Vegetables with Garlic, White Beans, and Olives could be in the vegetable chapter as well as the bean chapter. I chose to place it in the bean chapter because the beans give the dish a special character and they come to mind first when I think of that dish. When recipes can be categorized a number of ways, I have generally relied on the strongest association the recipe conjures up to help define it. Because of the inevitable arbitrariness of some of the placements, it is a good idea to check the index as well as the individual chapters if you are looking for a specific recipe or want to cook with a certain ingredient.

NOTES ON INGREDIENTS

To make your meal planning easier, stock your cupboards with the following nonperishable items; you'll find that your work in the kitchen will be simplified immensely:

- **couscous**
- **cornmeal**
- **white and brown rice**
- **bulghur**
- **lentils, both red and brown**
- **canned chickpeas**
- **canned black, kidney, and pinto beans**
- **canned whole tomatoes and crushed tomatoes**
- **tamari soy sauce**
- **assorted pastas**
- **olive oil**
- **a favorite tomato sauce**

I included an extensive glossary of ingredients in my first book, *Vegetarian Pleasures: A Menu Cookbook*, and a number of sidebars on ingredients in my second book, *Quick Vegetarian Pleasures*. In order to help you with shopping, I am going to repeat some of that information here.

BEANS To cook dried beans, either soak them overnight in plenty of water or boil them for 2 minutes and let them soak 1 hour in that water. They will then be ready to cook. Drain them, add plenty of fresh water, and cook at a lively simmer until tender. Canned beans vary in quality—some are overcooked and too soft, especially kidney beans. Try different brands, and look for ones without disodium EDTA added. Always rinse canned beans in a strainer before using them.

CHILI PASTE WITH GARLIC A concentrated mixture of ground chilies and garlic used in Chinese cooking. A little goes a long way. It can be found in most supermarkets and specialty food stores, and lasts a long time in the refrigerator.

COUSCOUS This "grain" is created by mixing semolina (coarse flour made from hard durum wheat) and water to form tiny granules. There's nothing quicker to cook than couscous; you just pour boiling stock or water on it and let it sit for 5 minutes. Do try the various recipes in this book using couscous; it has a delicate texture and flavor.

LENTILS, RED These tiny orange seeds are popular in Indian cooking. They cook quickly, turning a rich tan color. Their delicious, buttery flavor is enhanced when they are combined with Indian spices. They can be purchased in natural foods stores, specialty food shops, and Indian grocery stores.

MISO A naturally fermented Japanese soybean and/or grain purée that is filled with friendly bacteria and digestion-aiding enzymes. It comes in various colors and strengths. I prefer barley miso, which is sweet, mild, and light in color. Always dilute miso with a little water before adding it to stocks; this will prevent clumping. Purchase unpasteurized miso; it is found in the refrigerated section of natural foods stores.

OLIVES Can be divided into four basic categories—ripe (black) or unripe (green), and oil-cured or brine-cured. Generally speaking, brine-cured olives are saltier with a more assertive flavor than oil-cured varieties. Greek kalamata olives are a well-known example of brine-cured olives. My favorite oil-cured olives from France are soaking in an herb-strewn olive oil when I purchase them. This keeps them plump and moist. Many oil-cured olives are packed in a drier state, resulting in wrinkled skins. When I purchase such olives, I cover them with olive oil, herbs, and a generous slice of orange peel and store them in the refrigerator. After I've eaten all the olives, I use this delicious marinade in cooking, such as in a tomato-garlic sauce for pasta or drizzled on French bread slices.

RED BELL PEPPERS I am including a note on these flaming wonders because they enhance so many dishes with their vibrant color and flavor. Red bell peppers are green peppers that have ripened on the bush. They are not at all spicy or hot. I have found a way to avoid their oftentimes outrageous price in the market, and I want to pass it on to you.

In August or September, when they are most abundant and at their lowest cost, I purchase large quantities and freeze them. They can be frozen raw, which preserves some of their crunchiness and saves a lot of time. Just core the peppers and remove the inner white membrane that is attached. Cut the peppers into large chunks, small dice, or thin strips. Place one cut-up pepper in a small freezer bag and push out as much air as possible before sealing. Freeze flat so that the pepper pieces are spread out and can freeze evenly. When you need one red pepper in a recipe, just remove one bag from the freezer. Let it thaw, then pat the pepper pieces dry before using them. They will have lost some of their crunchiness, so cook them less than you would fresh peppers.

SESAME OIL Oriental sesame oil is dark brown, strong-flavored, and made from toasted sesame seeds. It is not the same as light-colored, cold-pressed sesame oil found in natural foods stores. Oriental sesame oil has a hauntingly good flavor for which there is no substitute. It lasts indefinitely in the cupboard, so always keep some on hand. It can be purchased in most supermarkets, specialty food stores, natural foods stores, and Asian grocery stores.

SOBA These long, flat Japanese noodles made from buckwheat cook quickly and are rather delicate, so take care not to overcook them. Their nutty flavor is unique and might take a little getting used to. Although soba is expensive, I think it is well worth the price.

TAMARI SOY SAUCE Tamari (and shoyu soy sauce made from soy and wheat) is an aged soy sauce that has a full-bodied flavor and is preservative-free. It can be purchased in natural foods stores and will last indefinitely in the refrigerator.

TEMPEH Ground soybeans and a living culture are fermented and then pressed into a cake to form tempeh. Like most soybean products, it is packed with nutrients: protein, iron, and vitamin B-12. When it is fresh, there are oftentimes black spots on it. These are part of the tempeh and are harmless. When tempeh is spoiled it will have an acrid smell, be slimy, and have blue, green, pink, or yellow mold on it. Tempeh must be cooked before eating. Because it freezes so well, it is easy to always have some on hand. Tempeh can be purchased in natural foods stores.

TOFU Also called bean curd, tofu is a type of soybean cheese. Soybeans are cooked and mashed, then their liquid (soy milk) is pressed out of them and mixed with a coagulant to separate the curds from the whey. The curds are then pressed into cakes to form tofu. It is an excellent source of protein and iron, and a good source of calcium. I always purchase extra-firm tofu because I prefer its texture. To fry tofu, you must pat the pieces very dry with paper or cotton towels, or else the tofu will stick to the pan. If you are using a cast-iron pan and you heat the oil until it is very hot (but not smoking), it is unlikely the tofu will stick. Using a nonstick pan is also an easy way to get crisp, perfectly fried tofu.

TORTILLAS These thin Mexican "pancakes" vary greatly from brand to brand. Some brands make thick, dry tortillas that break easily; others produce flaky, delicate ones. Flour tortillas, especially, need to be moist and supple. Try different brands, and when you discover a winner, freeze a few packages so you will have them on hand.

VEGETABLE STOCK

I rarely make my own vegetable stock because of the time and forethought needed to prepare a full-bodied stock. I purchase powdered vegetable stock base from my local health food store, and it makes a delicious stock. Most supermarket brands have ingredients in their stocks that you can't pronounce—beware! Powdered stock base or cubes last a long time in the refrigerator, so you can always have it available. Should you want to make your stock from scratch, here is a recipe for a delicious vegetable stock:

8 cups water

¼ cup tamari soy sauce

3 unpeeled carrots, washed and diced

3 celery ribs, diced

4 cups chopped cabbage

½ bunch parsley (stems included), chopped

3 onions, diced

6 garlic cloves, coarsely chopped

2 bay leaves

1 clove

Generous seasoning of freshly ground pepper

Dash of nutmeg

Makes 7 cups

1 Place everything in a large stockpot and bring to a boil. Reduce to a simmer and cook 1 hour, stirring occasionally.

2 Remove the bay leaves and discard. Strain the stock and discard the vegetables. Let the stock cool. Store in a tightly covered jar in the refrigerator, or pour into ice cube trays and freeze. When frozen, remove the cubes from the tray and store them in a plastic bag. Use as needed. The stock will stay fresh in the refrigerator for 1 week. After a week, bring the stock to a boil, then simmer for 10 minutes. The stock will keep fresh for 1 more week.

HEARTY SOUPS AND THICK STEWS

If you can spare an hour or so on weekends to make soup, you will benefit the whole week long. Soup improves as it stands, and most of these recipes produce a large pot, which enables you to freeze a portion. Soup lasts a number of days in the refrigerator and it reheats well, making it possible for you to get a few meals out of one batch. For convenience, soup can't be beat.

To make a great soup, you have to follow a few rules. When onions and garlic are called for, they must be sautéed before any liquid is added. This heightens their flavors and gives the soup dimension. If you were to just drop the onions and garlic into the stock, you'd have a weak-flavored soup. Also, make an effort to find a good vegetable stock base, whether powdered or

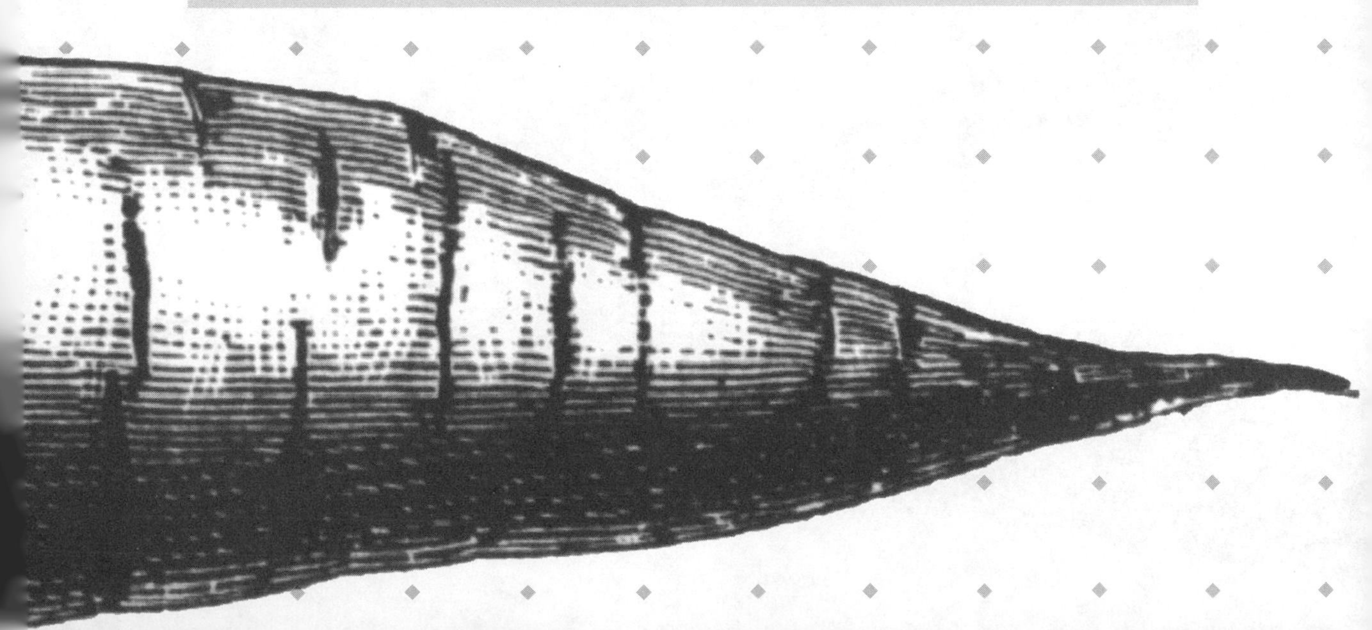

cubed, or make your own stock, for stock is the foundation from which all the other flavors build.

I try to prepare my soups at least a few hours in advance, but preferably the day before. Freshly made soup often lacks depth, and just a few hours of sitting can make it swim with flavor.

These soups are substantial and are meant to be main courses. If you serve a tantalizing salad made with assorted greens and some whole grain or crusty French bread alongside, you'll have a heavenly, wholesome meal.

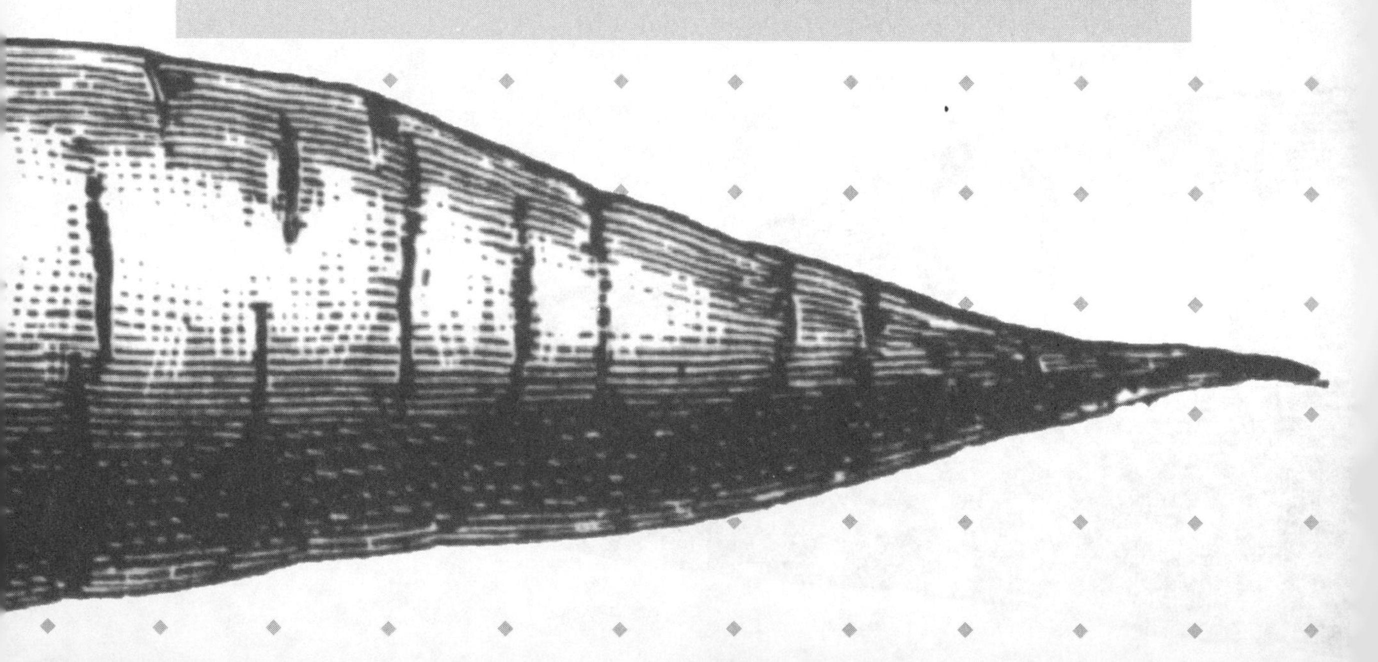

Quick PUMPKIN AND CORN CHOWDER

Cooked pumpkin, a great source of beta carotene, is very mild and it gives wonderful body and color to this delicious chowder. Don't hesitate to make this soup a few days in advance because, as with most soups, it benefits from sitting.

2 medium-large leeks

¼ cup olive oil

2 carrots, finely diced

10 cups vegetable stock

2 medium boiling potatoes, peeled and finely diced

1½ teaspoons salt

Generous seasoning of freshly ground pepper

¼ teaspoon ground cloves

Dash of cayenne

2 16-ounce cans pumpkin

½ cup heavy cream

2 cups fresh or frozen corn kernels

Minced fresh parsley for garnish

Serves 6 as a main course

1 Cut the root ends off the leeks. Cut a slit vertically along the entire length of each leek, cutting *almost* all the way through to the back. Rinse the leeks under cold running water, flipping through each layer to look for any hidden dirt. Thinly slice the white part of each leek plus about 3 inches of the green part. You should have about 3 cups.

2 Heat the olive oil in a large stockpot over medium heat. Add the leeks and carrots and sauté for 15 minutes. Pour in the vegetable stock and bring to a boil. Add the potatoes, salt, pepper, cloves, and cayenne; cook the soup for 30 minutes.

3 Place the pumpkin in a large bowl. Ladle about a cup of soup onto the pumpkin and stir it together to liquefy it. Pour it into the soup along with the heavy cream and corn. Cook 5 more minutes (or longer if the chowder is too thin). Serve in bowls with minced parsley sprinkled on top.

ROASTED RED PEPPER SOUP WITH DILL DUMPLINGS

Start this tasty soup early in the day so all you'll have to do at dinnertime is drop in the dumplings. And when you purée the soup, use a blender, if possible, rather than a food processor for a silkier finish.

4 to 5 large (2 pounds) red bell peppers (or 2 cups purchased roasted red peppers)

3 tablespoons olive oil

4 garlic cloves, minced

2 onions, finely diced

6 cups vegetable stock, plus more for thinning soup

1 celery rib, thinly sliced

2 carrots, thinly sliced

2 medium potatoes, peeled and finely diced

1 teaspoon salt

Generous seasoning of freshly ground pepper

Dash of cayenne

1½ tablespoons balsamic or red wine vinegar

DILL DUMPLINGS

1 cup unbleached flour

1¾ teaspoons baking powder

½ teaspoon salt

1 teaspoon sugar

1 Roast the peppers on a baking sheet close to the flame or heating element of a broiler. As they blacken, turn with tongs until evenly charred all over. This will take about 20 minutes. When done, place the peppers in a plastic bag and close the bag. Let them steam 10 minutes. Remove and discard the cores and seeds of the peppers, then peel off the blackened skin. (This can be done under cold running water.) Pat the peppers dry with paper towels. Dice the peppers; you should get at least 2 cups. If you are using purchased roasted peppers, dice them.

2 Heat the olive oil in a large stockpot. Add the garlic and onions and cook until the onions begin to brown, about 15 minutes.

3 Add the stock, celery, carrots, potatoes, salt, pepper, and cayenne. Bring the soup to a boil, then reduce to a simmer. Cook for about 20 minutes, or until the vegetables are tender. Stir in the reserved roasted peppers and cook 10 more minutes.

4 Let the soup cool 10 minutes, then purée it in batches in a blender or food processor. Return it all to the large pot. (The soup must be in a large, wide pot so there's room to cook the dumplings.) Stir in the vinegar, then stir in enough stock to

1½ teaspoons minced fresh dill, or 1 teaspoon dried

1 tablespoon chilled butter

¾ cup cold low-fat milk

2 tablespoons minced fresh parsley

Serves 4 to 6 as a main course

thin the soup to a heavy-cream consistency. The soup will thicken while the dumplings cook in it.

5 To make the dumplings, combine the flour, baking powder, salt, sugar, and dill in a medium-size bowl. Cut the butter into bits, then toss it into the flour mixture. With your fingertips, rub the butter into the flour until it forms coarse crumbs. Stir in the milk just until blended. Cover and chill the dumpling batter for 30 minutes, or up to 1½ hours.

6 Return the soup to a boil. Reduce the heat to a simmer. Drop in teaspoonfuls of dumpling batter to form 1½-inch dumplings (you should have about 16). Immediately cover the pot and simmer the soup 10 minutes, or until the dumplings are puffed. Do not remove the cover until the 10 minutes are up. Serve the soup with some dumplings in each bowl and garnish with parsley.

VEGETABLE CHOWDER

You can't beat the flavor or the great palette of colors in this chowder.

2 tablespoons unsalted butter

2 onions, very finely diced

3 garlic cloves, minced

½ pound mushrooms, thinly sliced (3 cups)

5 cups vegetable stock

2 carrots, thinly sliced

2 celery ribs, thinly sliced

2 cups finely shredded cabbage

1 medium-size potato, peeled and thinly sliced into bite-size pieces

2 tablespoons converted white rice

1 medium-size zucchini, quartered lengthwise and thinly sliced

½ cup fresh or frozen corn kernels

2 tablespoons minced fresh basil, or 1½ teaspoons dried

3 cups milk

½ cup heavy cream

½ teaspoon salt

Liberal seasoning of freshly ground pepper

Serves 4 as a main course

1. Heat the butter in a large stockpot over medium heat. Add the onions and garlic and sauté for 5 minutes. Stir in the mushrooms and sauté 10 minutes more, stirring often.

2. Pour in the stock, then add the carrots, celery, cabbage, potato, and rice. Cook at a lively simmer for 20 minutes.

3. Add the zucchini, corn, and basil; cook for 10 minutes. Mix in the milk, cream, salt, and pepper and cook an additional 5 minutes, but don't let the soup boil. Remove 2 cups of soup and purée it in a blender or food processor. Return it to the pot. Taste for salt before serving.

BLACK BEAN SOUP

A full-flavored, delicious soup that is smooth with bits of bean throughout. A salad with orange sections, black olives, and red onions would be a great starter.

1 pound (about 2¼ cups) dried black beans

½ cup olive oil

4 garlic cloves, minced

3 medium-large onions, diced

2 teaspoons ground cumin

1 teaspoon dried oregano

2 bay leaves

1 green pepper, cored and diced

2 celery ribs, diced

¼ cup tomato sauce

½ cup chopped fresh parsley

10 cups vegetable stock

1 tablespoon apple cider vinegar

½ teaspoon Tabasco sauce

1½ teaspoons salt

Generous seasoning of freshly ground pepper

1 tablespoon cream sherry or sweet vermouth

Sour cream for garnish

Serves 4 as a main course

1 Rinse the beans in a colander, then place them in a large pot and cover with water. Let soak overnight. (Alternatively, bring the beans to a boil and cook for 2 minutes. Remove from the heat, cover the pot, and let soak 1 hour.) Drain the beans in a colander and set aside.

2 Heat the olive oil in a large stockpot over medium heat. Add the garlic, onions, cumin, oregano, and bay leaves and sauté for 10 minutes, stirring often.

3 Stir in the beans, green pepper, celery, tomato sauce, parsley, vegetable stock, vinegar, Tabasco, salt, and pepper. Bring to a boil, then reduce the heat to a lively simmer. Cook, uncovered, stirring occasionally, for 1½ hours, or until the beans are very tender. Discard the bay leaves.

4 Remove about 4 cups of the soup and purée it in a blender or food processor. Return it to the pot. Stir in the sherry and cook 5 minutes more. The soup should have a consistency similar to heavy cream; boil a few more minutes if it is too thin, add a little stock if too thick. Serve in bowls with a small dollop of sour cream on top; it doesn't need much.

Quick

SWEET POTATO AND VEGETABLE STEW WITH FRESH GREENS

Sweet potatoes as the base of this stew not only lend a distinctive brilliance but also give it a wondrously rich flavor. If you are not fond of cilantro, just omit it, or substitute fresh parsley.

¼ cup olive oil

3 onions, finely diced

4 garlic cloves, minced

2 celery ribs, thinly sliced

8 cups vegetable stock or water

1½ cups finely chopped canned tomatoes with their juice

2 medium-large sweet potatoes, peeled and cut into 1-inch dice

1 carrot, thinly sliced

¼ teaspoon nutmeg

2 tablespoons minced cilantro (optional)

1½ teaspoons salt

Dash of cayenne

Generous seasoning of freshly ground pepper

5 cups (5 ounces) lightly packed fresh spinach, kale, or Swiss chard, torn into small pieces

Serves 4 to 6 as a main course

1. Heat the olive oil in a large stockpot over medium heat. Add the onions, garlic, and celery and sauté, stirring often, for 10 minutes. Stir in all of the remaining ingredients except the greens.
2. Bring the soup to a boil, then reduce the heat to a simmer. Cook, stirring occasionally, for 45 minutes, or until the sweet potatoes are tender. Remove 2 cups of the soup and purée it; then return it to the pot.
3. Stir in the spinach, kale, or Swiss chard and cook the soup about 5 more minutes, or until the greens are tender.

AUTUMN VEGETABLE SOUP

Root vegetables, winter squash, and kale combine to make a soup that evokes the essence of autumn and winter. If time allows, make it the day before; sitting will intensify these heartwarming flavors. As with most soups, this one cries out for peasant-style bread to serve alongside.

¼ cup olive oil

2 medium onions, finely diced

4 garlic cloves, minced

2 large parsnips, thinly sliced

2 carrots, thinly sliced

1 tiny (1 pound) butternut squash, peeled and cut into ½-inch dice (2 cups)

12 cups vegetable stock

2 medium red-skinned potatoes, cut into ½-inch dice

½ teaspoon dried thyme

1 teaspoon salt

Generous seasoning of freshly ground pepper

½ pound fresh kale (weight with stems), torn into tiny pieces (about 4 cups)

1 16-ounce can Great Northern (small white) beans, drained and rinsed

Serves 8 as a main course

1 Combine the oil, onions, and garlic in a large stockpot. Cook over medium-high heat for 5 minutes, stirring often.

2 Stir in the parsnips, carrots, and squash and sauté, stirring often, until the vegetables begin to brown, about 15 minutes. This step adds depth to the soup's flavor, so be certain not to skip it.

3 Stir in the stock, potatoes, thyme, salt, and pepper and bring the soup to a boil. Reduce to a simmer and cook about 45 minutes, or until the vegetables are tender.

4 Stir in the kale and beans and cook about 10 more minutes, or until the kale is tender. Remove about 3 cups of the soup and purée it in a blender or food processor. Return to the pot and stir to blend.

Quick CURRIED CAULIFLOWER AND POTATO SOUP

Here's a low-fat soup that's teeming with flavor. A spoonful of yogurt on top is indispensable, adding a delightful tang and welcome creaminess. Be careful with the cayenne: a little goes a long way.

1 tablespoon unsalted butter

1 tablespoon oil

2 garlic cloves, minced

2 medium onions, finely diced

1 red bell pepper, finely diced

2 celery ribs, thinly sliced

1 tablespoon curry powder

2 teaspoons ground coriander

1 teaspoon ground cumin

1 teaspoon turmeric

A few dashes of cayenne

1 medium-size (2 pounds) cauliflower, cut into small pieces

3 medium-size potatoes, peeled and finely diced

6 cups vegetable stock

1½ teaspoons salt

2 tablespoons minced cilantro (optional)

Plain yogurt (essential)

Serves 6 as a main course

1. Heat the butter and oil in a large stockpot over medium heat. Add the garlic and onions and sauté, tossing often, until the onions are tender and golden, about 10 minutes. Add the red pepper and celery and sauté 5 minutes.
2. Sprinkle on all the spices and stir to evenly coat the vegetables. Cook, stirring often, for 2 minutes to toast the spices. Stir in the cauliflower and potatoes and coat them well with the spices.
3. Pour in the stock and salt and raise the heat to high. Bring the soup to a boil, then reduce the heat to a simmer. Cook 20 minutes, or until the vegetables are tender.
4. Ladle half of the soup into a bowl or saucepan, purée it in a blender or food processor, then return it to the soup pot. Stir in the optional cilantro. Serve in bowls with a generous dollop of yogurt on top.

Quick LENTIL SOUP WITH SWEET POTATOES

Each one of my cookbooks has a recipe for a different rendition of lentil soup, and I'd be hard-pressed to choose my favorite among them. In this tasty version, sweet potatoes lend a rich flavor as well as color, and their high vitamin A content gives this already nutritious soup an added boost.

¼ cup olive oil

4 garlic cloves, minced

2 large onions, diced

1 teaspoon dried thyme

2 bay leaves

10 cups vegetable stock

1¼ cups lentils

2 celery ribs, sliced

½ cup minced fresh parsley

¾ teaspoon salt

Liberal seasoning of freshly ground pepper

2 medium (1 pound) sweet potatoes, peeled and cut into ¾-inch dice

Serves 4 to 6 as a main course

1 Heat the oil in a large stockpot over medium heat. Add the garlic, onions, thyme, and bay leaves and sauté for 10 minutes.

2 Raise the heat to high. Stir in the stock, lentils, celery, ¼ cup of the parsley, salt, and pepper. Bring to a boil, then reduce the heat to a lively simmer. Cook, uncovered, for 30 minutes.

3 Add the sweet potatoes and cook 20 more minutes, or until the sweet potatoes are tender. Discard the bay leaves. Remove 2 cups of the soup and purée in a blender or food processor. Return it to the pot with the remaining ¼ cup parsley. Cook 1 more minute before serving.

MINESTRONE SOUP

This is the perfect soup to choose when you want something full-bodied yet low in fat. This recipe makes a big potful, so don't hesitate to cool off a portion thoroughly and freeze it for future use; you'll be glad you did.

¼ cup fruity olive oil

2 large onions, finely diced

6 garlic cloves, minced

1 28-ounce can tomatoes, finely chopped with their juice

12 cups (3 quarts) vegetable stock

1 carrot, thinly sliced

2 celery ribs, thinly sliced

1 cup diced green beans

1 medium potato, cut into ½-inch cubes

1 16-ounce can chickpeas, rinsed and drained

2 bay leaves

3 tablespoons chopped fresh basil, or 1½ teaspoons dried

1 teaspoon dried oregano

A few pinches of saffron

Generous seasoning of freshly ground pepper

1½ tablespoons tamari soy sauce

1 Heat the oil in a large stockpot over medium heat. Add the onions and garlic and sauté, stirring often, until tender, about 10 minutes.

2 Stir in the tomatoes and their juice and cook 5 minutes. Add all the remaining ingredients except the zucchini, pasta, and cheese, and bring to a boil. Reduce to a lively simmer and cook 30 minutes, stirring occasionally.

3 Add the zucchini and pasta and cook 5 to 10 more minutes, or until the pasta is just tender. Pass the Parmesan cheese at the table, if desired.

1 small to medium zucchini, quartered lengthwise and thinly sliced

⅓ cup macaroni or spaghetti broken into 1-inch pieces

Grated Parmesan cheese (optional)

Serves 10 as a main course

Quick

SOBA SOUP WITH VEGETABLES AND TOFU

Soba served in broth is a traditional Japanese dish. It is a great choice when you want something light and revitalizing.

8 ounces soba (buckwheat noodles; see note)

5 cups water

⅓ cup tamari soy sauce

2 carrots, very thinly sliced

½ pound firm tofu, cut into ½-inch cubes

½ cup miso (see note)

2 tablespoons Oriental sesame oil

2 scallions, very thinly sliced

Serves 3 to 4 as a main course

1 Bring 3 quarts of water to a boil and cook the soba about 5 minutes, or until al dente. Do not overcook it. Drain in a colander, rinse under cold running water, drain again, and set aside.

2 In the same pot, bring the 5 cups of water and the tamari to a boil. Drop in the carrots and simmer 5 minutes. Stir in the tofu and cook 1 minute. Place the miso in a bowl, then remove about ½ cup of the broth and stir it into the miso to dilute it. Pour the mixture into the broth. Remove the pot from the heat so the miso doesn't boil. Stir in the sesame oil.

3 Place some soba in large soup bowls and ladle the soup over it. Sprinkle on the scallions.

Note: Soba and miso can be purchased at natural foods stores. My favorite variety of miso is the light-colored sweet miso.

Quick CURRIED RED LENTIL SOUP WITH VEGETABLES

Prepare this soup at least 2 hours before serving so the flavors mingle to produce a rich-flavored soup. If you are not familiar with red lentils (they are actually tiny orange lentils), you'll be glad to discover this tasty legume. Red lentils cook quickly, turn a golden color, and have a wonderful buttery flavor.

6 cups water

1½ cups red lentils, rinsed

1 tablespoon vegetable oil

½ teaspoon salt

1 medium potato, peeled and cut into ½-inch dice

2 tablespoons butter

2 garlic cloves, minced

1 small red bell pepper, finely diced

1 celery rib, thinly sliced

1 apple, peeled, cored, and cut into ½-inch dice

1½ tablespoons curry powder

½ teaspoon ground cumin

Dash of cayenne

1 tablespoon tamari soy sauce

4 ounces fresh spinach, torn into tiny pieces (4 cups)

Serves 4 to 6 as a main course

1 Bring the water to a boil in a 3-quart saucepan. Stir in the lentils, oil, and salt. When the water returns to a boil, reduce the heat to a simmer. Cook 20 minutes, stirring often. Scrape off and discard any foam that accumulates.

2 Stir in the potato and cook 20 more minutes, stirring frequently.

3 Meanwhile, melt 1 tablespoon of the butter in a medium-size skillet over medium heat. Add the garlic and cook 2 minutes. Stir in the red pepper, celery, and apple and sauté until tender, about 10 minutes. Sprinkle on the curry powder, cumin, and cayenne and cook 2 minutes, stirring often.

4 Scrape the vegetable mixture into the soup. Add the tamari, spinach, and remaining tablespoon of butter. Cook about 10 more minutes, or until the soup is the consistency of heavy cream—not watery or pasty. Stir often. Let the soup sit a few hours before serving. Reheat and check the consistency. Add a bit more water if it is too thick.

Quick FOUR-BEAN CHILI

Here is a tempting variation on chili that has vegetables in it. As with traditional chili, corn bread is the perfect accompaniment. Don't hesitate to make this large portion if you are feeding only a few people. Leftover chili can be served as another meal a few days later, and a portion can also be frozen.

3 tablespoons oil

2 large onions, diced

4 garlic cloves, minced

1 tablespoon chili powder

1 tablespoon ground cumin

½ teaspoon dried oregano

⅛ teaspoon cayenne

1 28-ounce can imported plum tomatoes, finely chopped with their juice

1 6-ounce can tomato paste

6 cups water

1 tablespoon tamari soy sauce

½ teaspoon salt

Freshly ground pepper

2 carrots, thinly sliced

2 green peppers, cored and diced

1 15-ounce can kidney beans, rinsed and drained

1 15-ounce can pinto beans, rinsed and drained

1 15-ounce can chickpeas, rinsed and drained

1 Heat the oil in a large stockpot over medium heat. Add the onions and garlic and sauté 10 minutes. Sprinkle in the chili powder, cumin, oregano, and cayenne. Cook, stirring constantly, for 2 minutes.

2 Stir in the tomatoes, tomato paste, water, tamari, salt, and pepper and blend well. Bring to a boil over medium-high heat, then add the carrots and green peppers. Cook, stirring occasionally, until the carrots are tender, about 30 minutes.

3 Add the beans and zucchini and cook until the zucchini is tender, about 10 more minutes. If the chili is too thin, cook a little longer; if it is too thick, add a bit more water. Stir in the butter just before serving.

1 15-ounce can black beans, rinsed and drained

1 medium zucchini, diced

1 tablespoon unsalted butter

Serves 6 to 8 as a main course

MAIN-DISH SALADS

As hot weather creeps lazily into my life and the steamy kitchen becomes less and less inviting, composing dishes with a minimal amount of cooking takes on a new urgency. Main-course salads based on grains, pasta, or beans are my solution to cooking, though listless from summer heat.

It's odd that I usually wait until warm weather to serve such fare because I so thoroughly enjoy it, and it is just as delicious in fall and winter. Colorful assortments of fresh vegetables and herbs are the mainstay of these salads, making them appealing to create and serve. Olive oil and garlic-based dressings usually provide the crowning touch, and the fruitier the oil, the more savory the salad. These creations are great vehicles for improvisation. You can substitute vegetables and herbs with equal

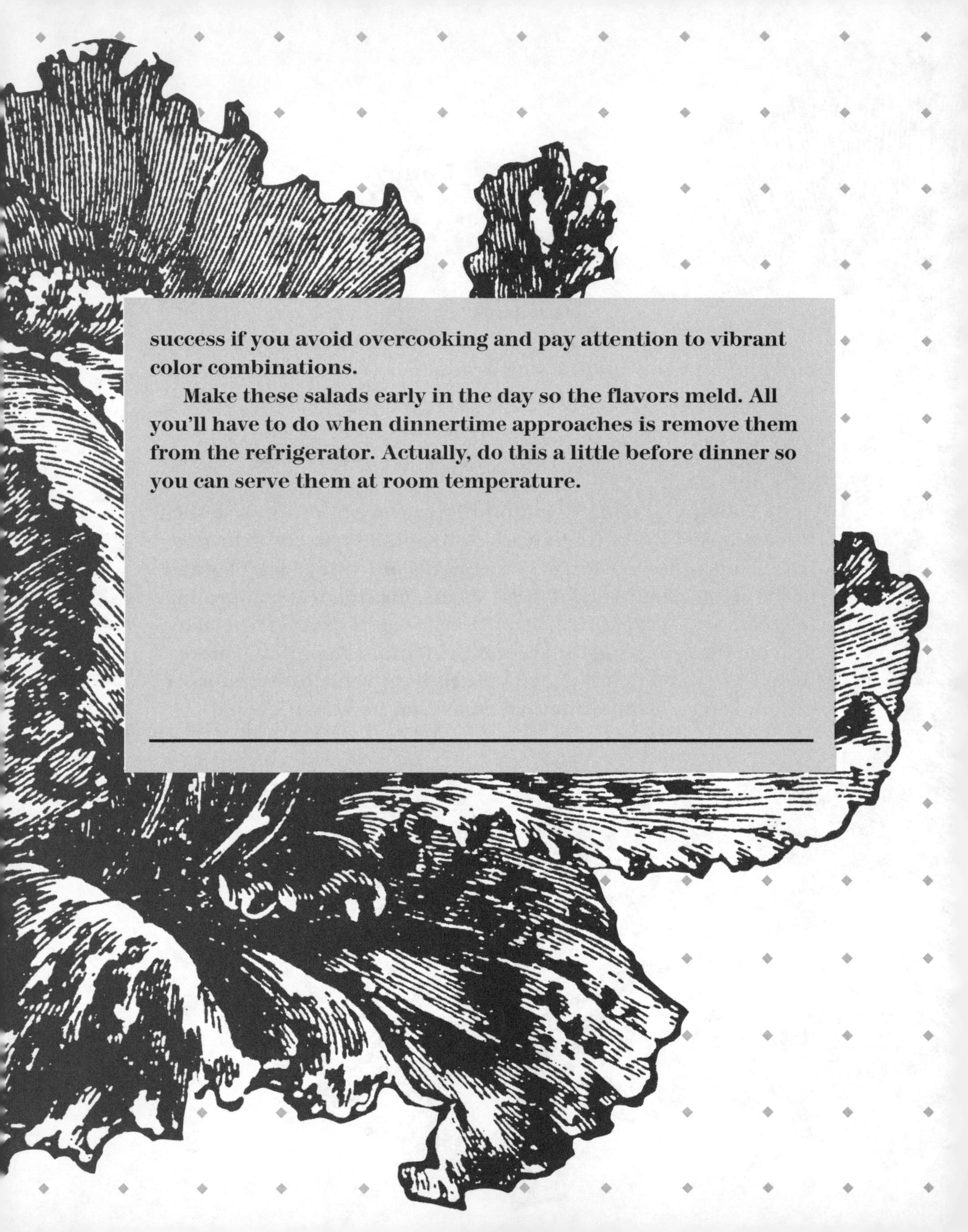

success if you avoid overcooking and pay attention to vibrant color combinations.

Make these salads early in the day so the flavors meld. All you'll have to do when dinnertime approaches is remove them from the refrigerator. Actually, do this a little before dinner so you can serve them at room temperature.

Quick

PENNE WITH GREEK-STYLE VEGETABLE MARINADE

This "sauce" requires no cooking; just marinate everything in one bowl and toss it onto the hot pasta. Great for summer because of the minimal amount of cooking involved.

⅓ cup olive oil

3 garlic cloves, pressed or minced

1 medium zucchini, halved lengthwise and very thinly sliced

2 tomatoes, finely diced

12 kalamata (Greek) olives, pitted and chopped (see note)

6 scallions, very thinly sliced

2 tablespoons finely chopped fresh dill, or 1½ teaspoons dried

1 cup finely diced feta cheese

Generous seasoning of freshly ground black pepper

1 pound penne or mostaccioli (quill-shaped pasta)

Salt to taste

Serves 6

1 Combine all the ingredients except the pasta and the salt in a medium-size bowl. Toss and let sit for 30 minutes or up to 4 hours. Cover and chill if held longer than 1 hour; bring to room temperature before cooking the pasta.

2 Bring a large pot of water to a boil. Add the pasta and cook until tender yet chewy, about 10 minutes. Drain thoroughly in a colander. Return to the pot or place in a large bowl.

3 Pour on the vegetable marinade and toss. Serve slightly warm or at room temperature, tasting to see if salt is necessary.

Note: To pit the olives, place them one by one on a cutting board. Lay the flat surface of a large chef's knife on the olive and give a thump with your fist. The pit will pop out. Cut the flesh into quarters.

Quick ORZO PESTO SALAD

Orzo salads pair particularly well with creamy dressings and this pesto sauce lends just the right balance, while diced vegetables and walnuts add some welcome crunch.

PESTO

1 well-packed cup fresh basil

¼ cup olive oil

3 garlic cloves, minced

½ teaspoon salt

Generous seasoning of freshly ground pepper

¼ cup grated Parmesan cheese

....

1½ cups orzo (rice-shaped pasta)

1 celery rib, thinly sliced

1 red bell pepper, finely diced

1 cucumber, peeled, seeded, and finely diced

⅓ cup slivered red onion

½ cup chopped walnuts

Serves 4

1 To make the pesto, combine the basil, olive oil, garlic, salt, and pepper in a blender or food processor and purée. Scrape into a bowl; stir in the Parmesan cheese. Set aside.

2 Cook the orzo in rapidly boiling water for 6 to 8 minutes, or until tender but not soft or mushy. Drain thoroughly in a colander, then place in a large bowl. Spoon on the pesto and toss well. Let cool.

3 Stir in the remaining ingredients, breaking up any clumps of orzo. Cover and chill at least 2 hours. Bring to room temperature before serving.

Quick TORTELLINI AND SPINACH SALAD WITH SESAME DRESSING

Fresh spinach adds wonderful color and texture to this special salad. Sesame lovers take note.

SESAME DRESSING

⅓ cup canola oil

2 tablespoons Oriental sesame oil

2 tablespoons lemon juice

1 teaspoon tamari soy sauce

2 garlic cloves, minced

½ teaspoon salt

Freshly ground pepper

1 pound frozen cheese tortellini

1 yellow bell pepper, cut into thin strips

1 tomato, cut into small cubes

⅓ cup slivered red onion

2 teaspoons sesame seeds

4 cups fresh spinach torn into small pieces, washed and spun dry

Serves 4

1 Combine all the ingredients for the sesame dressing in a screw-top jar and shake vigorously. Set aside.

2 Bring a large pot of water to a boil. Drop in the tortellini and cook until al dente, about 5 minutes. Do not overcook. Drain in a colander. Run cold water over the tortellini until they are cold, then drain again very well. Pour into a large serving bowl.

3 Stir in the pepper, tomato, and onion, then pour on half of the sesame dressing and toss well. Let marinate at least 30 minutes, or up to 8 hours. Cover and chill if longer than 1 hour. Bring to room temperature before serving.

4 Place the sesame seeds in a dry, small saucepan and toast them over medium heat until they begin to pop and smoke slightly, about 3 minutes. Pour into a little dish and let cool.

5 Just before serving, stir the spinach into the tortellini mixture. Pour on the remaining dressing and toss well. Sprinkle on the sesame seeds and toss again.

Quick TORTELLINI AND GREEN BEAN SALAD WITH TOMATO PESTO

I am exceptionally fond of the tomato pesto sauce that dresses hot capellini in my second book,* Quick Vegetarian Pleasures, *and I have found a wonderful way to adapt it to this cold tortellini salad. Paired with bright, crunchy green beans, this becomes a perfect pasta salad for a summer picnic.

THE PESTO

½ cup good-quality tomato paste

⅓ cup olive oil

¼ cup grated Parmesan cheese

2 garlic cloves, pressed or minced

2 tablespoons pine nuts

3 tablespoons finely chopped fresh basil, or 1½ teaspoons dried basil *and* ¼ cup chopped fresh parsley

¼ teaspoon salt

Freshly ground black pepper

....

1 pound green beans, each cut in half (about 4 cups)

1 pound frozen cheese tortellini

Serves 4

1 To make the pesto, whisk the tomato paste and olive oil together in a medium-size bowl. Whisk in the cheese, garlic, pine nuts, basil, salt, and pepper. Set aside.

2 Bring a stockpot of water to a boil. Drop the green beans in and cook until tender yet slightly crunchy and still bright green, about 5 minutes. Remove with a slotted spoon and immerse in cold water to stop further cooking. Pour out the water and replace with more cold water. Remove the green beans and place on a cotton kitchen towel. Pat dry.

3 Drop the tortellini into the boiling water and cook until tender yet firm, about 5 minutes. Drain in a colander and shake out any excess water. Place in a large serving bowl.

4 Mix in the green beans. Scrape the pesto onto the mixture and toss to coat well. Serve at room temperature. The salad can be prepared up to 24 hours in advance; bring it to room temperature before serving.

SOBA SALAD

The nutty flavor of soba is delicious in a cold salad. Because both soba and tofu are delicate and break easily, you must handle them gingerly (good pun!) and not toss too much.

The soba and tofu can be prepared up to 4 hours in advance but should be kept separate until serving time.

8 ounces soba (buckwheat noodles)

½ cucumber, peeled, seeded, and julienned

1 carrot, julienned or grated

1 scallion, very thinly sliced

½ pound extra-firm tofu

3 tablespoons tamari soy sauce

2 tablespoons Oriental sesame oil

1 tablespoon mirin (sweet sake) or sherry

1 tablespoon balsamic or red wine vinegar

2 teaspoons sugar

½ teaspoon minced fresh ginger

Serves 3

1 Bring a large pot of water to a boil. Drop in the soba and cook until al dente, no longer than 5 minutes. Be certain not to overcook the soba; it should be chewy. Drain in a colander and run cold water over it, tossing gently. Shake the colander and drain very thoroughly. Place in a large serving bowl. Place the cucumber, carrot, and scallion on top of the noodles. Don't mix in yet.

2 Slice the tofu into ½-inch-thick slices, then pat with a cotton towel or paper towels until very dry. Press lightly to extract as much moisture as possible. Cut the tofu into ½-inch cubes and place them in a medium-size bowl.

3 Combine the tamari, sesame oil, mirin, vinegar, sugar, and ginger in a cup. Drizzle about 1 tablespoon over the tofu and very gently toss to coat evenly. Let sit a few minutes to absorb the dressing.

4 Pour the remaining mixture on the soba and vegetables and toss gently but thoroughly. Let sit a few minutes so the sauce will be absorbed. Serve the soba on large plates with some marinated tofu placed on top.

Quick

ROTINI, ASPARAGUS, AND ALMOND SALAD WITH SESAME DRESSING

This light and flavorful salad is perfect for a summer day when you want to avoid heavy foods.

THE DRESSING

2 tablespoons tamari soy sauce

3 tablespoons Chinese rice vinegar or red wine vinegar

1½ tablespoons brown sugar

1½ tablespoons Oriental sesame oil

¼ cup vegetable or peanut oil

Liberal seasoning of freshly ground pepper

....

1 pound asparagus, bottom of stalks peeled, then cut diagonally into 1½-inch pieces

½ pound rotini (short corkscrew pasta)

4 scallions, thinly sliced

6 radishes, thinly sliced

½ cup sliced almonds, lightly toasted

Serves 4

1 Combine all the ingredients for the dressing in a screw-top jar and shake vigorously. Set aside.

2 Bring a large pot of water to a boil. Drop in the asparagus and let return to a boil. Cook until the asparagus is tender yet still slightly crunchy, about 3 minutes. Remove with a slotted spoon and immerse in cold water to stop further cooking. Drain, pat dry, then place the asparagus in a large bowl.

3 Stir the rotini into the boiling water and cook until tender yet still a little chewy, about 5 minutes. Drain thoroughly in a colander, then mix the rotini into the asparagus. Stir in the scallions, radishes, and almonds.

4 Pour on the dressing and toss. Serve at room temperature, or cover and chill up to 8 hours. Bring to room temperature before serving.

SUMMER EGGPLANT AND PENNE SALAD

I love to make this colorful salad at the end of summer when vegetables are plentiful and at their peak. Serve it with grilled garlic bread or baked French bread with Parmesan cheese.

1 medium (1¼ pounds) eggplant, peeled and cut into 1-inch cubes (no smaller)

6 tablespoons olive oil

2 yellow peppers, thinly sliced into strips

½ pound penne (quill-shaped pasta)

2 medium ripe tomatoes, cut into small cubes

4 garlic cloves, minced

2 scallions, very thinly sliced

1½ cups frozen peas, thawed

1 cup shredded fresh basil

2 tablespoons balsamic or red wine vinegar

1 teaspoon ground cumin

¾ teaspoon salt

Very generous seasoning of freshly ground pepper

2 cups arugula leaves, each cut in half (optional)

Serves 4 to 6 as a main course

1 Preheat the oven to 450 degrees.

2 Place the eggplant cubes in a large bowl, then pour 2 tablespoons of the olive oil over them. Toss quickly to coat evenly. Spread the eggplant cubes on a baking sheet so they rest in one layer. Bake 10 minutes, tossing a few times, or until the eggplant is tender but not at all mushy. The eggplant will continue to cook as it cools. Set aside to cool.

3 Heat 1 tablespoon of the olive oil in a large skillet over high heat. Add the peppers and sauté quickly for 2 to 3 minutes, or just until they are heated through. Scrape into a very large bowl and let cool.

4 Bring a medium-size saucepan of water to a boil. Drop in the penne and cook until tender yet chewy, about 10 minutes. Drain thoroughly in a colander, then run under cold water to cool. Drain again, shaking out as much water as you can. Stir the penne into the peppers.

5 Pour on the remaining 3 tablespoons of oil, toss, then mix in all the remaining ingredients except the arugula. Let sit 1 to 4 hours to marinate. Cover and chill if longer than 1 hour. Bring to room temperature before serving. If you are using the arugula, mix it in at serving time.

Quick

CURRIED COUSCOUS SALAD WITH GINGER-LIME DRESSING

This salad has a marvelous blend of tantalizing flavors and textures, and the only cooking involved is boiling water, so it's a great choice for summer weather.

1½ cups couscous

½ cup golden raisins

2 teaspoons curry powder

2 cups boiling water

½ cup coarsely chopped roasted (unsalted) cashews

1½ cups frozen peas, thawed

1 red bell pepper, cut into small dice

⅓ cup slivered red onion

2 tablespoons finely chopped fresh mint or cilantro

THE DRESSING

⅓ cup fresh lime juice (3 limes)

½ teaspoon ground cumin

1 teaspoon minced fresh ginger

2 garlic cloves, minced

½ teaspoon salt

Generous seasoning of freshly ground pepper

⅓ cup olive oil

Serves 4

1 Place the couscous, raisins, and curry powder in a large serving bowl. Pour on the boiling water, stir, and tightly cover with foil or a large plate. Let sit 5 minutes, then fluff with a fork. Cover again and let sit 10 more minutes. Fluff again, then let the couscous sit uncovered until it has cooled to room temperature.

2 Stir in the cashews, peas, red pepper, onion, and mint.

3 Combine all the dressing ingredients in a screw-top jar. Shake vigorously, pour onto the couscous, and toss. Let the salad sit at least 30 minutes, or cover and chill up to 24 hours. Bring to room temperature before serving, then taste to correct the seasoning.

CURRIED FOUR-GRAIN SALAD

Packed with grains yet amazingly light, this salad is equally great as summer picnic food or as an entrée in winter with some coarse bread alongside.

½ cup barley

½ cup wild rice or brown rice

½ cup bulghur, preferably dark, coarse-cut

½ cup couscous

1½ cups frozen peas, thawed

8 radishes, thinly sliced

2 scallions, very thinly sliced

1 cup raisins

⅓ cup chopped walnuts

1 tablespoon finely chopped cilantro or fresh parsley

THE DRESSING

¼ cup fresh lemon juice

⅓ cup olive oil

3 garlic cloves, pressed or minced

1 tablespoon curry powder

1 teaspoon salt

Liberal seasoning of freshly ground pepper

Serves 4 to 6

1 Bring about 2 quarts of water to a boil in a 3-quart saucepan. Drop in the barley and rice and cook, uncovered, for 40 minutes, or until tender when tasted. Stir occasionally. Drain thoroughly in a colander and let cool.

2 Meanwhile, place the bulghur in a medium-size bowl. Pour on boiling water to cover by 1 inch. Let sit for 25 minutes. Taste a few grains for tenderness. If they are still too hard, let sit for 5 minutes more. Place in a strainer and press out all of the liquid with the back of a spoon. Let cool.

3 Place the couscous in a medium-size bowl. Pour on ¾ cup boiling water, stir, and cover. Let sit for 10 minutes. Fluff with a fork and let cool.

4 Combine the barley, rice, bulghur, and couscous in a large bowl. Stir in the peas, radishes, scallions, raisins, walnuts, and cilantro.

5 Combine all the dressing ingredients in a screw-top jar and shake vigorously. Pour onto the salad and toss well. Let marinate at least 2 hours before serving. Chill if marinating longer. Serve at room temperature so that the grains are tender; they become firm when cold.

Quick

BLACK BEAN SALAD WITH PINEAPPLE AND HOT PEPPERS

This marinated bean salad juxtaposes sweet pineapple with zesty hot peppers to make a spunky, colorful main course that is peppered with crunchy vegetables. Crusty bread and a soft cheese such as Brie or chèvre would be welcome companions to this salad entrée.

THE MARINADE

3 tablespoons fresh lime juice (1½ limes)

4 tablespoons olive oil

½ teaspoon ground cumin

2 garlic cloves, pressed

½ teaspoon crushed red pepper flakes

¼ teaspoon salt

4 cups cooked black beans (see note)

½ tablespoon olive oil

1 small red bell pepper, cored and cut into ½-inch dice

1 small green bell pepper, cored and cut into ½-inch dice

1½ cups diced (¾ inch) pineapple, fresh or canned

3 scallions, very thinly sliced

1. In a small bowl, whisk together all the ingredients for the marinade. Place the beans in a large bowl and pour half of the marinade on them. Stir occasionally to coat.

2. Heat the ½ tablespoon of oil in a skillet. Add the red and green peppers and sauté for 5 minutes, or until tender yet still quite crunchy. Spoon into a medium-size bowl and let cool completely.

3. Stir the pineapple, scallions, celery, optional cilantro, and pepper into the cooled peppers. Pour on the remaining marinade. (The beans and the vegetable mixture can be prepared and chilled up to 4 hours in advance. They should be kept separate so the beans don't discolor the vegetables. Bring to room temperature before serving.)

4. Just before serving, gently mix the vegetables into the beans. Place a bed of lettuce leaves on each plate. Remove the vegetables and beans from the marinade with a slotted spoon and mound on the lettuce leaves.

Note: If you want to use dried beans, soak

1 celery rib, very thinly sliced

1 tablespoon finely chopped cilantro (optional)

Freshly ground pepper

Green leaf lettuce leaves for garnish

Serves 3 to 4

1½ cups dried black beans overnight. Drain. Cover with fresh water and cook 30 to 40 minutes, or until tender but not mushy. Drain and cool completely. If you want to use canned black beans, rinse and drain two 1-pound cans.

WARM LENTIL SALAD WITH WALNUTS, GREEN BEANS, AND RED ONION

The generous addition to this salad of lightly cooked red onion adds not only a deep flavor but also vibrant color. Sautéing red onion with just a splash of vinegar sets its color at a dazzling purple—a trick worth knowing for the charm it lends a dish. If timing makes it too difficult to serve this salad warm, it is also delicious at room temperature.

THE DRESSING

¼ cup olive oil

2 tablespoons red wine vinegar

½ teaspoon Dijon mustard

2 garlic cloves, pressed or minced

2 teaspoons fresh thyme, or ½ teaspoon dried

½ teaspoon salt

Liberal seasoning of freshly ground pepper

....

1 teaspoon olive oil

1 large red onion, halved vertically and thinly sliced

1 teaspoon red wine vinegar

½ pound green beans, cut into 2-inch lengths (2 cups)

1½ cups lentils

½ cup chopped walnuts

1 Combine all the ingredients for the dressing in a screw-top jar and shake vigorously. Set aside.

2 Heat the teaspoon of oil in a medium-size skillet. Add the red onion and sauté 2 minutes. To set the color, sprinkle the vinegar over the onions and toss well. Sauté about 5 more minutes, or just until they become tender yet still crunchy. Remove from the heat.

3 Bring about 6 cups of water to a boil in a 3-quart saucepan. Drop in the green beans and let the water return to a boil. Cook 5 minutes, or until tender yet still bright green. Remove the green beans with a slotted spoon and place in a medium-size bowl. Pour on about 1 tablespoon of dressing and set aside. Keep the water in the saucepan boiling.

4 Drop the lentils into the boiling water. After the water returns to a boil, cook the lentils, partially covered, for 15 to 20 minutes. Stir occasionally. The lentils are done when they are tender but still a tad crunchy. Do not let them get at all

¼ cup chopped fresh parsley

Lettuce leaves (optional)

Serves 4

mushy. Drain in a colander, then transfer to a large serving bowl. Pour on the dressing, toss well, and stir in the walnuts.

5 When the lentils are warm, not hot, stir in the green beans, red onions, and parsley. Serve as is or on a few lettuce leaves.

GRAINS

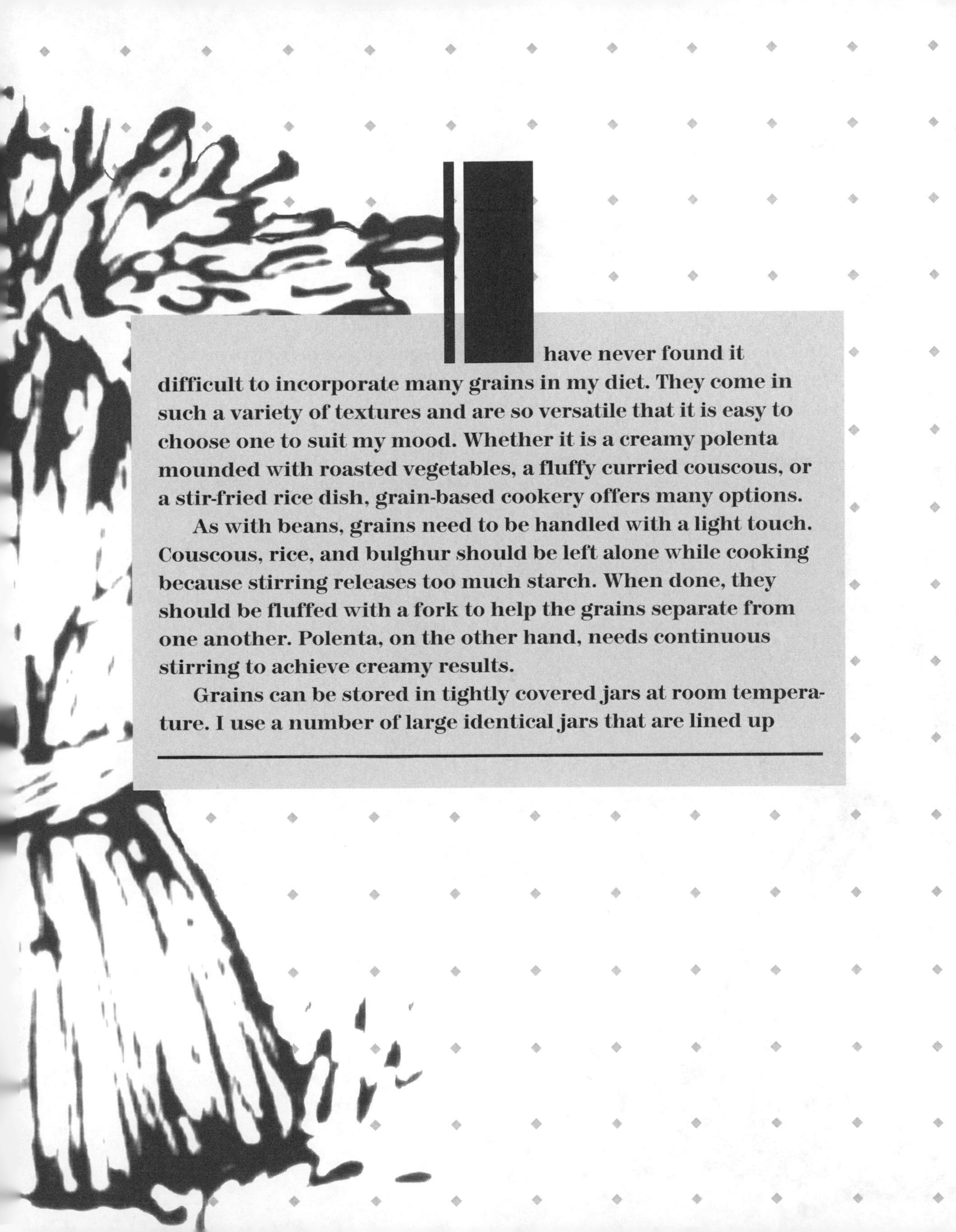

I have never found it difficult to incorporate many grains in my diet. They come in such a variety of textures and are so versatile that it is easy to choose one to suit my mood. Whether it is a creamy polenta mounded with roasted vegetables, a fluffy curried couscous, or a stir-fried rice dish, grain-based cookery offers many options.

As with beans, grains need to be handled with a light touch. Couscous, rice, and bulghur should be left alone while cooking because stirring releases too much starch. When done, they should be fluffed with a fork to help the grains separate from one another. Polenta, on the other hand, needs continuous stirring to achieve creamy results.

Grains can be stored in tightly covered jars at room temperature. I use a number of large identical jars that are lined up

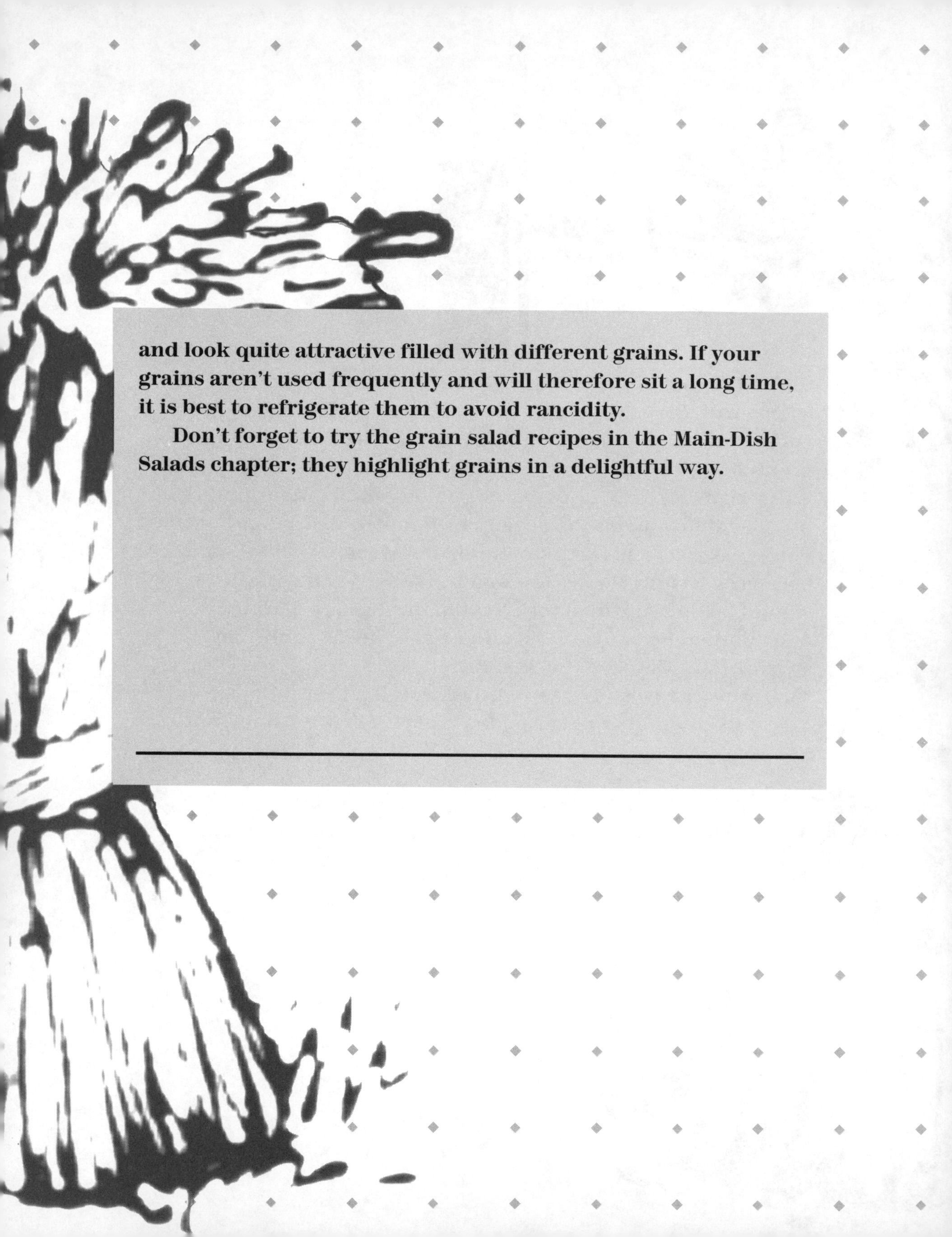

and look quite attractive filled with different grains. If your grains aren't used frequently and will therefore sit a long time, it is best to refrigerate them to avoid rancidity.

Don't forget to try the grain salad recipes in the Main-Dish Salads chapter; they highlight grains in a delightful way.

ROASTED VEGETABLES WITH POLENTA

Roasting large chunks of vegetables imparts them with a deep flavor and an alluring brown coating. Garlic cooked by this method becomes sweet and mellow, so be sure to include it.

2 small zucchini, sliced diagonally ¾-inch thick

1 red bell pepper, cored and cut into 1½-inch-square pieces

1 green bell pepper, cored and cut into 1½-inch-square pieces

1 large tomato, cored and cut into eighths

2 celery ribs, sliced diagonally ½-inch thick

8 garlic cloves, peeled

1 teaspoon dried thyme

Freshly ground pepper

3 tablespoons olive oil

2 medium onions, sliced ½-inch thick

Salt to taste

THE POLENTA

4 cups water

½ teaspoon salt

1¼ cups cornmeal

1 tablespoon butter, cut into bits

⅓ cup grated Parmesan cheese

Serves 4

1 Preheat the oven to 425 degrees.

2 Place the zucchini, peppers, tomato, celery, and garlic cloves in a large bowl. Sprinkle on the thyme and season with black pepper. Pour on two tablespoons of the oil and toss to coat. Spread the vegetable mixture onto a large baking sheet so that it is in one layer. Set aside.

3 Pour the remaining tablespoon of oil into a pie plate or 9- to 10-inch shallow pan and spread evenly. Carefully place the sliced onions in the dish, keeping them intact. Rub the bottom of the onions in the oil to coat them, then turn each slice over. Place the vegetables and onions in the oven and cook 25 to 30 minutes. Remove after 15 minutes and turn the vegetables and onions over with tongs. They are done when tender and brown. Season the vegetables with salt. Let cool while making the polenta because the vegetables are more flavorful served warm, not piping hot.

4 To make the polenta, bring the water and salt to a boil in a medium-size saucepan. Reduce the heat to medium and slowly drizzle in the cornmeal, whisking all the while. Continue to whisk until the polenta is thick and begins to tear away from the sides of the pan, about 7 minutes. Stir in the butter and cheese. Serve some polenta on each plate and top with the roasted vegetables.

Quick BROCCOLI RABE WITH TOMATO-CHEESE POLENTA

Richard Sax, in his much-treasured book* From the Farmers' Market*, recommends the Sicilian trick of pairing raisins with broccoli rabe to sweeten the slight bitterness of the greens. Here, a dynamic blending of spiciness, sweetness, and mild bitterness is the backdrop for an intriguing vegetable topping for the cheesy polenta, which is interlaced with bits of tomato.

3½ cups vegetable stock

¼ teaspoon salt

....

1 pound broccoli rabe

2 tablespoons olive oil

6 garlic cloves, minced

¼ teaspoon crushed red pepper flakes

¼ cup raisins

¼ teaspoon salt

1 tablespoon water

THE POLENTA

1¼ cups cornmeal

¼ teaspoon salt

1 tablespoon unsalted butter

3 tablespoons grated Parmesan cheese

½ cup seeded and diced canned or fresh tomatoes, well drained

Serves 3

1 In a medium-size saucepan, bring the vegetable stock and salt to a boil for the polenta. Meanwhile, chop off all but 1 inch of the broccoli rabe stems and discard. Wash the greens and coarsely chop them. You should get about 8 cups.

2 Heat the oil in a large skillet over medium-high heat. Add the garlic and red pepper flakes and sauté 2 minutes. Do not let the garlic brown.

3 Add the broccoli rabe, raisins, salt, and water. Toss well, then cover the pan. Cook 3 to 5 minutes, or until the broccoli rabe wilts yet still retains some crunch. Remove the cover and keep warm.

4 When the vegetable stock boils, reduce the heat to a simmer. Very slowly drizzle in the cornmeal, whisking all the while. Continue to whisk until the polenta thickens and begins to pull away from the sides of the pan, about 5 minutes.

5 Remove from the heat, then whisk in the salt, butter, and Parmesan cheese. Very gently stir in the tomatoes. Serve a generous portion of polenta on each plate and top with the broccoli rabe mixture.

Quick POLENTA AND GORGONZOLA "PIZZA"

This polenta dish cuts like a pie and the slices nicely retain their shape. Topped with mozzarella cheese, tomato slices, and crumbled blue cheese, these hearty wedges need just a salad to accompany them—perhaps one made with arugula and other greens.

3 cups water

½ teaspoon salt

⅛ teaspoon grated nutmeg

1 cup cornmeal

1 tablespoon unsalted butter

¼ cup grated Parmesan cheese

1 cup (3 ounces) grated part-skim mozzarella

1 medium-size tomato, cored and thinly sliced

½ cup (about 2 ounces) crumbled Gorgonzola or other blue cheese

Freshly ground pepper

Serves 4 to 6

1 Butter a 9-inch pie plate and keep near the stove.

2 In a 2½- to 3-quart saucepan, bring the water, salt, and nutmeg to a boil. Reduce the heat to low and then drizzle in the cornmeal, whisking all the while to prevent clumping. Cook about 5 minutes, constantly whisking, or until the polenta begins to pull away from the sides of the pan.

3 Remove from the heat and whisk in the butter and Parmesan cheese. With a rubber spatula, scrape the polenta into the baking dish, smoothing the top. Let sit 10 minutes, or cover and chill up to 4 hours. Bring to room temperature before beginning step 5.

4 Preheat the oven to 400 degrees.

5 Cover the top of the polenta with the grated mozzarella. Lay the tomato slices over the cheese. Sprinkle the Gorgonzola over the tomatoes, then season with the pepper.

6 Bake 20 minutes, or until hot and sizzling. Cut into wedges.

Quick

POLENTA WITH CAULIFLOWER, TOMATOES, AND HOT PEPPERS

The trio of tomatoes, garlic, and hot peppers is a natural match for cauliflower, highlighting its delicate flavor. When paired with polenta, this becomes a noteworthy dish.

1 tablespoon olive oil

6 garlic cloves, minced

¼ teaspoon crushed red pepper flakes

1½ cups finely chopped canned tomatoes, with their juice

1 medium (2 pounds) cauliflower, cut into small florets

4 cups vegetable stock

¼ teaspoon salt

1¼ cups cornmeal

1 tablespoon unsalted butter

⅓ cup grated Parmesan cheese

¼ cup minced fresh parsley

Serves 4

1 Heat the oil in a large skillet over medium heat. Add the garlic and pepper flakes and sauté for 2 minutes. Stir in the tomatoes and simmer for 5 minutes.

2 Mix in the cauliflower and toss to coat thoroughly with the sauce. Cover the pan and cook 5 minutes. Remove the cover, then continue to cook the cauliflower, tossing occasionally, until it is tender and the juices have thickened slightly, about 5 more minutes.

3 Meanwhile, bring the vegetable stock and salt to a boil. Very slowly drizzle in the cornmeal, whisking continuously with a wire whisk. Immediately reduce the heat to low; continue whisking the polenta until it is thick like mashed potatoes, about 5 minutes. Whisk in the butter and Parmesan cheese.

4 Stir the parsley into the cauliflower mixture. Serve the polenta on the center of each plate with a mound of cauliflower on top of it.

Quick CORN AND SCALLION SPOONBREAD

Spoonbread is a cross between polenta and a corn soufflé, and it's best eaten with a spoon. For a harmonious side dish, try some sautéed broccoli or kale with a good dose of garlic.

3 cups low-fat milk

½ teaspoon salt

1¼ cups cornmeal

4 tablespoons unsalted butter, cut into pieces

3 eggs, separated

1½ teaspoons baking powder

1 cup frozen corn kernels, thawed

2 scallions, very thinly sliced

Serves 4

1. Butter a deep 2-quart baking dish or soufflé dish and set aside.
2. Bring 2½ cups of the milk and the salt to a boil in a medium-size saucepan. Reduce to a simmer, then slowly sprinkle in the cornmeal, whisking all the while. Cook about 5 minutes, whisking constantly. It will be thick. Whisk in the butter, then scrape into a large bowl. Let cool.
3. Preheat the oven to 350 degrees.
4. Beat the egg yolks into the cornmeal mixture. Combine the remaining ½ cup of milk with the baking powder, then beat it in.
5. Whip the egg whites until they hold stiff peaks. Spoon them onto the cornmeal mixture, then gently fold them in.
6. Pour half the batter into the prepared baking dish. Sprinkle on the corn and scallions. Top with the remaining batter. Bake 60 minutes, or until a knife inserted in the center comes out clean. Serve immediately.

Quick COUSCOUS WITH PROVENÇAL VEGETABLES

A delicious vegetable concoction with green beans, tomatoes, red peppers, olives, pine nuts, and basil is mounded on a bed of couscous to make a light but intensely flavored dish. French bread is all you need to round off the meal.

2 tablespoons olive oil

3 garlic cloves, minced

¼ teaspoon crushed red pepper flakes

1½ cups finely chopped canned tomatoes with their juice

½ pound green beans, cut diagonally into 1½-inch lengths (3 cups)

1 red bell pepper, cored and cut into 1-inch dice

1½ cups vegetable stock

¼ teaspoon salt

1 cup couscous

1 tablespoon unsalted butter, cut into bits

10 kalamata olives, pitted and coarsely chopped (see note, page 25)

2 tablespoons pine nuts

2 tablespoons minced fresh basil

Serves 3

1 Heat the oil in a large skillet over medium heat. Sauté the garlic and red pepper flakes for 1 minute, then stir in the tomatoes and their juice. Bring to a boil, mix in the green beans and red bell pepper, then cover the pan. Cook, stirring occasionally, until the green beans are tender, 10 to 15 minutes.

2 Meanwhile, make the couscous. Bring the vegetable stock and salt to a boil in a medium-size saucepan. Stir in the couscous, cover the pan, and remove from the heat. Let sit 5 minutes, or until all the stock is absorbed. Fluff with a fork, then stir in the butter. Cover again and let sit until ready to serve.

3 When the green beans are tender, check to see that there is enough liquid to make a sauce. If not, stir in a few tablespoons of water. Mix in the olives, pine nuts, and basil. Serve a bed of couscous on each plate and top with a mound of the vegetable mixture.

Quick SKILLET CURRIED VEGETABLES AND COUSCOUS WITH ALMONDS

Everything is cooked together in one pan, which makes this colorful dish a snap to prepare.

2 tablespoons unsalted butter

2 garlic cloves, minced

2 teaspoons minced fresh ginger

4 teaspoons curry powder

Dash of cayenne (or more to taste)

1 red bell pepper, cored and cut into ½-inch dice

1 carrot, very thinly sliced

2 cups tiny broccoli florets

1 small apple, peeled, cored, and cut into ½-inch dice

2 scallions, thinly sliced

½ cup frozen peas, thawed

¼ cup raisins

⅓ cup sliced almonds

2½ cups vegetable stock

1½ cups couscous

½ teaspoon salt

Serves 3 to 4

1 Melt the butter in a large skillet over medium heat. Add the garlic, ginger, curry powder, and cayenne and sauté for 1 minute. Stir in the red pepper, carrot, broccoli, and ¼ cup of water. Cover the pan and steam the vegetables until almost tender, about 3 minutes.

2 Mix in the apple, scallions, peas, raisins, and almonds. Pour in the stock and bring to a boil. Stir in the couscous and salt, cover the pan, and remove it from the heat. Let sit for 7 minutes. Remove the cover, fluff the couscous with a fork, then cover again. Let sit 2 more minutes before serving.

Quick MIXED GREENS WITH GARLIC ON COUSCOUS

I love to combine kale with escarole in this dish, but feel free to substitute other fresh greens, such as spinach, broccoli rabe, collards, or mustard greens.

2 pounds fresh greens (weight with stems), such as kale, escarole, or spinach

2 tablespoons olive oil

6 garlic cloves, minced

¼ teaspoon crushed red pepper flakes

Salt

....

1½ cups vegetable stock

¼ teaspoon salt

1 cup couscous

Serves 3

1 Remove the coarse stems from the greens and discard. Thicker greens such as kale and collards will take longer to cook, so if you are using those greens in combination with more delicate greens, keep them separate. Wash the greens by dunking them in a large pot of cold water. Place the greens in a colander; discard the water. Repeat until no sand remains on the bottom of the pot.

2 Place the thicker greens in the pot with only the water that clings to them. Cover and cook over medium heat just until they begin to wilt. Add the more delicate, quicker-cooking greens, cover the pot, and cook quickly, until everything is wilted. Drain in a colander, pressing out excess liquid with the back of a spoon.

3 Heat the oil in a large skillet over medium heat. Add the garlic and red pepper flakes and cook 2 minutes—do not let it brown. Add the greens, mix well, and cook until the greens are tender yet still a bright color, about 3 minutes. Season rather generously with salt.

4 To make the couscous, bring the stock and salt to a boil in a small saucepan. Pour in the couscous, cover the pot, then remove from the heat. Let sit 5 minutes, then fluff with a fork. Serve the couscous on each plate with the greens mounded in the center.

Quick MEXICAN RICE WITH VEGETABLES AND CILANTRO

***I** often choose this rice dish when I crave something that's low-fat and basic, yet hearty. Everything is cooked together in a large skillet, making it a breeze to prepare. Don't hesitate to make this in advance because it is actually fluffier if it cools and is then reheated. Just sprinkle on a few tablespoons of water and reheat slowly.*

2 tablespoons olive oil

1 medium onion, finely diced

2 garlic cloves, minced

1 green pepper, finely diced

2 cups (½ pound) diced green beans

1½ cups converted rice

1 tablespoon chili powder

½ teaspoon salt

Generous seasoning of freshly ground pepper

3 tablespoons tomato paste

3 cups water

2 cups cooked kidney beans, either home-cooked or canned, rinsed thoroughly if canned

3 tablespoons finely chopped cilantro

½ teaspoon dried oregano

Serves 4

1 Heat the oil in a large skillet over medium-high heat. Add the onion and garlic and sauté 2 minutes. Stir in the green pepper, green beans, rice, chili powder, salt, and pepper and, tossing often, cook 2 minutes.

2 Combine the tomato paste with about ½ cup of the water and stir to thin out the tomato paste. Stir in the remaining water and mix well. Pour into the skillet and cover the pan. Bring to a boil, then reduce to a simmer. Cook 20 minutes, or until all the liquid is absorbed.

3 Remove from the heat. Gently stir in the kidney beans, cilantro, and oregano. Cover again and let sit 5 minutes. Serve immediately or let cool, uncovered, and reheat.

SPINACH, RICE, AND FETA CHEESE GRATIN

This delicious blending of flavors is reminiscent of the filling in spana-kopita—Greek spinach pie. I prefer to use white rather than brown rice in this gratin because it adds to the creamy, delicate texture.

2½ cups water

¼ teaspoon salt

1 teaspoon olive oil

1 cup basmati or converted white rice

2 teaspoons olive oil

1 medium-large onion, finely diced

1 red bell pepper, cored and finely diced

2 10-ounce packages frozen chopped spinach, thawed and squeezed dry

1 cup (5 ounces) finely diced feta cheese

¼ cup grated Parmesan cheese

1 tablespoon minced fresh dill, or 1 teaspoon dried

Generous seasoning of freshly ground pepper

1 egg, beaten

1 cup low-fat milk

1 tablespoon bread crumbs

1 tablespoon olive oil

Serves 4

1. To cook the rice, bring the water, salt, and oil to a boil in a medium-size saucepan. Add the rice, cover the pot, and reduce the heat to a simmer. Cook until all the water is absorbed, about 20 minutes. Spoon the rice into a large bowl and let cool.
2. Meanwhile, heat the 2 teaspoons of oil in a large skillet over medium heat. Add the onion and sauté until it begins to brown, about 10 minutes. Stir in the red pepper and cook until tender, about 7 more minutes.
3. Preheat the oven to 375 degrees. Lightly grease a 2½-quart oval gratin or other shallow baking dish.
4. Stir the onion and pepper mixture into the rice. Mix in the spinach, feta cheese, Parmesan cheese, dill, pepper, egg, and milk.
5. Spoon the rice mixture into the prepared gratin dish and smooth the top. Sprinkle on the bread crumbs, then drizzle on the olive oil. Bake 30 minutes, or until bubbling on the edges and golden on the top.

VEGETABLE FRIED RICE

This tasty rendition of the traditional Chinese dish is filled with vegetables and bits of fried tofu. Don't omit the sesame oil because it is indispensable for flavorful fried rice. Also, be certain to cook the rice well in advance—even the night before—to make sure it is cold when you begin stir-frying.

1½ cups long-grain brown rice

3 cups water

1 teaspoon vegetable oil

½ teaspoon salt

....

2 tablespoons vegetable oil

½ pound extra-firm tofu, cut into ½-inch dice and patted very dry

3 celery ribs, thinly sliced

¼ pound (about 20) snow peas, de-strung and cut diagonally into thirds, *or* 2 cups shredded cabbage

1 carrot, grated

3 scallions, thinly sliced

¼ cup tamari soy sauce

1 tablespoon Oriental sesame oil

Serves 3 generously

1 Combine the rice, water, oil, and salt in a medium-size saucepan. Cover and bring to a boil. Reduce the heat to a simmer; cook, undisturbed, until all the water is absorbed, about 45 minutes. Spoon the rice onto a large platter or shallow dish and let cool. Cover and refrigerate until cold, at least 2 hours.

2 Heat the oil in a large skillet or wok over medium-high heat until it is hot but not smoking. Add the tofu and stir-fry until golden, about 5 minutes. Spoon onto a plate, leaving any oil behind; set aside.

3 Add the celery, snow peas, and carrot to the skillet and stir-fry 2 minutes, or just until hot. Reduce the heat to low, then stir in the tofu, rice, and scallions. Pour on the tamari and sesame oil and toss well. Cook slowly, tossing frequently, until hot throughout, about 10 minutes.

Note: You can make this fried rice in advance with very successful results. Just undercook the vegetables and when it is time to reheat, sprinkle a few tablespoons of water on the rice mixture to create steam while reheating.

TRICOLOR PEPPERS AND RICE WITH FRESH BASIL

This peasant-style rice dish, studded with mozzarella, is a feast for the senses. Bursting with color, this low-fat sauté would be an ideal summer dish when peppers and fresh basil are in abundance. Start your rice early in the day or the night before so it is cold before you add it to the vegetables; this ensures fluffy results.

1 cup long-grain brown rice, rinsed

2 cups vegetable stock or water

1 teaspoon vegetable oil

½ teaspoon salt

....

1 tablespoon olive oil

4 garlic cloves, minced

1 green bell pepper, cored and cut into ¼ × 2-inch strips

1 red bell pepper, cored and cut into ¼ × 2-inch strips

1 yellow bell pepper, cored and cut into ¼ × 2-inch strips

2 scallions, thinly sliced

10 French oil-cured olives, pitted and halved (see note, page 25)

2 tablespoons water

½ cup chopped fresh basil

½ cup (2 ounces) very finely diced part-skim

1 Combine the rice, stock, vegetable oil, and salt in a medium-size saucepan. Cover and bring to a boil; reduce the heat to a simmer. Cook, covered, until all the water is absorbed, about 45 minutes. Gently spoon the rice into a shallow dish and let cool. Refrigerate until cold, about 2 hours.

2 Heat the olive oil in a large skillet over medium-high heat. Add the garlic and cook 1 minute. Do not let it brown. Stir in the three peppers and sauté until very tender, about 10 minutes.

3 Reduce the heat to medium. Stir in the cold rice, scallions, and olives and toss well. Sprinkle on the water and cover the pan. Cook a few minutes until the rice gets piping hot. Remove the cover and stir in the basil, mozzarella, Parmesan cheese, salt to taste, and pepper. Let cook 1 more minute. Serve immediately.

mozzarella cheese

2 tablespoons grated Parmesan cheese

Salt

Generous seasoning of freshly ground pepper

Serves 3

MOCK VEGETABLE RISOTTO

When I want a special main-course rice dish but don't have the time to labor over a traditional risotto, I use this short-cut method to obtain a rich and creamy rice that is filled with colorful vegetables and has its own cheese "sauce." A light salad is all you need to make it a meal.

1 tablespoon unsalted butter

1 medium onion, minced

1 cup converted white rice

2¼ cups vegetable stock

½ teaspoon salt

....

2 tablespoons olive oil

2 garlic cloves, minced

1 red bell pepper, cored and finely diced

1 medium zucchini, cut lengthwise into sixths and thinly sliced

¼ teaspoon fennel seeds, crushed

½ cup seeded, diced tomato, either fresh or canned

½ cup frozen peas, thawed

Liberal seasoning of freshly ground pepper

....

2 tablespoons white wine or dry vermouth

½ cup grated Parmesan cheese

1 Heat the butter in a 3- to 4-quart saucepan over medium heat. Add the onion and sauté for 5 minutes. Stir in the rice and sauté for 2 minutes, stirring often. Pour in the vegetable stock and salt and cover the pan. Bring to a boil, then reduce the heat to a simmer.

2 Meanwhile, heat the olive oil in a large skillet over medium-high heat. Add the garlic and cook 1 minute. Do not let it brown. Stir in the red pepper and sauté 3 minutes. Add the zucchini and fennel and cook 5 minutes, stirring often. Add the tomato and sauté 2 minutes. Stir in the peas and a generous seasoning of freshly ground pepper. Remove the pan from the heat.

3 After the rice has cooked about 17 minutes, it should be tender, not mushy, and there should be a little stock left over that has not been absorbed. At this point, stir in the wine and then all the sautéed vegetables.

4 Sprinkle in the two cheeses and the basil, then gently stir to incorporate them. Cook 1 minute and serve.

½ cup grated part-skim mozzarella cheese

1 tablespoon minced fresh basil

Serves 3 to 4

VEGETABLE PAELLA

Saffron permeates this low-fat paella, lending it its distinct flavor and golden color. A good choice when you want something light but special.

- ¼ teaspoon saffron
- ½ cup boiling water
- 2 tablespoons olive oil
- 4 garlic cloves, minced
- 1 red bell pepper, cored and cut into ½-inch dice
- 1 10-ounce package frozen baby lima beans, thawed
- 1 tomato, cored, seeded, and finely diced
- 1½ cups converted white rice
- 1 teaspoon paprika
- 2½ cups vegetable stock
- ½ cup dry white wine
- ½ teaspoon salt
- 1 cup frozen peas, thawed
- 1 6½-ounce jar marinated artichoke hearts, drained
- 3 scallions, very thinly sliced
- ½ cup finely chopped fresh parsley

Serves 3 to 4

1 Place the saffron in a teacup or small bowl and pour the boiling water over it. Cover it and let steep 10 minutes.

2 Heat the oil in a large skillet over medium heat. Add the garlic and sauté for 1 minute. Add the red pepper, lima beans, and tomato; sauté, stirring frequently, for 5 minutes.

3 Stir in the rice and paprika. Cook 2 minutes, stirring often. Pour in the stock, wine, saffron water, and salt and stir to blend. Cover the pan and bring to a boil. Reduce the heat to a simmer and cook 15 to 20 minutes, or until the liquid is absorbed.

4 Turn off the heat. Stir in the peas, artichoke hearts, scallions, and parsley and cover the pan. Let sit 5 minutes, or until heated through.

Quick

GREEK-STYLE BULGHUR AND VEGETABLES WITH FETA CHEESE

Many wonderful flavors of Greek cooking permeate this dish. Hot pita bread as an accompaniment would nicely continue the theme.

1 cup golden bulghur (see note)

2 tablespoons olive oil

2 medium onions, finely diced

1 cup seeded, diced tomato, fresh or canned

2 medium zucchini, quartered lengthwise and thinly sliced

1 red or green bell pepper, cored and cut into ½-inch dice

1½ teaspoons dried oregano

¼ teaspoon thyme

Generous seasoning of freshly ground pepper

10 kalamata olives, pitted and quartered (see note, page 25)

1 cup (about 5 ounces) finely diced feta cheese

Salt

Serves 3 to 4

1 Rinse the bulghur in a sieve. Place it in a medium-size bowl and pour in enough boiling water to cover by 2 inches. Let sit 20 minutes, or until the bulghur is tender when a pinch of it is tasted.

2 In batches, place some bulghur in a strainer and press out as much water as possible with the back of a large spoon. Place this dry bulghur in a bowl and repeat the procedure with the rest.

3 Heat the oil in a large skillet over medium-high heat. Add the onions and sauté 10 minutes. Stir in the tomato and sauté 5 minutes.

4 Mix in the zucchini, bell pepper, oregano, thyme, and pepper and sauté, tossing often, until the vegetables are tender yet crisp, about 10 minutes.

5 Stir in the bulghur and olives. Cook a few more minutes, stirring frequently, until the mixture is piping hot. Sprinkle on the feta cheese and gently toss to combine. Cook 1 more minute, then taste for salt; it might need a bit. Serve immediately.

Note: For this recipe I prefer the medium-grain golden bulghur to the coarse dark kind.

MIXED GRAINS BAKED WITH HERBS, VEGETABLES, AND CHEESE

Sometimes I crave grains, the heartier the better. This casserole offers four grains with varied textures and colors combined with herbs, vegetables, and cheese to make a savory, wholesome dish.

4 cups vegetable stock

½ cup barley

¼ cup wild rice

¼ cup brown rice

....

1 tablespoon olive oil

1 medium onion, diced

½ pound sliced mushrooms (3 cups)

1 cup finely chopped canned tomatoes, with their juice

Grated peel of 1 lemon (about 1 teaspoon)

½ cup sliced black olives (California-style)

½ cup chopped fresh parsley

2 teaspoons finely chopped fresh thyme, or ½ teaspoon dried

1 tablespoon finely chopped fresh basil, or ½ teaspoon dried

Generous seasoning of freshly ground pepper

1 Bring the vegetable stock to a boil in a medium-size saucepan. Add the barley and wild rice and simmer, covered, for 15 minutes. Stir in the brown rice and cook 10 more minutes. If you are going to cook the casserole immediately, pour the entire contents of the pot into a large, shallow 2½-quart baking dish, such as a 10 × 10-inch or 12 × 7 × 2-inch Pyrex dish. If you are not cooking right away, scoop out the grains with a slotted spoon and place them in the baking dish. Reserve the stock.

2 Preheat the oven to 350 degrees.

3 Heat the oil in a medium-size skillet. Add the onion and sauté 5 minutes. Stir in the mushrooms and cook until they begin to get brown and juicy, about 10 minutes. Scrape the mixture into the grains.

4 Stir in the tomatoes, lemon peel, olives, parsley, thyme, basil, and pepper. If you have separated the grains from the stock and you are now ready to bake the dish, bring the stock to a boil and pour into the casserole. Cover the dish and bake 30 minutes.

½ cup bulghur

1 cup frozen peas, thawed

1 cup (4 ounces) finely cubed Cheddar cheese

Serves 4 to 6

5 Remove the casserole from the oven and stir in the bulghur. Cover again and return to the oven. Cook 25 more minutes, or until all the liquid has been absorbed and the grains are tender.

6 Fluff the mixture with a fork; gently stir in the peas and cheese. Cover again and let sit outside the oven for 10 minutes before serving.

Quick

GARLICKY SWISS CHARD SAUTÉ ON BULGHUR

Garlic and hot peppers team with Swiss chard and pinto beans to make an extremely tasty and nutritious topping for bulghur. Try to get young Swiss chard with slender stalks so it will be extra tender.

2 cups vegetable stock

1 cup golden bulghur (see note, page 59)

....

2 tablespoons olive oil

4 garlic cloves, minced

¼ teaspoon crushed red pepper flakes

1¼ pounds Swiss chard (with 2-inch stems), washed and coarsely chopped (12 cups)

1 16-ounce can pinto beans, rinsed and well drained

Serves 4

1 Bring the vegetable stock to a boil in a medium-size saucepan. Add the bulghur and cover the pot. Reduce the heat to a simmer and cook until all the water is absorbed, about 20 minutes.

2 Meanwhile, heat the olive oil in a large skillet over medium-high heat. Add the garlic and pepper flakes and cook 1 minute, or until the garlic begins to turn golden but not at all brown. Drop in the Swiss chard with any water that clings to it, and with 2 large spoons, carefully toss it with the garlic mixture. Cover the pan and let the Swiss chard steam until it wilts, about 7 minutes. Toss again.

3 Stir in the pinto beans and cook 1 minute more, or until heated through. It's okay if a little liquid remains in the pan; this will serve as a sauce.

4 When the bulghur has absorbed all the stock, fluff it with a fork. Remove the pan from the heat and keep covered for 5 minutes. Serve some bulghur on each plate with a mound of the Swiss chard mixture in the center.

PASTA

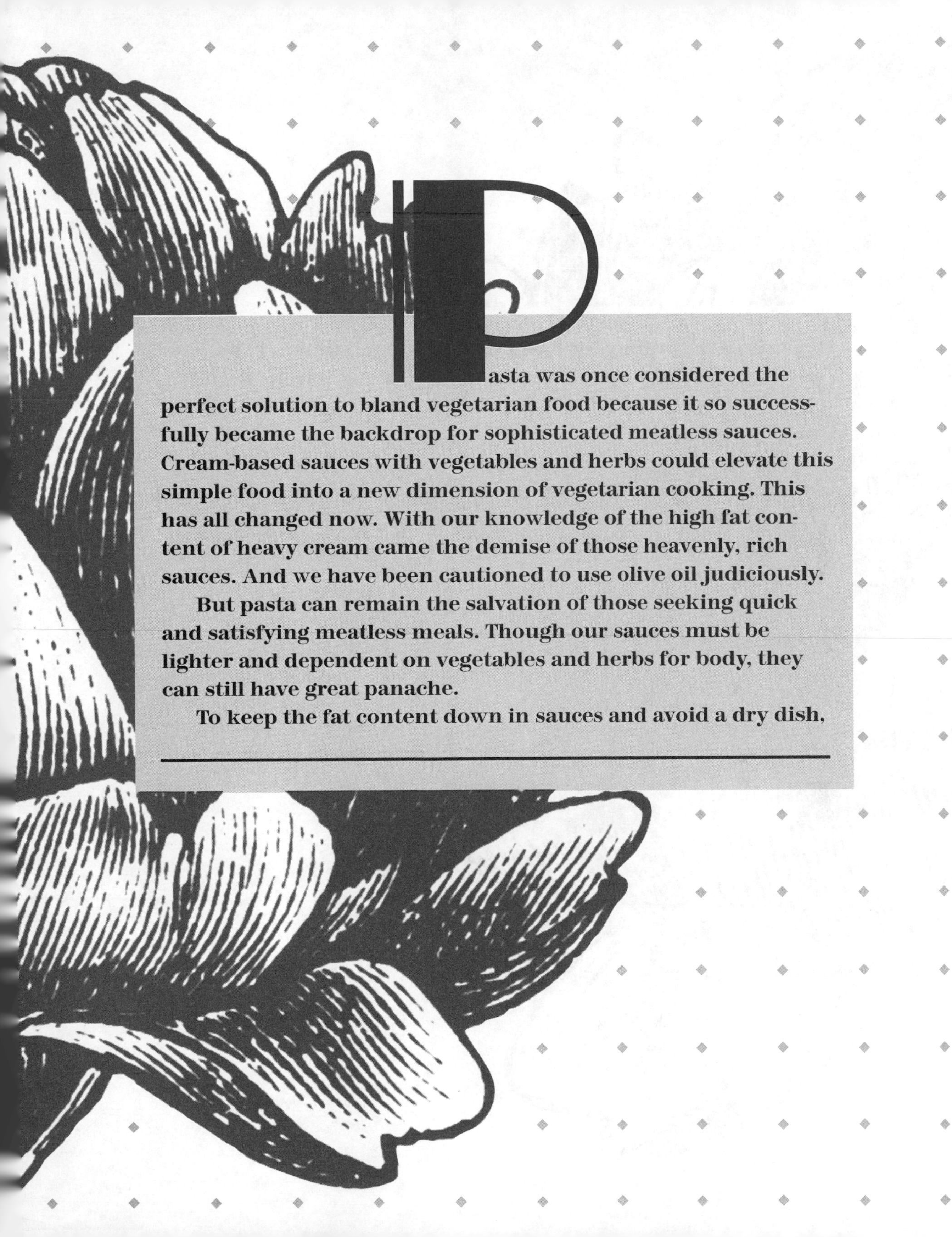

Pasta was once considered the perfect solution to bland vegetarian food because it so successfully became the backdrop for sophisticated meatless sauces. Cream-based sauces with vegetables and herbs could elevate this simple food into a new dimension of vegetarian cooking. This has all changed now. With our knowledge of the high fat content of heavy cream came the demise of those heavenly, rich sauces. And we have been cautioned to use olive oil judiciously.

But pasta can remain the salvation of those seeking quick and satisfying meatless meals. Though our sauces must be lighter and dependent on vegetables and herbs for body, they can still have great panache.

To keep the fat content down in sauces and avoid a dry dish,

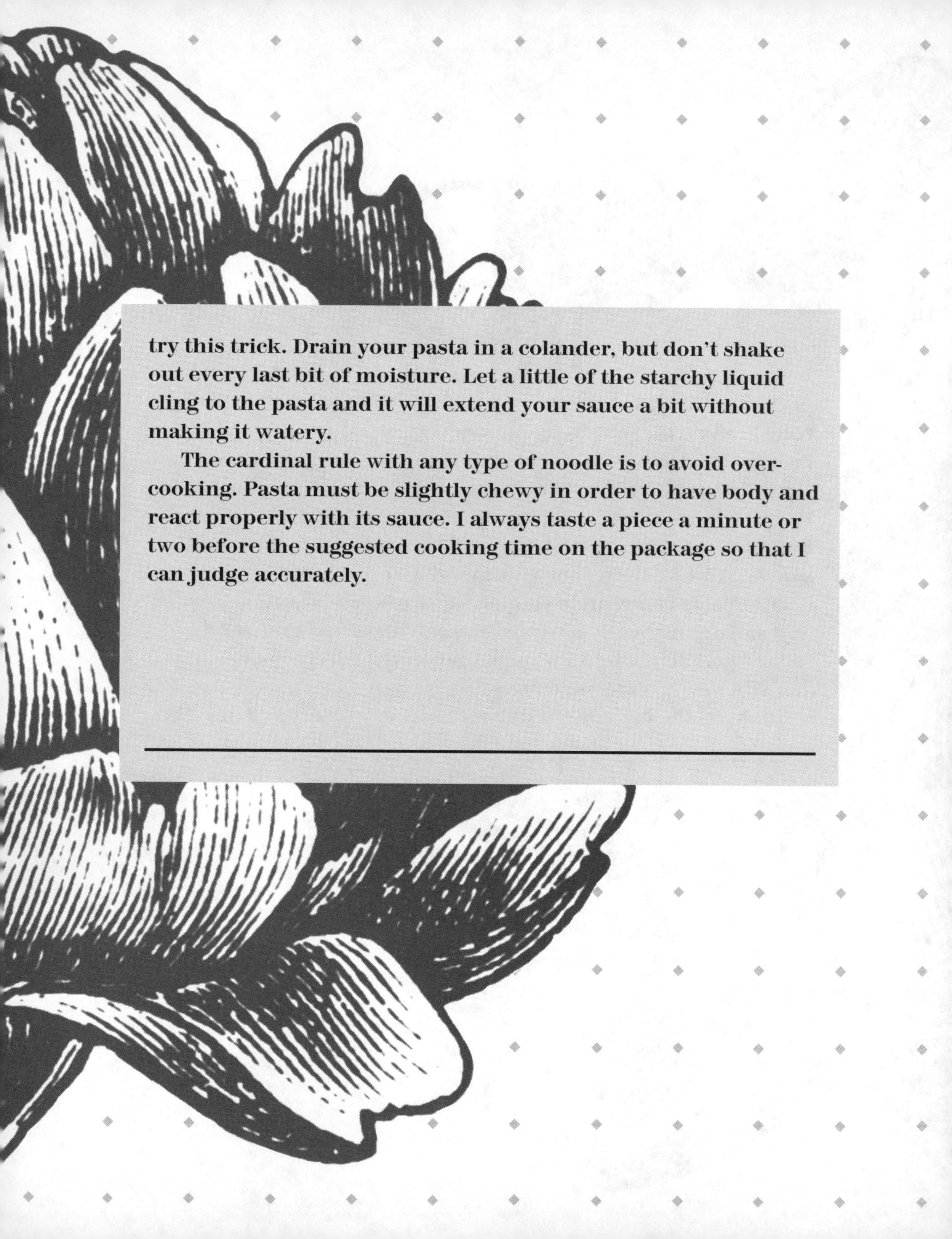

try this trick. Drain your pasta in a colander, but don't shake out every last bit of moisture. Let a little of the starchy liquid cling to the pasta and it will extend your sauce a bit without making it watery.

The cardinal rule with any type of noodle is to avoid over-cooking. Pasta must be slightly chewy in order to have body and react properly with its sauce. I always taste a piece a minute or two before the suggested cooking time on the package so that I can judge accurately.

Quick LINGUINE WITH PEPPERS AND GOAT CHEESE

This simple preparation with goat cheese as the basis of the sauce is especially elegant when paired with fresh pasta, although dried pasta is also delicious. The tang and creaminess of goat cheese in this sauce is unmatched.

2 tablespoons olive oil

2 garlic cloves, minced

1 red bell pepper, cored and cut into thin strips

1 green bell pepper, cored and cut into thin strips

2 scallions, thinly sliced

¼ cup minced fresh parsley

1 tablespoon minced fresh basil, or 1 teaspoon dried

¼ teaspoon dried oregano

....

16 ounces fresh linguine, or 12 ounces dried

4 ounces garlic and chive goat cheese or plain goat cheese, cut into small pieces

Serves 3

1. Bring a large pot of water to a boil.
2. Meanwhile, heat the olive oil in a large skillet over medium heat. Add the garlic and bell peppers and sauté 10 minutes, or until the peppers are tender.
3. Add the scallions, parsley, basil, and oregano and heat through. Keep warm while cooking the pasta.
4. Cook the pasta in boiling water until it is al dente. Taste a piece to avoid overcooking. Remove ½ cup of the pasta water and stir it into the pepper mixture. Drain the pasta in a colander. Place in a large bowl and toss with the sauce. Sprinkle on the goat cheese and toss again. Serve immediately.

Quick LINGUINE WITH SPICY ARTICHOKE SAUCE

Garlic, hot peppers, and the artichoke marinade bolster this spunky tomato sauce, making you want to brazenly lick your lips.

1 tablespoon olive oil

6 garlic cloves, minced

¼ teaspoon crushed red pepper flakes

1 28-ounce can plum tomatoes, finely chopped and well drained

½ teaspoon dried basil

½ teaspoon dried oregano

½ teaspoon salt

1 pound linguine

1 6-ounce jar marinated artichoke hearts

¼ cup minced fresh parsley

Grated Parmesan cheese

Serves 4

1. Heat the oil in a large skillet over medium heat. Add the garlic and pepper flakes and cook 2 minutes, tossing often. Stir in the tomatoes, basil, oregano, and salt and bring to a boil. Reduce to a simmer and cook, stirring often, for 15 minutes.
2. Meanwhile, bring a large stockpot of water to a boil. Drop in the linguine and cook until al dente. Taste a piece to avoid overcooking.
3. Add the artichokes and their marinade to the sauce. Stir in the parsley. Simmer about 5 minutes.
4. Drain the linguine and place it in a large bowl or return it to the pot. Toss with the sauce. Serve sprinkled with Parmesan cheese.

SMALL PASTA SHELLS WITH ROASTED VEGETABLES AND FETA CHEESE

This brightly colored pasta dish captures the glorious colors and seductive flavors of the Mediterranean. Garlic bread alongside adds the perfect touch.

1 small red bell pepper, cored and diced into 1-inch

1 small yellow bell pepper, cored and diced into 1-inch

1 small green bell pepper, cored and diced into 1-inch

2 tomatoes, cored, seeded, and cut into 1-inch dice

1 medium-large onion, cut into 1-inch dice, sections separated

2 celery ribs, thinly sliced on the diagonal

5 garlic cloves, coarsely chopped

1 teaspoon dried basil

1 teaspoon dried oregano

4 tablespoons olive oil

1 pound small pasta shells

1 cup (4½ ounces) finely diced feta cheese

20 black oil-cured olives, halved and pitted (see note, page 25)

Salt to taste

Generous seasoning of freshly ground pepper

Serves 4 to 6

1 Bring a large pot of water to a boil for the pasta. Preheat the oven to 425 degrees for the vegetables.

2 In a large bowl, combine the peppers, tomatoes, onion, celery, garlic, basil, oregano, and 2 tablespoons of the olive oil. Toss to coat the vegetables thoroughly with the oil. Spread the vegetables on a baking sheet so they rest in one layer. Bake for 20 minutes, or until the peppers are tender. Toss with a spatula once during baking.

3 Once the water starts boiling, drop the pasta in and cook until tender yet chewy, about 12 minutes. Drain thoroughly in a colander and either return to the pot or place it in a large bowl.

4 Spoon the vegetables onto the pasta along with the remaining 2 tablespoons of oil. Sprinkle on the feta cheese, olives, salt, and pepper (be very generous with the pepper) and toss. Serve hot or warm.

Quick RAVIOLI WITH TOMATO–BLUE CHEESE SAUCE

Uncooked sauces are a great time-saving method of dressing pasta with choice ingredients (see also Penne with Greek-Style Vegetable Marinade, page 25). This ravioli dish is best served warm, so there's no need to rush it to the table after it's been combined with the sauce.

¼ cup olive oil

1 medium-large tomato, cut into small dice

3 scallions, thinly sliced

3 tablespoons finely chopped walnuts

¼ cup finely chopped fresh parsley

Generous seasoning of freshly ground pepper

Salt to taste

1 pound frozen cheese ravioli

½ cup (2 ounces) crumbled blue cheese

Serves 4

1 In a large bowl, combine the oil, tomato, scallions, walnuts, parsley, pepper, and salt. Let sit for 30 minutes, or up to 4 hours. Cover and chill if longer than 1 hour, but bring to room temperature before the next step.

2 Bring a large pot of water to a boil. Drop in the ravioli and cook until tender yet still slightly firm, about 5 minutes. Drain thoroughly in a colander.

3 Toss the ravioli with the tomato mixture. Sprinkle on the blue cheese and gently toss again. Serve warm, not piping hot.

Quick

RAVIOLI WITH TOMATO CONCASSÉ

Roughly chopping tomatoes and sautéing them quickly with shallots or onions makes them delightfully sweet. They serve as a tantalizing base for this simple sauce.

2 tablespoons olive oil

4 shallots, finely diced

1 16-ounce can tomatoes, finely chopped and drained

1 tablespoon minced fresh basil, or ¾ teaspoon dried

¼ teaspoon salt

Freshly ground pepper

1 pound frozen cheese ravioli

1 tablespoon butter, cut into bits

Grated Parmesan cheese

Serves 3 to 4

1 Bring a large pot of water to a boil for the ravioli.

2 Meanwhile, make the sauce. In a large skillet, heat the olive oil over medium heat. Add the shallots and sauté for 5 minutes. Add the tomatoes, basil, salt, and pepper and cook, stirring frequently, for 10 minutes.

3 Drop the ravioli into the water and cook until al dente, about 5 minutes. Drain and then add to the sauce. Toss to coat thoroughly. Add the butter bits and toss again. Serve with Parmesan cheese sprinkled on top.

Quick

SPINACH FETTUCCINE WITH FRESH SPINACH AND GOAT CHEESE

The double impact of spinach pasta with fresh spinach is extremely flavorful as well as a great color combination.

1 pound loose fresh spinach, or 1 10-ounce package fresh spinach, stems discarded and leaves torn into small pieces (8 to 10 cups)

3 tablespoons olive oil

6 garlic cloves, minced

¼ teaspoon crushed red pepper flakes

1 pound spinach fettuccine

½ teaspoon salt

6 ounces goat cheese, crumbled

Serves 3 to 4

1. Bring a large pot of water to a boil for the pasta.
2. Wash the spinach in batches by dunking it in a large bowl of cold water. Remove and place in a colander.
3. Heat the oil in a large skillet over medium heat. Add the garlic and red pepper flakes and sauté 2 minutes, stirring frequently. Add the spinach with the water that clings to it and cover the pan. Cook for about 5 minutes, or until the spinach wilts.
4. Drop the fettuccine into the pot of rapidly boiling water. Cook until al dente, about 10 minutes. Remove ½ cup of the pasta water and pour it into the spinach mixture along with the salt; this will create a sauce.
5. Drain the fettuccine in a colander and return to the pot or place in a large bowl. Pour on the spinach and its liquid. Toss. Sprinkle on the goat cheese and toss again. Serve immediately.

Quick TORTELLINI WITH RED PEPPER SAUCE

Puréed red bell peppers make an extremely tasty sauce with a fiery color. For a beautiful color contrast and a nice balance of flavors, serve these tortellini with steamed, whole green beans.

THE SAUCE

1 tablespoon olive oil

1 medium onion, diced

2 garlic cloves, minced

1 large red bell pepper, cored and diced

2 fresh or canned plum tomatoes, seeded and diced

¼ cup dry red or white wine

¼ cup vegetable stock

A few dashes of cayenne

¼ teaspoon salt

1 tablespoon unsalted butter

....

1 pound frozen cheese tortellini

Grated Parmesan cheese

1 tablespoon minced fresh parsley

Serves 3

1 Bring a large pot of water to a boil for the tortellini.

2 To make the sauce, heat the oil in a medium-size skillet over medium heat. Add the onion and garlic and sauté for 5 minutes. Add the red pepper and tomatoes and cook 10 minutes more, or until the peppers are tender.

3 Pour in the wine and stock and cook at a lively simmer for 7 minutes. Purée in a blender or food processor, then return the sauce to the pan. (You should have about 1¼ cups sauce.) Stir in the cayenne, salt, and butter. Keep warm.

4 Drop the tortellini into the boiling water and cook until al dente, about 5 minutes. Drain thoroughly and return to the pot or place in a large bowl. Spoon on the sauce and toss to coat. Sprinkle on the Parmesan cheese, then top with the parsley. Serve immediately.

Quick

TORTELLINI WITH BROCCOLI, WALNUTS, AND OLIVES

This dish very nicely juxtaposes an array of flavors with the spiciness of garlic and hot peppers, the deep flavor of toasted walnuts, and the saltiness of olives. A nice choice for entertaining on a moment's notice.

¼ cup olive oil

6 garlic cloves, minced

¼ teaspoon crushed red pepper flakes

½ cup chopped walnuts

1 large bunch broccoli, cut into small florets, stalks peeled and diced (about 6 cups)

1 pound frozen cheese tortellini

12 kalamata or other brine-cured olives, pitted and quartered (see note, page 25)

¼ teaspoon salt

¼ cup grated Parmesan cheese

Serves 4

1 Bring a large pot of water to a boil.

2 To make the sauce, heat the oil in a large skillet over medium heat. Add the garlic, red pepper flakes, and walnuts. Sauté, tossing often, for 5 minutes.

3 Stir in the broccoli with ½ cup of water. Cover the pan and cook until tender yet still bright green, about 5 minutes.

4 Drop the tortellini into the boiling water and cook until tender yet firm, about 5 minutes. Drain thoroughly in a colander.

5 Mix the tortellini into the broccoli sauce along with the olives, salt, and Parmesan cheese. Serve immediately.

Quick CAVATELLI PUTTANESCA

Spicy and bold, this sauce is worthy of its name—puttanesca means "whore-style." Try it also with cheese ravioli for a nice match.

2 tablespoons olive oil

6 garlic cloves, minced

¼ teaspoon crushed red pepper flakes

1 green pepper, finely diced

1 28-ounce can whole tomatoes, drained and finely chopped with their own juice

8 black olives (preferably kalamata), pitted and quartered (see note, page 25)

2 teaspoons capers

Freshly ground pepper

1 pound frozen cavatelli

Grated Parmesan cheese (optional)

Serves 3 to 4

1 Bring a large pot of water to a boil.

2 Heat the olive oil in a large skillet over medium heat. Add the garlic and red pepper flakes and cook 2 minutes, stirring often. Add the green pepper and cook 5 minutes.

3 Stir in the tomatoes, olives, capers, and ground pepper and cook 15 to 20 minutes, or until the sauce has thickened and the green pepper is very tender.

4 Cook the cavatelli according to the package directions. Drain thoroughly in a colander, then return it to the pot or place in a large bowl. Stir in the sauce. Serve with a little Parmesan cheese, if desired; it won't need much.

Quick PENNE WITH KALE AND WHITE BEANS

The kale and white beans dominate this garlicky dish in which pasta plays only a supportive role. If you are not acquainted with kale, here's a great opportunity to discover this wonderful vegetable. It's packed with vitamin A, has a delicious flavor, and is a breeze to prepare.

1½ pounds kale

3 tablespoons olive oil

6 garlic cloves, minced

¼ teaspoon crushed red pepper flakes

⅓ cup vegetable stock

1 16-ounce can cannellini beans, rinsed and drained

½ teaspoon salt

½ pound penne (quill-shaped pasta)

¼ cup grated Parmesan cheese

Serves 3 to 4

1 Bring 3 quarts of water to a boil in a saucepan.

2 Prepare the kale by ripping it off its stems. Tear the leaves into bite-size pieces. You should have about 12 cups. Rinse by immersing in a large bowl of cold water. Remove and drain in a colander.

3 Heat the oil in a large skillet over medium-high heat. Add the garlic and red pepper flakes and sauté for 2 minutes. Stir in the kale and vegetable stock and cover the pan. Cook until wilted and tender yet still bright green, about 7 minutes. Gently stir in the beans and salt and keep warm over low heat.

4 Drop the penne into the boiling water and cook until tender yet chewy, about 10 minutes. Drain thoroughly, then carefully stir it into the kale mixture along with the Parmesan cheese. Serve immediately.

Quick SPINACH TAGLIATELLE WITH CORN, RED PEPPERS, AND HERBS

The natural sweetness of corn pairs wonderfully with the red peppers and spicy herb blend, giving this dish a charming Southwestern touch and a great splash of color.

¼ cup olive oil

1 red bell pepper, cored and cut into thin strips

¼ teaspoon crushed red pepper flakes

4 scallions, thinly sliced

2 cups frozen corn kernels, thawed

1 teaspoon dried oregano

1 tablespoon minced fresh basil, or ½ teaspoon dried

2 tablespoons minced fresh parsley

½ teaspoon salt

....

1 pound spinach tagliatelle (or spinach fettuccine)

¼ cup grated Parmesan cheese

Serves 4

1. Bring a large pot of water to a boil.
2. Heat the oil in a large skillet over medium heat. Add the red pepper and crushed pepper flakes and sauté for 5 minutes, or until just about tender. Add the scallions and cook 2 minutes, stirring occasionally. Mix in the corn, herbs, and salt. Keep warm over low heat.
3. Drop the tagliatelle into boiling water. Cook until tender yet chewy, about 7 minutes. Remove ½ cup of the pasta water and stir it into the vegetable mixture.
4. Drain the pasta. Return it to the pot or place in a large bowl. Spoon on the sauce and sprinkle on the cheese. Toss and serve immediately.

SPAGHETTINI WITH ZUCCHINI AND ROSEMARY

Rosemary gives this savory pasta sauce a distinct, yet not overpowering, flavor. Garlic bread is the perfect accompaniment.

2 tablespoons olive oil

2 medium onions, diced

4 medium zucchini, halved lengthwise and thinly sliced

1 teaspoon chopped fresh rosemary, or ¼ teaspoon dried, crumbled

½ teaspoon salt

Very generous seasoning of freshly ground pepper (about 20 turns of the peppermill)

1 pound spaghettini

½ cup grated Parmesan cheese

Serves 4

1. Bring a large pot of water to a boil.
2. To make the sauce, heat the olive oil in a large skillet over medium-high heat. Add the onions and sauté for 10 minutes, or until tender.
3. Mix in the zucchini, rosemary, salt, and pepper. Sauté, tossing often, until the zucchini is tender but not mushy, about 10 minutes. Keep warm over low heat.
4. Drop the pasta into the boiling water and cook until al dente. Remove ½ cup of the boiling pasta water and stir it into the zucchini mixture. Drain the spaghettini very well in a colander.
5. Place the spaghettini in a large bowl or return it to the pot. Spoon on the zucchini sauce and sprinkle on the Parmesan cheese. Toss to coat. Serve immediately.

Quick BAKED ZITI

Here's a quick and hearty dish that I love to assemble on a moment's notice because I always seem to have these ingredients on hand. This is my idea of comfort food.

1 pound ziti or penne

2 tablespoons olive oil

1½ cups tomato sauce (homemade or store-bought)

½ teaspoon dried basil

½ teaspoon oregano

2 tablespoons dry red wine

Freshly ground pepper to taste

2 cups (6 ounces) grated Muenster cheese

¼ cup grated Parmesan cheese

Serves 6

1 Cook the ziti in a large pot of boiling water until al dente, 12 to 15 minutes. Drain thoroughly in a colander and place in a large bowl. Pour on the olive oil and toss to coat well. Let cool.

2 Combine the tomato sauce, basil, oregano, red wine, and pepper. Pour onto the pasta and mix well.

3 Preheat the oven to 350 degrees.

4 Spread half the pasta in a large, shallow baking dish, such as a 9 × 13-inch (3-quart) Pyrex. Sprinkle on half the Muenster cheese. Spread on the remaining pasta, then top with the remaining Muenster cheese and finally the Parmesan cheese. Cover the dish with foil.

5 Bake for 30 to 40 minutes, or until hot and bubbly. Remove foil and bake 5 additional minutes.

Note: The dish may be prepared in advance through step 4 and refrigerated for up to 8 hours. Bring to room temperature before baking.

Quick BAKED ZITI WITH RICOTTA

This stick-to-your-ribs version of baked ziti is reminiscent of lasagne. A good choice to serve a crowd.

1 pound ziti or penne

1½ cups tomato sauce (homemade or store-bought)

1 egg

1 15-ounce container part-skim ricotta cheese

2½ cups (8 ounces) grated part-skim mozzarella cheese

¼ cup grated Parmesan cheese

Serves 6

1. Bring a large pot of water to a boil. Cook the ziti until al dente, 12 to 15 minutes. Drain thoroughly in a colander, then place in a large bowl. Pour on the tomato sauce to coat well. Let cool.
2. Beat the egg in a medium-size bowl. Beat in the ricotta cheese and 2¼ cups of the mozzarella.
3. Preheat the oven to 400 degrees.
4. Spread half the ziti in a 9 × 13-inch (3-quart) baking dish. Spread the ricotta mixture evenly on top. Spoon on the remaining ziti, sprinkle on the reserved ¼ cup of mozzarella, then finish with the Parmesan cheese. Cover the dish with foil.
5. Bake 40 to 45 minutes, or until hot and bubbly. Remove the foil and bake 5 additional minutes.

Note: The dish may be prepared in advance through step 4 and refrigerated for up to 8 hours. Bring to room temperature before baking.

Quick SESAME ASPARAGUS AND NOODLES

Assemble all the ingredients for this tasty dish before you begin cooking and it will be a breeze to prepare.

2 tablespoons sesame seeds

2 tablespoons Oriental sesame oil

¼ cup tamari soy sauce

2 tablespoons vegetable stock

2 tablespoons Chinese rice wine or dry sherry

½ teaspoon chili oil

1 pound linguine or vermicelli

1 tablespoon vegetable oil

2 garlic cloves, minced

1 teaspoon minced fresh ginger

1 pound asparagus, cut diagonally into 2-inch lengths

¼ cup water

1 teaspoon tamari soy sauce

4 scallions, thinly sliced

Serves 3 to 4

1. Bring a large pot of water to a boil for the noodles.
2. Toast the sesame seeds by placing them in a small skillet over medium heat. Swirl the pan occasionally until the seeds begin to smoke and become fragrant. Immediately pour them into a small bowl to cool.
3. Combine the sesame oil, tamari, vegetable stock, wine, and chili oil in a measuring cup and set aside. This will be the sauce for the noodles.
4. When the water is at a rolling boil, cook the noodles until tender yet chewy.
5. Heat the vegetable oil in a large skillet or wok over medium-high heat. Add the garlic and ginger and cook 1 minute. Add the asparagus and stir-fry 1 minute. Pour in the water and cover the pan. Cook until the asparagus pieces are tender, about 5 minutes.
6. Drain the noodles and return them to the pot. Pour on the prepared sauce and toss with tongs to coat.
7. Remove the cover from the asparagus. Pour on the teaspoon of tamari and the scallions and toss for 1 minute. Serve on the noodles. Garnish with the sesame seeds.

SOBA WITH ROASTED VEGETABLES

Roasted root vegetables caramelize and develop a marvelous taste as well as texture. When paired with soba, a full-flavored dish is created that also maintains the characteristic lightness of Japanese cooking. Hauntingly good.

2 tablespoons vegetable oil

1 tablespoon tamari soy sauce

2 purple-top turnips (about ¼ pound each), peeled, halved, and cut into ¾-inch slices

1 large (¾ pound) sweet potato, peeled, halved lengthwise, and cut into ½-inch slices

2 carrots, peeled, cut in half crosswise, thick top part cut in half lengthwise

2 medium onions, peeled and quartered lengthwise with root intact

....

8 ounces soba (buckwheat noodles)

½ cup vegetable stock

1 tablespoon tamari soy sauce

1 tablespoon Oriental sesame oil

Sesame seeds (optional garnish)

Serves 2

1. Combine the oil and tamari in a large bowl. Mix in the vegetables and toss to coat them thoroughly. Marinate for at least 30 minutes, or up to 2 hours.
2. Preheat the oven to 400 degrees.
3. Spread the vegetables on a baking sheet so they rest in one layer. Bake, tossing twice, for 25 to 30 minutes, or until the vegetables are tender.
4. Meanwhile, bring water to a boil in a 3-quart pot. Cook the soba until tender yet chewy, about 5 minutes.
5. While the soba is cooking, combine the vegetable stock, tamari, and sesame oil. Drain the soba and return to the pot. Pour on the liquid and toss gently. Serve the soba immediately in large bowls with the vegetables on top. If desired, garnish with a few sesame seeds.

BEANS

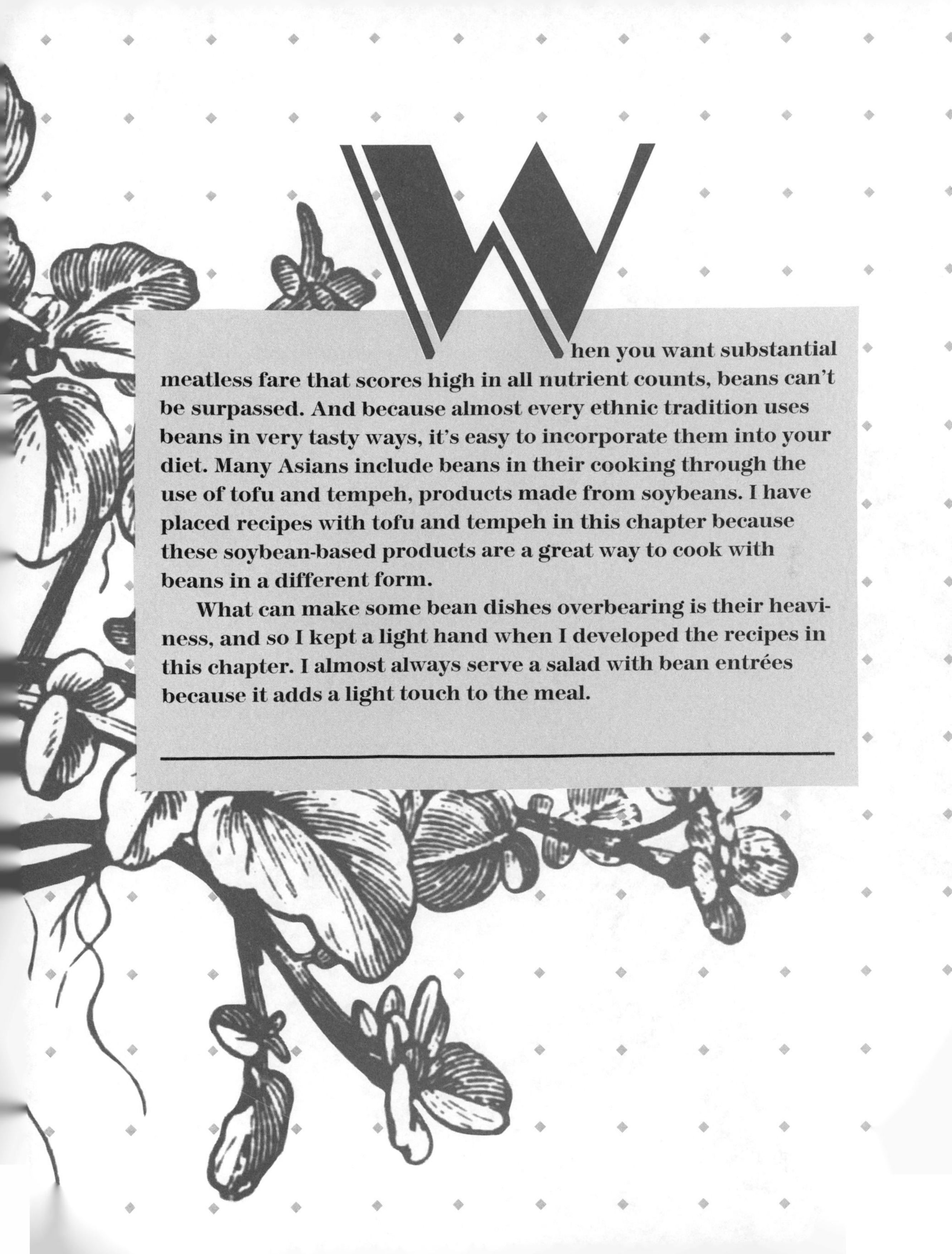

When you want substantial meatless fare that scores high in all nutrient counts, beans can't be surpassed. And because almost every ethnic tradition uses beans in very tasty ways, it's easy to incorporate them into your diet. Many Asians include beans in their cooking through the use of tofu and tempeh, products made from soybeans. I have placed recipes with tofu and tempeh in this chapter because these soybean-based products are a great way to cook with beans in a different form.

What can make some bean dishes overbearing is their heaviness, and so I kept a light hand when I developed the recipes in this chapter. I almost always serve a salad with bean entrées because it adds a light touch to the meal.

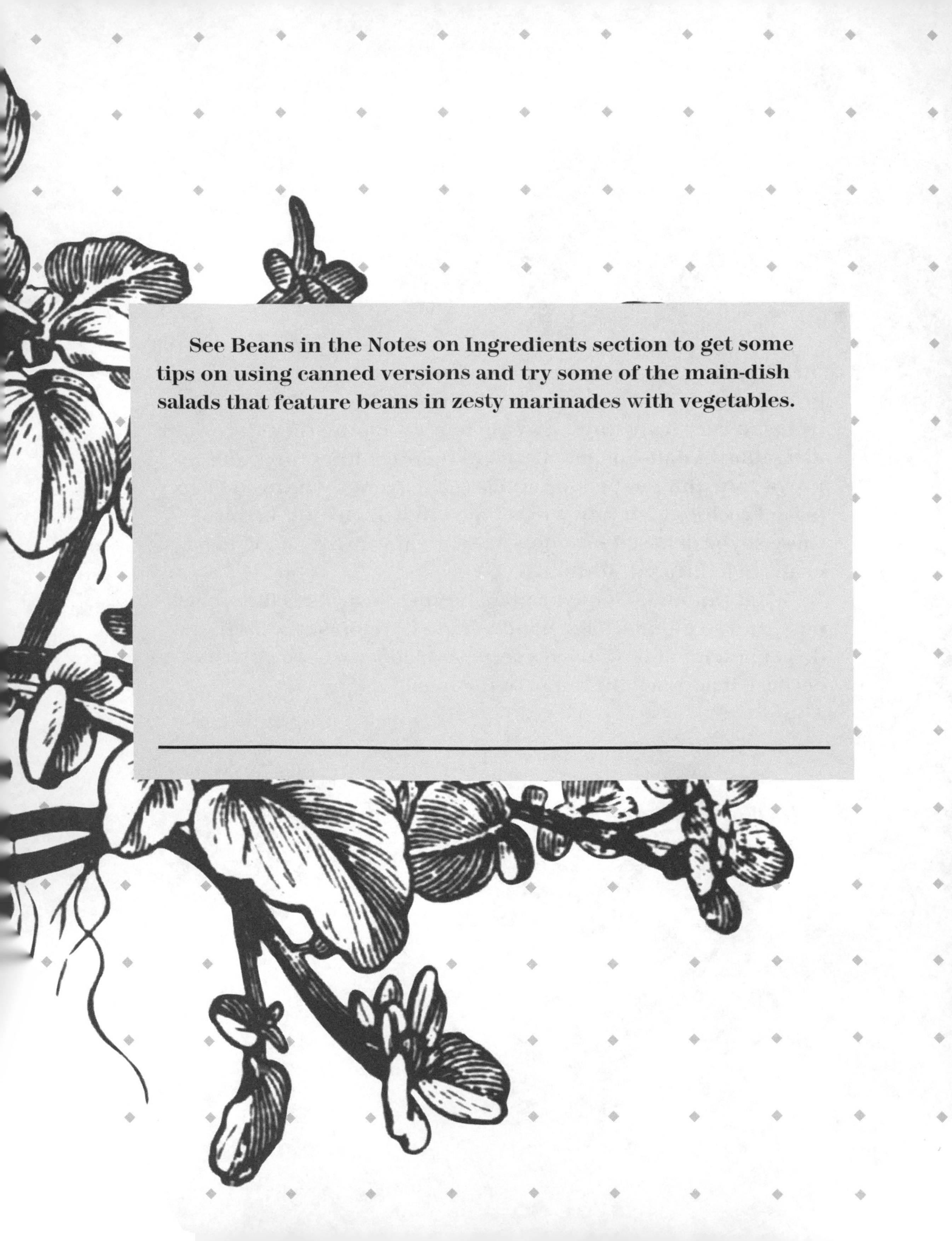

See Beans in the Notes on Ingredients section to get some tips on using canned versions and try some of the main-dish salads that feature beans in zesty marinades with vegetables.

Quick CHEESE AND BEAN QUESADILLAS

When quesadillas are filled only with cheese, they are too rich for me. Adding beans, olives, and scallions improves the texture and flavor of the filling. The recipe can be easily multiplied (make sure you have 2 baking sheets) and makes wonderful informal party food.

2 cups grated Monterey Jack cheese with jalapeño peppers

1 cup cooked kidney beans, rinsed and drained if canned

1 scallion, very thinly sliced

10 pitted black olives (California-style), thinly sliced

1 tablespoon finely chopped cilantro

4 8-inch flour (wheat) tortillas

Serves 2

1 Preheat the oven to 375 degrees.

2 In a large bowl, combine the cheese, beans, scallion, olives, and cilantro.

3 Place 2 tortillas side by side on a baking sheet. Divide the mixture and spread onto each tortilla, leaving a 1-inch border. Press the filling down with your fingers. Cover with the remaining 2 tortillas and press down again.

4 Bake 10 minutes, or until the cheese is thoroughly melted. Cut each quesadilla into 4 wedges before serving.

Quick

VEGETABLE AND BLACK BEAN BURRITOS

Mixing vegetables with beans makes these delectable burritos significantly lighter than traditional bean burritos, while the inclusion of orange in this spicy filling adds a dazzling touch. I have come to enjoy making burritos a lot more since some friends showed me this clever method of steaming wheat tortillas. It's easy and quick, and it makes the tortillas very tender. Lay out the fillings for the burritos and let each person make his or her own, steaming the tortillas as needed.

1 tablespoon vegetable oil

1 medium onion, finely diced

1 large red or green bell pepper, cored and finely diced

1 16-ounce can black beans, rinsed and drained

1¼ cups frozen corn kernels, thawed

5 orange sections, each cut into ½-inch dice

1¼ cups salsa, medium or hot

....

8 wheat (flour) tortillas (about 8 inches in diameter)

1½ cups grated sharp Cheddar cheese

Sour cream

Serves 4 (8 burritos)

1 Heat the oil in a large skillet over medium heat. Add the onion and pepper and sauté until very tender, about 10 minutes.

2 Add the black beans, corn, and oranges and cook 2 minutes, or until heated through. Stir in the salsa, then remove the pan from the heat.

3 Fill a pot that is at least 8 inches in diameter with about 2 inches of water. Cover the pot with a piece of foil, making it tight and secure. With a knife tip, poke holes all over the top of the foil. Bring the water to a boil, then place a tortilla on the foil. Steam it for about 1 minute, flip it over, and steam it on the other side for about 30 seconds, or just until hot. Repeat with the remaining tortillas as needed.

4 To serve, place a tortilla on a large plate. Spoon an eighth of the bean mixture along the center of the tortilla, then top with some cheese and a bit of sour cream. Roll, eat, and enjoy.

See Beans in the Notes on Ingredients section to get some tips on using canned versions and try some of the main-dish salads that feature beans in zesty marinades with vegetables.

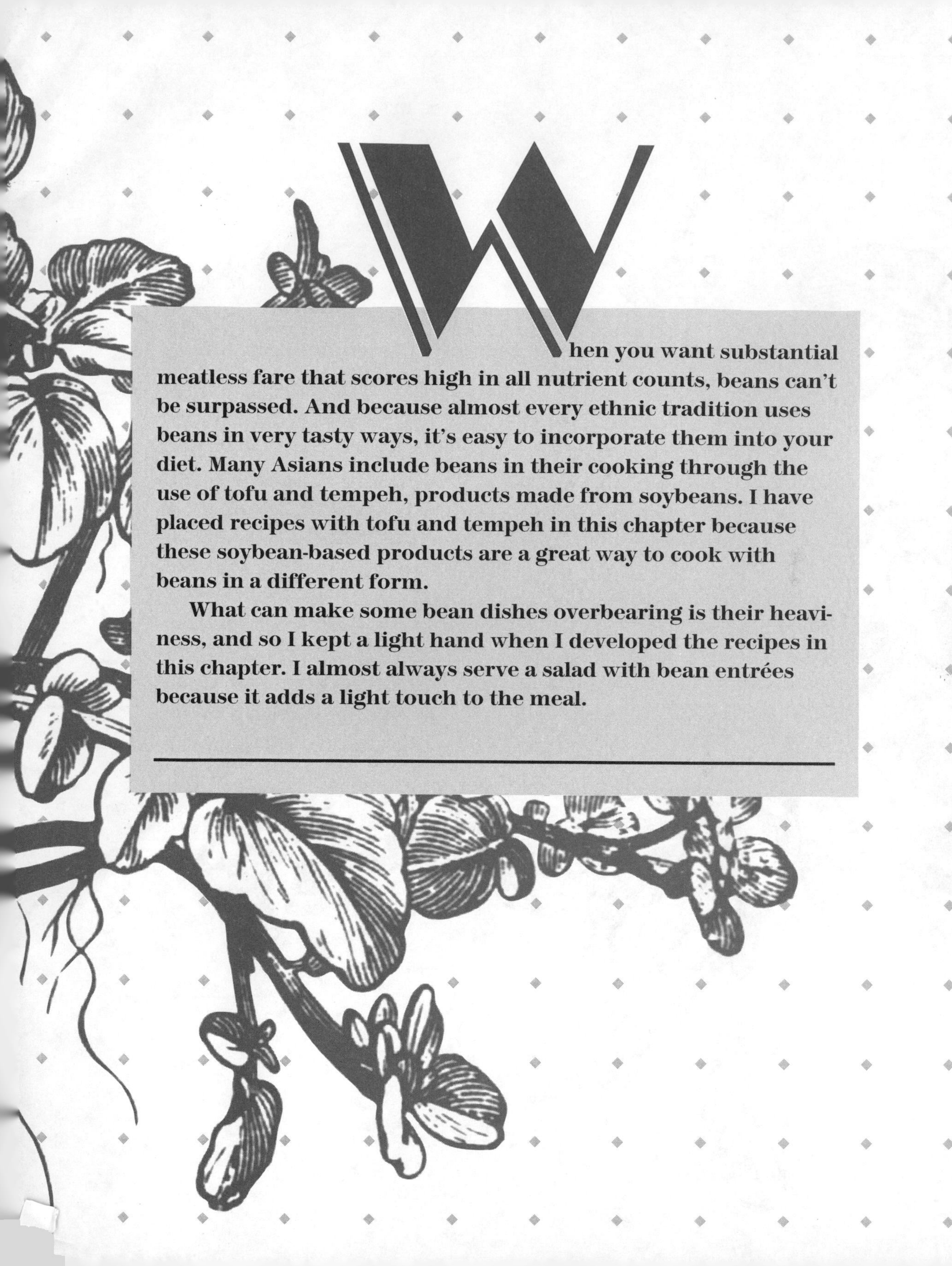

When you want substantial meatless fare that scores high in all nutrient counts, beans can't be surpassed. And because almost every ethnic tradition uses beans in very tasty ways, it's easy to incorporate them into your diet. Many Asians include beans in their cooking through the use of tofu and tempeh, products made from soybeans. I have placed recipes with tofu and tempeh in this chapter because these soybean-based products are a great way to cook with beans in a different form.

What can make some bean dishes overbearing is their heaviness, and so I kept a light hand when I developed the recipes in this chapter. I almost always serve a salad with bean entrées because it adds a light touch to the meal.

Quick

BAKED VEGETABLES WITH GARLIC, WHITE BEANS, AND OLIVES

This Mediterranean-style casserole, layered with cheese, needs only some crusty bread to accompany it and to sop up any garlicky juices left on your plate.

1 large bunch broccoli, cut into small florets

3 medium-large boiling potatoes, peeled and cut into 1-inch chunks

1 28-ounce can tomatoes, finely chopped and well drained

1 15-ounce can cannellini (white beans), rinsed and drained

½ cup pitted black olives, halved (any style; see note, page xx)

2½ tablespoons olive oil

4 garlic cloves, minced

¼ teaspoon crushed red pepper flakes

Salt

1¼ cups (4 ounces) grated Muenster cheese

Serves 3 to 4

1 Bring a 3-quart saucepan of water to a boil. Blanch the broccoli for 2 minutes, or until tender yet still crunchy. Remove with a slotted spoon, then plunge into a bowl of cold water to stop the cooking. Drain well and pat dry. Place in a large bowl.

2 Drop the potatoes into the boiling water and cook until tender, about 7 minutes. Drain well and add to the broccoli.

3 Stir in the tomatoes, cannellini, and olives. Combine the olive oil, garlic, and red pepper flakes. Pour over the vegetables and toss gently to coat. Season with salt to taste.

4 Preheat the oven to 400 degrees.

5 Spread half the vegetable mixture in a shallow casserole, such as a 12 × 7 × 2-inch Pyrex dish. Sprinkle on half the Muenster cheese. Spoon on the remaining vegetables, then top with the remaining cheese. Cover the dish with foil.

6 Bake 30 minutes, or until hot and bubbly. Remove the foil and bake 5 additional minutes for a golden crust.

CORN PANCAKES TOPPED WITH BLACK BEANS

Ruth Bronz, chef at the Bronze Dog Cafe in Great Barrington, Massachusetts, serves a fabulous combination of buttery corn pancakes topped with a mound of creamy black beans. After indulging in that great dish, I rushed home and created this version.

THE BLACK BEANS

1 tablespoon olive oil

1 garlic clove, pressed or minced

½ teaspoon ground cumin

2 16-ounce cans black beans, rinsed and drained

A few dashes of Tabasco sauce, or to taste

¾ cup water

CORN PANCAKES

1½ cups unbleached flour

2 tablespoons sugar

2 teaspoons baking powder

1 teaspoon salt

3 eggs

1¼ cups low-fat milk

2 tablespoons butter, melted

2 cups frozen corn kernels, thawed

Oil for greasing

Sour cream

Serves 4 (12 4-inch pancakes)

1 Heat the oil in a medium-size saucepan over medium heat. Add the garlic and cumin and sauté 1 minute. Stir in the black beans, Tabasco, and water and bring to a boil. Reduce the heat to a lively simmer and cook the mixture 5 minutes. Remove from the heat and let cool slightly.

2 Pour the contents of the pot into a food processor or blender and process until the beans are creamy yet still chunky. Scrape the mixture back into the saucepan and keep warm over low heat.

3 To make the pancakes, combine the flour, sugar, baking powder, and salt in a large bowl and mix well.

4 In a blender or food processor, thoroughly blend the eggs, milk, and melted butter. Add the corn and process a few seconds until almost puréed. You want to retain some chunks. Pour this mixture into the flour and stir just until blended. Do not overmix.

5 Lightly coat a griddle or large skillet with some oil and heat over medium heat until a drop of water dances when flicked on the pan.

6 Drop tablespoons of batter onto the griddle to make 4-inch pancakes. Cook until golden brown on each side; to make sure they are cooked through, make a slit in the center and peek at them. The batter should yield about 12 pancakes.
7 Meanwhile, check the consistency of the black beans; they should be like very soft mashed potatoes. If they are too thick, stir in a little water; if they are too soupy, cook them a little more.
8 On each plate, arrange 3 pancakes slightly overlapping in the center. Spoon some of the black beans onto the center and garnish with a small spoonful of sour cream.
Note: If you have leftover batter, cover and refrigerate; it will keep for 48 hours.

Quick

BAKED TOFU SZECHUAN STYLE

I came across this idea of baking marinated tofu at a health food supermarket. It is so easy and so flavorful that it has now become my favorite way to prepare tofu. Serve it with a grain dish such as couscous, rice, or bulghur pilaf.

THE MARINADE

2 tablespoons tamari soy sauce

1 tablespoon Oriental sesame oil

1 tablespoon vegetable oil

½ teaspoon minced fresh ginger

1 pound extra-firm tofu, cut into ¾-inch cubes and patted very dry

THE SAUCE

½ to 1 teaspoon chili paste with garlic

1 tablespoon tahini or natural-style peanut butter

2 tablespoons dry sherry, rice wine, or vermouth

Serves 3

1. In a medium-size bowl, combine the marinade ingredients. Gently stir in the tofu and coat well. Let marinate for 30 minutes, or up to 8 hours. Cover and chill if longer than 30 minutes.
2. Preheat the oven to 450 degrees.
3. Pour the tofu and its marinade into a shallow baking dish in one layer. Bake for 15 minutes, tossing once with a spatula.
4. Combine the sauce ingredients and pour over the tofu. Toss to coat evenly. Return to the oven and bake 10 more minutes, or until golden brown. Let sit 10 minutes before serving; it should be served warm, not piping hot.

Quick STIR-FRIED BROCCOLI AND TOFU IN PEANUT SAUCE

This spicy peanut sauce laced with ginger and garlic is the perfect foil for mild tofu. Cook 1 cup of rice before you begin stir-frying and keep it warm on the back burner.

THE SAUCE

¼ cup natural-style peanut butter

3 tablespoons tamari soy sauce

3 tablespoons Chinese rice wine or sherry

2 tablespoons water

1 tablespoon Oriental sesame oil

....

2 tablespoons vegetable oil

1 pound extra-firm tofu, cut into ½-inch cubes and patted very dry

3 garlic cloves, minced

1 teaspoon minced fresh ginger

¼ teaspoon crushed red pepper flakes

1 bunch broccoli, stalks peeled and cut into small pieces (about 5 cups)

¼ cup water

Hot cooked rice

Serves 4

1 Combine the peanut butter, tamari, and rice wine or sherry in a small bowl or large measuring cup and beat with a fork until smooth. Stir in the water and sesame oil, then set aside.

2 Heat 1 tablespoon of the vegetable oil in a large skillet or wok over medium-high heat until it is very hot but not smoking. Make sure the tofu is very dry, then drop it in the pan. Stir-fry until golden all over, about 10 minutes. Remove to a platter.

3 Add the remaining tablespoon of oil to the pan. Stir in the garlic, ginger, and crushed pepper flakes. Cook 2 minutes, stirring constantly. Do not let the garlic brown.

4 Add the broccoli, toss, then pour in the ¼ cup water. Cover the pan and cook the broccoli about 5 minutes, or until bright green and slightly crunchy. Remove the cover occasionally to toss the broccoli.

5 Return the tofu to the pan and toss. Pour on the peanut sauce and stir-fry 1 minute. Serve on rice.

Quick BARBECUED TOFU WITH PEPPERS AND ONIONS

The surprise ingredient in this barbecue sauce is a small amount of peanut butter, which helps the sauce adhere to the tofu and make it crispy. This treatment also works well on the grill. Cook the tofu and vegetables on skewers, rotating occasionally until evenly browned.

1 pound extra-firm tofu, cut into ¾-inch cubes and patted very dry

1 green pepper, cored and cut into 1-inch squares

2 small onions, quartered vertically, sections separated into halves

2 tablespoons tamari soy sauce

1 tablespoon vegetable oil

THE SAUCE

1 tablespoon natural-style peanut butter

1 teaspoon vegetable oil

2½ tablespoons ketchup

1 teaspoon mustard

2 teaspoons apple cider vinegar

2 garlic cloves, pressed

2 teaspoons chili powder

1 teaspoon molasses

A few dashes of Tabasco sauce

Generous seasoning of freshly ground pepper

Serves 3

1 Place the tofu in a large bowl with the pepper and onions.

2 Combine the tamari and oil and pour over the vegetables. With a rubber spatula, toss gently to coat. Let marinate for at least 30 minutes, or up to 4 hours.

3 Mix together all the ingredients for the sauce. Let sit at least 30 minutes to allow the flavors to meld.

4 Preheat the oven to 450 degrees.

5 Scrape the tofu and vegetables into a 9 × 13-inch baking dish, or similar large, shallow baking dish, ample enough for everything to rest in one layer. Bake for 15 minutes, tossing once with a spatula.

6 Remove the baking dish from the oven. Spoon on the sauce and gently toss to coat evenly. Return to the oven and bake 15 more minutes, or until lightly browned. Let sit 10 minutes so it can be served warm, not hot.

Quick TOFU HOISIN WITH BROCCOLI, RED PEPPER, AND WALNUTS

The garlic and hot pepper flakes are a nice foil for the sweetness of the hoisin sauce. To organize yourself, cook 1½ cups rice before you begin stir-frying and keep it warm on the back burner; the stir-frying will take only a few minutes.

THE SAUCE

⅓ cup hoisin sauce

2 tablespoons Chinese rice wine or dry sherry

1 tablespoon Oriental sesame oil

1 tablespoon tamari soy sauce

....

2 tablespoons vegetable oil

1 pound extra-firm tofu, sliced, patted very dry, then cut into 2 × ½-inch logs

6 garlic cloves, minced

⅛ teaspoon crushed red pepper flakes

1 red bell pepper, cut into 3 × ½-inch strips

1 bunch broccoli, cut into small florets, stalks peeled and sliced (about 5 cups)

½ cup walnut halves

⅓ cup water

Serves 3 to 4

1 Combine all the sauce ingredients in a small bowl and set aside.

2 Heat the oil in a wok or large skillet over high heat until it is hot but not smoking. Make sure the tofu is patted very dry to prevent sticking. Add the tofu and stir-fry until lightly golden all over. Remove to a platter and reduce the heat to medium-high.

3 If there is no oil left in the pan, add a teaspoon or so. Add the garlic and crushed pepper flakes and cook 1 minute. Stir in the red bell pepper, broccoli, and walnuts and toss to coat with the garlic. Pour in the water, toss, then cover the pan. Cook 5 minutes, or until the vegetables are tender yet still crunchy.

4 Stir in the tofu, then pour on the sauce mixture. Stir-fry 1 minute, or until the sauce coats everything and is thickened. Serve on rice.

Quick TEMPEH FAJITAS WITH CUCUMBER SALSA

Marinated tempeh and peppers are "roasted" to fill these fajitas, making them a very nutritious choice for either lunch or supper.

THE MARINADE

3 tablespoons tamari soy sauce

Juice of ½ lime

1 teaspoon brown sugar

2 tablespoons vegetable oil

3 garlic cloves, minced

¼ teaspoon crushed red pepper flakes

THE FILLING

8 ounces tempeh, cut into 3 × ½-inch strips

1 yellow bell pepper, cut into ½-inch strips

1 red bell pepper, cut into ½-inch strips

1 green bell pepper, cut into ½-inch strips

1 medium red onion, halved vertically and thinly sliced

CUCUMBER SALSA

⅔ cup low-fat yogurt

½ small cucumber, peeled, seeded, and finely diced (about ⅓ cup)

1 Combine the marinade ingredients in a large bowl. Stir in the tempeh, bell peppers, and onion. Marinate for at least 30 minutes, or up to 2 hours.

2 In a small bowl, combine the salsa ingredients. Cover and chill until ready to use.

3 Preheat the oven to 450 degrees.

4 Sprinkle a little water on each tortilla and rub it around the tortilla with your fingers. Stack the tortillas, then wrap the bundle in foil. Set aside.

5 Spread the marinated tempeh and vegetables on a baking sheet in one layer. Bake 15 minutes, or until the vegetables are tender and the tempeh begins to brown. Do not toss while cooking.

6 Place the tortilla packet in the oven for about 7 minutes. This will heat the tortillas with a little "steam" to soften them.

7 To serve, place a tortilla on each plate. Spoon some of the tempeh mixture along the center, cover with a little cucumber salsa, then fold and roll to enclose the filling.

¼ teaspoon ground cumin

1 tablespoon minced fresh parsley

....

8 8-inch flour tortillas

Serves 4

BLACK BEAN CAKES WITH ORANGE BASIL SALSA

Tomatoes and oranges together in salsa make a great match both for flavor and dynamic color. Serve these hearty bean cakes with a rice pilaf sprinkled with scallions.

SALSA

2 navel oranges, sections separated and cut into small dice

1 large tomato, cored, sliced, and finely diced

1 scallion, very thinly sliced

1 tablespoon minced fresh basil

1 garlic clove, minced

1 tablespoon lime juice

2 teaspoons olive oil

1 small jalapeño pepper, seeded and minced (wear gloves), or ¼ teaspoon crushed red pepper flakes

Salt

THE BEAN CAKES

4 cups cooked black beans, rinsed and drained if canned

2 eggs

½ cup bread crumbs

1 tablespoon olive oil, plus oil for greasing pan

1 Combine all the salsa ingredients in a bowl. Let sit at least 1 hour, or up to 8 hours, before using.

2 Place 3 cups of the black beans in a large bowl. Process the remaining 1 cup of beans with the eggs until smooth. Stir this mixture into the whole beans along with the bread crumbs.

3 Heat the oil in a medium skillet over medium heat. Add the onion, garlic, and celery and sauté until very tender and beginning to brown, about 10 minutes. Sprinkle on the cumin and cook 1 more minute.

4 Scrape the vegetables into the bean mixture and add the salt and pepper. Stir to mix well.

5 Preheat the oven to 375 degrees. Lightly oil a baking sheet.

6 Using a ⅓ cup measuring cup, scoop up 12 portions of the bean mixture and place on the baking sheet. With a knife or your hands, flatten into patty shapes. Bake 10 minutes, flip with a spatula, and bake 10 more minutes. Serve the bean cakes with a spoonful of salsa on each.

Note: The dish may be prepared in advance through step 4. Cover and refrigerate for up to 8 hours.

1 medium onion, very finely diced

2 garlic cloves, minced

1 celery rib, very thinly sliced

1 teaspoon ground cumin

¼ teaspoon salt

Liberal seasoning of freshly ground pepper

Serves 4 to 6

Quick SAVORY WHITE BEANS WITH RED ONION AND FRESH HERBS

I love white beans, especially cannellini and Great Northern. This easy method of serving them as a main course accentuates their buttery flavor. I serve this dish with sautéed spinach, which adds just the right color and texture.

1½ tablespoons olive oil

2 celery ribs, thinly sliced

1 medium red onion, quartered and cut into ¼-inch slices

1½ teaspoons red wine vinegar

1 tomato, cored, seeded, and finely diced

6 fresh sage leaves, finely chopped, or ¼ teaspoon powdered dried

2 sprigs fresh thyme, finely chopped, or ½ teaspoon dried

¼ cup chopped fresh parsley

4 cups freshly cooked white beans, such as cannellini or Great Northern, or 2 15-ounce cans white beans, rinsed thoroughly and drained

Salt

Generous seasoning of freshly ground pepper

Serves 4

1 Heat the oil in a large skillet over medium heat. Add the celery and sauté 5 minutes, stirring often.

2 Add the onion and cook 2 minutes. Pour the vinegar over the vegetables to set the color of the red onion; toss to coat well. Sauté about 5 minutes, or until the onion is tender.

3 Stir in the tomato and cook 2 minutes. Mix in all the remaining ingredients and cook about 5 more minutes, or until piping hot. If the mixture is dry, sprinkle on a few teaspoons of water and toss to blend. The beans should be moist and juicy, not dry.

Quick CORN AND BEAN TOSTADAS

Mexicans cleverly use nuts in their main-course cooking, especially as thickening agents. Here, walnuts add a delightful crunch to this flavorful topping. A light salad is all you need to accompany this dish.

1½ tablespoons vegetable oil

4 8-inch flour (wheat) tortillas

1 15-ounce can kidney beans, rinsed and well drained

1 cup frozen corn kernels, thawed

½ cup sliced black olives

¼ cup finely chopped cilantro

⅓ cup finely chopped walnuts (not ground)

½ cup mild or medium salsa

2 cups (6 ounces) grated Monterey Jack cheese with jalapeño peppers

Serves 2 to 3

1. Preheat the broiler.
2. With a vegetable brush, lightly coat 2 tortillas on both sides with some of the vegetable oil. Place on a baking sheet and broil until lightly golden on one side. Flip over and broil again until golden. Repeat with the remaining tortillas. Let cool on a rack. (You can prepare the tortillas up to 24 hours in advance; keep them covered in the refrigerator.)
3. Preheat the oven to 375 degrees.
4. In a large bowl, combine the kidney beans, corn, olives, cilantro, walnuts, and salsa.
5. Using two baking sheets or cooking just 2 tortillas at a time, divide the bean mixture and spread on each tortilla. Sprinkle on the cheese.
6. Bake 7 to 10 minutes, or until hot and bubbly. Slice in half before serving.

VEGETABLE DAL

Dal is an Indian purée made of lentils or split peas and spices. Here it is prepared like a stew with vegetables (called sambaar) and served on rice. If you have never eaten dal, you're in for a taste awakening. The blending of flavors is dazzling. Cook about 1 ½ cups rice (preferably basmati rice) to serve with this sambaar, and don't hesitate to make the sambaar up to 24 hours in advance; its flavor will be heightened as a result of sitting.

1 cup yellow split peas

4 cups water

1 teaspoon salt

2 tablespoons vegetable oil

2 medium onions, finely diced

2 garlic cloves, minced

½ teaspoon turmeric

1 teaspoon ground coriander

1 teaspoon ground cumin

¼ teaspoon cayenne

1 tomato, cored, seeded, and finely diced

1 cup water

2 medium potatoes, peeled and cut into ½-inch dice

8 ounces fresh spinach, stems discarded and leaves chopped into small pieces (about 8 cups loosely packed)

1 teaspoon lemon juice

1 Rinse the split peas in a sieve under cold running water. Pick out and discard any stones or foreign particles. Place the split peas in a 3-quart saucepan along with the water and salt. Bring to a boil, then reduce the heat to a simmer. Cook, stirring occasionally, for 45 minutes. Skim off and discard any foam that rises to the surface.

2 Meanwhile, heat the vegetable oil in a large skillet over medium-high heat. Add the onions and garlic and sauté until they begin to turn brown, about 15 minutes. Stir often. Mix in all the spices and cook 2 more minutes. Add the tomato and cook 2 minutes.

3 Pour in the cup of water and bring to a boil. Stir in the potatoes, cover the pan, and reduce the heat to a simmer. Cook until the potatoes are just about tender, about 10 minutes.

4 When the split peas are very soft and almost a purée, stir vigorously to make them smoother. Carefully stir in the contents of the skillet along with the spinach and lemon juice. Cook, stirring frequently to prevent sticking, 10 to 15 more

1 tablespoon finely chopped cilantro

2 tablespoons unsalted butter

Serves 4 to 6

minutes, or until the dal is the consistency of a thick stew and the vegetables are tender. (If too thick, add a little water.) Stir in the cilantro and butter and cook 2 more minutes. Serve on rice.

VEGETABLES

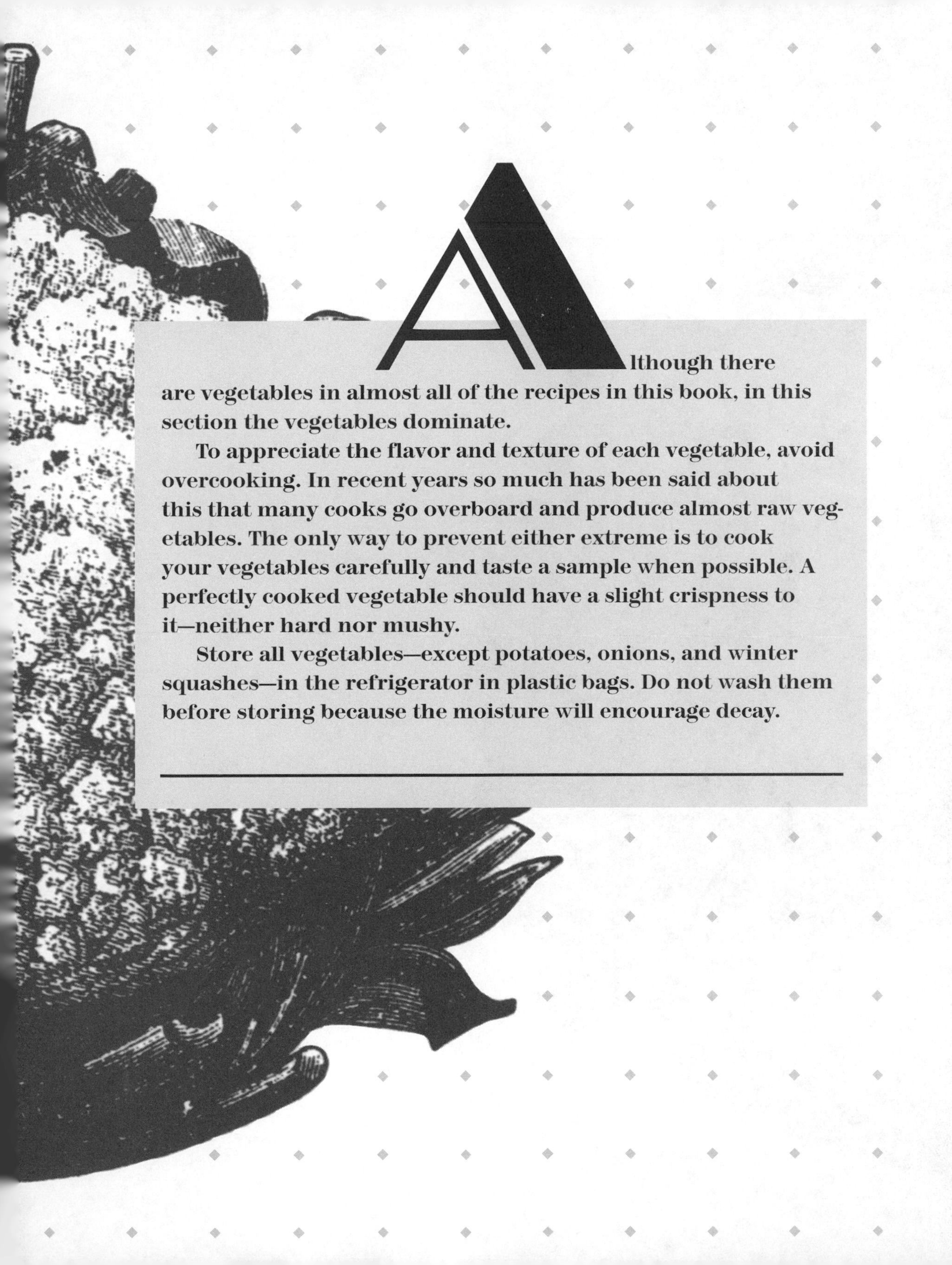

Although there are vegetables in almost all of the recipes in this book, in this section the vegetables dominate.

To appreciate the flavor and texture of each vegetable, avoid overcooking. In recent years so much has been said about this that many cooks go overboard and produce almost raw vegetables. The only way to prevent either extreme is to cook your vegetables carefully and taste a sample when possible. A perfectly cooked vegetable should have a slight crispness to it—neither hard nor mushy.

Store all vegetables—except potatoes, onions, and winter squashes—in the refrigerator in plastic bags. Do not wash them before storing because the moisture will encourage decay.

Quick BAKED GARLICKY BUTTERNUT SQUASH

Here is a variation of a recipe that the late Laurie Colwin wrote in** Gourmet. **This crusty, garlic-scented dish needs just a salad to make it a completely satisfying and delicious meal, although a close friend of mine says it is absolutely spellbinding served on a golden bed of polenta.

1 large (3½ pounds) butternut squash, peeled and cut into 1-inch dice

⅓ cup fruity olive oil

2 garlic cloves, minced

2 tablespoons minced fresh parsley

Salt to taste

Liberal seasoning of freshly ground pepper

⅓ cup grated Parmesan cheese

Serves 4

1 Preheat the oven to 400 degrees.

2 In a large bowl, toss together the squash, olive oil, garlic, parsley, salt, and pepper.

3 Spoon the vegetables into a 12 × 7 × 2-inch Pyrex dish or other shallow 2½-quart baking dish. Sprinkle on the Parmesan cheese. Bake for 1 hour, or until the squash is tender, not mushy.

CRUSTLESS SPINACH AND MUSHROOM PIE

This easy pie goes well with a potato side dish. It's just as delicious reheated, so look forward to a tasty lunch of leftovers.

2 10-ounce packages fresh spinach, washed and chopped, or 2 10-ounce packages frozen chopped spinach, thawed and squeezed dry

½ tablespoon unsalted butter

¼ cup bread crumbs

1 tablespoon olive oil

12 ounces (4½ cups) sliced mushrooms

2 scallions, thinly sliced

3 eggs

¾ cup low-fat milk

1 cup grated extra-sharp Cheddar cheese

⅛ teaspoon grated nutmeg

½ teaspoon salt

Freshly ground pepper

Serves 4

1 Prepare either the fresh or defrosted spinach as directed and set aside.

2 Preheat the oven to 375 degrees. With the butter, coat the inside of a 9-inch pie plate, then sprinkle with bread crumbs, rotating the plate to cover the sides. Let the extra crumbs fall to the bottom; this will form the crust.

3 In a large skillet, heat the olive oil over medium-high heat. Add the mushrooms and sauté until brown and the juices have evaporated, about 10 minutes. If you are using fresh spinach, add it with just the water that clings to it. Cover the pan. Cook until the spinach just wilts, about 5 minutes. If you are using frozen spinach, stir it into the mushrooms.

4 Stir in the scallions, then remove the pan from the heat and let cool.

5 In a large bowl, beat the eggs. Beat in the milk, all but 2 tablespoons of the Cheddar cheese, the nutmeg, salt, and pepper. Stir in the cooled spinach mixture.

6 Scrape everything into the prepared pie plate. Sprinkle the remaining Cheddar cheese evenly over the top.

7 Bake 30 minutes, or until a knife inserted in the center of the pie comes out clean. Cool for a few minutes before serving; cut into wedges.

Note: May be prepared up to 8 hours in advance through step 5 and refrigerated. Bring to room temperature before baking.

BROCCOLI AND RED PEPPER PIE

This colorful pie with a bread crumb "crust" has an added boost of protein from the chickpeas sprinkled throughout. For a pleasing accompaniment, try serving it with buttered egg noodles.

1 tablespoon olive oil

2 garlic cloves, minced

2 medium onions, finely diced

⅛ teaspoon crushed red pepper flakes

5 cups tiny broccoli florets (from 1 large bunch)

1 large red bell pepper, cored and diced

½ cup cooked, rinsed chickpeas (see note)

1 tablespoon unsalted butter, softened

¼ cup plus 1 tablespoon bread crumbs

3 eggs

½ cup milk

¼ cup grated Parmesan cheese

¼ teaspoon dried oregano

1 Heat the oil in a large skillet over medium-high heat. Add the garlic, onions, and red pepper flakes and sauté for 10 minutes.

2 Stir in the broccoli, red bell pepper, and chickpeas. Pour on 2 tablespoons of water, cover the pan, and cook for about 7 minutes, or until the broccoli is tender yet still bright green. Remove the cover and cook away any remaining liquid. Place the mixture in a bowl and let cool.

3 Preheat the oven to 375 degrees.

4 To make the "crust," butter a 9-inch pie plate with ½ tablespoon of the soft butter. Sprinkle ¼ cup of bread crumbs on the bottom of the pie plate. Rotate to cover the bottom and sides of the plate with the crumbs.

5 In a large bowl, beat the eggs. Beat in the milk, Parmesan cheese, oregano, salt, and pepper. Stir in the vegetable mixture. Spoon half the mixture into the pie plate. Sprinkle on the Muenster cheese. Spoon on the remaining mixture, then sprinkle the remaining tablespoon of bread crumbs over the top. Dot with the remaining ½ tablespoon butter.

¼ teaspoon salt

Liberal seasoning of freshly ground pepper

1 cup (3 ounces) grated Muenster cheese

Serves 3 to 4

6 Bake 30 to 35 minutes, or until a knife inserted in the center of the pie comes out clean. Let sit 5 minutes before serving.

Note: Leftover chickpeas can be marinated in an herb vinaigrette and served in a salad at another time.

Quick VEGETABLE TIAN

A tian is a Provençal shallow earthenware casserole, which gives this vegetable dish its name. Other shallow baking dishes can do a similar job of slowly baking a vegetable concoction in olive oil and herbs.

Try to make this dish as is without improvisation because the balance of juicy and dry vegetables provides just the right amount of moisture to ensure even cooking. The heavenly crumb topping made of fresh bread crumbs gives this tian added depth, so be sure to include it. To add to the meal, try a side dish of egg noodles. My husband and I are so enamored of this tian that the two of us can polish off the whole thing with just a bit of French bread as an accompaniment.

2 slices good-quality white bread

1 tablespoon plus ¼ cup olive oil

1 garlic clove, minced

1 pound green beans, tips removed

12 ounces mushrooms, halved or quartered, depending on size

1 red bell pepper, cut into 2-inch chunks

1 tomato, seeded and finely diced

1 large red onion, cut into eighths

½ teaspoon dried basil

½ teaspoon dried oregano

1 teaspoon dried dill weed

Generous seasoning of freshly ground pepper

Serves 4

1 Preheat the oven to 375 degrees.

2 Tear the bread into pieces. Place them in a blender or food processor and make bread crumbs.

3 Heat 1 tablespoon olive oil in a small skillet over medium heat. Add the garlic and sauté 1 minute. Stir in the crumbs and toss to coat thoroughly with the oil. Cook, stirring frequently, until the crumbs begin to turn golden and crisp, about 5 minutes. Remove from the heat.

4 In a large bowl, combine all the remaining ingredients, including the remaining ¼ cup olive oil. Toss well. Scrape the mixture into a shallow 2½-quart baking dish and smooth over the top. Sprinkle on the bread crumbs and press them down evenly. Bake 1 hour, or until the vegetables are very tender.

Quick TWICE-BAKED POTATOES STUFFED WITH CHEESE AND SALSA

Even though these potatoes must be cooked an hour before being stuffed, I think of them as very quick to prepare because they take only 10 minutes of my time. This low-fat, high-protein version of stuffed potatoes needs just a salad to complete the meal.

2 large baking potatoes, scrubbed

½ cup low-fat cottage cheese

1 tablespoon low-fat milk

½ cup grated part-skim mozzarella cheese

3 tablespoons mild, medium, or hot salsa

2 tablespoons minced fresh parsley

Serves 2

1 Preheat the oven to 400 degrees.

2 Poke the potatoes a few times with the tip of a knife. Place them directly on the rack in the oven and bake until tender when pierced through the center, about 1 hour.

3 Meanwhile, blend the cottage cheese and milk together in a blender or food processor until perfectly smooth. Scrape into a bowl and stir in the mozzarella, salsa, and parsley.

4 When the potatoes are done, slice them in half lengthwise. Scoop the flesh into a medium-size bowl. Mash it with a fork, then stir in the cheese mixture. Fill each potato shell with some filling.

5 Place the stuffed potatoes on a baking sheet. Bake 20 minutes, or until brown on top.

MUSHROOM ENCHILADAS

Cottage cheese enhances the tasty filling in these enchiladas. Because they are so satisfying, a salad is all you need to balance the meal.

1 tablespoon olive oil

2 garlic cloves, minced

1 pound mushrooms, thinly sliced (about 6 cups)

½ teaspoon dried oregano

1 16-ounce can pinto beans, rinsed and well drained

1 cup low-fat small curd cottage cheese

½ cup finely chopped fresh parsley

2 cups mild or medium salsa

8 8-inch flour (wheat) tortillas

1 cup grated sharp Cheddar cheese

Serves 4 to 6

1 Heat the oil in a large skillet over medium-high heat. Add the garlic and cook 1 minute. Do not burn it. Stir in the mushrooms and cook until the juices are released and then evaporate, about 10 minutes. The mushrooms should begin to stick to the pan.

2 Add the oregano and pinto beans and cook 1 minute. Remove the pan from the heat and let the mixture cool.

3 Preheat the oven to 375 degrees.

4 Stir the cottage cheese and parsley into the bean mixture. Place the pan in front of you to begin rolling the enchiladas. Place the salsa in a bowl in front of you, along with the tortillas and a pastry brush.

5 Spread a thin layer of salsa in a 9 × 13-inch baking dish. Lay a tortilla on a plate, then brush both sides of the tortilla with a little bit of salsa. This will moisten the tortillas and prevent them from breaking. Divide the mushroom mixture into 8 portions and place 1 portion along the bottom of a tortilla. Roll tightly. Place the enchilada seam side down in the baking dish. Repeat with the remaining tortillas.

6 Spoon the remaining salsa all over the enchiladas. Neatly place the Cheddar cheese along each enchilada. Cover the baking dish tightly with foil.

7 Bake 30 minutes, then remove the foil and bake 5 more minutes. The enchiladas should be piping hot, but be careful not to dry them out through overcooking.

Note: The enchiladas can be prepared up to 8 hours in advance through step 6. Bring to room temperature before baking.

Quick MIXED PEPPER QUESADILLAS

The filling in these quesadillas is scrumptious. They make a great choice for lunch or dinner.

1 tablespoon olive oil

1 red bell pepper, cored and cut into very thin strips

1 yellow bell pepper, cored and cut into very thin strips

1 green bell pepper, cored and cut into very thin strips

1 tomato, cored, seeded, and finely diced

8 pitted black olives, thinly sliced

1 teaspoon red wine vinegar

1 teaspoon oregano

Salt

Generous seasoning of freshly ground pepper

....

4 8-inch flour (wheat) tortillas

1¼ cups grated Monterey Jack cheese with jalapeño peppers

Serves 2 to 3

1 Heat the oil in a large skillet over medium-high heat. Add the peppers and sauté, tossing often, for 10 minutes, or until the peppers are tender.

2 Stir in the tomato, olives, vinegar, oregano, salt, and pepper and cook until the peppers are very soft, about 10 more minutes. Remove from the heat and let the mixture cool.

3 Preheat the oven to 375 degrees.

4 Place 2 of the tortillas on a baking sheet. Sprinkle a quarter of the cheese on each tortilla, leaving a 1-inch border. Spread half the pepper mixture on each tortilla, then sprinkle on the remaining cheese. Top with the remaining tortillas, gently pressing down to make the filling adhere.

5 Bake 10 minutes, or until the cheese is thoroughly melted. Cut each quesadilla into 4 wedges before serving.

Quick LEEK FRITTATA

It's unfortunate that leeks aren't as popular in the United States as they are in Europe because their sweet delicate flavor is incomparable. Serve this delicious frittata with home fries and toasted peasant-style bread for a great trio.

3 large leeks

1 tablespoon unsalted butter

6 eggs

¼ cup low-fat milk

2 tablespoons grated Parmesan cheese

¼ teaspoon salt

Freshly ground pepper

Serves 3 to 4

1. Cut the roots off the leeks. Cut off all but about 3 inches of the dark green part and discard. Make a vertical cut down the length of the leeks almost through to the back. Wash the leeks very thoroughly under cold running water, separating the leaves to reveal any hidden dirt. Pat the leeks dry, then thinly slice them, discarding any tough green part if necessary. (You should have about 3½ cups.)
2. Preheat the oven to 350 degrees. Butter a 9-inch pie plate and set aside.
3. Melt the tablespoon of butter in a large skillet over medium heat. Add the leeks and sauté, stirring often, until tender, about 10 minutes. Set aside to cool.
4. Beat the eggs in a large bowl. Beat in the milk, cheese, salt, and pepper, then stir in the leeks. Pour this mixture into the pie plate.
5. Bake 20 to 25 minutes, or just until a knife inserted in the center comes out clean. Do not overcook. Serve immediately.

Quick SUMMER FRITTATA

This frittata is light on eggs and chock-full of vegetables—a good choice when you have small amounts of several vegetables on hand. Plan ahead so you can serve it warm, not hot; the texture and flavor will be improved.

1 tablespoon olive oil

1 small zucchini, finely diced

1 small yellow squash, finely diced

1 red bell pepper, finely diced

1 tomato, cored, seeded, and finely diced

4 scallions, very thinly sliced

¼ cup shredded fresh basil, or ½ teaspoon dried

Butter for greasing

4 eggs

¼ teaspoon salt

1 cup grated Monterey Jack cheese with jalapeño peppers

Serves 4 generously

1 Heat the oil in a large skillet over medium-high heat. Add the zucchini, yellow squash, and red pepper and sauté until the vegetables begin to get tender, about 7 minutes.

2 Add the tomato and continue to cook the mixture, tossing often, until the vegetables are tender and the mixture begins to stick to the pan. Raise the heat to evaporate any excess juices. Remove from the heat, then stir in the scallions and basil. Let the mixture cool.

3 Preheat the oven to 350 degrees. Butter a 9-inch pie plate.

4 Beat the eggs and salt in a large bowl. Stir in the cheese and vegetable mixture and pour into the pie plate.

5 Bake 25 to 28 minutes, or until a knife inserted in the center of the frittata comes out dry. Cool the frittata on a rack and serve it warm, not hot.

Quick BROCCOLI AND RICOTTA OMELET

Your omelet will be a glowing success if the filling is hot before you place it in the eggs. Also, make two omelets to better control the texture of the eggs.

2 cups tiny broccoli florets

½ cup part-skim ricotta cheese

1 tablespoon minced fresh basil, or ½ teaspoon dried

2 tablespoons grated Parmesan cheese

Salt

Freshly ground pepper

Butter for greasing

4 eggs, well beaten

Serves 2

1 In a medium-size saucepan, steam the broccoli in a vegetable steamer or with just a little bit of water until it is tender yet still bright green, about 5 minutes. Taste to see if it is cooked properly. If it is too crunchy, cook a few minutes more. Drain thoroughly and return to the pot.

2 In a small bowl, combine the ricotta, basil, Parmesan cheese, and salt and pepper to taste. Gently stir into the broccoli. Cover the pot and keep warm over low heat.

3 Lightly coat an omelet pan with some butter and heat the pan over medium-high heat. Pour in half the eggs and stir with a fork until curds begin to form. Shake the pan a little to distribute the liquid. When the omelet begins to set but is still slightly wet, spoon on half the hot broccoli mixture. Immediately fold over the omelet and serve. Repeat with the remaining eggs and filling.

Quick

ZUCCHINI, CHEDDAR, AND SALSA OMELET

Here's a tasty omelet that can be easily put together at a moment's notice. Cooked rice is a suitable side dish.

2 teaspoons olive oil

2 cups thinly sliced zucchini (from 2 small zucchini, quartered lengthwise and thinly sliced)

½ teaspoon dried oregano

¼ cup mild or medium salsa (homemade or store-bought)

Freshly ground black pepper

Butter for greasing

4 eggs, well beaten

1 cup (3 ounces) grated Cheddar cheese

Serves 2

1 Heat the oil in a small skillet over medium heat. Add the zucchini and oregano and sauté until almost tender, about 5 minutes. Stir in the salsa and black pepper and cook until the zucchini is tender, not crunchy or mushy. The mixture should not be watery at this point. If there is any liquid, raise the heat and boil to evaporate. Keep the zucchini hot on low heat while you make the omelet.

2 Lightly grease an omelet pan with some butter and heat the pan over medium-high heat. When it is hot, pour in half the beaten eggs. Stir the eggs with a fork just until curds begin to form. Tip the pan slightly to cause the liquid eggs to run to the sides. Cook until set but slightly wet, about 1 minute total.

3 Place half the cheese on one side of the omelet. Spoon on half the zucchini mixture, then flip the omelet over to cover it. Slide the omelet onto a serving plate. Repeat to make another omelet.

Quick SZECHUAN CABBAGE AND MUSHROOMS IN CHILI SAUCE

When I want a low-fat dish with a lot of kick, I inevitably turn to spicy Chinese food. Serve this with rice (cook about 1 cup), which should be completely cooked and kept warm on the back burner when you begin stir-frying.

THE SAUCE

1½ teaspoons cornstarch

1 teaspoon water

1 tablespoon chili paste with garlic

3 tablespoons tamari soy sauce

¼ cup Chinese rice wine or dry sherry

1 teaspoon sugar

2-pound head napa (Chinese) cabbage

2 tablespoons vegetable or peanut oil

4 cups (about 12 ounces) sliced mushrooms

2 scallions, very thinly sliced

Serves 3

1 Stir the cornstarch and water together in a small bowl. Stir in all the remaining sauce ingredients and set aside.

2 Chop the root end off the cabbage and discard. Wash the leaves thoroughly. Chop the cabbage into 1½-inch pieces. It should yield 8 to 10 cups.

3 Heat the oil over medium-high heat in a wok or large skillet until hot but not smoking. Add the mushrooms and stir-fry until brown and juicy, about 5 minutes. Raise the heat to high. Add the cabbage and stir-fry, using 2 spoons or spatulas to toss it, for about 3 minutes, just until it wilts.

4 Stir the sauce once more. Pour onto the vegetables. Sprinkle on the scallions. Toss a few seconds, or until the sauce thickens. Serve on rice.

STUFFED ZUCCHINI WITH CHUNKY TOMATO SAUCE

Stuffed vegetables make a very attractive and satisfying main course. Serve these stuffed zucchini with buttered egg noodles for a good match.

4 medium zucchini

1 tablespoon unsalted butter, cut into bits

Salt

Freshly ground pepper

2 tablespoons olive oil

2 garlic cloves, minced

1 medium onion, finely chopped

1 egg, beaten

½ cup diced roasted red peppers (from a 7-ounce jar)

¼ cup minced fresh parsley

1 cup bread crumbs

1 cup grated Swiss or Cheddar cheese

1 tablespoon minced fresh basil, or ½ teaspoon dried

½ teaspoon dried oregano

THE SAUCE

1 tablespoon olive oil

1 medium onion, finely diced

2 cups canned plum tomatoes, finely chopped,

1 Cut the ends off the zucchini. Halve lengthwise, then with a teaspoon carefully scoop out their centers, leaving a ¼-inch-thick wall. Finely chop the centers and set aside. Place the zucchini boats in a large skillet (you will have to do this in batches) with ½ inch of water. Cover the pan and bring it to a boil. Cook about 5 minutes, or until the zucchini are tender but not at all mushy. Place them on a cotton kitchen towel to drain.

2 Lightly oil a baking dish large enough to hold the zucchini. Place them in the dish, cavity side up, then sprinkle the butter bits in the shells. Season with salt and pepper to taste.

3 Drain the water and wipe the skillet dry. Pour in the oil and heat over medium heat. Add the garlic and onion and sauté until the onion is tender, about 10 minutes. Add the chopped zucchini and sauté about 10 minutes more, or until the zucchini is just tender. Scrape into a large bowl.

4 Mix in the egg, roasted peppers, parsley, bread crumbs, cheese, basil, oregano, and salt and pepper to taste. Stuff the zucchini boats with the mixture, carefully pressing it down to make it compact.

with their juice

Salt

Freshly ground pepper

Serves 4

5 Preheat the oven to 375 degrees.

6 Bake the zucchini, uncovered, for 30 minutes, or until golden brown and sizzling.

7 Meanwhile, make the sauce. Heat the olive oil in a medium-size skillet. Add the onion and sauté until tender, about 10 minutes. Stir in the tomatoes along with salt and pepper to taste. Cook, stirring occasionally, until the sauce begins to thicken, about 10 minutes. Put a few spoonfuls of sauce in the center of each serving plate and spread it out. Place the stuffed zucchini on the sauce.

Note: May be prepared through step 4 up to 24 hours in advance and refrigerated. Bring to room temperature before baking.

SPICED CAULIFLOWER WITH FRAGRANT RICE PILAF

Here are two Indian dishes that complement each other with a mélange of spicy, tangy, hot, and sweet flavors. A few spoonfuls of plain yogurt on the side add a soothing touch and a delightful contrast.

THE PILAF

1 tablespoon vegetable oil

1 onion, diced

1 cup basmati or converted rice

2 cloves

1 cinnamon stick

1 bay leaf

¼ teaspoon ground cardamom

¼ cup sliced almonds

⅓ cup raisins

½ teaspoon salt

2 cups water

THE CAULIFLOWER

2 tablespoons vegetable oil

1 large onion, diced

2 garlic cloves, minced

½ teaspoon minced fresh ginger

1 teaspoon ground coriander seed

1 teaspoon turmeric

½ teaspoon ground cumin

1 In a medium-size saucepan, heat the oil over medium heat. Add the onion and sauté for 5 minutes. Stir in all the remaining pilaf ingredients except the water and cook 2 minutes more, stirring often.

2 Pour in the water, cover the pot, then bring to a boil. Lower the heat to a simmer and cook over low heat until all the water is absorbed, about 20 minutes.

3 Meanwhile, make the cauliflower. Heat the oil in a large skillet over medium heat. Add the onion, garlic, and ginger and sauté for 5 minutes, tossing often. Stir in all of the spices and cook for 2 minutes, again stirring often.

4 Add the tomatoes; cook 2 minutes. Thoroughly mix in the cauliflower and salt and cover the pan. Cook, stirring occasionally, until the cauliflower is tender, about 7 minutes. Remove the cover. (If the sauce is watery, cook at high heat for a few seconds until it thickens.) Stir in the peas and cilantro and cook 1 minute more.

5 Return to the rice pilaf. When all the water is absorbed and the rice is tender, remove the cinnamon stick and bay leaf, then fluff the rice with a fork. Let sit, covered, for 2 minutes before serving. Serve the rice alongside the cauliflower.

¼ teaspoon ground cardamom

⅛ teaspoon cayenne, or more to taste

1½ cups finely chopped canned tomatoes, with their juice

1 medium cauliflower, cut into small florets (about 6 cups)

¼ teaspoon salt

1 cup frozen peas, thawed

1 tablespoon minced cilantro or fresh parsley

Serves 4

PIZZAS, CALZONES, FOCACCE, AND BOBOLI

To my mind, pizza and its relatives are superlative foods. With a crisp, well-made crust as a base, they become ideal vehicles for combining your favorite cheeses, vegetables, and herbs.

A calzone is actually a pizza folded over to make a turnover. These self-contained stuffed pouches can be made any size, so if you want party food that's easy to eat, you can make them smaller than my recipes suggest.

Focaccia (pronounced fo-KAH-cha) is another cousin to pizza. Its thicker, often herb-laced crust can be lightly dressed with just a sprinkling of Parmesan cheese and served as one would serve bread, or it can be covered with a more substantial topping and made into a meal, as I have done here. I have gotten great results using frozen bread dough as a quick and easy base for focaccia. Seek out a good-quality dough, additive-free and containing just flour, water, yeast, and salt.

To incorporate herbs and oil in a thawed dough, make sure your dough is at room temperature, then knead in the added ingredients as best you can. Let the dough rest 10 minutes or so, then knead again until evenly blended.

If you want to make your focaccia dough from scratch, follow the recipe for pizza dough (page 132), using 1 tablespoon oil in the dough; omit incorporating more oil in the dough if the recipe calls for it.

PROVENÇAL VEGETABLE PIZZA WITH GOAT CHEESE

This is a fabulous pizza—both to look at and to savor. First, a layer of cheese is sprinkled on the dough, then a very garlicky tomato-zucchini mixture, and finally spoonfuls of creamy goat cheese. It's easy to make, and becomes even easier if the zucchini mixture is made early in the day.

THE DOUGH

1 cup warm water

2 teaspoons active dry yeast

½ teaspoon sugar

2 tablespoons olive oil

2½ cups unbleached flour

1 teaspoon salt

....

Oil for greasing bowl and pizza pans

THE TOPPING

2 tablespoons olive oil

6 garlic cloves, minced

¼ teaspoon crushed red pepper flakes

6 cups thinly sliced zucchini (from 3 medium zucchini, quartered lengthwise and thinly sliced)

1 teaspoon dried oregano

2 tablespoons shredded fresh basil, or 1 teaspoon dried

1 To make the dough, combine the water, yeast, and sugar in a small bowl and stir to mix. Let sit 10 minutes. Stir in the olive oil.

2 Combine the flour and salt in a large bowl. Pour in the yeast mixture and stir until a ball of dough is formed. Turn onto a floured surface and knead until smooth, about 5 minutes.

3 Very lightly oil a large glass or ceramic bowl. Place the ball of dough in it, rotating the dough so the entire ball is oiled. Cover the bowl with plastic wrap and put in a warm place until the dough rises to double its size, 1 to 1½ hours. (Sometimes I heat my oven for a minute—just until it is warm, not hot—then turn it off and place the bowl in the oven.)

4 Meanwhile, make the topping. Heat the olive oil in a large skillet over medium-high heat. Add the garlic and red pepper flakes and sauté for 2 minutes. Stir in the zucchini, oregano, dried basil (if using fresh basil, see step 9), thyme, salt, and ground pepper. Sauté until the zucchini is tender but not mushy, about 10 minutes.

¼ teaspoon dried thyme

Salt

Generous seasoning of freshly ground pepper

½ cup canned crushed tomatoes

10 oil-cured olives, pitted and quartered (see note, page 25)

3 cups (9 ounces) grated part-skim mozzarella cheese

6 ounces goat cheese

Serves 4 to 6 (1 17 × 11-inch pizza or 2 9-inch pizzas)

5 Mix in the crushed tomatoes and olives and cook 2 minutes more. Remove from the heat and let cool. (The vegetable mixture can be made and kept refrigerated for up to 24 hours in advance. Bring to room temperature before assembling the pizza.)

6 Preheat the oven to 450 degrees. Lightly oil a 17 × 11-inch baking sheet or 2 9-inch pizza pans.

7 When the dough has doubled its size, punch it down to its original size and remove all the air bubbles. (If you are not ready to cook the pizza, chill the dough.) Roll the dough to fit the pans or baking sheet, stretching the edges as necessary once in the pan.

8 Sprinkle on the mozzarella cheese. Spread the zucchini mixture evenly over the cheese.

9 Bake the pizza for 17 minutes, or until the crust is golden underneath. (Use a spatula to help you peek.) If you are using fresh basil, sprinkle it on the pizza now. Place small spoonfuls or chunks of goat cheese evenly over the pizza and bake 2 additional minutes. Slide the pizza onto a large cutting board and cut it into squares. Serve immediately.

Quick

QUICK PIZZA

This alternative to a yeast pizza dough is delicious. A delicate, crisp crust is created with baking powder as the leavener, making it ultraquick to prepare and lending itself to a variety of imaginative toppings. Below are some of my favorite choices. Feel free to improvise.

Oil for greasing pan

THE DOUGH

2 cups unbleached flour

½ cup whole wheat flour

1½ teaspoons baking powder

½ teaspoon salt

4 tablespoons unsalted butter, chilled and cut into pieces

1 cup low-fat milk

TOPPING SUGGESTIONS

Sliced tomatoes, grated Muenster and mozzarella cheeses (or crumbled Gorgonzola), topped with dried basil and oregano

Grated mozzarella cheese and strips of roasted red peppers, then gobs of goat cheese and shredded fresh basil once removed from the oven

Grated fontina cheese, then diced tomatoes, minced garlic, and cooked broccoli bits, with little spoonfuls of ricotta cheese all over the top, finally sprinkled with dried basil

1 Preheat the oven to 450 degrees. Lightly oil 2 17-inch-long baking sheets.

2 Place the two flours, baking powder, and salt in the container of a food processor and pulse until mixed. Drop in the butter pieces and pulse until large crumbs form. With the motor running, pour in the milk and process just until a clump of dough forms. (Alternatively, combine the dry ingredients in a large bowl. Add the butter pieces and rub into the flour with your fingertips until coarse crumbs form. Pour in the milk and stir just until combined.)

3 Scrape the dough onto a lightly floured surface. Gather it into 4 balls. Roll out each ball with a lightly floured rolling pin into an 8-inch circle. Place two circles on each prepared baking sheet.

4 Top with the toppings of your choice and bake 12 to 15 minutes, or until golden on top and bottom. Peek underneath the crust to make sure it is golden brown.

Grated Jarlsberg cheese, sautéed mushrooms, and minced garlic sprinkled all over

Grated Muenster cheese topped with sliced cherry tomatoes and little spoonfuls of pesto

Tomato sauce, chopped cilantro, spoonfuls of goat cheese, then grated Parmesan cheese sprinkled all over

Serves 4 (4 8-inch pizzas)

PIZZA WITH ROASTED RED PEPPER SAUCE AND JALAPEÑO CHEESE

No tomatoes on this pizza—the incomparable flavors of roasted red peppers and basil make up the delectable sauce, and the jalapeños give the pizza some kick without being overbearing.

Pizza dough (page 132)

1 7-ounce jar roasted red peppers, thoroughly drained and patted dry

2 garlic cloves, minced

2 tablespoons olive oil

½ teaspoon dried basil

Dash of cayenne

1½ cups (4½ ounces) grated Monterey Jack cheese with jalapeño peppers

1½ cups (4½ ounces) grated part-skim mozzarella cheese

Serves 4 (1 17 × 11-inch pizza or 2 9-inch pizzas)

1 While the pizza dough rises, make the sauce. Combine the roasted peppers, garlic, olive oil, basil, and cayenne in a blender or food processor and purée. Scrape it into a bowl.

2 Preheat the oven to 450 degrees. Lightly oil a baking sheet or pizza pans and proceed to line them as in step 7, page 133.

3 Spread the red pepper sauce on the dough. Sprinkle the two cheeses evenly over the dough. Bake 15 minutes, or until the crust is golden underneath.

ZUCCHINI AND RED PEPPER CALZONES

Crunchy pine nuts enhance this aromatic filling, adding both texture and flavor. Remember these calzones for a special luncheon; they'll be a big hit.

THE FILLING

1 tablespoon olive oil

4 garlic cloves, minced

2 medium zucchini, quartered lengthwise and thinly sliced (4 cups sliced)

1 red bell pepper, diced

1½ tablespoons pine nuts

½ cup tomato sauce (homemade or store-bought)

Freshly ground black pepper to taste

Pizza dough (page 132), or 1 pound frozen bread dough, thawed

½ pound thinly sliced or 2½ cups grated Muenster cheese

1 egg, beaten with 1 teaspoon water (egg wash)

Serves 4 to 6 (6 7-inch calzones)

1. Heat the oil in a large skillet over medium-high heat. Add the garlic and cook 1 minute. Stir in the zucchini, red pepper, and pine nuts. Sauté until the vegetables are tender yet still slightly crisp, about 7 minutes. Stir in the tomato sauce, season with the black pepper, then cook 1 minute more. Remove from the heat and let cool completely. The filling can be made up to 24 hours in advance and chilled. Bring to room temperature before using.
2. If you are making the dough from scratch, prepare the pizza dough as directed. After it has risen, punch it down and knead it a few times. If you are using purchased bread dough, go to the next step.
3. Preheat the oven to 375 degrees.
4. Continue with steps 5, 6, and 7 on pages 138 and 139 (Eggplant and Smoked Cheese Calzones).

EGGPLANT AND SMOKED CHEESE CALZONES

These folded pizzas are not difficult to make and are especially easy if you make the filling early in the day. If you are in a hurry, you can use a 1-pound package of store-bought frozen pizza or bread dough, thaw it, and proceed with step 5.

THE FILLING

1 tablespoon olive oil

1 medium onion, finely diced

2 garlic cloves, minced

1 16-ounce can tomatoes, finely chopped and drained, or 2 medium tomatoes, cored, seeded, and finely chopped

1 medium (1 pound) eggplant, peeled and finely diced

1 green pepper, cored and finely diced

½ teaspoon dried oregano

½ teaspoon salt

½ teaspoon sugar

Generous seasoning of freshly ground pepper

1 teaspoon balsamic or red wine vinegar

....

Pizza dough (page 132), or 1 pound frozen bread dough, thawed

2½ cups (about 8 ounces) grated smoked Gouda or

1 Heat the oil in a large skillet over medium heat. Add the onion and garlic and sauté, tossing often, until the onion is very tender, about 10 minutes.

2 Stir in all the remaining filling ingredients. Cover the pan and cook for 15 minutes, or until the eggplant is very tender. Stir occasionally. Remove the cover and cook away any juices that may have accumulated. Remove from the heat and let cool. The filling may be prepared and chilled up to 24 hours in advance. Bring to room temperature before using.

3 If making the dough from scratch, prepare the pizza dough as directed. After it has risen, punch it down and knead it a few times.

4 Preheat the oven to 375 degrees.

5 Divide the dough into 6 pieces, then roll each piece into a ball. With a rolling pin, flatten one ball into a 6- or 7-inch circle. Place a small cup of water beside you, dip your finger into the water, and moisten the outer edges of the circle. Place a sixth of the eggplant filling on half of the circle, then top with a sixth of the grated cheese. Fold the dough over the filling to make a turnover or half-moon shape. Pinch and roll the edges closed.

smoked mozzarella cheese

1 egg, beaten with
1 teaspoon water (egg wash)

Serves 4 to 6 (6 7-inch calzones)

6 With a pastry brush, lightly brush the top of the calzone with some of the beaten egg wash. Place on an oiled baking sheet, then make 5 more calzones. (You will probably need two baking sheets. In this case, bake on two oven racks, then switch halfway through cooking.)

7 Bake 25 minutes, or until golden brown. Let sit at least 20 minutes before serving. They should be served warm, not piping hot.

Note: Leftover calzones can be refrigerated and reheated a few days later; they'll still be great.

Quick PEPPER-OLIVE FOCACCIA

Rosemary-flecked dough makes a savory bed for a Mediterranean-style mélange of peppers and olives. This focaccia is my favorite.

1 tablespoon olive oil

4 garlic cloves, minced

1 large red bell pepper, thinly sliced into strips

1 large green bell pepper, thinly sliced into strips

8 oil-cured or 6 kalamata olives, pitted and sliced (see note, page 25)

....

1 pound frozen bread dough, thawed and at room temperature

½ teaspoon dried rosemary, crumbled

Generous seasoning of freshly ground pepper

2 tablespoons olive oil

½ cup plus 2 tablespoons grated Parmesan cheese

Serves 4

1 Heat the oil in a large skillet over medium heat. Add the garlic and cook 1 minute. Do not let it brown. Mix in the peppers and cook, stirring often, until very tender, about 10 minutes. Remove from the heat and stir in the olives. Let cool.

2 Place the thawed dough in a large bowl. Sprinkle on the rosemary, pepper, and 1 tablespoon of the olive oil; knead these into the dough until incorporated.

3 Preheat the oven to 400 degrees.

4 Roll and stretch the dough into a 9 × 12-inch rectangle, then place on a baking sheet. Spread the remaining tablespoon of olive oil all over the surface of the dough. Sprinkle on ½ cup of the cheese, then pat it down with your hand to help it adhere.

5 Place in the oven and bake until the cheese is a rich golden brown, about 12 minutes. Remove from the oven and spread the peppers all over the focaccia. Sprinkle on the remaining 2 tablespoons of cheese. Bake 7 more minutes. Cut into 4 squares and serve.

Quick SPICY EGGPLANT FOCACCIA

The crust in this focaccia develops a nutty flavor by having part of the Parmesan cheese kneaded into the dough before baking. For best flavor, serve this one warm rather than hot.

2 tablespoons olive oil

4 garlic cloves, minced

½ teaspoon crushed red pepper flakes

1 small (¾ pound) eggplant, peeled and cut into ½-inch dice

1 small green pepper, cut into ½-inch dice

1 cup tomato sauce, homemade or store-bought

½ teaspoon dried basil

2 teaspoons water

Salt

Freshly ground pepper

....

1 pound frozen bread dough, thawed and at room temperature

5 tablespoons grated Parmesan cheese

Flour for dusting

Serves 4

1 Heat the oil in a large skillet over medium heat. Add the garlic and red pepper flakes and cook for 1 minute, stirring constantly.

2 Stir in the eggplant, green pepper, tomato sauce, basil, water, and salt and pepper to taste. Cover the pan and cook, stirring occasionally, 15 to 20 minutes, or until the eggplant and pepper are tender and not at all crunchy. Because there isn't much liquid in this mixture, it will "steam" rather than simmer. Remove from the heat and let cool.

3 Preheat the oven to 400 degrees.

4 Place the thawed dough in a large bowl. Sprinkle on 2 tablespoons of the cheese and knead it into the dough. Roll the dough into a 9 × 12-inch rectangle, flouring the work surface as necessary. Place it on a baking sheet.

5 Bake the dough 10 minutes. Remove from the oven, then spread the eggplant mixture all over the dough. Sprinkle the remaining 3 tablespoons of Parmesan cheese on top of the eggplant.

6 Bake 10 more minutes, or until the dough is golden brown. Place the focaccia on a cutting board and cut into squares. Let cool about 15 minutes, serving it warm, not hot.

Quick LEEK AND GOAT CHEESE FOCACCIA

Madeleine Kamman, on her first-rate cooking show* Madeleine Cooks*, once used a combination of leeks, walnuts, and goat cheese on a pizza and thus inspired me to try it here. It is a fabulous medley of flavors, making a memorable focaccia. Don't hesitate to pack it for a picnic; it is delicious at room temperature.

2 medium-large leeks

2 teaspoons plus 1 tablespoon olive oil

¼ cup heavy cream

Salt

Freshly ground pepper

1 pound frozen bread dough, thawed and at room temperature

½ teaspoon dried thyme

Flour for dusting

2 tablespoons finely chopped walnuts

4 ounces garlic and herb or plain goat cheese, cut into small pieces

Serves 4

1 To clean the leeks, make a vertical slit in each along its length through to the back. Rinse under cold running water, flipping through the leaves with your fingers to rid them of all sand and dirt. Thinly slice the leeks, using as much green as possible, but avoiding the extra-thick outer leaves.

2 Heat the 2 teaspoons of olive oil in a medium-size skillet over medium heat. Add the leeks and sauté until tender, about 10 minutes. Add the cream and salt and pepper to taste and cook 2 minutes more, or just until the cream thickens.

3 Preheat the oven to 400 degrees.

4 Place the thawed dough in a large bowl. Evenly sprinkle on the thyme, then the remaining tablespoon of olive oil. Knead until incorporated. You can let it rest after a few minutes of kneading and it will absorb some oil, then knead a bit more. Roll the dough into a 9 × 12-inch rectangle, flouring the work surface as necessary to prevent sticking. Place the dough on a baking sheet.

5 Bake the dough 10 minutes. Remove from the oven, then spread the leeks all over the dough to within ½ inch of the edges. Sprinkle on the walnuts. Bake 10 more minutes. Remove from the oven and drop on the pieces of goat cheese. Bake 3 additional minutes, or until golden. Let cool a few minutes before serving. Serve cut into squares.

Quick BROCCOLI AND RICOTTA BOBOLI

Purchasing a premade boboli (cheese crust) makes this a snap to prepare.

1 tablespoon olive oil

4 garlic cloves, minced

4 cups tiny broccoli florets (from 1 small bunch broccoli)

⅓ cup water

2 scallions, very thinly sliced

Salt

Generous seasoning of freshly ground pepper

1 cup part-skim ricotta cheese

2 tablespoons chopped fresh basil, or 1 teaspoon dried

1 large (1 pound) boboli

1 cup grated part-skim mozzarella cheese

Serves 4

1 Heat the oil in a large skillet over medium heat. Add the garlic and sauté 2 minutes. Stir in the broccoli and toss to coat with the garlic. Pour in the water and cover the pan. Steam the broccoli until tender, still bright green but not crunchy, about 7 minutes.

2 Remove the cover and stir in the scallions, salt, and pepper. Cook until all the liquid has evaporated, just a few more minutes. Set aside to cool.

3 Preheat the oven to 450 degrees.

4 Combine the ricotta and basil in a small bowl. Spread it on the boboli, then place the boboli on a baking sheet. Spoon the broccoli all over the top; cover with the mozzarella cheese.

5 Bake 10 to 12 minutes, or until the crust is golden and the cheese is sizzling. Cut into 8 wedges.

SUMPTUOUS SANDWICHES

A great sandwich needs great bread—there's no getting around it. Lackluster bread that isn't engaging enough to be enjoyed alone won't be much improved with a filling between slices. Whether it's French bread, slices of loaf bread, or rolls, bread must have texture and substance along with a fresh flavor.

Vegetarian sandwiches do take a little more time to prepare than traditional cold-cut fare, but the results are worth the effort. The vegetables, cheeses, and herbs impart wonderful flavors, making these sandwiches appealing enough for light dinners.

Strive for an attractive presentation when you prepare a sandwich. Curly green-leaf lettuce that extends outside the

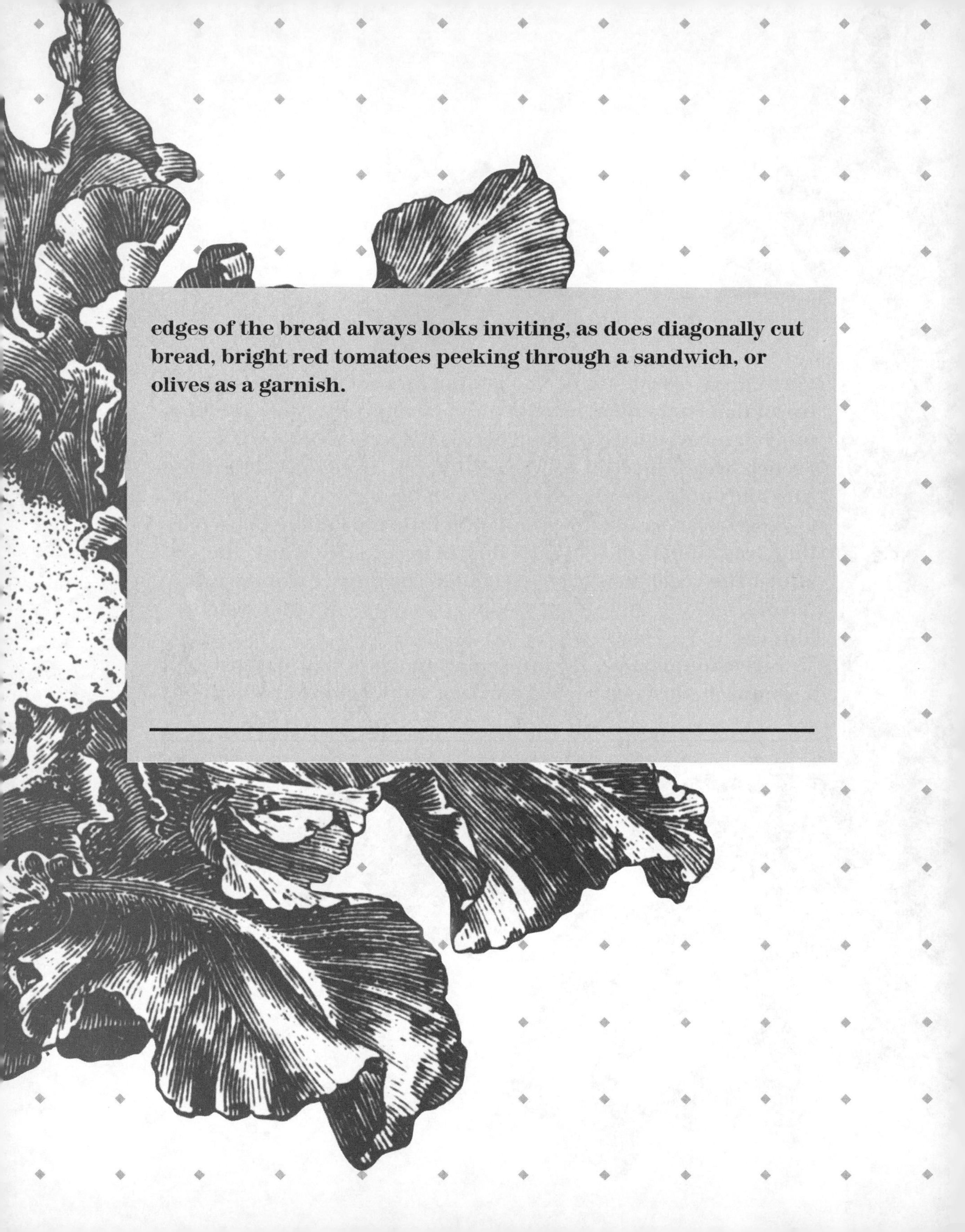

edges of the bread always looks inviting, as does diagonally cut bread, bright red tomatoes peeking through a sandwich, or olives as a garnish.

Quick

EGGPLANT, FETA CHEESE, AND TOMATO SANDWICHES

Layered with fresh basil, this sandwich's outstanding flavor will please you for days.

¼ cup bread crumbs (approximately)

1 medium (1 pound) eggplant, skin left on and cut into ¼-inch slices

7 tablespoons olive oil

1 loaf French bread or crusty peasant bread

Freshly ground pepper

4 ounces feta cheese, thinly sliced

2 medium tomatoes, thinly sliced

16 fresh basil leaves

Serves 4

1 Preheat the broiler. Place the bread crumbs on a small plate. Brush both sides of each eggplant slice with oil, using 3 tablespoons in all. Press both sides of the eggplant into the bread crumbs, then place on a baking sheet. Broil until golden brown, turn, and brown the other side. Set the eggplant aside to cool.

2 Cut the bread in half horizontally so the crust makes up the top and bottom of each sandwich. Cut the loaf into 4 portions.

3 To assemble each sandwich, drizzle 1 tablespoon of the olive oil on the inside of the bread, then season generously with pepper. Place a quarter of the feta cheese slices on the bread, top with a quarter of the tomato slices, tear up 4 basil leaves into small pieces and sprinkle them on the tomato, then place a few eggplant slices on top. Cover with the top of the bread and slice the sandwich in half.

CORNBREAD AND JALAPEÑO PEPPER CHEESE SANDWICHES

Here is a simple idea for a sandwich that works well because the foods it combines—cornbread and jalapeño pepper cheese—are perfectly compatible. Make the cornbread the night before or early in the morning so it has ample time to cool. The sandwiches can be served alone or accompanied by some marinated vegetables or lightly tossed greens.

THE CORNBREAD

Butter for greasing

¾ cup unbleached white flour

¼ cup whole wheat flour

1 cup cornmeal

1 tablespoon baking powder

½ teaspoon salt

¼ cup sugar

1 egg, beaten

1¼ cups low-fat milk

3 tablespoons butter, melted and cooled

....

8 ounces (brick) Monterey Jack cheese with jalapeño peppers, thinly sliced (about 32 slices)

Serves 6 to 8

1 Preheat the oven to 400 degrees (375 degrees if your baking dish is glass). Butter a 12 × 7 × 2-inch baking pan or dish (see note) and set aside.

2 In a large bowl, combine the two flours, cornmeal, baking powder, salt, and sugar.

3 Thoroughly combine the egg, milk, and melted butter in another bowl. Pour this mixture into the dry ingredients and stir just until blended. Do not overbeat. Scrape into the prepared pan and bake 20 to 25 minutes, or until golden on top. Cool completely on a wire rack.

4 Cut the cornbread into 16 pieces about 2 × 3 inches. Cut each piece in half horizontally, then place a few thin slices of cheese on each bottom half. Cover with the top slice of bread to make small sandwiches.

Note: This makes a low cornbread, suitable for sandwiches. If you want to make it to serve plain rather than in sandwiches, use an 8 × 8-inch pan and cook 25 minutes.

PORTOBELLO MUSHROOM, TOMATO, AND BASIL SANDWICHES

You can grill these giant Portobello mushrooms instead of sautéing them by removing the stems and brushing both sides with olive oil. Grill them about 3 minutes on each side. Whether you sauté or grill them, you'll have a knockout of a sandwich.

4 tablespoons olive oil

8 ounces Portobello mushrooms, sliced ½-inch thick

2 teaspoons balsamic vinegar

1 small garlic clove, pressed or minced

3 7-inch pieces narrow French bread, each sliced horizontally

6 tomato slices, each cut in half

9 basil leaves

Salt

Freshly ground pepper

Serves 3

1 Heat 1 tablespoon of the olive oil in a large skillet over medium heat. Add the mushrooms and sauté until brown and juicy, about 10 minutes.

2 Meanwhile, in a small dish combine the remaining 3 tablespoons oil with the vinegar and garlic and stir to blend.

3 If the French bread isn't absolutely fresh and crisp, heat it in the oven a few minutes, until just hot.

4 To assemble the sandwiches, spread ⅙ of the oil and vinegar mixture on each half of French bread. On each bottom half of the bread, layer ⅓ of the mushrooms, tomato slices, and basil leaves. Season with salt and pepper and top with the remaining bread. Slice the sandwiches in half and serve immediately.

Quick

HUMMUS-STUFFED PITA BREAD SANDWICHES

This sandwich has become almost standard fare on menus in vegetarian restaurants, and because it is so good when well made, I decided to include it here. When hummus is used as a spread, it should be thicker than the traditional dip consistency, so be cautious when adding the water to avoid making it too thin. Conversely, if you want to turn the leftover hummus spread into a dip, thin it with a little water.

1 cup cooked chickpeas (either home-cooked or rinsed canned chickpeas)

½ cup tahini

1 large garlic clove, minced

Juice of 1 lemon (3 to 4 tablespoons)

¼ teaspoon salt

¼ to ⅓ cup cold water

....

4 6-inch pita breads (see note)

Thinly sliced cucumber

Thinly sliced red onion

Thinly sliced tomato (optional)

Alfalfa sprouts or leaf lettuce

Serves 4

1 To make the hummus, combine the chickpeas, tahini, garlic, lemon juice, and salt in a food processor. Process until smooth. Slowly pour in ¼ cup water and process again. Check the consistency; it should be spreadable, not runny. Add more water if it is too thick. Scrape into a bowl.

2 Cut the pita breads in half to make two pockets. Heat in a toaster or oven just to soften. Let cool slightly.

3 Spread hummus in each pocket. Fill with some cucumber slices, red onion, tomato, and sprouts.

Note: This sandwich is also delicious on sliced whole grain bread.

FRENCH BREAD WITH GOAT CHEESE AND RED PEPPER RELISH

This winning combination can be turned into hors d'oeuvres by slicing the French bread intothin rounds and making a small version of this open-face sandwich.

1 tablespoon olive oil

2 medium onions, finely diced

2 red bell peppers, finely diced

1 teaspoon sugar

2 teaspoons balsamic or red wine vinegar

Salt

Generous seasoning of freshly ground pepper

½ to 1 teaspoon capers

....

1 loaf French bread

4 ounces goat cheese

Serves 4

1 To make the pepper relish, heat the oil in a large skillet over medium-high heat. Add the onions and sauté until tender and beginning to brown, about 10 minutes.

2 Stir in the peppers and cook 10 more minutes, stirring often. Mix in the sugar, vinegar, salt, and pepper. Reduce the heat to medium, cover the pan, and cook until the mixture is very soft and the juices are somewhat caramelized, not watery, about 20 more minutes. Stir occasionally.

3 Scrape the mixture into a bowl, then stir in the capers. Let cool completely; chill until ready to use. Bring the relish back to room temperature before serving.

4 Slice the French bread horizontally and cut into 3- to 4-inch lengths. Heat in a 400-degree oven until slightly crisp (not hard).

5 Spread some goat cheese on each piece, then top with a spoonful of the pepper relish.

Quick HERBED MUSHROOM SPREAD SANDWICHES

Succulent mushrooms laced with herbs make a sumptuous base for sandwiches. I especially like this spread on toast made from a good-quality Vienna or Italian bread.

2 teaspoons olive oil

12 ounces mushrooms, finely chopped (about 4 cups)

1 teaspoon tamari soy sauce

¼ teaspoon dried thyme

¼ teaspoon dried oregano

¼ teaspoon dried dill

Freshly ground pepper to taste

1 tablespoon mayonnaise, plus extra for spreading

1½ tablespoons very thinly sliced celery

6 slices bread (preferably Vienna or Italian)

3 pieces green leaf lettuce

Serves 3

1 Heat the oil in a large skillet over medium-high heat. Add the mushrooms and sauté them, tossing often, until their juices have been released and then evaporate, about 10 minutes.

2 Stir in the tamari, herbs, and pepper to taste and cook until the mushrooms begin to stick to the pan, about 2 minutes more. Scrape the mixture into a bowl and cool to room temperature. Stir in the tablespoon of mayonnaise and the celery and chill until ready to serve.

3 Lightly toast the bread. Spread each piece with a very thin layer of mayonnaise. Divide the mushrooms and spread on 3 of the bread slices. Top with the lettuce and remaining bread. Slice the sandwiches in half diagonally and serve.

Quick Broiled Tomato and Mozzarella Sandwiches

These open-face sandwiches capture the fresh taste of the tomatoes and herbs with sweet mozzarella cheese as the perfect backdrop. Be certain to serve them right from the oven so the cheese stays soft.

French bread sliced horizontally, or slices of firm bread such as sourdough

Olive oil

Very thinly sliced part-skim mozzarella cheese

Thin tomato slices

Dried basil

Dried oregano

Freshly ground pepper

Grated Parmesan cheese

1 Preheat the broiler. Lightly toast whichever bread you choose, then brush the top of each piece with a little olive oil. Place the bread on a baking sheet.

2 Place a few slices of mozzarella cheese on the bread (you don't need much). Top with the tomato slices. Generously sprinkle basil, oregano, and pepper on the tomato. Sprinkle Parmesan cheese all over the tomato. Broil the sandwiches until the mozzarella is melted and bubbly and the Parmesan cheese has turned golden brown. Serve immediately.

Quick VEGETABLE SUBS

These submarine (hero) sandwiches are a staple in my family. We rely on them for lunch more than any other sandwich because they are so easy and so satisfying. The added bonus is that they are equally popular with any meat lover who joins us for lunch.

Submarine, grinder, or hero rolls

Vinaigrette salad dressing

Mayonnaise

Freshly ground black pepper

Thinly sliced Muenster, Swiss, or provolone cheese

Thinly sliced tomato

Thinly sliced red onion

Thinly sliced green or red bell pepper strips

Romaine or leaf lettuce

Optional additions: sliced black olives, sliced pickles, sliced pickled peppers

1 Slice the rolls almost all the way through. Heat them briefly in a 350-degree oven if they are not perfectly fresh.

2 Open the rolls and spread a very thin coating of vinaigrette on each half, then top with a thin layer of mayonnaise and some black pepper. Layer all the remaining ingredients on the rolls, being careful not to overstuff them. Close the sandwiches and slice in half.

Quick

CUCUMBER, RED ONION, AND SPROUTS SANDWICH

Here is another sandwich that I frequently serve my family. It is especially convenient because we always seem to have the ingredients on hand. This trio of vegetables works well together, and it is enhanced in a sandwich made with whole grain toast, although other breads such as crusty rolls work well, too. If you are not an onion lover, just omit it and you'll still have a delicious sandwich.

Sliced whole wheat or sourdough bread

Mayonnaise

Cucumber, peeled and cut into ⅓-inch slices

Freshly ground black pepper

Red onion, very thinly sliced

Alfalfa sprouts

Toast the bread. Spread with some mayonnaise. Layer on the cucumber, black pepper, onion, and sprouts. Top with slices of toast to make sandwiches. Slice in half diagonally and serve.

Quick

HERBED CREAM CHEESE SPREAD AND CUCUMBER SANDWICHES

You can certainly experiment with different combinations of herbs, but my favorite mixture is the one below where the flavors blend and none is too overpowering.

8 ounces Neufchâtel (light cream cheese), at room temperature

1½ tablespoons low-fat milk

2 scallions, very thinly sliced, or 3 tablespoons very finely chopped red onion

2 tablespoons minced fresh parsley

1 teaspoon minced fresh dill, or ¼ teaspoon dried

1 teaspoon minced fresh thyme, or ¼ teaspoon dried

1 teaspoon minced fresh basil, or ¼ teaspoon dried

Generous seasoning of freshly ground pepper

Dash of salt

8 slices whole grain bread

1 cucumber, peeled and cut into ¼-inch slices

Serves 4

1 In a large bowl, work the cream cheese and milk together with a fork until blended, then beat it until smooth. Stir in the scallions, herbs, pepper, and salt. Cover and chill at least 1 hour for the flavors to meld.

2 To make each sandwich, spread the mixture on both slices of bread and place the cucumber slices in between.

BREAKFAST AND BRUNCH

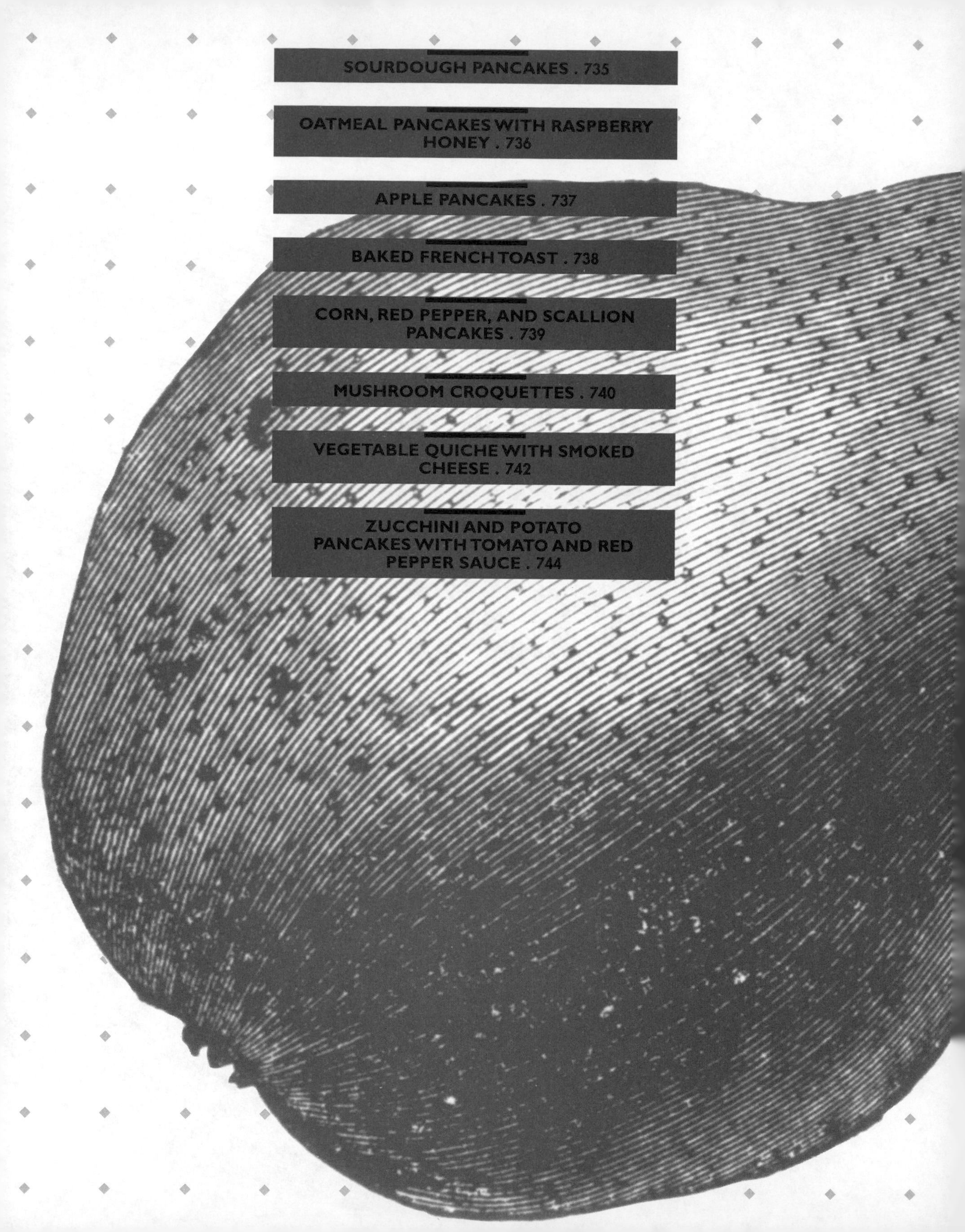

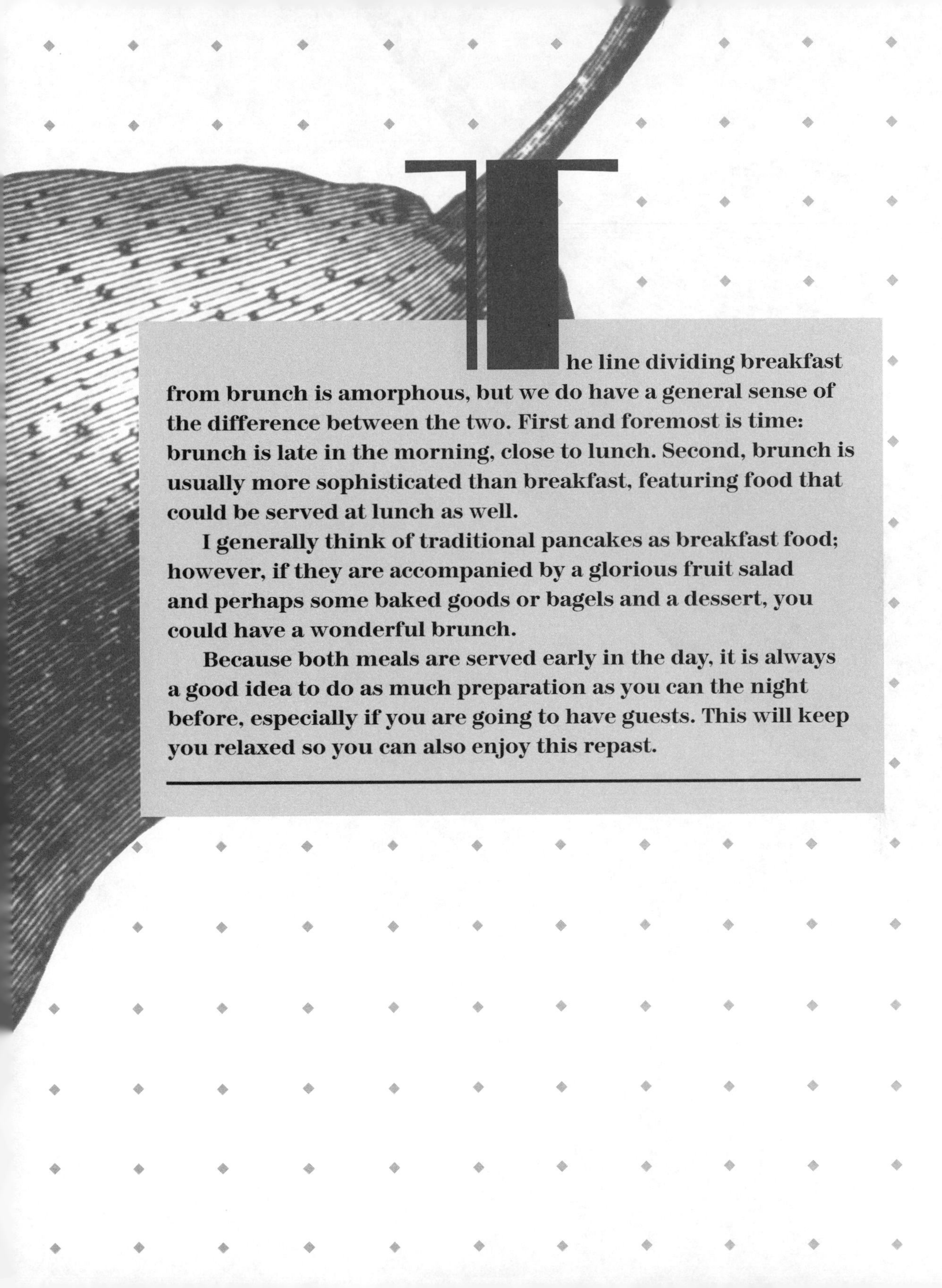

The line dividing breakfast from brunch is amorphous, but we do have a general sense of the difference between the two. First and foremost is time: brunch is late in the morning, close to lunch. Second, brunch is usually more sophisticated than breakfast, featuring food that could be served at lunch as well.

I generally think of traditional pancakes as breakfast food; however, if they are accompanied by a glorious fruit salad and perhaps some baked goods or bagels and a dessert, you could have a wonderful brunch.

Because both meals are served early in the day, it is always a good idea to do as much preparation as you can the night before, especially if you are going to have guests. This will keep you relaxed so you can also enjoy this repast.

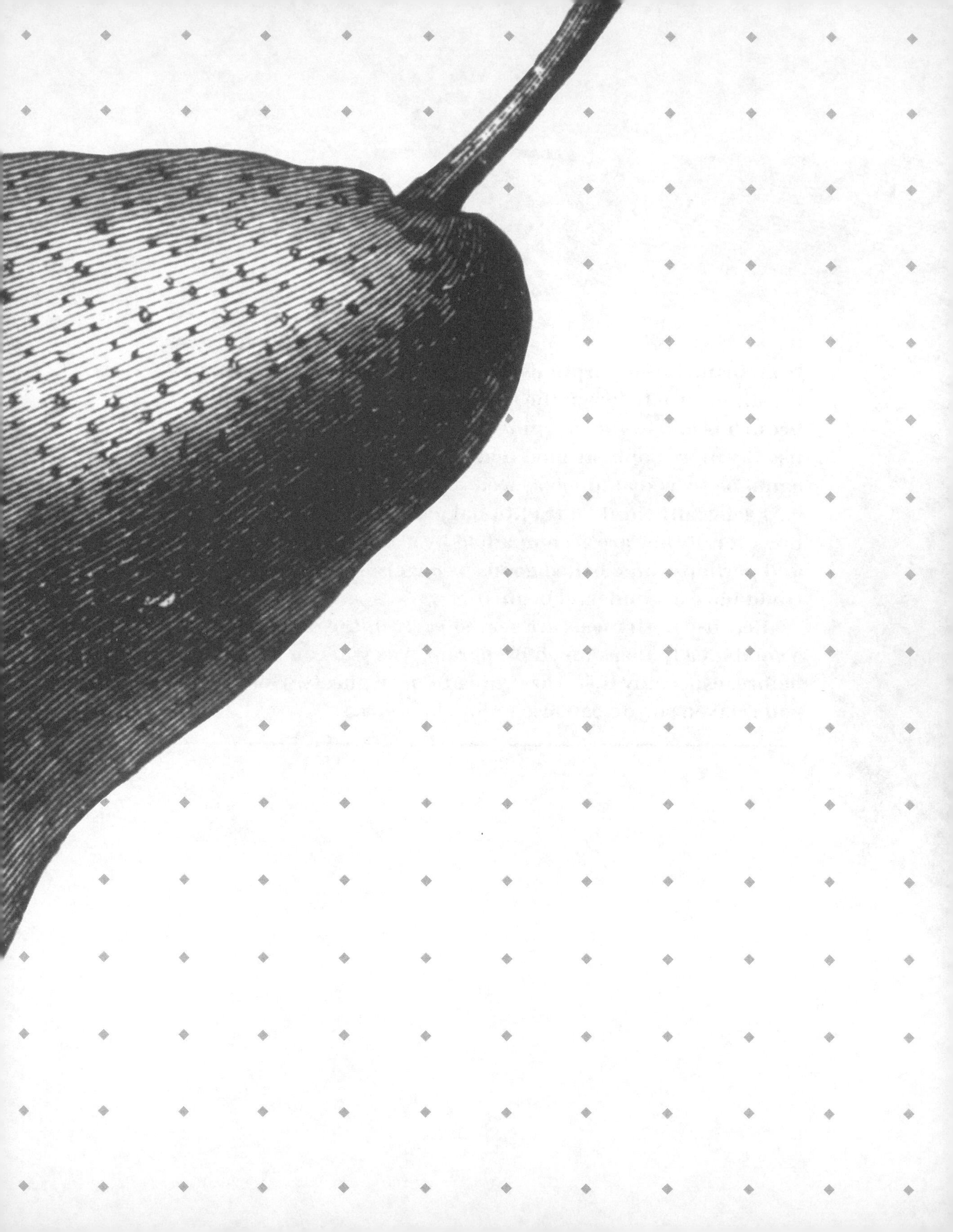

SOURDOUGH PANCAKES

These light, tasty sourdough pancakes are quicker to prepare in the morning than traditional pancakes because half the work is done the day before.

THE STARTER

1 tablespoon active dry yeast

1½ cups warm water

2 teaspoons sugar

1 cup unbleached white flour

½ cup whole wheat flour

THE ADDITIONS

¾ teaspoon baking powder

¾ teaspoon salt

4 teaspoons sugar

2 eggs, lightly beaten

2 tablespoons milk

3 tablespoons butter, melted

Serves 4 to 6

1 Combine the yeast, water, and sugar in a large bowl and stir to blend. Let sit 5 minutes. Stir in the two flours and mix until smooth. Let sit, uncovered, for 2 hours. Cover the bowl with plastic wrap and refrigerate for 24 hours.

2 Whisk in the baking powder, salt, and sugar, then whisk in the eggs, milk, and butter; beat until smooth.

3 Heat a lightly greased skillet or griddle over medium heat. Add enough batter to make 4-inch pancakes and flip when bubbles have burst on the top of each pancake. They should be golden brown on each side when done. Serve with maple syrup.

OATMEAL PANCAKES WITH RASPBERRY HONEY

Adding oat flour to bread products gives them a wonderful flavor and texture, and these pancakes are a good example of that. In the past, only maple syrup would adorn my pancakes because I love its flavor so much, but this raspberry honey is so delicious and has such a captivating color that it has become a competing favorite.

RASPBERRY HONEY

1 cup fresh or frozen raspberries

1 cup honey

3 tablespoons water

½ teaspoon grated lemon rind

THE PANCAKES

½ cup oats

1 cup unbleached flour

½ teaspoon salt

3 tablespoons sugar

1¾ teaspoons baking powder

1 egg

3 tablespoons butter, melted and cooled

1½ cups low-fat milk

Serves 3 to 4

1. To make the raspberry honey, combine the berries, half the honey, and the water in a medium-size saucepan. Bring to a simmer and cook, stirring often, for 15 minutes.
2. Strain the honey through a sieve and press as many solids through as possible. Discard the seeds. Beat in the remaining honey and the lemon rind and let cool.
3. To make the pancakes, place the oats in a blender and grind until powdery. Pour them into a large bowl, then thoroughly mix in the flour, salt, sugar, and baking powder.
4. Beat the egg in a medium-size bowl. Beat in the butter and milk until blended. Pour this into the flour mixture and stir until thoroughly combined, but don't overmix it. Let the batter sit 5 minutes.
5. Heat a large skillet or griddle over medium heat until a drop of water sizzles when flicked on it. Make 3½-inch pancakes, flipping them over once bubbles have burst on the top. Serve with the raspberry honey.

APPLE PANCAKES

The memorable apple pancakes at Martin's restaurant in Great Barrington, Massachusetts, are the inspiration for these pancakes. They are always a big hit because the caramelized apples give them so much flavor. If you sauté the apples the night before, it will simplify your morning work. Also, don't hesitate to serve these for supper; they are the perfect comfort food.

THE APPLES

3 medium-size apples (any variety except Granny Smith or Golden Delicious, which are too firm)

1 tablespoon unsalted butter

1 tablespoon firmly packed brown sugar

½ teaspoon cinnamon

¼ teaspoon grated nutmeg

½ teaspoon vanilla extract

THE PANCAKES

1½ cups unbleached flour (or substitute ½ cup whole wheat flour for ½ cup white flour)

1½ teaspoons baking powder

1 tablespoon sugar

½ teaspoon salt

1 egg

1½ cups low-fat milk

3 tablespoons butter, melted and cooled

Serves 3 to 4

1 Peel and core the apples, then very thinly slice them.

2 Melt the butter in a large skillet over medium heat. Add the apple slices and sauté until they begin to soften, about 5 minutes. Add the brown sugar, cinnamon, and nutmeg and sauté, tossing often, until very tender, about 7 more minutes. Sprinkle on the vanilla, toss, then spoon onto a plate and let cool.

3 To make the batter, thoroughly combine the flour, baking powder, sugar, and salt in a large bowl. In a separate bowl, beat the egg, then stir in the milk and melted butter. Pour this into the flour mixture and stir until combined. Stir in the cooled apples.

4 Lightly oil a griddle or large skillet and heat over medium heat until it is hot enough for a drop of water to dance on it. Spoon on some batter to make 3-inch pancakes. Flip when bubbles form and burst on top. Cook until golden. Serve with maple syrup.

Quick BAKED FRENCH TOAST

This has become one of my favorite breakfast preparations when entertaining because the little time needed to prepare this dish is spent the night before, thereby allowing me a hassle-free morning with a substantial breakfast. Great when you have houseguests.

Butter for greasing

6 slices firm bread (such as sourdough)

5 eggs

1½ cups low-fat milk

2 teaspoons vanilla extract

1 teaspoon ground cinnamon

⅛ teaspoon grated nutmeg

THE TOPPING

4 tablespoons unsalted butter, softened

⅓ cup firmly packed light brown sugar

½ cup finely chopped walnuts

Serves 4 to 6

1 Generously butter a 12 × 7 × 2-inch baking dish (such as a rectangular Pyrex). Lay the bread slices in the dish, cutting slices to fill the spaces.

2 Beat the eggs in a large bowl. Beat in the milk, vanilla, cinnamon, and nutmeg. Pour over the bread, making sure it is submerged. Cover the dish and refrigerate overnight.

3 To make the topping, combine the butter, brown sugar, and walnuts in a small bowl. Keep at room temperature until you are ready to bake the French toast.

4 Preheat the oven to 350 degrees.

5 With a knife, spread the topping all over the bread. Bake 40 minutes, or until puffed and golden. Let sit 10 minutes before cutting. Cut into squares and serve with maple syrup. (Leftover French toast is delicious reheated; just bake until hot.)

CORN, RED PEPPER, AND SCALLION PANCAKES

Jam-packed with vegetables, these tasty pancakes need only a spoonful of salsa and a dot of sour cream for a special brunch or dinner offering. Great served with home fries.

1 tablespoon vegetable oil

1 medium red bell pepper, cored and finely diced

4 scallions, thinly sliced

4 eggs

⅔ cup milk

1¼ cups unbleached flour

1¼ teaspoons baking powder

¾ teaspoon salt

1 teaspoon sugar

Freshly ground pepper

2 cups frozen corn kernels, thawed

Vegetable oil for frying

Salsa

Sour cream

Serves 3 to 4 (9 4-inch pancakes)

1 Heat the oil in a large skillet over medium heat. Add the bell pepper and scallions and sauté just until the pepper is tender, about 7 minutes. Set aside to cool.

2 Beat the eggs in a large bowl. Beat in the milk. Add the flour, baking powder, salt, sugar, and pepper and mix just until combined. Stir in the cooled vegetables and the corn.

3 Coat a large frying pan with a very thin layer of oil and heat over medium heat until hot. Cook about 3 pancakes at a time using about ¼ cup batter per pancake. The pancakes are done when they are golden brown on both sides and cooked through. Serve with a large spoonful of salsa on top of each pancake and a tiny spoonful of sour cream on the salsa.

Note: Leftover uncooked batter can be refrigerated and used the next day.

MUSHROOM CROQUETTES

A crisp coating encases a creamy center of mushrooms in a cheese sauce, making these croquettes a wonderful alternative to eggs for brunch. Make the filling the night before so you can have an easy morning before the guests arrive. For an accompaniment, toss diced sweet potatoes with oil and bake for 30 minutes.

1 tablespoon olive oil

1 medium onion, very finely diced

1 pound mushrooms, finely chopped (4 cups)

½ teaspoon dried thyme

3 tablespoons unsalted butter

5 tablespoons unbleached flour

¾ cup low-fat milk

1 egg yolk

¼ cup grated Parmesan cheese

½ teaspoon salt

Freshly ground black pepper

Pinch of grated nutmeg

2 tablespoons minced fresh parsley

---

1 egg, beaten

1 cup bread crumbs

Oil for frying

Serves 4

1 Heat the oil in a large skillet over medium-high heat. Add the onion and sauté until tender, about 5 minutes. Stir in the mushrooms and thyme and cook, stirring often, until the mushrooms release their juices and then the juices evaporate, about 15 minutes. The mushrooms are done when they begin to stick to the pan. Remove the pan from the heat and let the mushrooms cool.

2 Melt the butter in a medium-size saucepan over medium heat. Whisk in the flour and cook, whisking constantly, for 2 minutes. Whisk in the milk and cook until it gets very thick, about 2 more minutes. Remove the sauce from the heat and let cool 5 minutes.

3 Whisk the egg yolk into the sauce. Using a spoon, stir in the Parmesan cheese, salt, pepper, nutmeg, and parsley. Stir in the mushrooms, then cover the pot and chill until very cold, at least 2 hours or up to 24 hours.

4 To bread the croquettes, place the beaten egg in a small soup bowl and place the bread crumbs in another small bowl. Using a ¼-cup measure, scoop up a scant ¼ cup of the mushroom mixture, roughly shape it into a 2½ × 3-inch log with your hands, then place it in the beaten egg. Roll it over to coat evenly, then roll it in the bread crumbs. Place the croquettes on a large plate as you finish breading them. These can be kept at room temperature for an hour before you fry them.

5 Pour about ¼ inch of oil into a large skillet. Heat over medium-high heat until the oil sizzles when a tiny bread crumb is dropped into it. In batches, fry the croquettes on both sides until golden brown. Drain on paper towels. You can keep the croquettes warm in a 325-degree oven up to 30 minutes.

VEGETABLE QUICHE WITH SMOKED CHEESE

Almost any combination of precooked vegetables would be delectable in this quiche. Strive for contrasting colors, and don't hesitate to try spinach, mushrooms, red pepper, or zucchini.

THE CRUST

Ice cubes

1 glass water

1 cup unbleached flour

¼ cup whole wheat flour

¼ teaspoon salt

5 tablespoons unsalted butter, chilled and cut into bits

2 tablespoons vegetable oil

THE FILLING

1 tablespoon olive oil

1 medium onion, finely diced

1 garlic clove, minced

½ cup diced yellow squash

1 cup tiny broccoli florets

1 tomato, seeded and diced

¼ teaspoon dried basil

¼ teaspoon dried marjoram

3 eggs

1¼ cups milk

½ teaspoon salt

1 To make the crust, place some ice cubes in a glass of water and set aside. In a large bowl, combine the two flours and salt. Add the butter bits and toss to coat. With your fingertips, quickly rub the butter into the flour until coarse crumbs form. You don't want the butter to be perfectly blended. Pour on the oil and toss to blend.

2 Sprinkle on 3 tablespoons of the ice water, toss, then gather the dough into a ball. If it is too dry, sprinkle on an additional tablespoon of water. Knead the dough two or three times to make it smooth. Gather it into a ball, flatten it into a disk, then wrap with plastic wrap. Chill 10 minutes, or until slightly firm.

3 On a lightly floured surface, roll the dough large enough to fit a 10-inch quiche pan. Fill the pan with the pastry, pushing it ¼ inch above the rim of the pan to allow for shrinkage. Prick all over with a fork. Freeze the crust for 30 minutes, or cover and freeze up to 1 month.

4 Preheat the oven to 375 degrees.

5 Line the piecrust with foil. Cover the bottom with pie weights or dried beans to prevent shrinkage. Bake the crust for 12 minutes, remove

Freshly ground pepper

½ cup grated smoked Gouda cheese

½ cup grated Swiss cheese

Serves 4

the foil and weights, then bake 3 minutes more. Let cool while making the filling.

6 Heat the oil in a large skillet over medium heat. Add the onion and garlic and sauté for 5 minutes. Stir in the squash, broccoli, and 2 tablespoons of water. Cover the pan and steam until tender. Remove the cover and boil away any remaining water. Stir in the tomato and herbs and sauté 1 minute. Set aside to cool.

7 Beat the eggs in a large bowl. Beat in the milk, salt, and pepper.

8 Sprinkle the smoked and Swiss cheeses over the bottom of the piecrust. Arrange the vegetables over the cheeses. Carefully pour in the egg mixture, being certain not to overfill the pie. (Leftover custard can be baked in a buttered custard cup.) Bake for 35 to 40 minutes, or until a knife inserted in the center of the quiche comes out clean and the top is golden. Let the quiche sit for 15 minutes before cutting and serving. Quiche is most delicious served warm, not hot.

ZUCCHINI AND POTATO PANCAKES WITH TOMATO AND RED PEPPER SAUCE

You can grate the zucchini in advance, but don't make the batter until you are ready to start cooking. I like to serve egg noodles with these pancakes.

THE SAUCE

1 tablespoon olive oil

1 small onion, minced

1 small red bell pepper, cored and finely diced

1 large tomato, cored, seeded, and diced (1 cup)

Salt

Freshly ground pepper

THE PANCAKES

3 cups grated zucchini (2 medium)

1 8-ounce baking potato, peeled and grated

2 tablespoons grated onion

3 tablespoons unbleached flour

1 tablespoon grated Parmesan cheese

1 egg, beaten

½ teaspoon dried basil

½ teaspoon salt

Freshly ground pepper

Oil for frying

Serves 3 (12 3-inch pancakes)

1 To make the sauce, heat the oil in a medium skillet over medium heat. Add the onion and red pepper and sauté 5 minutes. Stir in the tomato and salt and pepper to taste and cook until there is a nice sauce consistency and the juices have thickened, about 15 minutes. Keep warm until needed.

2 To make the pancakes, place the zucchini in a cotton kitchen towel and gather it into a ball. Squeeze out all the juices. Place the zucchini in a large bowl.

3 Stir in all the remaining pancake ingredients except the oil. Heat a very thin layer of oil in a large skillet over medium-high heat. Fill a ¼-cup measure with batter for each pancake and drop on the skillet. Flatten with a spatula to make thin pancakes. Fry on both sides until a rich golden brown. As they finish cooking, keep warm on a baking sheet in a 350-degree oven until completed. Serve with a spoonful of sauce on each.

ESPECIALLY FOR ENTERTAINING

Although I have been exceedingly fond of quick recipes in recent years, every now and then I get the yen to prepare an elaborate meal for friends and immerse myself in the process of cooking. The recipes in this section are generally more involved than others in this book and are good choices when you want to serve something extra special.

When I taught cooking, I would always encourage my students to divide time-consuming recipes into segments. Rather than feel you have to cook uninterruptedly, start early in the day and perform a few steps like chopping vegetables and grating cheese, then come back to the recipe later. This approach makes demanding recipes quite easy.

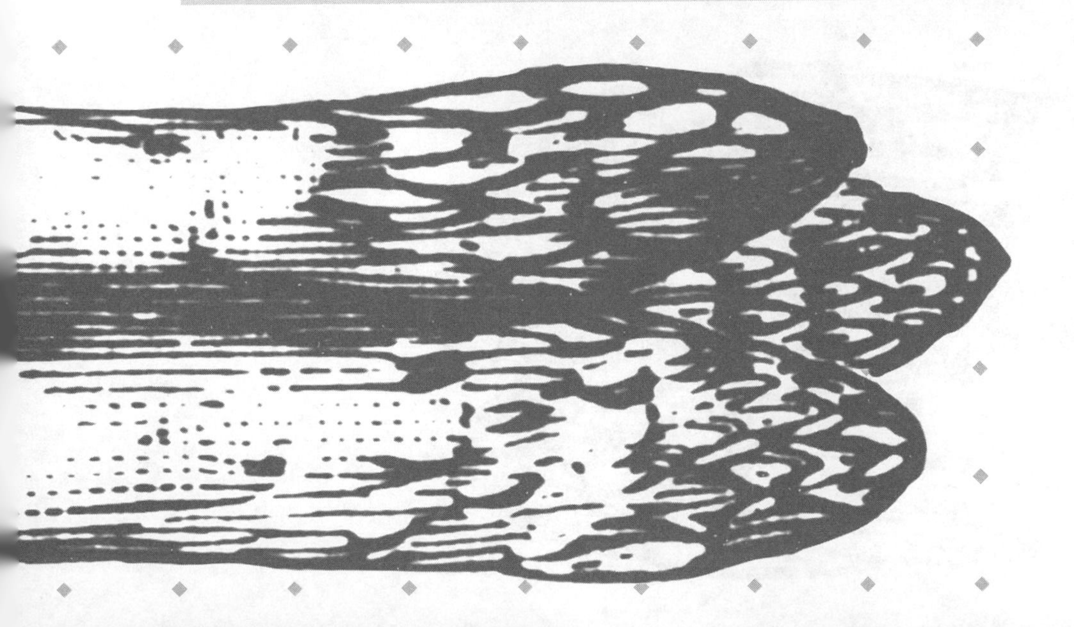

I have given suggestions for side dishes for most of these recipes. Add a salad and a special dessert and you'll have elegant meatless dinners.

CARAMELIZED ONION TART

Long slow cooking gives the onions a rich brown color and a fabulous sweet flavor. Serve this tart alongside a pilaf and perhaps a colorful steamed vegetable such as green beans or carrots.

3 tablespoons unsalted butter

4 pounds onions, thinly sliced (about 16 cups)

¼ teaspoon dried thyme

½ teaspoon salt

Freshly ground pepper

1 sheet frozen puff pastry (half a 17¼-ounce box), thawed

Serves 4 to 6

1 Melt the butter in a large pot over medium heat. Stir in the onions and thyme and cook, stirring frequently, until the onions are brown and jam-like, about 1 hour. Season with salt and pepper and scrape into a bowl to cool. (Can be prepared, cooled, covered, and chilled for up to 24 hours.)

2 Roll the puff pastry sheet into an 11-inch square. Place it in a 9-inch tart pan with a removable bottom and trim off the excess. Freeze 30 minutes, or place in a plastic bag and freeze up to 24 hours.

3 Preheat the oven to 425 degrees.

4 Scrape the onion mixture into the tart shell. Bake 25 minutes, or until the crust is golden brown. Cool slightly, then remove the outer rim. Serve warm rather than piping hot.

HOMEMADE MUSHROOM AND GOAT CHEESE RAVIOLI WITH GINGER CREAM SAUCE

The person who first thought of using wonton wrappers to make homemade ravioli and tortellini is brilliant. They are easy to use and make a delicate casing, thereby allowing you time to experiment with fillings. This is a wonderfully elegant dish—a good choice for a special occasion. Serve it with a salad of baby greens and some hot, crusty bread.

1 tablespoon olive oil

4 garlic cloves, minced

1 pound mushrooms, minced (about 4½ cups)

¼ teaspoon dried thyme

Pinch of grated nutmeg

⅛ teaspoon salt

Generous seasoning of freshly ground pepper

1 tablespoon minced fresh parsley

⅓ cup (packed) goat cheese

1 16-ounce package wonton wrappers (about 60 wrappers)

1 egg yolk, beaten with 1 teaspoon water (egg wash)

THE SAUCE

½ tablespoon unsalted butter

1 tablespoon minced fresh ginger

1 garlic clove, minced

1 To make the filling, heat the oil in a large skillet over medium-high heat. Add the garlic and cook until lightly golden, about 2 minutes. Do not let it brown. Stir in the mushrooms, thyme, nutmeg, salt, and pepper and sauté until the juices are released and then evaporate, about 15 minutes. The mixture will begin to stick to the pan when it is done.

2 Scrape the filling into a bowl and let it cool completely. Stir in the parsley and goat cheese.

3 Place the wonton wrappers and egg wash in front of you. Place one wrapper on a cutting board. Measure out 1 teaspoon of filling and put it on the center of the wrapper. Form it into a neat ball with your fingers. With a pastry brush, lightly brush some egg wash along the perimeter of the wrapper. Place another wrapper on top, then with your fingers seal the dough, keeping the ball intact while pressing out any air pockets.

4 With a 2½-inch round biscuit (pastry) cutter (or knife), cut out the ravioli and discard the scraps. Repeat with the remaining filling and wrappers.

½ tablespoon unbleached flour

2 tablespoons pale dry sherry, dry vermouth, or dry white wine

⅔ cup whole milk

Salt

Freshly ground pepper

1 tablespoon minced fresh parsley for garnish

Serves 4

You should have about 30 ravioli. As they are completed, place them on a large platter, then cover with plastic wrap. The ravioli can be prepared up to 8 hours in advance and refrigerated. Bring to room temperature before cooking because they should cook for 1 minute only and cold ravioli requires longer cooking time.

5 To make the sauce, combine the butter, ginger, and garlic in a small saucepan over medium heat. Cook until the garlic begins to turn golden, about 2 minutes. Whisk in the flour and cook 1 minute. Whisk in the sherry, milk, and salt and pepper to taste and bring to a boil. Strain the sauce into a small bowl and discard the ginger and garlic.

6 To cook the ravioli, bring a large pot of water to a boil. Drop in the ravioli, and after the water returns to a boil, cook the ravioli just 1 minute. Carefully pour the ravioli into a colander and let drain.

7 Pour the sauce into the pot and heat just until it begins to simmer. (If it is too thick, add a few drops of milk.) Return the ravioli to the pot and gently toss to coat. Serve garnished with the parsley.

EGGPLANT ROLLATINI

This is a delicious dish. Its filling is somewhat firm compared to the traditional ricotta filling found in most eggplant rollatinis, and is far superior, I think. Because its preparation can be separated so easily into stages, it can be a hassle-free meal if you take advantage of these do-ahead tips. Up to 24 hours in advance, make the sauce, then cook the eggplant. Chill. Finally, make the filling and then assemble the rollatini. And don't hesitate to freeze the entire dish because it won't suffer a bit from it.

Steamed diced green beans or sautéed zucchini are lovely with this dish. You could also try buttered and parsleyed egg noodles for a more substantial addition.

THE SAUCE

2 tablespoons olive oil

3 garlic cloves, minced

1 28-ounce can crushed tomatoes

2 tablespoons red wine

1 teaspoon dried oregano

1 teaspoon dried basil

½ teaspoon salt

Liberal seasoning of freshly ground pepper

....

2 medium-size eggplants (about 2 pounds)

¾ cup bread crumbs

½ cup olive oil

THE FILLING

4 eggs

1 garlic clove, minced

1 To make the sauce, heat the olive oil in a medium-size saucepan over medium heat. Add the garlic and sauté just until it begins to turn golden. Do not let it get brown. Immediately stir in the tomatoes, wine, oregano, basil, salt, and pepper. Partially cover the pot to prevent the sauce from splattering all over the stove. Simmer, stirring occasionally, for 20 minutes. Set aside to cool.

2 To prepare the eggplants, cut off their ends. Cut them lengthwise into ¼-inch slices, keeping the skin on.

3 Preheat the broiler.

4 Pour the bread crumbs onto a large plate. With a pastry brush, coat both sides of each eggplant slice with a thin layer of olive oil, then dip the slices into the bread crumbs to coat them completely. In batches, place them on a cookie sheet and broil on both sides until golden brown

¾ cup finely chopped fresh parsley

¼ cup minced fresh basil, or 1 teaspoon dried

½ cup bread crumbs

¾ cup grated Parmesan cheese

1 cup grated part-skim mozzarella cheese

Serves 6

and very tender. Stack them on a platter after each batch is finished.

5 To make the filling, beat the eggs in a medium-size bowl. Beat in all the remaining filling ingredients except ½ cup of the mozzarella cheese.

6 Preheat the oven to 375 degrees.

7 Put a thin layer of the tomato sauce on the bottom of a 13 × 9 × 2-inch baking dish. Divide the stuffing to match the number of eggplant slices. Place one portion of the stuffing at the end of an eggplant slice, then roll to cover. Place seam side down in the baking dish and proceed with the remaining eggplant slices.

8 Pour the remaining sauce over all the eggplant rolls, then sprinkle the remaining ½ cup of mozzarella on each roll. Cover the dish with foil.

9 Bake for 30 minutes, then remove the foil and bake an additional 10 minutes, or until hot and bubbly.

Note: This dish may be prepared through step 8 up to 24 hours in advance and refrigerated, or frozen up to 2 weeks in advance. If frozen, let thaw in the refrigerator overnight before baking.

GRILLED POLENTA WITH ZUCCHINI AND SUN-DRIED TOMATOES

Adding a touch of heavy cream to this sauce makes it truly luscious and fit for a special occasion. If you don't have a grill, you can broil the polenta with equally good results.

THE POLENTA

3½ cups vegetable stock

½ teaspoon salt

1 teaspoon finely chopped fresh rosemary, or ¼ teaspoon dried, crumbled

1 cup cornmeal

2 tablespoons unsalted butter

¼ cup grated Parmesan cheese

1 cup grated part-skim mozzarella cheese

2 tablespoons olive oil

THE SAUCE

½ cup sun-dried tomatoes (see note)

1 tablespoon olive oil

2 garlic cloves, minced

1 medium onion, finely diced

3 medium zucchini, cut in half lengthwise, then thinly sliced on the diagonal

⅓ cup heavy cream

1 To make the polenta, set aside a 10 × 10-inch shallow baking dish or other comparable dish. Bring the vegetable stock, salt, and rosemary to a boil in a medium-size saucepan. Reduce the heat to a simmer, then gradually sprinkle in the cornmeal, whisking constantly. Cook the polenta, whisking all the while, until it begins to pull away from the sides of the pan, about 7 minutes. Whisk in the butter, Parmesan cheese, and mozzarella cheese.

2 Scrape the polenta into the reserved baking dish and smooth over the top. Let cool for 10 minutes, then cover and chill for at least 1 hour, or up to 24 hours. When you are ready to begin cooking, cut the polenta into 12 squares. Lightly brush each side with the olive oil and place the squares on a baking sheet. Set aside while you make the sauce.

3 To make the sauce, place the sun-dried tomatoes in a bowl. Pour boiling water on them to cover. Let sit 10 minutes. Drain, then pat dry with paper towels. Slice the tomatoes into thin strips.

4 Heat the olive oil in a large skillet over medium-high heat. Add the garlic and onion and sauté

Salt

Liberal seasoning of freshly ground pepper

Fresh rosemary sprigs for garnish (optional)

Serves 6

for 5 minutes. Stir in the zucchini and sun-dried tomatoes and sauté until the zucchini is tender yet still slightly crunchy, about 7 minutes.

5 Meanwhile, grill or broil the polenta until golden brown on each side, about 10 minutes total. Place 2 squares of polenta on each serving plate.

6 Pour the cream into the zucchini mixture along with the salt and pepper. Let boil just until the sauce begins to thicken, about 1 minute. Spoon onto the polenta and garnish with fresh rosemary sprigs.

Note: If your sun-dried tomatoes are packed in oil, use only ⅓ cup. Omit cooking them in step 3; just slice them into strips.

SPINACH ENCHILADAS WITH ALMOND RED SAUCE

The addition of ground nuts to sauces is a Southwestern technique, which lends the sauce extra body and a richer flavor. I love these enchiladas and hope you will, too.

THE SAUCE

½ cup almonds

1 tablespoon olive oil

1 medium onion, minced

2 garlic cloves, minced

¼ teaspoon crushed red pepper flakes

2 cups tomato sauce (homemade or store-bought)

⅔ cup water

2 teaspoons paprika

THE FILLING

1 egg

1 15-ounce container part-skim ricotta cheese

1 10-ounce package frozen chopped spinach, thawed and pressed dry in a strainer

1 4-ounce can chopped green chilies, drained

2 tablespoons finely chopped cilantro

¼ teaspoon salt

Freshly ground pepper

1. Preheat the oven to 375 degrees.
2. To make the sauce, place the almonds in a shallow dish and toast until they are fragrant and begin to turn golden, about 5 minutes. Let cool, then grind until powdery in a blender. Set aside. Keep the oven on if you plan to cook the enchiladas right away.
3. Heat the oil in a medium-size saucepan over medium heat. Add the onion, garlic, and red pepper flakes and, stirring often, cook until the onion begins to brown, about 10 minutes. Stir in the tomato sauce, water, and paprika. Boil 2 minutes, then stir in the ground almonds. Remove from the heat.
4. To make the filling, beat the egg in a large bowl. Beat in all the remaining filling ingredients. Divide the filling into 8 portions.
5. Spoon a thin layer of sauce in a 9 × 13-inch baking dish. Place a tortilla on a plate, spoon a little sauce on it, and spread it around with the back of a spoon. Flip the tortilla over and repeat (this softens the tortilla and helps prevent it from breaking). Place an eighth of the spinach mixture along the edge of the tortilla, then roll it up to form a cylinder. Place in the baking dish, seam

8 6½-inch flour tortillas

1 cup grated Monterey Jack cheese

Serves 4

side down, and repeat with the remaining tortillas and filling.

6 Pour the remaining sauce over the enchiladas, then sprinkle on the grated cheese. Cover the dish with foil.

7 Bake for 30 minutes, or until bubbly.

Note: May be prepared up to 8 hours in advance through step 6. Bring to room temperature before baking.

STUFFED BASIL CRÊPES WITH ROASTED RED PEPPER SAUCE

Stuffed with a zucchini and goat cheese filling, these crêpes can be prepared in stages, making this elegant dish seem easy. Couscous is a good side dish.

THE CREPES

1 egg

½ cup unbleached flour

¼ teaspoon salt

½ cup plus 2 tablespoons milk

2 tablespoons butter, melted

1½ tablespoons minced fresh basil, or 1 teaspoon dried

Butter or oil for greasing pan

THE FILLING

1 tablespoon olive oil

2 garlic cloves, minced

1 medium onion, finely diced

1 tomato, cored, seeded, and finely diced

¼ teaspoon fennel seed, crushed

2 medium zucchini, cut lengthwise into sixths and thinly sliced (4 cups)

Salt

Generous seasoning of freshly ground pepper

1 To make the crêpes, combine the egg, flour, salt, milk, and melted butter in a blender and blend until smooth. Pour the batter into a bowl and stir in the basil.

2 Heat an 8-inch omelet pan or nonstick skillet over medium-high heat and lightly grease the pan. With a measuring spoon, pour a scant 2 tablespoons of batter into the pan and swirl it around to coat the entire surface. Cook the crêpe for about 2 minutes, or until lightly browned. Flip and cook about 1 more minute. Place the cooked crêpe on a sheet of wax paper and repeat until all the batter has been used. You should have 8 crêpes. They can be stacked on each other to cool. (The crêpes may be prepared up to 48 hours in advance, wrapped, and refrigerated.)

3 To make the filling, heat the olive oil in a large skillet over medium-high heat. Add the garlic and onion and sauté for 5 minutes, or until the onion begins to get tender. Stir in the tomato and fennel and cook 1 minute. Stir in the zucchini and cook, stirring often, until tender, about 10 minutes. Season with salt and pepper to taste. (The filling may be made up to 48 hours in advance and chilled.)

THE SAUCE

1 7-ounce jar roasted red peppers, well drained and patted dry (1 cup)

¼ cup tomato sauce (homemade or store-bought)

1 garlic clove, minced

Dash of cayenne

Salt

....

6 ounces goat cheese, crumbled (about 1 cup)

Serves 4

4 To make the sauce, combine the peppers, tomato sauce, garlic, cayenne, and salt in a blender and purée. Pour into a small saucepan to heat at serving time.

5 Preheat the oven to 300 degrees.

6 To assemble the crêpes, lightly butter a 12 × 7 × 2-inch baking dish or one of similar size. One side of each crêpe will be more attractive and herb-flecked. Place this side down on a surface so it is on the outside. Spoon an eighth of the zucchini mixture along the center of the crêpe. Place some goat cheese on top of the filling, then roll the crêpe to make a log. Place seam side down in the baking dish. Repeat with all the crêpes.

7 Lay a lightly buttered sheet of wax paper on the crêpes. Cover the dish with aluminum foil. Bake 20 to 30 minutes, or until hot throughout.

8 Meanwhile, gently heat the sauce just until hot. Serve 2 crêpes on each plate with some sauce spooned on.

POLENTA TIMBALES WITH SPICY MUSHROOM SAUCE

These timbales are an ideal dish for entertaining because they are at once beautiful and delicate and also very satisfying. The bonus is that almost all the steps can be prepared in advance.

THE POLENTA

2 cups low-fat milk

2 cups water

1¼ cups cornmeal

¼ cup sour cream

¼ cup grated Parmesan cheese

½ teaspoon salt

⅛ teaspoon grated nutmeg

Freshly ground pepper

1 cup (4 ounces) finely diced Italian fontina cheese, plus 8 thin 1-inch-square slices Italian fontina cheese

THE SAUCE

2 tablespoons olive oil

1 medium onion, minced

4 garlic cloves, minced

¼ teaspoon crushed red pepper flakes

1 pound mushrooms, quartered or cut into eighths (about 7 cups)

1 28-ounce can imported plum tomatoes, finely chopped with their juice

1 Place 8 custard cups or ramekins in a handy spot to pour the polenta into when it's cooked. Arrange all the polenta ingredients in front of you before you begin cooking. Bring the milk and water to a boil in a medium-size heavy-bottomed saucepan. Reduce the heat to low, then slowly drizzle in the cornmeal, beating all the while with a wire whisk. Whisk constantly until the polenta tears away from the sides of the pot, about 5 minutes.

2 Remove from the heat and whisk in the sour cream, Parmesan cheese, salt, nutmeg, and pepper. Stir in the cubed fontina just until the cubes are evenly distributed (they shouldn't melt much). Quickly spoon the mixture into the custard cups, then smooth over the tops of the timbales with the back of a spoon, or overfill them and scrape off the excess with a knife. Let the timbales sit for 15 minutes. (The timbales may be prepared in advance up to this point, covered, and refrigerated for up to 24 hours.)

3 To make the sauce, heat the olive oil over medium-high heat in a large skillet. Add the onion, garlic, and red pepper flakes and cook, stirring often, until the onion is tender, about 7 minutes. Add the mushrooms and sauté until

1 tablespoon tomato paste

½ teaspoon salt

Liberal seasoning of freshly ground pepper

1½ tablespoons minced fresh parsley

Serves 4

the juices are released and then evaporated, about 15 minutes.

4 Stir in the tomatoes, tomato paste, salt, and pepper. Cook, stirring occasionally, until the sauce is thick, about 25 minutes. (The sauce may be prepared up to 24 hours in advance and refrigerated.)

5 Preheat the oven to 400 degrees. Generously butter a shallow broilerproof baking dish that's large enough to hold the 8 timbales.

6 Run a knife around each timbale to loosen it from the custard cup, then invert into the baking dish. Place a slice of the remaining cheese on top of each timbale. Bake for 15 minutes, then place under the broiler for 3 minutes, or until the cheese is bubbly. Remove from the oven and spread the cheese more evenly over the timbales. Broil 2 minutes more, or until golden.

7 If the sauce has become too thick again, thin it with a few more tablespoons of water. Stir in the minced parsley. Serve 2 timbales per person with the mushroom sauce surrounding them.

SPINACH AND GORGONZOLA RISOTTO

The characteristic creaminess of a risotto is achieved by ladling small amounts of stock into rice and stirring until it is absorbed before adding more stock. It is not difficult to do, but it is a last-minute dish that requires your full attention for about 40 minutes. You can chat with guests while performing this task, or pull up a stool and read a good book while stirring with your book-free hand. A special salad made with baby greens is all you need to accompany this luscious dish, but plan to serve it after the risotto.

4½ cups vegetable stock

⅛ teaspoon grated nutmeg

½ teaspoon salt

Freshly ground pepper

1 tablespoon unsalted butter

1 medium onion, minced

2 garlic cloves, minced

1 cup (3 ounces) thinly sliced mushrooms

1 cup arborio rice (see note)

3 cups (3 ounces) lightly packed spinach leaves, torn into small pieces

2 tablespoons golden raisins

2 ounces (about ½ cup) crumbled Gorgonzola cheese, or other blue cheese

½ cup grated Parmesan cheese

1 Combine the stock, nutmeg, salt, and pepper in a medium-size saucepan and heat just until hot. Reduce the heat to low and keep hot while you make the risotto.

2 In another medium-size, heavy-bottomed saucepan, melt the butter over medium-high heat. Add the onion and garlic and sauté, tossing often, until the onion begins to brown, about 7 minutes.

3 Stir in the mushrooms and cook until the mushrooms are brown and their juices have been released and then evaporated, about 10 minutes. Stir often. Stir in the rice and cook 2 minutes, stirring constantly to coat the grains evenly and cause them to become almost translucent.

4 Reduce the heat to medium. Fill a ½-cup ladle with hot stock and pour it on the rice mixture. Stir constantly until the liquid is absorbed, about 4 minutes. Add another ½ cup of stock and stir until it is absorbed. Keep repeating this procedure, making sure not to add stock until the

Serves 3 (can easily be doubled)

previous ladleful of stock has been absorbed. Each ladleful should take about 4 minutes.

5 When about two-thirds of the stock has been used, stir in the spinach and raisins. Continue to add the stock as described above. When 1 ladleful of stock remains, taste the rice. The grains should be tender but still slightly chewy—that is, al dente. If they are hard, add a ½ cup of warm water and test again after it has been absorbed. Before the last ladleful of stock has been added, stir in the Gorgonzola, Parmesan cheese, and last bit of stock. Stir 1 to 2 minutes, or until thick and creamy. Serve immediately.

Note: Arborio is an imported Italian rice with short, fat grains and a lot of starch. It's available at specialty food shops and many natural foods stores.

RISOTTO PRIMAVERA

Asparagus and peas lend a spring accent to this colorful risotto, but actually it can be made during any season now that asparagus is practically a year-round vegetable.

4½ cups vegetable stock

½ teaspoon salt

Generous seasoning of freshly ground pepper

2 tablespoons olive oil

1 carrot, very thinly sliced

5 asparagus stalks, peeled and cut into 1-inch pieces

1 red bell pepper, cut into ½-inch dice

½ cup fresh peas or thawed frozen peas

1 medium onion, minced

2 garlic cloves, minced

1 cup arborio rice (see note, page 191)

1 tablespoon finely shredded fresh basil, or ½ teaspoon dried

½ cup grated Parmesan cheese

Serves 3

1. Combine the stock, salt, and pepper in a medium-size saucepan (on a back burner) and bring to a simmer. Reduce the heat to low and keep hot while making the risotto.
2. Heat 1 tablespoon of the oil in a medium-size skillet over medium heat. Add the sliced carrot and sauté 1 minute. Stir in the asparagus and sauté 2 more minutes. Add the red pepper and fresh peas (if you are using them) and cook about 3 more minutes, or until the vegetables are tender but not mushy. If you are using frozen peas, add them now, then remove the pan from the heat. They do not need to cook.
3. In a heavy-bottomed medium-size saucepan, heat the remaining tablespoon of olive oil over medium heat. Add the onion and garlic and cook, stirring often, until the onion begins to brown, about 7 minutes. Stir in the rice and sauté 2 minutes, stirring constantly.
4. Fill a ½-cup ladle with stock and pour it on the rice. Stir constantly until the liquid is absorbed, about 4 minutes. Add another ½ cup of stock and stir until it is absorbed. Keep repeating this procedure, making sure not to add stock until the previous ladleful has been absorbed. It should take about 4 minutes for each ladleful of stock. Regulate the heat accordingly.

5 When one ladleful of stock remains, taste the rice. The grains should be tender but still slightly chewy. If they are hard, add ½ cup of warm water and test again after it has been absorbed. Before adding the last ladleful of stock, stir in the vegetables, basil, and Parmesan cheese, then the remaining stock. Stir 1 to 2 minutes, or until thick and creamy. Serve immediately.

BAKED STUFFED RED PEPPERS

Spinach fettuccine and smoked cheese are the main components of this highly flavorful stuffing, making these brilliant red peppers a feast for the eyes as well as the appetite. Because they are so substantial, all you need is some steamed summer squash to sit alongside them.

4 large red bell peppers

¼ pound spinach fettuccine

1 cup part-skim ricotta cheese

¼ cup plus 2 tablespoons low-fat milk

1 cup grated smoked cheese (such as smoked Gouda)

1 cup grated part-skim mozzarella cheese

2 scallions, very thinly sliced

½ teaspoon salt

Generous seasoning of freshly ground pepper

Olive oil for greasing

Serves 4

1 Slice the tops off the peppers (save these scraps for another use). Pull out the seeds and fibrous insides of each pepper and discard. To make each pepper sit steadily upright, slice a very thin piece off each bottom.

2 Bring a large pot of water to a boil. Drop the peppers in and let the water return to a boil. Cook 5 minutes, then remove the peppers with tongs. Invert them on a kitchen towel and let them drain and cool.

3 Return the water to a rapid boil. Cook the fettuccine for 7 minutes, or until al dente. Drain in a colander. You need about 2 cups fettuccine.

4 To make the stuffing, beat the ricotta with the milk in a large bowl. Stir in both cheeses, the scallions, salt, and pepper. Cut the fettuccine a few times with two knives to shorten the strands. Stir the fettuccine into the cheese mixture.

5 Preheat the oven to 375 degrees.

6 Rub a little olive oil all over the outside of each pepper. Stuff each pepper with the fettuccine mixture. Smooth over the tops by pressing down the stuffing. Place the peppers in a lightly oiled, shallow baking dish, such as a 12 × 7 × 2-inch

Pyrex dish. Bake for 30 minutes, or until hot, bubbly, and lightly browned.

Note: May be prepared, covered, and refrigerated up to 24 hours in advance. Bring to room temperature before cooking.

STUFFED YELLOW PEPPERS WITH TOMATO-BASIL SALSA

I like to make this tasty dish at the height of summer when the cost of yellow peppers is reasonable and tomatoes and basil are at their prime. The white bean and zucchini stuffing makes them substantial, so all you need for accompaniments are a salad and some crusty bread.

4 large yellow bell peppers

1 tablespoon olive oil, plus extra for greasing

3 garlic cloves, minced

2 medium zucchini, cut lengthwise into sixths and thinly sliced (2 cups sliced)

1 15-ounce can cannellini (white kidney beans)

¼ teaspoon powdered sage

⅓ cup grated Parmesan cheese

⅔ cup grated fontina, Monterey Jack, or Muenster cheese

Salt

Generous seasoning of freshly ground black pepper

THE SALSA

1 large ripe tomato, very finely diced (1 cup)

1 garlic clove, minced

½ cup finely shredded fresh basil

1 Cut the tops off the peppers. Cut any flesh away from the stem, finely dice it, and set aside. Discard the stem. Pull out the seeds and fibrous interior of the peppers and discard them.

2 Bring a large pot of water to a boil. Drop in the pepper shells and let the water return to a boil. Cook the peppers for 5 minutes. Remove them with tongs and let drain upside down.

3 Preheat the oven to 375 degrees.

4 Heat the tablespoon of oil in a large skillet over medium heat. Add the garlic and cook 1 minute. Stir in the zucchini and diced peppers and cook until tender yet still slightly crunchy. Remove from the heat, then stir in the cannellini, sage, two cheeses, salt, and pepper.

5 Lightly oil a shallow baking dish large enough to hold the peppers. Divide the vegetable-bean mixture into four, then stuff each pepper with it. Place in the baking dish. (May be prepared to this point and chilled up to 24 hours in advance.) Bake 30 minutes, or until piping hot and beginning to brown.

8 oil-cured black olives, pitted and chopped (see note, page 25)

2 teaspoons olive oil

2 teaspoons balsamic vinegar

Salt

Freshly ground black pepper

Serves 4

6 Meanwhile, combine all the salsa ingredients in a bowl. Let sit at room temperature until ready to use. Pass the salsa at the table to spoon onto the peppers.

EGGPLANT TART IN PUFF PASTRY

The deep meaty flavor and garlicky overtones of this eggplant filling are a nice match for delicate puff pastry. Pasta would make a great side dish; try angel hair with minced parsley or orzo with bits of sautéed tomato mixed in.

1 sheet frozen puff pastry (half a 17¼-ounce box), thawed

2 tablespoons olive oil

1 medium onion, very finely diced

4 garlic cloves, minced

1 16-ounce can tomatoes, finely chopped and well drained

1 large (1½ pounds) eggplant, peeled and cut into ¼-inch dice

1 green pepper, cut into ¼-inch dice

¼ cup finely chopped fresh basil, or 1½ teaspoons dried

¾ teaspoon salt

Generous seasoning of freshly ground pepper

2 eggs

¼ cup grated Parmesan cheese

1 Roll the puff pastry into an 11-inch square. Place it in a 9-inch tart pan with a removable bottom and trim off the excess. Cover and freeze for 30 minutes, or place in a plastic bag and freeze up to 24 hours.

2 To make the filling, heat the olive oil in a large skillet over medium heat. Add the onion and garlic and cook 5 minutes, tossing often. Add the tomatoes and sauté 5 more minutes.

3 Stir in the eggplant, green pepper, basil, salt, and pepper and toss well. Cover the pan and cook about 20 minutes, or until the eggplant is tender. Remove from the heat and cool slightly.

4 Place two-thirds of the eggplant mixture, the eggs, and the Parmesan cheese in a food processor or blender and purée. Scrape the mixture back into the skillet and mix with the reserved eggplant.

5 Preheat the oven to 425 degrees.

6 Spoon the eggplant mixture into the frozen tart shell and smooth over the top. In a small bowl, combine the bread crumbs, Parmesan cheese, garlic, parsley, and melted butter. Sprinkle evenly over the tart.

CRUMB TOPPING (PERSILLADE)

1 tablespoon bread crumbs

1 tablespoon grated Parmesan cheese

1 garlic clove, minced

2 tablespoons minced fresh parsley

1 tablespoon unsalted butter, melted

Serves 4 to 6

7 Bake 25 minutes, or until a rich golden brown. Remove the outer rim of the tart pan and let the tart sit for 10 minutes before cutting into wedges.

SPINACH LOAF WITH CURRIED CREAM SAUCE

Buttered egg noodles go very well with this savory loaf. Try sautéing bits of red pepper or tomato and adding them to noodles before serving; this will lend an attractive splash of color.

2 pounds loose fresh spinach, or 2 10-ounce packages fresh spinach, or 2 10-ounce packages frozen chopped spinach, thawed

1 tablespoon unsalted butter

1 medium onion, minced

1 carrot, grated

3 eggs, beaten

1 cup low-fat milk

½ cup bread crumbs

3 tablespoons grated Parmesan cheese

¼ teaspoon grated nutmeg

½ teaspoon salt

Freshly ground pepper

THE SAUCE

1½ tablespoons unsalted butter

1 teaspoon curry powder

2 tablespoons unbleached flour

2 cups milk

Dash of cayenne

Salt

Serves 4 to 6

1. If you are using fresh spinach, discard the stems, wash the leaves thoroughly, and drain them. Place the spinach in a large covered skillet or pot with only the water that clings to them. Cook until the spinach just wilts. Let cool; squeeze out the moisture with your hands. Finely chop the spinach. If you are using frozen spinach, just squeeze out all the moisture between your hands. Put it in a large bowl.
2. Heat the butter in a small skillet. Sauté the onion until tender. Combine with the spinach. Stir in the carrot, eggs, milk, bread crumbs, cheese, nutmeg, salt, and pepper to taste.
3. Preheat the oven to 375 degrees. Generously butter a 9 × 5-inch loaf pan. Line it with wax paper, then butter the paper.
4. Spoon the spinach mixture into the pan and smooth the top. Cover loosely with foil. Place the dish in a larger baking dish and fill with 1 inch of hot water.
5. Bake for 1½ hours, or until a knife inserted in the center of the loaf comes out clean. If a lot of water evaporates before the cooking time is up, add more hot water to keep it at a depth of 1 inch. Let sit for 10 minutes before unmolding onto a platter.

6 To make the sauce, melt the butter in a medium-size saucepan over medium heat. Whisk in the curry powder and flour and cook for 2 minutes, whisking constantly. Whisk in the milk, cayenne, and salt. Cook, whisking often, until the sauce comes to a boil.

7 Slice the loaf and serve with sauce spooned on each slice.

EGGPLANT STEAKS WITH PEPPERS AND TANGY BASIL SAUCE

Here's an attractive and delicious dish that can be prepared in easy stages and reheated. Rounds of crumb-coated broiled eggplant are topped with a colorful pepper sauté, then drizzled with a spoonful of garlicky basil sauce. Serve with a lightly buttered starch such as egg noodles, rice, or couscous.

THE PEPPERS

1 tablespoon olive oil

4 garlic cloves, minced

1 medium onion, halved and thinly sliced

1 green bell pepper, cored, halved, and thinly sliced

1 red bell pepper, cored, halved, and thinly sliced

2 tomatoes, cored, seeded, and finely diced

2 teaspoons drained capers

Salt

Generous seasoning of freshly ground pepper

THE SAUCE

1 cup low-fat yogurt

1 garlic clove, pressed or minced

¼ cup finely chopped fresh basil

Salt

Freshly ground pepper

1 To make the pepper sauté, heat the olive oil in a large skillet over medium-high heat. Add the garlic and onion and sauté, tossing often, for 10 minutes, or until the onion is tender.

2 Mix in the peppers, tomatoes, capers, salt, and pepper and cook about 20 minutes, or until the peppers are very tender and the mixture is jamlike. Stir often so that everything cooks evenly. The peppers can be cooked up to 8 hours in advance and reheated. Add a few drops of water if the mixture sticks to the pan.

3 Meanwhile, make the basil sauce by combining all the sauce ingredients in a small bowl. If made well in advance, keep chilled; otherwise, keep at room temperature to serve cool, not cold.

4 To cook the eggplant, preheat the broiler. With a pastry brush, lightly coat both sides of each eggplant slice with some olive oil, then coat the slices with the bread crumbs. Place on a baking sheet. Broil until golden brown on both sides, turning over as necessary. The eggplant can be prepared up to 24 hours in advance and reheated before serving.

THE EGGPLANT

1 medium (1¼ pounds) eggplant, skin left on and sliced ¾ inch thick

3 tablespoons olive oil

⅓ cup bread crumbs

Serves 4

5 To serve, place a few eggplant "steaks" on each serving plate. Top with some pepper mixture, then drizzle with a spoonful of sauce.

MUSHROOM CUTLETS WITH SPICY CREAM SAUCE

These tasty pancakes remind me of sausage patties because of their texture and spicy overtones. You can serve them with a vegetable or noodle side dish, or alongside scrambled eggs for a breakfast treat. In either case, don't omit the sauce; it is simple yet hauntingly good.

1 tablespoon unsalted butter

2 medium onions, finely chopped

1 pound mushrooms, finely chopped

1 cup diced cooked potato (1 medium)

2 eggs

1¼ cup bread crumbs

2 tablespoons minced fresh parsley

1 cup grated Swiss cheese

½ teaspoon dried thyme

⅛ teaspoon celery seed

¾ teaspoon salt

Liberal seasoning of freshly ground pepper

Dash of cayenne

Oil for greasing

THE SAUCE

½ cup sour cream

½ cup medium-hot salsa

Serves 4 (11 to 12 cutlets)

1 Heat the butter in a large skillet over medium heat. Add the onions and sauté until tender, about 10 minutes. Raise the heat to medium-high and stir in the mushrooms. Cook, stirring often, until the juices have evaporated and the mixture begins to stick to the pan, 10 to 15 minutes.

2 Place in a food processor along with the potato and eggs and process until smooth. Scrape into a large bowl and let cool to room temperature. Stir in the remaining pancake ingredients except the oil.

3 Preheat the oven to 350 degrees. Generously oil a baking sheet.

4 Scoop the mixture into a ⅓-cup measure and scrape off the excess. Drop onto the baking sheet and flatten slightly. (You might have to use two baking sheets or cook these in two batches.) Bake 15 minutes, flip, then bake 15 additional minutes. They should be golden brown when done.

5 To make the sauce, beat together the sour cream and salsa. Serve a spoonful of sauce on each cutlet.

Note: May be prepared through step 2 up to 24 hours in advance. Keep covered and refrigerated.

INDEX